HISTORY OF THE OLD TESTAMENT

III

VOL. III

HISTORY OF THE
CLAUS SCHEDL

OLD TESTAMENT

THE GOLDEN AGE OF DAVID

alba house

A DIVISION OF THE SOCIETY OF ST. PAUL
STATEN ISLAND, NEW YORK 10314

First published under the title: **Geschichte des Alten Testaments** by Tyrolia-Verlag, Innsbruck, Austria

Library of Congress Cataloging in Publication Data

Schedl, Claus.
  History of the Old Testament.

  Translation of Geschichte des Alten Testaments.
  Includes bibliographical references.
  CONTENTS: v. 1. The ancient Orient and ancient Biblical history.—
v. 2. God's people of the covenant.—v. 3. The golden age of David. [etc.]
  1. Bible.   O. T.—History of Biblical events.
I. Title.
BS1197.S3213   221.9   70-38990
ISBN 0-8189-0231-0 (set)
ISBN 0-8189-0208-6 (v. 3)

Nihil Obstat:
  Donald A. Panella, M.A., S.T.L., S.S.L.
  Censor Librorum

Imprimatur:
  Joseph P. O'Brien, S.T.D.
  Vicar General, Archdiocese of New York
  March 19, 1971

Designed, printed and bound by the Fathers and Brothers of the Society of St. Paul as part of their communications apostolate.

THE THEOLOGIAN AND
THE OLD TESTAMENT

BY theologian we understand not merely the professional theologian who studies the Bible in connection with his vocation in order to qualify himself for the exercise of his office, but every believer for whom the Bible is an interesting and venerable document of the history of the ancient Eastern mind and religion. The Bible is not the private literature of a specially elect band of devotees, but the life book of God's people. It is in this book that the Word of God, binding on all men, has become flesh.

Just as the person of Christ "who, though he was in the form of God, did not count equality with God a thing to be grasped, but emptied himself, taking the form of a servant, being born in the likeness of men" (*Phil.* 2, 6-7) is the key to all theology, it is also the only approach to the Bible. Just as the God-man Jesus spans a mighty dichotomy in his person, by uniting what appear to be strictly disparate elements in one divine-human unity, so the word of the Bible is filled with a dynamism which surpasses human measurement. Are we now about to do away with this involvement in the sphere of human affairs by advancing a theology of the word of the Bible that concentrates too heavily on the overpowering splendor of that Word which was in the beginning with God and which is incapable of being incorporated into "the shards of letters"? [1]

Not at all. Just as the man who repudiates Christ's bodily

---

1. Origen, *Commentary on St. John*, Migne, PG 13, 29B-32B.

existence and ascribes only a phantom human existence to the Incarnate Word is guilty of seriously misinterpreting Christ, so the man who refuses to recognize the fact of the Incarnation entirely misses the mystery of Scripture. Just as Christ was a true man of his times, speaking the Galilean dialect and wearing the dress of his century, so every word in the Bible is spoken in a concrete, unique, and historical setting. This very fact determined its fate. The dust of centuries has grown heavy upon it. The Word has made its way into history, as every other, earlier or later, profane document of history.

If we mean to approach this word, we must face the difficult task of entering into all the stipulations of historical development and not rest comfortably in our secure position by pointing to the fact of inspiration. Whoever wishes to approach the Bible in a scientific manner necessarily takes on the total load of a profane exegesis. The Old Testament is a written document of the Ancient Near East, and it has undergone a development over the course of more than a thousand years before reaching its present form. For the most part it is written in the Hebrew language. A scientific examination of the Old Testament, therefore, becomes impossible without the study and knowledge of this language. The man who bases his approach only on translations is always something of a stranger to the concrete call of the revealed word; for every translation is, in some respects, a betrayal. Only the original text is inspired, and not the translations, no matter how venerable they might be.

The Old Testament is also a literary document. Thus we are also obliged (and it would be a serious error to omit this task) to approach the text in terms of the principles of philology and literary criticism in order to critically test every passage. But a literary criticism always runs the danger of being too removed from life and reality, unless it constantly keeps in sight the *Sitz im Leben* — its position in actuality.

The written document thus appeals to the mute witnesses of ancient history, which are made articulate by archaeological excavation. Philology, literary criticism, archaeology, and the history of the Ancient Near East are the guideposts for this pro-

fane exegesis; without them we are irrevocably lost in the realm
of unreality, and we miss the full "incarnation of the Word."
The personal religious conviction of the investigator plays no
role in this. In fact, we might go so far as to claim that if there
were one ideal technique for carrying out this methodology of
examination, then the results of a study by an atheistic philologist
and a believing theologian would be completely in agreement.
And, in practice, to a large extent, this is exactly what happens.

But if we mean to rest content with this *profane exegesis,*
we fail to recognize the inexhaustible reality of the Bible word.
Profane exegesis must be enlarged upon, not only as a mere
supplement, but as an ultimate fulfillment, by "pneumatic" exegesis. The primary source of Scripture is at once both human
and divine. If one of the pillars is missing here, the whole construction collapses in ruin.

This is not the place to fully treat on the nature of inspiration,[2]
although the study of Scripture wanders about blindly without
a clear idea of it. Both Church and synagogue have always
attested to the fact that the Bible contains God's word. Disagree-
ments were only on questions concerning how the authorship of
Scripture was to be ascribed to God, and how it was possible
to speak of human authorship. The Patristic age [3] was fond of
parables: the Holy Spirit, it was claimed, used the human author
like a musical instrument (organ, flute, lyre, etc.). Though it is
an attractive metaphor, it runs the risk of considering human
cooperation too exclusively in terms of a dead "instrument,"
without any proper activity of its own. When God overshadows
a human author, he does not extinguish human existence; he
elevates it into greater light, into a freedom untrammeled by sin.
Inspiration is the elevation of the human faculties. If God calls
upon man to compose a book, he directs this call to a concrete,
historically qualified man, who, under the divine impulse, takes up
the historical source material available and forms it into a unity
that has been revealed to him. In this process, it is only too easy

---

2. A. Merk, *De Inspiratione S. Scripturae,* Biblical Institute, Rome 1951.
3. Cf. J. Schildenberger, *Vom Geheimnis des Gotteswortes,* 1950, p. 17.

to recognize the awkward hand of the human author, who was obviously not always an accomplished literary artist. But it is from this very defect that God's power sounds its clearest note. Thus the word formed by man becomes the true "bounty of the divine Word." [4] We can then speak of personal literary style, power of poetic expression, artistic or faulty composition without thereby calling into question the divine reality of inspiration.

Once the divine origin of Scripture is properly grasped, there are some ponderable conclusions. The basic concept of this book is divine and grandiose. It lays bare the deepest abysses of sin and judgment; but it also discloses the glories of forgiveness and grace. There is nothing superficial or monotonous about this book. It sounds depths of such great dimensions that they shine like lightning "from the beginning to the end of days." This book was not composed without a plan; it storms along towards its goal. The "shards of the individual words" announce the irresistible and passionate arrival of the Eternal Word. The words are all oriented towards *the* Word. The Old Testament is the "educator towards Christ." Thus, if you tell how you look at Christ, I will tell you how you read the Old Testament. The ultimate understanding of Scripture comes only from faith and Spirit. Once a man has tasted the "sweetness of the word" (*Ps.* 34, 8), he is awake to the "passion of the divine." Since the Spirit who has inspired this book is passion and love, the man who has once experienced this "divine taste" can never again turn away. Even the mighty waters of boredom, which every study necessarily involves, will not be able to destroy this love. The final object of theological instruction does not consist in the imparting of knowledge, but in the development of the "theological eros." If this succeeds, the small spark becomes a conflagration which can inflame the entire world.

Thus we raise our voice in a complaint which is perhaps also an accusation: Why is there so much weakness and fragility in Christianity? Obviously, because the word has been dulled. We are taken up with New Testament exegesis and frequently

---

4. Origen, *Commentary on Jeremiah*, Migne, PG 13, 544C.

lose ourselves in spiritualistic conclusions. The bread of the Old Testament is not broken enough. And still the Catholic Church is, much more than we dare to realize, *the* Church of the Bible. The liturgical missal is almost exclusively Old Testament in its sung texts. If we would remove the Old Testament from our liturgy the Church would be without song. Take away the powerful' readings from Law and Prophets from the liturgical year, and Christianity is made incomplete. The Old Testament is neither old nor ancient; it is a living reality in our midst. But how many of us recognize the power coming from this book? Today, more than ever, we must call upon the tidings of the Old Testament, in order to recognize the hand of Yahweh in a world on the verge of collapse. Yahweh is a God of history, and he directs the chaos of human history towards a goal and purpose he has set.

The concluding words of this introduction are taken from Origen, one of the greatest Scripture scholars and interpreters of the Greek Church, and for that matter, the whole Church: "If we have once admitted that these writings owe their origin to the creator of the world, we must be convinced that whatever is encountered by those who examine into the fundamental meaning of the world will also be met with in the study of Scripture. The further we progress in reading, the higher the mountain of mysteries towers above us. And just as a man who sets out upon the sea in a tiny ship is unafraid so long as he is close to the land but, when he gradually approaches the high seas and the waves begin to swell and he begins to be lifted high upon their crests or, when they gape open and he begins to be swarmed under into the abyss, it is then that his spirit is seized by a monstrous fear and anxiety for having entrusted such a tiny ship to such monstrous floods — this is the experience we seem to have when, from the smallness of our merit and the narrowness of our spirit we dare to approach so wide a sea of mysteries." [5]

---

5. Origen, *Homily on Genesis.*

CONTENTS

FOREWORD   v
ABBREVIATIONS   xvii
INTRODUCTION   xxi

SECTION ONE
SAMUEL, THE LAST OF THE JUDGES

Chapter I: At the Portals of Destruction   5
  A) Samuel, The "Child of God"   5
  B) The Sons of Belial   14
  C) The Catastrophe   19
    1) The war with the Philistines   19
    2) The loss of the Ark (1 S 4, 3-22)   22
    3) The Ark of the Covenant among the Philistines   24

Chapter II: Prophet and Reformer (1 S 7, 2–8, 22)   29
    1) Opposition to the Gods of Canaan   29
    2) The war with the Philistines   32
    3) The demand for a king   34

Chapter III: The Books of Samuel   39
    1) Name and position in the canon   40
    2) Literary genre   41
    3) The author   42
    4) History of the text   45

SECTION TWO
THE KINGSHIP OF SAUL

Chapter IV: Saul's Election (1 S 9–12)   53
    1) Anointed by Samuel (1 S 9, 1–10, 16)   55
    2) The royal election at Mizpah (1 S 10, 17-27)   60
    3) The deliverance of Jabesh-Gilead (1 S 11, 1–12, 25)   62
    4) Samuel's abdication — confirmation of Saul's kingship in Gilgal   67

Chapter V: Saul's Rejection (1 S 13—15)   71
   1) Saul's war against the Philistines (1 S 13—14)   72
   2) The war against the Amalekites and Saul's rejection (1 S 15)   79

Chapter VI: Saul and David between Love and Hate   87
  A) David at Saul's Court (1 S 15, 35—21, 1)   90
   1) Anointed by Samuel (1 S 16, 1-3)   91
   2) David before Saul (1 S 16, 14-23)   97
   3) David's fight with Goliath (1 S 17, 1-54)   103
   4) The rival (1 S 18, 1—12, 1)   114
  B) David as Fugitive (1 S 21, 2—27, 12)   125
   1) David in Nob (1 S 21, 1-10) and the blood-bath in Gibeah
    (1 S 22, 6-23)   126
   2) The fool at Gath (1 S 21, 11-16)   132
   3) Outlaw chief in the wilderness (1 S 22, 1—27, 12)   132
   4) David as vassal of the Philistines   143
  C) The Catastrophe on Mount Gilboa (1 S 28 — 2 S 1)   145
   1) Full scale attack by the Philistines   145
   2) Saul and the medium (1 S 28, 5-25)   148
   3) The battle on Mount Gilboa (Gelboe)   153
   4) David's lament   155

SECTION THREE
DAVID'S KINGDOM

Chapter VII: David, King of Judah   163

Chapter VIII: David, King over All Israel   175
  A) War with the Philistines (2 S 5, 17-25)   176
   1) The battle at Baal-Perazim (2 S 5, 12-21)   176
   2) The battle at Bekaim (2 S 5, 22-25)   178
  B) Jerusalem as Capital   179
   1) The conquest of Jerusalem   182
   2) Construction of David's city   187
   3) David's family   190
  C) Entry of the Ark of the Covenant   191
  D) The Great Promise and Covenant with David   196
   a) "House" (bayit)   200
   b) "Seed" (zera')   201
   c) "Son of God"   201
   d) "Forever" ('ôlām)   203

Chapter IX: Securing the Kingdom from Without   207
   1) Push to the Mediterranean   207
   2) War with Moab   209

3) War with Ammon and Aram (2 S 8, 1-12; 10, 1-19)   210
    a) The battle at Rabbath-Ammon (2 S 10, 1-4)   212
    b) The battle at Ḥelam (2 S 10, 15-19)   214
    c) The battle at Hamath (2 S 8, 1-12)   215
4) The war with Edom (2 S 8, 13-14)   216
5) Subjugation of the Canaanite cities   217
6) The treaty with Hiram of Tyre   218

Chapter X: The Internal Organization of the Kingdom   221
    1) The captain of the army   222
    2) The Mazkir   222
    3) The priest (kōhᵃnîm)   223
    4) The scribe (sôphēr)   224
    5) Forced labor   224
    6) The privy council   225

Chapter XI: Family Tragedy and Crisis in the Kingdom (1 S 9–74) 227
    A) Family Tragedies   230
    1) David's adultery with Bath-Sheba (2 S 11)   230
    2) The rape of Tamar (2 S 13, 1-22)   238
    B) Crisis in the Kingdom   241
    1) Absalom's revolt   243
        a) Absalom's family (2 S 14, 25-27)   243
        b) Preparation for the revolt (2 S 15, 1-12)   244
        c) David's flight from Absalom (2 S 15, 13–17, 29) 246
        d) Absalom's seizure of power (2 S 16, 15–17, 23)   249
        e) The end of Absalom (2 S 17, 24–29, 9)   252
    2) Revolt of the Benjaminite Sheba (2 S 20, 1-22) 255
    3) The end of Saul's posterity (2 S 21, 1-14)   258
    4) Census and pestilence (2 S 24)   262
    5) "The last words of David" (2 S 23, 1-7)   268

SECTION FOUR

SOLOMON IN ALL HIS GLORY

Chapter XII: Theology of History   277
    A) The Books of Kings   278
    1) Title and content   279
    2) The sources   279
    3) Composer and date of composition   280
    B) The Books of Chronicles   282
    1) Title and content   282
    2) The sources   283
    3) Author and time of composition   284
    4) Historical value of Chronicles   285

Chapter XIII: The Battle for Succession   287
   1) Adonijah's attempted coup (1 K 1, 5ff.)   288
   2) David's testament and death (1 K 2, 1-12)   291
   3) Settling with the conspirators (1 K 2, 13-46)   294

Chapter XIV: The Sun King of Israel   297
   1) "A wise and discerning mind" (1 K 3, 12)   298
   2) The new administration   300
   3) The Solomonic kingdom in the midst of the Ancient
      Near East   309
   4) Trade and mining   313
      a) Commerce in horses and chariots (1 K 10, 28-29)   314
      b) The Queen of Sheba (1 K 10, 1-13)   316
      c) Caravans to Tarshish (?) and Ophir   317

Chapter XV: Solomon the Builder   323
  A) Construction of the Temple   323
   1) The house of Yahweh   324
   2) The Cherubim   328
   3) The "Pillars of the World"   332
   4) The "Mountain of God"   336
   5) The "Primordial Sea"   341
   6) Yahweh's kingship and cosmic symbolism   343
   7) The consecration of the Temple   347
  B) Palace Construction   350

Chapter XVI: Signs of Collapse   355
   1) Pagan sacrifice in Jerusalem   355
   2) Mortgage of Israelite cities with Hiram   357
   3) Revolt of Edom   358
   4) The revolt of Damascus   358
   5) The revolt of the forced laborers   360
   6) Solomon's death and burial   361

Chapter XVII: Divided Kingdom and Divided Faith   365
   1) Political division   365
   2) Division in faith   368
Appendix: The Chronology of the United Kingdom   374
   1) Reckoning time in terms of the "Year of Salvation"   375
   2) Secular chronologies   377

SECTION FIVE
THE GOLDEN AGE OF HEBREW LITERATURE

Chapter XVIII: "The Psalms of David"   385

A) Post-Reformation Interpretation of the Psalms   385
   1) Word and history   388
   2) God's spirit and human congeniality   388
   3) "Pneumatic exegesis"   389
   4) The "de-sanctification" of scripture   390
   5) "Sitz im Leben"   392
   6) Cult and song   394
   7) Catholic interpretation of the Psalms   397
B) Evolution of the Psalter   400
   1) The five books of Psalms   400
   2) The Yahwistic and Elohistic redaction   401
   3) Collections of Psalms   402
   4) The dating of the individual Psalms   403
C) The Psalms as Poetry   409
   1) Rhythmic laws   409
   2) Headings and titles   411

Chapter XIX: The Solomonic Wisdom Literature   417
A) The Proverbs of Solomon   420
   1) Structure of the Book   421
   2) Appropriation of foreign culture   423
   3) The Solomonic collections (H and V)   427
   4) The house of wisdom (Collection I, Ch. 1–9)   429
B) Solomonic Lyric: The Song of Songs   434
   1) Mystical and mythical interpretation   435
   2) Collection of popular love songs   437
   3) Solomonic courtly song   438
   4) Prophetic mystique of love   443

INDEX   447

ABBREVIATIONS

AASOR	Annual of the American School of Oriental Research
ABEL	F. M. Abel, *Géographie de la Palestine* (Études Bibliques), Paris, vol. I, 1933, vol. II, 1938
AfO	E. Weidner, *Archiv für Orientforschung*, Graz
AJA	American Journal of Archaeology
ANEP	J. P. Pritchard, *The Ancient Near East in Pictures relating to the Old Testament*, Princeton Univ. Press, 1954
ANET	J. P. Pritchard, *Ancient Near Eastern Texts relating to the Old Testament*, Princeton Univ. Press, 1955
AnglTR	Anglican Theological Review
Ann. PEF	Annual of the Palestine Exploration Fund, London
AnOr	Anacleta Orientalia, Rome
Ant.	Flavius Josephus, *Antiquitates Judaicae, Jüdische Altertümer*
AO	Alter Orient
AOB	H. Gressmann, *Altorientalische Bilder zum Alten Testament*, Berlin/Leipzig, 1927
AOT	H. Gressmann, *Altorientalische Texte zum Alten Testament*, 1926
APAW	Abhandlungen der Preussischen Akademie der Wissenschaften, Berlin
ARM	Archives Royales de Mari, Paris
Arch	Archaeology
ArOr	Archiv Orientálni
AT	Altes Testament
ATD	Hentrich and Weiser, *Das Alte Testament Deutsch*, Göttingen
BA	The Biblical Archaeologist
BASOR	Bulletin of the American Schools of Oriental Research

BB	Bonner Bibelkommentar
Bibl	Biblica
BiblArch	The Biblical Archaeologist
BibLex	H. Haag, *Bibellexicon*
BibLit	Bibel und Liturgie
BHK	R. Kittel, *Biblica Hebraica*, adapted by Stuttgart, 1954
BJRL	K. Galling, The Bulletin of the John Rylands Library
BK	M. Noth, *Biblischer Kommentar, Altes Testament*, Neukirchen
BRL	Biblisches Reallexicon
BZ	Biblische Zeitschrift, Neue Folge, Paderborn
BZAW	Beihefte zur ZAW
CalwK	Calwer Kommentar: Die Botschaft des Alten Testaments, Stuttgart
CBQ	The Catholic Biblical Quarterly
ClamB	Pirot-Clamer, *La Sainte Bible*, Latin and French text with both exegetical and theological comment, Paris
DB	Vigouroux, *Dictionaire de la Bible*, Paris, 1861-1912
DBS	Supplément au Dictionaire de la Bible, Paris, 1926
DOT	Winton-Thomas, *Documents to the Old Testament*
EB	Echter Bibel, Würzburg
EinlAT	O. Eissfeldt, Einleitung in das Alte Testament unter Einschluss der Apokryphen und pseudepigraphen sowie der apokryphen und pseudepigraphenartigen Qumrān-Schriften. Entstehungsgeschichte des Alten Testaments, Tubingen, 1956
EnchBibl	Enchiridion Biblicum. Documenta ecclesiastica Sacram Scripturam spectantia, Rome, 1956
EncMikr	Encyklopaedia Mikra'it. Encyclopaedia Biblica. Thesaurus rerum biblicarum, Hebrew University, Jerusalem, 1950
EphThLov (ETL)	Ephemerides Theologicae Lovanienses
ET	The Expository Times
EvT	Evangelische Theologie
FF	Forschungen und Fortschritte, Berlin
Fs	Festschrift
GAV	H. Schmökel, *Geschichte des Alten Vorderasien*, Leiden, 1957

GTT	J. Simons, *The Geographical and Topographical Texts of the Old Testament*, Leiden, 1959
GVA	A. Moortgat, *Geschichte Vorderasien bis zum Hellenismus*, Munchen, 1950
HAT	Handbuch zum Alten Testament
HistM (HM)	Fritz Kern, *Historia Mundi*, 1952
HUCA	Hebrew Union College Annual, Cincinnati
IEJ	Israel Exploration Journal, Jerusalem
IntBib	The Interpreters Bible. A Commentary in twelve volumes, New York
JAOS	The Journal of the American Oriental Society
JBL	The Journal of Biblical Literature
JEArch	Journal of Egyptian Archaeology
JerB	Jerusalem Bible
JNES	The Journal of Near Eastern Studies
JSS	The Journal of Semitic Studies
KAT	E. Sellin, *Kommentar zum Alten Testament*, Leipzig
KB	Keilschriftliche Bibliothek
LexVT	L. Koehler – W. Baumgartner, *Lexicon in Veteris Testamenti Libros*, Leiden, 1953
LXX	Septuaginta
Migne, PG	Migne, *Patres Greci*
Migne, PL	Migne, *Patres Latini*
MiscBibl	Mischellania Biblica
MT	R. Kittel, *Masoretischer Text nach der Biblica Hebraica*, 1954
NouvRevThéol	Nouvelle Revue Théologique
OLZ	Orientalische Literaturzeitung, Leipzig
Or	Orientalia, Rome
PEQ	Palestine Exploration Quarterly, London
PG	Migne, *Patres Greci*
PL	Migne, *Patres Latini*
RA	E. Eberling and Br. Meisnner, *Reallexicon der Assyriologie*
RB	Revue Biblique, École Biblique, Jerusalem
RCB	Rivista di Cultura Biblica
REHM	Die Bücher der Könige, Echter Bibel, Würzburg, 1949
RSR	Recherches de Science Religieuse

Rev HistRel	Revue de l'Histoire des Religions, Paris
SAT	Gunkel — Gressmann, *Die Schriften des Alten Testaments,* Göttingen
ST	Studia Theologica
TGI	K. Galling, *Textbuch zur Geschichte Israeis,* Tubingen, 1950
ThLZ	Theologische Literaturzeitung, Leipzig
ThZ	Theologische Zeitschrift, Basel
TTZ	Trierer Theologische Zeitschrift
UM	C. H. Gordon, *Ugaritic Manual,* Rome, 1955
VD	Verbum Domini
VT	Vetus Testamentum
WTJ	Westminster Theological Journal
ZAW	Zeitschrift für Alttestamentliche Wissenschaft
ZDMG	Zeitschrift der Deutschen Morgenländischen Gesellschaft
ZDPV	Zeitschrift des Deutschen Palästinavereines
ZKT	Zeitschrift für Katholische Theologie, Innsbruck
ZTK	Zeitschrift für Theologie und Kirche

THE SACRAMENT OF THE WORD

JUST as Genesis does not present a natural science account of
the origins of the world, the historical books of the Bible do not
mean to portray the profane-history evolution of Israel in the
world picture of the Ancient Near East. The presentation is far
too incomplete for that. Idyll-like narrative sections, which have
lost their orientation for the totality, stand side by side with annal-
like lists of regnal years, which only hint at the manifold course
of actual history. And still these varied sources are animated by
a unified trait. It is not the history of the Ancient Near East that
is written here, history that would be of interest only to the
professional historian or the specialist; in the historical books of
the Bible it is God's activity with man, particularly with the
people of God, that is presented in all its sublimity and despair. In
Israel, it is true, "we see the blossoming of a youthful historical
composition which finds no parallel in the entire realm of the
Ancient Near East," [1] but the "words of the days" (*dibrê hayyāmîm*), as the Israelites named their historical books, are only
the body into which the inspired Spirit breathes the soul of
God's word.

It is thus the object of the Biblical historical books to portray
both the human "days and works," as they are recognizable

---

1. A. Alt, *Kleine Schriften,* II (1953), 34.

against the background of the Ancient Near East, and the eternally valid word of God, which appeals to every age. Biblical historical narrative necessarily turns into a theology of history.

The problem of Old Testament theology has been directed along new paths primarily by the works of Gerhard von Rad.[2] Everything historical, no matter how important or worthy of knowing it is in itself, belongs, in his judgment, to the realm of history of religion, as the study developed prior to the first world war. It is not the historical element in itself, the event which actually happened in human history, according to von Rad, which was of interest to the writer of Biblical history; "the actual course of this history was now beyond the memory of any man" (p. 14). Behind the sources there were, he claims, various cult texts, liturgies, and creed formulas, which had already transformed profane history and interpreted it in terms of salvation history. The Bible does not present immediate historical recollections, but rather the expression of credal elements; it is not so much a document of ancient history as a creed of Old Testament faith. Obviously, these credal elements presuppose historical facts, which, however, have been transformed by faith and elevated to a higher plane. The Old Testament is thus, primarily, kerygma, witness, and not so much a witness to history as a witness to Old Testament faith. The course of ancient history can no longer be grasped in terms of this witness; as such it had no real interest for the Biblical "history writers." A chronological ordering of the course of ancient history can no longer be drawn up on this basis; the creed formula is not interested in describing the historical event; its purpose is rather to describe and celebrate the salvific deeds of God, continually reenacted in liturgy and cult. To sum it up in its simplest formulation, Gerhard von Rad regards the Old Testament historical books as credal writings and witnesses to faith. This is his greatest merit. The Old Testament books are thus rescued from their literary and religion-history isolation and introduced into the community of Old Testament faith. The books of the Old Testament are owing to the faith of the Old Testament "church." It is true that von Rad is adamant in defending the historicity of these credal elements; this involves the further question of why he does not equally stress the historicity of the facts that they celebrate. His answer: "The search for the historicity of what is testified in faith can never be given up; otherwise this purely theological kerygma is left hanging in the air and it turns into blind faith, divorced from all reality." [3]

---

2. G. von Rad, *Theologie des Alten Testaments*, I: *Die Theologie der geschichtlichen Überlieferungen Israels* (Munich, 1957).

3. V. Hamp, *Besprechung des Werkes von Rad*, BZ, NF 2 (1958), 307.

The object of our investigation can never be merely to examine into the "credal myths of ancient Israel," but rather the actual course of the history of the Old Testament people of God. This objective, furthermore, is actually achievable in terms of the Old Testament documents of faith. To inquire merely into the testimony of faith and not to examine the realities attested would be going only half way into the problem. Obviously we must avoid a one-sided, rationalistic historical methodology, treating only those elements as actual facts which are verified in history, which are significant in the broader area of humanity. We must never forget that history has windows and doors which are always open to the intervention of the divine. It is only in our attempt at a full synthesis of divine revelation and human history together that the full testimony of the Old Testament, in all its "divine-human" magnitude, can ever be grasped. "The work of the Biblical theologian is accomplished along the outer margins of human existence. He must attempt something that must seem impossible to many, and blasphemy to some. He can only accomplish his purpose when he remains constantly aware of the mandate which is imposed by the nature of his objective." [4] The Biblical theologian must combine two elements; he must be an historian who delves into the testimony of times past with all the means at his disposal; but even more so he must be a theologian, always prepared, but never over-hasty, to recognize the openness of history, the unexpected emergence of something new in the world.

The divine-human dynamic which is thus involved is, according to Cardinal Newman, to be ascribed to the "sacramental character" of Scripture.[5] The written word is the veil and sign of the hidden, divine reality and, when it is approached in the proper spirit of faith, it is a source of grace. The ideal Scripture scholar is not the philologist who has no religious orientation, but rather the scholar who is also a man of faith, who stands in

---

4. M. Diberius, *Wozu Theologie?* ThLZ (1949), 140.
5. Seynaeve, *Cardinal Newman's Doctrine on Holy Scripture*, ThR 50 (1954), 131-136.

spiritual relationship with the entire Church. The inspiration of
Scripture, it is true, is the extraordinary endowment of a human
author which enables him to compose literary works under
divine guidance and enlightenment; but for a book to become
part of Holy Scripture, there must also be the testimony of its
divine authorship and origin, pronounced by the Church of Old
or New Testament. Inspiration and canonicity are two concepts
which need to be distinguished, but they are intimately bound up
together. God makes use of both of them in forming his Church.
K. Rahner [6] refers to the inspiration of Scripture as Church
recognition of divine authorship, which is not restricted to the
Church of the New Testament but, with equal right, applies to
that of the Old Testament. In both Testaments it is the history of
one and the same salvation which is revealed. The foundation of
Israelite historical writing is faith in the one God, and thus a faith
in the unity of history. The one God, however, at various and distinct times, has spoken into human history; the Bible thus becomes
a continuing "address of God" [7] to his people, who are called to
response and responsibility. This concept lays bare the ultimate
foundation of human history. "God's word and God's heart" (2
S 7, 21) move human history towards its goal. It is a genuinely
Biblical expression when we say that God's own heart is beating
in the midst of history. In the prophetic interpretation of history,
history turns into one single drama of love between Yahweh and
his chosen bride-nation, a drama which, in large part, turns into
a moving tragedy of human faithlessness. God is a jealous God,
and he will not suffer any rival to his love. Consequently, history
turns into a constant cycle of rejection and election. It is the
"mouth of Yahweh" (1 S 15, 24) which determines the rise
and fall. The succeeding epochs are determined by "the mouth,
the word, and the heart of God." [8] This implies an abbreviation of

---

6. K. Rahner, *Über die Schriftinspiration*, ZkTh 78 (1956), 137-168. / Claus
   Schedl, *Die Inspiration der Bibel, neu durchdacht*, BibLit 22 (1954/55),
   33-38.
7. W. Zimmerli, *Das AT als Anrede. Beiträge zur evangelischen Theologie*
   24 (1956), 9-36.
8. G. Oestborn, *Yahweh's Words and Deeds: A Preliminary Study into the
   OT Presentation of History*, Uppsala Univ. Arsskrift 7 (1951), 3-80.

the historical point of view, if we want to interpret the Old Testament one-sidedly in terms of its fulfillment, and transpose later, more developed concepts into an earlier age. This would lose sight of the inner divine-human drama. It must rather be our objective to portray this "ascent from the heights" in terms of its gradual growth and development. This objective already determines the self-contained acts of the divine drama. Prehistory forms the great overture to the whole of human history; in the patriarchal era, the horizon narrows from universal history to the history of one people, Israel; the formation of this people, the federation of the twelve tribes at Sinai, up to the entry into the promised land, makes up a further act; from the end of the era of judges down to the fall of the Davidic-Solomonic kingdom, we have a distinct unit, a compact historical epoch.

The Book of Judges ends on a shrill note of dissonance. Samson, it is true, in a final fury of spirit, did succeed in uprooting the pillars of the temple of Dagon, so that the whole edifice collapsed. But he himself perished in the ruins. All his heroic deeds have left no visible trace behind. Despite his manifold accomplishments, he was a solitary warrior at an all but abandoned post. On Israel as a whole he had hardly any effect at all. The other tribes soon lost their feeling of mutual solidarity to such a point that they began waging war against each other. Idolatry, violence, rape, civil war, and constant threats from the enemy outside the boundaries combined to make the final years of the era of the judges into a nadir of national and religious despair. Individual men, it is true, acting under the impulse of the Spirit who had fallen upon them, did manage to wring a temporary freedom from their oppressors and to accomplish certain religious reforms, but all this was only a temporary success, destined to pass without lasting issue.

The condition is well described in the sad sentence of Jg 21, 24: "And the people of Israel departed from there at that time, every man to his tribe and family, and they went out from there every man to his inheritance. In those days there was no king in Israel; every man did what was right in his own eyes." This internal division in Israel was seized upon primarily by

the Philistines. The stormy inroads of the Sea Peoples had dealt
them a severe defeat along the Asiatic coast. Along the coastal
plains they founded their cities, from which they sought to
penetrate into the mountain country. In terms of world history,
there are only two possible solutions to this tension: Either
Palestine must become, as its name implied, completely Philistine,
or, if the Israelites could succeed in uniting to a common purpose,
Israelite. The odds were all with the Philistines. But in an hour
in which the cause of Israel seemed to be completely lost, the
people called for a king who would weld them together into a
national power and achieve a victory over the Philistines. Kingship in Israel was not the result of any internal development. It
certainly did not correspond to the divine kingship of Yahweh,
which had been established on Sinai; it was rather the consequence of a hostile pressure threatening from without.

Samuel, as the last of the judges, is also the prophet of this
great political change. He succeeded in initiating the religious
reform, in renewing the ancient faith in Yahweh, in once again
making Israel fit for military service. His most difficult mission
was the transition of the free federation of the twelve tribes into
a kingdom. The first king he anointed, Saul, stirred up the
greatest expectation, which quickly succumbed to an even bitterer
disillusionment. The figure of Saul is clouded by a note of un-
speakable tragedy. It is only with the second anointed one, with
David, that Israel entered upon an unparalleled era of religious
and political ascendancy. David created a mighty empire whose
sphere of influence extended from the stream of Egypt to the
great river. In the west, he opened the way to the Mediterranean.
By the incorporation of Edom, he achieved an access to the Red
Sea and, beyond that, into the fable-shrouded land of Ophir. The
hostility against the ancient hereditary enemies was forgotten,
the Canaanite cities were incorporated into the new kingdom,
the twelve tribes were united under the elective monarchy of
David, and a world empire was created such as Israel was never
again to experience in all her later history. Mighty treasures,
trophies of war and payment of tribute, flowed into Jerusalem.
David laid the foundation upon which Solomon continued to

build. It was Solomon, in his building of the Temple, who gave religious splendor to the kingdom. Under Solomon, the court of Jerusalem was not only the political, but also the intellectual center of the Ancient Near East. Under him, wisdom poetry and lyric flourished to an unheard of degree. The great promise of the prophet Nathan, foretelling the abiding permanency of the house of David, was a foundation for the future messianic promises of the prophets. It is no wonder that the era from the end of the judges down to the splitting of the kingdom has always been considered the most splendid era of Israel's history, and can truly be called the "Golden Age of David."

After the death of Solomon, the mighty kingdom collapsed, not only politically, but also in the sphere of religion. From this time on, the history of the kingdoms of Judah and Israel runs along separate paths. We are fully justified in treating the preceding "Golden Age of David" as a compact unity, in one volume.

The extent to which this epoch has determined the historical thinking of later ages can be seen from the fact that its two principal characters, David and Solomon, are interpreted as types of Christ; David symbolizes the struggle and the Passion, while Solomon symbolizes the triumph of Christ.[9]

Such considerations abstract completely from the historical reality and turn into a symbolical expression of faith. It must be the constant preoccupation of the Biblical theologian to abandon all this symbolism, listening instead to the reality of the word, just as it first came from the "mouth and heart of God" towards the end of the first millennium before Christ, addressed to God's chosen ones, in an ancient language, in a time that has slipped away from us; but at the same time, as a faithful "meditator upon the word" (Ebener) he will realize that these words are "silver refined in a furnace on the ground, purified seven times" (Ps 11/12, 7), actually a "sacrament," in which the presence of God tents among humanity.

---

9. J. M. Congar, *David et Salomon, types du Christ en ses deux avènements*, La Vie Spirituelle, 400 (1954), 323-340.

FOR THE HISTORY OF THE ROYAL ERA

In this connection, only the most important treatments of the history of the kings of Israel are mentioned; special commentaries and studies are listed in the course of the individual sections:

B. Stade, *Geschichte des Volkes Israel* (Berlin, 1887). (Extremely rationalistic concept of history, frequently with a depreciatory attitude towards the Bible.) / B. Baentsch, *David und sein Zeitalter* (Leipzig, 1907). / J. Hastings, *The Greater Men and Women of the Bible* (Edinburgh, 1914). (Extensive biographies of Samuel, Saul, David, etc., scientifically established, but designed for edification.) / L. Denoyers, *Histoire du peuple hebreu des Juges a la captivite* (Paris) I (La periode des Juges) 1922; II (Saul et David) 1930; III (Salomon — la religion et la civilisation sous les trois premiers rois) 1930 (Exhaustive work on this period, written with scientific acumen and brilliant style.) / A. Bertholet, *Kurturgeschichte Israel* (Göttingen, 1920) (rationalistic). / R. Kittel, *Geschichte des Volkes Israels* (Gotha, 1925) (a standard work). / J. Pedersen, *Israel: Its Life and Culture* (Copenhagen I-II, 1926; III-IV, 1940). / W. O. E. Oesterley, *A History of Israel, I: From Exodus to 586* (Oxford, 1932). / A. Allgeier, *Biblische Zeitgeschichte* (Freiburg i. Br., 1937). / W. F. Albright, *From the Stone Age to Christianity,* 2nd ed. (New York, 1957). / W. Vischer, *Das Christuszeugnis des Alten Testaments* (II, Die Propheten) Zurich, 1942 (Valuable biblical-theological orientation). / M. Noth, *Geschichte Israels* (Göttingen, 1950) (Vast and frequently tendentious overall study, hypercritical on Israel's earlier history). English: *History of Israel* (New York, 1960). / P. Heinisch, *Geschichte des Alten Testaments* (1949). (The best, if somewhat conservative, overall presentation in German Catholic circles). / C. H. Gordon, *Geschichtliche Grundlagen des Alten Testaments* (1956). / R. de Vaux, *Les Institutions de l'Ancient Testament, I: Le nomadisme et ses survivances, institutions familiales, institutions civiles* (Paris, 1958) (A new view on Israel's earlier history).

Geography of Palestine

G. A. Smith, *The Historical Geography of the Holy Land* (London, 1931). (The many editions the book has gone through are sufficient evidence of indispensable value). / F. M. Abel, *Géographie de la Palestine* (Études bibliques) (Paris, 1. Bd. 1933). (Recognized today as the classical work on the geography of Palestine). / G. E. Wright and F. V. Filson, *The Westminster Historical Atlas to the Bible* (Philadelphia, 1953). / L. H. Grollenberg, *Bildatlas zur Bibel.* English: *Atlas of the Bible* (Nelson, 1956). (Indispensable tool). P. Lemarie and D. Baldi, *Atlante storico della*

Bibbia (1955). / Knaur, *Länder der Bibel. Mit 180 Farbbildern und Reliefkarten* (Munich/Zurich, 1958). / R. P. Tellier, *Atlas Historique de l'Ancien Testament* (Paris, 1948). / E. G. Kraeling, *Rand McNally Bible Atlas* (USA, 1956). / M. du Buit, *Géographie de la Terre Sainte* (École Biblique Jerusalem, Paris, 1958).

Biblical Archaeology

Fr. Noetscher, *Biblische Altertumskunde* (Bonner Bibel, 1940). / G. A. Barrois, *Manuel d'archéologie biblique* (Paris I, 1939; II, 1952). / W. F. Albright, *The Religion of Israel in the Light of Archaeological Excavations* (New York, 1969). / A. Jirku, *Die Ausgrabungen in Palästina-Syrien* (Halle, 1956). *Die Welt der Bibel* (Stuttgart, 1957). An inexhaustible source for biblical history and archaeology is the *Encyclopaedia Biblica, Thesaurus rerum biblicarum.* Hebrew title: *Encyclopaedia Miqra'it,* published by the Hebrew University in Jerusalem, I, 1955; II, 1954; III, 1958.

SECTION ONE

SAMUEL, THE LAST OF THE JUDGES

THE author of the Book of Samuel is masterful in presenting the introduction of kingship into Israel. He is fond of contrast; on the one hand he describes the idyll in the house of Elkanah, the pilgrimages, the barren Hannah. This brings the story to its first moving climax. Hannah regards her barrenness as a punishment from God. In an effort to escape this curse, she seeks help in prayer before the face of Yahweh. Her prayer is heard, and she gives birth to a son who is to have far-reaching influence on the future history of Israel. For Samuel is the man whose mission it is to accomplish the transition from the kingship of Yahweh to an earthly kingship. His figure shares the spotlight of two distinct epochs. The simple appeal of the story of Samuel's childhood is all but irresistible. Despite the much suffering there is perfect harmony in subjection to the will of God. It is not too difficult to decide whether this family from Ramathaim represents a rare exception in the midst of a brutal era, or whether the families of Israel all lived in a like reverential fear of God.

Our narrator contrasts this strongly religious rural family idyll in Ramathaim with the situation at the sanctuary in Shiloh, which cries to heaven for vengeance. In terms of pure narrative, this contrast achieves the background he requires to motivate the introduction of kingship into Israel. In the sanctuary of God there is pure godlessness. From this central point, it was eating its way into the body of the nation, like a devastating plague. It called down the judgment of God upon it. Like a scourge of God, the Philistines overran the country. As a last resort, the Israelites brought up the Ark of the Covenant. But even this was no longer in a position to save them. Israel was beaten, the sanctuary at Shiloh was destroyed, the Israelite tribes in the Palestinian mountain country were completely disarmed and subjugated to the hard rule of the Philistines. There was little prospect of shaking off this distasteful yoke. Then Yahweh, the God of Israel, stirred up, in Samuel, a man of God, a prophet and judge, who was destined to lead his people from the depths of their humiliation to their most glorious hour, in the kingship of Saul and David. Samuel was still a figure of the older generation, one of the charismatic leaders like the judges. In his eye, kingship was a hateful thing. And still he bowed to the demands of the people and the express will of Yahweh; he anointed the new king. The deeper the religious and national crisis — the sanctuary destroyed, the Ark in the hands of the enemy, the people's capacity for defense successfully broken — the more impressive and significant appears the work which Samuel accomplished in the course of "forty" years, as prophet and judge in Israel.

CHAPTER I

AT THE PORTALS OF DESTRUCTION
A) SAMUEL, THE "CHILD OF GOD"

THE Hebrew text of the first Book of Samuel begins with these words: "And there was . . . ." Many authors think that the word "and" implies that the narrative of the Book of Judges is being continued here. But the Books of Ezekiel and Esther also begin with the word "and." This is merely the Hebrew style of narrative, and it does not permit any conclusions on the subject of the Book's connection with what precedes or follows. Despite the fact that this Hebrew idiom does not authorize any such conclusions, the Book of Samuel, in terms of content, does take up the narrative of the Book of Judges; the first principal figure is Samuel, a judge, just like the other heroes of the Book of Judges.

The first person to be named is a certain Elkanah. His name means: "God has acquired" or better "God has accomplished." Similar names appear also in the Accadian texts.[1] His genealogy is traced back through Jeroham, Elihu, and Tohu as far as Zuph. The same genealogy, with a few variants, is presented by the

---

1. Accadian Ilu-ka-na-a. Cf. K. S. Tallqvist, *Neubabylonisches Namens-buch zu den Geschäftsurkunden* (Leipzig, 1905), 75. Eve too heard the verb *qānâh* in the name of her first son Cain: "I have gotten a man with the help of Yahweh" (Gn 4, 1).

Book of Chronicles, which traces the ancestry further back, as far as Levi (1 Ch 6, 18-23). Upon the occupation of the Promised Land, various cities throughout the whole district of the twelve tribes were assigned to the Levites for their residence. In the mountain country of Ephraim, the city of Ramathaim fell to the Levite Zuph, whose name apparently means "honeycomb." From him stems the family of the Zophites, whose ancestral seat received the epithet Ramathaim-zophim,[2] to distinguish it from other places with similar names. Samuel, the son of Elkanah, thus belongs to the order of the Levites,[3] and by his very birth he was already obligated to serve the Ark of the Covenant. One of Samuel's grandsons later appears in the list of temple singers whom David organized for the service at the sanctuary (1 Ch 6, 16).

Since there are several Ramah's in Palestine, many claim to have been the birthplace of Samuel. The mountain country of Ephraim, in which the village must be situated, extends from Shechem to Bethel. In this general area, some authors have identified Samuel's native city as Ramle, southwest of Lydda, while others identify it with Nebi Samwil, which dominates so much of its surrounding territory, and still others locate it with the Ramah located in the neighborhood of Jerusalem. These are fruitless efforts. Only the two locations of Bet Rima, 20 km, and Rentis, 13 km northeast of Lydda, in the Ephraimite hill country, have any real claim to genuinity. The greater probability centers upon Rentis. The Hebrew text uses the dual form Ramatayim in referring to the place; we may thus conclude to the presence of two (twin) peaks. Modern-day Rentis is actually built upon such a hill with two peaks. On the eastern peak the city was built, and on the western peak was situated the sacrificial site to which Samuel went up. 3 km northeast of Rentis is located, even today, a Mohammedan sanctuary (Wely) called Rigal Sufa, "the men of Zuf," which has perpetuated the memory of the Zophites.[4]

---

2. Unless *sôpîm* is an archaic singular form, a Sophit from Ramathaim. VT 7 (1957), 392.

3. For the Levitical derivation of Samuel's ancestry, cf. E. Tobac — J. Coppens, Les Prophètes d'Israel (1932), I, 124 G. Bressan, 56ff. / Also W. F. Albright, Archaeology and Religion of Israel (1946), 109, 205.

4. H. M. Wiener, The Ramah of Samuel, IPOS 7 (1927), 109-111. / A. Fernandez, La patria di Samuel, Bibl 12 (1931), 119-123. / Abel, II, 428 with bibliography.

Elkanah had two wives. The one was called Hannah (Anna) "grace, graciousness, beauty," and the other Peninnah (Phenenna), "coral pearl." Although Genesis (2, 24) had established monogamy, the taking of several wives seems to have been normal. Particularly when the first wife was childless, a man would take a second. The possession of several wives was considered a sign of wealth. The official law took cognizance of this circumstance and regulated the polygamy by a series of legal norms (Dt 21, 15-17). In such marriages, as we shall later experience in the case of David and Solomon, it was the favorite wife who enjoyed the greater influence. The other wife was the "hated" (Dt 21, 5) or the "provoker and irritator" (1 S 1, 6). Jealousy, constant slighting, and perpetual rivalry did much to disturb the family peace, and the lot of the second wife appears to have been a very bitter one.

The logical development of such a marriage — and we must remember that Elkanah's marriage with his two wives was one of the more successful — is clearly narrated in the account of the annual pilgrimage to the sanctuary at Shiloh. The distance involved is approximately 50 km. The road literally involves a "going up": "Now this man used to go up year by year from his city to worship and to sacrifice to the Lord of Hosts at Shiloh" (1 S 1, 3). Ramathaim lies on a spur of the western chain of hills, with an elevation of approximately 209 m above sea level, while Shiloh is some 680 m above sea level. Shiloh lies in the district of the tribe of Ephraim, "north of Bethel on the east of the highway that goes up from Bethel to Shechem" (Jg 21, 19). Excavations [5] have confirmed its identification with modern Khirbet Selun. The ancient city lay in the midst of a small and fertile plain, surrounded by a rampart of protective hills. Joshua had the Ark of the Covenant set up here, because the place was centrally located and could easily be reached by

---

5. The excavations conducted in 1929 by the Dane H. Kjaer show that Shiloh, in the 12th century B.C., had reached its greatest level of development. For the accounts, cf. A. Mallon, *Les Fouilles danaises de Silo*, Bibl 10 (1929), 370-375. / W. F. Albright, PEQ, (1927), 158.

the tribes from both north and south, as well as those who lived in Transjordan (Jos 18, 1). What Delphi was for the Greeks, Shiloh was for Israel, "the navel of the nation." [6] It was here, despite all the national abuses, that the spiritual weapons of belief in Yahweh were forged. It was no accident that Samuel, the great reformer of faith in Yahweh, came out of Shiloh.

The text of the narrative means to characterize Elkanah as an Israelite faithful to the law; it speaks of his making only one annual pilgrimage to the sanctuary, although the Law prescribes three such pilgrimages (Ex 23, 17): on Easter, Pentecost, and for the Feast of Tabernacles. But in these less refined times, this and other prescriptions of the Law could not be fully carried out. The favorite pilgrimage time was in the fall, after the grape harvest (Jg 21, 19-23).

It is in connection with this pilgrimage narrative that we first encounter the name for God which is the most frequently used: *Yahweh ṣᵉbā'ôt* (Sabaoth). In the Old Testament, this name occurs 260 times, 11 times in the Book of Samuel. The full form of the name is used by David in his battle with Goliath: "You come to me with a sword and with a spear and with a javelin; but I come to you in the name of the Lord of Hosts, the God of the armies of Israel" (1 S 17, 45). The name designates Yahweh as the war God of Israel [7] through whose irresistible power

---

6. C. Toussaint, *Les Origines de la Religion d'Israel* (Paris, 1931).

7. Sᵉbā'ôt is the plural of sābā' and originally means: gathering, crowd, people. In Accadian, sabu, in the singular, means man, soldier. In Israel too ṣᵉbā'ôt was no longer understood as a multitude of people in general; it referred rather to the military band of men, setting out to battle. In an applied sense, it was used to refer to the orderly host of stars (Is 24, 4; Jg 5, 14), the host of heaven and earth (Gn 2, 1). The prophets Amos and Hosea use the expression to refer to Yahweh as the almighty Lord of all the powers of heaven and earth, the creator of the world. LXX translates the word with *Kyrios dunameon,* and the Vulgate with *Dominus virtutum;* there is also the form *Kyrios pantokrator,* "almighty Lord." The form Sabaoth has passed into the English of Church usage, and into many other modern tongues as well. V. Maag, *Jahwäs Heerscharen.* SchweizTheolUmschau 20 (1950), 74-100; especially p. 79. / The most comprehensive analysis of "Lord of hosts" is by B. M. Wambacq, *L'épithète divine Jahve Seba'ot* (1947).

the tribes of Israel were able to subdue the Promised Land. He was their own personal battle lord and king of their nation. As such, it was his to command that the hosts of Israel make an annual appearance before his face.

Shiloh was the home of the high priest Eli (Heli), together with his two sons Hophni and Phinehas (Ophni and Phinees).[8] Eli held the position of high priest and was also judge in Israel; he enjoyed complete religious and political power. But in reality he was only a shadow of what he should have been. We shall soon witness the arbitrary arrogance with which his two sons abused the power entrusted to them.

Elkanah and his family sacrificed a peace offering before the face of Yahweh. It was customary to slaughter the sacrificial animal, the bull, sheep, or goat, in the sanctuary, pour the blood upon the altar, and burn the fat parts upon the altar. The priests received their portion and the rest of the animal was eaten by those who offered the sacrifice, in a sacred banquet, before the

See the evaluation by R. de Vaux RB 55 (1955), 587-590. / O. Eisfeldt, *Jahwe Zebaoth*, MiscAcademica Berolinensia (Berlin, 1950), 128-150. / W. F. Albright understands Yahweh as a hiphil form of the verb: "call into existence, bring forth, create"; Yahweh Sabaoth would thus be the Lord who calls forth and creates the army hosts. JBL 67 (1948), 377-381. / J. Obermann translates: "Rouser of the hosts." JBL 68 (1949), 309-314.

8. The name Eli is probably the abbreviated vocative form of $Y^e\d{h}aw'\bar{e}l\bar{\imath}$, "Long live the All-high!" (cf. 2 Ch 29, 14). The names of his two sons might be of Egyptian origin. Aaron's grandson, who was so adamant in his vengeance on the illicit relationship with the Moabites in Transjordania (Ex 6, 25) was also called Phinebas (Nb 25, 6ff). Phinebas might also be the Hebraized form of the Egyptian name Pi-Nehase, "to be a Moor or Nubian." Moses' wife, too, was a Cushite (Nb 12, 1). The derivation of the name of the second son is not so evident, but it might well mean something like "athlete, warrior," $\d{h}\hat{o}fen$ in Egyptian, "hollow of the hand," or $hfnr$, "hard-headed." Finally, the name of Moses himself is Egyptian in origin. All this goes only to establish the Egyptian tradition within the high-priestly family of Shiloh: W. Spiegelberg, ZDMG 53 (1899), 634; W. F. Albright, *From the Stone Age to Christianity* (1944), 254. / Ricciotti, *History of Israel*, I, 340.

face of Yahweh. This banquet had a festive character, but every year, for Hannah, it was an occasion for despondency and sorrow. Elkanah could give several portions to his second wife Peninnah, according to the number of her children, but Hannah received only one portion; for Yahweh had closed her womb. In the bitterness of her heart, Hannah abandoned the community banquet and went into the temple, to pour out her sorrow in the presence of Yahweh (1 S 1, 9ff). We have here an indication of the fact that individuals were also allowed to appear before Yahweh in his sanctuary, to pray to him.

Eli was sitting on a seat at the door post of the temple of Yahweh (1 S 1, 9), apparently not only to supervise the official worship, but also to fulfill his office as judge, in case suppliants came to seek his decision. It was there that he saw Hannah praying, and first took her for a useless, drunken woman. But when she had revealed the sorrow of her barrenness, he dismissed her with words of consolation.

Hannah corroborated her prayer by a vow. This was in perfect keeping with Old Testament practice. Jacob, on his flight, in Bethel, had pronounced a vow in praying for his speedy return home (Gn 28, 20-22). Jephthah did the same before his campaign against the Ammonites (Jg 11, 30ff). Hannah vowed that if she bore a child and it were a boy, he would belong entirely to Yahweh his whole life long. As a Levite,[9] Samuel was already obligated to service in the sanctuary, but only from his 30th to his 50th year (Nb 4, 23), and then only on specially determined occasions. What Hannah vowed was much more than his mere duty. She also promised that no razor would ever touch the head of her child; she made him a Nazirite. The law for the Nazirites is set down in Nb 6, although the practice does not originate with Moses; it dates back to the most ancient traditions. "The Naziricy was a vow and it implied a special and ir-

---

9. The Levitical background of Samuel is contested by some authors: 1 Ch 6, 22ff is explained in the sense that Elkanah, Samuel's father, has been confused with the Kahathite Elkanah, and accordingly a Levitical genealogy has been constructed for Samuel. The possibility must be admitted, but there is no convincing proof. At all events, Samuel was a *lēwî*, a Levite in the most proper sense of the word, a man bound by vow to the service of the temple. On the derivation and position of the Levites, cf. Albright, *Religion of Israel*, 124, 128, note 42.

revocable belonging to Yahweh. The Hebrew expression *nezîr 'elōhîm* (Jg 13, 5; 16, 17) is to be translated as "consecrated of God." The man who had given himself over to Yahweh was to abstain from certain things, especially the use of wine, and was to guard himself against all uncleanness (touching the dead). Such vows were very widely practiced, either in the sense of a temporary assumption of these obligations, or in the sense of a life-long consecration."[10] The origins of the Naziricy are perhaps to be sought in the concept of sacred war, in which certain individuals dedicated themselves by a vow, which was extremely recognizable in their flowing hair, to wage an unconditioned war against the enemies of Yahweh. This warlike ideal was transformed by the Law into an ascetic concept, which was based upon the priestly laws of abstinence (Nb 6). In the case of Samuel, who was destined to wage war for Yahweh, we can recognize a trace of the ancient Nazirite ideal, consecration to a sacred war.[11]

A year later, Hannah bore a son and gave him the name Samuel. Elsewhere in Scripture it is also customary for the mother to name her child (Gn 4, 25; 32, 31; 41, 51; Ex 18, 4). Here too the mother offers an interpretation of her child's name which cannot be entirely substantiated in terms of our modern linguistic science: "She called his name Samuel, for she said, 'I have asked him of the Lord'" (1 S 1, 20). Many explanations have been advanced for the name Samuel.[12] In comparison with the Ac-

10. G. von Rad, *Theologie des Alten Testaments I* (1958), 71.
11. W. Eichrodt, *Theologie des Alten Testaments I* (1957), 200ff. / M. Noth, Geschichte Israel (1950), 93.
12. The Bible identifies the name of Samuel with the verb *šā'al*, "to ask, to obtain." R. Kimhi postulates a composition with *šā'ûl mē'ēl*, "begged of God": but such a contracted form would be at variance with normal Hebrew practice. / Other authors have divided the name into *šemû-'ēl*, "Name of God." Similar formations would be *penû-'ēl*, "countenance of God," *re'û-'ēl*, "friend of God." Samuel would thus be an abbreviated reference to the miraculous birth of the child. "The name of (him who has presented us with this child) is God." / Jastrow points to Assyrian-Babylonian parallels. The Accadian word *šumu*, name, can also mean "posterity, son"; e.g., *Nabu-šum-ukin*, "Nabu has prepared a name (a son)": *Marduk-šum-ibno*, "Marduk has created a name (son)." Accordingly, Samuel would be called "Son of God," because he was born in a miraculous manner. / G. Bressan, 67ff. / M. Jastrow, *The Name of Samuel and the Stem Sa'al*, JBL 19 (1900), 82-105. / L. Kopf, *Arabische Etymologien und Parallelen*, VT 8 (1958), 209,

cadian name formations, the translation as "son, child of God" appears to be the most probable. Hannah could not find a more suitable name for her child, who was born by the miraculous intervention of God, than "son of God." Samuel was a child of prayer and miracle, a gift of Yahweh himself.

Hannah kept her child at home until his weaning, which, in the Ancient Near East, took place in the third or fourth year of the child's life; [13] she then brought the child into the sanctuary at Shiloh, in order to offer sacrifice and fulfill her vow. She left him there in the keeping of the high priest Eli. God had given her a child and she returned the gift, with equal magnanimity, completely to God. Hannah belongs among the great women of the Bible who were privileged to experience God's miraculous powers in their behalf. The Bible ascribes a song of praise to her composition, a song which she sang to Yahweh in the joy of her heart (1 S 2, 1-10). Since Hannah's song of praise has strongly influenced the New Testament *Magnificat,* it deserves a more thorough examination here.

The song of Hannah, by reason of its poetic power, might well be compared to the song of Deborah. Both are impetuous in their construction, full of bold images, and even bolder in their invincible faith in the power of Yahweh. Hannah's song consists of 17 double verses, each with three accents. This is the classical verse form which is used elsewhere as well in songs of praise, thanksgiving, and triumph. The song is divided into four strophes:

a) INTRODUCTION (1 S 2, 1-2): Three double verses, radiant with jubilation, victorious power over the enemy, and joy at the grace of salvation. All this was possible only because Yahweh is the Holy One, the unshakable rock, who has no equal.

b) PRAISE OF YAHWEH'S WISDOM (2, 3-5): Yahweh is not a distant God who has no care for the history of the world. The Psalm calls him a "God of knowledge." His vision penetrates the world of created things

---

proposes a derivation from the Arabic *sama,* "to be high, exalted." Samuel, accordingly, would mean "God is exalted." / E. Zolli, *Da Eva a Maria,* VD 34 (1956), 127 derives it from the Babylonian *semu simu,* destinatus ad Deum; id quod terminus technicus esset; "puer a Deo in oratione imploratus et ideo destinatus ad Deum."

---

13. E. Neufeld, *Ancient Hebrew Marriage Laws* (London, 1944), 258, 8.

and humanity, to its ultimate depths. Under his penetrating eye, the values of the world begin to falter. The man who is full today will be hungry tomorrow, and the man who is hungry today will feast tomorrow; the man who is a hero today, with his powerful weapons, will stand there tomorrow with his power broken; the lame and halt will be girt with strength. The barren woman, who is despised today, will be the mother of seven. The woman who is surrounded by a throng of children today will be a widow tomorrow. The values of the world are unmasked in all their nothingness. Only the man who has built his life upon Yahweh will be great.

c) PRAISE OF YAHWEH'S OMNIPOTENCE (2, 6-8): Man experiences death and life, the rise and fall of kings, wealth and poverty all about him. All this is not really the world's activity; the only actor in this grotesque world theater is, in the last analysis, Yahweh himself. "The Lord kills and brings to life; he brings down to Sheol and raises up. The Lord makes poor and makes rich; he lifts the needy from the ash heap, to make them sit with princes and inherit a seat of honor." All this he can do only because he is the creator of the world: "For the pillars of the earth are the Lord's and on them he has set the world."

d) YAHWEH JUDGE OF THE WORLD (2, 9-10): It is not a matter of indifference whether man is good or evil. Yahweh's eye is upon the righteous. He protects them along their way, while the path of the godless ends in the night of death. For God thunders down from heaven and holds judgment over all the earth. — The song concludes with a prayer for the king: "May he give strength to his king, and exalt the power of his anointed."

The ideas that this song expresses concerning God, the almighty creator of the world, the redeemer and the judge, are not alien to the religious consciousness of the era of the Judges. The poetic form is no matter for surprise either. The song of Deborah is universally considered to belong among the oldest songs of Israel. As we see from the epics of Ugarit, the poetic art reached a high point of development in Canaan of the second millennium. The author of the books of Samuel, who made frequent use of more ancient sources, also had this ancient hymn at his disposal, and he freely worked it into his historical narrative. Especially verse 5b: "The barren has borne seven, but she who has many children is forlorn," may have been the factor which prompted him to put it in the mouth of Hannah. The petition for the king was, obviously, added to the more ancient hymn only after the introduction of monarchy. A messianic interpretation of the concluding words "May he exalt the horn (power) of his anointed (Messiah)" was certainly not within the horizons of Israelite faith at the time of Hannah. It is only in the retrospect of the New Testament, where Zachary praises the raising of the "horn of salvation" (Lk 1, 69) in the Benedictus, that the song of Hannah can be reinterpreted in messianic terms. Particularly it is the *Magnificat* (Lk 1, 46) that takes up the ideas of the song of Hannah and applies them to the beginnings of the messianic era of salvation.[14]

B) THE SONS OF BELIAL

The description of the rural religious idyll of Ramathaim is now followed, in vigorous strokes and sharp contrasts, by the description of conditions at the sanctuary in Shiloh. The first narrative reached its climax in the birth of Samuel, the "son of God." The life of his parents and his own early life were entirely permeated and determined by the Law of Yahweh. Life and activity at Shiloh, on the other hand, is given its characteristic stamp by the sons of Eli, who are called "sons of Belial" (1 S 2, 12). Whether this word Belial [15] means merely "good for nothing" or is actually to be interpreted as "sons of hell," there is no harder judgment that the Old Testament could speak upon the sons of Eli than these terrible words: "They have no regard for the Lord" (1 S 2, 12). As the sons of the high priest, they should have known Yahweh and his law, and recognized it. But they had no concern for God or God's law and they lived as if there was no punishment for rejecting God. Their undoing has already begun. Unavailing were the repeated warnings of their aged father (2, 22-26), unavailing the threats of the man of God (2, 27-36), unavailing the word of God itself, spoken through the boy Samuel (3, 1-18). Their ears had become deaf, because Yahweh meant to destroy them (2, 26).

---

14. G. Bressan, *Il Cantico di Anna,* Bibl 33 (1952), 76-89. / E. F. Sutcliffe, *Beziehungen zum Magnificat. Scripture I* (1947), 56ff. / F. Stummer, *Die Vulgata zum Canticum Annae. Ein Entwurf zu einem wissenschaftlichen Kommentar,* TheolZ 1 (Munich, 1950), 10-19.
15. Belial is a composite Hebrew noun, *beli,* negation form, "nothing," and *yā'al,* "to do, to be worth": hence, "Good for nothing, scoundrel." In this sense LXX translates it as "worthless scoundrel." — Jerome, however, heard a deeper reference in the word: Belial is a person, the devil, the *diabolus.* In 2 S 22, 5, Belial is used as a parallel to *še'ôl,* "underworld, death." 2 Cor 6, 15 uses the same word for the devil. There is also a Babylonian netherworld deity called *belili.* P. Jouon, Bibl 5 (1924), 178-183. / H. Kaupel, *Die Damonen im AT* (1930), 124.

This infernal storm of perdition is momentarily interrupted and we see Samuel, the servant of Yahweh (2, 11. 18. 26; 3, 1. 19). We can only admire the narrative skill which has created a work of such great dramatic power. The catastrophe, however, is in the making.

The sons of Eli had no regard for the sacrificial laws. Modern scholarship had recognized the fact that the sacrificial laws of the Book of Leviticus are not the result of later, post-exilic legislation, but rather present a very ancient cultual practice. In peace offerings and sacrifices of praise, the fat parts were burned on the altar, while the brisket and the right shoulder went to the priest. Eli's sons, however, were not satisfied with the portion that was legally theirs; they sent a servant to seize the best portions from the very kettles of the sacrificers.[16] In fact, they were not even willing to wait for the sacrifice to begin; they reserved whatever portions they wanted before the sacrifice. Thus, they became a scandal before all Israel. Behavior like this was certainly not calculated to promote satisfaction among the pilgrims to the sanctuary.

Their contempt for the sacrificial laws was further aggravated by the improprieties they committed with the women who were serving at the sanctuary (2, 22). Some scholars have interpreted this as evidence of the fact that a Canaanite fertility cult had crept into the sanctuary of Yahweh in Shiloh, and that God was venerated in the practice of the sacred wedding ceremony. But if this was part of the divine services at Shiloh, why would Eli have rebuked his sons? It is easier to understand this abuse if we suppose that, side by side with the male Levites, there were also female servants who were in charge of many of the details of worship at the sanctuary. The text expressly states that they "served at the tent of meeting." [17]

---

16. In 1 S 2, 12-17, there are a series of sacrificial vessels and implements which cannot be clearly identified today. Large pots, with tripod bases, were discovered at Beth-Shan and Ras-Shamra (Galling BRL 342); a three-pronged fork in Gezer and Byblos (Galling BRL 169), a two-foot long fork in Lachish (ill. RB 48 [1939], 408).

17. Elephantine papyri attest to the probability of temple singers being employed in the Yahweh cult. LHN-Chantreuse, VT 5 (1955), 83-88.

Eli did indeed protest against these abuses, but his words were spoken in the wind. All he really did was to hide the guilt of his sons behind his threatening words (2, 23-25). His words are composed in a certain rhythm. It is possible that he is quoting an ancient proverb. "If a man sins against man, *'ĕlōhîm* will mediate for him; but if a man sins against Yahweh, who can intercede for him?" (2, 25). If we translate this word *'ĕlōhîm* as God, this means that, in case of any legal contention between two men, an appeal to God's judgment is always possible; *'ĕlōhîm,* however, according to Biblical usage, can also refer to a human judge (cf. Ex 21, 6; 22, 7; Ps 57/58, 2). Whenever there is any contention or legal claim taken up in the human realm, it is always possible to appeal to a court of higher instance. But what happens in the case of a sin against Yahweh himself? Here man is delivered simply to the inexorable justice of God. There is always the possibility of placating Yahweh by offering sacrifice. But this the sons of Eli refused to do. As a consequence, it is the terrible judgment of God himself which now thunders out against them.

The prophets were the conscience of the nation. We read that one day a "man of God" appeared before Eli and delivered an oracle from God (*nĕ'ûm yahweh*). In Christian usage, the term "man of God" refers to the holy and perfect man who lives his life completely in accord with God's will. A man can be a saint without having any particular mission to his fellow men. But in the Biblical "man of God" (*'îs 'elōhîm,* 1 S 2, 27), the characteristic element is that of mediatorship between God and man.[18] He is a mouthpiece for God, announcing the mysteries of Yahweh, a prophet who can give orders as to what man is to do. Such "prophesying men" must always have existed in Israel. We read already of Rebecca that she went out "to inquire of Yahweh" when the children struggled together within her (Gn 25, 22). The angel (or Yahweh himself) who appeared one day to a woman of the tribe of Dan, in order to announce the birth of Samson, is referred to by her as a "man of God" (Jg 13, 6). Samuel, too, will bear this name (1 S 9, 6). Later Biblical usage refers to such men of God as prophets (*nĕbî'îm*). Even though the term "prophet" is more familiar to us, the more ancient name "man of God" is a better insight into the character and mission of these men.

---

18. P. Joüon, *Locutions hébraiques, 'is'ĕlōhîm,* Bibl 3 (1922), 53.

They were to represent the interests of God, to announce his word, no matter how hard this word might be, even if it made men's ears "to tingle" (3, 11). Thus they also turn into the heralds of disaster, hovering like vultures in advance of the threatening doom of Israel; but they are also the angels of good tidings, pronouncing, even in the face of disaster, the new beginnings of God's work of salvation.

The message of this man of God (1 S 2, 27-36) is a sample of this prophetic sermon. Three elements must be stressed: a) The prophet recalls everything that Yahweh has done in the past; he has been prodigal with his gifts and graces. b) Against this magnificent background, the miserable response of human rejection takes on an ever darker hue. Man has abused the great and powerful deeds of God, man has dissipated God's graces. c) Consequently, God now passes judgment through the mouth of the prophet, proclaiming the imminence of judgment, while, on the other hand, pointing the way to new works of grace.[19]

The unknown and unnamed man of God appears suddenly from the shadows to announce God's judgment to the high priest Eli. Yahweh had mighty plans for the house of Eli, when he called upon it, in Egypt, to supply his priesthood. But Eli and his sons rejected Yahweh and his law. "Behold, the days are coming, when I will cut off your strength and the strength of your father's house, so that there will not be an old man in your house" (2, 31). The priesthood is taken away from the house of Eli. The members of his household who reach old age will be so wretched that they will have to beg before they are allowed to perform the humblest service at the sanctuary, in order to earn a crust of bread to prolong their life. In place of the faithless house of Eli, Yahweh "will raise up a faithful priest, who shall do according to what is in my heart and in my mind" (2, 35). As a sign that these words are true, the two sons of Eli will, in the not too distant future, both perish on the same day (2, 34).[20]

The third prophecy of doom came from the mouth of the

---

19. For further examples of a prophetic message, cf. Is 5: a. God's message, vs 1-2; b. Man's refusal 3-4; c. Judgment and salvation 8-23, 24-30.
20. The judgment on the house of Eli was shortly carried out. Phinehas and Hophni fell in the battle against the Philistines (1 S 4, 11). As further vengeance, Saul had 84 priests cut down in a single day at Nob (22, 16-19). Only Abiathar escaped the massacre, fleeing to

boy Samuel. He grew up in the care of Eli at the sanctuary, where he performed services in keeping with his tender age. His clothing was a linen ephod (2, 18), a word which refers to the common priestly garment as distinguished from the high-priestly ephod (1 S 22, 18).[21]

Probably this was a linen apron, such as David wore when he danced before the Ark of the Covenant (2 S 6, 14). In addition to this, Samuel's mother, upon the occasion of her annual pilgrimage, would bring an outer garment ($me^{\cdot}il$), the garment worn by people of rank. It is one of the miracles of grace that Samuel remained untouched by moral decay rampant at the sanctuary.

Samuel slept in the "Temple of Yahweh" (3, 3), as the text expresses it in general terms, apparently in a room added on to the sanctuary. From this position he was able to observe, by looking through the window, whether the seven-branched candle stick was still burning. Eli was already almost blind, and could no longer attend to this work himself; that is why Samuel was always at his side. While Samuel was engaged in this customary service, something quite extraordinary took place. He made his first acquaintance with the "word of Yahweh" (3, 1). The expression "word of God" is familiar also in the preceding books of Scripture (Nb 15, 31; 23, 16; Jos 3, 9; 24, 27); it is generally used in the same sense as "law of Yahweh," but from this time forward it takes on a new meaning. It refers to Yahweh's word of revelation, proclaimed through the mouth of his prophet. To oppose this word means to forfeit one's life (1 S 15, 23-26). From the time of Samuel onward the "word of Yahweh" is the decisive power in the history of Israel.[22]

David who established him as high priest. In connection with his accession to the throne, Solomon had him put aside and transferred the high-priesthood to Zadok (1 K 2, 27). The descendants of Eli do not maintain their posterity in Israel.

---

21. The high priest's ephod was a breastplate with the Urim and Thummim. Quite distinct from this is the ordinary ephod. Linguistically, ephod appears to mean "that which one bears" (cf. Arabic *'afada, wafada*).

22. On the development of the concept, "word of God," see G. Kittel,

Samuel had never before experienced the call of Yahweh. Yahweh's word came to his ear like a human word. At the first call, he ran to Eli and asked what he wanted. Only upon the third call did Eli realize that it was Yahweh who was calling the boy, and he advised him to answer the next time he was called: "Speak, Lord, for thy servant hears" (3, 9). Then Yahweh appeared, "and stood forth, calling as on the other times" (3, 10). Scripture is very brief on this point. There is no description of the divine apparition, only the proclamation of the words of judgment. Samuel remained in his cell until morning, when he opened the gates of the house of Yahweh and was afraid to tell Eli what had happened during the night. Only when the high priest threatened him did the boy tell the old man the divine sentence of punishment that had been pronounced against him. Eli might be a very questionable figure by reason of his negligence and weakness, but he achieves full spiritual greatness in the humility with which he accepts the pronouncement of Yahweh: "It is the Lord, let him do what seems good to him" (3, 18).

This chapter of catastrophe closes with a final statement on the career of Samuel: "And Samuel grew, and the Lord was with him and let none of his words fall to the ground" (3, 19). No matter how powerfully sin asserted itself, grace was even more powerful. The judgment of God was hovering on the near horizon, but the man was already approaching maturity who was to change the history of human doom into a history of divine salvation.

C) THE CATASTROPHE

1) THE WAR WITH THE PHILISTINES:

The Philistines [23] were the great adversaries of Israel. At almost the same time that Israel entered Palestine from the eastern desert, the Philistines took possession of the Palestinian coastland,

---

ThWNT IV (1942), 94ff. / O. Grether, *Name und Wort Gottes im AT* (1934), 64, Anm 3.

---

23. On the origin, nationality, and political organization of the Philistines, see Vol. I, p. 173ff.

making their way in the storm of the sea peoples, across the sea or by the land route over Syria. They settled in five cities: Gaza, Ashkelon, Ashdod, Ekron, Gath. The contemporaneity of the possession of the Promised Land, from both east and west, was, however, not one and the same phenomenon. Each ethnic group had developed its own political system. The Philistines, for the most part, simply took over the administrations of the Canaanite city-states. Even before the invasion of the Philistines, Canaan was split up into several small autonomous units, each with its own stronghold as a central point, and, as a rule, governed by an individual dynasty of its own.[24] Even the Egyptian sovereignty, under the Pharaohs of the New Kingdom, had introduced no essential changes into this political structure. The Egyptians wanted only their tribute; they allowed the Canaanite princes and kings to exercise the greatest possible freedom. When, with the descendancy of the New Kingdom in Egypt, the power of the Pharaohs in Canaan began to dwindle, the old system of small individual political centers continued to flourish in the country. It was into this long established tradition that the Philistines now made their way. They established themselves in the ancient cities, reducing other settlements to ruins; but, to a great extent, they are the heirs and successors to the ancient Canaanite system of city-states.

Only one element distinguished them from their Canaanite predecessors. Without detriment to their individual autonomy as city states, they freely banded together in decisive moments of crisis, for common activity. One or another of the city-state-kings would then take command of the Philistine city federation. The roots of this common military and political effort are to be sought in the inbred military construction of the Philistines themselves. Throughout the long history of their warlike migrations, common effort in all their more important undertakings was, quite simply, a prerequisite for survival. This element, which represents some progress over the former system of Canaanite city-states, developed the Philistines into a formidable aggressive power.

---

24. A. Alt, Kleine Schriften, II (1953), I-II: Staatenbildung der Israeliten in Palästina.

It was this factor which, at a time when Egyptian sovereignty in Palestine was practically meaningless, won the political hegemony for the Philistines. In this respect, it is no great exaggeration to refer to them as the heirs of the Pharaohs.[25] Even though the sphere of Philistine influence was much narrower than that of the Pharaohs, it appears all the more active within these narrower limits. This was a fact that the Israelites experienced above all others: they had no corresponding military organization to oppose to the combined forces of the Philistines.

The Philistines, operating from their coastal plains, sought to reduce the hill country to their sovereignty. This must not be understood in the sense that they meant to acquire territories for settlement; on the contrary, they were concerned only with establishing sovereignty after the example of their predecessors the Pharaohs of Egypt. By exacting tribute of cattle and agricultural products, they sought to make the mountain countries serve their needs. "For themselves the authority and the military profession, for the Israelites and the Canaanites the dependent position of working class — that is how, in the mind of the Philistines, the functions of the country of Palestine were to be divided." [26] This claim was supported by their professional soldiery, and the military experience that had become second nature from the days of their migrations.

The Israelite possession of the land took on an entirely different character. The under-equipped Israelites, were not in a position, as they entered the Promised Land, to deal with the fortified Canaanite cities. It is true that they overcame Jericho and Ai, that they undertook battle with the league of Canaanite cities and managed to achieve individual successes, but the principal district of Israelite settlement remained the citiless and unfortified hill and mountain country. Consequently, they did not take over the system of Canaanite city-states; even after taking possession of the country, they retained the old patriarchal formation of individual tribes. There was no professional soldiery and no central power. Only in times of crisis was it possible for a charismatic

25. *Ibid.*
26. *Ibid.*

leader to sound the general summons to arms. Then, when the war was concluded, each one returned to his own tent. The only element which held Israel together was its belief in Yahweh. In Yahweh the Israelite national consciousness found its true roots.[27] The covenant concluded by Moses on Mount Sinai bound the twelve tribes into a religious and national unity, but, after the occupation of the Promised Land, it allowed the individual tribes such great autonomy that even the military undertakings recorded in the Book of Judges could hardly be said to involve Israel as a nation. The time for a political consolidation of all Israel was not yet ripe. Only the overpowering oppression of the Philistines managed to achieve the formation of the Israelite state; and after this formation, in a very short time, the history of all Palestine begins to follow a different course.

Even though it says in 1 S 4, 1b that Israel took the field against the Philistines, it must be the Philistines, once again, who started the war, and forced Israel to her own defense. The Philistines assembled their military power in Aphek, which is known already in the Egyptian Execration texts and the lists of the Tuthmoses III.[28] The Israelites encamped at Ebenezer (*'Eben hā'ezer*), "Rock of help," so named after a later victory of Samuel's.[29] The text does not say where the battle took place. Israel suffered a terrible defeat. The number of 4000 casualties sounds somewhat improbable. But Israel would not admit defeat. The broken army reassembled, to carry its desperate battle to the very end. This time, they hoped for salvation by bringing up the Ark of the Covenant.

2) THE LOSS OF THE ARK (1 S 4, 3-22):

As we already discussed, in the time of the Judges, the name Yahweh *Ṣebā'ôt,* Yahweh of hosts, must have come into general

---

27. *Ibid.*
28. The Egyptian form of Aphek is written *'pgwm*: Gressmann, AOT 105, ANET 242. Aphek is commonly identified with Ras *el-'Ain*, 15 km NE of Tell-Aviv.
29. Ebenezer might well be sought in Ain Sinia, 15 km NNE of el-Bireh in the central mountains.

use for the God of Israel. Wars were looked upon, not as profane affairs, but as sacred undertakings. The beaten army would not ask by what type of weapon or by what manner of military strategy they had been overcome; they phrased it as a religious question: "Why has the Lord put us to rout today before the Philistines?" (4, 3). They ascribed their defeat to the absence of Yahweh of hosts and his Ark of the Covenant. The elders of Israel — it is important to note, once again, that there are no generals or leaders as such — decided to have the Ark of the Covenant brought into the camp.

The Ark of the Covenant was not only the repository for the Tables of the Law, but also the throne of Yahweh himself. With the Ark, the war God of Israel came into the camp. He was received not only with great joy, but the text also speaks of a *terû'â,* that is, the battle cry with which the battle was initiated or which was taken up in pursuing the enemy (cf. Jos 6, 5; Jg 7, 20; 1 S 17, 20, 52 etc.).[30] The arrival of the Ark in the Israelite camp also made a telling impression upon the Philistines. They finally determined to make a final stand against the "Hebrews" (1 S 4, 9). In the ensuing battle, Israel lost not 30 "thousand" (*'eleph*) men, but the 30 "tribal levies" (*'eleph*) were mercilessly beaten. Israel's temporary military conscription was not on a par with the professional soldiery of the Philistines. The defeat turned into a religious and national catastrophe by reason of the fact that not only the two priests Hophni and Phinehas fell in battle, but also the Ark of the Covenant itself fell into the hands of the enemies. This meant, in terms of contemporary attitude, that not only Israel itself, but Israel's God had been vanquished. A runner brought the news of the defeat to Shiloh. The old high priest Eli fell backwards from his seat, broke his neck, and died. The wife of Hophni, who was about to deliver, was seized by her labor pains and died. To the child she bore she gave the name Ichabod, "departed is the glory (of the Ark)."[31]

---

30. P. Humbert, *La teru'a, Analyse d'un rite biblique* (Neuchâtel, 1946).
31. The interpretation which the dying mother sets on the name of her child is, like most etymologies in the Bible, popular rather than scienti-

This victory opened the mountain country to the Philistines. They made their way to Shiloh and destroyed the sanctuary. The extent of this destruction can still be appreciated from an examination of the excavations.[32] In the twelfth century, as determined on the basis of the pottery finds, Shiloh enjoyed its greatest period of prosperity. In the middle of the eleventh century, catastrophe burst upon the city. Great mounds of ashes testify to the destruction of the city by fire. It was razed to the very ground, and remained a ruin until the Hellenistic era. The Christians built a basilica there, which also succumbed to the ravages of time. Today there is hardly a more abandoned place in all of Palestine than Khirbet Selûn, the ruins of Shiloh. For the subsequent history of the Old Testament, these ruins serve as a solemn warning (cf. Jr 7, 12; 26, 9; Ps 77/78, 59-64).

With the destruction of Shiloh, the Philistines had attained their objective. Israel had been dealt a mortal wound. It was the covenant with Yahweh alone which had, heretofore, held the twelve tribes together. Now the Ark of the Covenant was lost and the central sanctuary had been destroyed. It seemed that Israel's final ruin had been accomplished. History had decided in favor of the Philistines. But Israel's God was not a God like the gods of the other conquered peoples; this the Philistines were soon to learn, to their great distress.

3) THE ARK OF THE COVENANT AMONG THE PHILISTINES:

It was only to be expected that the Philistines would set up the Ark of the Covenant as a victory trophy in the temple of their god Dagon in Ashdod. Although the Philistines had con-

---

fic. Names compounded with a negative prefix are most unusual. In terms of comparison with other names, such as *'itāmār, 'izebel, 'icezer*. Some authors think that *i* is an abbreviation for *abî* — "My father, God, is glory, help."

---

32. Shiloh was excavated by the Dane H. Kjaer in 1926 and 1929. IPOS 10 (1930), 87-114. / Briefer account by J. C. Nagele, *De prima siluntis destructione effosionibus recentibus illustrata,* Antonianum 6 (1931) 401-416. / L. Hennequin, DBS III (1938), 377ff.

quered the Canaanite cities militarily and politically, they were soon conquered themselves in the domain of race and religion. They lost their own language and, in terms of religion, they were completely assimilated into the Canaanite beliefs. The most widely venerated God seems to have been Dagon.[33] Originally he was an ancient Semitic storm God, but, in the course of his westward migration, he turned into an agricultural and fertility god, and eventually into a sea god. The Philistines built a great temple to him in Ashdod (5, 1-7), as well as in Gaza (Jg 16, 23).

Yahweh's superiority over Dagon was apparent the first night. The statue of Dagon fell face downward on the ground before the Ark of the Lord. When they put the statue of their god back upon his throne, the following night witnessed an even clearer demonstration. The next morning they found Dagon's head and hands cut off and lying on the threshold of the temple. These mysterious goings on in the temple of Dagon seized the inhabitants of Ashdod with a terrible fear. This fear was further aggravated by an outbreak of tumors, so that the inhabitants of Ashdod had no further recourse but to send the Ark of the Covenant into the neighboring city of Gath. The plague of tumors followed the Ark into Gath, and the people there sent it on, after a brief interval, into the city of Ekron. Here too the hand of Yahweh lay heavy on the inhabitants of the city. In order to rid the country of this plague, the priests and sooth-sayers advised that the Ark of the

---

33. F. J. Montalbano, Canaanite Dagon, *Origin and Nature*, CBQ 13 (1951), 381-397. Comprehensive presentation of the dragon cult from the Accadian time onward. From the 24th century on, the dragon was venerated in Mesopotamia as a war and storm god. The name is probably connected with the Accadian root *dq*, "cloudy, rainy." The cult quickly spread to Phoenicia, where we find evidence of its popularity in texts and votive columns. Cf. ANET 130, 139-144. / According to the Amarna Letters, there was a Canaanite prince with the name Dagan-Takala (Letter 317, 318). The word appears in the place name Beth-Dagon in Asher, and in a similarly named location in Judah (Jos 15, 41). Because of the close verbal association with *dāgan*, grain, the deity was also venerated as a fertility god and eventually, by the reason of the similarity with *dāg*, fish, a sea god. Dagon coins, half man and half fish, have been discovered in Arvad, Beirut, and Ashkelon. Bressan, 113.

Covenant together with propitiatory offerings, be sent back to the Israelites. But, in order to be certain that the catastrophes actually came from Yahweh, the Philistines decided to wait for a clear sign from God. The Ark of the Covenant was loaded onto a wagon,[34] together with the golden sacrificial gifts, according to the number of the five Philistine cities, five golden images of tumors, and five mice. Mice, in the Ancient Near East, were regarded as bearers of pestilence.[35] The wagon was hitched to two milch cows, whose calves had been locked in their stalls at home. The cows were allowed to choose their own path. Following their natural impulses, they would have immediately returned to their home barns, but they actually bore the cart in the direction of the Israelite district, towards the city of Bethshemesh.[36] This was the sign of divine intervention. The Philistines realized that it was actually Yahweh's hand that had struck them.

The people of Bethshemesh were in the valley harvesting wheat when they saw the cart approaching with the Ark of the Covenant. The distance from Ekron to Bethshemesh is about 20 km. The Philistine leaders stayed at the border. The arrival of Yahweh's Ark of the Covenant could only be greeted by sacrifice. There was a great rock in that place. Such rocks were frequently used as places for sacrifice (cf. Jg 6, 19-21; 1 S 14, 33). The cows were slaughtered, the wood from the wagon was used for a sacrificial fire, and the animals were burned and offered to Yahweh as a holocaust. The stone upon which the Ark of

---

34. A Philistine cart is depicted in R. Kittel, *Kriege in biblischen Landen* (1918), 27. Two-wheeled wagon with a square box on the axle, drawn by four cows.

35. Many authors think that the "mice" are merely symbolic reference to the disease from which the Philistines suffered, such as "cancer (crab), or wolf," but there is no convincing argument to support this view. E. K. Harrison, *Disease, Bible and Spade*, BA 16 (1953), 88-92, thinks it is the bubonic plague.

36. Modern Tell er-Rumeileh, 25 km due west from Jerusalem. The ancient name is still retained in the nearby location of 'Ain Šem, where Byzantine ruins can be discovered. For the excavation account, cf. under Beth-shemesh in DBS I (1928), 975-981, 3 (1938), 331-335. / E. Grant, G. Wright, *Ain Shems Excavations*, Haverford, vol. 1-5, 1931-39. / I (1939), 152-156. / Bibl 21 (1940), 429-437.

the Covenant was set down lay in the field of Joshua of Beth-shemesh (6, 18). From this point it was the Levites who once again took custody of the Ark (6, 15). Some people from Beth-shemesh "looked into the Ark of the Lord," not maintaining the proper respect; as a consequence, just as in the Philistine cities, a great number of people shortly died.[37] Then they were all seized with fear of God and they said: "Who is able to stand before the Lord, this holy God?" (6, 20). They sent messengers into the city of Kiriat-Jearim (Cariathiarim)[38] asking them to take charge of the Ark.

Men from Kiriat-Jearim came and brought the Ark of the Covenant into their city. They set it up on the hill of Abinadab and consecrated his son Eleazar for the service at the sanctuary. It was here that the Ark of the Covenant remained until David had it brought into Jerusalem.

The fear of Yahweh fell not only upon the Philistines, but upon the Israelites as well. Yahweh was not a God like the other gods. Conquered and all but annihilated, he had still achieved the final victory. If his people would sincerely repent and turn to him, a new national rise to power would result. The only strength of Israel was its belief in Yahweh.

---

37. The numbers in the text, "70 men from the people, 50,000 men," is a corrupt reading. N. H. Tur-Sinai, *The Ark of God at Beit Shemsh.* VT I (1951), 275-286, suspects the error is an incorrect reading of *šb'm*, "seventy," which is to be read as two words, *šb*, "old man," and *'m* "people": He struck old men and warriors alike in the people, a thousand men."

38. Kiriath-Jearim means "woods city" and recalls the ancient times in Palestine when there were still forests to be felled and cities to be settled. It is situated 20 km ENE of Beth-shemesh and belonged to the tribe of Judah. When the land was occupied, it belonged to the confederation of the Gibeonite cities and thus escaped destruction (Jos 9). The city also called by other names, such as *kiriath-baal,* "Baal city" (Jos 18, 14), or *sedê-ya'ar,* "forest tract" (Ps 131/132, 6).

CHAPTER II

PROPHET AND REFORMER

(1 S 7, 2-8, 22)

1) OPPOSITION TO THE GODS OF CANAAN:

WE do not know the young Samuel's reaction to the destruction of Shiloh. Probably he escaped the catastrophe by taking refuge in his home city of Ramathaim. It is not until some 20 years later (1 S 7, 2) that he once again appears in public life. This time he already stands at the head of Israel, as prophet and religious reformer. The great day of the Mizpah (Misphat) (7, 5), is inconceivable without a lengthy and thorough period of preparation. Even the young Samuel, in the years of Philistine oppression, must have worked tirelessly as a preacher of repentance throughout the country (such activity is explicitly recorded of his later years — 7, 16), in order to lead his people back to their faith in Yahweh. The fundamental theme of his prophetic preaching was the following: the national catastrophe did not come upon Israel without reason. Yahweh sent it as a punishment for Israel's defection to the *Be'ālîm* and the *'aštārôt*. You must destroy the idols in your midst and make room again for Yahweh; then he himself will take away the yoke of foreign hegemony.

Finally, after much disillusionment and many bitter defeats,

Samuel was privileged to experience the great day at Mizpah. He must have been in his thirty's. "So Israel put away the Baals and the Ashtaroth, and they served the Lord only" (7, 4). During the days of the Judges, Israel had served the Aramaean Cushan-Rishathaim for 8 years (Jg 3, 7-9), Eglon king of Moab for 18 years (Jg 3, 12-15), Jabin, king of Hazor, for 20 years (Jg 4, 1-3). The 20 years of the new oppression by the Philistines after the destruction of the sanctuary at Shiloh were also years in which the faith in Yahweh deteriorated while foreign gods made inroads into the conscience of Israel.

The Book of Samuel refers to the *be'ālîm* and *'aštārôt* (7, 3-4). Both words are plural in form, apparently a general term for gods and goddesses. But closer examination reveals a clear reference to the religion of Canaan. *Ba'al* means "lord, owner"; in married living it refers to the husband who possesses a wife. Religious thought of those days conceived of a divinity as possessing a certain place, a mountain, or a country, and, consequently, spoke of the *ba'al-pe'ôr* (Nb 25, 3), the Ba'al of Pe'or, or *ba'al-sāphôn* (Ex 14, 2), the north Ba'al, or the god was conceived of as the protector of covenant fidelity, thus *ba'al-berît* (Jg 3, 33), Baal of the covenant. In the time of the Judges and the early kings, the name baal did not yet have any explicit pagan significance. David himself addresses Yahweh as baal (2 S 5, 20). Names compounded with baal were common in Israel. Saul's son was called *'iš-ba'al*, "man of baal" (2 S 2, 8), Jonathan's son was called *meri-ba'al* (2 S 4, 4; 9, 6; 1 Ch 8, 34; 940), "beloved of Baal," and David's councillor bore the name *'ahi-ba'al* (2 S 15, 12), "baal is my brother." With the growing inroads of paganism, baal became the proper name of the Canaanite gods, and was thus proscribed in Israel as a name for god. The Israelites went so far as to replace the personal names compounded with *-ba'al* with the word *-bôšet*, "shamefulness, idolatry." This gave rise to the transformed names *'išbôšet, mepîbôšet*. Another substituted form is *-tôpel*, "foolishness, folly," accordingly *'ahi-tôpel*.

The female goddess *'aštarte*, in the Masoretic pointing, bears the vowels of *bôšet*, "shamefulness," and is, accordingly, read as *'aštôret*. In Mesopotamia this corresponds to the goddess Istar, in Ugarit *'ttrt*, the most widely venerated female goddess of the Ancient Near East. She was the throne consort of the storm god Ba'al-hadad. She was venerated as the source of growth and prosperity in field and meadow, fertility in man and beast. In the intoxicating rites of temple prostitution, her worshippers sought to plunge deep into the divine mysteries of life.

By the word *'aštārôt*, it is probably the small figurines of the goddess that we are to understand;[1] these were carried as amulets or preserved in the home. The figurines represented the goddess, in starkly realistic form, completely naked, and with pronounced sexual characteristics. Since the Bible frequently confuses the two goddesses *'ašērâh* and *'aštarte,* which are not clearly distinguished in the Canaanite pantheon, and frequently even equivalates them, the word *'aštārôt,* in the present case, could mean the same thing as *'ašērôt.*[2] These powers are thoroughly familiar from the battle of the prophets against the inroads of Canaanite paganism. The *'ašērâh* must have been a wooden cult object which could be burned or felled like a tree. The precise nature of this cult object cannot be more definitely ascertained; most probably it was some kind of wooden emblem for which we have contemporary Babylonian examples. If, accordingly, the *'aštārôt* refer to the wooden cult pillars erected on the sacred high places, then it is a logical conclusion that the *beʿālîm* refer to the stone *maṣṣēbôt* on the sacred high places, which, presumably, represent the male phallus. What we are to understand by these sacred high places (*bāmâh*) has been clarified by the excavation in Nehariya.[3] The *bāmâh* was a large stone, or group of stones, upon which sacrificial gifts, previous objects, pearls, cult figurines, vessels, were deposited. The fact that oil was poured out in these sacrifices is abundantly attested to by the stains on the excavated stones. Near these sacrificial high places stood an altar for the ritual sacrifices, together with the wooden pales and the stone pillars. Sacred groves were particularly popular for the location of such high places.

During an era in which the central sanctuary lay in ruin and the entire country was under the sovereignty of the Philistines, the Canaanite idol worship must have spread like a plague through Israel. A conquered people is freely inclined to change its faith for that of its victors. Against this background, the reform activity

---

1. In the excavations of Mizpah, modern Tell en-Hasbeh, were discovered a great number of Astarte figurines, as well as the remains of a temple of Astarte, which, however, dates to a later period although it casts much light on events of Samuel's time. DBS III (1938), 408. / Grollenberg, *Atlas* (1958), 56.
2. For more detailed information on the gods of Canaan, cf. Albright, *Religion of Israel,* 55, 93, 121. / Cf. Jg 3, 7; 2 Ch 19, 3; 33, 3.
3. Excavation report in RB 63 (1956), 91-93. / Detailed account of the present state of the problem, cf. L. H. Vincent, *La notion biblique du haut-lieu.* RB 55 (1948), 245-278; 438-445 u. / W. F. Albright, *The High Place in Ancient Palestine,* vol. du Congr. (Strassbourg, 1956). Suppl. to VT IV (1957), 242-258.

of Samuel cannot be praised highly enough. He was the precursor of the great prophets of Israel, who all fought to uphold the prerogatives of Yahweh. Samuel must have preached the fiery words of a Savonarola. The people did away with the *be'ālîm* and the *'aštārôt,* cleansed the land, and renewed their covenant with Yahweh. Then Israel was once again, spiritually, ready for war. The Philistines observed the events at Mizpah with uneasy suspicion. They regarded Mizpah as a threat and hoped to put a speedy end to the affair by a sudden *coup de main.*

2) THE WAR WITH THE PHILISTINES:

The propitiatory assembly at Mizpah (Masphat) soon turned into a military summons. Samuel poured out water in the presence of Yahweh, an ancient ritual of purification, in order to atone for the people's sins.

The Philistines were already upon them. In this moment of extreme crisis, the elders of Israel made the prophet Samuel their judge: "And Samuel was judge of the people of Israel at Mizpah" (7, 6b). Prior to this time, as Levite and prophet, Samuel had been the spiritual leader of his people; now he also became their political and military head. These heroes of antiquity were called "judges" (*šōpeṭîm*) not because they pronounced sentence primarily, although they did this too, but because they were to accomplish the sentences of Yahweh upon his enemies and liberate Israel from the crisis of foreign attack. In this present crisis, all Israel's hope was riveted upon Samuel.

This was a holy war and needed to be "sanctified" by a sacrifice. That is why Samuel sacrificed a lamb as a whole burnt offering to Yahweh and cried to heaven in prayer. This "crying" is an important word in the context: it refers to the battle cry which signaled the beginning of the holy war. Yahweh had witnessed the conversion of Israel, and he turned to his people with a shower of graces. Already under Joshua, the battle at Gibeon (Gabaon) had been decided by thunder, lightning, and hailstorm; a second time, the bloody chariot battle at the torrent of Kishon was decided, amid thunder and lightning, in favor of Barak. This time too "Yahweh thundered with a mighty voice against the

Philistines" (7, 10) with the result that the Israelites beat them decisively and pursued them back to the coastal plains. In remembrance of this victory, Samuel erected a great stone and called it the stone of helping (7, 12), *'eben hā'ezer,* Ebenezer. This practice of erecting large stones to commemorate a significant event was a familiar one. Jacob erected a memorial in Bethel, when he was fleeing from his brother Esau (Gn 35, 14), and he erected another in commemoration of his alliance with Laban (Gn 31, 45). Joshua did the same thing at Shechem, when he erected a stone as the memorial of the covenant between Yahweh and his people (Jos 24, 26). Such memorial stones, which are called by their celtic names, dolms, menhirs, and cromlechs or cairns, are to be seen everywhere in Palestine, although it is not always possible to determine the historical event they are meant to commemorate.[4]

This victory not only freed Israel from foreign occupation, but also enlarged her territory. The country as far as Gath and Ekron returned to Israelite possession. In terms of territory, the boundary was pushed only some 10 km to the west; but the less tangible fruits of the war were much greater in scope. For the years that followed, Israel lived in peace not only with her Philistine neighbors, but also with the Canaanites who still dwelt in the land (7, 14).

With this victory over the Philistines, Samuel had actually completed his mission as judge. The people had been liberated and each man returned to his own tent. Samuel, however, retained the spiritual leadership of his people. His activity as judge now concentrated on the three centers of Bethel, Gilgal, and Mizpah, as well as his home city of Ramathaim. He was constantly traveling between these various points, watching over the sacred fire of national faith in Yahweh. These city names, however, which describe the district of Samuel's influence and activity, circumscribe a very narrow district, essentially only the mountain country of Ephraim. When the Bible says that Samuel assembled "all Israel" (7, 5) at Mizpah, this can certainly not refer to all twelve tribes. Transjordania and Galilee lay outside his sphere of influence and

---

4. Bressan, 136.

activity. The same is true in the case of the narratives of the Book of Judges; each individual judge could hardly be expected to have worked outside the district of his own tribe.

Samuel, in the full strength of his years, had indeed succeeded in moving the heart of his people to shake off the Philistine yoke. But as he grew old, one piece of his work after another fell away, and the Philistine peril was more threatening than ever before, on the political and religious horizon of Israel. It was this extreme crisis which moved the elders of Israel to approach the aged prophet and demand the institution of a monarchy, a king who would unite the national powers of all Israel and effect a decisive liberation from the constant pressure of her enemies.

3) THE DEMAND FOR A KING:

It must have taken a long time before the elders of Israel decided to approach Samuel at Ramathaim. It was the crisis that impelled them. Samuel's two sons, Joel and Abijah, were associated with their aged father in his office as judge, but they could easily be bribed, and "perverted justice" (1 S 8, 1). It was impossible to think of Samuel being succeeded by his sons. Samuel's declining days were embittered by his experience with his sons. In order to decide the matter definitively, the elders of Israel made this proposal to Samuel: "Appoint for us a king to govern us like all the nations" (8, 5).

The military kingship of the Philistines has already been described. It was precisely this strict organization to which they owed their repeated successes. In Transjordania, the territories of Edom, Moab, Ammon, and Aram, which had established their tribal possessions at about the same time as Israel, had early gone over to monarchical government. Our knowledge of these kingdoms is almost exclusively dependent upon the Bible, and thus we never see them in their stage of growth; they are always represented as mature powers which already existed when the Israelites first immigrated into the settled country. It is surprising to note that Israel was the last to form a monarchy. Certainly Israel had made the furthest westward advances into the ancient territory of Canaan, but she did not succeed in possessing the entire country.

The territory of Israelite settlement was broken by a ring of
Canaanite cities. Israel, accordingly, was lacking in the political
prerequisites for the establishment of a national monarchy. The
kingdoms east of the Jordan were in a much better position. But
their kingship, too, seems to have been, at the outset, not a
dynastic but an elective monarchy.[5]

If Israel's political dismemberment made it difficult to achieve
the formation of a monarchy, there were also religious complica-
tions. Already in the days of Gideon, the possibility of a monarchy
was clearly felt. After his brilliant victory over Amalek, Gideon
was approached with the proposition that he undertake an hereditary rulership over Israel (Jg 8, 22). This was his answer to
the proposal: "I will not rule over you, and my sons will not rule
over you; the Lord will rule over you" (Jg 8, 23). Gideon does
not use the expression "to be king" (*mālak*), but only the expression "to be ruler" (*māšal*). Actually, however, it was a real
hereditary monarchy that was offered him. This he refused, on
religious grounds. Noth [6] is of the opinion that this passage
echoes the resentment of the later monarchical era, simplified,
however, by its historical perspective. In Israel, there must have
been, above all, prophetic circles, who saw the monarchy as a
defection from the rule of Yahweh.

The "royal law" which Samuel proclaimed (1 S 8, 10-22) is
the best expression of this resentment. Even though its precise
formulation no doubt stems from the era in which the Books of
Samuel were finally set down in their definitive form, that is,
the time of the monarchy, even the most dedicated textual criticism
cannot circumvent the clear fact that Samuel had a very negative
view of the monarchy. The picture he draws could well have been
gathered, even before its introduction, from the experiences of
the neighboring peoples.[7] First of all, a king would create a

---

5. On the political tendencies in the "primitive state of the Kingdom of
   Israel," cf. A. Alt, *Kleine Schriften*, II (1953), 28ff.
6. M. Noth, *Geschichte Israels* (1950), 142ff.
7. J. Mendelsohn, *Samuel's Denunciation of Kingship in the Light of the
   Akkadian documents from Ugarit*. BASOR 143 (1956), 17-22. The
   king's law is not a retrospective reconstruction, but a contemporary
   critique in the light of prevailing conditions in the Canaanite kingdoms.

standing army, with professional soldiery; then he would introduce forced labor, he would enlarge his own possessions at the expense of his subjects, until they cried out under his lash. The ancient freedom would, once and for all, have disappeared.

This picture of the monarchy as portrayed by the aged Samuel was dismissed by the representatives of the people with a simple "No" (8, 19). Samuel was a wise and religious enough man not to insist obstinately upon his own point of view. The great decisions of his life all belonged to God. Once again he called to Yahweh for a decision (8, 6). Whether he directed a formal question to God, through the high priest, by the Urim and Thummim, or attempted to learn Yahweh's will by some other means is not mentioned in Scripture. Yahweh's decision was affirmative, for the monarchy; but we catch an echo of the bitterness of the rejected divine king: "They have not rejected you, but they have rejected me from being king over them" (8, 7).

Samuel repressed his own personal opinion and declares his readiness to fulfill the people's will as represented by their elders. We cannot, however, entirely avoid the impression that monarchy, in Israel, made its way into history under a heavy load of religious opposition. The crisis of the age, the war with the Philistines, and the threatening war with the Ammonites all seemed to demand the immediate unification of Israel's national forces under a single king, as the ultimate and indispensable condition of national survival. Monarchy in Israel, from its very beginnings, bears the stamp of a military kingship;[8] it was born, not of dynastic grounds, but from the will of the people. It is and remains an elective monarchy, open to the criticism of its subjects, and thus it bears within itself the seeds of its own destruction (1 S 8, 18). But despite all its questionable merit, Yahweh himself has bent to the will of his people. This is the theology-history significance of this section. Even though it was introduced against his will, it is precisely this kingship of David that Yahweh makes the recipient of his greatest promises.

---

8. A. Alt, *Kleine Schriften*, II (1953), 24.

Samuel was a great man, as religious reformer, as victor over the Philistines, as judge of his people. But the greatest mission that he ever accomplished was to find the right king for his people. His first attempt did not succeed. Saul's kingship remains only an episode. But when Samuel anoints David to be king of Israel, he establishes a dynasty which is to have no end.

CHAPTER III

THE BOOKS OF SAMUEL

Commentaries: KAT: Caspari 1926 / SAT: Gressmann 1921[2] / BB: Leimbach 1926 / HBK: Ketter 1940 / EB: Rehm 1949 / ClamB: Médebielle 1949 / SBB: Goldmann 1951 / GarB: Bressan 1954 / JerB; de Vaux 1953 / ATD: Hertzberg 1956 / IB: Caird, Schroeder, Little 1953.

Introductions: Cornely-Merk 1940,[12] 377-386 / Simon-Prado I, 1941[4], 251 — 254 / Höpfl-Miller-Metzinger 1946[5], 149 — 158 / Pfeiffer 1948[2], 338 — 373 / Kuhl 1953, 130 — 147 / Eissfeldt 1956[2], 322 — 339 / Weiser 1957[4], 130 — 140 / Robert-Feuillet 1957, 414 — 434 / DBS II (1934), 240 — 256.

Patristic Literature: Origen, Homily on Elkanah, Anna and Samuel. MG XII, 991 — 995 / Chrysostom, De Anna sermones quinque; de Saul et Davide homiliae tres. MG 54, 631 — 675; 675 — 708 / Pseudo-Hieronymus, Quaestiones in libros Regum. ML 23, 139ff. / Gregory the Great, Commentary on 1 Sm 1 — 16. ML 79, 17 — 468 (examples of allegorical exegesis).

IN our presentation up to this point, we have used, almost exclusively, the Book of Samuel as our source material, with the implicit presupposition of its historical reliability. Since the greater part of Samuel's activity is already well known, we might reasonably be expected to ask whether this man, who figured so prominently as Levite, reformer, prophet, general, and judge, in the destiny of his people, actually left an historical work behind him. The name of the book might suggest this possibility. How correct, or incorrect, this opinion might be is a problem that needs to be examined more closely in terms of Old Testament literary history.

1) NAME AND POSITION IN THE CANON:

In our modern editions of the Old Testament, we have two Books of Samuel. This division is not original. The Masoretes, who definitively established the present-day Hebrew text in the early Middle Ages, counted these two Books as one; at the end of the second book they present the total number of 1506 verses, and they reckon the middle of the Book at 1 S 28, 23.[1] How are we to explain its current division into two Books? The answer might well lie with the ancient methods of publishing books. Since, in the Hebrew text, only the consonants were written, without the vowels, the text as such was brief and it could easily fit into one scroll. But when the Bible was translated into Greek, it was no longer convenient to write the text on one single roll, the text now being significantly longer since Greek writes also the vowels. On these technical grounds, not only the Books of Samuel, but also Kings, Chronicles, and Ezra and Nehemiah, were very early divided in two. The Septuagint refers to these Books not as the Books of Samuel, but rather as βασιλειῶν α'β' "Books of the Kingdoms, one and two," while the modern-day two Books of the Kings were counted as "kingdoms, three and four." This division into four Books passed into the old Latin translation. The designation, "Books of the four Kingdoms," was unsatisfactory to St. Jerome, who considered it misleading. Consequently, in his new translation, he divided the Books according to the Hebrew text: *Liber Samuelis* and *Liber Malachim*. In Church parlance, the numbering in terms of the "four Books of the Kings" (*quattuor regum*) has prevailed to our own day. The new critical edition of the Vulgate, however, once again recommends the numbering in terms of 1 and 2 Samuel and 1 and 2 Kings, a practice which we follow in this book.[2]

The Hebrew canon counts the Book of Samuel among the "former prophets," a category to which the Books of Joshua, Judges, and Kings also belong, the four Books together comprising, as it were, the four Gospels of Old Testament history.

---

1. BHK
2. Biblia Sacra iuxta Latinam Vulgatam Versionem ad codicum fidem, Liber Samuelis 1944, Liber Malachim 1945, edited and published by the Benedictine Fathers of the Abbey of St. Jerome in Rome.

2) LITERARY GENRE:

The two Books of Samuel are indeed permeated by the unifying leit-motiv of the introduction and establishment of monarchy in Israel. As a prelude to this story, and at the same time as a somber background, the sad story of Eli is first presented; next Samuel is characterized as the man of transition, and finally, in Saul, the story of the first abortive attempt at monarchy is narrated, until the crown finds its abiding place of rest in the house of David. Each individual episode is oriented towards this primary leit-motiv. Is this "youthfully vigorous work of history, which has no parallel in the historical writing of the Ancient Near East," [3] to be ascribed to one single author, or have several hands, separated by intervals of many years, worked together to bring it to its present state?

Despite its uniform orientation, the work does show evidence, even upon superficial examination, of surprising inequalities. For example, the characteristics of family life are portrayed down to the most inconsequential details of daily living. There is a charm and freshness in the idyll of Ramathaim. We can still sense the joy that pervades the narrative. It is a portrait, compact in its own unity, which seems to lack the feeling for larger historical frames of reference. An equally explicit attention is devoted to the anointing of Saul (1 S 9, 1-10, 16), David's marriage with Abigail (1 S 25), and the description of David's life at court (2 S 9-20). Despite the individualized and careful attention of these miniature tableaux, the Books of Samuel do not represent a complete biography of either Samuel or Saul or David. It is rather like a small family portrait gallery, in which each individual subject is free to enjoy his own existence.

In sharp contrast to this style, the great events of history which reach far beyond the realm of family life are recorded only in their essential features, with unconcerned brevity. Samuel's activity as judge, which lasted for "forty years," is summarily dismissed in three verses (1 S 7, 15-17), and three verses are enough to describe his prophetic mission, which was the wonder of all Israel (1 S 3, 19-21). In like manner, the wars and conquests, which seem so important for our understanding of the course of history, as well as the political and social reform in Israel, are all dismissed in the most general terms (1 S 14, 47-52: Saul's campaigns; then 2 S 8, 1-18; 20, 23-26: David's wars and rule).

Finally, the last four chapters (2 S 21-24) give the impression of an appendix which appears to be out of character to the otherwise compact construction of the entire work.

These variations in content are heightened by divergences in style. We find the greatest literary unity and compactness in the sections which portray David's court (2 S 9-20). The first Book, on the other hand, gives the impression of a mosaic, composed of a great variety of undoubtedly

---

3. A. Alt, *Kleine Schriften*, II (1953), 34.

precious stones. What is more, some episodes are recorded twice, each time differently: for example, David's introduction to the court of Saul (1 S 16, 14-23; 17, 55-58).

The same event is frequently judged from an entirely different point of view, as, for example, the introduction of the monarchy is either received with wild enthusiasm or rejected with devastating criticism (1 S 8, 1-22 with 9, 1-10).

3) THE AUTHOR:

Who is the author of this historical Book, a work which is obviously a masterpiece of composition on the one hand, and which, on the other hand, gives clear evidence of being pieced together from various unequal blocs and remnants?

The Talmud attributes the work to Samuel: "Samuel wrote the Books of Judges, Ruth, and his own Book."[4] With respect to the Book of Samuel, this is clearly impossible; Samuel's death is described half-way through the Book (1 S 28, 3). According to the Talmud, it is the prophets Nathan and Gad who completed the Book. This opinion was also shared by the Christian exegetes of the early Church, although Theodoret of Cyrus already expresses a contrary position: "It is clear that the individual prophets set down the events of their times in writing; only later were their various accounts collected and formed into the Book of Kings."[5]

It is impossible for the Book of Samuel to be the work of eye-witnesses, since it recounts events which extend over an interval of 120 years. Obvious differences in literary form and content suggest a collective work, the present form stemming from the efforts of the final editor. The Books of Samuel, however, must not be written off as pure fabrication; they bear clear traces of genuine historicity, a narrative in which the various sources have been worked into a higher unity, into a "masterpiece of ancient historical writing." Next we must examine the sources distinguished by literary criticism.

Only one source is explicitly cited, the "Book of the Jashar" (Book of the Just) (2 S 1, 18), an anthology of heroic songs. The other sources can only be determined on internal grounds.

The section in 2 S 9-18 is an obvious eye-witness account; in its description of life at David's court in Jerusalem and Solomon's succession to the throne, it is one of the most beautiful pieces of Old Testament prose, the work of one single hand, sustained by one central idea, David's kingship. The predominant name for God is Yahweh. It is thus called the Yahwist account. This same artistic touch is to be

---

4. *Bara bathra* I, IV, fol 14b; cf. L. Goldschmidt, *Der Babylonische Talmud,* VI, 976, 977.

5. Theodoret of Cyrus, *Migne,* PG 80, 529.

observed in other parts of the Book, for instance in 1 S 9; 14; 25; 38 etc. There is the same perspicuity in the narrative, the same historical leit-motiv. Taken together, these sections present a compact picture of the rise of monarchy: a description of the Philistine crisis (1 S 1, 4-6), Saul's rejection, and, finally, the abiding choice of the House of David. This Yahwist historical tapestry lacks only the figure of the prophet Samuel. Criticism has attempted to identify its author with any of several persons in David's immediate circle, such as the high priest Abiathar or the prophet Nathan, who is supposed to have written this Book in justification of Solomon's succession to the throne.

At all events, there is no difficulty in assigning such an historical work to the tenth century. In the days of Wellhausen, who assigned a much later date to these Books, the Ancient Near East was largely still unknown. Today, however, we know that already in the fourteenth century men were writing with ink in Canaan, and that around 1100 B.C. papyrus was introduced from Egypt. The Bible itself clearly states that many events were recorded in writing (2 S 8, 17; 20, 25). The very important discoveries at Ugarit are further confirmation of the flourishing state of literature in Canaan at the end of the second millennium. There is no reason why the writing of history should not have flourished at David's court.[6]

Side by side with this Yahwist "history of David," there are other texts which are less enthusiastic about the introduction of the monarchy, which they see as a defection from Yahweh. These sections do not seem to accommodate to the main lines of the work. They obviously proceed from a different line of tradition. They are generally referred to as the Elohist sources. Matters of religious import occupy the foreground here. The texts concentrate about the figure of Samuel. In prophetic circles, the monarchy was not so welcome as at the court of Jerusalem. It is thus entirely possible that the prophetic circles developed a parallel picture of contemporary history, and, in keeping with their philosophy, described the individual events in quite different colors.

The great Yahwist and Elohist sources were further amplified by individual sources which are generally grouped together as source X. Among these we must mention particularly the documents in 2 S 21-24 which are added as an appendix.[7]

Does this mean that the Book of Samuel is simply a plaything in the hands of history? That it is merely a formless composite of Yahwist, Elohist, and other sources? Actually, we should be more disturbed if we

---

6. M. Smith, *The so-called "Biography of David" in the Books of Samuel and Kings*, HarvardTheolRev 44 (1951), 167ff. / R. H. Pfeiffer, *The Hebrew Illiad* (1957). Composed already during Solomon's lifetime by the high priest Abiathar.

7. Division according to individual sources in Bressan, 26.

failed to note the hand of several editors in reworking this Ancient Near East historical document. As we have already mentioned in the section of Pentateuchal criticism, the ancient copyists were not content with a slavish reproduction of their sources. Old Babylonian texts were thus worked over in Neo-Babylonian times, and the Egyptian Book of the Dead appears in a whole series of new recensions. It is only logical to expect the same thing in Israel, with the constant ups and downs of its political and religious history. The division of the Pentateuch into various independent and parallel sources (JEPD) has been called into serious question today. The Bible certainly did not develop in an editor's office. It is hard to believe that two historical works, a Yahwist and an Elohist account, existed side by side. The predominant element is the Yahwist account from the royal court in Jerusalem. His work was then augmented by the traditions of the prophetic circles, possibly from the Northern Kingdom, and several other popular accounts were also worked into the narrative.[8] The date of this final form of the Book is a hotly

8. The "classical" source theology is by J. Wellhausen, in the 4th edition of his *Einleitung in das AT*, by Fr. Bleek (Berlin, 1878). (Samuel is composed like the Heptateuch, of source J. and E., which were combined by a deuteronomic redactor.) / The source theology was carried further by K. Budde, *Die Bücher Richter und Samuel, ihre Quellen und ihr Aufbau* (Giessen, 1890). / *The Books of Samuel, Critical Edition of the Hebrew Text printed in Colors* (Baltimore-Leipzig, 1894). / *Die Bücher Samuel* (im Kurzer Handkommentar AT, publ. Marti) (Tübingen-Leipzig, 1902). / With a few individual variations, the other commentaries follow this same general point of view: Nowack, Sellin, Corhill, Kittel, Driver, Smith. / A new and radical position is proposed by G. Holscher: *Die Anfänge der hebraischen Geschichtsschreibung* (Heidelberg, 1942) (J. dates from the year 800 B.C.; the historical content of the books is very meager; they are mostly legends or etiological sagas). / H. M. Wiener, *The Composition of Judges 2, 11 to 1 Kings 2, 46* (Leipzig, 1929) (Source N is the work of Nathan, source G dates from the first half of the 9th century).

Fragment hypothesis: H. Gressmann, *Die älteste Geschichtsschreibung und Prophetie Israels* (v. Samuel bis Amos und Hosea) (Göttingen, 1910) (divides the whole book into individual sections and examines into their *Sitz im Leben*. The individual sections have unequal historical value. We must distinguish among idylls, legends, and historical accounts.) / W. Caspari, *Die Samuelisbücher* (KAT Sellin) (Leipzig, 1926) (distinguishes three principal documents, three fragments). / L. Rost, *Die Überlieferung v.d. Thronnachfolge Davids* (Beiträge zur Wissenschaft v. AT, F. 3, H. 6), (Stuttgart, 1926) (shatters even the unity of 2 S 9-20). / I. Hylander, *Der literarische Samuel-Komplex*

contested question. The dates suggested extend from the time of David to after the exile. Most probably, the Book achieved its present form shortly after the split of the kingdom, in the ninth century. It was this time that showed the greatest interest in establishing the legitimacy of David's dynasty. At that time, also, the ancient source material was still readily available.

This conception of the Book of Samuel does not contradict the concept of inspiration, which can easily extend over the course of several centuries and several authors. Inspiration does not mean mere mechanical dictation; it implies an incarnation of the word, and with respect to historical writing, the source material needs to be thoroughly penetrated by the revealing spirit. Various hands may have worked upon this Book at various times; but it is the Spirit of God, impregnating these historical sources with interpretation, order, and judgment, that makes them Scripture.

4) HISTORY OF THE TEXT:

There is hardly another Book of the Old Testament in which the text is as badly damaged as in the two Books of Samuel. The original was written in the old Semitic alphabet. Shortly before the turn of the millennium, quadratic script made its appearance in Palestine. During this transition from one script to the other, similar letters were easily confused.[9] The ancient Semitic script preferred the "incomplete writing" (*scriptio defectiva*), as witness the Mesha inscription.[10] Then too, as in the other Books, many mistakes can be assigned to the fatigue of the copyist. Similar beginnings or endings of words easily led to abbreviations or repetitions of the same word. This is a fate which the Book of Samuel must necessarily share with every literary product that has been handed down in manuscript. Many misunderstandings can be explained on the basis of the Hebrew consonant alphabet. It was not until the sixth century after Christ that Jewish scribes called the Masoretes ("handers down of tradition"), supplied the consonant text with vowel points, thereby creating an official norm for the Hebrew text, which was printed from the fifteenth century onwards.

(*1 S 1-15*) *traditionsgeschichtlich untersucht* (Uppsala, 1932). R. Press, *Der Prophet Samuel. Eine Traditionsgeschichtl. Untersuchung,* ZATW 56 (1938), 177-225. / J. Schildenberger, *Zur Einleitung i.d. Samuelbücher,* Misc. Miller (1951), 130-168 establishes the fundamental units on the basis of the principle of form history: they have been combined by the author in a sort of free historical composition.

---

9. Numerous examples of this in the Commentary by Bressan, 7.
10. Thus, e.g., originally David's name was written *dwd,* and only later, for the sake of greater clarity, a *yod* was introduced, *dwyd.*

The problem of text history can be appreciated only by a comparison with the ancient versions (translations). These go back to an era more ancient than the present Hebrew text (Masoretic text). The Books of Samuel were translated into Greek already in the second century B.C., and they have come down to us in various recensions.[11] The Greek translation is much more prolix than the Hebrew, but there are some omissions. The commentary of N. Peters lists 71 omissions and 123 additions.[12] It is not difficult to understand how sentences and words could be omitted, but how are we to explain the additions in the Greek text? De Boer, in his critical investigation of the Book of Samuel, arrives at the conclusion that the Septuagint does not present a literal translation of the original Hebrew, but a free reworking, so that both the additions and the omissions are to be explained in terms of Greek style.[13] This position does not hold up against closer examination. The translator did not take a free and liberal attitude towards his work; quite the contrary, he was slavishly faithful to his original, and frequently sacrificed intelligibility to faithfulness.[14] In fact, where it was possible, he attempts to find a Greek word which contains the same or similar consonants as the Hebrew word.[15] He holds fast to the Hebrew sentence construction, which may certainly have sounded alien to an ear which was attuned to the Greek language; the words which he could not understand he simply reproduced in Greek letters, and, on the other hand, he constantly translated Hebrew names and places.[16] This certainly does not make for a free and artistic reproduction of the original text. We are rather forced to the conclusion that the differences between the Greek and Hebrew text as we know them are not the product of the translator's work; they must be attributed to the presence of a different Hebrew recension of the original text.

All this presupposes the fact that our present-day Hebrew Masoretic

---

11. A. Rahlfs is one author who has devoted himself to the study of the Septuagint text. On the basis of the three ancient recensions, the Hexapla of Origen, the Lucan and the Hesychian, he has developed an "original text," which probably best reproduces the original Hebrew. His text is based primarily on the Codex Vaticanus (B). A. Rahlfs, Septuagint (Stuttgart, 1935, 1945).

12. N. Peters, Beiträge zur Text — und Literarkritik sowie zur Erklarung der Samuelbücher (Freiburg, 1899), 158-167.

13. A. H. de Boer, Research into the Text of 1 S 1-16 (Amsterdam-Paris, 1928).

14. 1 S 8, 3; 14, 38; 18, 31, etc.

15. In 1 S 1, 4 the Hebrew 'āhēb is given in Greek as ἠγάπα and in 5, 4 raq is translated ῥάχις; in 10, 1 pak is φάκος and in 13, 21 dorbān is translated as δρέπανον.

16. Cf. 1 S 13, 3; 14, 1; 20, 19, etc.

text is not identical with the original. The variants must, in each individual case, be critically examined, and in this work the more ancient reading is frequently to be substantiated on the basis of the Septuagint. This fact is further confirmed by the recent discoveries along the Dead Sea. Cave 4 yielded an almost complete manuscript of the Book of Samuel, together with fragments from the other caves. The text shows variants from the Masoretic text in favor of the Septuagint.[17]

The reconstruction of the original text is further aided by the ancient versions (translations). When the Greek Septuagint text was taken over by the Church and used as a proof of the messianic character of Jesus, the Jews quickly produced several new translations. The best known of these are the three versions of Aquila, Symmachus, and Theodotion. Unfortunately they have almost completely disappeared. The few extant fragments largely confirm the readings of the Septuagint. Of greater importance is the Aramaic translation, which is called simply Targum (translation). The Book of Samuel was translated by Jonatan Ben 'Uzzi'el in the second century after Christ, although its present form dates back only to the fourth century. The Syrian version, the Peshitta, is dependent upon Jonatan's Targum. This group of texts, however, possesses no great critical value. When the common people in the synagogue no longer understood the Hebrew text, the text was freely interpreted by the reader without any critical substantiation. The Targum thus has the character of an explanatory and paraphrasing translation. It is to be expected that in difficult passages the text is enlarged upon (for example in the Song of Hannah — 1 S 2, 1-10). Because of their venerable age, however, both Targum and Peshitta offer valuable hints towards a better understanding of the original text.

The old Latin translation, insofar as it is preserved, is, ultimately, based on the Septuagint text. In restoring the Bible to the *hebraica veritas,* St. Jerome made abundant use of existing translations in the Book of Samuel. These books were Jerome's first efforts, and they do not present the polished style achieved in his later work on the Pentateuch. Nor was Jerome in a position to make any critical studies of the Hebrew text; he merely used the Hebrew version available at his time. This fact seriously lessens the critical value of his translation, although it has lasting merit for the history of text criticism.

The science of text criticism, which has long advanced beyond the stage of mere arbitrary alterations and improvements of diffi-

---

17. F. M. Cross, Jr., *A Report on the Biblical Fragment of Cave Four in Wadi Qumran,* BASOR 141 (1956), 9-13. Of the 33 columns of the First Book of Samuel, 23 are preserved, and the whole of the Second Book, Bibl 35 (1954), 263-266; BASOR 132 (1953), 15-26.

cult readings and has attained the rank of a generally acknowledged scientific discipline, with established working principles and
methods, has done its utmost to reestablish the probable original
text despite the manifold varieties in the present text form. In
their totality, the two Books of Samuel portray the story of the
rise of monarchy in Israel, a story that could hardly be more
perceptive, dramatic, or convincing. By means of the excavations
to which we shall constantly refer in the course of our presentation,
the text is consistently vindicated as a faithful witness to its
time.

Though we cannot say that the prophet Samuel wrote these
Books, investigation of the text does yield the fact that the accounts of his activity as judge and prophet must have been set
down in writing not long after his time, and thereupon worked
into the historical Book as we know it today.

SECTION TWO

THE KINGSHIP OF SAUL

THERE is hardly a more consummate tragedy than the kingship of Saul. The account of his brief reign is summed up in the two words *bāḥar* and *mā'as,* choice and rejection. It was upon Saul that the hope of the people threatened by his existence all centered; it was from him that they expected something superhuman. His rise was rapid, almost too rapid to maintain itself. It was Yahweh's own election that lay upon him. He is a man marked by God, anointed by the prophet Samuel, chosen by the people, confirmed in his kingship by successful campaigns and victories. Victorious in the political realm, he collapses in the religious sphere. In the story of the very first king, we clearly see that kingship in Israel is not like kingship in any other nation. The king of Israel belongs to two worlds, religious and political: the two are inseparable. In terms of religion, the kingship is the kingship of Yahweh's favor, for it is Yahweh, even after the institution of an earthly king, who is and remains the true and only Lord of the host of Israel. When the earthly king takes a position "against the word or mouth of Yahweh," it is the sheer weight of nature itself which precipitates his collapse. The external political collapse is only the visible expression of the tragedy that has already been enacted within.

CHAPTER IV

SAUL'S ELECTION

(1 S 9 — 12)

OUR narrator sketches a new family picture, just as perceptive, vital, and filled with personal characteristics as the two he has already presented, the idyll of Ramathaim and the tragedy of Shiloh. The new family is also introduced by a genealogy.[1] The story begins with Kish of the tribe of Benjamin, who had a son named Saul.[2] The tribe of Benjamin was well known for its warlike character. In the era of the Judges, all the other tribes joined against it in order to subdue Benjamin (Jg 19-21). The tribe was almost completely rooted out of Israel. Although seriously weakened as a result of this civil war, Benjamin seems to have largely maintained its warlike disposition. It was not in vain that the patriarch Jacob gave Benjamin the ravenous wolf as his heraldic animal (Gn 49, 27). Kish too seems to have been a true son of

---

1. The genealogy can be found, with slight variations, in 1 Ch 8, 29-33; 9, 35-39 as well. Dhorme makes an attempt to harmonize the texts, but this is not entirely successful. Apparently the genealogies are based on different lines of tradition. There is an Assyrian eponymous official in 755 B.C. who has the name Qi-i-$šu$, which apparently means "gift" (of God).

2. $šā'ūl$, "the man got by prayer." There is a scarab of reddish brown limestone from the 8th century with the inscription lš'l, "belonging to Saul." IEJ 4 (1954), 236-238.

Benjamin; he is called *gibbôr hāyil*,[3] literally, "man of power" (9, 1). It is true that this same expression can describe a man who is rich and "powerful in possessions" like Boaz (Rt 2, 1; 2 K 15, 20; 24, 14), but this cannot be its meaning in the case of Saul's father. In the era of the Judges, this expression was generally understood as "mighty hero of war," like Jephthah (Jephte) (Jg 11, 1). It seems, thus, to be no accident that it was precisely from this warlike tribe and from this family in which military prowess was a long tradition, that the first king of Israel was chosen.

The home of this family of Benjaminites was Gibeah (Gabaa), that is, "heights, mountain." In order to distinguish it from other mountain locations, it was called *gib'at šā'ûl* (1 S 11, 4; 2 S 21, 6; Is 10, 23) or *gib'at binyāmîn* (Jg 20, 4; 1 S 13, 2; 1 K 15, 22). Excavations [4] have clearly shown that Gibeah is to be identified with the modern Tell-el-Ful. 5 or 6 km north of Jerusalem, rising like a step pyramid, there is a mountain 839 m in elevation. The heights afford a splendid view of the surrounding country. To the south lies Jerusalem, in those days still in the possession of the Jebusites; to the southwest, looking out across Anatot, the mirror of the Dead Sea is visible; towards the north-

---

3. J. van der Ploeg, *Le sense de gibbor hajil*, in *Vivre et Penser* (Revue Biblique) 1 (1941), 120-125. / P. Joüon, Bibl 7 (1926), 164.

4. In the years 1922-23 and 1933 it was excavated by W. F. Albright. Comprehensive account in C. C. McCown, *The Ladder of Progress in Palestine*, (1943), 205-209. / Abel II, 334. / DBS 3 (1938), 404ff. / Galling, BRL, 101ff. The name Tell-el-Gul means "bean-hill" and today it is entirely uninhabited. The hillside was parcelled into fields which were planted especially with beans. In 1951 I wanted to visit the mountain of Saul from Jerusalem. I made my way freely, traveling on foot: in the Bible countries, it is best, where possible, to travel in the ancient manner. My only companion on the journey was a small Hebrew Bible, and I was attempting to test the narratives of the Book of Samuel, *in situ*. But as I made my way from the main road into the mountain country, I was arrested by an Arab military detachment and returned to Jerusalem as a Jewish spy (Hebrew Bible!). Once again I attempted the expedition, this time dressed as an Arab, but to no avail. At Nebi Samwil I was once again taken prisoner and managed to get free only after some lengthy negotiations.

east the cities of Geba and Michmash are close at hand (1 S
13, 16; 14, 16). Towards the north the view stretches for some
12 km, before it is cut off by an horizon of higher mountains.
The present-day sites of Ramallah and el-Bireh are 893 m in
elevation. The western horizon is formed by the Nebi Samwil, with
an elevation of 895 m. The foot of the Tell-el-Ful is the crossing
for the highways which join south and north Palestine. The traveler
from the coastal plain to the Jordan Valley must also cross the
mountains in the vicinity. Nature predestined these mountain
heights to a position of dominion, a truly royal mountain, buffeted
by wind and weather, providentially chosen, in a stormy time, to be
the first royal city of Israel.

1) ANOINTED BY SAMUEL (1 S 9, 1 – 10, 16):

Two lines are enough to sketch a royal portrait of Saul: "Saul
was a handsome man. There was not a man among the people
of Israel more handsome than he; from his shoulders upward he
was taller than any of the people" (9, 2). The Hebrew language
has few words to express character; in this portrait we have simply
the word "good" (ṭôb), which appears to say everything that
is implied in the concept of a perfect man. The young Saul was
a royal character, a truly majestic figure.

What a contrast in the narrative! We have just been favored
with a presentiment of the glory of the future ruler of Israel, and
now comes the sober narrative of his search for the lost she-asses.
The narrative is not set in a dream land, but on the mountains
and valleys of the Palestinian farmer and shepherd. His father's
misfortune with his cattle is what brings Saul to his throne. The
asses had wandered astray. Their number is not mentioned, but
at any event their loss would have been a serious matter for the
not particularly wealthy family of Kish. There is a hint of this in
the father's words to his son: "Take one of the servants with you,
and arise, go and look for the asses" (9, 3). Thus begins a
three day's search through the district of Benjamin and Ephraim.
The path that they took is described in terms of places which

cannot be precisely located today.[5] When they were searching through the territory of Zuph his kin, without any further success, Saul had already decided to give up the search and return home, lest his father also begin to worry about his lost son.

Once again the element of chance enters. The servant has one last hope to suggest. He knows that in the city "there is a man of God, and he is a man that is held in honor; all that he says comes true" (9, 6). Saul decides, against his will, to seek out this man of God, and see if he might know where the asses are. They start along the path to the city. They are met — a genuine touch of Ancient Near East color — by maidens coming out to draw water. In response to Saul's question they answer immediately, as maidens are so likely to do, with more information than had been requested. In one breath they hear how the man of God had come into the city, that sacrifice is being offered on the high place, and that they must hurry if they mean to overtake him (9, 11-13).

A later glossator has here added the information that in ancient times people went to consult a "seer" (rō'eh), when they wanted to ask questions of God. Later the seer was called "prophet" (nābî') (9, 9). The word "seer" occurs only rarely in the Bible, a total of 10 times, 7 of these in the Books of Samuel. This information clearly shows that there was a "seer cult" in ancient Israel. Perhaps this name came into disrepute, so that the expression nābî', "herald, proclaimer (of the word of God)" was preferred.[6] In visiting a seer, it was imperative to bring a gift. The

---

5. Saul begins his search in the neighborhood of šālišāh, a locale which cannot be more definitely identified, although it must be situated north of Gibeah. The name of the second valley, ša'alim, probably "field of jackals," is still retained in the modern 'Araq dār eš-Šu'alek, that is, "the rocky dens of the jackals," some 25 km north of Gibeah. The second day they looked further in the country of Yemini and the territory of the Zophites. These last were settled around the city of Ramathaim, the home of Samuel. The country yemini is, accordingly, to be sought not far from this region: Ramathaim is about 30 km from Gibeah. The two men had made a circle of some 30-35 km in their two days' search and found nothing. / L. Heidet, Le voyage de Saul à la recherche des ânesses de son père, Bibl 1 (1920), 532; 2 (1921), 363-368. / For a good map, cf. Bressan, Appendix 2.

6. M. A. van den Oudenrijn, De vocabulis quibusdam termino nabi' synonymis, Bibl 6 (1925), 294ff.

elders whom the king of Moab had sent to the seer Balaam brought with them "the fees for divination in their hands" (Nb 22, 7, 17). King Jeroboam sent his wife to the prophet Ahijah with ten loaves of bread and a jar of honey, to inquire into the fate of his sick sons (1 K 14, 1-3). Saul, unfortunately, had no gift to offer. The bread was all used up. But his servant came to the rescue with the "fourth part of a shekel of silver." [7]

At the city gate they actually met Samuel, who took them along to the high place (bāmâh); at that time the Israelites worshipped Yahweh on sacred high places, which, however, in the era of the Kings, were abrogated because of the dangers of defection to the Canaanite cults. At the sacrificial banquet, Samuel assigned the place of honor to Saul, and served him with the largest and choicest portion.[8] This extraordinary behavior of Samuel shows that he had already anticipated these events: he treated Saul as Yahweh's chosen one.[9]

After the banquet, Samuel brought Saul and his servant into his house, and spread a bed for them upon the roof. Early next morning he awakened them and led them out of the city. As they approached the gate, Samuel told Saul to send his servant on ahead. In the early morning solitude of the city gate, Samuel poured oil upon Saul's head. Then he kissed him and said: "The Lord has anointed you to be nāgîd over his inheritance" (19, 1). Ritual anointing was a regular practice in the Canaanite world of that day. In one of the Amarna letters,[10] the Hittite King Addu-Nirari writes this to the Pharaoh: "Manahbirria, King of Egypt, your grandfather, made my grandfather Taku king of Nuhasse, and poured oil upon his head . . . ." By this anointing Saul be-

---

7. A silver shekel weighed about 14.55 g. (c. 1½ ounce). Minted coinage was in common circulation only during the Persian era.
8. The fat pieces were considered the best (Ex 29, 22; Lv 3, 9; 7, 3).
9. M. Buber, *Die Erzählung von Sauls Königswahl*. VT 6 (1956), 113-173, feels that the scene was prepared well in advance. There would have been "conspirators" assembled on the heights, and Samuel would have presented the future king to them. But there are no traces of, any such "conspiratorial atmosphere" (148) in the text.
10. J. A. Knudtzon, *Die El-Amarnatafeln* (Leipzig, 1915), I, 319; table 51, lines 4-7.

came a "messiah" (*māšîªḥ*), an anointed (*christos*). It is only in the prophetic writings that this word acquires its "messianic" meaning. In ancient times it referred simply to the king who was elevated above the ranks of ordinary men by his anointing. One astonishing note is the fact that Samuel anointed Saul, not to be a king (*melek*), but as *nāgîd*. As reformer, Samuel had fought against the inroads of Canaanite paganism, and had the *beʿālîm* and *ʿaštārôt* removed. He himself had no doubts as to the necessity of kingship in Israel, although the royal ideal he envisioned, the product of Israel's religious heritage, was different from that of the representatives of his people, who looked beyond their national frontiers and sought to introduce a pagan ideal. The spiritual conflict which ensued played about the two ideals, either *nāgîd* or *melek*. The Hebrew word *nāgîd* is related to the Ugaritic word *nōqēd,* shepherd, as well as the Accadian *naqid ṣalmat qaqqadi,* "shepherd of the black heads." [11] The concept of shepherd of the people, together with the symbolism of shepherd's staff and scepter, was familiar in Israel since the time of Jacob's blessing (Gn 49, 19). In Samuel's opinion, Israel had no reason to borrow from the pagans. In the era of the Judges, Yahweh constantly provided a savior for his people, endowing him with his own Spirit; in this present hour of national crisis he would also send his people a shepherd (*nāgîd*).[12] The contradiction which appears in the narratives of the introduction of monarchy is thus not the result of a later interpretation of history;[13] it is founded in the historical position of Samuel himself. Time was pressing forward; new solutions must be sought to control the situation. Samuel, as prophet, wanted to draw upon the religious depths of his people, but the elders were looking to the pagan world about them. After the introduction of monarchy,

---

11. H. Cazelles, VT 8 (1958), 321-326, Besprechung von R. de Vaux, *Les Institutions de l'At* (1958).
12. The introduction of kingship has much in common with the elevation of the charismatic leaders of the people, during the era of the Judges: a. election by Yahweh, b. gift of the Spirit, c. heroic deeds, RB 61 (1954), 585.
13. W. Eichrodt, *Theologie des AT,* 1 (1957), 298. Divided judgment of the kingship, in the sources.

along pagan models, the *malkût,* the monarchy, had to be incorporated into the community of Israel's religious beliefs. This was accomplished by men like the prophet Nathan, who pronounced divine promises to this same *malkût,* the kingship of David. But even in the days of the kings, the title *nāgîd* is still retained as the name for the designated, future king.

The title *nāgîd* is thus surrounded by a religious halo, whereas *melek* describes the profane sphere of kingship. As Yahweh's specially designated representative, Saul is called *nāgîd,* the shepherd consecrated and chosen and proclaimed by Yahweh; it is only the free choice of the people which confers the royal title *melek.* Divine consecration and human dignity are clearly distinguished.[14]

In the Old Testament, when God presents a revelation, he supports its credibility by subsequent signs. The anointing of Saul is followed by three such signs, by which Saul is to recognize the genuinity of his election. At Rachel's tomb [15] he will meet two men who will tell him that the asses have been found (10, 2). At the oak of Deborah [16] he will meet three men who are making a pilgrimage to Bethel and they will give him two loaves of bread (10, 3-4). Finally, at Gibeah, he will meet a group of prophets [17] whereupon he himself will be seized by

---

14. A. Alt, *Kleine Schriften,* II (1953), 23.
15. The tomb of Rachel would be located, accordingly, in the mountains of Ephraim and is not to be identified with the Kubbet Rahil, located in the neighborhood of Bethlehem. This would more probably be the Mausoleum of Archelaus. Bressan, 164.
16. Instead of Tabor in the text we are probably to read Deborah.
17. Hebrew *ḥebel-nᵉbi' îm,* "band, group, society of prophets." The origin of prophecy is treated more explicitly in the following volume. Here it is sufficient to point up the fact that this is the first passage in Scripture where the *nᵉbi'îm* make their appearance. In the time of Samuel there must have been religious societies (*ḥᵃbālîm*) of men who acknowledged Yahweh's sovereignty by solemn sacrifices on the sacred high places, by procession with music and song, and who preached the Yahweh faith, so that they came to be known as "preachers, heralds" (from *nābā',* "to preach," *nābî',* "preacher, herald"). The practices of these "preacher-brotherhoods" seem, frequently, to have taken on an ecstatic character.

the Spirit of Yahweh and begin to "prophesy" (10, 5-6). If these signs are verified, then he may do "whatever his hand finds to do," for God is with him (10, 7), that is, God's help will crown his every undertaking, everything that he has "under hand," with sure success.

The three signs all appeared in the manner foretold by the seer. These events all produced a profound effect upon Saul. He became a different man, for God "gave him another heart" (10, 9). From this moment on, he bore the special predestination of Yahweh in himself, but he told no one of his experience (10, 16).[18]

2) THE ROYAL ELECTION AT MIZPAH (1 S 10, 17-27):

"If there is a single scene in the Biblical narrative of the introduction of kingship into Israel that bears the clear stamp of Ancient Near East living, then it is certainly the popular assembly at Mizpah (Maspha) where the king was chosen by sacred lot." [19] Samuel had assembled the representatives of the tribes at the memorable location of Mizpah. It was from here that reform had first spread; it was from here that Israel had begun its victorious battle against the Philistines. This location, rich in memories, was now to witness the decision for or against

---

18. M. Bič, *Saul sucht die Eselinnen*, VT 7 (1957), 92-97, considers the account of the search for the lost asses as a document of religious syncretism, dating from an era in which Israel had gradually grown into the Canaanite world of ideas. Kish would belong to a sanctuary, the *gibbôrē ḥayil* would have been the bodyguard of the divinity. The search for the lost animals is interpreted as simply the festival of a lost and searched for divinity, reminiscent of the festival of the dying and resurgent deity. The place names, and the whole geography, would accordingly have a mystical meaning, and should be so interpreted. / H. J. Stoebe, *Noch einmal die Eselinnen des Kiš*, VT 7 considers the account as a legend, meant to glorify the hero by means of the "humility motif," composing a free narrative of his original vocation. Even though the account has clear literary leanings, this still speaks more for historical reality than freely composed legend.
19. L. Desnoyers, *Histoire du peuple hébreu*, II, 39.

the kingship. Samuel himself was the chief speaker against the kingship. In his great "election discourse" (10, 18-19) he explained that the election of a king is actually a defection from God, who, since the exodus from Egypt, had constantly proved to be the Savior of his people. But when the representatives of the tribes, despite his address to them, insisted upon their demand: "Set a king over us" (10, 19), he had the individual tribes approach in order, and cast the sacred lot upon them.

Israel still practiced a patriarchal form of popular assembly. The twelve tribes (šebātîm) were divided into clans (mišpāḥôt or 'ªlāpîm), and these were further divided into individual families or clans (battîm or bêt'ābôt — literally, "houses of fathers"): Joshua, after the failure of the expedition against Ai, also cast the lot according to tribes, families, and households, in order to determine the guilty parties (Jos 7, 14-18). In electing the king, this same ancient pattern was followed. Our narrator presupposes a knowledge of this practice and recounts only the result: "The tribe of Benjamin was taken by lot, the family of the Matrites, and from among them Saul." The precise manner of casting the lot is open to conjecture. The text says repeatedly that the individual groups "entered before the presence of Yahweh." The decision could thus be arrived at by the Urim and Thummim, which were found in the high priest's oracle pouch; they answered either yes or no, or frequently refused an answer. The lot may have proceeded in something like the following manner: Samuel would admit, for example, the tribe of Benjamin to the presence of Yahweh, perhaps before the Ark of the Covenant, before which the high priest was standing, and ask: "Is the king to come from the tribe of Benjamin?" Then the high priest would take a stone from the oracle pouch with the answer yes. In the same way, the lot would be taken over the various families, and households until it came to Saul.

Saul, knowing what was coming, had hidden among the "baggage," by which we are to understand the wagons, tents, and equipages of the travelers who had come from a great distance (10, 22). The assembly once again had recourse to lot, to see whether Saul was present or not. When it was discovered that he had hidden among the baggage, they went to look for him. When he made his way into the midst of the people, a truly royal apparition, a new cry rang out for the first time in the history of Israel: "Long live the King!" (10, 24). Samuel presented the new king to the people with these words: "Do you see him whom the Lord has chosen?" (10, 24).

Kingship makes its first appearance in Israel as an elective monarchy. The king was demanded by the assembly of elders which had gathered at Ramathaim to speak to Samuel, and now he was chosen by God in Mizpah. It was not plurality of votes that decided, but the word of Yahweh. Samuel recorded the whole proceedings in writing, and left the record in the presence of Yahweh, that is, in the Ark of the Covenant (10, 25). Samuel then dismissed the assembly.

Saul too returned to Gibeah. He was joined by several "men of valor whose hearts God had touched" (10, 26). They formed the bodyguard of the king and the nucleus of the future professional army.

On this very day of general enthusiasm, it was obvious that not all were in accord with the principle of monarchy. Samuel was opposed on religious grounds, but among the people there were circles who not only were unenthusiastic about the new king, but actually said contemptuously: "How can this man save us?" (10, 27). They refused to bring him any presents. Saul pretended not to notice this omission, but this fact clearly shows how insecure was the foundation of this new monarchy. Before it was completely recognized, Saul would have to achieve some significant success.

3) THE DELIVERANCE OF JABESH-GILEAD (1 S 11, 1-12, 25):

When we read the account of the Ammonite war, we feel that we are back in the Book of Judges. The situation is the same: Israel is critically oppressed by her enemy, and there is little hope for deliverance; but then the Spirit of Yahweh comes upon Saul, and with unexpected strength he strikes down the enemy and frees his people from their time of crisis. Saul's kingship had been prophetically foretold by Samuel and confirmed by the people through the medium of sacred lot, but before achieving general recognition, it needed the test of battle.

After his election as king, Saul returned to his farmer's work as if nothing had happened. Meantime, storm clouds were gathering in the land across the Jordan. The Ammonite king Nahash (serpent) had taken advantage of Israel's political weakness and her subjugation under the yoke of the Philistines, in order to occupy Israelite territory across the Jordan. Opposition was currently centered about the city of Jabesh-Gilead. The entire district of Gilead (Galaad)[20] was the settlement of three Israelite tribes, Ruben, Gad, and half of Manasseh. To the tribe of Gad belonged the eastern bank of the Jordan, from the Lake of Gennesaret down to the Red Sea, and thus also the threatened city Jabesh-Gilead (Jabes Galaad).[21]

Already in the days of the Judges the Ammonites had attempted to occupy sections of Gilead, but they were beaten back by Jephthah (Jg 10, 6-12, 7). The fact that the Ammonites were now in a position to pursue their claims to the very banks of the Jordan must be interpreted as a sign of Israel's complete national descendancy.

The inhabitants of Jabesh felt themselves too weak to directly oppose the Ammonite demands. They chose the lesser evil and offered Nahash a treaty and military service (11, 1). In the event of a war, in which they would certainly be defeated, their

---

20. Perhaps from the Arabic *ǧalʿad*, "hard-stony," thus mountain country, or from *ǧaʿuda*, "uneven, rough." Steep valleys have been eroded into the mountain country, attaining an elevation of 1261 m in the *Umm ed-Daraǧ*. Bressan, 179.

21. The name is preserved in modern Wadi Jabis, between the Yarmuk and the Jabbok, a deep and beautiful valley, abounding in vegetation, which empties into the Jordan. On the southern entrance to the valley, modern *Der Ḥalāwa*, at an elevation of 500 m were discovered ruins which, however, date to Roman times. According to the investigations of Nelson Glueck, Jabesh Gilead, BASOR 89 (1943), 2-5; 91 (1945), 7 (photographs!), the ancient Jabesh is to be located on the northern entrance to the valley, at modern Tell-el-Mekbereh. This locale affords a fine panoramic view to north and west. Beth-shan is only 15 km distant, some four hours (31, 12). The pottery remains attest to Israelite settlement from the 13th to the 6th centuries.

city would be destroyed, men, women, and children would be slaughtered, while the maidens would be divided among the victors as booty. If, however, Nahash was willing to accept the treaty of alliance, then they would at least have saved their lives, even though it would have been the end of their freedom. As it turned out, Nahash pressed his demands, which, in keeping with the brutality of that age, are terrible to relate. He demanded that all the men have their right eye gouged out, making them unfit for military service; the left eye was covered by the shield in battle. Reduced to this defenseless position, the city would necessarily remain in subjection to the Ammonites. At the same time the treaty conditions involved a crude jest which would have made a laughing stock of the town's inhabitants. Mockery and ridicule seemed to have run in this people's blood. In David's time, they sent his ambassadors back with half-shaven beards and half torn clothing (2 S 10, 4; 12, 16-31).

The people of Jabesh asked for seven days to consider the proposal, and began casting about for help among their fellow tribesmen. Their request was magnanimously granted, in the full realization that no help would be forthcoming. The hour was ripe for Saul. The envoys from the threatened city directed their path immediately to the newly elected king, at Gibeah. Saul was just coming back from the field where he had been plowing with the oxen. When he heard the shameful news, the Spirit of God came upon him (11, 6); he slaughtered the oxen, cut them into twelve pieces, and sent the pieces to the twelve tribes of Israel with this threat: "Whoever does not come out after Saul and Samuel, so shall be done to his oxen!" (11, 7).[22]

---

22. The dismemberment of animals, human beings, and other things was not alien to the Ancient Near East. The Levite cut the body of his ravaged wife into twelve pieces, at Gibeah, and sent them out as a summons to a war of vengeance against Benjamin (Jg 19, 29). According to a text from Nari, an official demanded that a captured criminal be killed and his head cut into pieces and sent into the city, to inspire terror to all. Text in G. Wallis, *Eine Parallele zu Richter 19, 29 und 1 S 11, 5 aus dem Briefarchiv von Mari*, ZATW 64 (1952), 57-61.

In a treaty between Assurnirari (753-746) and Mati'-ilu of Bith-

The city of Jabesh was allied to Gibeah by a covenant of blood. When all Israel swore together to avenge the shameful deeds at Gibeah, Jabesh alone did not take part in the punitive expedition, which spelled almost the complete extermination of the tribe of Benjamin. As punishment for having failed to join the expedition, Jabesh was made war upon, destroyed with fire and sword, men and women killed; only 400 maidens were allowed to survive, and those were given to the Benjaminites as wives, to assure the continued existence of the tribe of Benjamin (Jg 21, 8-14).

Saul's envoys went out to the individual tribes with the bloody pieces of meat. Together with them went the *pahad Yahweh*. Commentators are not agreed as to whether this is an objective genitive, that is "fear of Yahweh, fear in the face of Yahweh," or a subjective genitive, that is, "the fear that Yahweh inspires." The former might well be the more probable solution. The unmistakable threats from Saul filled all with fear of the king and, at the same time, fear of Yahweh, since the king of Israel was Yahweh's anointed one. At all events, "the people came out as one man" (11, 7).

Now Saul could show whether he was capable of delivering Israel from the threats of her enemies. That was the primary reason for demanding a king. Saul set the city of Bezek [23] as mustering point, situated 15 km west of the Jordan, on the same heights as Jabesh, some 20 km away from the threatened city, a distance which could be covered in a single night's march. The number of the assembled warriors, 30,000 from Judah and 300,000 from Israel (11, 8) is based upon a misunderstanding of the word *'eleph*, "thousand," which also means "household."

Agusi, we read: "Just as the head of this ram has been cut into pieces, so shall the head of him who breaks this covenant be cut into pieces." Text *ibid.* The Hittites seem to have made use of similar expressions. / A. Goetz, *The Hittite Ritual of Tunnawi* (N. Haven, 1938); W. F. Albright, JBL 59 (1940), 316.

---

23. Modern Khirbet Izbik, which has preserved the ancient name, on the road which joins Schechem to Beth-shan.

From Judah came 30 household levies, and from Israel 300. The problem will come up again in our consideration of David's census. The seventh day arrived. The envoys had all returned to Jabesh. This was their answer to Nahash: "Tomorrow we will give ourselves up to you, and you may do to us whatever seems good to you" (11, 10). Saul had completed his plan of attack. During the night he would march from the mustering camp, and at the time of the "morning watch" [24] he would arrive at Jabesh and take up battle. On tactical grounds, he divided his army into three divisions, just as Gideon (Jg 7, 16) and the Philistines (13, 17) had done. The battle began in the early dawn and by the midday heat it had been decided, as the messenger announced in Jabesh (11, 9). It was harvest time, and Saul had to hurry in order to avoid the unbearable midday heat. Mesha (9th century) king of the Moabites, used the same tactic in his war against the Israelites: "I went by night and I fought against it from the break of day until noon and I took it and I killed all the people . . . ." [25]

The campaign went off according to plan. When the sun was high in the heavens, the Ammonites had been beaten and put to flight, "so that no two of them were left together." Saul made a triumphal entry into the liberated city. The unbelievable had happened. The short span of seven days had seen the rise of a powerful military levy, which, under the adroit leadership of King Saul, had driven the enemy from the land. The new monarchy had proved itself successful. Saul's over-enthusiastic followers wanted to turn this very victory into an act of vengeance, and remove the opposition which had shown itself contemptuous when Saul was chosen at Mizpah. Saul, however, showed greater depth of soul, and was unwilling to desecrate the day of his first triumph with the blood of his fellow countrymen (11, 13).

But the iron must be forged while it is still glowing. Samuel,

---

24. The Israelites divided the night, not like the Romans into four vigils, but into three vigils of four hours each. The third vigil would thus be equivalent to the early morning hours of 2 − 6:00.

25. Mesha inscription, line 15: Galling, TGI 48.

still the spiritual leader and perhaps even the political head of the nation, was quick to seize the opportunity: "Come, let us go to Gilgal, and there renew the kingdom!" (11, 14).

4) SAMUEL'S ABDICATION — CONFIRMATION OF SAUL'S KINGSHIP IN GILGAL:

After the warriors had rested from the exertion of battle, they marched down from Jabesh to Gilgal (Galgala) [26] near Jericho, in two clear and refreshing summer night's marches. What was to take place there, since Saul had already been chosen king by the assembled tribes at Mizpah? The text is uncertain. It might mean either "renew the kingship" (*haddēš*) or "sanctify" (*qoddēš*). The solemn ceremonies at Gilgal fall into two distinct parts, the offering of sacrifice and the abdication of Samuel. The sacrifices after the military campaign were expiation offerings.[27] But the sacrifices at Gilgal have a further and deeper meaning; they are a joyous festival in the presence of Yahweh, thanksgiving for the confirmation of Saul's kingship. At Mizpah there had been no sacrifices; Saul had been proclaimed king by lot, but his "solemn enthronement" takes place only at Gilgal.[28]

It was also Samuel's hour to step down, to entrust his power as judge into the hands of the new king. First he exonerated himself in the presence of all the people. "I have walked before you

---

26. Muilenburg, *The site of ancient Gilgal*, BASOR 140 (1950), 11-27. Examination of the ancient and medieval accounts and prospective diggings at the site confirm the *khirbet el-mefjir* as ancient Gilgal.
27. Cf. Nb 31, 19; 19, 12 (after the battle against the Midianites).
28. The later history of the kings makes it clear that the new king's accession to power was achieved in various stages. In the case of David and Solomon, and other kings as well, there was a rather lengthy interval between official naming and eventual enthronement. Thus, we need not explain the anointing by Samuel, the royal election at Mizpah, and the anti-royalist harangue of Samuel as mere historical legend. The accounts may well have derived from various sources: 8, 1-22; 10, 17-27 and 12 from source E; 9, 1-10, 16; 11, 1-15 from source J. Their very divergencies help to lay bare the opposing forces which led to the formation of kingship in Israel.

from my youth until this day," and have represented the public interest of Israel. But now he has grown old — in his seventy's — and from now on "the new king walks before you," that is, attends to the business of state. Looking back upon his long activity as judge, he asks the people, in the presence of Yahweh and his anointed one: "Whose ox have I taken? Or whose ass have I taken? Or whom have I defrauded? Whom have I oppressed? Or from whose hand have I taken a bribe to blind my eyes with it?" And the whole people, in the presence of Yahweh, had to give public testimony to the pure and blameless manner in which he had fulfilled his office. But there is one thing that the old man and prophet cannot forget. Although he himself had assembled the people to elect a king at Mizpah and to confirm the kingship at Gilgal, he could still not rest content with kingship as such. For him it was always a defection from Yahweh's kingship (12, 12). Now that the inevitable had happened, and Israel had her king, king and people alike could face the prospect of a future blessed by God only if they kept faith with Yahweh. But if they should refuse to hear Yahweh's voice and rebel against the "mouth of Yahweh," then the hand of Yahweh would destroy them (12, 15). This was no address of flattering congratulation for the enthronement of the new king; it was a statement in every way worthy of the incorruptible man of God, as Samuel truly was.

The military relief of Jabesh implied not only a military victory but also a psychological success. Israel's self-awareness as a nation was reawakened. The people had witnessed a solemn proof of the fact that they no longer needed to stand hopelessly under the oppression of foreign powers. The kingship of Saul achieved fulfillment in the manner of the charismatic leaders from the days of the Judges.[29] It takes on form and meaning from the gift of Yahweh and the choice of the people. From its very inception it was conceived of as a defensive kingship, and thus it was obligated to military pursuits. In individual cases, such as the siege of Jabesh, we read of a conscription of all the tribes. But as a lasting institution, this was insufficient. If the king

---

29. M. Noth, *Geschichte Israels*, 146ff.

was to hold his enemies in check, he must take the further step and build a standing army. This is the new element which distinguishes Saul's activity from that of the Judges. The Judges, acting upon God's own impulse, had achieved their successes by means of a military conscription. "Saul quickly managed to augment the military proscription by a corps of standing troops, constantly prepared for battle and especially suited to small scale engagements. Tradition gives ample evidence of how he formed a body of constantly available troops, and employed them in engagements in which the tribal levy was not called upon. It is particularly owing to these troops that, so long as Saul was king, the Philistines could be kept at a considerable distance from the Israelite frontier; adaptation to their adversary's tactics, in this one point, produced abundant fruit." [30]

---

30. A. Alt, *Kleine Schriften*, II (1953), 27.

CHAPTER V

SAUL'S REJECTION

(1 S 13-15)

IT is clear that the Books of Samuel do not mean to present a complete account of Saul's reign, and yet it certainly is strange that the enthusiastic confirmation of Saul's kingship in Gilgal is immediately followed, in the same chapter, by the account of his rejection. The accounts are presented side by side, in anecdote form, and this further complicates the problem of temporal succession. 1 S 13, 1 does offer an historical reference, but it seems to be hopelessly corrupt: "Saul was one year old when he became king, and he ruled two years over Israel." On the basis of this text, M. Noth [1] concludes that Saul's kingship was an episode of only two years. But this would certainly be too short to admit the various military campaigns (14, 47-48). The *Biblia Hebraica* of R. Kittel proposes emendations. In the first member of the sentence, the number has been lost, whereas in the second member we are to read "20" and not "2" since the symbol for "2" (*beta*) is similar with the numerical symbol for "20" (*kaph*) and the two can easily be confused. This would assign a reign of 20 years to Saul. Most commentators avoid the difficulty by regarding the sentence as a marginal gloss which found its way into the text at a later date, no doubt occasioned by the stereotypically repeated

---

1. M. Noth, *Geschichte Israels*, 153.

introductory formula from the Books of the Kings: "NN was so many years old when he began to reign and he reigned so many years." Correspondingly, there would have to be a notice for Saul: "He was . . . old when he became king, and he ruled 20 years over Israel." [2]

The Apostle Paul, in his sermon in Antioch, assigns Saul a reign of 40 years (Ac 13, 21). As we shall discuss more explicitly in our appendix on chronology, 40 belongs to the symbolic numbers and makes no real statement about the actual number of years. We thus have no criteria for establishing a more precise dating of Saul's reign. Only with the help of excavations can we arrive at some approximate values. On the basis of successive excavation strata, the destruction of Shiloh can be assigned to the time around 1050 B.C., or somewhat later.[3] Samuel's activity must have reached its climax about 1030 B.C., and Saul must have become king around 1020 B.C. The first events of his reign must have followed in quick succession: the liberation of Jabesh and the defeat of the Philistines. After this, Saul had time to erect a citadel, to organize his army, and to conduct his various campaigns against Moab, Ammon, Edom, and Aram. The assumption of the 20 years would thus be not too far from the truth.

1) SAUL'S WAR AGAINST THE PHILISTINES (1 S 13 – 14):

Saul's success after the battle at *'eben hā'ezer* was not a lasting one. Saul did manage to arrest the furthest advances of the Philistines and to secure a few years of peace; but when Samuel became an old man, the Philistines seemed to have achieved control of the entire mountain district, without any great show of resistance. They even managed to establish outposts (*nāṣîb*)[4] which

---

2. H. J. Schöps, *Symmachusstudien III*, Bibl 29 (1948), 31-51, explains "one year old" as equivalent to "innocent, free of sin." He quotes the *Deutsche Historienbibel* of Petrus Comestor.

3. Albright, *Religion of Israel*, 119.

4. The expression *nāṣîb* is not clear; the word is generally *maṣṣāb*. The translation as "military post" is based on Targum and Jerome (statio philistinorum). LXX has ἀνάστημα, "columns, statues," literally "something set up," a warning marker, indicating Philistine territory?

were apparently military garrisons, in the neighborhood of Saul's home city of Geba (13, 3), from which point they controlled the surrounding country. It is possible that such outposts were spread throughout the country. Their principal objective was to keep Israel weaponless and defenseless. With this end in view, they achieved a monopoly of iron working. There was no smith in Israel (13, 19). The Book of Judges recounts that the Israelites had swords (Jg 3, 12; 8, 20; 9, 54) in their wars against the Moabites (Jg 3, 12), Midianites, and Amalekites (Jg 7, 13). In their war against the Philistines, however, they no longer had them. Shamgar fought with an oxgoad (Jg 3, 31), and Samson fought the Philistines with the jawbone of an ass (Jg 15, 15).[5] The Philistines allowed the Israelites to use iron only for their agricultural implements. If they wanted to sharpen a plowshare, they had to go to a smith in Philistine territory and pay him a high price (31, 21);[6] it must have been the Philistines themselves who first introduced the use of iron in Palestine. The Iron Age in Palestine begins with the migration of the sea peoples. This fact is further confirmed by archaeology.[7] The first iron instruments and vessels came from the Philistine excavations of the twelfth

---

5. Excavations in ancient Jaffa have cleared up this puzzle. The excavator, Dr. Kaplan, unearthed an actual jawbone of an ass, the tooth cavities supplied with razor-sharp metal inserts, a very formidable weapon.

6. To sharpen a plowshare required the payment of one *pym* (*payim*). This hitherto unintelligible measure of weight has recently been confirmed as correct by excavation finds. Jerusalem yielded a bronze weight, and Gezer a marble weight, and further weights appeared in Tell en-Nasbeh and Beth-Sur, all with the inscription *pym*, probably a dual of *peh*, "mouth, piece," thus two thirds of the normal monetary unit, the shekel. It is quite understandable that the farmer would allow his implements to grow dull before going to the smith. Bressan, 208ff. / B. N. Wambacq, in VD 29 (1951), 48. / Galling, BRL 187. / W. F. Albright, BAZOR 68 (1931), 9. / G. R. Driver, *On the Hebrew peṣîrâh* (1 S 13, 21). Alternate form for *peʳrûṣâh*, "order, command, prescription, price." Afo 15 (1945-51), 68.

7. On the iron monopoly, cf. G. E. Wright, *Iron in Israel*, BA 1 (1938), 5-8. / Archaeological observations on the period of the Judges and the early Monarchy, JBL 60 (1941), 27-42. / Barrois, I (1930), 370ff.

and eleventh centuries. The Philistines used iron primarily for weapons, and only secondarily for agricultural implements. The first iron plowshare was discovered in Gibeah, Saul's city, and it dates back to the time of Saul himself. Only during the age of David do we discover more iron implements, a clear proof of the fact that the Philistine monopoly had been broken. The working of iron has frequently been reserved by conquering nations.[8]

Saul's primary objective was to eliminate the Philistine outpost in Geba. He did not call out three "thousand" ('eleph) men, but rather set up three "battle companies" ('eleph); one of them he left behind at Gibeah under the command of Jonathan, while he himself, with the other two, took up a position north of Geba in Michmash, on the mountains near Bethel. This maneuver caught the Philistine outpost from north and south in a pincer movement. Jonathan took the initiative and overcame the Philistine outpost in Geba. This was the beginning of Israel's revolt against the Philistines. Saul had to face the fact that the Philistines would not submit passively to this attack, but would return in greater strength. Accordingly, he had the trumpets blown throughout all the land, and assembled the entire military strength of Israel at Gilgal (13, 3-4).

The Philistines actually did attack in fearsome numbers. According to the Hebrew text, they had 30 "thousand" ('eleph) war chariots, an unbelievable number. The number 3000 would already be too many for even a major power. Darius could send only 200 chariots into the field at Arbela. But if we interpret 'eleph in its more ancient meaning of kin, relationship, the account becomes historically more credible. The Philistines, just like the Greeks at Troy, fought by clans and families. Accordingly,

---

8. Porsenna allowed the Romans to use iron only for agricultural implements. "In foedere, quod expulsis regibus populo romano dedit Porsina nominatim comprehensum invenimus, ne ferro nisi in agri cultu uteremur." Pliny, NaturHist 34, 14 cited in Bressan, 207. / O. Johannsen, *Probleme der älteren Geschichte des Eisens*, FF 21/23 (1947), 40-43. The smelting of iron began in Asia Minor: its substitution for bronze is to be explained in terms of an increased need for metal.

they sent not 30 "thousand" but 30 "clans" or "tribal levies" into the field with chariots. They camped principally at Michmash (Machmas), thereby sealing off access in the north (cf. Appendix, map 5).

The Israelites had nothing to oppose to such a force, which outnumbered them ten to one. Fear laid hold of all the land. People sought refuge in caves, cisterns, and inaccessible mountain heights. Many fled into Transjordania before the approach of the Philistine hordes. Saul, too, reversed his position. He withdrew the two companies from Michmash and Bethel and concentrated the resistance around Gibeah. Then he went down to Gilgal to assemble the troops. Speed was the order of the day. For the Philistines it would be an easy matter to break through into the Jordan Valley from their mountain position. This is what Saul was afraid of. He was eager to seize the initiative for himself, but his hands were tied by the divine oracle. He had to wait for Samuel to come to Gilgal and make known Yahweh's directions (10, 8) and offer sacrifices. Saul waited seven days, but Samuel did not come. In human terms, this was sheer irresponsibility. The Philistine threat grew greater and greater, the poorly armed Israelites were hardly able to contain their anxiety, and a great number of the popular conscription had already fled.

Wars and battles, among ancient peoples, always began with sacrifice, in many cases human sacrifice.[9] According to the Israelite conception of things, the warriors were sanctified by the sacrifice; "Sanctify the war" and "declare war" are thus synonymous. It was customary to determine the will of the gods in advance by various signs. In Israel, too, it was customary to determine the will of Yahweh before any major undertaking, either by the sacred lot, or by the services of a man of God. In the case of Gilgal, Samuel had assured the king of a divine oracle. But when Samuel did not come, Saul himself offered the sacrifices in order to sanctify the war and thus open battle.

---

9. For a text which casts some light on the opening of wars, in Ugarit, cf. ANET 143c, d. / According to Porphory, *De Abstinentia II*, 56, the Greeks regularly offered human sacrifice before taking the field.

Hardly had this happened when the aged Samuel appeared before Saul, like the incarnation of his conscience. He had only one word: "You have done foolishly" (13, 13). The evil that Saul did in offering this premature sacrifice was so great that he must pay for it at the price of his kingship (13, 14). We find it difficult to determine the precise nature of this outrage. The offering of sacrifice was conceded to later kings. The outrage in question could, accordingly, hardly have been the arrogation of a priestly prerogative. We are more inclined to justify the actions of Saul than those of Samuel. But Samuel lays bare the sore point, the failing that will lead to Saul's final tragedy. Despite the explicit announcement of a divine oracle, Saul had not waited; he had acted according to his own plan, which demanded speed and initiative, and thus he had rejected the direction of Yahweh. It was no wonder that Yahweh should take the kingship away from him.[10]

It must have been with a sense of inner bitterness that Saul made his way back to Gibeah. When he assembled his warriors there, there were only 600 men left. With such a force he could hardly chance an open battle against the superior power of the Philistines, and on the other hand the Philistines themselves were somewhat hesitant to attack Saul directly in Gibeah, where he would be on more familiar ground. Gibeah has an elevation of 839 m, whereas Michmash is only 607 m; this fact must not be overlooked in assessing the military tactics of those days. There could be no question of a direct attack upon Michmash. The Philistines would have had to cross the deeply furrowed Wadi Suwenit and the Wadi Fara in order to arrive at Gibeah. In this case, Saul, from his position of vantage, could have easily observed the movements of the Philistine troops. For the time being, his only alternative was to await the initiative of the Philistines.

---

10. H. Wilderberger, *Samuel und die Entstehung des israelitschen König-tums*, ThZ 13 (1957), 442-469. Saul, even as king and commanding general, was subject to the laws of the Yahweh amphictyony. He runs into immediate opposition whenever he acts according to his own good pleasure instead of following the divine law.

The Philistines did not remain idle. According to the ancient
military maxim: "Lay waste the country and the cities will fall
like ripe fruit," they sent out three "heads" of raiding parties
(13, 17), one headed north towards Ophrah, a second westward
into the region of Beth-Horon, and the third southwards into the
desert of Judah. In the face of these destructive hordes, burning
and laying waste the countryside, it is only natural that the
Israelites sought refuge wherever they could find it, in caves,
cisterns, and mountain heights.

The two main bodies of troops also seemed to have gradually
drawn closer together. Saul descended from Gibeah and concentrated his power at Geba,[11] while the Philistines advanced their
outposts as far as Wadi Suwenit. The location is precisely described.
There were two great rock outcroppings there, one on the northern
side of the valley and the other on the southern. The names are
bôṣēṣ, shining, white rock, and *senneh, thorn.*

It was Jonathan who actually started the battle. Together with
his shield-bearer, and in a spirit of youthful adventure which was
not, however, without its religious enthusiasm — "It may be
that the Lord will work for us; for nothing can hinder the Lord
from saving by many or by few" (14, 6) — he climbed up the
rock, dispatched the Philistine outpost, and began battle. From
his observation spot, Saul witnessed the beginning of the tumult.
Uncertain as to whether or not he should join battle, he had
Yahweh's will determined by the high priest's ephod. Before
the high priest could give an answer, however, Saul had already
delivered a sign. Once again he did not wait for the oracular
decision. Immediate action was necessary if Jonathan was not to
be lost. Saul gave the signal for the attack. The "Hebrews" who
had taken the field with the Philistines saw a splendid opportunity
to deal with their oppressors; they joined Saul's forces. Attacked
from within and without, the Philistines sought safety in flight.
This was the perfect moment for those who had sought refuge
in hiding to come out and join the pursuers; they chased the

---

11. General opinion favors the reading Geba' instead of Gibeah in 1
    S 14, 2. From Gibeah it would have been impossible for Saul to
    follow the movements of the enemy camp: the distance is too great.

Philistines down the high road along which they had entered the country, beyond Beth-Horon as far as Aijalon, a distance of 20 to 25 km. In order to take full advantage of his victory, Saul commanded his people, under threat of curse, to eat nothing along the way, but to pursue the enemy without rest (14, 24). This command proved to be most unwise. Saul meant to gain time, but actually lost time. In the evening, his people were so hungry and fatigued that they slaughtered their animals and ate their flesh with its blood. Saul wanted to spend the night in further pursuit of the enemy. But the divine oracle refused an answer. Somebody in the party must have contracted guilt. Saul became very angry. He could see the enemies escaping his hand. And now this further obstacle. In his wrath, he swore that the guilty party, must die, even if it be his own son Jonathan.

The lot was cast again and it fell upon Jonathan, who, during the pursuit, unaware of his father's prohibition, had stopped to eat some honey. Saul persevered obstinately in his oath and wanted to have Jonathan put to death. Thereupon, the entire army rose up against him and "ransomed" Jonathan, probably by some substitute victim (14, 45).

Jonathan condemned his father's way of acting in hard terms: "My father is ruining this land" (14, 28). The day had begun so splendidly, with Jonathan's heroic adventure. The victory had been won, but in the evening there was no joy at the victory. Saul was no longer master of the situation. Through lack of moderation he had not only failed to follow up his victory, but, by hazarding even the life of his own son, he had lost the sympathy of his warriors. It is understandable that, after his encounter with Samuel at Gilgal, Saul should have lost his sense of moderation. The threatened rejection was gnawing at his soul. His rash oath, that no one dare to eat anything, that even Jonathan himself must die, is only an expression of his inner insecurity. By the heroic excess of the dedication demanded of his people, he meant to assure himself of Yahweh's favor. His figure thus enters into a peculiar twilight.

There are some writers [12] who feel that they must attempt a

---

12. Duff Cooper, *David* (1946), 68.

vindication of Saul. They feel that his image has been caricatured by religious fanatics until it is unrecognizable. He was a clever politician, but he had too little insight into the sensitivities of contemporary religious circles, and this spelled his ruin. But all this is too modern a conception. The Ancient Near East, and Israel too, were aware of no such distinction between secular and religious spheres. Saul's religious collapse came first; his political and military decline were only the necessary consequence. His soul was not endowed with the power it takes to constantly venture his kingship upon the word and mouth of Yahweh. He reckoned too heavily upon human potentials, and left too little room for the divine potential; in a word, he had too little faith. That such a man could not remain Yahweh's anointed one is obvious. The war against the Amalekites is the final stage in his rejection.

2.) THE WAR AGAINST THE AMALEKITES AND SAUL'S REJECTION (1 S 15):

The successful campaign recorded above did not completely remove the Philistine peril. The defeated army began regrouping their strength, against the favorable moment in which they could attempt a counter-offensive. In the meantime, Saul was free to consolidate his power. It is in this period that we must assign the construction of the royal citadel in Gibeah, which, from this time on, is called Gibeah of Saul. In the years 1922-1923 and 1933, Gibeah was excavated by W. F. Albright.[13] The destruction recounted in the Book of Judges 19-20 was substantiated by a thick stratum of ashes, dating from the twelfth century. After this destruction, Gibeah remained a simple village, until Saul enlarged and fortified it. At Tell-el-Ful, the lower sections of strong fortification walls, constructed of massive stones, are still visible. The foundations of the palace have also been laid bare. The rich pottery finds dating from 1050-1000, show that this location enjoyed its most flourishing era under King Saul. After Saul's death, the government was centered about the new royal city of Jerusalem.

After the enemy had been driven from the land, Saul was also in a position to improve the construction of his army. Wherever he saw a strong man (literally, "a son of strength"), someone suited to bearing arms, he called him to his bodyguard. This was something new in the history of Israel. Side by side with the general popular levy, we now note the

---

13. Ground plan of Gibeah in Galling, GRL 191.

appearance of a standing royal army, always ready for battle, with Saul's cousin Abner acting as commander-in-chief.[14] It is quite in keeping with Ancient Near East custom to entrust this important position to a close relative. After the expulsion of the Philistines, Saul also organized the smiths and systematically began to arm his people. Previously only Saul and Jonathan had been armed with lance and spear, but now the entire army was equipped with the same weapons (12, 22; 14, 52).

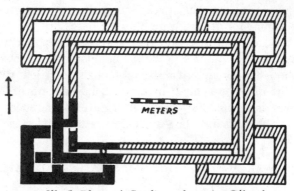

Ill. 1 Plan of Saul's palace in Gibeah.

The glory of an Ancient Near East ruler demanded not only a victorious battle campaign, but also a large harem. In this respect the kings of Israel are no different from their neighbors. Numerous wives and children were considered a sign of wealth and position. The wives were divided into those of first rank (*'iššâh*) and those of second rank (*pilégeš*). The second-rank wives are also frequently referred to as concubines although this does not adequately represent the nature of their positions. Concubine refers rather to an unlawful and unsanctioned form of cohabitation, whereas the position of the secondary wife was completely established by law. This distinction goes back into the most ancient times of the Old Testament. The patriarch Jacob had two wives of first rank, Rachel and Leah; their slave girls, Bilhah and Zilpah, were wives of second rank (Gn 29-30). Wives which were won as booty in war or acquired by alliances of friendship were also generally second-rank wives.

---

14. In Hebrew *śar ṣābā'*, "leader of the army, general." *śar* is probably derived not from the Accadian *šarru*, which always means "king," but from the Egyptian *śr*, "prince, leader." / The name *'ab-nēr* or *'abī-nēr* means: "The father (God) is light," in Accadian *abu-nu-ri*. Other composite forms are *nur-nergal*, "Nergal is light," of *nur-šamaš*, "The sun god is light." Bressan, 233.

So far as we know, Saul had only one wife of first rank, a woman named Ahi-noam ("my brother is a source of love") and one wife of second rank, named Zilpah (2 S 3, 7; 21, 7-11); it is possible that he had other wives as well (2 S 12, 8). At all events, Saul's harem did not rival the number or splendor of the harems of David and Solomon. From Saul's first-rank wife was born his son Jonathan ("Yahweh has given him"), Isba'al [15] ("the Lord exists"), and Malkishua ("the king saves"), as well as the daughters Merab ("may God increase") and Mikal [16] ("the almighty one"?), who became David's wife.

Saul's years were filled with wars. The historian depicts him on campaigns against Moab, Ammon, Edom, and against the kings of Aram-Zobah (1 S 14, 47), without giving any further details as to his success. These campaigns seem to have had little influence for the religious development of the country. Into this same era, although we cannot be more precise in our dating, must fall the campaign against the Amalekites, which spelled Saul's definitive rejection. That is why this campaign is described in great detail (1 S 15, 1-35).

The command to undertake this campaign is given by Samuel, who suddenly steps out of the background once again and passes on the word of God to Saul: "Thus says the Lord of hosts, I will punish what Amalek did to Israel in opposing them on the way, when they came up out of Egypt" (15, 2). The land of the Amalekites borders, in the south, along the wilderness of Shur, against Egypt. Since šûr means simply "wall," this district is clearly outlined. It refers to that desert territory which extends from the Egyptian boundary wall into the Sinai Peninsula (cf. Ex 15, 22). Havilah is assigned as the eastern boundary (Gn 25,

---

15. In the Masora we read yišwî, which is a late rewriting of 'išba'al. In the early royal period, ba'al, "lord," was also used in reference to Yahweh, but later it meant only the Canaanite gods, and accordingly the ancient names were all rewritten. Perhaps it was the abbreviated form of the divine name Yô that was first substituted for ba'al, 'iš-yô, "Man of Yahweh, Yahweh exists." Later, the name of the idol was dropped and replaced by bôšet, "abomination." M. Jastrow, however, thinks bešet is to be derived from the Accadian word baštum, "property, possession, one who is mighty." Accordingly, 'išbôšet would mean: "The Mighty One exists." Cf. The element bšt in Hebrew proper names, JBL 13 (1894), 19-30.

16. From mî-yākôl, "Who is the Mighty One?" Derivation based on a stele found in Beth-Shan on which there is reference to an Egyptian god m'k'r, "the conqueror, the almighty." Bressan, 233.

18), a territory which cannot be more precisely determined, although it is most probably to be sought in the trench of Aqaba, which divided the district of Edom and Amalek. The Amalekites thus, for the greater part, are inhabitants of the desert territory which extends southward from Palestine to the boundary of Egypt, across the Sinai Peninsula. This could very well explain their name. Amalek is derived from *meluh, meluhha*,[17] which is approximately equivalent to "salty," hence a salty desert country. The Amalekites are simply desert dwellers. As such, they control the whole of the caravan traffic along the Sinai Peninsula. When Israel marched out of Egypt, they felt threatened by the new arrivals, and thus they attacked them at Rephidim (Ex 17, 8-16; Dt 25, 18). This was the first battle that the young nation of Israel had to face. The battle was successful for Israel, but Moses, upon his death, left a strict command that, when the moment was ripe, Israel should take vengeance upon Amalek and blot it out from the face of the earth (Dt 25, 17-19). Hordes of Amalekite robbers probably were making repeated attacks on southern Palestine, burning and pillaging, during the days of Saul; Samuel then seized upon this opportunity to order Saul, in the name of Yahweh himself, to settle the long-standing account.

Yahweh's command is phrased in terms of complete annihilation. Saul was to execute the *herem,* the ban, upon Amalek. It was to be a holy war; pronouncing the ban upon persons or things caused them to be withdrawn from profane usage, they belonged to God alone and must be annihilated.[18]

The practice of "sacred annihilation" is not an invention of Israel. It is to be found among the other peoples of the Ancient Near East, and among western peoples as well.[19] The closest related example for this is King Mesha of Moab whose god Chemosh ordered him to execute

---

17. Bressan, 235.
18. "To place under the ban" is, in Hebrew, *heḥerîm* (hiphil of *ḥāram*), in Arabic the word *ḥarama* means, in modern times, "forbid." The harem is the "forbidden, inaccessible place," whether the reference is to a sanctuary or to the women's quarters.
19. Cimbri, Teutons, and Ligurians dedicated the conquered city to their god by complete annihilation and destruction. Bressan, 236.

the *herem* upon Israel: "Chemosh said to me: Go! Capture (the city of)
Nebo from Israel! And I went ... and I killed all the people, 7000 men
and boys, and women and girls and maid-servants, for I had sworn
to Ashtar-Chemosh to destroy it." [20]

The basis for the "ban" is perhaps to be sought in the popular belief
in magic. It was thought that a magical and injurious power dwelt within
one's enemies, and in all his possessions. In order to protect against this
power, it was necessary to annihilate everything. Although Israel imitated
her Ancient Near East neighbors in this tactic of military procedure,
the ban took on a new significance by virtue of her belief in God. By
the utter destruction of the servants of the idols, belief in Yahweh was
to be preserved in all its purity (Dt 20, 10-19). This theological foundation
of a later age was probably intended to explain and excuse the severity
of earlier practices. But the very fact that the Bible records such annihilation campaigns is proof of the fact that Israel is a genuine people of
the Ancient Near East and that its historical tradition is reliable and
worthy of faith.[21]

Upon Samuel's orders, Saul undertook the execution of the
ban against the Amalekites. As the base of his operations he chose
Telaim or Telam, a name which is preserved in present-day et-
Tilma,[22] some 40 km southwest of the southern end of the Dead
Sea. But before the beginning of the punitive expedition, Saul
sent a message to the tribe of the Kenites, advising them to
split from the Amalekites if they wanted to escape destruction.
The Kenites were a part of the Midianite tribe, and they had
shown themselves friendly to the Israelites upon their leaving
Egypt. Among their numbers had been Hobab, the son of Jethro,
who showed the Israelites the way through the desert (Nb 10,
29-32; Jg 1, 16). One part of the Kenite tribe returned to its
former homeland after the occupation of Palestine, while another
established itself in the southern country, in the territory of the
related Amalekite tribe, and another seemed to have settled in
Galilee (Jg 4, 11). It was thus an ancient debt of gratitude — for
history imposes its obligations — which prompted Saul to warn

---

20. Mesha stone, lines 14-17; Galling TGI/ANET 320.
21. H. Stieglecker, *Härte und Grausamkeit im AT*, ThPQ (Linz) 98
   (1950), 9-30. / H. Kruse, *Conceptus interdicti*, VD 28 (1950), 43-50.
22. Abel II, 477.

the Kenites of the southern country; they followed his advice and split with the Amalekites.

The text states that Saul went through the entire district of Havilah, down to the wilderness of Shur, putting everything under the "ban." This is a territory of some 40,000 sq. kilometers. Most probably he concentrated only on the principal settlements, and was content to take King Agag prisoner. He marched northward with abundant booty; he could not bring himself to "ban" the valuable herds and the person of the king himself. In the neighborhood of Carmel, a location in the desert of Judah, he had a victory monument erected, a "hand" (*yād*) pointing up to heaven (15, 12).

The returning troops assembled at Gilgal, apparently to be purified after their campaign. Samuel heard in Ramathaim that Saul had not completely executed the ban. This was the final judgment over Saul. A word from Yahweh came upon him: "I repent that I have made Saul king" (15, 11). All night long Samuel cried out in prayer to Yahweh for grace for Saul. In the morning he set out and climbed to Gilgal, not to bless Saul for his successful campaign, but to pronounce his complete rejection. Saul came to meet him with a bad conscience but a friendly expression, only to hear the words of judgment. The sheep which had been preserved from the ban and brought home by Saul were bleating and the cattle were lowing. Saul attempted to put the blame on the people (15, 21, 24). But Samuel would have no part of this. As king, Saul should have been in a position to insist. It is understandable enough to want to spare the booty for human consumption and not unreasonably annihilate it. It could always be offered in sacrifice to Yahweh, as part of a victory festival. But Samuel would have none of all these compromise proposals. He opposed them all with the inexorable word of Yahweh, who wants not sacrifice but obedience: "Behold, to obey is better than sacrifice, and to hearken than the fat of rams. For rebellion is as the sin of divination, and stubbornness is an iniquity and idolatry! Because you have rejected the word of the Lord, he has also rejected you from being king" (15, 22-23).

With these hard words, the aged seer made to depart from Saul. In the anguish of his despair, Saul laid hold of Samuel's cloak and sought to hold him back. The cloak ripped, a further sign that Yahweh had torn away the kingship from Saul. From now on, Saul would preserve only the external trappings. If Samuel had not returned to camp with him, his authority would have been completely destroyed. Samuel thus escorted him, in order to avoid the worst. Arrived at the camp, he demanded that the captive king Agag be led before him. Agag hoped that the hour of his liberation was at hand: "Surely the bitterness of death is past." But Samuel answered him with an ancient proverb: "As your sword has made women childless, so shall your mother be childless among women" (1 S 15, 33). And Samuel cut Agag in pieces before the Lord in Gilgal, a grisly scene. Samuel returned to Ramathaim, and Saul to Gibeah. They never met again in life.[23] Samuel mourned for Saul, because Yahweh had rejected him.

This last encounter with Saul shows Samuel in all his austere grandeur. Aged, weak, weaponless, he has the courage to face this victorious king [24] and make him bow before the word of God. Even though the people had demanded a king like the kings of the nations, Israel's kingship was still essentially different from the pagan concept. Despite the presence and activity of the earthly king, it is Yahweh who remains supreme Lord and king of his people. The "mouth of Yahweh" continued to give orders through his heralds, the prophets, orders which even the king must follow if he wanted his kingship to perdure. Saul had rebelled against "the mouth of Yahweh and against the word of Samuel" (15, 24), and thus he must perish.

Sovereign and solitary, above all human activity, stands the inexorable claim of Yahweh to be sole ruler, a claim to which every man must submit against his own better judgment; otherwise Yahweh would not be the Lord who probes the heart and soul of man. Just as inexorably Samuel stands as Yahweh's herald. It was not envy or jealousy that prompted him to break his staff

---

23. 1 S 19, 24 is a reference to a further confrontation. It is possible that the story of the prophets should be located prior to the Amalekite campaign.
24. Gressmann, 52.

over Saul. Night after night he had prayed for Saul, and for years he mourned for him. The evil premonitions which had forced hard words about Israel's kingship from his soul before the elders at Ramathaim, at the election in Mizpah, and finally at the confirmation of Saul's kingship in Gilgal had now, unfortunately, come to fulfillment. The chosen one of Yahweh had risen against Yahweh's command. Saul's crown was broken in two. Even though the breach was not immediately visible from without — before and after, Saul remained in command — still the splendor of Yahweh had departed from him. Inner reproach gnawed at his life's marrow. An "evil spirit from the Lord" tormented him (16, 14). The further accounts of his life tell only of the hate and love that waged a constant struggle in Saul's soul, until hate gained the upper hand and Saul cast his lance at his rival David, in an effort to kill him. This life, which began so splendidly in the glory of Yahweh's election, ends in a night of despair. In the ill-fated battle of Gilboa he falls deliberately upon his own sword.

Against this somber background, the figure of Samuel stands out all the more splendid. He let not a single word of Yahweh "fall to the ground" (3, 19). He announced the word of Yahweh to the high priest Heli as unafraid and resolutely as he later proclaimed it to King Saul. His is a character of sterling and iron, a precursor of those prophets who, without fear or trepidation, forced kings and rulers under the judgment of Yahweh's word, that word which is as sharp as a two-edged sword, which penetrates to the separation of bone and marrow.

CHAPTER VI

SAUL AND DAVID BETWEEN LOVE AND HATE

THE breach between Samuel and Saul was a definitive one. Each returned to his own place, "Samuel to Ramathaim, and Saul to his house in Gibeah" (1 S 15, 34). Neither saw each other again.[1] The man who towered above all others, not only head and shoulders, but also by the measure of his divine election, was not equal to his mission. Was it just perhaps that too much was demanded of him, too much expected, more than he could bear? Or was he perhaps a sacrifice to the vengeful spirit of the aged Samuel, who took advantage of Saul's descendancy to prove to the people that kingship was not for them, thus initiating a secret

---

1. According to 1 S 19, 18-24, Saul once again sets out in pursuit of David and is seized by an ecstatic experience in the midst of the "prophets" of whom Samuel was in charge. The expression "and Samuel did not see Saul again until the day of his death" means either that the two men, in general, had no further dealings with each other (in sharp contrast to their former close relationship) — and in this case the encounter would be purely incidental and unintentional, with the two parties making every effort to avoid each other — or else this contradictory textual evidence is to be explained in terms of difference in the sources. It is best to retain the present state of the text, with its apparent inconsistencies.

plan of defamation and attack until one day he was in a position
to pronounce Saul's final rejection.[2] Such an insidious and deliberately malevolent course of intrigue is not in keeping with the
character of the prophet Samuel as the Bible portrays him. If
Samuel had been an abject intriguer, then he would have certainly rejoiced at Saul's decline. But as it was, he took no joy
in the tragedy; day and night he mourned for the rejected king
(1 S 15, 34).

It is precisely in Saul's eventual collapse that the course of
salvation history is more visible than ever before. No matter how
clearly we examine and portray the play of human motivation
in the history of the kings — various political ideologies, the
struggle for power, jealousy, court intrigue, etc. — no matter
how thoroughly and perceptively we manage to fit them into the
framework of Ancient Near East history, according to the clear
testimony of the Bible there is always an open question that can
never be interpreted in terms of merely profane history. A supra-
historical power also demands to be taken into account. God
himself is always involved. The fate of Saul does not leave him
indifferent. Yahweh's heart beats in the rhythm of history. Obviously this conception of history is anthropomorphic, but how
is man to speak of God if not in human terms! The statement of
1 S 13, 34b retains its full validity: "The Lord repented that he
had made Saul king over Israel." The same expression occurs
before the story of the deluge: "Yahweh repented that he had made
man upon the face of the earth" (Gn 6, 6). At all the great
turning points of the history of human ruination, Yahweh always supplies a new beginning. From the deluge, which would
have spelled the end of human existence, a new humanity rises in
the person of Noah, to carry on God's covenant with humanity.
Now the divine judgment is slowly realizing its threats in Saul,
the person of David is rising like a new dawn on the horizon,

---

2. Duff Cooper, *David* (1946). The author is, by profession, a diplomat
and as such had new and different insights into various aspects of
David's life; the picture drawn by Samuel on the other hand, is
dismissed as the unfavorable report (9-68) of an embittered old man
who was overly concerned with maintaining his own position.

David whom "God chose for his privileged instrument, who accomplished his divine plan of preparing for the work of redemption." [3] If the life of every individual man is planned by God, then there is a special plan behind the life of those whom God entrusts with special missions in the history of salvation. It is the Bible's primary preoccupation — for the Bible is primarily a religious book — to follow out the many steps of God's directing providence; this does not free us of our obligation to examine the Biblical narratives in terms of human credibility, to find a place for them within the framework of Ancient Near East history, and thus to prepare the necessary earthly material for the incarnation of God's Word. David was a man of ancient Israel. His anointing will not elevate him to a realm of perfection. He had to mature into his mission. "How flat and artless it would be to paint the picture of this great man in such a way that all the shadows disappeared." [4] We must attempt to delineate his character with all its passion, love and hate, that make him stand out above the measure of ordinary men. But what makes David imperishable is not the fact that he lived at the beginning of the first millennium before Christ and was an extraordinary ruler in the Ancient Near East, but rather the fact that, in his person, there shines forth something of the glory of Him who was to come and establish the kingdom of God, something of the glory of the great son of David, Jesus of Nazareth, bound by ties of blood to his great ancestor. The blessing pronounced upon Judah settled upon the tent of David. In terms of salvation history, there is hardly a more significant new beginning than the call of David. We must not be surprised at the space and importance which the Books of Samuel assign to the life story of David.

David's rise is described in three sections, like a mighty triptych,[5] in 1 S 15, 35 — 2 S 1 etc. Each section contains five chapters, three epic strophes, beginning with the idyllic shepherd life in the hills of Bethlehem, from which our hero, as if by accident of chance, was called to sing and play at the royal court

---

3. DBS III, 819.
4. Duff Cooper, *David* (1946), 276.
5. Bressan, 251.

(15, 24 — 21, 1). Here develops the conflict between love and hate, a conflict which eventually drives David into the desert, fugitive and despised (21, 2-27, 12). The third "strophe" sings of Saul's tragic demise on Gilboa, and David's lamentation (1 S 28 — 2 S 1).

A) DAVID AT SAUL'S COURT
(1 S 15, 35 — 21, 1)

The "first epic strophe" sings of three events which are meant to characterize David's rise, but which at the same time pose many problems of textual criticism. The section (15, 35 — 16, 3), which recounts David's anointing by Samuel, contrasts well with the preceding account of Saul's rejection. But there are two contradictory accounts of how David came to the royal court. According to 16, 14-23, Saul's courtiers hit upon the idea of finding a singer and player for the sick king. The choice falls upon David, who already had a name as warrior and singer. According to 17, 1-18, 5, Saul meets the young David, unfamiliar with the ways of war, only after his battle with Goliath. He acts as if he had never heard of the young singer. How is this possible? — Attempts have been made to harmonize the inconsistency in the two sources: David had already come to court as a harp player, but Saul, in his mental condition, did not recognize him. That is why he needed to inquire into David's name after the battle with Goliath. This solution is too comfortable to be correct. The historian had several sources at his disposal. On the one hand he could turn to the traditions of the prophetic circles that surrounded Samuel, traditions which made a special point of preserving those moments in Israel's history which were marked by Yahweh's choice and intervention. The accounts from the royal court tell the story of David's youth quite differently. The editor of the Books of Samuel was already faced with divergent accounts, and he put them together without any attempt at harmonization. It is precisely in these inconsistencies in his source material that he merits a greater faith in his reliability than he could have accomplished by any attempts at harmonization. In like manner, the Synoptics recount similar episodes from the life of Jesus in terms of different, and apparently contradictory details. Just as these discrepancies among the Synoptics enrich our knowledge of Jesus' activity, the same can be said about the author of the Books of Samuel.[6] There are many episodes which we can describe only in coarse outline; the individual details escape not only our grasp today but they were also beyond the grasp of the contemporary reader.

---

6. DBS II (1943), 296ff.

1) ANOINTED BY SAMUEL (1 S 16, 1-13):

For Samuel it was a mortally dangerous undertaking to go to Bethlehem and anoint the new king there. If Saul should hear about it, it might mean Samuel's life. That is why Samuel hesitates at Yahweh's order: "How can I go? (that is, I cannot possibly go)[7] If Saul hears it, he will kill me" (16, 2). Where human planning can find no way to succeed, the divine command opens new possibilities. The narrative is presented in such a fashion as to present the impression that Samuel is acting under the direct address of God. Yahweh "says to him" (*'āmar*), what is to happen here and now. Is this merely a question of narrative style, or does the formula clothe some special reality? If so, what was the special manner of this "speaking of Yahweh" to Samuel?

This problem touches upon the boundaries of religious knowledge and experience, an area in which Scripture itself has little to say. Scripture presents the lapidary facts in all their sobriety, without describing the course of religious phenomena. Scripture does not describe the motives of human activity in describing the actions of its principal figures; man is presented as standing in the immediacy of Yahweh's address. By means of this systematizing style, which deliberately ignores all human agency, the Scripture writer achieves that solemn tone which is proper to religious "saga." And when this "saga" treats of heroes and saints, cowards and sinners, the Books of Samuel are not the history of heroes, but the story of Yahweh himself, guiding, by his word, the fates of his chosen ones and all his people. In this is visible something of the kingship, something of the *malkûd* of Yahweh. He alone is Lord and king who has something to "say," that is, something to command.[8] By delivering his word into the world,

---

7. Adversative *'êk*: Such questions, which begin with "How," always imply that the opposite of the question expressed is the actual reality. "How shall I go?" is thus equivalent with "I cannot possibly go." Cf. Castellino, *Libro dei Salmi* (1955), 270, in the critical apparatus to Ps 11/10. / For other examples, cf. Gn 26, 9; 39, 9; 44, 8; Jr 48, 14. Cf. Mary's question in Lk 1, 34.

8. In Arabic the word for prince is "Emir" — "speaker," someone who has something to say.

choosing and rejecting, Yahweh realizes his kingship. Since the call of David involves the typical representation of God's own kingship in Israel, Yahweh himself is so intimately interested in the success of this work that he advises the aged Samuel to set about his work with diplomacy and circumspection.

Upon Yahweh's command that he anoint a king, Samuel sets out for Ramathaim; with him he leads a heifer, for sacrifice (16, 2), to camouflage his subversive mission. People were quite accustomed to see the aged prophet making his way through the tribes of Israel to rekindle faith in Yahweh and conduct divine services. That was precisely how, in his youth, he had gradually made the people ripe for their war of liberation against the Philistines. The fact that Bethlehem was deeply aroused (16, 4) at the prophet's arrival leads us to suspect that these religious pilgrimages were no longer expected of the aged Samuel. With the election of Saul, the aged precursor had stepped into the background. But now his hour had come again; Yahweh's kingly rule, which had been condemned by Saul, was to be reestablished.

Samuel's path led him by Saul's citadel,[9] from where Saul could look out like an eagle from his nest and observe what went on in the country beneath. Did he perhaps notice that the aged seer was carrying a "horn" with him (*qeren* 6, 1)? The expression "horn" is hardly accidental here. The activity involved is the anointing of a king. The ancient popular presentations are all in harmony. The hero Gilgamesh is recounted to have killed the bullock of the sky, the bull with the long horns, which held six guru of oil. Such a horn was used in anointing King Lugalbanda.[10] The Ancient Near East "horn" is a direct reference to kingship and kingdom. The account of David's anointing also shows how Yahweh raised up "a horn of salvation" in Israel.[11]

Yahweh's choice and election strikes upon Bethlehem in the tribe of Judah, a not insignificant location, which might well

---

9. The distance between Ramathaim and Bethlehem is given at about 50 km.
10. Gilgamesh, ANET 85.
11. Lk 1, 69: Zechariah's Canticle: Κέρας σωτηρίας "horn of salvation," and hence a messianic theme.

have been the principal city of Judah before the elevation of Jerusalem to the rank of capital.[12] The name is pre-Israelite.[13] In the Amarna letters [14] the name appears in the form Bet-Lahamu; it is one of the Canaanite place names which are called after the house (*bêt*), that is, the temple of a divinity. Lahamu is one of the chaotic gods of the Enuma-elish epic,[15] venerated as a war-god. The Hebrews interpreted the name Bet-Lehem as a reference to bread (*leḥem*) "house of bread." [16] Through David and the great son of David, the name of this ancient Canaanite and later Judaite cult location became the symbol of the messianic time of salvation, a gospel of peace and joy for all men, adorned with shepherd idyls and angel songs.

After the place is determined, the persons are introduced. Being god means to choose and reject. The city elders (*ziqnê hâ'îr*), the city council, composed of the heads of the leading families, came to meet Samuel; a man like Samuel could not be ignored. Because of the nearness of Saul, however, the meeting was uncomfortable. Hence the first question: "Do you come peaceably?" (*šâlôm*). And he answered: "Peaceably" (16, 4). A man who comes to offer sacrifice can only give the impression of peace. Hence Samuel's invitation: "I have come to sacrifice to the Lord; consecrate yourselves, and come with me to the sacrifice." [17] The sacrifice was to have a joyous character, since it was connected with a sacrificial banquet. Samuel demands the ritual purification which was necessary preparation for a sacral meal (16, 15). The cult was not yet centralized in Jerusalem. Bethlehem

---

12. F. Willesen, *The 'PRTJ of the Shibboleth Incident*, VT 8 (1958), 97, claims that Ephratha refers not only to the city of Bethlehem, but is meant to express the whole of Judea: this would clearly establish the predominant position of Bethlehem during the era of the Judges.

13. *EncMikr* II, 86-88.

14. Amarna 290, 16 in ANET 489.

15. ANET 61-70.

16. The Arab hears "house of meat (*laḥm*)" in the word *bet-laḥm*. *lḥm*, in Semitic languages means the principal food of a region: in agricultural country, bread; in steppe country, meat; along the coastland, fish.

17. LXX: "Rejoice with me." MT: "And come to the sacrifice with me."

too must have had its sacred heights. This fact is not to be interpreted as a defection against Yahweh, as was the case later in the era of the kings, but rather as a legitimate adjunct to the Yahweh cult.

Among the inhabitants of Bethlehem, Samuel invites especially the family of Jesse (Isai).[18] The invitation also extended to his sons, among whom the chosen one was expected to be. But the decision is based this time on different principles than those which governed the election of Saul, who towered above the others head and shoulders. Eliab had a kingly stature and appearance, but an inner voice told Samuel that Yahweh's choice had not fallen upon him. And so it went until all seven sons had been led before the prophet. Yahweh had chosen none of them (16, 10). Only the eighth son was missing, David. Is there perhaps some textual inconsistency here? According to 1 S 16, 10 Jesse had eight sons, according to 1 Ch 2, 15, seven sons. Is there a question of two distinct sources here? Most likely not. The inconsistency is more easily explained in terms of the Canaanite manner of speech and expression, as it is known from Ugarit. For the modern man, number is a definite magnitude, but for the Ancient Near East man it is more a poetry, a play of thought and words. It is obvious that Jesse had several sons. Without meaning to commit himself to a definite number, the narrator says simply: "He had seven sons and an eighth one too." Or he might say "six sons and a seventh son too," which could both mean the same thing. Jesse might actually have had ten or more sons.[19] Among his daughters Zeruiah (Sarvia) and Abigail are

---

18. The Hebrew name *yišay* was transcribed in LXX as Ἰεσσαι, hence our familiar form Jesse, since, in Hellenistic times, the *ai* was pronounced as *e*. The derivation and meaning are not certain. Proposed interpretations: "man of Yahweh," "brave, strong," "Yahweh exists." Bressan, 255.

19. On number proverbs, cf. Am 1; 3, 6, 9: "For three outrages, and for four ..." Pr 30, 18: "Three things there are and a fourth as well." In the Ugaritic texts, number plans are very popular. Thus in the epic of Kuriti and Ḥuraja we read: "The wife that you have taken ... will bear you seven sons and an eighth she will bring as eighth into the world." A. Jirku, *Die Ausgrabungen in Palästina und Syrien* (1956),

mentioned by name (1 Ch 2, 16); their sons help to determine the fate of David.

The narrator is fond of monotonous repetition: "Then Jesse called NN and made him pass before Samuel. And he said, 'Neither has the Lord chosen this one.'" But there is one son who has not yet been taken into account. His father calls him the "little one" (*haqqāṭan* — 16, 11), that is, the youngest, who is out in the field with the sheep. Samuel insists that they fetch the young boy, or else the sacrificial meal cannot begin. They do his bidding. When the young boy comes in from the field and stands before the old prophet, he immediately wins Samuel's complete sympathy. The young shepherd boy is described in short brief strokes. Three traits are especially called to attention. David was *'admônî*, which is translated in the LXX as πυρράκης, "fire-colored," and in the Vulgate as *rufus*, "red-blond." Esau, in Gn 25, 25, is also called *'admônî*, especially because of his red hair. David would thus have red-blond hair, which must have been a startling exception in his neighborhood, since the Semites are generally presented as black-haired on the ancient pictures. Whether any conclusion as to his racial stock can be determined on the basis of this fact is largely a matter of speculation. The narrator also describes the beauty of David's eyes. He adds a third trait: David was handsome, that is, of pleasant external appearance. Red-blond, bright-eyed, quick at counting sheep, sharp at marking the far horizon, nimble and well-formed — that is the picture of David's external appearance which won the heart of all.

Impelled by the spirit, Samuel immediately acknowledged: This is the one. He anointed him in the midst of his brothers. From this very moment, "the Spirit of the Lord came mightily upon David" (16, 13). His whole life, hereafter, is under the direction of the "Spirit." Anointing and endowment with the Spirit go together. Each is a realization of Yahweh's election.

---

54. Also ANET 146, 153. This is in perfect keeping with Semitic usage. In order to suggest an approximate number, it is customary to give two successive numbers. Meyer, *Hebräische Grammatik* I (1952), par. 60, 6.

The man whom Yahweh chooses he will also prepare for the mission he entrusts him with. The anointed no longer belongs to himself, he is "seized by the Spirit of God, taken possession of, and impelled."

The scene closes with a mention of Samuel's return to Ramathaim (16, 13). There is no further account of what took place in Bethlehem, what was the result of this unexpected anointing of the "little one." Apparently, the anointing was not recognized as a substitute for King Saul; the anointing could only signify a religious consecration and office, an official designation. Father and brothers must have realized that Yahweh had some special plans for this boy. But what these plans were they could not suspect in any detail. Thus the feast was passed, the prophet was back in his home, and in Bethlehem everyone set about his customary activities. David himself went back to his herd just as before. And yet he was different: the spirit of the anointing was soon destined to lead him away.

The interpretation of the name David has been the object of renewed discussion. Among the excavated texts at Mari,[20] the title *da-wi-du-um* (*dawidum*) occurs in the meaning "leader, commander." It is possible that David first received this name from his followers in the desert, who referred to him as "*dawid*," "leader." What, then, was his personal name? In 2 S 21, 19 we read of a second combat with Goliath. The hero is not David this time but Elhanan.[21] Many authors take this for the King's personal name, while "David" is his throne and royal name. This is, of course, a possibility; but it cannot be clearly demonstrated.

The traditional derivation of the root *dwd*,[22] "beloved, favored," is a good expression of the applicability of an ancient adage to David: *Nomen est omen*. Solomon, as the sun-king of Israel, did indeed outrank his father David in wisdom and splendor. His majesty came to nothing, and

---

20. A. Jirku, *David der "Hauptling,"* FF 27 (1953), 28.
21. A. M. Honeymann, *The evidence for regnal Names among the Hebrews*, JBL 67 (1948), 13-25.
22. From the stem *dwd*, from the qatil form *dāwîd* = "beloved, darling." Meyer I, 37, 4. Likewise, the form *dôd* = "uncle, darling, champion" is also used as a divine epithet (Is 5, 1; Am 8, 14). Mesha, King of Moab, boasts on his stone inscription: "I took from there the altar of your '*dod*' (i.e., your patron god)." Mesha Inscription, line 12. Text in Galling, TGI 48 (Hebrew text) and ANET 320.

the enthusiasm of the people cooled; but David, the young shepherd boy and singer, the brave hero and warrior, king and judge, won the hearts of his people and in their history he is and remains the "beloved," the darling of his people, until the time that all their love was to flare out anew to greet the great "son of David" from Nazareth.

2) DAVID BEFORE SAUL (1 S 16, 14-23):

The narrative of David's anointing and Saul's rejection comes to a climax in the assertion of the Spirit. After his anointing, David is seized by the Spirit, and from one wonder to another, he is impelled towards his goal. He is the man who follows the impulse of the Spirit, who gives God free hand, and thus proceeds from one success to another. He becomes a "man of success," like Joseph in Egypt, because Yahweh was with him (Gn 39, 23).

The sad fate of a man who rebels against the "Spirit" is clearly portrayed by the account of Saul's sickness and "possession." For the Biblical narrator, there is no neutral man. Either a man is led by the Spirit of God or he is tossed about violently by the "evil spirit." "Now the Spirit of the Lord departed from Saul, and an evil spirit from the Lord tormented him" (16, 14). Our narrator is attempting to lay bare the cause of Saul's change in behavior. The ultimate explanation lies in the fact that "an evil spirit of Yahweh" had been sent upon Saul, and he succumbed to its attack after he had resisted the impulse of the Spirit of God. What does this mean? What kind of sickness is described here?

a) DEMONIC POSSESSION: The ancient commentators [23] interpreted the passage as clear proof of the existence of demonic possession. According to Augustine,[24] "God also makes use of evil spirits for the punishment of the wicked." In terms of theology, such an interpretation cannot be challenged. The man who closes himself to God is always open to demonic forces. In extraordinary cases, this turning away from God can take the form of direct possession. Was this the case with Saul? The text speaks of periodic attacks, which grow more frequent and violent. The activity

---

23. Bressan, 264.
24. Ad Simplicianum: "Utitur enim Deus etiam spiritibus malis ad vindictam malorum." Migne, PL 40, 131.

of the evil spirit is described by the verb *bāʿat* [25] which expresses the sudden and unexpected onset of a surprise attack. Saul seems to have been otherwise normal and healthy. Then suddenly this uncanny secret power would come upon him, disturbing him, so that he no longer seemed master of himself. His courtiers attributed these attacks to actual inroads of an evil power. In fact, they went so far as to name Yahweh himself as the sender of this evil power. "An evil spirit from the Lord tormented him" (16, 14), says the narrator; and the people at court said: "Behold now, an evil spirit from God is tormenting you" (16, 15). Is this perhaps a combination of contradictory positions? God is good; how can he send an evil spirit (*rûaḥ ʾelōhîm rāʿâh*)? [26] The difficulty can be obviated by realizing that *ʾelōhîm* does not mean "God" in the proper sense of the word, but merely "power." Since all extraordinary events in nature and history were ascribed to the activity of *rûaḥ*, the expression *rûaḥ ʾelōhîm rāʿâh* is equivalent to "a mysterious evil power fell upon him." But how can our narrator persist in saying that this mysterious evil power came from Yahweh and was sent by him? Whatever the case may be, we are here faced with a clumsy and not clearly stated form of expression. The narrator refers the activity back to Yahweh as the ultimate source, the only true efficient cause of all human happenings.

b) DESCRIPTION OF THE SICKNESS: [27] It is surprising to note the manner in which the court people sought to control the attacks "of the evil spirit." They do not think of prayer and sacrifice and ritual purification, as was the common usage in expelling evil spirits throughout the Ancient Near East. They do not turn to any religious remedies, but seek help in a purely natural sphere. They advise the disturbed king to have a harp player brought to court, so that he can soothe the king's spirit by song and music as soon as an attack approaches. All this suggests a psychic condition rather than a demonic possession. But the ancient historian simply had no terms at his disposal to describe a psychic malady.

---

25. In S 16, 14 we have the piel form: *ûbiʿatattú*. The corresponding Arabic form *bġt* refers to the suddenness of an attack, or some news, or some deed. The old translator no longer understood the original meaning of the verb. They translated it to fit the context: LXX: επνιγεν "he choked"; Vulgate: *exagitabat*, "it drove him about."

26. Kaupel, *Die Dämonen im AT* (1930), 59-70. Best and most complete exposition of the physical and psychic effects of the *rûaḥ yahweh* in R. Koch, *Geist und Messias* (1950), 4-58.

27. H. C. Ackermann, *Saul, a psychotherapeutic analysis*, Anglican Theol Rev 3 (1920/21), 114124. / A. Machabey, *Notes sur les repports de la musique et de la médicine dans l'antiquité hebraique*, Rev. de l'Hist. de la Médicine Hébraique, Paris 5 (1952), 117-135. Saul was a Neuropath.

Still, on the basis of the text recorded, we can reconstruct a working picture of Saul's psychic condition. Even before his rejection from Samuel, Saul does not seem to have been a man with good psychic balance. Despite his physical size and strength, he was shy and fearful. On his election day, he was hiding among the baggage, so that he had to be looked for. Elected king, he still remained a farmer. Informed of the threat against the city of Jabesh-Gilead, he falls into an uncontrolled wrath, hacks the oxen into pieces and sends them throughout the tribes as a declaration of sacred war. In the Philistine war he turns into a Cunctator, unable to decide upon a consistent strategy until he is forced by Jonathan's attack. Here again, he knows no measure; he takes a rash oath and thus himself neutralizes the success of his victory. This is the picture of Saul when he is well. He is indeed a man with great capacity, but also a man of serious liabilities: he is a man of inner contradictions, easily jumping from inactivity to exaggerated demands upon his strength. Even in his well days, Saul was a hard man to put up with. He seems to have been a person who could not be guided by clear reason, a man given to unforeseen outbursts of feeling. Even for a character that enjoyed good psychic balance, the prospect of rejection would have been a serious trial; for a person like Saul it could easily lead to collapse. The news of his rejection gnawed at his soul, a wound without remedy. His defense reactions suggest delusions of persecution. He must have felt that everything he now undertook was meaningless. His kingship would not last, since Yahweh had rejected him. All this must have driven him to the point of madness. The attacks described in the text would thus be the delirium of a man sick with delusions of persecution. The fact that Saul could still be active during these attacks is further confirmation of our assumption that he considered himself a persecuted man, and felt the need to put up some defense. Saul was a sick man, very sick; he was seriously shaken in heart and head. Rejection tormented his thinking and wore down his nerves. He was on the road to complete mental and physical collapse.

c) Attempts at Remedy and Pacification: The court people chose a favorable opportunity to suggest to the sick king that he call in a harp player to soothe his sick mind. The old warrior (*gibbôr ḥāyil* — 1 S 9, 1) had apparently not yet found time to devote himself to these more leisurely arts. He did, however, accept the proposal. The court people already had a candidate in mind, one of the young squires (*ne'ārîm*). The name David is to be found nowhere in this entire narrative. The story mentions only a son of Jesse, who is best fitted for the position in question (16, 18). He is a good musician and a good singer. The Hebrew text expresses both concepts with the same simple word *naggēn*, which means "play on a stringed instrument" and also "sing." [28] The instrument

---

28. Albright, *Religion of Israel* (1956), 141. "In those days there was no

is called *kinnôr* (16, 23).[29] His musical accomplishments were further enhanced by his early reputation as a warrior. Ben-Jesse was already well known as a "man of valor, man of war" (16, 18). Battle and song, in ancient times, were not mutually exclusive; they went together, complementing each other. When Ben-Jesse is also called "prudent in speech," the picture outlined in Scripture is in perfect keeping with the times. Hostile armies frequently spent whole days encamped against each other without activity, as in the case of Michmash (1 S 13-14). The monotony of the campfires was dispelled by young and old singers. This could well be the background for the accomplishments of Ben-Jesse. It was in camp that he had developed his gift for singing and speaking; apparently telling stories of ancient days, of battles and victories, of the pride of Israel, of the glory of Yahweh, God of hosts.

The young harp player at the royal court has thus had a previous history. He does not come directly to court from his herds; he has

---

sharp distinction between poet, composer, or performer." Representation of lyre players in the tomb of Beni-Hassan. Among the immigrating Bedouins there is one who carries a lyre. Bossert, *Altsyrien,* 913.

---

29. Popular conception represents David as a harp player. The Psalter is also called "harp of David." But, in terms of music history, this is a false conception. A *kinnor* is not a harp. Harps have been found in Mesopotamia (from Ur, illustrated in H. Schmökel, *Ur, Assur und Babylon,* 1955, T 34) and Egypt (ANEP, ill. 207, 208), in illustrations and remains, but never in the area of Syria-Palestine. Music performers from this territory are always portrayed with the lyre. Cf. Gressmann, AOB 51: Semitic caravan making its way across the Egyptian border. Behind the donkey walks a man with a lyre. Ill. 151: three captive lyre players from Lachish. The distinction between harp and lyre consists in the size and also in the way the strings are mounted. "The harp strings are mounted obliquely to form a bow, parallel to each other, while the lyre's strings are arranged in parallel horizontally or vertically in a trapezoid shaped frame or else in a bunch" (Galling, BRL 390). The harp was played while sitting, because of its size, while the lyre could be held in the hand and played while dancing. Illustrations in Galling, BRL 393; ANEP 199: four musicians, three of them with lyres. Also 204, 205, 206. Neither can David be properly referred to as a zither player, since such instruments did not exist at his time (Galling, BRL 390). David was, accordingly, a lyre player; the lyre was the best known and best loved instrument of Syria-Palestine. On the development of these musical instruments in general, see the explicit account by Gerson-Kiwi in DBS (1957), 1422ff. (les instruments).

already experienced his first days in camp. The fact that he was also stately to look upon was a further recommendation for the royal service; kings have always preferred physically well developed men for their service.

Accordingly, the royal messengers one day came to the aged Jesse at Bethlehem, demanding that he send his son to the court. The messengers mentioned the son of Jesse whom they desired by name. It was David, "who is with the sheep" (16, 19). Jesse makes no resistance to the royal command. It was no small honor for the family of Jesse in Bethlehem that a member of their clan and household had been chosen for the royal service. The aged Jesse tries to express his gratitude. He has David bring a gift along to the king. In their very simplicity, the gifts seem to have a symbolic character. David brings [30] ". . . bread, and a skin of wine" (16, 20). He also brought a kid. He thus brought all the elements of a simple meal. The essential elements David brought with him, bread, wine and meat; as further ornament he could produce song and music.

Whenever the "evil power" came upon Saul (16, 23), and a feeling of depression made him sad and moody, David would take the lyre and play and sing. The song and music restored calm to the anxious soul of the king and Saul "was refreshed, and was well" (*rāwaḥ*). David also had to "stand before the face of the king" (16, 21), a common expression for service in the royal court. An ivory sculpture discovered in Megiddo,[31] dating from the twelfth century, shows a man with a lyre playing before a king seated upon his throne. Similarly, harp players are represented

---

30. MT reads "an ass of bread," which makes no sense. Vulgate interprets: "asinum plenum panibus," "an ass loaded with bread," LXX uses the measure gomer (c. 4.1 liters), "a gomer of bread," which is also meaningless. Probably it is a copyist's error. Instead of "ass" (*ḥamôr*) we are to read "five" (*ḥ*ᵃ*miššâh*), hence "five loaves." BHK as loc.

31. Portrays the king's victory over his vanquished enemy. The king seated on his throne, the queen standing before him, and behind her a man with a lyre, followed by a warrior who leads in the captive and bound kings. Jirku, *Die Welt der Bibel*, plate 63. On a potsherd from Megiddo there is a poor picture of a lyre player. *Ibid.*, plate 78. / Ricciotti, *History of Israel*, I (1952), 361 presents illustrations of six Egyptian musicians with harps.

in the Nimrud gallery, playing in the presence of Assur-Nasirpal. There were court musicians in Mesopotamia as well as in Egypt. And in the small principalities of Syria and Palestine, the example of the great powers was imitated. Formerly, Saul had no time for such things. It was only his sickness that forced him to find leisure for it. The young musician quickly won his favor, "and Saul loved him greatly, and he became his armor-bearer" (16, 21). Since General Joab (2 S 18, 15) had as many as ten armor-bearers it is probable that King Saul had several, too. David was not the only one. This leads us to conclude that David was accepted into the ranks of squires, in order to have a definite position at court. As such, he would be expected to participate in various programs of exercise and weapons training. But he would always have to be prepared for his special office as Saul's musician.

David brought extraordinary musical talents and also great military prowess to the court of Saul. Does the text mean to describe nothing more than the rise of a man highly favored by fate? Obviously, the human prerequisites for success are here present in a more than ordinary measure. But we cannot escape the religious echo. The narratives of David's anointing and Saul's sickness are joined together by the concept "spirit." In one case it is the "spirit" in decline and destruction, and in the other it is "the Spirit of Yahweh" in the ascendancy. It is no mere chance that the two are linked together; it was the Spirit of Yahweh that combined the two to achieve his mighty mission.

Even though we thus conclude that Saul's condition can be described as a genuine psychic malady (psycho-neurasthenia) — at any event the text does not force us to assume direct possession — the indication of his mental disorder does not explain everything. We are faced with a sickness, but the form of this sickness is not to be explained merely in terms of some functional or organic disorder. The reference to the "evil spirit of Yahweh" indicates that the malady was caused by Yahweh's withdrawal from Saul and conversely, it is rooted ultimately in the religious sphere. Saul's soul could have found a remedy, if he had bowed beneath God's judgment of rejection. As it was, he sought for some defense against this barb, and he was completely destroyed.

3) DAVID'S FIGHT WITH GOLIATH (1 S 17, 1-54):

The success of Michmash had not completely done away with the Philistine peril. It is true that the Philistines had been thrown back from the high country of the Ephraimite Mountains into the coastal plains, but they had not abandoned their objective. This time they centered their attack upon the more southerly district of the tribe of Judah. In Samson's day, they had already established their hegemony here, but their control had been momentarily shaken by the successes of Samuel and Saul. It may have been strategic considerations which primarily determined this military objective. The serious losses of their previous campaigns were ascribed to the circumstance that the battle had to be fought so far away from Philistine territory. In the event of a similar disaster in their attack upon Judah, they could quickly beat a retreat to their fortified cities, Gath first of all, and somewhat further distant but still within marching distance, Ekron, Ashdod, Ashkelon, and Gaza.

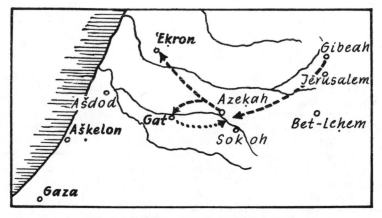

Ill. 2. David's Battle with Goliath
(Bressan, Samuele, Appendix, map 5)

The Philistine army actually assembled at Socoh, from where it marched to Ephes-dammim. Distinction between mustering point and battle scene was a common strategy (1 S 11, 8). Ephes-dammim is located between Socoh and Azekah,[32] some 7 km distant from each other. Between these two locations the Philistines drew up their position. Why precisely here? Coming down from Bethlehem, and passing the Pool of Solomon, the road leads next along the Wadi el-Gindi. After some 25 or 30 km the valley widens, from which point it bears the name Wadi es-Sant. The Philistines thus occupied the entrance to the valley, before the very gates of the mountain country of Judah. If they could succeed in effecting a breakthrough here, the mountain country lay open to them as far as Hebron and Bethlehem.

Saul quickly mustered out the levies and took up his position in Wadi es-Sant, the Biblical valley of Elah.[33] Here the two armies encamped in good positions, facing each other on opposite sides of the valley, neither of them attempting an attack, for a span of some 40 days, according to 1 S 17, 16.[34] The only activity reported was a warrior who proceeded from the Philistine ranks and challenged the Israelites to single combat. His name was Goliath [35] and he is called *'iš habbēnayim*.[36] This is how the

---

32. Of the three locations named, *śôkôh* can be most certainly identified with the greatest certainty. If we draw a straight line from Bethlehem to the Mediterranean, Khirbet Suwekeh, with its ruins from Roman and Byzantine eras, would lie right in the middle. The Arabic name recalls the old root *śwk*. The name, however, could very well have changed, as so often happens. Ancient *śôkôh* is generally located today on the nearby ruin mound of Khirbet 'Abbad, 400 m in elevation, where excavation has unearthed remains of fortifications dating from the 13th-6th centuries. Bressan, 269. / *'azeqâh* is, most probably, to be located at Tell-Zakariyah, 7 km distant. By reason of their strategic location both places were fortified and strengthened by Rohoboam (2 Ch 11, 7, 9). *'efes-dammîm* might well have got its name, which means "end of the blood" (i.e., bloody defeat), only after the memorable battle.

33. The meaning of *'ēlâh* fluctuates. GesB gives it as "large tree, such as oak or terebinth." The Arabic name *es-Ṣant* points to "mimosa" or "acacia," and thus "Oak or Acacia Valley."

34. I.E., "a long time," unless we are to read 40 instead of 4.

35. The name Goliath, since it ends in -*at*, can be neither Philistine nor Canaanite. Nahat and Manahat are Edomite names; Basemat, Esau's wife, is a Hittite (Gn 26, 34). Neither are there any parallels among the Illyrian names. Bressan, 112, 271. It is probably a remnant of

"War Book" of the Dead Sea discoveries [37] refers to warriors who take a position between two hostile forces. This time it was an individual man, and his challenge was to settle the battle by single combat. Because of his gigantic size and awe-inspiring armament, no Israelite dared to face him in battle. His size is given as six cubits and a handsbreadth,[38] a giant stature for a man. Computing the cubits according to the Egyptian measure which was customarily used in Canaan, this gives a height of almost ten feet. It is possible that this measure also included the characteristic Philistine helmet plume,[39] but this still describes a giant size of almost nine feet. We know that the pre-Israelite population included a tribe of bᵉnê-'anākîm (Dt 1, 28; Jos 11, 21)[40] that far surpassed the Israelites in size and development. Joshua had destroyed all remnants of them in the territory settled by the Israelite tribes. But some remnants had been preserved in Gath (Goliath's home city), Gaza, and Ashdod. The giant from Gath had a score to settle with Israel. This might well have prompted him to represent the Philistines in making this general challenge to Israel. His armament and weapons were in keeping with his giant stature. His head was protected by a bronze helmet,

---

an ancient lost language, perhaps hurrite. *EncMikr* II (1954), 508.
36. Dual form of the substantive *bayin* "distance," in the present case, "the distance between the two camps," Zorell, Lex 106.

---

37. "War of the Sons of Light against the Sons of Darkness." Cf. K. G. Kuhn, *Beiträge zum Verständnis der Kriegsrolle von Qumran*, ThLZ 81 (1956), 25-30.
38. It is not entirely clear what is the cubit employed here. The unit of measurement was "a finger"; 4 fingers equal one handsbreath or span, and 6 spans equal one ell (elbow) or cubit. Both in Egypt and Babylon it was customary to distinguish the regular (smaller) and Royal (larger) cubit. The normal Egyptian cubit equals 24 fingers (45.8 cm); the royal Egyptian cubit equals 28 fingers (52.5 cm); in Babylonia the ordinary cubit was 30 fingers (49.5 cm) and the royal cubit was 33 fingers (55 cm). Since the prophet Ezekiel measures the larger cubit at 28 fingers, we might well presume that the Egyptian measure was predominant in Canaan up to the exile.
39. Beecher, *Hasting's Dictionary of the Bible* 2, 227a.
40. Among these we must assign also the "giants" with whom David's heroes had to fight (2 S 21:16, 18, 20, 22).

his body by a coat of mail, with greaves of bronze upon his legs.[41] His shield-bearer carried a great shield before him,[42] big enough to cover an entire man. He was armed like a mobile fortress, unassailable and invulnerable. His offensive armament consisted of two weapons, a bronze sword (kîdôn)[43] and a lance (h^{a}nît), whose shaft looked like a weaver's beam,[44] and whose

41. Philistine with helmet on a painting from the palace of Ramses III. Gressmann, AOB 111 (oxcart with Philistines), 112 (naval battle). Same in Bossert, Altsyrien 947, 948, 949. The Hebrew word širyôn is generally translated as "coat of mail." In the Nuzi texts it occurs 23 times in the form ZA-ri-a, and refers to a leathern protective piece worn by men and horse alike. The word is not Semitic, but probably a loan word from Mitanni. A leathern coat was covered with rows of metal plates, varying in size, so that the result was like a coat of scales. Such a coat of mail afforded the required protection and still afforded the desired mobility. Illustrations from Nuzi in ANEP 161, reconstruction of the armor in Galling, BRL 417. / R. H. Pfeiffer and H. A. Wolfson, Excavations at Nuzi, Vol. XV, besprochen von F. R. Kraus in VT 8 (1958), 107. / Two such "scales" with holes for attaching them to the coat were discovered in Gaza. Bressan, 273. The word for these metal scales (qašqaššim) is also to be found in texts from Ugarit. EphTheolLov 28 (1952), 405.

42. There were two kinds of shields, the great defensive shield (ṣinnâh) which covered the entire body, and the smaller battle shield (māgēn) which the warrior carried on his left arm. Galling BRL 457.

43. G. Molin, What is a kîdôn? JSemStud 1 (1956), 334-337 deutet kîdôn als Sichelschwert. / O'Callaghan, The Word ktp in Ugaritic and Egypto-Canaanite Mythology. Or 21 (1952), 42, "long shafted weapon" at all events, this weapon was not carried "between the shoulders" (bên k^{e}tēphaw); ktp does originally mean shoulder, but it is used in a transferred sense for weapons. Based on precise figures from the Qumran texts, such a kîdôn was 69 cm in length and 6 cm across. Goliath's sword might well have been much bigger. RB 64 (1957), 590.

44. Yigael Yadin, Goliath's Javelin and the "Menor Oregim," PEQ 86 (1955), 58-69, m^{e}nôr is probably not the heavy lower beam of a loom, but the "yoke shaft" which was fastened to the middle of the warp-beam and was thrust back and forth in rhythm with the weaving. Goliath's lance also had a "sling loop" in which the warrior would insert his fingers in hurling the weapon, thereby attaining a much greater distance in the cast: some 20 m without such a sling, some 80 m with it. This form of javelin was well known both in the Aegean and in the Egyptian world. 15 illustrations.

head weighed some 600 shekels.[45] Against a man so equipped, no one on the Israelite side dared to stand. Up to the time of Saul, iron working was the monopoly of the Philistines. In Israel there were no smiths (1 S 13, 19). Only Saul and his son Jonathan were privileged to own a coat of mail. The position was hopeless for Israel. Hence the despair of the Israelites, who did not dare to make an attack, while the Philistines lorded it over them with their giant hero Goliath.

Single combat, in warfare, was a common practice among the ancient peoples, sometimes as an exhibition of prowess at the beginning of a battle, like the fight between Hector and Ajax Telamon,[46] and sometimes, as here, in an effort to decide the entire war on the basis of single combat, like the challenge that Paris made to the Achaeans.[47] In Palestinian history, the duel of Sinuhe is an obvious parallel.[48]

Just as with the Homeric heroes, the actual fighting is preceded by a word duel. Goliath challenges the Israelites. If only one of them will come out and kill him, then the Philistines will be Saul's slaves, just as now the Hebrews are slaves of the Philistines. The man is confident of his victory: "Am I not a Philistine?" (17, 8). From the Israelite side came only silence, terror, and despair. This was the moment at which David appeared in the camp.

The narrative in 1 S 17, 12-30, which is missing in the Septuagint, must obviously preserve an ancient source, and is thus very informative on the subject of ancient warfare. The three eldest of Jesse's sons had answered the king's call to arms. Their father now sends his youngest son to camp, with provisions

---

45. Weight of the suit of armor 5000 shekels, and the lance head 500. This based on the smaller, ordinary shekel 40 and 4 kg; the temple shekel would be about twice that. Such lance heads have been discovered in Palestine: Jirku, *Die Ausgrabungen in Palästina-Syrien* 1956, table 12.
46. Iliad 7, 67-92.
47. *Ibid.*, 3, 86-93.
48. Text in Galling, TGI 5: The Egyptian Sinuhe was forced to flee for political reasons and withdrew Retennu (Syria, Palestine). Here he was one day challenged to a duel by a "strong man," whom he overcame in the fight. ANET 18.

for them: An *epha* (38 or 39 liters) of parched grain [49] and ten loaves (17, 17). This seems to have been only supplementary provisions; otherwise David would have had to travel this long road every three or four days. The text, however, suggests the impression that Jesse was sending his youngest son to camp in a special effort to determine his sons' welfare. In the war against Gibeah (Jg 20, 10), all the tribes had assembled to avenge the blood-guilt on the wife of the Levite. On this occasion 10 were chosen for every 100 to see to the provisioning of the troops. Something similar may well have been the case in the Philistine war. It is unlikely that each individual soldier had to provide for himself. But supplementary provisions were always welcome. Jesse would show particular kindness to the commander, the "commander of the tribal levy" (not the "commander of their thousand"), by sending him ten cheeses. David was to bring his brothers' *ᵃrubbâh* (some token) home from the camp. Was this to be a "token" [50] for their aged father to recognize that they had received the gift, or is it a reference to the pay [51] which the brothers received and did not want to keep at camp? The question cannot be resolved. Jesse's concern for his sons off in the army afforded David his first opportunity to prove the fact that the "Spirit" would lead him to extraordinary deeds. His insistent questions about the impious Philistine, and the rewards offered by the king, made his eldest brother Eliab angry. But David would not be shut up. He kept asking. He felt a very keen sense of shame when no Israelite dared to face the armor of the Philistines. The proffered reward also had its attractions: wealth, the King's daughter, freedom for his family;[52] but these con-

---

49. Roasted grain was the first food the Israelites ate after crossing the Jordan (Jos 5, 11); Boaz entertained Ruth with the same food (Rt 2, 14); Judith took a supply along with her when she went to Holofernes (Jg 10, 5). The Arabs still make extensive use of it.

50. Zorell, Lex 626.

51. In Ugarit the soldier's wages were paid to them. Barrois II, 88.

52. His father's house would become a *ḥophŝi* in Israel (17, 25). In other connections, *ḥophŝi* (Ugaritic *ḥpt*, Amarna *ḥubŝu*) refers to a manumitted slave (Ex 21, 2, 5), but here it refers to freedom from royal taxation. This shows that Saul had already introduced royal law (1 S

siderations, splendid as they were, were not enough to make David wager his life. There was something higher at stake here. It is characteristic of David that, on the occasion of his first public appearance, there is evidence of that depth of insight that determines his whole life. The battle between Israel and the Philistines is not merely a national test of strength. They are fighting for the "living God" (*'elōhîm ḥayyîm*). Goliath had attacked the hosts of the living God. According to David's faith, he must necessarily fall. For the living God is stronger than spear and coat of mail.

David goes before King Saul and declares himself ready to face combat with the Philistine. The words he speaks on that occasion would have to be taken as sheer arrogance, as the presumptuous boast of youth, if it were not for David's tremendous faith: "Your servant will go and fight with this Philistine" (17, 32). Saul wants to keep the young man from certain death. From the human point of view, there can only be one issue to this combat. David, on the other hand, goes on to describe his skill and strength as a fighter. He has already fought with bear and lion as a shepherd,[53] and he will have a like success against the Philistine. The final argument is once again his faith in Yahweh. Saul is eventually convinced and says: "Go, and the Lord be with you" (17, 37).

The scene that follows is not without its humor. Saul offers David his own coat of armor. This included a long robe,[54] a helmet, and a coat of mail, together with a belt and sword. David tried to walk wearing the armor, but he could not. Is this proof

---

8, 11-17) with taxes and tribute. Indemnity from such tribute is equivalent to elevation to the ranks of the nobility. J. Gray, *Feudalism in Ugarit and Early Israel*, ZATW 64 (1952), 49-55. / J. Mendelsohn, *New Light on the Hupšu*, BASOR 139 (1955), 9-11. Refers to the middle class of free farmers, between the large estate owners and the slaves.

---

53. Well known is the "lion plate from Beth-Shan." Jirlu, *Die Welt der Bibel*, T. 29.
54. The Hebrew word *mad* or *madu* is not easy to explain. It probably means the long garment which kings and high officers used to wear, while the ordinary warrior wore a much shorter garment. Jouon, Bibl 1 (1920), 366-368.

of the folly of his presumption? Was he ashamed and forced to yield? No; he was not to be moved from his purpose. Instead of wearing the armor, he decides to face the Philistine with only his staff and his sling, just as he faced the wild animals as a shepherd.

He takes his shepherd's staff, called *maqqēl* in Hebrew, the short club-shaped staff, generally provided with a knot,[55] which could be used in fighting animals; he also takes his sling,[56] selects five smooth stones from the bed of a brook, and goes to face the giant. Apparently he was careful to conceal the sling, since otherwise Goliath could have found protection behind his great shield. It is understandable that such an unarmed opponent must have provoked the superbly equipped giant to fury: "Am I a dog, that you come to me with sticks?" (17, 43). But David has a coat of mail of his own, which far surpasses the giant's armor in splendor. He comes armed "in the name of Yahweh of hosts, the God of the armies of Israel" (17, 45). What a contrast. On the one side a picture of outraged fury, and on the other a quiet and victorious faith. In this decisive moment, where so much is at stake, the name of Israel's God occurs for the very first time in Scripture. It is Yahweh of hosts, the war God of Israel, who is fighting for David.

When David approached to within proper range, he quickly took a stone from his shepherd's bag, whirled his sling through the air, and the stone was off towards its goal. The giant was struck in the forehead and fell on his face. Whether the stone penetrated his forehead is not clearly indicated. But it had done its work. The colossus lay unconscious on the ground. David ran up, drew the giant's own sword from its sheath, and struck off his head. Then, with his foot on the fallen warrior,[57] he held the

---

55. Hence to be distinguished from the *maš'ēnāh* or *miš'éneh*, literally "support" the long staff upon which the shepherd could lean. Cf. Ps 22/23, 4. There is an Arab shepherd boy with both long and shorter staff in Guthe, *Palästina*, ill. p. 51, 86.

56. There is a braided sling in Guthe, *Palästina*, Abb. 100, S. 109. Dazu Galling, BRL 459. / H. Bonnet, *Die waffen der Völker des AO*. (1926), 114. / Illustrations in: E. Wright, BiblArch (1958), 120.

57. Cf. The duel of Sinuhe: "I pierced him so that my arrow stuck in

severed head in his hands and raised a victory shout (17, 51). When the Israelites saw this, they took up the battle cry (*yārî'û*) and set out in pursuit of the confused and terrified Philistines. The narrative mentions three locations which pinpoint the path of their flight. The nature of the terrain suggested an obvious course of retreat. Refuge in the surrounding mountain country was too difficult of access. Besides, the Israelites controlled the heights. The Philistines had only one objective, to reach their fortified citadels as quickly as possible. They fled from the valley of Elah as far as *sa 'arayîm,*[58] that is, "double gate," so called because it stood at the entrance to the valley and controlled the approach to the mountains, some 10 km distant from the battle field. There the stream of fugitives split. One group turned towards Gath,[59] some 15 km away; the others quickly lost themselves along the 20 km long retreat towards Ekron.

After the enemy had been successfully overcome, the Israelites returned and plundered their camp. The concluding sentence of the narrative presents some problem: "And David took the head of the Philistine and brought it to Jerusalem; but he put his armor in his tent" (17, 54). Jerusalem was then still in the possession of the Jebusites. We must assume that David later brought these trophies with him when he made Jerusalem his capital.[60] At the time this narrative was recorded, the author might still have been able to see the head of Goliath there. The giant's weapons, however, were not deposited in David's own tent, but in the tent or tabernacle of Yahweh,[61] which was then

---

his neck; he cried out and fell upon his face. I smote him with his axe and raised my victor's cry upon his back." Galling, TGI 5ff.

58. Modern Tell eṣ-Ṣafijeh. Formerly the reputed location of Gath; today this hypothesis is unsupported by the tradition of the text. The statement may come from the author himself, writing in Davidic or post-Davidic times, and presuming that Jerusalem was already the capital of the kingdom.

59. Modern *'Araq el-Menšije*. O. Proksch, ZDPV 66 (1943), 174-191.

60. De Boer, *1 S 17: Notes on the Text and the Ancient versions*, OTST 1 (1941), 79-104 holds that instead of Jerusalem we are to read Nob. This, however, is pure hypothesis, unsupported by the tradition

located at Nob. It was from there, according to 1 S 21, 8ff., that
he took Goliath's sword back, when he was being pursued by
Saul. It was a general practice in antiquity to deposit victory
trophies in sanctuaries. The victory had been won in the name of
Yahweh. The trophies in Yahweh's tabernacle were to serve as
a perpetual witness to this fact, so that all Israel would recognize
"that the Lord saved not with sword and spear; for the battle
is the Lord's and he will give you into our hands" (17, 47). A
conviction of faith which does full justice to that ancient time
with its victorious faith in Yahweh.

Elhanan and Goliath

2 S 21, 19 also recounts a victory over a giant from Gath: "And there
was again war with the Philistines at Gob, and Elhanan the son of Jaareor
Egim, the Bethlehemite, slew Goliath the Gittite, the shaft of whose
spear was like a weaver's beam." — The same narrative occurs in a
somewhat different form in 1 Ch 20, 5: "And there was again war with the
Philistines; and Elhanan the son of Jair slew Lahni the brother of
Goliath the Gittite, the shaft of whose spear was like a weaver's beam."
The accounts appear to be contradictory. According to 1 S 17, 4, it was
David who slew Goliath; according to 2 S 21, 19, however, it was
Elhanan, and according to 1 Ch 20, 5 Elhanan killed not Goliath, but
his brother Lahmi. The most recent text is the one from Chronicles,
which regularly uses the books of Samuel and Kings as sources. The
reading is easily explained as a faulty copy of the original. Instead of
bêtlahmi, "the Bethlehemite," it reads an accusative, *'et-lahmi*, "Lahmi,"
and thus arrives at a new name for a giant, who, since he could not
be Goliath himself, had to be introduced as his brother. The Book
of Chronicles thus presents the same narrative, but in a corrupt reading.
But what is the relationship between 1 S 17, where David killed
Goliath, and 2 S 21, where this same heroic deed is ascribed to Elhanan.
Whose son was Elhanan? Was he the son of Jaare or Jarr? Among
the 30 heroes in David's company (2 S 23, 24) there is also mention
of an Elhanan, son of Dodo of Bethlehem. Since in the ancient Hebrew
manuscript form, the letters *ayin* and *resh* are frequently interchanged with

---

of the text. The statement may come from the author himself, writing
in Davidic or post-Davidic times, and presuming that Jerusalem was
already the capital of the kingdom.
61. This is the meaning we get if we merely leave off the final *waw*
in the Hebrew text. Instead of *'hlw*, "His tent," merely *'hl* "the tent."

daleth (and there are many examples to prove this fact),[62] the forms *yā'rê* and *yā'îr* are only variant writings of *dôdô*. It would follow from this that Elhanan, son of Dodo of Bethlehem is the man who overcame Goliath.

Does the credit for this victory, accordingly, belong to someone other than David? Gordon [63] has this to say: "It is more probable to suppose that an heroic deed can be transferred from a person of lesser rank to a better known hero, than conversely. The situation may have been as follows: Elhanan slew Goliath, but the feat was ascribed by the people to King David. In the Books of Samuel, we find both the correct and the altered version of the story. The Biblical chronicler discovered the contradiction and attempted to harmonize the version." This solution on the basis of one man's heroism attributed to another is both too simple and too arbitrary. Such a striking victory could never have been attributed to David if it had not actually taken place as recorded. The real solution to the problem must be sought elsewhere.

The rabbinic tradition [64] which St. Jerome follows in his Vulgate translation,[65] attributes both battles with Goliath to David, as one and the same battle. Jerome translates Elhanan as Adeodatus, "given by God," and takes this as a cognomen of David's; *ben-ya'rê* is literally translated as *filius saltus*, "son of the woods," which Jerome takes to be a reference to David's life as a shepherd.

The discoveries at Mari, in which the word *dawidum* [66] occurs in the general meaning of "leader, commander, chief," has recently suggested the opinion that Elhanan is David's real name, before he was called "David, leader," by his followers. If this is true, then this brief narrative at the end of the Book of Samuel is doubly valuable, since it preserves a record of the ancient name Elhanan, which was later overshadowed by the royal name "David" and gradually forgotten. It would thus be Elhanan, that is, the young David, who actually overcame the giant Goliath.[67]

---

62. Bressan, 696.
63. C. H. Gordon, *World of the OT* (1956), 158.
64. V. Aptowitzer, *Rabbinische Parallelen und Aufschlüsse zu LXX und Vg* (I. Die Bücher Samuels), ZATW 29 (1909), 251.
65. F. Stummer, *Einige Beobachtungen über die Arbeitsweise des Hieronymus bei der Übersetzung des AT*, Bibl 10 (1929), 14ff.
66. Cf., above, the discussion of the name of David.
67. This would mean that David's father Jesse would have had a second name, Dodo, which is most unlikely. I suggest rather that *dwdw* means David himself, generally written "*defective*," as *dwd*. Goliath was overcome by Elhanan, that is, David. It was only after David's original name had been forgotten that the explanatory addition *ben-dôdô* was added.

4) THE RIVAL (1 S 18, 1-12, 1):

His victory over Goliath was the beginning of David's ascendancy. Saul, who was not even sure of the courageous shepherd's name and origin before the duel, has David called after the victory.[68] Now it would be the king's part to make good the promised rewards for victory: wealth, the king's daughter, and freedom from taxes for the family. There is no express mention of this being done. But from the fact that from now on David is regularly found at the royal court we can conclude that, after his victory over Goliath, he had a permanent position in the king's retinue. And that was not all. Because of his brilliant military capacity, Saul soon began to entrust him with special missions, and put him in command of a division of soldiers. With David's repeated success, the love and enthusiasm of the people continued to grow; even among the court circles he continued to win greater and greater sympathy (18, 5).

At the very first meeting, David won the full sympathy and respect of Jonathan, son of Saul, who was marked as successor to the throne. In David, Saul recognized a kindred soul. He too, on the great day at Michmash (1 S 14), joined battle against the Philistines in the name of Yahweh, with the bold and reckless enthusiasm of youth. Two bold and courageous men met each other here: brave, spirited, faithful, and true. It could not be any other way: "The soul of Jonathan was knit to the soul of David" (18, 1). The Hebrew word *qāšar* is also used to express man's love for a woman. But the love between friends, and the faithfulness that marked the lasting friendship between David and Jonathan, who, according to every law of nature, should

---

68. The divergencies in the sources have already been pointed out. The LXX already appreciated this condition and, accordingly, simply dropped the sections 17, 55-58 (Saul inquires into the name of the man who slew Goliath) and 18, 1-6 (bond of friendship with Jonathan). It is true that the Greek translation does gain in conciseness by these omissions, but is such a violent method really faithful to the truth? We are here faced with an historical work in which several traditions have been worked together, and not all their contradictions can be easily harmonized.

have been rivals and mortal enemies, is stronger than love for a woman, even stronger than death. In his lament for his dead friend David will sing these words: "I am distressed for you, my brother Jonathan; very pleasant have you been to me; your love to me was wonderful, passing the love of women" (2 S 1, 26).

Since Jonathan loved David "like his own soul" (18, 3) he wanted to make some external expression of this sentiment. He made a covenant with David (*kārat bᵉrît*). This was no mere friendship, sealed by a handshake; in 20, 8 the covenant is expressly called a sacred covenant, literally a covenant of Yahweh. Yahweh himself is witness and guardian of their friendship. This presupposes that the covenant was concluded under oath in the name of Yahweh.[69] It was Jonathan who took the initiative in this case. He took off his own *mᵉ'îl*, a robe or outer garment which was worn over the tunic, the mark of nobility and rank.[70] He also removed his long *mad,* or war coat, together with girdle, sword, and bow. Homeric heroes are also described as exchanging their weapons,[71] but such a complete changing of clothes, which is actually equivalent to an exchange of personalities, is to be found nowhere else in ancient literature.

David could not have wished for anything more splendid. The hearts of all the people were his. His battle with Goliath was only the beginning of a long series of victorious campaigns against the Philistines. Upon his return, maidens and women came dashing to meet him, playing on timbrels and cymbals.[72] They

---

69. The Ugaritic correspondence casts new light on the concept *bᵉrît*. International treaties, based on bilateral stipulations, seem to have been unknown. The normal case was for the stronger party to offer his "stipulations" (*rakašu*) to the weaker. Such a treaty procedure was called *ina beri*. Parties who were equal in strength and position obligated themselves by swearing an oath. Cf. J. Nougayrol, *Le palais royal d'Ugarit IV* (1956). H. Cazelles in VT 8 (1958), 104.

70. Saul wore such a *mᵉ'îl* (1 S 24, 5, 12), and so did the spirit of the departed Samuel (28, 14), Tamar the daughter of David (2 S 13, 18), and the high priest (Ex 28, 31).

71. Glaukos and Diomedes exchange weapons on the battlefield (II, 6, 230).

72. *tôph* is the small hand drum which was struck in rhythm during the

also sang a song, which was clearly dictated by the inspiration of the moment, although it was formulated according to the pattern of ancient victory chants. The regularly repeated refrain,[73] which turned into something of a slogan,[74] has been preserved, a distich with three *arses* in each member, and final rhyme:

hikkâh šā'ûl ba'ᵃlapâw
wᵉdāwîd bᵉribᵉbôtâw.
"Saul has slain his thousands,
and David his ten thousands."

This was a severe blow to Saul. Jealousy, suspicion, and a constantly growing hate laid hold of his soul. "They have given me only thousands. What more can he have but the kingdom?" (18, 8). In such an unbalanced and disturbed man as Saul, this must easily have led to new crises. From now on he must recognize this celebrated young warrior more and more as his own rival. No wonder that, in his state of depression, in a sudden attack of violence, he assaulted David.[75] Impelled by his evil spirit, he became violent in his throne room, and tried to run the young musician through with his lance. But David was quick to dodge the throw (18, 10-14). Saul could no longer abide his presence and did his best to keep him as far as possible from the court. In naming David as leader of a "company of a thousand" (*śar-'āleph*), a "clan levy," and entrusting him with

---

dance. *šalîš* is not clearly definable; apparently it is a percussion instrument similar to the Egyptian sistrum. Illustrations in Galling, BRL 393, Gressmann AOB 456ff.

---

73. The "catch-line" is introduced by the word '*ānâh*, literally "to answer," and it means to introduce a refrain. Examples: Pss 41/42, 6, 12; 42/43, 5.

74. The slogan is one of the most dangerous weapons in politics. Its origins are in the irrational, it cannot be silenced by logical argument, it hits the opponent hard and wounds him where it hurts. Even an adroit counterpropaganda cannot very easily reduce its effectiveness. ThPQ (Linz) 105 (1957), 273-299.

75. Many exegetes see the above account as a double for 19, 8-10. LXX, accordingly, has omitted the first account.

campaigns against the Philistines, Saul obviously had the ulterior motive of hoping that David would fall at the enemy's hand.

Meantime, it seems that the time had also come to attend to his promise of marriage with the king's daughter. The first-born daughter Merab (Merob) would have been the one in line. Saul offered her to David. It was for her that David had fought against Goliath. But when his dream was at the point of being fulfilled, the goal seemed too high for him, so that he answered in all modesty: "Who am I, and who are my kinfolk, my father's family in Israel, that I should be son-in-law to the king?" (18, 18). It is difficult to determine whether this is to be taken as indication of the fact that David was unable to raise the proper sum for purchasing a bride, or is merely an instance of Oriental politeness. At all events, Merab was given in marriage to a certain Adriel from Meholah.[76]

In the meantime, a new and very personal attachment had grown up betweeen David and Michal (Michol), Saul's second daughter. Michal's love for him must have been deep and genuine, since she dared to face the burden of her father's anger (19, 11 ff.). The narrative is extremely vivid and gives a clear picture of life in the royal court. Saul is informed of what is taking place between the two young people. He approved of this. Not that he was favorable towards the young people, but because he saw this as a welcome opportunity to have David destroyed. The wedding was to be a plot laid against him (18, 21).[77] Saul had the court people tell David, confidentially, that the king would have no objection to such a marriage. David answers: "Does it seem to you a little thing to become the king's son-in-law, seeing that I am a poor man and of no repute?" (18, 23). By this reply he means to indicate that he is not in a position to pay the

---

76. Ancient *'abél-mᵉḥôlâh* (probably "dance place"), home of the prophet Elisha (1 K 19, 16). The city belonged to the tribe of Issachar and must be located in the region of the Jordan, east of Bezeq, in modern Wadi el-Maliḥ, perhaps to be identified with Tell Abu Sifri. The tragic end of the five sons of Merab is recorded in 2 S 21, 8ff. Bressan, 306.

77. *môqēš* means the "sling" or "trap" with which birds and other animals are snared. Cf. Pss 90/91, 3; 123/124, 7.

established price for his bride.[78] The servant reports to the king. Now Saul has an opportunity to trap David. He demands the grotesque marriage price of a hundred Philistine foreskins,[79] to be delivered by a stipulated date.

Even before the appointed time has run out, David is able to bring not only 100, but 200 foreskins as the marriage price (18, 27). Saul had no other recourse than to master his wrath and give his daughter Michal to the successful hero for his bride. He began to feel strangely uncomfortable in the presence of David, and to fear him. Marriages frequently serve to unite dissident parties; but this marriage was not destined to seal their peace and good will: it was only a camouflage for the mortal hate of the king, stealthily awaiting the next, and better, opportunity.

---

78. The bridegroom paid this sum, not to his bride, but to her father. Hebrew *mohar*, Arabic *mohr* or *mohr el bint*. Shechem declared his willingness to pay an extraordinarily high *mohar* for Dinah after she had been shamed (Gn 34, 12). According to Ex 22, 15, in such a case the man is expected to both pay the bride price and also marry the woman. In Dt 22, 29 the price is set at 55 shekels. In Ugarit we find the same expression: *tmrh l abh*, "pay the bride price to the father." The *mohar* is not a "Morganitic gift" for the bride, but a sort of indemnification to the prospective father-in-law, who is deprived of the working power of his daughter by her marriage. Cf. E. Neufield, *Ancient Hebrew Marriage Laws* (London, 1944), 94-117. On the Ugaritic text see R. Dussaud, *Les decouvertes de Ras Shamra et l'Ancien Testament* (Paris, 1937), 83. Kornfeld, *Marriage*, DBS V (1954), 905ff.

79. It was an ancient custom to count one's fallen enemies. Gressmann AOB 113, presents a picture of Egyptian scholars collecting and counting the severed hands of their fallen enemies. From the time of the Assyrian king Sanherib we have a picture of soldiers, accompanied by a recorder, numbering the severed heads of their enemies. *Assyrian Sculptures in the British Museum* (London, 1938), Pl. XLVII. Flavius Josephus found the word "foreskin" unsuitable for his Greek audience and replaced it with "heads" — which David is said to have cut off. Cutting off and counting male members is noted on Egyptian representations of the Pharaohs Merneptah and Ramses III, as practiced on the sea peoples. E. Meyer, *Geschichte des Altertums* 1884, 312ff. — In some parts of Abyssinia the practice is still supposed to exist today. At all events, in the war of 1948, the Somali did the same thing to the fallen Italians. Bressan, 309.

Shortly afterwards, Saul dropped his mask and declared openly, in his royal council, "before his son Jonathan and all the servants" (19, 1), that he meant to get rid of David, his rival. Jonathan tried to intervene. Next day, when Saul was leaving the city, Jonathan joined him and looked for a favorable opportunity to broach the subject of David in their conversation. The king's anger had now lost its strength. Saul was approachable on the subject, when his son argued that David had really done nothing deserving of death. Quite the contrary, his successes had been successes for all Israel, and thus for the king too. It is quite in keeping with Saul's labile character that he immediately swears by Yahweh, "David shall not die" (19, 6). What contrast in this one man! The previous day he had pronounced a death sentence, and the very next morning he swore the exact opposite. For the next several days David came and went at the royal court as if nothing had happened. And yet, any moment might bring a sudden reversal of his position.

The high spirits in which Saul could be so immoderately good, had just as suddenly departed. Depression once again laid hold of him, the "evil spirit of Yahweh" (19, 9). It was now that he needed David to play for him. The young musician must have felt uncomfortable as he approached the king with his lyre on this occasion. As it actually turned out, Saul seized his lance, which he apparently always kept by his side, and hurled it at David, in an attempt to pin him against the wall. David, probably quite prepared for the maneuver, dodged the throw and escaped.

He returned to his home, apparently hoping that the king's attitude would soon improve. But this time there was no turning back. Saul sent his messengers to watch David's house and kill him next morning [80] (cf. Ps 58/59). Michal must have suspected something. She persuaded David to take flight, and let him down

---

80. Some surprise has been expressed that the policemen did not force their way into the house. The messengers in Gaza did not kill Samson, either, when they discovered that he had retired for the night. They planned instead to take him first thing in the morning (Jg 16, 1-3). Apparently, the night was considered as sacred. To kill a man at night, in his bed, was unheard of.

through the window of their upper room.[81] Her whole preoccupation was to afford David as much time as possible for his escape. She resorted to trickery. Next morning, when the messengers asked after David, she explained that he was sick. The report was carried back to Saul. In his wrath, Saul demanded that David be brought along with his bed, so he could kill him. Meantime, Michal had transformed the bedroom into a sickroom. Beside the bed she had placed the $t^e r \bar{a} p \hat{i} m$ [82] apparently small

81. "She let him down" (19, 12). On the ground storey, David could have jumped through the window by himself. The houses of the upper class had a second storey which was regularly used as sleeping quarters. Michol could have let him down by a rope, as Rahab did for the spies (Jos 2, 15). It is possible that the house was built along the city wall and thus David would have been free to escape at once. It is difficult to understand how he made his way through the city gate otherwise.

82. The word teraphîm has been interpreted, like 'elohîm, as a majestic plural with singular meaning. The teraphîm would thus have been a statue large enough to be laid in bed in David's place. These household gods and idols had been forbidden by the official religion, but they are frequently encountered in private cult and even in the royal court. Cf. Gressmann, 81ff. Ricciotti, History of Israel I (1953), #361. / This interpretation is contradicted by the evidence of excavations. Nowhere in Palestine have such large statues been unearthed, although hundreds of smaller statues of gods and goddesses have been discovered. "The representations of divinities in Canaanite temples are always outline figures on steles, which are cut into the stone." W. F. Albright, Religion of Israel, 129. Teraphîm would thus be a real plural. In these smaller terracotta figurines it was customary to venerate the household and tutelary deities (Lares), and also the spirits of the dead (Manes). Hence, Rachel's interest in the teraphîm. The teraphîm were used for prophecy, as well as for protection against sickness. The Babylonians buried such statuettes under their floors or thresholds. Similar practices have been unearthed in Gezer, in Palestine. Women apparently carried them to assure safe childbirth. Our text is unassailable evidence of the fact that these teraphîm were also used in cases of sickness. The Hebrew text clearly states that Michol put the teraphîm alongside ('el), and not upon ('al) the bed. It was the efforts of later correctors which changed the 'el into 'al, as if Michol had laid the teraphîm in the bed itself. Cf.: A. Gelin, DBS IV (1941), 178; G. Contenau, La magie chez les Assyriens et les Babyloniens (Paris, 1947), 232-264 (on the

statues of the household and healing gods, so that anyone who entered the room would expect to find a sick person there. The bed itself she arranged to look as if someone were actually lying in it. At the head of bed she placed a "goats'-$k^e b\hat{i}r$," [83] apparently an article of clothing woven from goats' hair. At all events, this $k^e b\hat{i}r$ must have been something that would cause a visitor to think that a sick person was actually in the bed.[84] This conviction was, apparently, further confirmed by the "garment" (*beged*) which she laid upon the bed.

Saul severely reproached his daughter when he discovered that all this had been done only to camouflage David's flight. But the clever woman attempted to excuse her actions by claiming

use of talismans and amulets): A. Jirku considers *teraphîm* as an ancient singular with archaic mimmation. Bibl 34 (1953), 78-80; but this can hardly be the case in the present text.

83. Jerome translates: "*pellem pilosam caprarum ad caput eius*," that is: "she laid a hairy goat's skin at his head." LXX presupposes the reading *kābēd*, "liver," which is easily explained on the grounds that *daleth* and *resh* are frequently transposed or exchanged. The root *kbr*, according to GesB, means "to weave," and *kebîr* would thus mean "something woven of goat's hair," some sort of "fly netting." Albright derives *kbr* from the Aramaic and Arabic root *kebir*, "big, old." *Kebîr-'izzîm* would thus mean "an old he-goat." "It is easy to imagine how his half-veiled head, with its black beard and burning eyes, could be substituted for the figure of an old man." Albright derives *teraphîm* from the Canaanite root *trp*, "to wear out clothes." In this interpretation, Michol would have wrapped an old he-goat in worn out rags and laid him in the bed. *Religion of Israel* (1956), 231, n. 65. / Apart from the questionable philological derivations appealed to here, we might also object to the practicality of the plan. How was Michol to get an old he-goat up the second floor and lay him in the bed without any commotion? / Perhaps some more recent investigation or discovery will cast further light on this word *kebîr*, which occurs only here in Scripture.

84. The common people slept on the ground or floor, on mats. Even the beds of the upper classes were very simple affairs, a four-footed frame lashed together. The boards were frequently decorated with inlay work (Am 6, 4). Remains have been unearthed in Palestine, in Beth-Peleth. There is a reconstruction in the archaeological museum in Jerusalem.

that David had threatened her with death if she were to betray him (19, 17). And thus the hoar-frost of paternal hatred had withered this genuine love which had begun to blossom between David and Michal. After David's flight, Michal was given to another man as wife. But this first love of David's never grew cold; after the capture of Jerusalem he expressly stipulated that Michal should be given back to him. Meantime, however, things had greatly changed. When David danced before the Ark of the Covenant, and Michal laughed at him for it, the couple was permanently alienated (2 S 6, 20-23).

Where was David to take refuge? Who could afford him protection? His kinsfolk in Bethlehem? They were too little and too weak in Israel to stand up against the king. But there was one man before whom even the wrathful Saul had respect, the aged Samuel. David fled to Samuel, in Ramathaim, and told him the evil Saul had threatened against him. They both retired to the nearby prophets' colony at Naith.[85] Spies quickly discovered where David had hidden. Saul immediately sent messengers, once, twice, three times. But each time they were "seized by the Spirit and began to prophesy," and completely forgot the true purpose of their mission. Saul became furious and made the trip himself. But when he came into the neighborhood of Naith, he too was seized by a *rûaḥ 'elōhîm,* and he began to act like a prophet (19, 23). "And he too stripped off his clothes, and he too prophesied before Samuel, and lay naked all that day and all that night. Hence it is said, 'Is Saul also among the prophets?' " (19, 24).

This proverb had already been mentioned in connection with Saul's vocation (10, 12), and thus many authors consider it a parallel account here.[86] But the differences between the two are so clear that we must think in terms of two separate incidents. Saul's

---

85. The name has been handed down in various traditions: MT *nayôt, naweyat,* or *nawît.* LXX *Nawiot,* Vulgate *Naiot.* On the basis of similar formations such as *ṣarephat, daberat,* etc., *nayat* might well be the most probable. Possibly the sacrificial heights in Ramathaim are a point of comparison.

86. Both accounts are explained as etiological versions to explain the popular quotation. Hence, Gressmann, 82: "This saga is extremely

behavior seems very curious. He had determined to kill David. But when he approached the neighborhood of David's hiding place, his whole attitude suddenly changes. Thoughts of David disappear from his mind, and, on the other hand, he is more and more completely possessed by a prophetic ecstasy.

The institution of ecstatic prophecy in Israel will be treated more expressly in the next volume. Here we must be content with stressing only those principal features which make it possible to understand Saul's behavior psychologically. We have already mentioned that, already in Saul's day, there were communities of prophets, who were taken up with promoting the cult of Yahweh (10, 5ff). The root meaning of the word "to act as a prophet" (*hitnabbē'*) is not "to proclaim" and not "to fall into ecstasy." This is secondary. The prophets proclaimed the glory of God, not only in word, but also in music, dance, and song. According to 1 S 10, 5 they came down from the high place "with harp, tambourine, flute, and lyre." Their sacred processional dance may have been joined by others who were seized by the same spirit. This required putting aside at least the outer garments — as king, Saul wore the *me'il* (24, 5, 12) — in order to have the hands free for the tambourine and the dance. This is what Saul did; but his preoccupation with the dance and his enthusiasm became so intense (as we might well expect from his characteristic lack of moderation) that he collapsed from sheer exhaustion and lay there naked for the whole day and night.[87] David once again had opportunity to flee.

The text now continues with the account of the last meeting between David and Jonathan, and the banquet scene with Saul, in which Jonathan attempts to discover the king's attitude towards David (20, 1-21, 1). But since the preceding narrative has made it quite clear that Saul means to be rid of David, this chapter must be incorporated earlier into the account. Once again we can recognize the seams where the various sources assembled by the historian do not perfectly match. The narrative does, however, retain a value of its own, even though we cannot fit it into the proper temporal succession of events.[88]

---

informative in many respects, but it can hardly rank as history." Bressan, 312, is close to the truth when he says that the events were there before the prophet. Later, the proverb was applied to both individual episodes.

---

87. Not "completely naked": a man was "naked" if he was without his upper garments. König, *Hermeneutik*, 91.
88. The problem of text transmission here is explicitly treated by Bressan, 311.

David and Jonathan met each other in the open country, so that no one could listen to them unobserved, and discussed the situation. David wanted to know, once and for all, where he stood. His friend, the king's son, was to help him in this. The new moon [89] with its festival time, was near at hand. All the court people had to be present at the banquet. David's place, however, would remain unoccupied. How would the king react to this situation? This would be the best opportunity to discover Saul's attitude. Jonathan clearly understood the seriousness of his position. He was under no illusions. He knew that Saul desired David's death, but he also knew that not he, but David was called to be king and successor to the throne. It is a mark of Jonathan's greatness of soul that he still refused to destroy his rival, preserving true friendship to the very end. Once again they swore their "Yahweh covenant" which had been established between them.[90] By this covenant, Jonathan sought to recommend himself and all his posterity to the favor and good will of the future ruler. Whenever a new dynasty was established, the new holder of power would generally try to root out the entire family of his predecessor (Jg 9, 5; 1 K 15, 28ff.).

The new moon came. The table was set. The places were laid. The king was in his place, as always, by the wall, with his commander-in-chief Abner at his right, Jonathan across from him; David's place, at the left of the king, remained empty. On the first day the king said nothing. He thought that David was perhaps unclean and, for religious grounds, was unable to take part in the feast. But on the second day, his pent up anger burst its bounds. He demanded an answer of his son Jonathan. Jonathan answered with the subterfuge they had agreed upon, that David

---

89. The Day of the New Moon was inaugurated by the observation of the first appearance of the lunar sickel, and celebrated by sacrifice and feasting; but it was not a day of rest (Nb 28, 11-15). The idea was to dedicate the whole month to Yahweh by offering sacrifice at the first of the month (Ex 29, 38-42).

90. An interesting parallel is to be found in a letter from Ishme Dagan from Mari to his "brother": "We have sworn the solemn oath of the gods between us, you and I; we will meet again and reestablish the brotherhood that is between us forever." RB 59 (1952), 301.

had a legitimate excuse, since he had to go to Bethlehem where his family was holding sacrifice.[91] Upon hearing this, Saul lost complete control of himself. Before the whole table, he insulted Jonathan, calling him "a perverse whoreson," [92] and reproached him for his narrow-mindedness in refusing to understand, even now, that he would never be king, as long as Ben-Jesse was alive. "Therefore send and fetch him to me, for he shall surely die" (20, 31). Jonathan tried once again to put off his angry father: "Why should he be put to death? What has he done?" But this was not enough. Saul seized his spear to throw at his own son. In "fierce anger" Jonathan left the table. The die was cast.

The next day Jonathan, together with a squire who was to hold his arrows, went outside the city to a little-frequented place. There, as if practicing, he shot an arrow beyond the target. When the boy ran after it, Jonathan called: "Is not the arrow beyond you? Hurry, make haste, stay not." Then Jonathan sent the lad back into the city. David had been anxiously waiting in his hiding place. Would Jonathan come, and thus withstand this crucial test of their friendship? He came; he was there. David was deeply moved. He threw himself prostrate before Jonathan three times. They kissed each other, they cried, each of them, but most of all David. It was over him that the staff had been broken. Finally Jonathan collected his wits. There is not a moment to lose! "Go in peace, for as much as we have sworn both of us in the name of the Lord, saying 'the Lord shall be between me and you, and between my descendants and your descendants forever.' " — Jonathan went back into the city. For David, however, this marked the beginning of his life as a hunted and persecuted man (20, 35 — 21, 1).

B) DAVID AS FUGITIVE

(1 S 21, 2 — 27, 12)

The "second epic strophe (1 S 21, 2 — 27, 17), seven chapters, describes David's life as a fugitive and outlaw in the desert. Literary criticism has

---

91. For the annual family sacrifice of Samuel's parents, cf. 1 S 1, 7ff.
92. Instead of "son of a whore," most versions read the milder form: "son of shame." Cf. BHK on this passage.

discovered the evidence of various sources, which the editor has worked
into his account. Scholars, however, do not agree in evaluating the sources;
what one regards as "a very recent source" is seen by another as "a
very ancient popular account." [1] In attempting to pass judgment, we must,
accordingly, steer our course between Scylla and Charybdis. All commentators, however, agree in their high esteem for these chapters. The
drama between Saul and David proceeds towards its climax. In the
crucible of suffering, David grows in maturity and is prepared for his life
mission; Saul too, on Mount Gilboa, reaps the fruits of his own unfortunate
life. His kingship ends with a complete collapse of Israel's power. According to Scripture, it was not so much a case of Saul being broken in
his political endeavors, as running aground in his relationship with God.
In terms of his bad end, we find it easier to understand how Samuel was
able, in fact, even forced, to reject this man as king. He was not the
man to represent Yahweh's kingship on earth. His first duty should have
been to accomplish Yahweh's will and his command. Instead, shortly after
his election as king, he had taken a stand against the divine will and
subsequent years had only hardened his choice. David, on the other
hand, celebrated as the victor over Goliath, envied as the son-in-law of
the king, proceeding from one success to another, but then suddenly
plunged into the deepest misery, a helpless fugitive in the wilderness,
persecuted, threatened in his very life, "a dog in the wilderness" (24, 14),
not even worth hunting down — this David possessed one quality: a
rock-bound faith in Yahweh's protection. Before taking any decisive step,
he inquired into the will of Yahweh, which he followed without quali-
fication, even in the midst of despair. The author of this narrative portrays
the events of David's career as a fugitive and outlaw in the wilderness
with epic scope and true dramatic tension; but these events, in the
meaning of Scripture, are written against the background of God's plan,
and it is only within this work that they can ever be properly evaluated.

1) DAVID IN NOB (1 S 21, 1-10) AND THE BLOOD-BATH IN GIBEAH (1 S 22, 6-23):

What was David to do, now that he had been as good as
condemned to death by Saul and then declared perfectly free?
He turned his fugitive path from Gibeah of Saul towards the
south. But Bethlehem could not be his destination. His kingship
was far too weak to take a stand against the king. First he had
to inquire into Yahweh's will, and he thus directed his step to-

---

1. More extensive examples in Bressan, 341.

wards Nob,[2] the priestly city in the neighborhood of Jerusalem. The cult objects (tent, holocaust altar, ark of the covenant, table of the show-breads, and the ephod with the Urim and Thummim) had been scattered in various places since the destruction of Shiloh. The ark of the covenant, after the Philistines returned it to Israel, was still in Kiriath-Jearim (1 S 7, 1). The tent and holocaust altar had been saved from the catastrophe and set up in Gibeon (1 Ch 16, 39; 2 Ch 1, 3. 5. 13). The ephod and table of the show-breads, on the other hand, were in Nob. It seems that Nob was regarded as a royal sanctuary, since it was customary to inquire into Yahweh's will through the use of the ephod before military campaigns. That is why Saul, and David too, frequently came to this sanctuary and were well known to the high priest. The high priest at that time was Ahimelech,[3] a son of Ahitub.[4]

The high priest came out to meet David in great concern. Something must be amiss, since David was coming alone. Where were the young warriors,[5] who always accompanied him on his

---

2. The prophet Isaiah describes the approach of the Assyrian army (10, 32) gradually drawing closer to Jerusalem. Among the place names mentioned there, Ramah, Gibeah, Anathoth . . . , Nob is mentioned last, as a position from which Sanherib could stretch out his hand against Jerusalem. Nob must, accordingly, have been situated in the immediate vicinity of Jerusalem. Modern-day Beth-Nuba, north of Amwas (Nicopolis) or the village of Annabe near Lydda have been considered, by ancient (Jerome, *Letter* 108, 8) and modern authors (Médebielle, *Samuel*, 434), as the location of the Biblical Nob. Today, however, these opinions are no longer defended.

3. That is, "my brother (God) is king!"

4. That is, "my brother (God) is good." A certain *'ahiyyah*, who was high-priest at the battle of Michmash, is also called *ben-'ahitûb*. Were *'ahimelek* and *'ahiyyah* brothers? Or is Ahijah the Yahwistic correction of the pagan-sounding name *'ahimelek* (which is an echo of the Canaanite divinity *molek*)? The question cannot be definitely settled. It is possible that both names refer to the same person.

5. *ne'arîm* (21, 3) does not mean merely "young men" in general: it has the further connotation of "young warriors." In Canaanite language there was a collective form *na'arôn*, "young manhood (youth) equipped for war." Similarly, in the Hyksos era, the warriors were called by

military expeditions? Could David risk telling the high priest the whole tragedy which had just occurred at the royal court? He was in flight, his life was threatened, and thus he had to carefully conceal his tracks. To keep from involving the priest in his own ruin, he tells him only as much as he needs to know, without forcing him to share any danger. It was indeed a "business of the king," and one which demanded the utmost speed, that brought David to the sanctuary. And yes, his warriors were in such and such a place. David spoke the truth, the complete truth, although the priest could not understand it since he lacked the necessary background. This is no attempt to make a saint out of David, merely to show him for the man he was, a true oriental, clever, crafty, sure to salvage the best from even the most dangerous situation. The fact that his conduct was condemning the priestly family to destruction was not a part of his plans, nor, for that matter, within his power to prevent. There was a higher plan at work here, and David was only an unconscious and innocent tool in its execution.

What David immediately required for his journey was food and weapons. In this capacity, the high priest was no immediate help. There was no ordinary bread in the house, only the "Bread of the Presence" (21, 7), that is, the twelve show-breads, which were laid on the table of show-breads, in the presence of Yahweh, one for each of the twelve tribes (Lv 24, 5-9; Ex 25, 23-30). But these were consecrated loaves, and only the priests of the sanctuary could eat them. Still, the high priest showed no hesitancy in setting aside the prescriptions of the law in this case of necessity. He was prepared to give David the bread, upon the one condition that David and his young men have kept themselves from women.[6] David's answer can be taken as a general principle.

---

the Indian name *marya, mariannu*, "young men." W. F. Albright, *Mitannian maryannu*. AFO 6 (1930), 217-221.

---

6. Cultic cleanness as a prerequisite for military campaigns which were always considered "sacred undertakings" (Dt 23, 10) is still demanded among the Arab tribes of today: "All who participate in a campaign must shave, purify themselves, and wash their clothing. In the night

It goes without saying that "women have been kept from us as always when I go on an expedition" (21, 5). David is speaking in generalities, but the high priest can only understand his words as being spoken with respect to the present case. After David's assurance, Ahimelech no longer hesitates to give David the holy bread.[7]

David also needed weapons. Characteristically enough, weapons were not to be found in the priest's house. Only the sword of Goliath was there, wrapped in a cloth, behind the ephod. Here were also the trophies from David's victory over Goliath, and perhaps trophies from other victories as well. David could hardly have chosen a better weapon for his fight. Goliath's sword was a clear pledge that Yahweh's help would not fail him even in these days of crisis. Probably he also inquired as to the outcome of his undertakings, and the high priest, by using the sacred ephod, perhaps gave him an encouraging oracle. In terms of cult history, the high priest's ephod was originally a broad waist-apron of wool and linen, richly adorned with gold. Along with the ephod went the breast plate (hôšen, a sort of oracle purse, with the Urim and Thummim stones). After the destruction of Shiloh, these cult instruments were brought by the priests to Nob.[8]

David had acted with a high degree of human cunning, cleverly concealing his true intentions. He would have succeeded had it not been for a traitor. An uncanny figure observed David and the high priest, Doeg the Edomite,[9] who must have enjoyed a

---

before the decampment no one is to sleep with his wife; for no one who is unclean may participate in the campaign." R. Kittel, *Geschichte des Volkes Israel,* II (1922), 115, note 3.

---

7. Christ approved of this decision: Mt 12, 1ff.
8. K. Elliger, *Ephod und Choschen,* VT 8 (1958), 19-35. / M. Haran, *The Ephod according to biblical sources,* Tarbis 24, 380-391.
9. In a variant reading (D and R being easily interchanged), an Aramaean. Saul waged war against Edom as well as against Aram (14, 47), and could thus have taken men from both territories into his service. His name is variously interpreted, either *dô'eg,* participle from *d'g,* a man who takes care of things (steward, majordomo), or from the Aramaic form *dôyeg,* "sinner."

very influential position in Saul's court as "the man in charge of the shepherds." [10]

What was Doeg doing at the royal sanctuary? Strangely enough, the text reads that on that day he was "closed in" before Yahweh.[11] Some scholars believe that he was locked in the sanctuary in order to obtain an oracle, in order to learn God's direction through dreams or some other source. But this custom of "incubation oracle" so widely spread in the Ancient Near East, has no other example in the Bible. Since Doeg was an Edomite or Aramaean, it is more probable that Saul, just like Joshua (Jos 9, 21-27), assigned the non-Israelite population for the more menial services at the sanctuary. This makes it easy to explain the presence of this man at the sanctuary; he was "locked in," that is, busy, with his official duties.

Meanwhile, Saul had assembled the council, a "royal diet." This time it was not in his fortress, but at the ancient meeting place under the oak (22, 6). This may also have been the case whenever matters of state were to be deliberated.[12] But on this occasion, Saul wanted to lay bare David's entire conspiracy. He accused his court of being entirely against him. He suggested that David had already promised each of them rewards, vineyards, fields, high position. "No one discloses to me when my son makes a league with the son of Jesse" (22, 8). Then Doeg, the traitor, stood up and announced that David was in Nob, where he had got bread and a sword from the high priest. That was enough. Even the priesthood was among the conspirators.

In his great wrath, Saul immediately sent for the priests. The examination he conducted over them was dictated by his de-

---

10. BHK, a variant reading: "leader of the runners."
11. The translation "festive assembly" has no foundation in the text: 'aṣar means "shut in, enclose, deprive of liberty." The same verb, in 1 S 21, 6, is used of women who are "forbidden." Médebielle, Samuel, 435, explains it as Doeg being "held fast" to the fulfillment of his vow in the sanctuary.
12. Deborah also holds judgment under the oak (Jg 4, 5). In the Ugarit epic, Daniel also judges near the city gate, under a large tree, on the threshing floor. ANET 151.

lusions of persecution. For him the case was a clear one. The entire priesthood had aided the man who meant to seize his throne. To the calm and reasoned words of the high priest he had only one answer: "The king said to the guard [13] who stood about him, 'Turn and kill the priests of the Lord' " (22, 17).

His guard refused to obey the order, since they did not dare to attack the priests of Yahweh. Doeg, the foreigner, showed no such hesitation. When the furious king gave him a like order, the command was carried out on the spot. "On that day, 85 [14] persons who wore the linen ephod were killed" (22, 18). The blood ban was executed against the priestly city of Nob and the city, with all its inhabitants, was annihilated. Only Abiathar escaped the ban,[15] and he fled to David with the ephod.

With this passage, the mystery of God's direction in human history is once again visible. The divine judgment upon the house of Eli, already proclaimed in 1 S 2, is now executed by the king, who himself stands under the judgment of God. What appeared to be mere chance, the path David chose to save his life, was the working out of the catastrophe decreed by heaven. Yahweh's words to the boy Samuel held true: "I am about to do a thing in Israel, at which the two ears of every one that hears it will tingle" (3, 11). The bloody sacrifice of the innocent priests of Nob was, at the same time, an expiatory sacrifice for the trespasses of their fathers. What a sobering insight into the mysteriously intertwining ways of divine judgment we have in these verses.[16] It is not men alone who make history; invisible, and yet at the very center of all activity, Yahweh is present, judging, rejecting, choosing. Human history is a continuous divine judgment (cf. Ps 51/52).

---

13. The runners (*raṣîm*) form a sort of bodyguard for the king.
14. The number 85 is suspect. It would appear more likely that only Eli and his sons were priests at Shiloh. The gematria, that is, the interpretation of the Hebrew letters of the word for "priests" (*khny*) as numerical figures, gives the number 85. (K + H + N + Y = 20 + 5 + 50 + 10). Kittel, *Geschichte des Volkes Israel*, 117.
15. "My Father (God) is mighty."
16. Gutbrod, *Das Buch vom König* (1956), 187.

2) THE FOOL AT GATH (1 S 21, 11-16):

Like all political fugitives, David seeks refuge and security with his enemies. He turns to Achish,[17] the king of the Philistine city of Gath. But here, the people had not forgotten the slayer of Goliath and the vanquisher of the Philistine army (21, 12). David's position there was extremely dangerous. In his crisis, he had recourse to a stratagem. He pretended to be mad. Literally, "he changed his behavior (reason, understanding)" and acted like a fool.[18] He drummed [19] as for the dance, not on a drum, but on the gates and door posts, and he let his spittle run down into his beard. Mentally disturbed people were regarded as holy, since their strange behavior could be explained only by the fact that they were possessed by a divinity.[20] Achish would have nothing to do with a madman. Thus David escaped without injury (cf. Ps 55/56).

3) OUTLAW CHIEF IN THE WILDERNESS (1 S 22, 1-27, 12):

With the road to his enemies thus barred against him, David had no other alternative than to lose himself in the wilderness and

---

17. The king of Amkaruna (Ekron) was an *ikašau*. Assurbanipal's Inscription DBS IV, 397. An *akašau* is to be found on an Egyptian list of the Keftiv (Crete?). According to Meisler, it is Hurrite in origin: composed of the elements *ak* (he has given) and either *šarru* (king, God) or *šenni* (brother). The Philistines would thus be taking over the names of the earlier inhabitants. Cf. *EncMikr* I, 281ff. / G. A. Wainwright, *Caphtor-Cappadocia* VT 6 (1956), 199-210.

18. *wayyithôlel*, Hitpo from *hālal*, related to the Arabic *hilal*, "lunar sickel": Hence, NT refers to mentally unbalanced persons as "lunatics" (MT 4, 24; 17, 15). M. Bič, *La folie de David. Quelques remarques en marge de I Sm 21*. RHPhR 37 (1957), 156-162, treats the account as a legend. David comes as ruler of the land, not as a fugitive. The making of signs is, accordingly, to be compared with the marking of the doorposts in Egypt. A very questionable position.

19. According to a variant reading, "he made marks on the door panels" (*wayyᵉtaw*: he made signs like the letter *Tau*). The Vulgate refers to epileptic attacks: "he collapsed in their midst" (*collabebatur*).

20. This conception is still current among the Arabs. A *meǧnûm* (unbalanced person) is a man who has a *ǧin* (spirit, demon).

in the mountains. From Gath he went into the Cave [21] of Adullam (Odollam)[22] originally a Canaanite city, which had fallen to the lot of Judah when the land was divided. The key position this city occupied on the Wadi es-Sur explains why it was constantly rebuilt in the course of Israelite history.[23] The city is built on a lone hill, in the midst of a labyrinth of caves and wadis. The slopes of the Jewish mountain country, formed largely of limestone, have been strongly eroded by rivulets to form many natural caves.[24] It was into one of these caves, called simply the Cave of Adullam after the neighboring city, that David retired.

For "his brothers and all his father's house," for the whole clan, this was the sign to assemble. Clan consciousness, even today, among the Bedouin tribes is so strong that, in good and bad alike, they all stand or fall together. Saul was thus to exterminate the house of Jesse of Bethlehem as cruelly and unfeelingly as he slaughtered the priests of Nob. Together with David and his clan, there was a constant threat to the existence of all who were not in sympathy with Saul's maladministration. The result was a real exodus into the wilderness. "And every one who was in distress, and every one who was in debt, and every one who was discontented, gathered to him; and he became captain over them. And there were with him about 400 men" (22, 2).

David quickly enough realized that he would have to reckon

---

21. BHK proposes the reading "mountain fortress" (*meṣûdah*) instead of "cave" (*me'arah*), in order to reconcile 22, 1 with 24, 4.
22. Arabic *'adula*, "achieve security," and hence Adullam: "place of refuge." Midway between Gath and Bethlehem, some 20 km WSW of Bethlehem, are the ruins of *'Id el-me* of *'Id el-mijeh*, which has preserved the ancient name.
23. Adullam was a Canaanite city. Judah took a wife there and she bore him three sons (Gn 28, 1-5). Joshua took the city and killed its king (Jos 12, 15). After the taking of the land, the territory was assigned to the tribe of Judah (Jos 15, 35); it was given new fortifications by Rehoboam (2 Ch 11, 5-11), and in the Maccabean era it was held by Judas (2 Mc 12, 38).
24. SSE of Bethlehem is the cave of Hareitun famous for its prehistoric yields. It is 220 m in length and has several chambers which are joined together by a series of passageways.

with Saul's continued persecution. In such a case, the older people would not only be subject to the greatest danger, but they would also be a heavy burden upon the others. He immediately decided to send his aged parents to Mizpah (Maspha)[25] in Moab, for security (22, 3). They remained there during the whole time of his sojourn as a fugitive in the wilderness.

David's feeling of insecurity drove him from one place to another. For his pursuers, he was everywhere and nowhere. In changing his location, he was always guided by direction from above, ascertained by use of the ephod. In this, the priest Abiathar, who had fled to join his company, was his faithful helper. There was also a prophet, whose name was Gad,[26] who had joined him. The prophetic words and the oracular direction assured him of Yahweh's presence and guidance, and he obeyed with unqualified submissiveness.

On the advice of the prophet Gad, David left the Cave of Adullam and headed south towards Jaar Hereth. The place cannot be precisely determined; at all events, what is today an unwooded region may have then enjoyed a stand of timber (ya'ar).[27] Forests, wildernesses, and caves have always been the place of refuge for shipwrecks or exiles. Despite his own insecurity, and the threats against his own life, David was concerned with the well-being of his company. With his 400 men who had nothing more to lose, he presented a not inconsiderable fighting power. When the city of Keilah [28] was threatened by the Philistines, the hour

---

25. Unknown location. Through his ancestor Ruth David is related to the Moabites.
26. Encountered again in 2 S 24, 11-14ff; 2 Ch 29, 25.
27. B. S. J. Isserlin, *Ancient Forests in Palestine. Some Archaeological Indication*. PEQ 86 (1955), 87-88: for the Early Iron Age fortress in Tell el-Ful (Saul's fortress), the builders had both cypress and pine at their disposal. The full-scale deforestation begins with the era of the kings.
28. Seven or eight km south of Adullam, 12 km NW of Hebron. In the Amarna letters it is called *ki-el-ti*. According to Jg 15, 44, assigned by lot to the tribe of Judah. Modern Khirbet Qila. A. Jirku, ZATW 48 (1930), 228ff.

for David's band to strike seemed to have arrived. Keilah was also a mountain fortress, built upon a lone hill, 400 m above sea level. Gentle plains extended from the foot of the mountain. In harvest time, the population generally stayed outside, in the fields. This may have been the time the Philistines chose for their attack, plundering the threshing floors, driving off the cattle, and instituting a general siege. David was determined to hasten to the assistance of the threatened city. His people, however, were not so enthusiastic as their leader: "Behold, we are afraid here in Judah; how much more then if we go to Keilah against the armies of the Philistines?" (23, 3). David inquired into Yahweh's will by the ephod of the high priest Abiathar. The manner of making this inquiry is characteristic for Old Testament oracle. The question had to be formulated in such a way that it could be answered yes or no. David asked: "Shall I set out?" Then the priest apparently shook the Urim and Thummim stones in the ephod purse, reached in to select one, and according as the stone with yes or no came out, the question was considered to be decided. In this case, the decision was in favor of the campaign against the Philistines. It is easy to understand that such a decision inspired the entire company with invincible spirit and power; Yahweh himself was marching with them to victory (23, 1-6).

But the inhabitants of the liberated city — as so often happens in history — were not so happy to receive the relieving forces. Quartering and maintaining 400 fighting men was a heavy demand upon the tiny city. In order to be rid of their liberators, the city elders of Keilah made a secret pact with Saul. There could be no more welcome news for the angry king. As long as David ranged freely about in the wilderness, he could neither be attacked nor captured. But as soon as he shut himself up within a fortress city, behind its walls and gates, it could turn into a disastrous trap for him. This time, in order to be certain of victory, Saul assembled the entire people for the campaign (23, 8). He meant to deal a devastating blow to the man who was set on stealing his throne. David himself was uncomfortable in the fortified city. Once again he inquired into Yahweh's will, and was directed to abandon the city. Saul came storming upon Keilah, but when he arrived at the city, the bird had already slipped through the net.[29] The number of David's faithful band had been increased by 200, and he now counted 600 followers. From this time forward, the wilderness of Judah became a "fortress" ($m^e\d{s}\hat{u}d\hat{a}h$) for him and for his people, a home grounds in which he felt secure for the time being.

David and his band turned from Keilah towards the southeast, passing Hebron with its vast vineyards and fields, lying directly against the peaks of the mountain range. Towards the west, the countryside dropped in gentle waves towards the coastal plain. Towards the east, however, it drops precipitously from 900 m to 400 m, the average elevation of the wilderness of Judah, and then, in a second precipitous drop, reaches the level of the Dead Sea. Between the cultivated land and the wilderness proper, there is a varying strip of steppe country (*midbar*), where grass grows and herds can be pastured during the rainy season. Beyond this yawns the desert proper, a rugged and foreboding country with its precipitous walls, deeply eroded gorges, and towering rock formations standing like citadels. From this height it is possible to look down on the blue mirror of the Dead Sea, covered, at noonday, with a thin veil of vapor.[30] This desolate belt, which begins at the north end of the Dead Sea and extends beyond its southern end — 80 km long and 20-25 km across — is known in Scripture as "wilderness of Judah" (Jg 1, 16). It is divided into several

---

29. A figure which frequently recurs in the Psalms: 90/91, 3; 123/124, 7; 139/140, 4.

30. In June of 1951 I was able to visit David's refuge in the wilderness of Judah: Ziph, Carmel, Maon, and as far as Eshtemoa, with a side trip to Beni-Nain. There is a fine view of the Dead Sea from here. At this time the steppe had been scorched into a complete desert. Without road or direction we drove straight through the desert country. Since we were moving about in Jordan-Israelite border territory, each car was accompanied by a heavily armed Arab. Today the sound of motors has invaded the wilderness and dispelled something of its loneliness, but even the modern man cannot help sensing something of the mystery and awe that pervades these secret recesses and hiding places that cannot be discovered without a guide.

districts: the wilderness of Tekoa (Thecue) between Bethlehem
and Hebron (2 Ch 20, 20), the wilderness of Jeruel (2 Ch 20,
16), the wilderness of Ziph, Maon, and En-gedi (Engaddi).
David kept primarily to the outlying districts, along the heights
of Maon, Ziph, and Carmel. When the hunt began in earnest,
he withdrew into the wilderness proper, all the way down to
the Dead Sea.[31]

David settled first along the mountain heights of Ziph,[32] 7
km southeast of Hebron (23, 14), but he was always on the
move. Jonathan met David some 3 km further southeast of Ziph,
on the mountain dome of Horesh, a most daring undertaking for
the son of the pursuer. But Jonathan had a clear appraisal of
the course of events and knew infallibly that his friend would
succeed to the kingship. He came into the wilderness to renew
his bond of friendship (23, 16-18).

The inhabitants of Ziph were not entirely comfortable with
the "bandits" so close at hand. They preferred to give their
loyalty to the king, who actually possessed the power, and not
to side with this questionable pretender. They sent messengers
to Saul, betraying David's location (cf. Ps 53/54). Saul was
determined to spare no effort, even if he had to fight his way
through all the clans [33] of the tribes of Judah. He covered the
distance in forced marches, guided by a man from Ziph who
knew the country. A running hunt ensued, unparalleled in Biblical history. David, naturally, did not remain in his "fortress" at
Horesh (wooded district). He passed over into the wilderness

---

31. On "wilderness of Judah," cf. G. H. Smith, *Historical Geography of
the Holy Land* (London, 1907), 13th Ed. B. Ubach, *Excursion aux
déserts d'Engaddi*, Zif, Maon. RB 53 (1946), 249-256. / Westminster
Atlas 63. / R. Köppel, *Palästina, die Landschaften in Karten und
Bildern* (Tubingen, 1930), Fig 74, 75, 101, 103, 111, 130-137.

32. At an elevation of 878 m. It affords a splendid view of all the surrounding wilderness of Judah as far as Engaddi. Modern Tell Zif, a
desolate mound of ruins. Assigned by lot to the tribe of Judah (Jos
15, 55), and fortified by Rehoboam (1 Ch 11, 8).

33. *'aleph* means, not only thousand, but also clan or family. Mi 5, 1:
"But you, O Bethlehem Ephrathat, who are little to be among the *clans*
(not *thousands*) of Judah . . . ."

of Maon.[34] Saul heard of this and pursued him there. He soon
had him contained; only one deeply eroded wadi divided the
two companies.[35] Saul and his people rushed headlong down the
one side of the valley, eager to find a suitable route of ascent,
and quickly fall upon his victim. David fled along the other
side of the valley, determined to escape his pursuers' hand. Then
came the news of a Philistine invasion. Saul was forced to give
up pursuit. The bird was almost in the net, so he believed, and
he had to let it slip away again; that is why the place is named
"Rock of Escape." [36] In order, finally, to achieve some security,
David withdrew to En-gedi (Engaddi) along the Dead Sea (24,
1ff.).

Hardly had Saul repulsed the Philistines when he returned
to the pursuit of David. In this next episode we can recognize
two distinct accounts which contain so many similarities that it
is easy to recognize them as different versions of the same event.
The first version, in chapter 24, tells of Saul's obstinate pursuit
of David, which was so insistent that David had no other recourse
than to hide in a large cave. Saul entered this very cave, to
satisfy the needs of nature.[37] It would have been a simpler matter
to strike him down on the spot. David's men were eager to do so,
but David prevented them. He did not want to sin against the
anointed of the Lord. Instead, he crept up and cut off a tassel
from Saul's cloak.[38] When Saul had left, David came out of

34. Modern Khirbet Ma'in; 7 or 8 km south of Ziph. RB 53 (1946), 256ff.
35. In this sense we are probably to understand the word *sela'*, rock
    (24, 26). Cf. de Vaux, *Samuel*, 11. Modern Wadi el-Malaqi, northeast
    of Maon.
36. Thus LXX, but MT: "rock of decision."
37. In Hebrew, the euphemistic expression: "cover his feet." Cf. Jg 3, 24.
    Even today, the Bedouin is accustomed to squat and let his flowing
    robes fall to the earth, bell-shaped, on all sides. De Vaux, *Samuel*, 11.
38. A tassle cut from the cloak (Accadian: *si-si-ik-tu*) is symbolic for
    the whole person. Possessing even a particle of the garment gives
    a man power over the whole person. When a sick man is unable
    to go to the temple, he sends the priest a piece cut from his clothing,
    to achieve a cure by magic. Similarly, in rites of propitiation in various
    sections of the kingdom, a piece cut from the royal cloak represents
    the presence of the king himself. It might well be that such Ancient

the cave, and, holding the tassel in his hand, attempted to convince his pursuer that he had no evil intention towards him. He is "only a dead dog, only a flea," and it was not worth hunting him. When Saul heard David's voice and recognized that his adversary had been in a position to take his life but had spared him instead, he was moved to tears and broke off the pursuit. Once again, in this man impelled by passion, delusion of persecution, and terrible anxiety, it was the element of good that had won the upper hand. But for how long? (cf. Ps 56/57).

The second account, in chapter 26, has a similar setting. David is being continuously pursued by Saul, when he slips into the slumbering camp one night, steals the king's lance and drinking cup, escapes undetected, climbs a nearby height, and sounds the alarm to the camp. He calls the commander of the army, Abner, and Saul too, by name, protesting his innocence. Once again, he points out, Saul's life had been in his hands, but he had spared the anointed of the Lord. Saul, too, should finally come to his senses. Overcome by his adversary's magnanimity, Saul abandoned his pursuit.

A comparison between the two accounts shows that there are many similarities, not only in the general outline, but even in the individual details. On the basis of this fact, Gressmann [39] claims that "there can be no doubt regarding the literary dependence of the two episodes." R. De Vaux [40] maintains the historicity of the narrative, but feels that there is only one episode, reported in two different manners. There must have been several anecdotes about David's magnanimity among the people. The historian took them as he found them and worked them into his narrative in a unified form. In terms of literary criticism,

---

Near Eastern customs also figure into the present account. J. de Fraine, VD 25 (1947), 218-230. / Very conclusive in this respect is a document from Mari: M. Noth, *Remarks on the Sixth Volume of the Mari Texts.* JSemStud 1 (1956), 322-333: Itur-Asdu assures us that he has cut neither hair nor seam from the cloak of the "dreamer" Malik-Dagan.

39. Gressmann, 98.
40. De Vaux, *Samuel,* 119.

according to Eissfeldt,[41] the two chapters are a distich within the Yahwist tradition: "They are masterpieces of the narrator's art. The material was not purely invented, but taken from popular accounts."

The similarities in the two accounts are indeed astounding. Already in the treatment of David's summons to the royal court we have left open the possibility that the same event might be presented here as two different episodes, based on different points of view. The court circles had different interests than the prophetic circles. Can this same criterion be applied to chapters 24 and 26? Or are the dissimilarities so considerable in this case that we must actually think of different events? The locale is different: the first episode takes place in En-gedi (24, 2), the second takes place in the wilderness of Ziph on the hill of Hachilah (26, 3). The first episode takes place in a cave (stealing the tassel of the cloak) during the day; it was only an accident; the second takes place in the camp, at night (theft of the lance and drinking cup), and was a bold and deliberate adventure. The literary similarity in the magnanimous words of David and the moving confession of guilt on the part of Saul are not so decisive as to force us to regard the two narratives as a double account of one and the same episode. We might thus come much closer to the reality of the matter if we actually suppose two encounters between pursuer and pursued.[42] The notice of Samuel's death (25, 1) occurs in the very midst of the time in which David is a fugitive in the wilderness. Samuel must have reached a very advanced age.[43] The stereotyped expression: "Now Samuel died; and all Israel assembled and mourned for him, and they buried him in his house at Ramah," [44] is the epitaph for a man who is one of the greatest in Israel. He stands at a pivotal point in

---

41. Eissfeldt, *Einleitung*, 329, 337.
42. Bressan, 402ff.
43. According to Calmet, 98 years. He died two years before Saul. *Commentaire littéral sur tous les livres de l'AT* (Paris), II, 1724. Quoted in Bressan, 385.
44. Similar formula used at the interment of Joshua, the bones of Joseph and the Highpriest Eleazar. Jg 24, 29-33.

history and his was the bitter mission, entrusted to him by Yahweh himself, of inaugurating the transition from a religious federation of tribes into a monarchy.

There remains the rather considerable problem of how David managed to live as outlaw chief in the wilderness. In the cities of Keilah and Ziph he was not welcomed. The strong man from the desert was a threat to them, and they made every effort to deliver him to the stronger man Saul. A single example casts some light on the methods employed not only by David, but other exiled men as well, in order to get their daily bread. "The story of the miserly Nabal the fool, and his beautiful and clever wife Abigail, is one of the masterpieces of the court narrator's art. What a marvelous progression from great and important to lesser and secondary events and circumstances, and what an abrupt alternation of the most profound and the most trivial details. Indeed, we must wonder at the narrative art of the many verses which rejoice in David's idyll with Abigail in the wilderness; but beneath this idyll shines the somber beauty of the austere life of a hunted and penniless man." [45]

David seems to have kept a tight rein upon his men. He would not allow wild plundering. He preferred to live on friendly terms with the population of the marginal districts. He sent word to Nabal: "Your shepherds have been with us, and we did them no harm, and they missed nothing, all the time they were in Carmel" (25, 7). The shepherds, on the other hand, must have recognized the presence of David's company as a protective wall against occasional attacks from robbers. For this protection he afforded them, David felt entitled to some remuneration. Nabal,[46] the wealthy shepherd, lived in Maon. He pastured his herds some 2 km to the north, on Carmel,[47] 3000 sheep and

---

45. Gutbrod, *Das Buch vom König*, 201, note 1.
46. *nābal*, fool, not only intellectually deficient, but also morally and religiously defective. Hence, equivalent to "stupid, vulgar, godless." P. Jouon, Bibl 5 (1924), 356-361.
47. *karmel* does not mean, as it is generally translated, "God's vineyard" (*kerem'el*), but simply: "fruit garden." The final "l" might be the Indo-Germanic diminutive ending. / Meyer, *Hebr. Grammatik* I (1952), 111. Modern Kermel. ABEL, II, 296.

1000 goats. Even if the number seems rather high, we cannot doubt that Nabal was one of the most powerful sheikhs of the area, which was in the tribe of Caleb. He had certainly profited from the protection afforded by David's company. And he certainly should be willing to show his appreciation. When David's messengers appeared in Carmel at the time of the shearing, the shepherds' harvest festival, to demand their tribute, Nabal had only harsh words for them. David, thereupon, decided to use force to seize what was rightfully his by the law of the wilderness. The undertaking would probably have ended in a blood bath and plunder, if the clever Abigail had not made her appearance. She had a presentiment of the coming ruin and tried to head it off. "Then Abigail made haste, and took 200 loaves and two skins of wine, and five sheep ready dressed, and five measures of parched grain, and a hundred clusters of raisins, and 200 cakes of figs, and laid them on asses" (25, 18). Thus equipped, she set out to David. Her diplomacy and feminine powers of persuasion succeeded in restraining David from the massacre which was on the point of breaking out.

Meantime, the "fool" was holding a revel that would have done a king proud. Since he was full of wine, Abigail did not immediately tell him that the danger had been turned aside. Next morning, when he was sober, she told him the whole story. "And his heart died within him, he became as a stone. And about ten days later the Lord smote Nabal; and he died" (25, 38). David saw this as God's own doing. Nabal's evil had fallen upon his own head. David wooed Abigail and took her for his wife. For David, this meant not only the acquisition of Nabal's considerable wealth, thereby assuring the support of David's company; according to the clan relationship of those days, this wedding established the most intimate bonds with the tribe of Caleb. The center of this tribe was Hebron. It was here that David was later proclaimed king. Family ties thus play a considerable role in establishing his kingship in Judah. By family descent he was bound to his kinship in Bethlehem, and now had married into the mighty tribe of Caleb. The fact that he also took a second wife Ahinoam [48] from Jezreel (Jezrahel) a city in the south,[49] is to be evaluated in the same sense. Marriage generally confirmed treaty alliances which were already existing or newly contracted. Without this family and tribal support David's rapid rise would not have been such an easy matter.[50]

For the time being, however, the kingship is not yet in sight. Abigail and Ahinoam apparently had to share David's fugitive life. It appeared that Saul, in a spirit of vengeance against this marriage, gave Michal, David's first wife, to a certain Paltiel.[51]

4) DAVID AS VASSAL OF THE PHILISTINES:

In order to put an end, once and for all, to Saul's further attempts to pursue him, David negotiated an alliance with the Philistine King Achish of Gath. This time he announced himself not as a solitary fugitive seeking political asylum, but, with his 600 followers, he represented a not inconsiderable military power. And this time he came with all his baggage and followers. David was seeking the protection of the Philistine king, but he wanted to have a free hand. He thus approached Achish with the proposal that he assign him and his people a residence city along the southern border district. Achish agreed to the proposal and gave David the city of Ziklag (Siceleg),[52] not only as a royal fief,[53]

---

48. "My brother is the charm of love."
49. Cf. Jos 15, 56, where, in connection with Carmel and Maon, there is also mention of a place called Jezreel. This must not be confused with the city of the same name on the Plain of Jezreel, which played an important role as the second city of the Northern Kingdom.
50. In summer of 1951 I was able to watch the flocks being watered. In the deepest point of the valley floor there is an abundant spring. The water is drawn into huge troughs. We admired the strict order and discipline which the shepherds maintained among their flocks. The individual groups were arranged in pyramid form, with the apex, the bell-wether, positioned near the water. Only when the one group was finished would the shepherd of the second group use his long shepherd's staff to yield the drinking position to the bell-wether of the second flock.
51. "My refuge is God" (2 S 3, 15).
52. The location of Ziklag is contested. Probably at Tell el-Huwêlfeh,

but as his personal possession. The only condition of the grant was, apparently, David's obligation to protect the border against invasion from the steppe. He probably also reckoned on the booty which David would acquire from his military campaigns primarily against the Israelite districts. But in this he was deceived. He had not reckoned with the real cleverness of his crafty vassal.

For David, together with his band of some thousand souls, to fall on the city of Ziklag and establish his headquarters there, is characteristic of that stormy century. In much the same way, the sea peoples no doubt established themselves in Asia Minor after their great migration of 1200. If a city offered resistance, it was stormed and annihilated; if it opened its doors, the conquerers entered as the new ruling class. The original population must be content with serving its new masters.

From Ziklag as a base, David led various razzias, not, as Achish had anticipated, into the district of Judah, but into the territory of southern Bedouin tribes. David, as a true son of the wilderness, followed the laws of the wilderness. A razzia [54] is a sudden attack upon an enemy tribe — never on a related or friendly clan — with the objective of carrying off flocks and possessions, everything that has any value. There need be no open hostility involved; the fact that a distant tribe or the farmer settlers of a cultivated area had no friendly relationships to one's own tribe was sufficient to justify such a raid. The raiders generally tried to avoid bloodshed, in order to escape the laws of blood vengeance. Prisoners, however, were treated with the utmost severity. They were buried up to their necks in the earth, to make flight impossible.[55]

These accounts are based on more modern Arab practices,

---

25 km south of Gath (*Arak al-Menšijeh*).
53. Kittel, *Geschichte des Volkes Israel*, II, 173.

---

54. Razzia is a loan word from the Arabic *razu*, and thus the most logical word to describe David's desert campaigns.
55. A. Jaussen, *Coutumes des Arabes au pays de Moab*, Etudes biblique (Paris, 1908), 165, 167.

but a comparison with the Biblical narratives would indicate that there has been little change. David led his raids with particular severity, since they were generally aimed against the ancient hereditary enemy of Israel, the tribe of Amalek (27, 8). His raids deserve to be compared to the blood ban (*herem*) whose object was the total eradication of an enemy tribe. This was to prevent Achish from receiving information as to the true objective of David's raids. He encouraged the Philistines in their belief that his campaigns were directed against Judah. Achish was happy with the rich booty that David assigned to him as his share and felt that David had been won over, once and for all, to the Philistine cause: "He has himself utterly abhorred by his people Israel; therefore he shall be my servant always" (27, 12). In this, of course, he was very much mistaken. It was by these campaigns that David defended the tribal territory of Judah from the predatory Bedouin hordes, thereby winning even greater sympathy among his fellow countrymen and laying an even firmer foundation for his future kingship. It is possible that during this same time he also established firm bonds of friendship with the Cherethites and Pelethites, a Philistine people in the southern territory, from whom he later formed his bodyguard (2 S 8, 18; 15, 18; 20, 7).

C) THE CATASTROPHE ON MOUNT GILBOA

(1 S 28 — 2 S 1)

1) FULL SCALE ATTACK BY THE PHILISTINES:

The war between Israel and the Philistines for the possession of the land between the Jordan and the Sea was a particularly vigorous contest. Israel was penetrating the country from the east, and the Philistines from the west. For a long time it was actually undecided whether Canaan would be Israelite or Philistine (Palestinian). Three principal attack routes can be distinguished in this Philistine penetration. During the days of Samuel, and at the beginning of Saul's reign, they attempted to force their way into the middle of the mountain country. There they succeeded in taking the mountain heights, where they established their outposts. But in the campaign of Michmash, Saul threw them back to the level country. Their attack against the southern territory of Judah was broken by the defeat of their champion Goliath. Since Israel was growing weaker and weaker, internally, as a result of Saul's maladministration, the Philistines undertook a final and full scale campaign directed against the plains which separate Galilee from the south. Here they could literally "roll over" Israel. They must have told themselves that their previous defeats were owing to the fact that their war chariots were unable to maneuver properly in the mountain country. Accordingly, they chose the great plain for their present battle field. Here they would be able to develop their striking power to better advantage. The fact that they were in a position to determine the battle locale in advance of their campaign is clear evidence of their vastly superior strength.

Mustering point and battle field are once again clearly distinct. The Philistines assembled their military levy at Aphek, the traditional mustering point for major campaigns.[56] When the army had assembled, in companies of 100 and 1000 men, the five Philistine kings who bear the title of $s^e r\bar{a}n\hat{i}m$ (related with a Greek word *tyrannos* — 1 S 5, 8; 29, 2), organized their individual troops. In the levy of King Achish of Gath they saw the Hebrews under David's leadership. This they would not accept: "What are these Hebrews [57] doing there?" (29, 3). Although Achish very convincingly vouched for the faithfulness of his Hebrew vassal, he was forced, under pressure from his allies, to dismiss David and his troops. Since the battle at Michmash, the Philistines were mistrustful of any Hebrews serving in their forces. On that occasion, at the decisive moment in the battle, they had gone over to their compatriots (14, 21). There was to be no such second occurrence.

David found himself in a very disagreeable position. It must

---

56. Cf. 1 S 4, 1: situated on the Plain of Sharon, modern *Ras el-'ain,* Antipatris of Herodean times.

57. The Philistines refer to their adversaries simply as Hebrews. Cf. the expeditions against the Habiri, in Vol. I, p. 161.

have been a difficult matter for him, as the Philistine vassal, to march against his own people and he may well have done so only with the intention of abandoning the Philistines at a decisive moment or even falling upon their rear. Now, by the mistrust of the Philistine princes, he was rescued from this uncomfortable position. And not only that. While Saul was being defeated in the north and the kingdom was falling to Philistine power, David, in the south, was free to lay the foundations for his new kingdom.

The Philistines apparently approached Israel along the ancient military route that led through the Wadi Ara[58] over the Carmel mountains, and took their position at Shunem,[59] a small village at the foot of Gebel Nebi Dahi. Saul's army, on the other hand, was encamped "by the fountain which is in Jezreel (Jezrahel)"[60] (29, 1), an extremely strategical point. This position is at an equal distance from Nazareth and Tabor in the north, Megiddo in the west, and Dothan in the south, and Beth-Shan to the east. The city controlled access to the vast Plain of Jezreel and the open country leading to the Sea; it was thus a control point for access to the Jordan Valley. The fountain along which Saul's army took up its position, is apparently the same fountain mentioned in the Book of Judges, Ain Harod (modern-day Ain Galud), only a few kilometers southeast of the city of Jezreel. Saul's rear was covered by the Gilboa Mountain range,[61] a mighty mountain chain 18 km long and 5 to 8 km in breadth, and some 518 m in elevation. The two hostile forces were separated by only 6 km. This time it would be a battle on the level

---

58. This is the same route taken by Thutmosis III, around 1480, in the battle of Megiddo. Galling, TGI, 12.
59. Modern *Sôlem* (or *Sûlam*), the *ša-na-ma* of the Thutmosis lists. From here also comes Abishag the Shunammite who was chosen to keep the aged King David warm (1 K 1, 3). Cf. also the Shulammite in Song of Songs, 7, 1.
60. The name of the city Jezreel means "May God sow." A reference to the fertility of the plain. Hosea interprets the name as an oracle of threatened punishment (Ho 1, 5; 2, 24) on the basis of the meaning: "May God scatter." As the second capital city, it plays a decisive role in the history of the Northern Kingdom. Modern Zer'in.
61. Modern *Ǧebel Fukû'a*.

ground, where the Philistines could develop their chariot formation to good advantage. A sad prospect for Israel.

When Saul observed the battle preparations in the Philistine camp, he was afraid "and his heart trembled greatly" (28, 5). What was he to do? In every military campaign it went without saying that Yahweh's direction must be ascertained (14, 18). Apparently, after the blood bath at Nob and the flight of Abiathar, Saul had provided for a new ephod. But the Urim-Thummim oracle refused an answer (28, 6).[62] Saul's next recourse was dream interpretation; Yahweh had, in times past, made known his will through dreams, even for pagans (Gn 40, 5; 41, 1). Neither was there any prophet to deliver Yahweh's word to him (28, 6). God had already abandoned Saul. The silence of death surrounded him on every side, even before the battle.[63] But Saul meant to force an answer out of God, and he thus turned to a medium (witch) in En-Dor.

2) SAUL AND THE MEDIUM (1 S 28, 5-25):

Saul was a man of great interior conflict and contradiction. He had forbidden sooth-saying and necromancy under pain of death (28, 3), and had literally attempted to root it out of Israel in order to apply the Mosaic law in its fullest severity: "A man or a woman who is a medium (*'ôb*) or a wizard (*yidde'onî*)[64]

---

62. Probably it was the non-committal stone that was drawn.
63. A Babylonian lament over the silence of a divinity runs as follows: "I called to my god, but he did not show his face; I prayed to my goddess, but the goddess did not raise my head. The seer gave me no word. I then turned to a conjurer (medium), but there was no answer for me." A. Jirku, *Altoriental. Kommentar zum AT* (Leipzig, 1923), 149.
64. Both terms occur regularly in reference to conjuring and mediums. But what is the original basic meaning? The root meaning of *'ôb* is uncertain. A few suggestions might be offered: from the Arabic *aba*, "to return"; hence *'ôb*, one who returns from the afterlife. / Perhaps related with the word *'ôb* in Jb 32, 19 (only occurrence), in the meaning of bottle. At any event, in the myth of Ishtar's descent to the netherworld the messenger of the gods proffers a bottle filled with the water of life, whereupon the goddess can once again rise

shall be put to death; they shall be stoned with stones, their blood shall be upon them" (Lv 20, 27). In his desperate circumstances, Saul had no other recourse than to worship what he had tried to ban, and to summon the very powers he had persecuted. He ordered his men to seek out a woman who was a medium (28, 7). This difficult task gives us an insight into the ancient Canaanite conceptions of the hereafter, which were also popular in Israel. We are in the presence of very somber and poorly defined concepts here.

The woman is called a *ba'ªlat'ôb,* literally "mistress or possessor of an *'ôb.* The Septuagint translates the word as "ventriloquist," [65] and thus produces a ridiculous situation. It is true that, in the performance of such mediums, ventriloquism and other artificial effects, and even direct influence on the part of the devil, may have played a role; but it is more important to examine the underlying concepts of the hereafter which figure in the situation. When the woman is called a "mistress of a seeking spirit of the dead," this presupposes the belief that the spirits of the dead would take possession of her, speaking and prophesying through her. We are dealing with a sort of possession by the spirit of the dead, who could be conjured up by magical rites.

Saul's men found such a woman in En-Dor.[66] Saul disguised

---

to the upper world. ANET 108. / The Odyssey records that Odysseus offered sacrifice at the entrance of Oceanos; the dead came to drink the blood and were restored to life. / It is possible that bottles with water or sacrificial blood were also used in conjuring up the spirits of the dead. For a more detailed treatment, cf. the article *'ôb* by Tur-Sinai in *EncMikr* I, 135ff. / The derivation from the Accadian is also deserving of attention. The root *aw* forms *awatum,* "word, affair, event," and *awum,* "speaker"; *'ôb* is thus someone who speaks. / *Yidde'onî* (piel form derived from *yada'*) means someone who informs.

---

65. ἐγγαστρίμυθος.

66. On the northern slope of the Gebel Dahi stands the modern village of *'Indur,* which preserves the ancient name — 15 km from Gilboa Mountains. The ancient En-dor — names fluctuate in their location — was located on a different hill, the *Khirbet es-Safsafeh,* some 5 km

himself and, with two companions, set out to consult her (28, 8). The clever woman wanted to be sure that this was not a trap and she forced the unknown man to swear that she would suffer no harm. In his desperate position, Saul was prepared to do the most contradictory things: to swear by Yahweh and at the same time to conjure up the spirits of the dead.

The course of the scene as presented in the text can be briefly outlined. As soon as the woman was pacified by the oath, she set about the practice of her art. Whether or not she wielded a leather bottle with living water or sacrificial blood is not said. First she asked whom she was to bring up. Saul answered: "Bring up Samuel for me" (28, 11ff.). But even before she could practice her magical arts, she unexpectedly saw figures beginning to rise, and she cried out in terror. At that same moment she realized that the man who called upon Samuel could be none other than King Saul himself. Saul allayed her fears and asked her further: "What do you see?" The figure was veiled from him. She answered: "I see a god (*'elōhim* — a figure of the hereafter)[67] coming out of the earth." — "What is his appearance?"[68] — "An old man is coming up; and he is wrapped in a robe" (*me'il*).[69] Then Saul knew it could only be Samuel; he fell prostrate and touched the earth with his face as a sign of reverence and obeisance. From this moment on, the woman was no longer required. The dialogue takes place only between the two men.

---

south of Tabor. The tribe of Manasseh had not succeeded in expelling the Canaanites from the territory. Hence, despite the strict royal edict, magic still flourished here (Jos 17, 12ff). N. Zori, *New Light on Endor*, PEQ 84 (1952), 114.

---

67. *'elohim* generally means God; but there is also a secondary meaning, not only beings from the afterlife, but also supermen or mighty heroes. The Vulgate translates literally, but incorrectly: *"deos vidi ascendentes."* Cf. O. Schilling, *Der Jenseitsgedanke im AT* (Mainz, 1951), 73. / H. Kruse, *Elohim non Deus*, VD 27 (1949), 278-286. / J. L. McKenzie, *The appellative use of El and Elohim*, CBQ 10 (1948), 170-186.

68. Despite the apparent plural which has preceded (*'elohim*), Saul asks his question in the singular.

69. *me'il*, the shawl-like cloak of the upper classes, the characteristic garment which Samuel received, every year, from his mother (2, 19).

Samuel asks reproachfully: "Why have you disturbed me by bringing me up?" Saul's extreme despair breaks through in his answer. God Elohim — he no longer uses the name Yahweh — has abandoned him, and refuses him an answer; he speaks neither by dream, nor prophet, nor by the ephod. What is he to do? The Philistines are attacking. Samuel has no answer either. He merely repeats the severe words of judgment which he must have spoken during his life. Yahweh has abandoned Saul, has even become his enemy, has wrested the kingship from his hands and entrusted it to his rival David. Saul has taken a stand against the explicit order of Yahweh and not carried out the ban against Amalek. In recompense, Yahweh would execute the ban upon the house of Saul in Israel, and this would take place the very next day. Yes, that very next day Saul and his sons and warriors would be with Samuel in Sheol.[70] There is no word of comfort and no word of encouragement. Perhaps, in some corner of his soul, Saul had cherished the hope that this very man who had once anointed and chosen him, would be able to help him in this moment of extremest crisis. But there were only words of inexorable divine judgment against him.

Then Saul fell full length upon the ground, literally prostrated by the answer. At first the woman could not understand. She speaks to Saul and manages to get him onto a bed. Eventually he takes some nourishment. She quickly slaughters a fatted calf and bakes some bread. This was Saul's last supper before his death.[71]

Examining this account simply in terms of style, we must concede that the story here reaches a moment of unexpected and supremely dramatic

---

70. The OT conception of the fate of the dead is somber and not well explored. The underworld (*še'ôl*) unites just and unjust, Samuel with Saul and his sons. But this same somber conception yields an important theological fact. Christ himself must descend to the gates of sheol, to shed light on the fate of the departed. Cf. Heinisch, *Theologie des AT* (Bonn) 1940, 244-254.

71. Reinach holds that the interrogation must be preceded by a ritual fast, which was followed, after the apparition, by a ritual banquet. *Le souper chez la Sorcière*, Rev. de l'Histoire des Religions 88 (1923/24), 43-50. Rejected by: Bressan, 425ff.

climax, before tragedy breaks upon Saul and his house. The one-sided rationalistic school of interpretation cannot assign any historical value to the narrative, but still marvels at the narrator's art: "From the outset, he knows how to heighten the feeling of suspense by his reserved statement. . . . The mystery is unveiled no more than absolutely necessary. The ultimate despair which impelled the king into this dubious undertaking, the ensuing dream which unnerved him to the point of complete collapse — these are masterfully painted. The catastrophe in the life drama of King Saul, which is now drawing to its end, is strikingly introduced by this chapter. We cannot refuse sympathy to this solitary, desperate, and abandoned king. Our only regret can be the fact that his figure is not raised to true tragic grandeur, such as might awaken our sympathies. The figure of Saul, broken within and despairing in the face of crisis, is utterly lacking in that titanic note of the ultimate defiance which could still win our honest applause." [72]

Guthrod, in his new commentary (1956), takes a different view: Since Gressmann's book, in 1921, many things had changed: "Gressmann's attitude must be considered as outdated. It is obviously the expression of that school of Western thought which subscribes univocally to the observation of natural-science phenomena, and, accordingly, must explain an oracle from the dead, since it is outside the framework of natural science, only as saga and poetic license. But our present-day encounter with the thinking and clear facts from the realm of Asiatic and African culture can only make us cautious in judging such an 'impossibility' out of hand." [73]

In the light of serious modern science, it is hardly possible to doubt the reality of these necromancy scenes. But for the Christian, it is unnecessary to appeal to the example of Asiatic and African people. In the lives of the saints, there are sufficient critically established examples,[74] in which the departed have spoken to living people. In itself, therefore, assuming a belief in the survival of the human soul after death, and this was the unshakable conviction of ancient peoples, there is no possible objection to be made to the appearance of Samuel's figure from the dead.[75] But he did not come in answer to the woman's conjuring; she

---

72. Gressmann, 115.
73. Guthrod, *Das Buch vom König*, 230. Also Kittel, *Geschichte des Volkes Israel*, II, 126 can find no grounds for doubting the actual occurrence of the facts. "We must recall that Saul is only permitted to speak to the spirit, but not to see him. The woman might have been a very clever master of deception."
74. Bressan, 430ff.
75. We deliberately use the word "figure" and not "soul," because our dogmatically oriented and developed concept of "soul" cannot be applied to this ancient text.

herself was terrified, as if something extraordinary were taking place. The framework of normal conjuring seems, accordingly, to have been violated here. Did God directly intervene here, and, despite all the power of magic, raise up the figure of Samuel to deliver a final judgment on Saul? This is the position taken by many exegetes, among them Médebielle,[76] and might be considered the *sententia communis* among Catholics.

There is also another opinion, represented by significant Fathers such as Basil and Cyril of Alexandria,[77] who maintain that it was not God, but rather the devil, who is at work here. For God does not surrender the soul of a just man to the power of the demons. Accordingly, it must have been the devil who took on Samuel's figure and imitated his voice, in order to drive Saul to the nadir of despair. For Yahweh abhors magic, and how could he possibly make use of it? This explanation, with its appeal to diabolical power, is not, in the last analysis, particularly convincing. There is nothing in the text to lend it substance. The serious words spoken by Samuel can hardly be put into the mouth of the devil.

No matter what opinion is eventually adopted, and despite all the uncertainties surrounding the account, there is no doubting the fact that the passage represents an ancient document for Israel's belief in a life after death. The dead are not dead. Their existence is not completely extinguished. They can, if God permits, rise up from the world of the dead and admonish the living (Si 46, 23).

3) THE BATTLE ON MOUNT GILBOA (GELBOE):

This terrible night could only be followed by an even more terrible day. Covering 30 km under cover of night,[78] going a whole day and night without eating anything (28, 20), burdened in soul by Samuel's ultimate sentence against him — such a man was incapable of directing his forces in battle. What led Saul to risk the formation of his troops on level ground near the fountain? Against the Philistine chariot forces he had no equivalent armament to oppose. Perhaps he had simply lost control of the situation and his own judgment as well. Perhaps the Philistines began

---

76. Médebielle, *Samuel,* 457ff.
77. Basil: Migne PG XXX, 497 and Cyril: PG LXVIII, 437.
78. The distance between Gilboa and En-dor is 15 km.

the battle before Saul had time to occupy a more favorable position on the heights. The text is silent regarding the precise circumstances of the battle. It records only the sober facts: "The Philistines fought against Israel; and the men of Israel fled before the Philistines, and fell slain on Mount Gilboa" (31, 1). The battle seems to have begun on the plain. The Israelites retreated before the press of the war chariots, and withdrew to the mountain country at their rear. But the advantage of the higher ground no longer served them: Israel had lost the battle. The only hope of salvation lay in immediate flight.

Against this somber backdrop, there is one picture which is drawn in more vivid strokes, the end of Saul. When the Philistine archers discovered Saul's position —he wore the crown and armlet as royal insignia (2 S 1, 10) — they aimed particularly at him. Together with him were fighting his sons Jonathan, Abinadab, and Malchishua. They covered their father with their own bodies and all fell in the battle. In these simple words, our historian establishes an imperishable monument to the sons of Saul.

The differences and quarrels of recent days were all forgotten. How greatly they all must have suffered, particularly Jonathan, at the prospect of their father's hopeless decline. And still they stood at his side and faced a hero's death.

Now Saul stood there alone, an unshielded target for the archers. Seriously wounded by several shafts, and suffering from an abdominal wound,[79] he still remained defiantly on his feet, leaning hard on his lance (2 S 1, 6). He knew that his end was upon him, but he still had strength. To keep from falling alive into the "hands of the uncircumcised" (31, 4), who would make sport of him and mock him, he ordered his armor bearer: "Draw your sword and thrust me through with it." The man was afraid to obey, however. Then Saul took his own sword and fell upon it. When his armor bearer saw that Saul was dead he also fell upon his own sword and died beside his master (31, 4ff.).

When the inhabitants of the Plain of Jezreel learned the outcome of the battle, they abandoned their cities and fled, panic-

---

79. According to the LXX translation: εἰς τὰ ὑποχόνδρια.

stricken, across the Jordan. The Philistines pursued them and occupied the entire district. On the city walls of Beth-Shan they hung the corpses of Saul and his sons. Saul's head and armor they sent home as victory trophies, to display in the temples of their gods (31, 9).

The inhabitants of Jabesh-Gilead had not forgotten that Saul had once liberated them. Some courageous men embarked upon a daring adventure. Under cover of night, they slipped up to the city walls of Beth-Shan, removed the dead bodies of the king and his sons, and brought them into their own city. There they cremated them,[80] held the customary lamentations, and buried their remains beneath the tamarisk tree, where, apparently, the city meeting place was located.

This spelled the ultimate failure of all the hopes that had been placed in Saul's kingship. He was to have freed Israel from the yoke of the Philistines (1 S 8, 21); but now the hand of the Philistines lay upon them heavier than before. There is an inexpressible note of tragedy about Saul's life, a mystery that can be penetrated only against the background of God's master plan. The first king of Israel was broken by his defiance of God, and there could be no other end.

4) DAVID'S LAMENT:

David could consider himself fortunate that the Philistines had dismissed him from their army so that he and his company

---

80. BHK conjectures, instead of "burn" (*yiśrephû*), "make a dirge" (*yiś-pedû*), since the Semites were accustomed to bury their dead, not cremate them. Only two instances of cremation are recorded in the Bible, the cremation of Achan and his family (Jos 7, 25) and that of the idolatrous priest from the time of Josiah (2 Ch 34, 5). Both of them were regarded as exceptionally severe punishments. To go unburied was regarded as a curse. The burning of the corpses at Jabesh was not a true cremation, but only a partial burning. Because of the advanced state of decomposition such measures were deemed necessary. / Partial cremation was also familiar to Homer. Since the Greeks before Troy were unable to bury their fallen warriors in their native land, they burned the bodies, gathered the bones, and took them back to Greece (Iliad 7, 334).

could return to Ziklag. He was thus spared what would have been the greatest tragedy of his life. Upon his arrival in Ziklag, he found only the charred remains of the town. The Amalekites had taken advantage of its unprotected position to conduct a razzia of gigantic proportions.[81] They had made a sudden raid on the southern territory of the Cherethites, the southern district of Judah, and the southern territory of Caleb (30, 14). As was customary in raids, they drove off everything of value, herds and property, women and children. What was left behind went up in flames. There were tears and bitter words of reproach for David, for having left the city without defense. It is understandable that they were on the point of stoning their otherwise so popular and beloved leader (30, 6). Finally, David made use of the ephod to determine whether or not he should pursue the raiding party. When the answer was affirmative, he set out with 600 men in pursuit. By the time he had reached the brook of Besor,[82] 200 of the men were so exhausted that they could not continue the pursuit. Since military campaigns generally took place early in the year, it is possible that the otherwise dry wadi was filled with great masses of water which made progress difficult. David immediately left the 200 men behind, not only because they could go no further, but also to serve as a rear guard. He also left the baggage train at this point, and continued the pursuit. They found an Egyptian slave, fatigued to the point of death, whom the Amalekites had abandoned in the wilderness. They gave him

---

81. The large-scale archaeological excavations in the Negeb, directed by Glueck, have proved that this district was anything but an uninhabited wilderness: there was extensive cultivation and animal industry. N. Glueck, *Further Exploration in the Negeb*, BASOR 137 (1955), 10-22; RB 63 (1956), 87ff.

82. The precise location of Besor is uncertain. Bressan, 441, identifies it with the *Wadi bir es-Seba'*, some 20 km south of Ziklag. It is small wonder that the men were exhausted. The march from Apheq back to Ziklag involved some 80 km. Apart from forced marches, the trip would require three days. Then one day of rest in the destroyed city and another 20 km to march. It is a testimony to the endurance and dedication of David and his 600 that they were inured to such hardships.

figs and raisins to eat and revived him. Under his guidance, David found the camp of the Amalekites who were drunk with victory; he fell upon them unawares, seized all their plunder, freed their prisoners, and returned to Ziklag. When a quarrel broke out among his warriors who were unwilling to share their plunder with the 200 who had been left as a rear guard, he decided that those who did the fighting and those who had to stay behind were to receive a like share. For later times, too, this became an inviolable law (30, 24).

History loves contrasts. In the north there is the devastating defeat of Saul; in the south an unexpected triumph of David. In the north the Israelites are forced to abandon house and home and live a fugitive life; in the south, David sends part of his plunder to 15 cities in Judah. Whether this was a calculated move on his part, or simply an age-old obligation that tribal relatives must have their share of military plunder, at any event, David succeeded in gaining more and more sympathy in Judah (30, 31).

Meantime, he was anxiously awaiting news as to the outcome of the battle. He was in Ziklag only two days, and then on the third day a man came from Saul's camp, with his clothes rent and earth upon his head (2 S 1, 1ff.). He had no good news to report: Israel was smitten, Saul and Jonathan were fallen. His account [83] of Saul's death is considerably different from the version described above. He had seen Saul leaning upon his spear, with the chariots and horsemen close upon him. Saul had asked him: "Stand beside me and slay me; for anguish had seized me, and yet my life still lingers." [84] The Amalekite did

---

83. Critics believe that two sources have been combined to produce this account. The similarities and differences are better explained perhaps by presuming that in 1 S 31 we have the report of the historian himself, while 2 S 1 gives the account of the messenger which need not be absolutely trustworthy in every detail. Bressan, 458; de Vaux, *Samuel*, 137.

84. The sentence contains a very hard word to translate: šabaṣ. In Ex 28, 39 the verb šbṣ means "to weave a sample." There is no point of comparison with the present text. The older versions are only poor attempts. LXX: "terrible darkness has encompassed me"; Vulgate: *"tenent me angustiae";* Targum and Peshitto: "convulsions, cramps have

as Saul requested, taking the dead man's crown and armlet as a gift and sign of allegiance to the new king. Apparently he expected a royal reward for this service. But he received quite the opposite. David had him cut down on the spot, because he had raised his hand against the anointed of Yahweh.

David then intoned his lamentation over Saul.[85] The song was included in the collection of the "Book of Heroes," [86] from which source the author of this narrative reports it. The lament is marked by a triple repetition of a refrain-like exclamation: "How are the mighty fallen!" (2 S 1, 19. 25. 27). This set the basic tone for the whole lamentation. David sees, in spirit, how they are rejoicing in the Philistine city, how women and maidens are hastening to meet the victors and sound the victory sounds. But in Israel, too, they are to sing a song and teach it to the sons of Judah,[87] not a song of jubilation but a song of deepest

---

seized upon me." The sense, at all events, is clear: "I am mortally struck."

---

85. Here we meet a form of song that is much used in later literature, the lamentation (Qînah), originally no doubt a dirge. The classical form of the Qînah strophe has three accents in the first member and two in the second (3 + 2). Cf. the song of Amos on the fall of the virgin Israel (Am 5, 2) or the lament of Isaiah over the fall of Babylon (Is 14, 4-21). In ancient Canaan, too (Ugarit), this strophe form was already known. Israel here exhibits her use of the ancient song forms. R. Dussaud, Les découvertes de Ras Shamra et l'AT (Paris, 1937), 76.

86. Hebrew: sepher hayyašar. Elsewhere yašar means "straight, upright, honorable." Accordingly, the translation: "Book of the Just." In the Kuriti epic of Ugarit, a yšr of the god El is a warrior who is to drive out the Terachites. Dussaud, 101. — yašar is thus equivalent to "warrior, hero." In this "Book of Heroes" the deeds of the "warriors of Yahweh" are sung. — Jos 10, 13 already quotes from it: "Sun, stand still." Also the "Book of the Wars of Yahweh" (Nb 21, 14).

87. Accordingly, David's lament was rapidly spread, by his own order. L. Auerbach (Enc. Judaica, s.v. David) interprets this as a political move on David's part. He publicly joins the general lamentation of the people in an attempt to win general sympathy.

national mourning. This was not a "bow song," [88] but a great elegy of the battle of Gilboa. Although David had suffered such bitter experiences at the hands of Saul, there is not a single note of reproach. Instead, he praises Saul as "splendor of Israel," the brave hero whose sword never came back empty. Like a double star, inseparable in life and faithful even in death, shines the image of Saul and Jonathan. They were swifter than eagles and stronger than lions. They brought home rich booty to the women of Israel, gold ornaments and precious apparel. But now they are fallen in battle. The glory of Israel lies smitten on the high places. Therefore, may neither dew nor rain fall on Gilboa again.

It was to be expected that David would find special words for Jonathan his friend, whose love was more than the love of women (2 S 1, 26). The song is obviously the spontaneous expression of genuine feeling, not a word of hatred or rejoicing at the demise of his enemy, but noble sentiment transfigured by a magnificent and forgiving love. David, who was unwilling to kill Saul when Saul was delivered into his hands, remained true to his commitment. Even after his death, he will not raise his hand against the anointed of Yahweh; rather, he bows in deepest reverence before the death of him whom the hand of Yahweh had struck down.

Yet, in the entire song, there is not a word of Yahweh, not a single religious sentiment. Why is this? Would it not have been a supreme irony, if David had reopened all the old wounds, by calling upon the name of Yahweh and making him a part of the song? This was the deepest root of the present catastrophe, the fact that Saul was broken by his faithlessness to Yahweh.

---

88. The word *qšt* (bow) 31, 18 is an example of how a marginal gloss can make its way into the text. In order to immediately identify the elegy in the text, a copyist wrote the letters: *q(inat) š(a'úl) wy (ehônatan)* — "Lamentation over Saul and Jonathan," in the margin. A later copyist, no longer understanding this abbreviation, introduced it as the word *qešet*, "bow," into the text itself, reading the letters *wy* as *tau*. V. E. Reichert, *A Note on "Qeshet."* JBL 70 (1951), 14.

But a lamentation is to heal wounds, not open them. And thus David sings only of the magnificent warriors, the unforgettable heroes, who lie fallen on the heights of Gilboa.[89]

After the defeat, the northern part of the country passes under Philistine control, but in the south everything is ready for David's rise to kingship. With infinite patience, with clever strategy and planning, David had managed to protect Judah from the inroads of the robber hordes from the south. His fellow clansmen in Bethlehem were bound to him by ties of blood; he had married into the clans people of Hebron; and by his gifts of booty he had won the sympathy of 15 cities. If anyone in Judah was to step forward as Saul's successor, it could only be the son-in-law of the fallen king, the victor, who had killed his "ten thousand" Philistines. Time had been working slowly but surely for David. Yahweh's master plan, which had become visible in Samuel's anointing of David, although it was not yet clearly intelligible, had reached maturity. The hour had come for the outlaw captain to be king of Judah and Israel.

---

89. Cf. the lament of Gilgamesh for his friend Enkidu: "My friend and brother, panther of the wilds, Enkidu, my friend and brother, with whom I went out, with whom I climbed the mountains, my friend, with whom I slew lions . . . ." ANET 87 (Gilgamesh Epic, Table VIII).

SECTION THREE

DAVID'S KINGDOM

CHAPTER VII

DAVID, KING OF JUDAH

DAVID is not to be ranked among the usurpers who force their way into power under any circumstances and by any means. Although he had been convinced of his divine call since the memorable occasion of his meeting with the prophet Samuel who had taken him from among the flocks and anointed him, he had made no attempt to remove his predecessor from the throne. But neither is David the type of the politician who can afford to stand calmly by and wait, well aware that time is working for him. If we were to understand his character in such a worldly light, we would lose sight of the great religious element which was the real, underlying power behind his activity and undertakings. The type of the irreligious and opportunistic politician is proper to a different era. The rulers of the Ancient Near East are described, in the historical documents we know, as being great in their political accomplishments, but having felt that they were even greater by their belief in the divinity in whose service and under whose explicit command they had entered upon their rule. Within this religiously oriented Ancient Near East, we meet the figure of David as that of a man who has ordered his life and activity completely after the direction of his God Yahweh. David becomes king, not by seizing the political power in Israel; the kingship is destined for him by Yahweh himself, gradually prepared and, at the opportune moment, committed into his hands. It would be a quite erroneous procedure to sketch a portrait of the historical David by striking the religious element out of the narrative; in terms of Ancient Near East history this could never be proper methodology. It would result in the caricature of a man who was supposed to have lived around the turn of the first millenium, but could certainly not have lived in this manner. The real David lived in constant encounter with his God. We might say that he knew how to exploit political advantages with a wisdom that approached genius; the decisive motivation for his political activity, however, came directly from the will of Yahweh.

After the catastrophe on Mount Gilboa, it was obvious that David's time had come to enter upon his heritage; still he asked Yahweh first: "Shall I go up into any of the cities of Judah?" And the brief response: "Go up!" David was not satisfied with this general answer; he wanted a more precise direction: "To which shall I go up?" The response from the lot oracle: "To Hebron." This divine decision directed David along his path, just like the pillar of cloud or fire on the exodus from Egypt. David knew that Yahweh was with him, and who could be against him?

He thus went up [1] from Ziklag 'to Hebron. Once again it was an expedition with retainers and weapons, family and baggage, a mighty caravan. But now it was no longer in flight; David was on the road to power. Hebron opened its gates and received David and his "company" into the city.[2] This time, David's followers were no longer considered an alien band; they were ac-

---

1. An actual ascent is involved here: from the flat country in the west (400 m) up to the mountain heights (1000 m). Ziglag to Hebron is approximately 50 km.
2. Hebron probably means "confederation, covenant, confederacy," from ḥabar, "to bind." This is understandable in view of the ancient epithet qiryat 'arba', which is generally translated as "four cities," a reference to the village and clan communities which were leagued together to form a city community. De Vaux, Samuel, 141. Other authors take 'Arba' as the name of a Hurrite (?) tribe which had settled in Hebron. Cf. II, 63, note 53.

cepted into the body of the citizens. The bandits and free booters of the wilderness now formed the "secure foundation of the new kingship."

We must not be surprised to note that the "men of Judah" unanimously came to Hebron to anoint David king. This was only the logical consequence of the political situation. After Saul's death a new king had to be chosen. There was no thought of going back to the harsh era of arbitrary power prior to the institution of the monarchy, where every man did what he thought best. The individual clans would have been constantly exposed to the raiding parties of their neighbors. The situation cried for a strong hand. Saul's dynasty was practically extinct, and the north had fallen under Philistine control. From that quarter, for the moment, there was little to be hoped. Apparently, tribal rivalries between north and south also had a role to play. If anyone was to be king in Judah, it could only be a Judaean. The person to be chosen was hardly subject to doubt; David was the obvious selection. His family ties had already made him the most powerful sheikh of the southland. His bravery and political acumen had been abundantly tested. If the men of Judah — that is, the sheikhs with their clans — were to commit themselves to any master, it could only be this man. Through the solemn act of royal anointing [3] David was confirmed in his actual position of power in Judah. But from the very outset, he had set his sights upon the goal of kingship over all of Israel.

This intention is already evident in his first official diplomatic act, the embassy to the city of Jabesh-Gilead. Externally, this was only a quite proper testimony of gratitude for the fact that the brave men of Jabesh had buried the remains of Saul and his sons. The gratitude was expressed in the form of blessing: "May you be blessed by the Lord, because you showed this loyalty to Saul your Lord, ('ādôn — sovereign, king!) and buried him . . . . And I will do good to you because you have done this thing" (2, 4). Reading between the lines, however, we can see David's

---

3. First anointing by the prophet Samuel (1 S 16, 13ff); second anointing as king of Judah (2 S 2, 4); third anointing over all Israel, likewise in Hebron (2 S 5, 3).

clear claim to represent Saul's legitimate successor. This diplomatic embassy seems to have had no tangible success; it was, however, at least a declaration of intention, and it prepared the way for David's rise in the north.

After the catastrophe of Gilboa, Saul's captain Abner arose as the strong man in Israel. He gathered together the scattered fragments and formed a new center of power in Mahanaim [4] in Transjordan. He set up Saul's son Ishbaal [5] as his successor. "He was 40 years old when he began to reign over Israel, and he reigned two years" (2, 10). This is a surprising piece of news. We read that David was king in Judah for seven and one half years before he was anointed king over all Israel. It would follow that the Northern Kingdom was five years without a king, in a state of complete dissipation, under the control of the Philistines. It speaks well for Abner's statesman-like ability that, despite this fact, he succeeded in bringing a large part of Palestine back under his control, operating from his base in Transjordan, from where he succeeded in uniting, for example, districts from the tribe of Asher, the Lake of Genesareth, the Plain of Jezreel, the mountains of Ephraim, and the whole tribal territory of Benjamin (2, 9). Apparently, under pressure from the Egyptians, the Philistines were forced to abandon their occupied territory to its own fate. Abner crowned his five years' work of liberation by placing Saul's son on the throne, thus publicly announcing the resurrection of the shattered kingdom of Saul. Only the territory of the tribe of Judah lay outside his control. But when Abner

---

4. Location uncertain. According to Gn 32, 22, the location must be north of the Jabbok (modern Narh ez-Zerqa, "the blue river"). Perhaps Khirbet el-Mahna, 700 m above the sea, 10 km southeast of Jabesh. Since Manahaim is a dual form ("twin camps"), other scholars identify the ancient site as Tulul ed-Dahab, "the mount of gold," some 10 km east of the Jordan on the right bank of the Jabbok, 118 m above sea level. Bressan, 475.

5. MT: *Ish-bosheth* — "Man of shame." This was clearly not the man's real name, but rather *Ish-baal* — "Man of God." Since Baal was, later, the exclusive name for the pagan god, the Masoretes carefully rewrote names compounded with Baal, substituting the word *bosheth*, "shame," for the name of the pagan deity.

organized the military preparations he required to incorporate Judah into the kingdom of Israel, he struck, understandably enough, upon energetic resistance. David is not personally leading his troops on this occasion; he entrusted the defense to his captain Joab. In Joab, one of the most striking figures besides David himself enters upon the scene. His was a quite different makeup than his uncle's. A warlike capacity and a strong ambition they had in common. But David understood how to observe the proper moderation, whereas Joab was hard, inexorable, unyielding, a soldier of the old school, a commander of genius, but a man who never hesitated in the face of bloodshed. With a certain undertone of bitterness, the Bible frequently refers to him as the son of Zeruiah (Sarcia).

The opponents met near the great Pool of Gibeon (Gabaon)[6] (2, 12ff.) and both sides drew up their forces. The Biblical account refers not only to a "war tournament" with twelve warriors on each side, chosen from the two camps, and later turning into a wild battle;[7] it was a true and proper "representative battle," [8] which was to decide the campaign. Upon Abner's proposal, twelve young warriors were chosen from either side.[9] This number may have been obligatory for the "game" ($\check{s}hq$). The rules of the battle were also determined according to ancient laws of war. The text is formidable in its very brevity: "Each caught his opponent

6. Jeremiah 41, 12 speaks of the "great waters of Gibeon." Modern ed-Jib, some 12 km north of Jerusalem, on the boundary of the tribal territory of Judah. Some 8 springs have their source here, feeding several pools, one of them hewn out of the stone, 17 x 12 m in dimension. Ill. in A. Jirku, *Welt der Bibel* (1957), 81. Ed-Jin has been under excavation by the Americans since 1956, under the direction of I. B. Pritchard. Current account in the *Biblical Archaeologist* 19 (1956), 66ff. Discovery of jar handles with the stamp gb'n. Identification as ancient Gibeon is contested by K. Elliger, *Beeroth und Gibeon* ZDPV 73 (1957), 125-132. The reservoir in question is the roman level inside the city and can thus not have been the scene of the combat recorded here.

7. Médebielle, Rois 471.

8. O. Eissfeldt, *Ein gescheiterter Versuch der Wiedervereinigung Israels* (2 S 2, 12; 3, 1), La NouvClio 3 (1951), 110-127; 4 (1952), 55-59.

9. Y. Yadin, "Let the young men . . . arise." JPOS 21 (1948), 110-116.

by the head, and thrust his sword in his opponent's side; so they fell down together" (2, 16). A relief from Tell Halaf (11th — 9th century) in northwest Mesopotamia depicts two warriors engaged in just such a combat. Each fighter had seized his adversary's head with one hand and is plunging his sword into his adversary's side with the other. The relief is an illustration of our text, and our text affords the commentary we need to understand the relief.[10]

Since all 24 warriors fell, the combat was undecided and had to be carried to a regular battle. Abner had chosen only the men from the tribe of Benjamin for this confrontation, and his troops were unable to withstand the wild assault of Joab. He was forced to give ground. Biblical battle accounts are generally very laconic; but one scene from this fight is presented with full particulars, since it has great significance for the future fate not only of Abner but of Joab as well. Joab's brother Asahel,[11] Zeriah's second son, was pursuing Abner as fleet as a gazelle. He would turn neither to right nor to left; Abner alone was his objective. The seasoned warrior, however, was unwilling to sacrifice this blossoming young life. He would have gladly spared the young man. How could he look Joab in the eye, or initiate further negotiations towards a united kingdom, if he killed the young man? But Asahel did not share the gazelle's timidity; he was bold as a young lion. He could not be shaken off — he had already overtaken Abner — and the old warrior struck him with the butt of his spear[12] which pierced him through, and he died on the spot. Part of the pursuing party stayed with the fallen warrior; but Joab no longer knew any moderation. He continued the pursuit in full fury. Abner succeeded in reaching the heights of Gibeath-

---

10. C. G. Gordon, *World of the O.T.* (1956), 29. On a Babylonian cylinder, a representation of three pairs of warriors. With their right hands they have grasped their adversary's beard, and with their left they are plunging their swords into his body. M. Jastrow, *Bildermappe zur Religion Babyloniens und Assyriens* (Giessen, 1912), 138. Ill. of two "young men at play" in *EncMikr* II, 19. The victor grasps his adversary by his hair and runs the sword through his neck.

11. "God (El) has made (created)."

12. Perhaps the spear was equipped with a striking head at either end.

Ammah with the rest of his men,[13] from which vantage point he called to the furious Joab to come to his senses and stop the pursuit: "Shall the sword devour forever!" (2, 26). Finally, Joab had the trumpet sounded and ended the battle. Under cover of night, Abner, with the rest of his people, withdrew through the Arabah (the Jordan Valley),[14] crossed the river, marched the entire morning, and reached Mahanaim about midday. The attempt to incorporate Judah into the kingdom by military power had to be considered a total shipwreck. In addition, the death of Asahel had involved the invocation of blood vengeance, which made it impossible to entertain a peaceful encounter between Abner and Joab, the most important representatives of Northern and Southern kingdoms. Was the kingdom to be split forever?

It was Abner who held the real power in the Northern Kingdom. Ishbaal, as his representative in the public eye, is only a puppet figure. An argument between the two cast the whole affair into a new state of flux. The object of the argument was Rizpah [15] (Respha), a concubine from Saul's harem, whom Abner had taken for his own (3, 5-11). The Ancient Near East did not customarily react so strongly to the possession of a woman. Why, then, did Ishbaal react so violently? There was more at stake here. The man who took over the harem of the deceased king thereby asserted his claim to succession to the throne.[16] Whether Abner actually thought

---

13. The precise site is not known. Probably one of the heights that look down precipitously upon the Jordan, in the vicinity of Geba', 8 km east of Gibeon. De Vaux, *Samuel*, 145.

14. *'ārabah* means, literally, "dry, waste territory." In the Bible the term is used for the whole of the Jordan trench from the Lake of Genesareth to the Dead Sea, and can also include its further extension down to the Gulf of Aqaba. In the era 3000-1200 B.C. the eastern bank of the Jordan was proportionately heavily settled. Glueck can point to some 70 archaeological sites. After this period the district turns more and more desert. N. Glueck, *The Jordan*, BiblArch 6 (1943), 62-67; RB 63 (1956), 89. / A. V. D. Oudenrijn, *Eber hayyarden Gegend am Jordan*, Bibl 35 (1954), 138. / B. Gemoer, *Be'eber hajjarden*: in Jordans Borderland, VT 2 (1952), 349-355.

15. Glowing stone, coal.

16. The harem of the deceased king passed on to his successor. Abner's conduct was not so much the free exercise of his sexual choice as it was a political maneuver. De Vaux, *Samuel*, 146.

of going so far as to set aside the puppet king and establish himself on Saul's throne is most improbable. That is why a reproach from Ishbaal, who owed him everything he had, must have made him very bitter. From this day forward, Abner was actually looking for a political maneuver which would deliver the Northern Kingdom into David's hands. As a realistic politician, he understood that the future of Israel lay in David's hands.

Accordingly, he sent secret messengers to David and proposed an alliance: "Make your covenant with me, and behold, my hand shall be with you to bring over all Israel to you" (3, 12). Such an offer must have been extremely welcome to David. But he did not accept immediately. He needed to have some pledge to guarantee the genuinity of Abner's good will. Once again, in this politically decisive moment, it is a woman who plays an important role, unawares. The condition David sets is this: his first wife Michal must be returned to him before further negotiations can be entertained. There is no doubting the fact that David's first love for Michal was very great and that, despite his harem, he longed for her. But since marriages, in the Ancient Near East and in the modern Orient as well, are frequently made to serve as confirmation of a treaty or alliance, the restitution of Michal would have political consequences. If Ishbaal actually restored his sister Michal to her husband David, this would be a public recognition of David's right to the throne. In a word, David's condition upon future negotiations was designed to discover whether the proffered alliance was seriously intended.

Ishbaal, who had made such sharp reproaches to Abner on Rizpah's account, did not dare to make any objections when Michal was restored to David. It was not easy for Michal to leave her second husband Paltiel, to whom Saul had given her after David's flight; she must have loved him very much. In tears, he accompanied her as far as Bahurim (Baurim)[17] at which point Abner strictly ordered him to return home. With some 20 men, Abner escorted Michal to Hebron and handed her over to

---

17. Probably modern Râs et-Tmîm, on the eastern slope of the Mount of Olives.

David. He had already cemented relationships with the "elders of Israel," the various tribal heads, and attempted to win them for David. But the most difficult objective was to win the sympathies of the tribe of Benjamin. This, too, had not proved beyond the capacity of Abner's adroit tactics. This news was more than welcome to David. There must be a celebration. Accordingly, David prepared a great banquet. Abner took leave with the promise: "I will arise and go, and will gather all Israel to my lord and king, that they may make a covenant with you, and that you may reign over all that your heart desires" (3, 21ff.).

Thanks to Abner's diplomatic activity, all the obstacles had been removed from the establishment of a united elective monarchy over all Israel and Judah. Abner could well be content with his successes. His life work was on the point of being crowned.

There was, however, an enemy in the background, one man who could not bring himself to rejoice at the course events had taken, and this was Joab, the son of Zeruiah. He thought only of his blood vengeance in behalf of his slain brother Asahel. David, apparently, had acted prudently in assigning him no active role in the negotiations with Abner. But when Joab, upon his return home, heard what had happened, he immediately sent a messenger to Abner and asked him to return. When the two met at the city gate, Joab asked Abner to come inside with him as if to speak privately. Abner did so without suspicion. Then suddenly Joab stabbed him in the belly and he died on the spot. This was full satisfaction of the law of blood vengeance: the blood of the slain Asahel was avenged (3, 20-27); but such a deed could not possibly win David's approbation. It cast him in a very suspicious light, as if he himself were privy to a deliberate plot to rid himself of the most powerful man in the Northern Kingdom.

David was not the man to soil himself with blood guilt. He made no common cause with the murderer. In his way of seeing it, this was not blood vengeance, but simple murder. David, however, was still too weak [18] to take a public stand against this

---

18. In another interpretation, this is not a reference to David's weakness, but rather to his kindness and willingness to forgive. In the interests of the state he had abandoned his own personal desires for vengeance

powerful son of Zeruiah. He did what he could: he decreed a "state funeral" for Abner, decked himself in sack cloth and ashes,[19] and sounded the lamentation (3, 33). Abner was easily one of the most capable men of his day. David himself refers to him as "great" (3, 38). He would certainly have brought the work of unification, which he had so successfully undertaken, to a happy conclusion. But his powerful position in the now united kingdom must have eventually led to some serious differences. Joab's murder thus produced a new political situation. David could not rejoice over Abner's demise, and yet his death would further hasten the unification of north and south. The north was now without a leader — Ishbaal's puppet rule was without significance — and more imperiously than ever before, it looked to David for its king.

In this fluid situation, two brothers, political adventurers, thought they might ingratiate themselves with David by the murder of Ishbaal. Both were captains [20] from the tribe of Benjamin, and their native city was Beerot.[21] Their names were Baanah and Rechab.[22] For their heinous crime, they chose the most favorable moment, the hour of the afternoon rest. In southern countries, the afternoon rest, or siesta, is an unvarying law.[23] Women were expected to watch at the door, and in this capacity

---

and negotiated with his political opponent. Joab had no appreciation of this kind of behavior. Bressan, 496.

19. The word "sack(cloth)" comes from the Sumerian *šak* and means a coarsely woven material, generally goats' hair. The penitential sack could not have referred to a garment woven of hair, however, but rather an apron worn about the waist, filled with dust and ashes to be strewn on the head. Bressan, 493.

20. *Śarê gedûdîm*, originally leader of a company or band that goes on raids. In this era, probably a lower rank of military service.

21. Be'erot is one of the four Canaanite cities which outmaneuvered Joshua after the entrance into the promised land and were thus spared (Jos 9). Saul probably drove the population into exile, whereupon they took refuge in Gath. Be'erot was incorporated into the tribe of Benjamin (2 S 4, 2). Modern El-Bireh, 15 km north of Jerusalem.

22. *bǎ'anah* "(born?) in pangs"; *rekab*, "chariot warrior" (?).

23. Even today we say: "During siesta time only mad dogs and Englishmen are on the streets."

they kept themselves busy at some task they could perform half asleep. Ishbaal's doorkeeper, accordingly, was sitting there gleaning wheat. But she became drowsy and soon fell asleep. Unnoticed, the two adventurers crept into the house, where they murdered Ishbaal in his sleep, cutting off his head and stealing away with this grisly trophy (4, 1-8). Under cover of night, they made their way to the Arabah, where they could easily take cover in the Jordan underbrush. Their feet could not carry them fast enough to deliver the welcome news to David:[24] "Here is the head of Ishbaal, the son of Saul, your enemy, who sought your life; Yahweh has avenged my lord and king this day on Saul and his offspring" (4, 8).

But they were mistaken in their man. David was not the type of an oriental despot, wading his way through blood. When the messengers from the battle of Gilboa had admitted his attack upon Saul, David had him cut down on the spot; could he now be expected to spare the lives of two adventurers who had perpetrated an obvious and open murder against an unarmed and defenseless man? David had them cut down on the spot, and had their severed hands and feet [25] hung up as a terrible example near the Pool at Hebron. He took Ishbaal's head and had it buried in Abner's grave.

Thus, without David's knowledge or complicity, the last two pillars of the Northern Kingdom had fallen. He could make way to the throne — a rare example in the grisly history of the Ancient Near East [26]— with clean hands, unsullied with the blood of his adversaries.

---

24. *běśôrah* means, in general, "joyous news." εὐαγγέλιον in Greek (Odyssey XIV, 152). Only in Christian usage does it take on the literary meaning of the four written Gospels.

25. Probably not only the severed members, but the entire corpses as well. Amen-hotep II (1448-1422), after a victorious campaign in Asia, had the bodies of six princes hung from the city walls of Thebes. Generally, the conquered enemies' hands and feet were cut off to be carried home as trophies of the victory. The goddess Anat thus hung the severed heads of her enemies upon her back, while tying their severed hands to her belt. ANET 136b.

26. Even Solomon ascended the throne over the dead body of his brother Adonijah (1 K 2, 13).

CHAPTER VIII

DAVID, KING OVER ALL ISRAEL

ABNER'S diplomatic preparations bore fruit. The sentence: "All the tribes of Israel came to David at Hebron" (5, 1) apparently means that, after Abner's murder, the negotiations had been taken up once again. Two important considerations are recorded here: already during Saul's lifetime, David had led out and brought in Israel, that is, he was intimately bound to the cause of the northern tribes. In addition, it was Yahweh's own promise that rested upon him, that he should one day be the shepherd who tended Israel.[1] After these preliminary negotiations, the day of the royal anointing and coronation could be determined. Now it was the elders of Israel, that is, the heads of the individual tribes (the sheikhs) who came to Hebron to strike a covenant (berît) with David first. This was not to be an absolute monarchy, but an elective kingship. The conditions set by the heads of the various tribes are not recorded. At all events,

---

1. Shepherd is a very ancient name for king. In the Code of Hammurabi, it is frequent: "Hammurabi, the shepherd (ri-ya-um, Hebrew rô'eh), called by Enlil, shepherd of the people am I." The expression corresponds to the theocratic ideal. The king is only the shepherd who pastures the human herd. God remains the true master; the human administrator of the state is only his representative. C. H. Gordon, World of the OT (1956), 167.

David acceded to their wishes, and they anointed him king (5, 3). This is the third anointing for David; the first was by the prophet Samuel, which, like a prophetic vision in symbolic ritual, anticipated the future course of events; his second anointing was as king over Judah: and now the third anointing consecrated him ruler over all twelve tribes. The official ceremony was, apparently, performed by the high priest Abiathar. Each of his anointings was a religious and political high point.

Such a ceremony commanded public celebration, and this time the banquet took three whole days. "They were there with David for three days, eating and drinking, for their brethren had made preparation for them. And also their neighbors . . . came bringing food on asses and on camels and on mules and oxen, abundant provisions of meal, cakes of figs, clusters of raisins, and wine and oil, oxen and sheep, for there was joy in Israel" (1 Ch 12, 40ff.). But after the banquet, the time was come to test the high hopes they entertained for the new king: the Philistines were making their presence felt.

A) WAR WITH THE PHILISTINES (2 S 5, 17-25)

When David withdrew from Ziklag and went to Hebron, to be anointed king there, the Philistines offered no opposition. They could only approve the course of events which led to one of their vassals rising to power. Moreover, they hoped to derive some advantage from the political division in Israel. But with David's position as king over all Israel, the situation had essentially changed. David was no longer their vassal; he had become a power to be reckoned with. In two obstinate campaigns, the Philistines make an attempt to smother David's new kingdom.

1) THE BATTLE AT BAAL-PERAZIM (2 S 5, 12-21):

David fell back upon his earlier tactics. He did not remain within the fortified walls of Hebron, where he could be captured. "He went down to the stronghold (*mesûdâh*) (5, 17), by which we are to understand, as in the story of David's persecution, not a citadel constructed by human effort, but rather a natural mountain fortress, something like the strongholds near Adullam.[2] The Philistines always had to search for his whereabouts (17). In his experience as an outlaw chieftain, David had learned the advantages of war on the move; he had also acquired a certain insight into the Philistine method of waging war. The Philistines finally established themselves in the neighborhood of Jerusalem. The objective was obvious: to drive a wedge between north and south and thereby isolate David. They spread out in the valley of Rephaim (Raphaim).[3] The guerilla warfare must have been rather extensive. It is to this campaign that we must assign the heroic exploit of the three warriors who fought their way through the Philistine ranks to bring David some drinking water from the fountain at Bethlehem. David, however, refused to drink; he poured the water out in the presence of Yahweh (2 S 23, 13-17).

David's extreme mobility kept the Philistines constantly on edge. Before the decisive battle, he inquired into Yahweh's will, which promised him victory. He attacked at a point where the enemy least expected. He must have marched around the Philistine camp. For his attack did not come from the south, but from the Baal-Perazim (Baal Pharasim),[4] some 2 km north of Jerusalem. David had occupied the heights and from there he stormed down upon the enemy with the fury of a mountain torrent ($p^e r\hat{a}\d{s}\hat{i}m$). God had granted him victory; hence the inter-

---

2. Cf. the name "Alpine fortress" from the last war.
3. Precise location uncertain; at all events, in the immediate vicinity of Jerusalem. Named after the fabled founders of the city. According to Joshua 15, 7-9; 18, 15-17, north of the valley of the Hinnom, modern Plain of Baqa' between Jerusalem and Bethlehem, where the last spur of the railroad line ends. Others locate the valley of Rephaim further to the north, in the continuation of the Hinnom Valley in the direction of Lifta (Nephtoah). This opinion is confirmed by American excavations. Some 5 km south west of Jerusalem three artificial hills were discovered, containing ostraca of foreign origin from the 12th — 11th centuries. Possibly the Philistines had secured this point of support for some time. J. Gray, *The Refaim*, PEQ 81 (1949), 127-139. Outline map by P. Vincent, DBS IV, 901, 911.
4. Modern Ras en-Nadir, on the road to Ain-Karim.

pretation of the place name Baal Perazim as "Lord God of the torrent." [5] It is also possible that Yahweh actually intervened from his superior position.[6] At all events, the attack came upon the Philistines so unexpectedly that they left their idols behind and sought safety in headlong flight.

2) THE BATTLE AT BEKAIM (2 S 5, 22-25):

The Philistines did not consider themselves defeated; they reassembled and strengthened their forces and then returned to the mountain country where they once again laid seige to the Plain of Rephaim. How was David to surprise his enemy a second time? He no doubt reconnoitered the position, with his experienced general's eye, to determine the most advantageous point of attack. But, as always, it was Yahweh's lot oracle that made the final decision. An attack in the valley itself would have been pointless. David and his warriors would have had to fight their way uphill and they could easily be overrun. Once again, he chose his familiar tactic of envelopment. This time he attacked, not from the north, but from the east, across from Bekaim.[7] An initial attack from this direction could result in the Philistines' being dislodged from their position in the valleys of Rephaim and Sorek, into the great plain below.

The signal for the attack, which David was to await according to Yahweh's instruction, is difficult to interpret: "When you hear

---

5. The place name might be pre-Israelitic and may be a reference to the streams of water located in the sanctuary built in honor of Baal. P. Vincent, *Jérusalem antique*, I (Paris, 1912), 118.

6. M. H. Segal, Jewish QuartRev 5 (1924), 210.

7. Bekaim is to be derived from *bakah*, "to weep." According to the Arab botanists, there is, in the neighborhood of Mecca, a balsam bush called *baka'*. When a leaf is torn from the plant, a small drop, or "tear," exudes. Possibly there was a similar plant in the Hinnon Valley. Today a giant nettle grows there, causing the Arabs to refer to the valley as *Wadi el-Meis*, "nettle valley." Bressan, 507. / R. Tournay, RB 53 (1947), 525 ff. / Map in P. Vincent, DBS III, 901.

the sound of marching ($ṣe'ādim$) on the heads (tops, — heights?)
of Bekaim (the balsam trees — RSV), then bestir yourself; for
then the Lord has gone out before you to smite the army of the
Philistines" (5, 25). Is this meant to indicate that a body of
David's troops was forming an ambuscade and had then reached
their superior position — "When you hear the sound of marching"
— and thus everything was ready for the attack? [8] And where
is the location of Bekaim? Or is this a reference to the sound
of the wind in the *bekaim* — trees (balsams), which sounded like
the marching of an army? [9] At all events, the Philistines are once
again overrun. This was the decisive stroke in the hundred years'
war. Palestine did not turn Philistine, as it so often seemed she
must; Palestine is wholly Israelite.

B) JERUSALEM AS CAPITAL

After the Philistine invasion had been definitively turned,
David was free to attend to the internal construction of his
kingdom. First he had to settle the question of his capital city.
The former royal city of Hebron was too far away from the
northern tribes. Saul's fortress city, which was situated like an
eagle's aerie to command the mountains of Ephraim, does not
seem even to have been considered. A king from the tribe of
Judah could not possibly take up residence within the tribal
territory of Benjamin. David's eventual choice is truly a stroke
of genius, further proof of his far-seeing natural gift of government. The royal city which ruled the tribes must not lie within
the territory of any tribe. Accordingly, already during the two
Philistine campaigns, David had been centering his attention
on the ancient Canaanite fortress of Jerusalem, which was, at
the time, occupied by the Jebusites. The city was centrally lo-

---

8. D. Yellin, JPOS 3 (1923), 191ff.
9. P. Jouon changes $ṣe'adah$ (steps) to $ṣē'aqah$ (outcry). Yahweh would
   thus be announcing his arrival by a battlecry which thundered above
   the tops of the *beka'* growth. The emendation is an arbitrary one,
   and not convincing. Bibl 9 (1928), 302-303.

cated, with good lines of communication in all directions, it belonged to no individual tribe in Israel, and it was, moreover,
a natural fortress.

Jerusalem belongs to the most ancient settled localities of Palestine.
Judging from archaeological finds, it must have been populated already
around 3000 B.C. It is first mentioned by name around 2000 B.C., in
the Egyptian Execration Texts,[10] under the form *'wš'mm* (*rušalimum*).[11]
In ancient Egyptian practice, one's enemy could be seriously harmed by
writing his name, together with a corresponding curse formula, on a
clay vessel and then shattering the vessel in a sacred place. The curse
was then thought to work upon the party execrated. These curses were
directed primarily against Egypt's various hostile neighbors, including
many Canaanite cities, among them Jerusalem. The Pharaohs of the Middle
Kingdom thought they could thus shatter the distant hostile cities, by a
form of analogous magic.[12]

In the Amarna letters, written in Akkadian,[13] we find the first occurrence of the form Urusalim, which is widespread in the Babylonian and
Assyrian texts in the form *Ur-ša-li-im-mu*. If we recall that the Semites
generally named their cities after a human founder or a divinity to

---

10. With untiring dedication, K. Sethe has put together and deciphered
the shattered remnants: *Die Ächtung feindlicher Fürsten und Völker
und Dinge auf altägyptischen Tongefässscherben des MR* (Berlin,
1926), e 27-28 and f 18. The work was continued by G. Posener,
Princes et pays d'Asie et de Nubie. Textes hiératiques sur des figurines
d'envoûtement du Moyen Empire. V (Brussels, 1940), E 45.
11. According to the judgment of the Egyptologists, a relatively accurate
transliteration of the Canaanite word, in which *mm* corresponds to
lm. A. Jirku, *Bemerkungen zu den ägyptischen sogenannten "Ächtungs-
texten."* ArchOr 20 (1952), 167-169, contests the equivalence of the
names, since *aleph* can transliterate a Canaanite *l*, but never an *r*.
Specifically on the question of name derivations, cf. *EncMikr* III
(1958), 791.
12. A. Scharff, *Geschichte Ägyptens von der Vorzeit bis zur Gründung
Alexandreias* (1950), 93.
13. These letters originate from the archives of the Egyptian heretic-
pharaoh Ikhnaton (1377-1358), who introduced the solar cult as
the only valid religion and built his residence in Amarna. The archive
contains a rich correspondence with countless Asiatic princes and
cities. The letters are written, not in Egyptian but Akkadian, the
current diplomatic language of diplomacy. Best edition is J. H.
Knudzton, *Die El-Amarna-Tafeln* (Vorder-asiatische Bibliothek) (Leipzig, 1915), 2 vols. The name Jerusalem occurs in letter 290, line 14.

whom the foundation of the city was ascribed, we are probably on the right path when we interpret the name Jerusalem in this same manner. It consists of two elements: *uru* and *šalim* (*šalem*). The first is developed from the verb *yārâh* — "to found."[14] Šalim must thus be the name of the founder or divinity. The city thus means "Šalim has founded" or "foundation of Šalim." But who is this Šalim? Since it is predominantly divinities who figure in the place names of this era,[15] we should expect the name of the founder to reveal a god rather than a man. Now, in the whole Semitic sphere of influence between Nile and Euphrates there is a much revered god named Šalim; in the ethnic disturbances occasioned during the Hyksos era he takes on the form *Šulman*. Šalim means "whole, sound, healthy," and *šulman* means "one who has to do with wellbeing (*šulmu*)." On the basis of the name we might thus conclude that Šalim was venerated as a healing god. In Jerusalem he must have been equivalated to the supreme deity El, as witness Abraham's encounter with Melchizedek (Gn 14, 18ff.). Thorough investigation has actually succeeded in establishing the universalistic character of this divinity.[16] It can only be that this god's temple was predominant in the city. King 'Abd-Hiba wrote to the Pharaoh[17] that Bit-Šulman, the temple of Šulman, had been destroyed. This might well establish the fact that the city name of Jerusalem is derived from the god Šalim or Šulman. David imposed a new name on the conquered Jebusite city, "city of David" (*'îr-dāwîd*), but the ancient pagan name still asserted itself. Numerous jar stamps [18] from the sixth and fifth centuries are witness to the fact that the form Jerušalem was the current name of the city. This form was preserved in the Hebrew consonant text (*yrwšlm*), but since the vocalization of the Masorete text,[19] the enlarged form *yerûšālayim* became more prevalent. It appears that the mysticism of late Judaism seized upon the name of the holy city. The form *šālēm* was developed into the artificial form *šālayim*, in order to give an echo of *šāmayim*, heaven.[20] In Jewish mysticism,

---

14. GB on *yarah* I, "lay a stone as foundation."
15. Cf. Beth-Lehem, "Temple of the God Lahamu"; Beth-El, "Temple of El"; Beth-Horon, "Temple of the God Horon."
16. J. Lewy, *Les textes paléo-assyr. et l'AT*, Rev. hist. des relig., 110 (1934), 60ff.
17. *The Sulman Temple in Jerusalem*, JBL 59 (1940), 519-522, Amarna-brief 290.
18. P. Vincent, DBS IV, 899.
19. The Biblical hebraica presents the text according to the codex of the family of Ben-Asher of Aleppo, from the year 1008 A.D.
20. H. Rust, *Warum Jerusalajim?* ThLZ (1949), 627-629. — According to *EncMikr* III (1958), 792, there is no mystical meaning, only an ancient locative form: cf. the place names Qarnaim, Eglaim, Shomraim.

the earthly Jerusalem thus turns into "the city of heaven." The New Testament grecized form' Ιεροσόλυμα would obviously recall the word ἱερός ("holy") to Greek ears, so that the further designation ἁγία πόλις ("holy city") is only a further development. In the modern Arabian world, Jerusalem is called simply *el-ḳuds,* that is, the "sanctuary" or "holy city."

The Bible contains two accounts of the conquering of Jerusalem (2 S 5, 6-16 and 1 Ch 11, 4-9). These accounts exhibit not only many points of agreement, but also significant variations. The account in the Book of Samuel numbers 55 words, while in 1 Chronicles there are 42 words, 20 of which are the same. How are these facts to be explained? It is generally admitted that the chronist,[21] in composing his history towards the end of the fifth century, made use of the Books of Samuel as a source and copied from them. But he did not copy in a mechanical manner; he fitted the text into the general outline of his own composition; he simply dropped episodes and accounts which were unfitted to his purpose, and enlarged other sections from various sources. Many geographical details might have been no longer understood in his day. Although the first stages of modern criticism generally placed little value on his chronicle as a tendentious historical composition, today we can recognize its true value, since we now have available sources which had been previously lost.[22] The following presentation is, accordingly, based on both accounts.

1) THE CONQUEST OF JERUSALEM:

At the time of entry into the promised land, the city was promised to the tribe of Benjamin; but the city proved to be impregnable and maintained itself as an erratic bloc in the midst of Israelite territory (Jos 18, 28). Concerning the Jebusites, we know nothing more than the fact that they belonged to the ancient and established Canaanite population (Gn 10, 15). We must not exclude the possibility that, in the ethnic disturbances of the Hyksos era, Amurru and Mitanni peoples got control of the city. One indication of this would be the destruction of the Bit-Sulman,

---

21. Historical value of the Chronicles discussed on p. 285.
22. Comparison of the various opinions in Bressan, 508ff.

as narrated in the Amarna correspondence.[23] Thus, the city would have already had a long and troubled history behind it when David addressed himself to the objective of making it the most significant city in the world, and in the history of humanity.

The conquest of Jerusalem was no small matter, even for a man as versed in warfare as David. Prior to this time, he had been used to facing his enemies on the open battle field. Now he was to take a fortified citadel. Like all ancient Canaanite cities, Jerusalem was built upon a rock pinnacle, protected on the one side by the deeply eroded Kidron Valley, and on the other by the Tyropoeon Valley, which, today, is almost completely filled. The location of the settlement was very circumscribed. The area was only four and one half hectares. The ground plan looked more or less like a protracted bottle, 400 m in length, and 70 to 120 m in width. From either side, in the valleys, an attack was virtually inconceivable. The only weak point was on the northern side, where the land rises towards the later terrace of the temple. A diagonal well, some 70 m in length, protected the city from this quarter. Ancient Jerusalem was not situated entirely on the highest of the surrounding hills; its elevation is 760 m, while the surrounding mountains are all higher, so that the mountains form a protective wall around Jerusalem (Ps 123/124). The traveler has to approach very close to the holy city before he can even see it. This was even truer of the ancient city of David on the Ophel hill, which today, lies outside the city walls, south of the former temple area of Haram eš-Šerif, today merely an uninhabited and much ransacked dumping ground of history.[24]

The city's life was dependent upon the spring (fountain) which arose at the foot of the Ophel in the Kidron Valley. The water emanates from a fissure in the rock, 4.80 m in length. Its name Gihon means "bubbly, sputtering"; the spring does not yield its water in a consistent flow; the water seems to gather in a subterranean reservoir whence it spurts forth from time to time, the frequency of the spurting being dependent upon the season of the year.[25] In order to assure themselves of a water supply even in times of war, — the resistance capacity of a besieged city was largely dependent upon its water supply — the Canaanites excavated water systems in various cities. Best known are the great Canaanite water tunnels in Gezer, Gibeon, and Megiddo.[26] In ancient Jerusalem, too,

---

23. Amarna letters, 290.
24. Recommended, in this respect, is the *Atlas of the Bible* of Grollenberg (Nelson, 1956), Ill., 191, 192.
25. C. E. Wright, *Biblical Archaeology* (1958), 123.
26. Noetscher, KAB, 164ff. Abbildungen der Tunnel von Megiddo und Gibeon bei A. Jirku, *Welt der Bibel* (1957), T. 76 u. T. 80.

such a system had been elaborated. "Eloquent testimony to this fact is the carefully planned network of tunnels in the immediate neighborhood of the fountain. One of the first attempts to bring the water closer to the city consisted in the construction of a passageway leading to a chamber above a deep shaft. From the chamber, a further passageway was extended, semi-circular in form and some 37 m in length, through the native rock in the direction of the spring. From this position, jars and cans could be let down to the spring through the shaft." [27] In times of war, this access to the water was filled up from outside, while the besieged city continued to receive its life's water through the well shaft. This shaft may have led either into the inside of the city or at least into the neighborhood of a strongly fortified tower.

Her natural position thus made Jerusalem all but impregnable. The situation was further aggravated by the contemptuous communication sent to David, which was at the same time a reference to the pointlessness of a siege: "You will not come in here, but the blind and the lame will war you off [28]— David cannot come in here" (5, 6). David must have assembled an impressive fighting force to take the city. The Book of Samuel (5, 6) speaks only of "David and his men," but the chronist (1 Ch 11, 4) enlarges upon this by adding the fact that "all Israel went up against Jerusalem." David obviously reckoned on a long siege. He knew the city could not be taken by storm. Accordingly, he outlined a plan upon whose execution he set a high price. That the city could continue to receive her water supply from subterranean sources was certainly well known to him. As long as the city had water he could never bring her to her knees. David had to strike the city in this one vital artery. Once again, just as in days when the youthful David first came to the camp of Israel, heralds were sent to make the public proclamation: "Whoever would fight the Jebusites and

---

27. C. E. Wright, Bibl. Arch. (1958), 125; ANEP 7, 44.
28. Vulgate translates: *Non ingrederis huc nisi abstuleris caecos et claudos*, that is, "You can't enter here unless you have removed the blind and the lame." This gives no meaning. H. P. Smith, *The Books of Samuel* (1904), 288, represents the position that the Jebusites had mockingly erected statues of the Israelite God on the city walls, one of which was blind like Isaac and the other lame like Jacob! Good imagination!

forces his way through the *ṣinnôr* (2 S 5, 6 — water shaft), he will be a chief and a prince" (1 Ch 11, 6).[29]

At all events, the undertaking called for a display of extra-ordinary heroism. The prize was claimed by Joab, son of Zeruiah, who thus achieved appointment to the highest military position. The reconstruction of his heroic enterprise is open to various possibilities, according to our interpretation of the word *ṣinnôr*. That we are, at all events, dealing with the water supply, is evident from Ps 41/42, 8: "Deep calls to deep in the thunder (literally, "with the voice") of your cataracts" (*ṣinnôrêka*).[30] These are the only two passages in which the word *ṣinnôr* occurs. It can refer either to the whole subterranean tunnel or only to the access passage. Hence the following two interpretations: Joab, together with a few daring followers, climbed up into the city through the water shaft, opened the city gates, and admitted the attacking forces. This sealed the fate of the city.[31] But since it is uncertain

---

29. The chronist has left out the reference to the *ṣinnôr*, since at his time the word was not widely understood. In the Book of Samuel, on the other hand, there is no mention of the reward promised to the victor. Bressan, 514, claims that the text is not in proper order.

30. Vulgate: *abyssus abyssum invocat, in voce cataractarum* (*ṣinnôrêka*) *tuarum.*

31. The location was rediscovered in 1867. An excellent account by the man responsible for the discovery himself: C. Warren, *The Survey of Western Palestine,* Jerusalem-London, 1886, 366-371. He made his way from the spring through the later tunnel of Hezekiah into the citadel itself, until he struck upon a 13 m high and 2-4 m wide shaft or chimney. Since no ladders were immediately available, it seemed that further penetration was impossible. Moreover, some of the rock threatened to collapse. With the aid of a few boards laid crosswise, the ascent was accomplished in relatively short order. The exploration was continued, in a most adventuresome manner, by Parker in 1909-1911. Two of his workmen negotiated the chimney in the same way. P. Vincent, RB 33 (1924), 365 for the account. In my journeys in Palestine in 1951 I attempted to climb the tunnel. As I prepared to make my unsuspecting way down the many stairs leading to the spring, I suddenly heard the cries of the women carrying water, coming up behind me. A man never goes down into the spring while women are drawing water. I let them all pass, carrying their ancient

whether the water tunnel ended within the city gates or outside them, in the vicinity of a fortified tower position, it would also be possible that Joab's heroic adventure consisted rather in a bold and unexpected attack which brought the opening of the water tunnel into his power and thus forced the city to capitulate for lack of water.[32]

The fact is that, through this bold undertaking of Joab's, David became master of "fortress Zion" (5, 7). This passage represents the first occurrence of the name Zion in Scripture. The original meaning of the Hebrew word ṣiyyon is much contested. Most probably it means "rock" or "citadel." [33] This would refer, original-ly, to the citadel within the Jebusite city. In the course of time, Zion refers to the whole city of Jerusalem and turns into the

---

water jugs on their heads, some of them with quite modern gas cans for water. Then I made my way down, together with two young Arab boys. The descent is narrow, the rocks damp and slippery. Leaning hard on both hands, and attempting to turn around in the narrow passageway, I slipped and fell into the water up to my waist, much to the delight of my young companions. But I was not to be stopped. In the tunnel itself, the water reached only to our knees. We kept on wading. When we reached the vertical shaft, I could only illuminate it with my lamp. We kept following the tunnel of Hezekiah. When we drew near to the exit, the boys began shouting "Ya-banat!" That is, "Look, out, girls!" When they had left the spring, we came back up to daylight. I dried myself in the sun and then returned to the city through the dung gate. — The question of the ṣinnôr is expressly treated in Bressan, 515ff. By the same author: L'espugnazione di Sion et il problema del "ṣinnôr." Bibl 25 (1944), 346-381. / H. J. Stoebe, Die Einnahme von Jerusalem und der ṣinnôr, ZDPV 73 (1957), 73-99.

---

32. J. Simmons, Jerusalem in the Old Testament. Researches and Theories (Leiden, 1952), 170ff.
33. Three derivations: a. "a place which is exposed to the sun." ṣahah, "shine, sparkle"; or ṣayah, "be dry"; hence ṣiyyôn, "arid land, rock." b. "the citadel," ṣiyyôn related to the Arabic sûn, "protect," or with the Hebrew ṣawah, "to be high, lofty, exalted." Hence ṣiyyôn, "for-tress, citadel." Cf. Médebielle, Rois 482. c. Since ancient Jerusalem housed a non-semitic population, the word ṣiyyôn could also be Hurrite. ṣeya, 'water, river": water city, city on the water? Very uncertain. DBS IV, 914.

splendid name for the religious center of God's people, finding
a ready echo in the full enthusiasm of psalmist and prophet.[34]

2) CONSTRUCTION OF DAVID'S CITY:

In the history of the city of Jerusalem, the name Zion has
undergone many changes. Present-day Zion, with the upper-room
of the Last Supper and the supposed grave of David, is situated
on the western hill. Ancient Zion occupied only the small territory of the Ophel hill between the Kidron and the Tyropoeon
Valleys. Since 1867, ancient Jerusalem has been the scene of
numerous excavations.[35] Although it is now demonstrable that
the Ophel was settled already around the year 3000 B.C., the
various strata which are otherwise so common in ancient settlements are almost entirely lacking here, so that as a result the
history of this very important city cannot be reconstructed on
the basis of stratigraphy. According to the account of Flavius
Josephus, in the era of the Macabees, this was the site of a
Syrian fortress, which had been conquered by the Jews around
140 B.C.; not only was it leveled to the ground, but the very
stones upon which the fortress stood were carried away, so that
Jerusalem could never again be threatened from that quarter. For
the contemporary political situation of the day, this was a great
advantage; but for the historian it is irreparable loss. The debris
was simply toppled down the hillside. Thus, the slopes of the
Ophel have yielded abundant masses of debris, mixed with ostraka
dating from the third millennium down to the third and second
centuries B.C.[36] There is hardly any accurate basis for reconstruc-

---

34. Pss 2, 6; 13/14, 7; 86/87, 1, 5; Is 18, 27; Jr 3, 14, etc.
35. The story of the excavations is briefly summed up in: Chester C.
    McCown, *The Ladder of Progress in Palestine* (1943), 227-243. /
    Original accounts are to be found in: F. J. Bliss, *Excavations at
    Jerusalem 1894-97* (London, 1898). / R. A. S. Macalister and J. G.
    Duncan, *Excavations on the Hill of Ophel* (Ann. PEF IV) (London,
    1926). / J. W. Crowfoot and G. M. Fitzgerald, *Excavation in the
    Tyropoean Valley* (Ann. PEF V) (London, 1929).
36. Absolutely indispensable for a more precise archaeological account of
    Jerusalem are the standard volumes of J. Simons, *Jerusalem in the*

ting life in Jerusalem during David's reign on the basis of stratigraphy, a source of such rich information for other ruins and
mounds. Still, the complicated labyrinth of fortification positions
on the Ophel does present some picture of the strength and
impregnability of the city. The hills were encompassed by defense
walls in the strength of 8 to 12 meters. Where this foundation
was considered insufficient to repulse a possible attack or withstand a siege, huge bastions were added as further support from
without.[37]

Such a fortress could obviously not be simply overrun; its
capture needed careful strategy. In keeping with the custom of
his time, David gave the vanquished city a new name " 'îr dawîd"
(city of David — 5, 9), which, however, did not prevail against
the ancient name. At the same time, David addressed himself to
the task of equipping Jerusalem for its new position as royal city
and capital of his kingdom. The text, with laconic brevity, presents this account of David's building activity: "David built the
city roundabout from the Millo inward" (5, 9). For our historian
and his first readers, who were familiar with the geography of
the city, this was no doubt intelligible, but for us it is the beginning of a riddle. Does this mean that David encompassed his new
royal city with a new city wall? Excavation does not seem to
bear this out. The strong fortification system on the Ophel is
generally referred to as "Jebusite." [38] It is only later repairs and

Old Testament, Researches and Theories (Leiden, 1952). For the
present discussion, cf. ch. IV: Sion, City of David and Phel, Excavations on the South-Eastern Hill, Millo and Acra. The Waterworks
of the City, pp. 60-193. The second work is from the grandfather of
Palestinian archaeology, P. Vincent, _Jerusalem de l'ancien Testament,_
I. La Ville (Paris, 1954). In addition, the Hebrew work _sepher
yerûšalayim,_ by M. Avi-Yonah: Jerusalem, its natural surroundings, history, and development from the beginning up to modern times. Numerous illustrated plates and maps. I (1956).

37. C. E. Wright, _Biblical Archaeology_ (1958). Figure 78 shows the
    remains of the city walls. Figure 79: remains of the fortifications of
    the Jebusite city.
38. N. Avigad, _The Fortification of the City of David,_ IsrExpl 2 (1952),
    230-236. In the year 1954, a street construction crew struck upon

additions that are ascribed to David, which is certainly understandable. David did not enlarge the conquered city; he merely
brought its defensive capacity up to date. Particular difficulty is
occasioned by the world Millo (Milo), literally "filling up, heap-
ing up." Solomon, in building his temple, enlarged the city to
the north (1 K 9, 15; 2 Ch 32, 5). This involved filling up the
small basin between ancient Zion and the temple site. This
work was, certainly, first carried out by Solomon. David himself
was not interested in filling up the natural sink on the northern
side of his new city, and thereby developing a weak point. Accordingly, the term Millo might be used anachronistically, the
place name Millo being dated back to an earlier time. Other
scholars ascribe the Millo to David himself, but give the word
a different meaning. According to this view, David would have
filled up a breach or a weak point in the wall of the ancient fortress by the addition of new defense positions. A further opinion
considers the Millo as the dirt heaped up for the foundation of
the new royal palace, or perhaps a sacrificial high place to receive
the Ark of the Covenant.[39]

Although we cannot precisely determine what David actually
built, it is obvious that his first preoccupation was to bring the
ancient defense system up to date. It is also obvious that he must
have undertaken some reconstruction within the city. One of the
projects was certainly the erection of his royal palace, for which
King Hiram of Tyre supplied the wood and stone workers (5,
11). There must also have been a barracks for "David's heroes,
the famous *gibbôrîm*" (2 S 23, 8-39; Neh 3, 16) and for the
600 men in his body guard, composed of Cherethites and Pelethites, together with their families (2 S 15, 18). After the trium-

the remains of the ancient Ophel walls. The wall was excavated
to a length of 30 m; sections of it were preserved to a height of 8 m.
RB (1956), 77.

39. The individual opinions are expressly discussed in Simons, *Jerusalem
in the OT* (1952), 131ff. His conclusion: "Be that as it may, it seems
impossible in this question of place to advance beyond a more or less
happy conjecture" 134. Cf. also P. Vincent, *La cité de David*, DBS
IV, 914ff.

phal entry of the Ark of the Covenant, many priests and Levites also transferred their homes into the new capital. Desnoyers [40] estimates the population as 7 or 8 thousand. This is more likely to be a low rather than a high estimate. Since the habitable area of the walled city was proportionately small, we must presume that the extensions of the city towards north and west had already begun at the time of David.

3) DAVID'S FAMILY:

Immediately after the royal anointing in Hebron, we find the statement that David continued to grow in strength and power (2 S 3, 1). In the parlance of the Ancient Near East, this would have included a corresponding harem. The king's reputation and power could be measured in terms of the number and beauty and importance of his wives, as well as by the number of his sons. King Priam of Troy boasted fifty sons.[41] In addition to his two wives Abigail and Ahinoam, while he was still in Hebron, David took four other wives of first rank and two of second rank (3, 2-5). Ahinoam presented David with a son Ammon ("the faithful one"), while Abigail gave him Dodijah ("my beloved is Yahweh"). After becoming king in Hebron, David married Maacah from Geshur, an Aramaean tribe north of the Lake of Gennesareth, between Hermon and Bashan; this was a political alliance. She bore him Absalom ("my father is peace"). This is the first son who was born to David as king. He was the one who was later destined to raise his hand against his father, in an attempt to topple him from the throne. A fourth son, born from Haggith ("the splendid"), bore the name Adonijah ("my Lord is Yahweh"); he was destined to be David's successor, but he was supplanted by Solomon. Two other sons, also born in Hebron, were called Shethatiath ("Yahweh has held judgment") and Ithream [42] ("my relative [God] has shown himself magnanimous").

The names which David gave his sons were not empty words in

---

40. L. Desnoyers, *Histoire du peuple Hebreu des Juges à la Captivité* (Paris), II: Saul et David (1930), 184.

41. Iliad, 24, 493.

42. Name formations with *'amm,* "relative" go back into the second millennium. In Old Babylonian and Old Assyrian, but seldom in Canaan. This compound form disappears around 1000. In Hebrew the meaning of "people" has won out: e.g., *Rehab'am,* "May he expand my people." / W. F. Albright, *From Stone Age to Christianity* (1949), 244ff. / G. Ryckmans, *Apropos de noms de parenté en safaitique.* RB 60 (1953), 524-525: *'m* - father's brother (uncle): *dd* - grandfather.

his mind. If we knew nothing of David from other sources, we could still recognize his confession of faith on the basis of these names. His Lord and God is Yahweh (Adonijah), whom he loves intimately (Dodijah); for God has passed judgment (Shethatiath) and shown himself magnanimous, like a relative and friend (Ithream). He is the faithful one, who has kept his word (Amnon).

David's succession to the rule of all Israel must have had its effect upon his wives as well. In 2 S 5, 13, we read: "And David took more concubines and wives from Jerusalem, after he came from Hebron." The Book of Samuel mentions 11; in the Book of Chronicles (1 Ch 3, 5-8; 14, 4-7), on the other hand, there are thirteen names of sons born to wives of the first rank; the sons of the concubines are not mentioned. The account presumes an acquaintance with earlier records, and thus presents only a summary of the number of members in the royal house. In this present context, we mean to call attention only to the religious content of the names, since they cast much light upon David's faith in Yahweh. They are a singular hymn of gratitude for Yahweh's intervention in David's life. Yahweh has heard him (Shammua) and made him "brilliant" among his people (Shobab); he gave him the promised throne (Nathan), chose him in preference to all (Ibhar), and rescued him from time of crisis (Eliphelet). Yahweh has made his face shine upon him (Japhia) and has loved and known him (Beeliada) and let him live in peace (Solomon).[43]

C) ENTRY OF THE ARK OF THE COVENANT

Psalm 131/132, 1-5 attempts to remind Yahweh of all David's efforts to bring the Ark of the Covenant into a secure resting place: "I will not enter my house or get into my bed; I will not give sleep to my eyes or slumber to my eyelids, until I find a place for the Lord, a dwelling place for the Mighty One of Jacob." After the political unification and the building projects within the royal city, David devoted his entire energy to establishing a religious center for the unified nation. The Ark of the Covenant was still in Kiriath-Jearim (Cariathiarim, "wood city," 1 S 7, 2). Saul himself had made no attempts in this direction, probably because this city, at the boundary of the mountain country, lay under the control of the Philistines. Israel's greatest sanctuary thus stood abandoned in this city, without cult, without

---

43. Derivations of the individual names in Bressan, 483ff, 520ff.

pilgrims. David felt this to be a national disgrace. Religious and national motives alike may have prompted him to bring back the Ark of the Covenant. In this project, however, he encountered unexpected difficulties. His first attempt was unsuccessful.

It appears that the priesthood, whom we might have suspected to adopt David's plans with the greatest enthusiasm, wanted to hear nothing of the project. The sanctuary at Gibeon, the site of the ancient tent, with the altar of holocaust, would have suffered seriously in importance if the Ark of the Covenant were carried off to the capital city. It was thus not purely religious grounds, but rather some very human considerations, jealousy and rivalry — how often this is true in sacred history — which prompted the priesthood to boycott the transfer of the Ark. But for David there was too much at stake. He ignored the resistance of the priestly class and was prepared to transfer the Ark into the capital city without the cooperation of the priesthood (2 S 6, 1-10).

Accordingly, he one day sounded the call for the solemn transfer of the Ark. "All the people" (6, 2), that is, large crowds from all the twelve tribes, followed his call and came to Kiriath-Jearim. But how were they to transfer the sacred Ark without priests? The best solution was to imitate the miraculous manner in which it had been returned from the country of the Philistines. The Ark was accordingly placed upon a new cart to which they hitched oxen. Then the procession formed. They brought it out of the house of Abinadab, which stood on a hill. The wagon was guided by two men. The one, Ahio (Yahweh is my brother), probably saw to the animals, while the other, Uzzah, apparently walked beside the cart (6, 4). David walked before the Ark with the musicians, who were playing on lyres and harps and tambourines and castanets.[44] A clear blue sky, so characteristic of the country, must have smiled down upon this solemn procession. The people all joined triumphantly in the train. Then, in the neighborhood of the threshing floor of Nacon, some un-

---

44. Regarding the various musical instruments, cf. E. Gerson-Kiwi: *Musique, les instruments*, DBS V, 1414-1435. / Noetscher, BAK 250.

foreseen accident made it appear that the Ark was about to slide from the cart. Uzzah reached out to steady it and fell instantly dead, as if struck.[45] The music stopped, and terror seized the entire procession. What next? Why this outburst of Yahweh's anger? David himself did not dare to continue bringing the Ark into his city; he left it in the house of Obed-Edom. Thus, the first attempt met with a tragic end. David called the place Perez-Uzzah, "the breaking forth upon Uzzah," and was forced to recognize that it was not Yahweh's will.

When David saw that the three months' stay of the Ark in the house of Obed-Edom was a source of blessing rather than misfortune, he decided upon a second attempt.

This time the Ark was borne, not on a cart, but upon the shoulders of the Levites, as the law demanded. In order to be assured of Yahweh's favor, after the Ark had been carried six paces, David offered an ox and a fatling in sacrifice. David himself walked before the Ark of the Covenant. It was no solemn and stately procession; it was an enthusiastic and inspired dance.[46] The verbs used in the Hebrew text make this very clear. He went back and forth (*me̱karke̱r* — 6, 14), he leaped (*me̱pazze̱r* —

45. Does this mean that Uzzah was struck down by Yahweh's unaccountable wrath despite his innocence? Many scholars believe that Uzzah reached out to touch the ark irreverently and thus caused the cart to topple. It is obviously an open intervention of God, making his people conscious once again of the *tremendum mysterium*, the awesome mystery of the supreme Lord who thrones above the Cherubim. Transfering the ark on an open cart was a public violation of the Mosaic ordinances. Such experiences make a lasting impression on the indifferent. God cannot be treated like an object that can merely be carried from one place to another. But side by side with the figure of the inexorable and unfathomable Master, there is the picture of the forgiving God. Cf. Sister M. Aloysia, *The God of Wrath?* CBQ 8 (1946), 407-415. / N. H. Tursinai, *The Ark of God at Beit Shemesh and Pere̱s 'Uzza,* VT 1 (1951), 275-286. Palestinian place names derived from plagues worked by God.

46. Sacred dance played a great role in the ancient cults. Cf. W. O. E. Oesterley, *The Sacred Dance. A Study in Comparative Folklore* (Cambridge, 1923). / J. Doeller, *Davids Tanz vor Jahweh,* ZkTh 29 (1905), 576-579.

6, 14), he turned about in a circle (1 S 18, 6). He had taken off his royal clothing (1 Ch 15, 27) and was clad only in the ephod,[47] a simple linen apron. For the first procession with the Ark, David had assembled a band of marching musicians. It is hardly possible that these were lacking on the occasion of the second procession.[48] The only difference was the fact that this time it was the Levites who saw to the music (1 Ch 15, 16). The Book of Samuel makes particular mention of an instrument which belongs to the most ancient and venerable instruments of Israelite worship, the shophar, originally a curved ram's horn. Since it was blown without a mouthpiece, it was possible to produce tones which were similar to a human voice. Hence the expression "with the sound (voice) of the horn" (6, 15). Only the priest could blow this instrument. Perhaps its original application, in primitive times, was to dispel the evil spirits.[49] Sinai was filled with the voice of these horns (Ex 19, 16; 20, 18), when Yahweh gave his people their law. The horn was sounded, in the wilderness trek, whenever the Ark of the Covenant was being carried; Jericho was conquered by the same sacred horns (Jos 6, 4). It must have filled the people with a sacred dread when they heard the horns sounding in the ancient battle cry: "Let God arise!" (Ps 67/68, 1; 131/132, 8).[50]

This festive act, which belongs among the high points of Israel's religious history, ended with a family quarrel. With joyous heart, after escorting the Ark to its resting place, David came to bless his own house. The royal harem had not taken part in the procession; only from the window could Michal observe the festivities. What could David more logically expect, upon this joyous day, than happy hearts and open arms? But Michal greeted him with hard and contemptuous words: "How the king of Israel

---

47. K. Elliger, *Ephod und Choschen*, VT 8 (1958), 19-35. / Noetscher, BAK 308.
48. E. Gerson-Kiwi: only "la voix protectrice et cultuelle de cors" accompanied the procession. DBS V, 1418.
49. On the apotropaic character of sounding the horn, cf. DBS V, 1417.
50. Even after the destruction of Jerusalem, the horns were preserved and, together with the seven-branched candle-stick, they were a symbol of Jerusalem. Galling. BRL, 390.

honored himself today!" A recognition of his successful undertaking? Hardly. The next words express the perfect contempt of
this proud daughter of Saul for the humble Ben-Jesse: "Un-
covering himself today before the eyes of his servants' maids"
(6, 20). She had no eyes for the glory of the day's achievement,
only for David's supposed shame. He should have come riding
in, resplendent in his purple robes, and yet he danced, clad only
in the priestly apron (ephod). Although Michal was David's first
love, this woman had never managed to understand the real David.
David had no eyes for human judgment; his heart burned for
Yahweh alone, and for Yahweh he was prepared to divest himself
of much more than his royal clothing.[51] It is understandable that,
after this reproachful greeting, the two had little to say to each
other. The proud woman remained unfruitful to the day of her
death, probably because David withdrew from her (6, 23).

The music was accompanied by song (1 Ch 15, 27). Although we do not know which of the psalms was sung on this
occasion, Ps 23/24, long attributed to the authorship of David,
is most fitting to the situation. As the procession made its way
up the mountain side, the singers raised the solemn question:
"Who shall ascend the hill of the Lord?" A second chorus answered: "He who has clean hands and a pure heart . . . ." As they
approached the city gates, they raised the imperative command:
"Lift up your heads, O gates! and be lifted up, O ancient doors!
that the King of glory may come in." Then the second chorus:
"Who is this King of glory?" And the answer of the first chorus:
"Yahweh, strong and mighty; *Yahweh ṣᵉbā'ôt*, Yahweh of hosts,
the war god of Israel, will make his entrance." Upon this, the
gates of the Jebusite fortress had to open; for no one can resist
Yahweh.[52]

---

51. A. Dodd sees this "self-divesting" as a type of the "self-emptying" of
    Jesus the Messiah, who did not think equality with God a thing to be
    clinged to, but laid aside the cloak of his glory and "emptied him-
    self" (*"ekénōsen"* Phil 2, 7). Benedikt. Monatschrift (Beuron) 22
    (1946), 292-295.
52. Ps. 67/68 also describes the course of a procession: first the singers,
    harp players in the rear, young maidens in the middle striking their
    tambourines. The individual tribes according to their clans and families;

David had the Ark of the Covenant set up in a new tent,[53] and then offered countless sacrifices and blessed his people. After this, he spread a royal banquet for the many pilgrims. They all received bread, a portion of meat, and a cake of raisins (6, 19). In offering sacrifice and blessing the people, David was not arrogating a priestly prerogative; his activity harked back to the ancient family and tribal rights, whereby the father of the family or the tribal head was at the same time the priest for the community under his care. Saul, David, and Solomon regularly exercised such priestly functions without hesitation and without encountering any opposition. Only in later times were the functions of the cult proper reserved for the priests.[54] In Israel, cult and king cannot be distinguished.[55] Even though the priests performed the cultic functions, it was always the king who established them in their office and ordained the temple cult. It is impossible to doubt the priestly character of the Israelite kingship, just as Melchizedek was both priest and king, just as the Messiah to come will share both offices (Ps 109/110).

D) THE GREAT PROMISE AND COVENANT WITH DAVID

With the promise of the abiding permanency of the rule of David's house, the Book of Samuel achieves its climax. The leit-motiv which makes up the entire work is the introduction

Benjamin first, as the youngest, then the tribal heads of Judah, Zabulon, Nephthali, etc.

---

53. The Mosaic tabernacle remained, meantime, in Gibeon, where Solomon venerated it (1 K 2, 28).
54. King Uzziah (Ozias) was struck with leprosy because he arrogated priestly privileges (2 Ch 26, 16-21).
55. A. Bentzen, *The Cultic Use of the Story of the Ark in Samuel,* JBL 66 (1947), 37-53 identifies the Ark narrative as an historizing of the mythical God-dragon-conflict, with the motif of the dying divinity having disappeared from the Israelite ritual. / J. R. Porter, *The Interpretation of 2 S 6 and Ps 132,* JtheolSt NS 5 (1954), 161-173 holds that David introduced a Canaanite New Year's festival on the occasion of his enthronement. Both opinions are little more than unsupported hypotheses.

of kingship into Israel. Against the somber background of the Book of Judges — "In those days there was no king in Israel; every man did what was right in his own eyes" (Jg 21, 25) — the figure of the first king Saul shines briefly as a man of mighty expectations, but a king who fell short of his mission. His house had no permanence. Now it was David's turn. Was his kingship also destined to be a transitory episode? Never. The prophet opens horizons of an "everlasting" kingship, a kingship that will have no end.

The occasion for this prophecy was David's plan to build Yahweh a temple; it was not right for the king to live in a magnificent palace while Yahweh continued to live in a tent, as in the days of the desert wanderings. David discussed his plan with the prophet Nathan,[56] who was obviously one of his intimate advisors. Nathan at first encouraged him in his proposals. But during the night, the word of Yahweh came upon the prophet, and the word of Yahweh was quite different.[57]

Yahweh rejects the plan of building a temple.[58] It is not David who is to build Yahweh a house. What had David done to deserve such an answer? He was thinking only of God's greater glory, and now God rejects his plan. But only at first examination does it appear to be a rejection; upon closer consideration it developed into God's grandiose response to David's plan for building a house. David is not the one to build a house for God; his hands have shed too much blood — it is Solomon who will complete the earthly temple (2 S 7, 13; 1 Ch 17, 12;

---

56. Nathan, according to 1 Ch 29, 29, composed a history of David which was probably used as a source for the Book of Samuel. Hence, this explicit record, even from a purely historical point of view, is deserving of full faith.

57. The prophet also thinks and judges like a normal man. He is a prophet in the proper sense of the word only when the spirit of God takes hold of him and reveals things that remain hidden to human reason.

58. M. Simon, *La prophétie de Nathan et le Temple*, RHPhR 32 (1952), 41-58 holds that Yahweh is fundamentally opposed to the building of the Temple and not only desirous of a postponement. — Arbitrary opinion.

22, 7-8). For David, Yahweh himself will build an "everlasting" house. The important text must be quoted in its entirety. Chapter 7, 12: "When your days are fulfilled and you lie down with your fathers, I will raise up your offspring after you, who shall come forth from your body, and I will establish his kingdom. 13: He shall build a house for my name, and I will establish the throne of his kingdom forever. 14: I will be his Father, and he shall be my Son. When he commits iniquity, I will chasten him with the rod of men, with the stripes of the sons of men. 15: But I will not take my steadfast love from him as I took it from Saul, whom I put away from before my face. 16: And your house and your kingdom shall be made sure forever before me; your throne shall be established forever."

This solemn prophecy to the house of David occurs in three different contexts, the one cited above from the Book of Samuel, the passage in 1 Ch 17 and the passage in Ps 88/89. The strictest form of the original has, apparently, been preserved in the Book of Samuel, while the chronist and the psalmist have already introduced theological meditations and amplifications. On the essential point of "the everlasting kingdom of the house of David," all three are in perfect harmony.[59] Because of the importance of this prophecy for the subsequent development of messianic faith, we must make a closer examination of the most important critical opinions.

For Gressmann,[60] we are dealing with a saga: "Traits of prefabrication are everywhere preponderant; precisely for that reason it is improper to excise what seems to be improbable particulars, or even to reinterpret them until they become probable. This was the method of the rationalist school, which was unable to comprehend the miraculous as the product of a form-creating force. The exegete of modern times is careful not to strip off the ornaments of popular narrative art; he treats miracle as miracle." If we are concerned merely with saga, then there is no further question of the messianic content of the passage; or for that matter, even of its historical setting. At most, a saga could express something of the religious conviction of the age and nothing more.[61]

---

59. Bressan, 542ff.: Critica letteraria.
60. H. Gressmann, *Die älteste Geschichtsschreibung und Prophetie Israels* (Göttingen, 1921), 138.
61. M. Noth, *David und Israel in 2 S 7*, Mélanges biblique (Robert, 1957), 122-130.

Morgenstern [62] thinks, however, that the messianic idea developed only in the days of Zorobabel (520-516), to serve as a support for the Jewish-national movement among the repatriated exiles. The Nordic school [63] stresses the etiological character of the narrative. The saga was developed as an afterthought, to explain why David had been unable to build the temple. Simon [64] locates the context in the internal conflict among the Jews, postulating the existence of an anti-deuteronomic group which saw the temple construction as an attack against the Yahweh religion. On the basis of stylistic and linguistic investigation, Driver attempts to date the account around the year 700 B.C. Wiener,[65] on the other hand, maintains that the prophecy could not have originated after the reign of Solomon, since it still glorifies his kingdom, and this would hardly have been possible after the division of the kingdom. Rost [66] also holds for the historicity of the nucleus of this account, although the narrative may well be enhanced by theological considerations. The author of the oracle would be the prophet Nathan, and the time of composition would be the beginning of Solomon's reign. Eissfeldt [67] pushes the dating even further ahead, claiming to find some favorite concepts of the deutero-nomic school worked into chapter 7: accordingly the account could not have been composed prior to the middle of the ninth century. McKenzie [68] takes a stand against this date: on the basis of the abundant material which

---

62. J. Morgenstern, *Two Prophecies from 520 - 16 B.C.*, HUCA 22 (1949), 365-431.

63. H. Ringgren, *König und Messias*, ZATW 64 (1952), 120-147. / S. Mowinckel, *He That Cometh*. English by G. W. Anderson, (Oxford, 1956). "The king was regarded as a divine being, of whom virtues and divine help were expected." Since this hope was never fully realized in any of the kings, the expectation was renewed on the occasion of every new accession to the throne, and thus developed into a faith in the Messiah as a figure to come in the future. The Nathan prophecy is a "narrative echo" of the good wishes of the cult prophets who prophesy all manner of good auguries for the new king. Both the assumption of the divinity of the Israelite king as well as the existence of cult prophets are undemonstrated presuppositions. 97, 100.

64. M. Simon, *La Prophetie de Natan et le Temple*, Rev. d'Hist. et de Phil, Rel. 32 (1952), 41-58.

65. H. M. Wiener, *The Composition of Judges 2, 11 to I Kings 2, 46* (Leipzig, 1929), 5.

66. L. Rost, *Sinaibund und Davidsbund*, ThLZ 72 (1947), 130-134.

67. O. Eissfeldt, *Einleitung in das AT* (Tubingen, 1956), 324, 327.

68. J. L. McKenzie, *The Dynastic Oracles II S 7*, Theol. Stud. 8 (1947), 187-218.

he has assembled from a variety of cultural backgrounds (Assyria, Babylonia, Rome, and even England), he demonstrates that oracles on the everlasting permanency of a dynasty originate during the high point of a dynasty, never in times of descendancy. He applies this same law to the promise made to David's house.

This brief selection of contrasting opinions is enough to confirm the fact that modern investigation is drawing closer and closer to the historical credibility of the ancient narrative.[69] The traditional interpretation of the faithful has never doubted the genuinity of the prophecy. But it is well that this vital text has had to stand the cross-fire of criticism; it has emerged purified and better established than ever before.

Our understanding of the entire prophecy hinges on the proper interpretation of the individual key words. It would be a serious error to apply our modern concepts to the ancient text. On the contrary, we must examine the impact and meaning of certain key words at the time of David: house (*bayit*), seed (*zera‘*), Son of God, eternity, everlasting kingship (*‘ôlām*).

a) "House" (*bayit*):

Bayit refers not only to a residence, but also to a family, parents together with children and kin. Noah was to go into the ark with "his whole house" (Gn 7, 1); Yahweh strikes the "house of Pharaoh" (Gn 12, 7) for his abduction of Abraham's wife; Jacob gives "his whole house" (Gn 35, 2) the command to stay away from foreign gods. In addition to the individual house community, *bayit* can also refer to the larger family, the clan or tribe. Joshua, after the destruction of Ai, had the individual tribes come before Yahweh "by houses" (Jos 7, 14). Similarly, the whole people is referred to as "house of Israel, house of Judah, house of Aram." This usage is not restricted to the Hebrew language; Assyrian documents refer to the kingdom of Israel simply as "house of Omri" (*bit-ḥumuri*). — The word "house" can also refer to posterity. The father of Moses is called simply "the man of the house of Levi" (Ex 2, 1). The word refers particularly to the posterity of a king, a dynasty. During the secession of the Northern Kingdom, the northern tribes asked "what portion they now have with David's house" (1 K 12, 16). The man of God in Bethel announces "behold, a son shall be born to the house of David" (1 K 13, 2). This usage was not restricted to the house of David; a prophet also announced to King Jeroboam "that Yahweh will build a sure house for him" (1 K 11, 38). These brief examples, which could easily be augmented from a concordance of the Book of Kings, are

69. W. F. Albright, *Stone Age to Christianity* (1949), 33-47.

sufficient to prove that "house" is equivalent in meaning to dynasty. Accordingly, the expression "your house will abide forever" can only mean that David's dynasty is to rule forever.

b) "Seed" (*zera'*):

The meaning of *zera'* lies in the same direction as that of *bayit*. The word seed is used in reference to an individual child. Accordingly, Eve names her son for the fact that God has granted her another seed in the place of Abel (Gn 4, 25). Hannah prays before the Ark of the Covenant at Shiloh for Yahweh to send her a seed (1 S 1, 11). The collective meaning of the word, however, in the sense of "posterity" (Gn 3, 15; 12, 7; 13, 15), is much more preponderant. The protoevangelium speaks of the "seed of the woman and the seed of the serpent." More precisely, seed can refer to family descent (Ezr 2, 59) and especially the royal dynasty (2 K 11, 1). Thus, Athaliah wanted to extirpate the "whole seed of the kingship," that is, the entire dynasty.[70] If, accordingly, Yahweh promises David that he will raise up seed out of his own body, this can only refer to David's first successor on the throne, Solomon; but since seed and house must be interpreted together, the only logical conclusion is that seed refers not only to the immediate successor, the temple-builder Solomon, but to the whole dynasty to come.

c) "Son of God":

The statement "I will be a father to him and he will be a son to me" should not be particularly surprising in this context. The fact that David worshipped God as his Father is evidenced from the name he gives his son: Absalom, "my Father (God) is peace." The concept of a divine sonship, in the proper sense of the word, is certainly not within the confines of Israel's theological speculation; it seems, in fact, to be excluded. Yahweh has shown himself to be a Father to Israel; he had chosen Israel, formed, loved, and led her (Dt 32, 6; Is 43, 6; 63, 16; 64, 9). Accordingly, the Israelites were the children of his creation. The above sentence can thus mean only that Yahweh will show his special paternal love and care to the dynasty of David.

The contemporary world about Israel was familiar with a theology of God as king; but this theology cannot be taken as a parallel to Israel's monotheistic beliefs, and thus it has left no traces in the Bible. It was actually believed that the Egyptian Pharaoh had been born of the union between a god and goddess. In a sequence of paintings in the temple at Luxor, the divine generation of the Pharaoh is clearly presented; the first picture portrays the earthly and heavenly parents, Queen Maut-m-ua and King Tuthmosis IV (1422-1413), together with the goddess Isis,

---

70. Assyrian Equivalent: *zer šarri* — royal name.

embracing the queen, and the god Amon. Picture 2: the god Amon
enters the queen's chambers. Picture 3: Amon sitting before the queen,
symbolic of the sex act. There is a text as commentary: "Amon speaks to
his maid servant: Amen-hotep-hiq-wast is the name (of the child whom
you will bear) in your womb. He will be great.... He will make his
kingship perfect upon earth; he will raise and bear the kingly crown that
rules the earth, just like the eternal sun." Picture 4: Amon goes to the
god Khnum, who forms both gods and men, and gives him the command
to form the future child. Picture 5: Khnum forms the living image of the
child, while the goddess Hathor forms a twin image.[71] That the Pharaoh
was actually held to be the real son of god on earth is demonstrated by
the statement of the Sun King Ikhnaton: "I am thy son, who came forth
from thy body." [72]

The Babylonian and Assyrian concept of divine sonship was quite
different from the Egyptian conception. There is no question here of any
direct generation by a divine father and mother; but the birth of the
future royal child is attended by the gods. The gods form the body of
the child in his mother's womb and, when the child is born, he drinks
the milk of a goddess upon whose breast he is laid.[73] Such ideas are
directly opposed to Israel's religious beliefs. Yahweh is one, and he will
tolerate no other god or goddess. Sexual generation by divine parents is,
accordingly, inconceivable in Israelite mentality. Obviously, then, the
"father-son relationship" could only be conceived of in a symbolic manner.

The Biblical idea of divine sonship is closest related to the conception
prevalent in the Canaanite kingdom. J. Gray [74] points out that the
Canaanite kings held themselves to be the sons of El, and that this
divine sonship was never conceived of as an incarnation of the dying and
resurgent god. There are no texts which clearly attest to the cultic
veneration of the king during his lifetime. The kings were only men who
bore the sovereignty of the great El, who enjoyed the supreme kingship
among the gods. The sky god made known his will to the king through

---

71. A. Moret, *Du charactère religieux de la Royauté Pharaonique.* Ann.
du Musée Guinet, (Paris, 1902), 48-59 (pictures of Luxor).

72. A. Weigall, *Le Pharao Akh-en-Aton et son époque* (Paris, 1936),
129 VD 29 (1951), 39; ANET 371: Thy son, who came forth from
thy body. / J. de Savignac, *Théologie Pharaonique et Messianisme
d'Israel,* VT 7 (1957), 82-90. Proceed on the presupposition that the
Egyptian court influenced the court of Jerusalem, not only in political
matters, but also in religion. Stylistic similarities demonstrated between
Ps 2 and the enthronement dialogue between Pharaoh and his god.

73. R. Labat, *Le charactère religieux de la Royauté Assyro-Babylonienne*
(Paris, 1939), 53-96.

74. J. Gray, *Canaanite Kingship in Theory and Praxis,* VT 2 (1952), 193-
220.

the oracle of the prophets (Ugaritic: *trrm*, Hebrew: *tûr*, "to see, to have a vision"). As in many other respects, the Hebrew religion exhibits similarities with the Canaanite neighbors in respect to the office of prophecy, similarities which might appear very strange at first. But closer examination reveals the fact that Biblical prophecy, in its basic concepts, is not a derived phenomenon. The prophetic office in Israel will be expressly treated in the following volume.

d) "Forever" (*'ôlām*):

When we translate the word '*ôlām* as "eternity," we have already introduced a meaning which, strictly speaking, it does not have. Our concept of eternity is a clearly developed one, opposed to the transitory character of time. The root of the word '*ôlām* (*'lm*) means: "concealed." Looking backwards it refers to the long recesses of primordial time, and looking forward, it refers to the most distant future. '*ôlām* thus embraces the totality of time from the first beginnings to the most distant future, without implying any end or terminus to the sequence. In his essence, Yahweh embraces both poles. He rules from '*ôlām* to '*ôlām*. Subsequent theological reflection obviously develops into our more definite concept of eternity. '*ôlām* does not exclude our concept of eternity, but neither does it directly imply eternity.[75]

What David understood by the promised "everlasting" dominion of his house, is best understood by way of contrast with the house of Saul, from whom the kingship was taken back. David's dynasty, on the other hand, will rule forever, to the most distant future. David, in his prayer, thanks Yahweh for "having spoken of his servant's house for a great while to come" (7, 19).

The meaning of the prophecy is quite simple. It refers not only to his immediate successor on the throne, King Solomon, who was to build a temple for Yahweh, but to the dynasty as a whole, including the future Messiah. There will be good and bad kings. For the evil kings there will be chastisement. But one fact remains: the kingship will never pass from the house of David.

---

75. '*ôlām* with reference to the past, Dt 32, 7: "Remember the days of '*ôlām*, consider the years of many generations." — Referring to the whole period of human life: Ex 21, 6: "His master shall bore his ear through with an awl, and he shall serve him for '*ôlām*." — The duration of the world, Ps 77/78, 69: "like the earth for '*ôlām*." — Referring to the beginning of the world, Ps 89/90, 2: "Before the mountains were brought forth, or ever thou hadst formed the earth and the world, from '*ôlām* to '*ôlām* thou art God." — L. Murillo, Bibl 5 (1924), 291; H. von den Bussche, *Le Texte de la Prophetie de Natan sur la Dynastie Davidique biblique du temps. Ausführliche Untersuchung zum Begriff* '*ôlām*, RevTheol. et Phil. III (1952), 120-123.

This promise is so great and overwhelming that David goes into the "temple" to prostrate himself in the presence of Yahweh, who is enthroned over the Ark of the Covenant, and stammer his inadequate words of gratitude for this unheard of favor. There are no words for such a grandiose concept. In his prayer, David confesses that God's own "word and heart" (7, 21) watch over not only his own path, but that of all his people. It is no mere clever phrase, but rather an essential point of Biblical theology when we use the expression that God's heart is beating in human history. The words make it clear that the course of history is dependent not only on its human protagonists; above all human activity stands the "plan of God" (*dābar* — word), who, with all his "heart" (*lēbāb*), that is, with all his divine passion and love, is vitally intersected in the course of history and directs it towards its final goal. Only a strong faith in this God, active in human history, makes possible the prophecy about the everlasting kingship of David's house. His kingship is firmly rooted in God's master plan and it can be circumvented by no human power.

The words which Yahweh announces to King David through the mouth of Nathan the prophet are not merely a promise for the future. The difficult verse 2 S 7, 19 has been the subject of various translations. "You have treated me like a great man" (AT Henne), or "This is the vision which you bestow upon man" (Rehm EB). In the Jerusalem Bible, there are, quite properly, a series of periods to mark an omission. The translator did not know what to do with the expression *tôrat hā'ādam*. But it is precisely these words which bear the whole leit-motiv of the statement. The expression is related to the Accadian *terît niše*, the oracle by which human fate is determined. *Tôrat hā'ādam* thus means nothing less than "the determination of human fate." [76] In making known his will to the prophets, Yahweh, at the same time, determined the fate of David's dynasty. The house of David is a divine institution, independent of all human interference, and thus everlasting.

By his free choice of David's house, God's great plan of history [77] has entered upon a new stage. From times primordial,

---

76. H. Cazelles, VT 8 (1958), 322: De Vaux, *Les institutions de l'Ancien Israel. tôrah* is to be derived from the root *yarah*, "cast." *'ûrîm* is to be "the sacred lot," further developed in the meaning of "law, doctrine." — The covenant with David is to be identified with the promises made to the patriarchs, referring to the whole progeny and not merely the immediately succeeding generations. Cf. J. Scharbert, *Solidarität in Segen und Fluch im Alten Testament und in seiner Umwelt*, I (1958), 144ff: *Königssegen und Natanweissagung.*

77. J. Schildenberger, *Weissagung und Erfüllung*, Bibl 24 (1943), 107; 205-230. Ps 2 u. Ps 109/10.

mankind had been supported by its expectation of a dragon-slayer, someone who would restore the paradise that had been lost. In the covenant with Noah, God's blessing entered into the tents of Shem; in the Abraham covenant, the circle was drawn more tightly about the children of Israel. The dying Jacob prophesied that the scepter will not depart from the tribe of Judah. In the Sinai covenant, Yahweh becomes, in a particular manner, the God of the Twelve tribes. In the covenant with David (2 S 23, 5) God's salvific activity reaches an unheard of climax. When Yahweh's prophet announces the everlasting dominion of the dynasty of David, he furnishes the spark that kindles the prophetic expectation of the Messiah.

That David's faith in this "everlasting covenant" (*berît 'ôlām* — 23, 5)[78] of Yahweh with his house continued to live in later history is amply evidenced by Ps 88/89. But it was precisely this course of history that was to lead to a serious crisis in faith. The destruction of Jerusalem meant the demise of the Davidic dynasty. There was no longer any king from the house of David. Hence the passionate question of the psalmist: "Thou hast cast off David and rejected him.... Thou hast renounced the covenant with thy servant David; thou hast defiled his crown in the dust.... How long, O Lord? Wilt thou hide thyself forever?" The promise made to David also needed to be purified in the crucible of suffering. God's thoughts are not the product of man. He keeps his word and follows out his plan, but not the way man expects. The Babylonian hegemony came upon Palestine; the Persians, Macedonians and Seleucid rule. In Jerusalem there arose a new kingship, that of the Maccabees, and Herod the Idumaean, while the house of David had run out, impoverished and lost to oblivion. Then suddenly, with new power and brilliance,

---

78. The Ancient Near East is familiar with two kinds of *berît*, generally translated as "covenant"; the one, in which two partners of equal position bilaterally bind and obligate themselves; the other in which a sovereign imposes obligations upon his subjects, thereby determining their conditions and order of life. *berît 'ôlam* would thus be equivalent to *tôrat hā'ādām*, an eternal ordinance proclaimed by God himself. G. E. Mendenhall, *Covenant Forms in Israelite Tradition*, BA 17 (1954), 50-76.

the prophecy of David's eternal house is rekindled, this time on the lips of the Angel Gabriel, announcing to Mary the virgin: "The Lord God will give to him the throne of his father David, and he will reign over the house of Jacob forever" (Lk 1, 32). The people loved to refer to Christ as the Son of David. But what a mighty difference between his concept of the kingship and that of David's. He does not deny that he is king, in fact he openly admits this before Pilate (Jn 18, 33); nor does he deny that he is David's son, in fact he reduces the question *ad absurdum*: "Whose son is the Messiah?" — "David's" — "But if David calls him his Lord (Ps 109/110, 1), how is he his son?" (Mt 22, 45).

On a much more magnificent scale than anyone in the year 1000 B.C. could possibly have imagined, the ancient prophecy becomes reality. David thought in national and dynastic terms; he thought like a man of his age; but God was thinking on a divine scale. In Jesus of Nazareth, the true Son of God and the real son of David's house, there is a bond between the eternity of God and the transitory course of a human, sinful, and shattered dynasty. His kingdom bursts the narrow framework of a single nation; it is the world kingdom of all tongues and tribes, and his kingship bursts the bounds of human time. Elevated to the right hand of the Father, Jesus, true Son of David, rules forever.

CHAPTER IX

SECURING THE KINGDOM FROM WITHOUT

1) PUSH TO THE MEDITERRANEAN:

WITH laconic brevity, the Book of Samuel, in a single verse, recounts the outcome of a further war against the Philistines: "After this David defeated the Philistines and subdued them, and David took Methegammah (the mother city Gath) out of the hands of the Philistines" (8, 1). According to this account, David was not satisfied with defending the territory of Israel from Philistine invasion; he actually penetrated into the heartland of Philistia itself and subjected it to his sovereignty. Even though the treaty "metropolis or mother city of Gath" [1] is contested, other accounts clearly

---

1. The Hebrew text is obviously corrupt: *meteg ha'ammah* "bridle of the ell." Vulg thinks of tribute: *frenum tributi. meteg* means literally "bridle," but in a transferred sense it can mean "authority, rule." *'ammah* is used in connection with *'em,* "mother," in the transferred sense of "metropolis, mother-city." 1 Ch 18, 1 adds the words "and her daughters (cities)." But this does not give any intelligible meaning. Accordingly, Bressan 550 proposes the conjectural reading of *'et gat ha'amah* (the metropolis of Gath) instead of *meteg 'ammah.*

refer to battles which took place in the district of Gath (2 S 21, 20). We must also recall that David recruited 600 men for his bodyguard from the city of Gath. If Sayce's interpretation is not linguistically certain, at least it properly assesses the situation: David had gained control of "the high road to the sea." [2]

Where the Biblical text abandons our scholarship to pure conjecture, the results of excavation are surprisingly fruitful. The excavations at Tell Kasîle, 6 km (c. 4.1 mi.) north of Jaffa, in the present territory of greater Tel-Aviv, have shown that this site on the mouth of the Yarkon has had a rich history of human settlement. Twelve strata were uncovered. The lowest three (12 — 10) were Philistine. Then the city was destroyed by fire. The next level, the 9th, already yields objects which are characteristic of the Davidic-Solomonic era.[3] It is archaeologically certain that, towards the turn of the first millennium, the Philistine culture lost its individual characteristics, and the fine pottery work began to disappear. This can be explained by the fact that the coastal plains had come under the control of new masters, and thus within the sphere of new cultural influences. "The significance of the Philistine decline and the strong central government can hardly be exaggerated. It is almost equivalent to an economic revolution.

— Worthy of some mention is the proposal of Tolkowsky, *Metheg ha-ammah.* JPOS 1 (1921), 195-201, suggesting that *meteg* is a Philistine word with the meaning "iron staff." In this sense, David would have taken the iron ell-measure from the Philistines and introduced it as the standard into his kingdom as a standard of measurement. The linguistic basis is very shaky. / W. F. Albright, *Dwarf Mythology,* Isr ExplJ 4 (1954), 1-4 claims that David had taken something related to horse breeding from the Philistines. The concept of dwarfs working in the mines is current even in Canaanite circles. *meteg ha'ammah* is merely an abbreviation for *meteg bene'ammah,* that is, the bridle of the sons of the ell, the dwarfs, and thus the horse bridle, whose invention was ascribed to these industrious workers of the mines (?).

---

2. A. H. Sayce, *The Expository Time* 17 (1906), 215 treats it as a Babylonian loan word, *metiq ammati,* a technical term for "the great city on the sea."

3. B. Maisler, *The excavations at Tell Qasile,* BA 14 (1951), 43-49; Bibl 33 (1952), 560ff.

The Philistine power was broken; the mystery of iron working became common knowledge. From the post-Davidic era onwards, practically every peasant could fashion his own iron axes, hoes, plowshares, and sickles. This obviously resulted in an improvement in agricultural proficiency." [4]

Israel's new position along the sea coast, and her possession of the Plain of Sharon were the occasion of mighty plans, which became reality under Solomon, with the building of a fleet. David had made the breach; he had opened the way to the sea. No enemy could ever again threaten from the west. David was now free to concentrate his entire forces on his less settled boundaries.

2) WAR WITH MOAB:

"And he defeated Moab, and measured them with a line, making them lie down on the ground; two lines he measured to be put to death, and one full line to be spared. And the Moabites became servants to David and brought tribute" (2 S 8, 2). Despite the relationship of their ancestors and the friendly relations that had bound David to Moab — one of his ancestors had come from Moab (Ruth), and his parents had found refuge there — war broke out between Israel and Moab. Political situations quickly change, like the weather. Before, David had been a fugitive outlaw captain in the wilderness, but now he is a mighty ruler of united Israel. The family histories are presented down to their least detail, but our historian is silent on the greater events that move in world politics. In the present account, he does not even mention the occasion of the war. Judging from the drastic measures which David employed against the prisoners, it must have been a very serious dispute. Two thirds of the prisoners were simply cut down, and only one third was spared.[5] It is

---

4. C. E. Wright, *Biblical Archaeology* (1958), 117.
5. The "line," (*hebel*) is a unit of land measurement. In Arabic it is called *habul*, a cord some 5 m in length. Sammas-Rimmon (9th cent.) says of himself: "I destroyed their cities, took 3000 prisoners, and measured them with the line." S. Tulkowsky, *The Measuring of the Moabites with the Line*, JPOS 4 (1924), 118-121. — Noteworthy is

possible that Moab had joined the great alliance against David, and made treaties with Philistia, Ammon, Edom, and Aram, in an effort to keep David from the throne. We might find an echo of this in Ps 59/60: "Moab is my washbasin; upon Edom I cast my shoes; over Philistia I shout in triumph." After giving his attention to the Philistine problem in the west, David was free to embark upon his punitive measures against Moab. The wheels were beginning to turn. The great political transformation of the territories between Egypt and Mesopotomia could no longer be held in check.[6] Whether David wanted it or not, the next step was war with the Aramaean states. In this strategy he was following the footsteps of the Egyptian conqueror-Pharaohs, who enforced their claim to sovereignty all the way to the great river, the Euphrates. The descendancy of Egyptian power had resulted in a political vacuum in the middle country, making it possible for both the Hebrews and various Aramaean states to establish themselves in the territory. The Philistines were the first to attempt the establishment of their own sovereignty in Palestine, following Egypt's example. In this attempt they were definitively defeated by David. Now it was the Aramaeans, in the north, who made their influence felt in the power politics of that time. The first question to be settled was: Philistia or Israel. Further centuries will sound a different battle cry: Israel or Aram — until both parties, in their turn, are overcome by the resurgent empires from the land between the rivers.

3) WAR WITH AMMON AND ARAM (2 S 8, 1-12; 10, 1-19):

The occasion for this many years' war was an event which generally binds men together with ties of friendship. But when relations are overstrained on both sides, the eruption occurs where it is least expected. Nahas (serpent), the king of Ammon, had

the fact that the chronist does not record the cutting down of the prisoners, and omits all negative features of David's character.

6. A. Alt, *Kleine Schriften*, II (1952), 1-11: Palestinian states.

died. In those days, too, it was customary for neighboring govern-
ments to send envoys to express their grief. David, accordingly,
dispatched an appropriate message to Ammon. Just as with the
Aramaean Geshur, one of whose women he married as a pledge
of their alliance, David must have maintained friendly relationships with the deceased king Nahas. In terms of contemporary
politics, Ammon could only welcome a treaty with the King of
Judah, as a control against Israel. But when David became king
over all Israel, the situation was different. His former friends saw
his rise to the throne as a threat. We have no good reason to
doubt the sincerity and genuinity of David's message of con-
dolence. He wanted the friendly relations to continue with the
dead king's successor Hamun (merciful, — i.e., merciful is God).[7]
But the embassy was in for a terrible shock. Their sentiments were
not honored in Ammon; quite the contrary. The young king was
convinced by his counselors that the ambassadors were merely
spies in disguise, and that David was intent only on the "over-
throw" (10, 4) of the political situation in Ammon. Accordingly,
the ambassadors were treated shamefully. Such cruel mockery
seemed to be an innate characteristic of the Ammonites. They
had threatened the people of Jabesh that they would put out their
right eye; they now mistreat David's ambassadors by cutting off
half their beard and half their clothing and sending them on their
way.[8]

David had desired peace, but this cruel mockery had made
the Ammonites his enemies. Such mistreatment of his personal

---

7. David speaks of the friendly relationship (hesed) with which Nahash
   had received him, and this is the reason why the king wants to
   preserve his friendship (hesed).
8. The jest is really significant. The beard was torn or cut as an
   expression of grief (Jr 48, 37). The Ammonites cut off the envoys'
   beards so that, at least externally, they would appear to be fellow
   sympathizers, even though there was some doubt about the sympathy
   they felt. / A. Musil, *Arabia Petraea* (Vienna, 1908), III, 161 records
   how the Bedouins who lived in the neighborhood of Hebron cut off
   half the beard of a drunken man, a jest which led to an all-out war
   between the two tribes involved.

envoy could only mean war. This the Ammonites knew. Accordingly, they cast about for allies, and found them in the north, among the Aramaeans.

a) *The Battle At Rabbath-Ammon* (2 S 10, 1-4):

At considerable expense (10, 6) — according to 1 Ch 19, 6, 20,000 talents of silver — the Ammonites hired the military assistance of four Aramaean states, who were under the leadership of Hadadezer,[9] King of Zobah (8, 3). He was dreaming of a Syro-Aramaean empire. He wanted to unite the various independent Aramaean principalities under his sovereignty. Assyrian sources [10] record that he directed his campaign against the great river, where he snatched the cities of Pitru and Mutkinu from King Aššurabi II (1010 — 991). Such a man had no use for a strong kingdom of Israel; it went counter to his own plans for power. That is why the confrontation in Ammon was a welcome opportunity to intervene.

Together with Aram-Zobah, Aram-Rehob, Aram-Maacah, and Ishtob are mentioned. Their geographical location is the following: at the foot of Mount Hermon lie the small principalities of Aram-Maacah, with its capital city of Abel-Beth-Maacah,[11] and Aram-Rehob, which extends from the sources of the Jordan

---

9. "Hadad has helped." — Names compounded with Hadad were very frequent: Ben-Hadad (Son of Hadad, 1 K 15, 18), Abd-Addi (Servant of Hadad), Haddu-ram (Hadad is exalted). Hadad was the principal god of the Arameans. They had discovered his cult during their immigration into Syria, where they adopted it. The Canaanites referred to Hadad simply as Ba'al (Lord-God). As the thunderer (Rammon, Rimmon), he was the sky lord. A stele from Ugarit portrays him as pharaoh, a thunderbolt in his right hand, with which he shatters his enemies, and in his left hand the spears and sheafs of lightning. Two bull's horns extend from his helmet (DBS III, 1938, 480). He was presented as the storm and sky god with his throne upon a bull. Divine steles from Ugarit in A. Jirku, *Die Welt der Bibel* (Great cultures of Antiquity) 1957, table 50.
10. Bressan, 553.
11. Modern Abil el-Qamh near Tell el-Qadi, in ancient Dan.

towards Damascus. Ishtob [12] is to be located in the same general
vicinity. Examination into the Assyrian provincial divisions [13] has
definitely established the fact that Zobah is equivalent to the Assyrian Ṣubatu, and thus occupies a territory which begins north
of Damascus and must have embraced the entire district between
the wilderness and the Antilebanon, as far as Ḥums; probably
the fertile basin between the two Lebanon ranges was within
their sphere of power. The two principal cities of Zobah, as mentioned in 1 Ch 18, 8 are, doubtless, to be identified with Tubiḫu
and Kunnu in the Egyptian catalogue of Syrian cities which were
conquered by the Pharaohs of the New Kingdom. Both lay in the
vicinity of Ḥums. It is possible that the ancient Tubiḫu is identical with the later Baalbek. The location of Zobah along the edge
of the wilderness is also suggested by the fact that, in the seventh
century, the same district was a constantly threatened portal for
the inroads of the Arab tribes. They were simply following the
same migration pattern as the Aramaeans before them.[14]

The four allies led a considerable force into the field. Here,
once again, the word *'eleph* is generally mistranslated as thousand;
the result is an impossibly high figure. *'eleph,* according to the
military usage of the time, as we shall discover in connection with
David's census, refers to a clan or tribal levy. Accordingly, Zobah
and Rehob produced 20 companies, Ishtob 12, and Maacah 1.

---

12. Literally, "the man from Ṭob." A. Jirku, *Der Mann von Ṭob,* ZAW
    62 (1949/50) points to the usage of the Amarna letters in which
    'iš corresponds to *amelu,* "man, ruler," and generally refers to a
    regent of lower rank, a noble. The precise location of the "master of
    Ṭob" is contested. It is to be sought in northern Gilead (Jg 11, 3),
    identified by many as Ṭajibeh in Dan.
13. E. Forrer, *Die Provinzeinteilung des assyrischen Reiches* (1921), 62,
    69.
14. Albright, *Die Religion Israels,* 148, 236, Anm 6-8. / T. O'Callaghan,
    Aram Naharaim (1948), 124ff. / Abel I, 248 locates Zobah on the
    bend of the Nahr Litani, the modern Angarr, the Greek Chalcis. This
    is improbable, since from such a southerly position access to the
    Euphrates is hardly possible. The name Zobah might go along with
    the invention of copper: ṣôbah being derived from ṣehôbah, "golden
    red."

Concerning the total figures, it is impossible to be more precise, since the individual levies could vary considerably in strength. At all events, there was a considerable body of troops, which must not be underevaluated. Accordingly, David committed his best soldiers, under Joab's direction. The confrontation occurred at Rabbath-Ammon, the Ammonite capital. The enemy attempted to trap the Israelite army in a pincer movement. The Ammonites were based on their own city, while the Aramaeans marched to battle from the waters of Rabbah.[15] If Joab attempted an attack against the city, the Aramaeans would fall upon his rear and cut off his retreat to the Jordan. Joab, accordingly, divided his forces. He committed one division against the city, under the command of his brother Abishai. He himself undertook the confrontation with the united Aramaean forces and put them to flight. Joab then broke off the battle. He was not equipped to undertake a siege. This would require much greater strength. The pause in fighting was utilized by both sides, to reassemble and re-arm their forces.

b) *The Battle at Helam* (2 S 10, 15-19):

The new campaign was preceded by a great political conference of the Aramaeans under the leadership of Hadadezer. It was resolved to undertake a full scale attack against the Israelites. Even the Aramaeans "who were beyond the Euphrates" (10, 16) were won over to this proposal.[16] The military command was entrusted to Shobach.[17] This time David himself led the entire

---

15. Not in Madaba (1 Ch 19, 7), some 30 km south of Ammon. The reading can be explained by the interchanging of D and R: instead of *mydbh* read *myrbh*, the "waters of Rabbah." The capital of the Ammonites was called, more fully, Rabbath-Ammon, that is Great Ammon.
16. "The River" always means the Euphrates. The Aramaeans had thus crossed over the Euphrates and were causing great trouble to the Assyrians. It is one of the great ironies of history that precisely David's victory over the Aramaeans made it possible for Assur to begin its ascendancy, which was later destined to annihilate the Kingdom of Israel.
17. *Shobak* is perhaps a Hebrew name for "turning around or back," and is meant as a mockery.

Israelite force into battle. The confrontation took place near Ḥelam,[18] an unknown locale in Transjordania. The Aramaeans suffered a devastating defeat. 700 chariots were destroyed and 40 "divisions" ('eleph!) were shattered. Shobach himself was taken and killed.

When the Aramaeans realized that David could not be forced, they turned to peaceful overtures and became subject to them. This apparently means that they had to pay tribute. Their further support of the Ammonite cause was out of the question. David thus orders his captain Joab to settle with the Ammonites. The siege of Ammon was a difficult undertaking, but Joab forced the citadel and destroyed the city. It is in connection with the siege of Ammon that we locate the story of David's adultery with the wife of Uriah (Urias), which will be treated later.

c) *The Battle at Hamath* (2 S 8, 1-12):

Hadadezer was still unwilling to admit defeat. He continued to dream of a great Syrian empire; "he went to restore his power at the river Euphrates" (8, 3). When the embassy from King Toi of Hamath on the Orontes informed David that "Hadadezer was a man of war against Toi" (8, 10), this laconic report conceals the history of several campaigns which Hadadezer had undertaken against northern Syria, in an attempt to encompass Hamath and establish himself on the great river. The actual grounds for the new war against Hadadezer is not mentioned. It is a sign of David's military strength that, this time, the battle is carried into the heartland of Hadadezer himself. The decisive confrontation occurred in the neighborhood of Hamath (1 Ch 18, 3), in northern Syria, in the territory of the friendly King Toi.[19] The number of prisoners was very large, although, once again,

---

18. Identified by some as Aleppo, Assyrian Ḥalma. But the Israelite armies surely did not penetrate so far to the north. Probably modern 'Elamûn, 40 km northwest of Ammon, on the right bank of the Jabbok. Abel II, 247.

19. Not to be confused with Ḥamat on the Nahr Litani, where Bressan 553 locates the battle. This time the northern provinces are concerned.

it is not 20 "thousand" (*'eleph*), but 20 companies that were taken captive. On the occasion of the first Aramaean war, 33 companies had taken the field; there were 40 companies in the second war. Accordingly, if David succeeded in capturing 20 of them, this means almost half the hostile forces, although a precise count of their strength cannot be determined. Not knowing what to do with the 1700 horses he took, David had them hamstrung, to render them useless for warfare. He kept only 100 of the captured chariots, destroying the others. There is an echo of this victory in Ps 19/20, 8: "Some boast of chariots, and some of horses; but we boast of the name of the Lord our God."

There were two sequels to the war against Hadadezer. First there was the campaign against the Aramaeans of Damascus,[20] who had supported Hadadezer (2 S 8, 5). David defeated the city and established garrisons (*n*e*ṣibîm*) there, just as the Philistines had established over Israel. The second sequel to his victory was an alliance with Toi, the king of Hamath on the Orontes. The defeat of Hadadezer was new life for Toi. In order to secure the future of his country, he sent his son Joram [21] with rich gifts to David's court, to conclude a treaty. This sealed Israel's leadership in the Aramaean territory.

4) THE WAR WITH EDOM (2 S 8, 13-14):

In this case, too, the account furnished by the Book of Samuel is very brief; from the context, however, we may be quite certain that the war against Edom was occasioned by the Aramaean campaigns. It was while David was fighting against the Aramaeans in the north that the Edomites seized the opportunity to invade the exposed kingdom. The decisive confrontation

---

20. Hebrew *dammeśeq*, or *dar-meśeq* (1 Ch 18, 6), that is, "habitation in irrigated country." Abel II, 301. Antilebanon and Hermon produce numerous brooks which unite in the two principal rivers Abana and Parpar and turn the desert into an oasis. 691 m in elevation, Damascus belongs among the most ancient inhabitated areas of the Ancient Near East. Named in the Execration Texts. ANET 242.
21. According to 1 Ch 18, 10, Hadoram, abbreviated form for Hadad-ram, Hadad is exalted.

took place in the Salt Valley (*gê'melaḥ*).[22] The glorious victory recorded in Scripture hardly alludes to the extreme peril involved in the campaign, although it clearly evidenced it in Ps 59/60. The obvious reference in the Psalm is to a rejection of Israel's military power. Yahweh had given them a sign, but a sign to retreat, to flight. "Who will bring me to the fortified city? Who will lead me to Edom?" Accordingly, the battle must have fluctuated in the extreme. But Joab was not the man to be overcome by difficulties. According to 1 K 11, 15-17 he must have acted with great vigor and decision. For six months he remained in Edom "until he had cut off every male in Edom." These measures were directed principally against the royal house. Only Prince Hadad succeeded in escaping. He found political refuge in Egypt. Edom became a province in the kingdom of Israel. Israel thus acquired access to the Red Sea, across the bay of Elath. It was from here, during the days of Solomon, that the fleets sailed for the land of Ophir. Furthermore, Israel's yield from the productive Edomite mines was considerable.

5) SUBJUGATION OF THE CANAANITE CITIES:

From the days of their first entrance into the Promised Land, Israel had not succeeded in asserting mastery over the strong Canaanite cities which formed a defensive belt between the northern and the southern tribes. David found a solution to this problem. Where the Bible is silent we can reconstruct the course of the events on the basis of excavation. Towards the turn of the millennium, the cities of Beth-Sham, Taanach, and Megiddo were destroyed and rebuilt, this time by the Israelites, as the various names in the corresponding excavation levels clearly show. It was in this same period that Geber must have been incorporated into the kingdom.[23]

---

22. In modern Wadi el-Milḥ, 20 km west of the Dead Sea, a secondary valley of the Wadi Bir-Sebaʿ. The ruins of Khirbet et-Milḥ (salt ruins) have preserved the ancient name. R. de Vaux, *Samuel*, 166, identifies the Salt Valley with the Arabah basin, which already belonged to Edom.
23. On Beth-Shan and Gezer, cf. G. E. Wright, *Epic of Conquest*, BA

6) THE TREATY WITH HIRAM OF TYRE:

The Phoenicians, by the very position of the land they inhabited, were forced to look to the sea. The narrow coastal plain did not afford sufficient room for development or sustenance. They were, accordingly, forced to become the seafarers and merchants of the Ancient Near East. Because of the jagged and broken coastline, they never developed a unified state. The individual city states continued to assert their autonomy. Trade produced wealth and comfort. The cedar forests of Lebanon not only supplied the essential material for the construction of their own navy; cedar wood was much in demand, both by the Pharaohs along the Nile and the rulers of the land between the rivers.[24]

Since a new king was now in the ascendancy in Jerusalem, the King of Tyre thought it an opportune moment to establish a lucrative trade relationship. The embassy which he sent to Jerusalem was primarily concerned with this objective. Tyre had become Israel's nearest neighbor on the sea coast. The city was named from a rocky island just off shore, upon which it was impregnably built. Tyre (ṣur) means rock. Alexander the Great succeeded in taking the city only by constructing a huge earthworks, half a kilometer in length, which bound the city to the mainland.

The King of Tyre offered not only to furnish the technical assistance, the carpenters and masons, which David needed for the construction of his palace, but also to furnish the cedar wood. For the main rafters he needed beams of 20 to 25 m in length, and these were to be found only in Lebanon. Cedar was not only prized as building material; it also exuded a most pleasant aroma (Song 4, 11). The account of David's trade relationships with

---

3 (1940). On Ta'anak and Megiddo, cf. R. de Vaux, DBS IV (1948), 744.

---

24. On the cedar trade with Egypt, cf. the travel diary of Wen-Amon. Galling, TGI 36ff. The demand for cedar wood, for temples and palaces, in Mesopotamia, can be traced over the course of several centuries. Cf. ANET 25-27; 134, 240, 275-277, etc.

Hiram of Tyre,[25] as recorded in the Book of Samuel, follows immediately upon the conquest of Jerusalem. Apparently, David set about the construction of his new palace immediately following his conquest. This presents some chronological difficulty, however. Hiram survived David and also entertained friendly trade relationships with Solomon his successor, whom he assisted primarily in the construction of the temple. Accordingly, he would have witnessed the completion of this building in the 24th year of Solomon (1 K 9, 10-12), and thus must have reigned for 50 years. Such a lengthy reign is, in itself, quite possible. Pharaoh Ramses II reigned 67 years. But these facts are contradicted by the testimony of Menander of Ephesus, according to whom Hiram lived 53 years and reigned only 34.[26] Accordingly, the building of David's palace must be assigned to the later years of his reign. This would, obviously, appear to be more probable. This supposition is, further, confirmed by more recent chronological studies, according to which Hiram ascended the throne in the year 979/978 and Solomon in the year 971/970. Accordingly, David and Hiram were contemporaries for only 10 years, a sufficiently long period for the establishment of the friendly relations which continued between Solomon and Hiram after David's death.[27]

---

25. Abbreviation for '*aḥi-ram*, "My brother (God) is exalted."
26. Quoted in Bressan, 519.
27. J. Liver, *The Chronology of Tyre at the Beginning of the First Millennium B.C.*, IsrExplJ 3 (1953), 113-120.

CHAPTER X

THE INTERNAL ORGANIZATION OF
THE KINGDOM

SAUL'S court was marked by no particular distinction among the various official positions. Only the military was assigned to Abner. Saul was a man of war, and in the pressures of his reign, he could not undertake the construction of a civil administration. After the happy conclusion to David's wars, however, the situation was different. If the kingdom was to survive, it must be held together by a strong internal administration. It seems that David did not so much rely upon his own invention in this respect; he was guided rather by the rich experiences of Egyptian imperial administration, either directly through Egyptian officials or, what is more probable, following the example of the Canaanite cities which had spent long centuries under Egyptian influence. The influence of Mesopotamia, at this point in history, was too weak to be seriously considered. The fact that there were intimate relations between Israel and Egypt — even apart from the time of Israel's sojourn in the land of the Nile — is amply demonstrated by Solomon's marriage with a daughter of the Pharaoh. In all events, in the internal construction of his administration, David could well have been guided by foreigners.[1]

The Book of Samuel is certainly not interested in providing a very detailed account of the interior administration; it does not even present an explicit history of David's wars. The wars are all recorded as briefly as possible, and made to serve the larger purpose of depicting David's rise. For the rest, it is his concern with building a temple which occupies a place of primary interest. The constitution and administration of his government is merely touched upon, when names of individual court officials are mentioned without a more explicit description of their spheres of duty. The names and offices were, for the readers of that age, very obvious and easily understood; for us they frequently present a serious puzzle. The following officials are mentioned (1 S 8, 15-18; 20, 23-26):

1. The captain of the army: the military sphere was assigned to Joab: "Joab, the son of Zeruiah, was over the army." This position, apparently, dates from the conquest of Jerusalem. Joab was a warrior through and through, unwearying in his physical endurance, hard, unyielding, to the point of cruelty. Without him, David would not have been so successful in his wars. The king's administrative talent appears primarily in the fact that he knew how to find the right man for the right place.

The bodyguard, consisting of the Cherethites and Pelethites, were in charge of Benaiah, son of Jehoiada. Saul had already formed his own bodyguard, composed of Israelites. David was here breaking with tradition. He took non-Israelites into his service, to assure himself of a personal corps independent of the twelve tribes.

2. The *Mazkir*: This word is frequently translated "chancellor," but our modern concept does not correspond with that of ancient times. The root meaning of this word admits of two possibilities: either "remind, bring to memory"[2] or "inform."[3] In Egypt there was a "speaker of the

---

1. The Egyptian patterns must have been taken over, not directly, but through the Canaanite influences. Albright, *Die Religion Israels*, 136. / S. Morenz, *Ägyptische und Davidische Königstitulatur. Zeitschrift für ägypt. Sprache und Altertumskunde*, 79 (1954), 73. / J. van der Ploeg, *Les Chefs du Peuple d'Israel et leurs Titres*, RB 57 (1950), 40-61. / Noetscher, BAK 114 (officials), 145 (military).

2. Participle *hiphil* from *zakar*, "remind."

3. Joseph in Egypt asks his fellow prisoners to inform him of their

king" (*wham. w*). His duties are described on the stele of Intef. He had to regulate the court ceremonial, present the desires of the people to the Pharaoh, and communicate the Pharaoh's decrees to the people. When the prince went outside the palace, he had to supply the police protection.[4] The Mazkir is thus the intermediary between king and people, chief steward and "chancellor" in one and the same person. This was the duty of Jehoshaphat Ben Ahilud.

3. The priests (*kōhanîm*): It is important to note that the priesthood was also subject to royal authority. The king gives them their official call and can also depose them. The two priests Abiathar and Zadok do not yet bear the title of "high priest," although the title *rabbu kāhinima,* "the great one among the priests," is verifiable in Ugarit.[5] Even though the title is not yet used, the presence of two high priests in the days of David is an uncontested fact, although it admits of various explanations. Abiathar was entrusted with the high-priestly office as the legitimate successor from the house of Eli. After the massacre of the priests at Nob he had fled to David and, after the solemn transfer of the Ark of the Covenant into Jerusalem, he had continued to function in his priestly office there. Together with Abiathar, there is a second high priest, enjoying a like position, Zadok, whose genealogy (1 Ch 5, 38) is traced back to Aaron through Eleazar. It is possible that Zadok had already taken over the high priesthood under Saul, after the massacre at Nob, and David, after his victory over Saul, had retained him in this office. In this explanation, the presence of two high priests at the time of David would represent a religious and political compromise. Other scholars believe that Zadok had been a priest of the pre-Israelite city god of Jerusalem,[6] but had then embraced the Yahweh faith and continued the cult of the god Zedek (justice?) in a new form. The Aaronitic genealogy would then be invented, as a demonstration of his legitimacy. Although Israel did take over various Canaanite cult elements, as we shall discover later in the story of the temple building, this attempt to derive the Zadokites from the Jebusite priesthood seems most questionable. This dual high-priesthood was not abrogated until the time of Solomon. In the internal difficulties occasioned by the succession to the throne, Abiathar had taken the side

---

fate after their liberation by the Pharaoh. Gn 40, 14; cf. also Is 43, 26; Jr 4, 16.

---

4. J. H. Breasted, *Ancient Records of Egypt* (Chicago, 1906) II, 764, with a complete translation of the stele.
5. W. F. Albright, *From Stone Age to Christianity* (1949), 281. *The Religion of Israel,* 123.
6. H. H. Rowley, *Zadok and Nehustan,* JBL 58 (1939), 113-141. Taken over by H. Haag, Bibellexikon. 1450.

of Adonijah, and was accordingly deposed by Solomon and exiled into Anatoth. From this time onward, the Zadokites retained the office of high priest until the time of the Maccabees.

4. The scribe (*sôphēr*): In the Egyptian court there was an office of "scribe" (Egyptian: *ss*). He saw to the king's diplomatic correspondence within and without the kingdom. It is worth noting that precisely this official bears the Egyptian name Shisha or Shusha.[7] This official, most probably, was also charged with keeping the royal annals, administering the archives and the library.[8] These official court documents are frequently drawn upon by the Biblical history writers: they are referred to as sources in these terms: "Words of the days of the kings" (1 K 14, 19, 29; 15, 7, 23, 31, etc.).

5. Forced labor: The man in charge of forced labor is not mentioned in the first list of officials (2 S 8, 16) but in the second list (2 S 20, 24). This apparently means that with the increase in construction and building, this office needed to be created. His duty was to force the people to participate in the public building projects. For these projects, the Israelites employed not only slaves and members of subject populations, particularly the Canaanites, but also their own countrymen. Particularly during the days of Solomon, this recruiting for forced labor took on immense proportions (1 K 5, 13ff.; 12, 4ff.). In this respect, David's kingdom was no different from the great kingdoms of Egypt or Mesopotamia. There were also state officials. The man who bore such an office must obviously reckon with the hate of the people. In David's day, Adoram[9] was the man in charge. How thankless this position was is clearly demonstrated by the fact that an official of the same name, if not the same person, was stoned to death by the rioting workmen (1 K 4, 6; 12, 18).

---

7. R. de Vaux, RB 48 (1939), 394-405. / B. Maisler, *The Scribe of King David and the Problem of the High Officials in the Ancient Kingdom of Israel*, JPOS 13 (1946), 105-147 derives the name from the Hurrite. The MT reading is present as a further, Yahwistic, elaboration, understanding Serajah as coming from *sa-wa-sarri*.

8. As excavations have elaborately demonstrated, every temple and royal court had its archives and library. The same thing can be presumed of Jerusalem. A. H. Sayce, *The Libraries of David and Solomon*, Journal of the Royal Asiatic Society (1931), 783-790. / S. Yeivin, *Social, religious and cultural trends in Jerusalem under the Davidic Dynastie*, VT 3 (1953), 149-166.

9. Short form from *'adonî-ram*, "My Lord (God) is exalted." B. Maisler, *Zur Erforschung der Eigennamen der Hl. Schrift*. Lesonenu 15 (1947), 37-44.

6. The Privy Council: The statement that David's sons were *kōhᵃnîm*, that is, "priests," is surprising (8, 18). In like manner, a certain Ira was a *kōhēn*, a "priest." Does this mean that, together with the official priesthood of Aaron's family, David also established a new priesthood composed of members of his own family members? It is certain that as supreme lord and king, based on the precedent of ancient tradition according to which the heads of family and state could also exercise priestly functions, he himself had performed cultic activities. But it is hardly conceivable that David should have included his own sons among the ranks of the priesthood. Either he assigned them as his representatives at official functions, which the king was expected to perform personally,[10] or else *kōhēn* must have had a further meaning. Albright proposes the translation of "seer." [11] On that same basis, Bressan [12] translates the word *kōhᵃnîm*, in our present passage, as "counsellor." Thus, David would have formed a "privy council" composed of his sons and perhaps also drawing on the services of other experienced priests and officials — to advise him in his more important affairs of state.[13]

David thus gave the new kingdom a new form of government; it continues to present the impression of a patriarchal rule, but it is in the process of transformation into a strong centralistic administration, such as Solomon was later to effect. David was particularly wise in doing nothing to alter the tribal structure of the nation. The individual tribes he governed conjointly with the "elders of Israel," the heads of the individual tribes and clans. It was Solomon's day which first witnessed the breach of this framework, which was then replaced by a centralistic government with a new system of district division.

---

10. R. de Vaux, *Samuel*, 166.
11. W. F. Albright, *From Stone Age to Christianity* (1949), 33, 409. Not a loan word from the Arabic, as formerly supposed, but Old-Canaanite.
12. Bressan, 559. — J. A. Montgomery, *The Year-Eponymate in the Hebrew Monarchy*, JBL 49 (1930), 311-319 maintains that David's sons were established as "priests of the year," and that the year was named after them, just like the eponymous annual officials of the Assyrians. Little support in the text.
13. It is possible that the text is corrupt here and that instead of *kōhᵃnîm* (priests) we are to read *sôkᵉnîm* (chamberlains). This reading is recommended by LXX αὐλαρχαί; cf. Is 22, 15, where Shobna, the chief chamberlain, is actually called *sôken*. Albright, *The Religion of Israel*, 229, note 46.

CHAPTER XI

FAMILY TRAGEDY AND CRISIS IN
THE KINGDOM
(2 S 9 — 24)

UP to this point, David's career had been a continual rise. He was a master at exploiting the political situation for his own advantage, but his hands were still clean of blood and crime. The further course of his history shows the power of evil making its sure inroads into this extraordinary character. Times of persecution generally effect a moral intensity, a climax in moral purity and concern. On the other hand, an era of secure control is likely to effect a gradual corruption and moral rot. The man who appears to be safe against every attack is threatened most by this security. This typically human fate, with its sin and failure, asserts its mastery over David, too, and the Biblical author records it with the same candor and objectivitity which were so evident in the story of David's ascendancy. It is only in his battle with his passions, in the cycle of defeat and victory, that David's character attains its final maturity, a maturity which raises him above the measure of the ordinary man. It is the family tragedies and crises in his kingdom which gave him his epic and tragic death.

Literary criticism recognizes chapters 10-20 of the second Book of Samuel as a unified complex of tradition. The narrative is so vivid that we are forced to postulate an eye witness as its author. Someone in the immediate vicinity of the court and David's family must have recorded the incidents. We think of the high priest Abiathar [1] or Ahimaas,[2] the son of the high priest Zadok, or the prophet Nathan. [3] Hence also the almost universal agreement regarding the early dating of this section which assigns it to the tenth century, the golden age of Hebrew literature.[4] It is a masterpiece of the narrator's art, and there is hardly a parallel in Biblical literature.[5] The title, "Father of History" might better apply to the author of these chapters than to the famous Greek Herodotus who lived some five centuries later.[6]

The historical character of these ten chapters has never been seriously doubted. This unanimity of opinion also extends to the narrative skill which comes to such a perfect blossom here. The narrator is not only a chronist, concerned with delivering the facts; he is a psychologist and artist as well, reading into the innermost souls of his characters, and masterfully recreating their ideas and sensitivities.

Although there can be no doubt as to the historicity of the events narrated here, these chapters possess something of the character of a novel.[7] In this respect, the word "novel" does not imply pure fabrication. The subject matter is reality and not invention. But it is an historical narrative that achieves great depths of psychology, a history presented with the novelist's consummate skill and art. The narrator is a master of characterization. The characters he introduces are perfect types. David is presented in clear, sharp lines, with all his passion and weakness. Inexorably at his side, at once his Mephisto, his worse

---

1. E. Auerbach, *Wüste und gelobtes Land. Geschichte Israels von den Anfängen bis zum Tode Salomons* (Berlin, 1932), 245.
2. R. H. Pfeiffer, *Introduction to the OT* (1948), 357.
3. H. M. Wiener, JPOS 7 (1927), 139ff.
4. W. F. Albright, *From Stone Age to Christianity* (1949), 292.
5. O. Eissfeldt, *Intro.*, 33.
6. Bressan, 561.
7. Gressmann, 163, 181.

and at the same time stronger self, his soldier and captain Joab. David's sons, although children of the same father, are so different that they soon come to battle and division. The voluptuary Amnon, overcome by his own passion, Absalom the silent, the one who cannot forget, ever conscious of his purpose. Then the men in the background, not mere walk-ons in this tragedy, but living people with their own individual destinies to pursue.

All this justifies us in accepting the judgments of literary criticism [8] to the effect that these chapters represent the historian's art to a degree of mastery that is unequaled in any later historical narrative. Only the circumstance that this masterpiece is contained in the Church canon of Sacred Scriptures can explain the fact that it has remained inaccessible for so many scholars of our sophisticated age.[9]

If the entire section is completely lacking in miracles and wonders — a fact which has made no small contribution to its merit in the eyes of critics, there is still an unmistakable and consistent leit-motiv to the whole narrative, an unshakable conviction in divine providence.[10] Psychological motives are presented as the forces which figure in human behavior, but our narrator is much more than a psychologist. The ultimate object of his attention is not the human psyche, but the activity of God which permeates all things, before whom man acknowledges his guilt and from whom he receives the free gift of forgiveness. This most human of all Biblical narratives, which seems to have so little theological preoccupation about it, thus reveals, in all its depths, the very essence of Israelite historical writing; it is always a theology of history.

It is impossible to be more expressive in this respect. Retelling the story would be an inspired imitation that could never recapture the original. We cannot absolve our readers of their need to let the original power of the Biblical text work upon themselves. The following explanations are only a guide to a deeper under-

---

8. R. H. Pfeiffer, *Introduction*, 359.
9. W. R. Arnold, *Ephod and Ark*, 118, 8 quoted in Pfeiffer, *Introduction*, 359.
10. Gressmann, 182.

standing that has been made possible by the recent discovery of more ancient sources.

A) FAMILY TRAGEDIES

In the Talmud,[11] the reading of sections on Bath-Sheba's adultery and the rape of Tamar are forbidden because of their allegedly provocative and seductive character. Apparently, this prohibition regards only public reading, and this is quite proper. The fact that such "scandal stories" appear in our Bible is only a further indication of the complete "incarnation of the word." The Bible, as a book of revelation, is not destined merely to glorify man's grandeur before God, but just as freely to lay bare his whole human misery, which becomes visible whenever the "evil impulse" [12] gains power over his heart.

1) DAVID'S ADULTERY WITH BATH-SHEBA (2 S 11):

Five brief verses are enough to outline the tragedy which, like a flood of passion, comes bursting down upon David's soul (2 S 11, 1-5): resumption of the war with Ammon (1), David in the palace (2), the possibility of sin (3), the deed (4), and the consequences (5). Whereas the progress of the Ammonite war is recorded in quick, sure strokes, almost too briefly, the events at the royal court are described in comfortable detail. In the one, it is only the course of the war that is important; in the other it is the exploration of human character.[13]

The introductory dating is characteristic of ancient warfare: "In the spring of the year, the time when kings go forth to battle." The ancient Hebrew year began in the spring month of Nisan

---

11. Mišna, Megillah 4 (3), 10. / A. Geiger, *Urschrift und Übersetzung der Bibel* (Frankfurt a. M. 1928), 368.
12. *Yĕser hāraʻ* Gn 8, 21.
13. Gressmann, 154.
14. *litešûbat haššanah* — "on the return of the year." Vulgate: "vertente anno," is thinking of the end of the year, which reading does not give the proper sense. Bressan, 573.

(March/April). The rainy season was past, the wadis no longer contained so much water, and the land was dry so that it was possible once again to bivouac in the open country. After the successful outcome of the campaign against the Aramaeans, all that remained was the final reckoning with Ammon, from where the spark of war had first originated. This campaign was left to Joab, David's captain. David set him in charge over "all Israel" (11, 1), that is, the entire military levy, in order to assure him of a speedy and certain victory. The military strategy of that day first laid waste the surrounding countryside and then encompassed the capital for a siege. The capital of the Ammonites is here called simply "Rabbah," the "great city." The full name is *Rabbath bene-Ammon,* the "great city of the sons of Ammon." Situated near the source of the Jabbok River (the present-day Nahr-ez-Zerqa, the Blue River), which flows in a long arc towards the Jordan, at a point where several valleys converge, the city was destined by nature itself to occupy a predominant position in the Transjordan. This is also the reason why ancient Rabbah rose to the position of capital city of the new state of Jordania, under the name of Amman. The Rabbah of the sons of Ammon was a twin city, the lower city on the river (749 m) and the citadel on the rock, modern el-Qalaah (850-860 m). It is 110 km from Jerusalem and 64 km from the Jordan.[15]

While the army was in the field, David remained in the city of Jerusalem. The circumstances which led to the adultery are interesting from the point of view of popular custom.[16] The noon rest period or siesta is part of the way of life in southern countries. In order to escape the oppressive hot air in the rooms, it was customary to take the siesta, where possible, on the roof terrace of one's home. David did the same thing. "He was walking upon the roof of the king's house." From here he could look down upon the lower courts and houses that surrounded the palace. As he did so, on this day, he saw a woman taking the

---

15. Outline of the city and description in R. Boulanger, *Moyen Orient* (Les guides bleus), Jordanie 466ff. / H. Haag, Bibellexikon 1396ff and Galling, BRL 432ff.
16. Gressmann, 155.

ritual purification bath.[17] "She was purifying herself from her uncleanness" (11, 4).[18] The name of the woman was Bath-Sheba (Bethsabee),[19] daughter of Eliam [20] and wife of Uriah (Urias),[21] a Hittite [22] in David's service. The lines of relationship are not clearly recognizable. If Eliam, Bath-Sheba's father, actually belongs to the Thirty (2 S 23, 24), then we have the psychological key for understanding many difficult changes of allegiance. In this case, a certain Ahibaal, David's counsellor, would also have been Eliam's father and Bath-Sheba's grandfather. On the occasion

---

17. Vulgate has misconstrued the situation, having the woman bathing on the roof terrace. The word "roof" is to be referred to David, who could see down into the other courtyards from his palace roof.

18. Sexual relations were veiled, among the ancients, with a very special reticence. They made one "unclean," that is, incapable of taking part in public worship. Thus, after the menstrual bleeding, women were obliged to undergo a ritual bath which "purified" them, that is, made them capable of partaking in public worship, seven days after the flow had ceased. These are the very days which modern biology considers as generally unfertile. Immediately after this period, the woman is most likely to conceive, and we can presume that this is the most likely explanation of Bath-Sheba's case (Lv 15, 19ff).

19. Bath-Sheba is interpreted in different ways: "daughter of the oath," daughter of the seventh day," "daughter of satiety," so far as the possible Hebrew roots are concerned. Other authors see Sheba as a reference to the Babylonian "seven divinity" (*ilu si-bi*), the seven winds, which were venerated in Canaan as well, as the bringers of fertility. A. Jirku, *AO Kommentar sum AT* (Leipzig, 1923), 64. — Since Bath-Sheba's husband was a Hittite, A. H. Sayce, HUCA (1942-43), 98 takes Bath-Sheba as the Hebraized form of the Hittite *bat-hepa*, "daughter of the goddess Ḥepa." The non-Israelite origin of the name is also advanced by *EncMikr* II, 379.

20. "El (God) is my relative."

21. From the sound of it, a genuine Hebrew and Yahwistic name: "My light is Yahweh." But a Hittite-Hurrite derivation is more probable. *ewri* (*ewar-ur*) is frequent in Hittite names, e.g.: *Ew(a)ri-Teshup*, "God Teshup is the Lord." Uri-yah, corresponding to "God Yahweh is my Lord." *EncMikr* I, 178ff.

22. Hittite need not be understood necessarily as National Hittite, a member of the Hittite nation, whose empire collapsed in the stormy period of the sea peoples' invasions; it is equivalent to non-Israelite. De Vaux, *Samuel*, 172.

of Absalom's revolt, Ahibaal would then have abandoned David and gone over to the revolutionary cause simply because he had not forgotten David's adultery with his granddaughter.

Meantime, destiny pursued its course. The love scene in the palace is recorded with all due reticence. Only the absolutely necessary information is presented. "The reader's suspense is carefully kept alive by Bath-Sheba's message to David. Now it is the king's problem to keep her from punishment and himself from public scandal." [23] In such cases there was a law regarding both parties: punishment by death (Lv 20, 10; Dt 22, 22; Code of Hammurabi n. 129).

David at first attempted to hide the fact. He had the soldier Uriah come back from the camp at Rabbath-Ammon and invited him to visit his wife and "wash his feet." [24] Such a visit, of course, would have concealed David's fatherhood of the expected child. Uriah, however, was too much a soldier to avail himself of this special privilege, while his comrades, and even the Ark of Yahweh, were living in tents in the open field. He spent the night at the door of the king's house and did not go down to his own home. David's second attempt, making Uriah drunk, met with no greater success. This put David in an extremely delicate situation. Public scandal seemed unavoidable. But one foul deed inevitably leads to another.

"The technique of our narrator is perfectly splendid. He understands how to keep his readers in a state of breathless suspense. The subtle way in which the contemplation of foul deeds slinks about in the darkness of human thinking is inimitably portrayed in the letter concerning Uriah and in Joab's reply." [25] David sent Uriah with the ill-famed letter back to camp. Joab was ordered to place this man at the most dangerous point of

---

23. Gressmann, 155 — W. Kornfeld, *L'Adultère dans l'Orient Antique*, RB 57 (1950), 82-109.
24. After a journey of 110 km Uriah had a right to rest. It was a characteristically oriental practice to invite someone to wash his feet after a long journey (Gn 18, 4; 19, 2; 24, 32). Uriah was expected, of course, to go home and visit his wife.
25. Gressmann, 155 .

battle, then to leave him without support so that he would be certain to fall. This, of course, is precisely what happened. The messenger who brought the report of the unsuccessful attack upon Rabbah provoked the king's criticism and anger. "Why did you go so near the city to fight? Did you not know that they would shoot from the walls?" (11, 20). But when the messenger, in conclusion, as an afterthought, mentioned that Uriah had also fallen, the king's attitude changed. No more fierce anger, merely the common expressions of sympathy: "Do not let this matter trouble Joab, for the sword devours now one and now another" (11, 25). As an official honor to the widow of a' great warrior, David now took Bath-Sheba into his harem. Thus the outward appearances were saved: the adultery and the murder which followed were not only sealed, but camouflaged under the cloak of royal benevolence. Evil, which makes its way in stealthy silence, seemed to be triumphant. Life would simply have returned to normal, as in so many Oriental court affairs, if there had been no prophet to take a merciless stand against evil, proclaiming it for what it is, unmasking the secret intentions of the human heart.

The prophet Nathan came before the king and proposed a case for judgment. Unsuspecting, the guilty king must now pronounce his own sentence. In open accusation the king might have brusquely turned aside. But Nathan's parable prepares him, interiorly, to recognize his own desperate situation. The parable is drawn from everyday life in Palestine. It smacks of the shepherd's life, and also testifies to the social distinctions and contrasts prevalent at David's time. Rich and poor are played against each other. It is not the social import, however, which interests the prophet, but the moral aspect. The evil heart of the rich man, who despite his many sheep, steals the one single and dearly beloved sheep that is the sole property of the poor man and slaughters it for his guests, so fires the righteous spirit of the king that he jumps up in anger and pronounces the sentence of death upon the cruelty of the rich man. What follows cannot be outdone for sheer dramatic impact. We hold our breath. The prophet says, short and simple: "You are the man" (12, 7). It was a test of Nathan's courage, and he proved to be a true precursor of those great prophetic figures of the past who did not shrink before the fearsome prospect of telling the truth to the mighty ones of this earth.[26] What will David do now? For a long moment, the decision hung on a single thread. Will he also silence the mouth of this unpleasant nemesis? But at that very moment David's spiritual grandeur stands revealed. He had had the courage to sin, but now he finds also the greater courage to confess his sin. "I have sinned against the Lord" (12, 13).[27] The death penalty, which David deserved for his sin, would not be required, but the child of that sin, according to the prophet's clear foretelling must die. As long as the child still lived, David fasted and prayed to preserve the spark of life. But when it died, he saw it as a judgment of God and surrendered himself to God's just disposition (12, 15-25).

"Then David comforted his wife, Bath-Sheba, and went into her" (12, 24). The women had their own quarters (Gn 24, 67; 31, 33; Jg 4, 17). It was an exceptional case for the man to bring the woman into his own room, like the bridegroom in the Song of Songs (1, 4). The narrative seems to give the impression that the second child born of their union was Solomon. In the list of Bath-Sheba's children in 2 S 5, 14 and 1 Ch 3, 5; 14, 4, however, Solomon is named as her fourth child. The historian has here omitted the names of the other children as unimportant.

---

26. The Hebrew text is composed in rhythmic prose, as it frequently is in the case of prophetic oracles. Many scholars, however, consider this as a secondary insertion into the text (Gressmann, 156; Pfeiffer, *Introduction,* 353). The alleged grounds are not convincing. We are willing to admit a certain literary stylizing by the author of the book, but the fact of prophetic confrontation cannot be simply interpreted out of existence. — Cf. the "Lamentations of the Garrulous Farmer" from Egypt, complaining that the powerful of this earth are seizing everything for themselves, contrary to all right and justice. ANET 409, Gressmann, AOT 33.

27. For the theology of sin the conception expressed in this passage is extremely important. Adultery is not merely a human affair; the man who sins attacks Yahweh. Cf. 2 S 12, 9: contempt for the voice of conscience is contempt for the words of Yahweh himself.

It is generally the mother's prerogative to name her child [28] (Gn
4, 1. 25; 19, 37; 1 S 1, 20; 4, 21). According to the present text,
however, it was David who gave his son the name *šelōmōh,* Solomon. For the Hebrew ear, the name clearly plays upon the concept of peace (*šālôm*), since Solomon's kingdom represents the
great and idealized era of peace for Israel. So much for the
popular etymology. Scientifically, the derivation of the name
points in a different direction. The city of Jerusalem, as we have
pointed out above, had been named for the healing god *Šalim*
(later form: *Šulman*) who was widely venerated between Asia
Minor and Egypt. Accordingly, we find a great variety of names
formed with the element *šalamu,*[29] for example, *a-bi-ša-la-mu* or
a-bu-še-lim (my father is *Šalim*), *i-li-ša-lim* (my god is *Salim*),
sa-lim-a-hu-um, (*Šalim* is my brother). The Hebrew *šelōmōh*
and the Grecized form Solomon would thus be an abbreviated
form of a longer name compounded with the divinity *Šalim-Šulman,*
with the meaning "consecrated or belonging to the god *Šulman.*"
Since David was such an ardent advocate of belief in Yahweh,
it is impossible to explain this name as a revision to the more
ancient pagan customs. Abraham had already identified the
god of Jerusalem with the supreme God, the creator of heaven
and earth.[30] It is in precisely such circumstances that we can
best see how the faith of ancient Israel stood squarely in the midst
of its Semitic environment, and still managed to rise above it.
The real Šulman-healing-god for David was Yahweh. David's
deeper religious convictions are expressed by the surname which
the prophet Nathan gave the child Solomon. Upon Yahweh's
command he called him *yedîd-yâh,* that is, "Yahweh's beloved."
But this surname no longer appears in the Bible. The omission
has been explained as the result of its holiness: it could not be

28. BHK suggests the conjectural reading: "*she* called his name . . . ."
29. K. L. Tallquist, *Assyrian Personal Names* (1914), 190b.
30. Cf. Gn 14, 19. The divine pithet *'elpkone 'ereṣ* "God, El, Creator
    of earth," or in the fuller form: "Creator of heaven and earth," is
    found already in the 14th century in the age of the Ugarit epic. W.
    F. Albright, Notes on Ps 68 and 134. Norsk teologisk Tidskrift 56
    (1955), 1-12.

used in everyday speech. But this is not a convincing argument.[31] Other scholars think that the kings of Israel all had two names, a private name and a throne name, which was given to them on the occasion of their succession to the throne.[32] But this can hardly be the case for Solomon; already at birth he is called Jedidiah. We must consider this not so much a symbolic surname, which did not find its way into everyday usage, as rather the vehicle of a prophetic promise.[33]

Meantime, Joab had succeeded in storming the capital of the Ammonites (2 S 12, 26-31). He had won control of the "city of waters." For us, the expression is no longer entirely clear. It can refer to the lower city, situated along the river; but the taking of the lower city would not yet make him master of the strongly fortified citadel. Scholars have thus been inclined to identify "city of waters" with the water supply system. Excavation has discovered a complicated network of tunnels, which supplied the beleaguered city with water.[34] Just as in the conquest of Jerusalem, Joab thus struck against their vital nerve, the water supply. Sooner or later the beleaguered citadel would have to capitulate. It was at this moment that Joab sent his messengers to David, inviting him to be present for the final storming of the city; it would then be not Joab's name, but David's which was imposed upon the conquered city.[35] Among the plunder from this city, the most precious treasure mentioned is the golden crown of the city god Milcom,[36] which weighed a talent of gold,

---

31. R. Flint in *Hasting's Dictionary to the Bible* IV, 559b.
32. R. de Vaux, *Samuel*, 179. / A. M. Honeyman, *The Evidence for Regnal Names among the Hebrews*, JBL 67 (1948), 13-25.
33. Prophetische Namengebungen Jes 7, 14 (Emmanuel); 60, 14, 18; 62, 4.
34. Abel II, 425 — Galling, BRL 433.
35. The victor imposed his name on the conquered city. Cf. Jerusalem gleich Davidstadt. / H. Kruse, *Ethos victoriae in VT*, VD 30 (1952), 71.
36. Today generally identified as the god Molok or Molek, derived from the original form Muluk, "king." A south Mesopotamia text from the 24th century records the offering of sacrifice, on the 27th of every month, in honor of ma-al-kum. A. Bea, *Moloch in den Marita-*

and was adorned with precious stones.[37] It was these precious stones and not the heavy crown itself which David placed upon his own head (12, 30). Concerning the manner in which David disposed of his prisoners, the present state of the Masoretic text is not sufficiently clear (12, 31). In view of the initial challenge and the embittered warfare, harsh treatment would not have been surprising. The Vulgate interprets the obscure text in the sense that David had the inhabitants of the conquered city led out to be "sawed and cut to pieces." [38] But this can hardly be the case. During the rebellion of Absalom, David was strongly supported by the King of Ammon. This presupposes much more lenient treatment in the present circumstances. Obviously, the "sawing and cutting into pieces" could not refer to the men themselves — this would have been an act of unheard of cruelty — but to the stone and wood on which the prisoners were forced to work as forced laborers. Hence we must translate: "He brought forth the people who were in it, and set them to labor with saws and iron axes, and made them toil at the brick-kilns." This would be the perfectly normal way of putting prisoners of war to work. The city itself — probably only the fortifications — was destroyed and the entire district of Ammon was incorporated into the kingdom of David. With the eventual collapse of the Davidic-Solomonic empire, the Ammonites later recovered their independence, rebuilt their fortress, and remained the hereditary enemy of Israel.[39]

2) THE RAPE OF TAMAR (2 S 13, 1-22):

Tamar is the only one of the apparently many daughters of David whose name had been handed down. The reason for this

---

feln, Bibl 20 (1939), 415. / N. Schneider, *Das Scheusal der Ammoniter*, Bibl 18 (1937), 337-343; 19 (1938), 204.

37. The weight of the Israelite talent is unknown; an Assyrian talent weighed 60 kg. De Vaux, *Samuel*, 190.
38. A. Condanim, *David cruel par la faute d'un copist*, RB 7 (1898), 253-258.
39. W. F. Albright, *Notes on Ammonite History*, Misc-Ubach (1953), 131-136.

was her tragic fate: "The tragedy that unfolds here only demonstra tes the powerful tension at work within the great family of David. Love, passion, hate, revenge, and murder are the destructive forces which, inevitably, reach the boiling point. David, in the forgiving kindness of his old age, appears almost as a weakling, left to the mercy of his wild son." [40] Once again we must marvel at the artistry of our author, who is not content with a mere record of the facts: he paints a psychological drama which remains without parallel. The characters are sharply defined: the young and innocent Tamar (palm), sister of Absalom, both of them children of Maacah from Geshur, and her half-brother Amnon, David's eldest son from his marriage with Ahinoam, and thus his destined successor to the throne, an unrestrainable young man who burns with a sick and impetuous love for his half-sister. This passion tormented him so much that he became ill.[41] Even for him, her half-brother, it was no easy task to gain access to Tamar, since the princess was well guarded and apparently lived in her own quarters within the palace. His "good friend" Jonadab had some clever advice to offer. He suggested that the young man, already consumed with the pangs of unrequited love, should actually pretend to be sick and ask for Tamar as his nurse. David was glad to grant the capricious patient his request.

The unsuspecting Tamar comes and prepares the desired "heart-shaped cakes." [42] While she is giving him this food, his passion erupts. The maiden attempts to defend herself. "Such a thing is not done in Israel" (13, 12). Having no other recourse, she suggests marriage; her father David would surely have no objection.[43] But he did not want to wait that long. He overpowers

---

40. Gressmann, 163.
41. Egyptian love poetry also makes frequent reference to being sick from love, the sickness being capable of cure only by the presence of the "sister." ANET 468.
42. Untranslatable word play in the Hebrew: *libbeb lebibôt,* "to heart heartlets," i.e., to make little cakes in the form of a heart.
43. Marriages between half-brother and sister were not extraordinary during the patriarchal era (Gn 20, 12), but were forbidden by the Mosaic law (Lv 18, 11; 20, 17; Dt 27, 22). From Tamar's words we can assume that such marriages were still allowed during the royal era.

his own half-sister. Who can understand the riddles of the human heart? No sooner was his will accomplished than the passionate young man no longer cared to see the woman he had shamed. His passionate love turned into an equally passionate hatred (13, 15). "Arise, be gone." He had no further words for her. This she could not understand. He called his slave: "Put this woman out of my presence, and bolt the door after her." Now she was only "this woman," shamed and desecrated. In her misery, the hapless maiden rent the long sleeve of her garment,[44] strewed dust over her head, and, crying and lamenting, laying her hand upon her head,[45] she ran to her brother Absalom. He was barely able to comfort her: "He is your brother; do not take this to heart" (13, 20). He himself, however, took the affair very much "to heart." Such an outrage must be avenged and expiated. Absalom knew how to wait and hold his peace. With uncanny dedication to his ultimate objective, he prepared for the day of vengeance.

It was some two years later that Absalom invited all the princes of the royal house to celebrate the shearing festival at his estate in Baal-Hazor.[46] Amnon was among the guests. He apparently felt that Absalom had already long since forgotten his affair with Tamar. But it was Absalom's characteristic way of acting that he prepared something long in advance and then, when the moment came, acted with lightning speed. When the hearts of

---

The rape of a virgin was, however, something unheard of in Israel. The meaning of the word *nebalah* extends from "vulgarity, baseness, pride," all the way to "godlessness." Cf. P. Jouon, Bibl 5 (1924), 357-361.

---

44. Illustration of a maiden similarly dressed on an ivory from Megiddo. *Westminster Atlas* (1953), 46, fig. 29.

45. The mourners on the Ahiram sarcophagus likewise have their hands placed on their heads. Gressmann, AOB 665, 666. – DBS III, 466.

46. Modern Tell 'Aṣur, about 10 km north-northeast of Bethel, modern Betîn, 1010 m elevation. Absalom's holdings were thus located 30 km north of Jerusalem, in the tribal territory of Benjamin. Was this perhaps proscribed property of King Saul's?

all the guests were "merry with wine," Absalom ordered his servants to strike Amnon dead. In his conception of things, this was not fratricide, but the performance of his sacred duty. For Amnon's crime, death was the penalty set by law (Lv 20, 17). The outrage was thus expiated, but now the law of blood vengeance applied. Absalom had to flee. He made his way into his mother's home country, Geshur, and stayed with his grandfather Talmai (13, 37).

B) CRISIS IN THE KINGDOM

The aged David must now think seriously of the problem of succession. He had the prophetic assurance that the throne would abide within his house, but no decision had been given as to who was to inherit this throne. According to the right of primogeniture, Amnon should have followed him upon the throne. But Amnon had been put to death by Absalom, in his revenge for the rape of his sister Tamar. It is possible that the expiation of this crime was not the only consideration which motivated Absalom in killing Amnon; after the death of Amnon, he was next in the line of succession. But as a fugitive in Geshur, he had very little chance. His father's wrath against him and his outlaw's status among the people effectively barred his way. Absalom, however, had friends in court. He himself was a man who knew how to wait and lay his plans, until the propitious moment came. His uncle Joab carefully prepared the way for his return. He could not present the problem openly before David. Accordingly, he sent a wise woman from Tekoa (Thecue), an ancient Canaanite settlement, some 9 km south of Bethlehem. As Nathan had done on a former occasion, she presented a case to David for his decision as supreme judge (2 S 14, 4ff.). As she begins to speak, she certainly gives the impression of describing a genuine family tragedy. Her husband is dead. Only two sons remain, and they begin an open war against one another. One of them is slain. Now, his relatives invoke the law of blood vengeance and demand the death of the second. But this would involve the complete extinction of "spark and name." In this case, *summum jus* would become *summa injuria*. The obligation of maintaining the family line is higher than the obligation of blood vengeance. Thus, David swore that not a hair of the surviving son's head should be harmed. This was a solution that might well make the woman happy. But she continued to speak, carefully spinning the situation, so that David soon realized that someone else was acting through this woman. Immediately he thought of Joab. Then the woman refers to him as an "angel of God," an exaggerated bit of politeness, but the statement that assured her goal. David begins negotiating with Joab regarding the prospect of Absalom's return. During the three years of exile, David had adopted a much more resigned attitude, but his righteous anger had not completely disappeared. He was willing to permit Absalom's return, but he forbade him all access to the court. But Absalom, from his new position of vantage close to home, was able to remove this obstacle as well. When Joab no longer wanted to represent his cause at court, after the course of two more years, he set fire to Joab's ripe barley field, thereby forcing him to act as intermediary once again. This time David capitulated completely. Absalom was free to come to court. The sentences that follow are like the return of the Prodigal Son. David was waiting upon his throne. For five long years he had not seen his son. Then Joab leads Absalom into the room; Absalom prostrates himself in reverence and touches the floor with his forehead. But his father David stands up from his throne, raises the lost son to his feet, and kisses him. In this kiss he has forgotten everything. He feels that he has once again won the heart of his son. But what tragedy is encompassed by this scene. If we only reflect that this son, welcomed home with open arms, is soon to stretch out his hand against his father's throne and, further, is destined to fall by the hand of Joab, the very man who has made possible his return and reconciliation, then we see the terrible evil and ruin that is set loose by Absalom's hunger for power. David had managed to unite the interests of the opposing tribes, and to erect a unified kingdom, acting with decisive bravery and great diplomatic skill. But Absalom's revolt was to cast this young and unsettled kingdom into a serious state of crisis (2 S 13, 29 — 14, 33).

1) ABSALOM'S REVOLT:

"This competely unified narrative is the longest in all the historical books of the Old Testament; the other narratives which might be compared with this have resulted only from the accretion of what were originally smaller individual units into one larger composition. A proportionally briefer span of time is here developed with greater attention to detail. The two days in which David flees from Jerusalem to Mahanaim embrace some twelve scenes. The constant change in situation, the great wealth of personalities, the frequent and sudden changes in mood — these reveal a well developed technique and an advanced degree of narrative art. Just as surely as the material treated can be considered as historically reliable, equally certain, on the other hand, is the fact that the historical facts are stylized. What we see is thus reality, but not the mere sober narrative of what took place; the events are all artistically enhanced. We thus have one of the most beautiful of all historical accounts, greatly enhanced by the skill of the novelist." [47]

a) *Absalom's Family* (2 S 14, 25-27):

In connection with Absalom's return to Jerusalem, our author provides a brief account of Absalom's family. Absalom himself is presented as a handsome young man, the ideal royal prince, a man without fault or failing. The proud glory of his head was his wavy hair, which he cut once a year. The weight of the hair cut off was 200 shekels by the king's weight.[48] As we gather from the narrative of the sheep shearing, Absalom had property of his own. According to 2 S 14, 27 he had three sons and a most beautiful daughter; according to 2 S 18, 18, while still alive, he had a monument erected so that his name would at least be

---

47. Gressmann, 181 .
48. An improbable figure! Based on the larger shekel weight, 16g, 8.4g on the smaller standard, about 1½ kilo. LXX gives only 100 shekels, which does not make the figure appreciably more credible.

preserved, since he had no children. We might thus conclude that his sons died at an early age. His only daughter Maacah was married to Rehoboam (Roboam), Solomon's son (1 K 15, 15).[49] The reason why Absalom had no further children is unknown to us. It lies like a dark shadow upon his family life. Lack of children could be interpreted as a curse from God.[50] But our narrator spends no further time on the subject; his interest is taken up with the coming revolt.

b) *Preparation for the Revolt* (2 S 15, 1-12):

As we have already seen, Absalom was a man who prepared his plans from afar and then, when the favorable moment had come, proved lightning fast in their execution. No one could have any further doubt that he meant to succeed David on the royal throne. His next move was, in terms of conditions in his day, a new and unheard of ostentation. He surrounded himself with a bodyguard of 50 "men to run before him" and appeared in public with a chariot and horses. He gradually began to win the heart of the people. There are discontents in every age. Their discontent may have grown in proportion to the length of David's reign. Problems continued to grow, and the administrative machinery of the young state was not equal to the increased demands. The normal suits and contentions were decided by local and tribal courts, as before. In more important cases, an appeal to the king may have been the rule. Whenever the discontents came to Jerusalem to have the king decide their case, Absalom was there to greet them at the city gate. This is the time-revered tactic of all demagogues who desire power. Absalom went among the people and spoke to every new arrival: "Where are you from? From what city? What brings you here?" He had no interest in achieving an objective decision. He was concerned only with power. He had an answer for everyone, but there

---

49. This presupposes that Maacah is older than her royal consort. This has led to the conjecture of an abbreviated expression here. Instead of daughter, we should translate granddaughter — there being no special word for this in Hebrew. But since kings attach great importance to marriages contracted with royal blood, this marriage with an older woman is certainly quite possible. Bressan, 621.

50. Cf. 1 S 1, 4ff. Hannah, the mother of Samuel.

was poison in his answer: "See, your claims are good and right; but there is no man deputed by the king to hear you. Oh that I were judge in the land! That every man with a suit or cause might come to me, and I would give him justice." With such tactics, he gathered all the discontents about him, men who hoped for a new and better future after his succession to kingly power.

After thus undermining David's position for four long years, he struck a decisive blow, disguised beneath the mask of religion. He asked David for permission to go to Hebron, in order to fulfill a vow he had made in the days of his exile. It is a puzzle that David should have agreed to this whole arrangement. Was he blind; was he no longer able to evaluate the political situation? The only really satisfying explanation is the fact that he was still Absalom's father, and that he simply could not believe in the revolt of his own son. David kissed his son and sent him away on his "pilgrimage."

The manner in which Absalom prepared for this "pilgrimage" must certainly have aroused the suspicion of an acute political observer. With Absalom some 200 men set out, all of them ostensibly invited to the "sacrificial banquet." David's best counsellor Ahibaal [51] was part of the "pilgrimage." The conspiracy had continued to grow in alarming proportions. A signal had been prearranged for the partisans throughout the entire kingdom: "As soon as you hear the sound of the trumpet, then say, 'Absalom is king at Hebron!' " (15, 10).

Absalom's rebellion shook the kingdom to its very roots. The situation is clearly recalled in Ps 3: "O Lord, how many are my foes! Many are riding against me; many are saying of me, there is no help for him in God." But in this very moment of extreme peril, the lion David rises once more. With his usual

---

51. "My brother is Baal." Since Baal (Lord, God) was later used exclusively of the Canaanite divinities, the Masoretes disfigured the name to form the word: Ahitophel, "my brother is abomination." Ahibaal comes from Giloh in the vicinity of Bethlehem. If he was really Bath-Sheba's grandfather, then his betrayal of David is easier to understand.

quick and decisive strokes, he very soon makes the necessary provisions and decisions to assure his eventual victory; meantime he must resort to flight.

c) *David's Flight from Absalom* (2 S 15, 13-17, 29):

Absalom had made good preparations. When David himself discovered that "the hearts of the men of Israel had gone after Absalom" (15, 13), this means that the *coup d'état* had been widely received with sympathy and enthusiasm. Under such circumstances, any defense of Jerusalem was inconceivable. Hence the decision to immediate flight. Only the ten wives of second rank remained in the city. In these hours of treason and defection, the characters all stand revealed for what they really are.

Could David rely on his bodyguard, the Cherethites and Pelethites? What would be the allegiance of the 600 mercenaries from Gath, under the direction of Ittai?[52] The mercenaries are not particular about what master they serve, provided they are well paid. But Ittai does not belong to the type of mercenary captain that is always bent on personal gain; in his eyes, faithfulness was more than silver. It is an irony of fate that Philistine mercenaries protect the king of Israel. David thus had a nucleus of faithful troops upon which he could build his resistance. He takes his stand in the Kidron Valley and lets the bodyguard and mercenaries march by.

The priesthood also kept faith with David. The high priests Zadok and Abiathar were prepared to bring the Ark of the Covenant up the Mountain of Olives (15, 23-29), but David turned them back to the holy city. The motives which prompted him are characteristic of both his faith and clever planning. Human wisdom told him that the Ark of the Covenant would only be a hindrance on the flight that lay before them. If the priesthood continued to hold faith with him, they would be of greater service to him by remaining in the holy city than by sharing in his flight. But David's faith is also in evidence. If

---

52. Abbreviated form for *itti-yah*, "with me is Yahweh." Maisler suggests a Hurrite origin. *EncMikr* I (1955), 791.

Yahweh has rejected him, the Ark will be of no avail. But if, on the other hand, Yahweh has truly chosen him, then Yahweh himself will lead him back into the holy city, to his holy tabernacle. The procession with the Ark of the Covenant thus withdraws into the city and David's first loyal followers make their way into the city abandoned by their king.

Now David sets out upon his *via dolorosa* along the Mount of Olives.[53] The way is stony. The fact that David goes barefoot, with veiled head,[54] is not so much a picture of the king cast down from his glory into the depths of misery, but rather that of a penitent. He sees his downfall in a religious light. Yahweh's hand is at work.

Dispatches of alarm follow close upon his flight: "Ahibaal is among the conspirators with Absalom" (15, 31). Nothing strikes closer than the betrayal. Even Ahibaal, his friend, table-companion, and counsellor had raised his heel against him.[55] But, on the other hand, an aged man — his clothing torn out of grief, his head strewn with dust — rushes up to meet the fugitive king. It is Hushai (Husai), the "friend of the king." [56] What was this old man to do on the flight? He would only be an obstacle. But he could be of real service to the desperate cause of his master if he went over to the rebels, made it a point to seek out Ahibaal's counsel, and then kept David informed of events in the rebel camp. Hushai, as David's second confederate, thus makes his way back into the very city into which Absalom is making his triumphal entry.

The events are closely crowded. David has only a few hours head start. His rebellious son is already in possession of the city as his fugitive father reaches the heights of the Mount of Olives. There are always people who know how to use times of crisis and upheaval for their own personal advantage. Such a man was

---

53. The difference in elevation from the valley to the Mount of Olives is 150 m.
54. "Veiling the head" is a sign of grief. Cf. 2 S 19, 5; Jr 14, 3; Est 6, 12.
55. An echo in Pss 40/41, 54/55.
56. "Friend of the king." Translation of the Egyptian court title: "who is known to the king." De Vaux, *Samuel*, 195.

Ziba, the servant of Mephibaal,[57] the crippled son of Jonathan, whom David had brought to the royal court (2 S 9, 1-13). Hardly had David crossed the heights of the Mount of Olives, when Ziba came to meet him with a couple of asses, saddled, "bearing 200 loaves of bread, a hundred bunches of raisins, a hundred of summer fruits, and a skin of wine." For David, at this point, it was a token of assistance which the clever Ziba meant to render him. Deceitfully, he claimed that his master Mephibaal had gone over to Absalom. David was hit hard by the news, but he could easily understand that Saul's family would adopt such a course of action. In gratitude for the proffered assistance, he assigned all Mephibaal's property to the clever servant. He acted most hastily in taking this man at his word, but in the press of the moment he had no time to verify the man's account and provide himself with accurate information.

The most bitter element in any human misery is mockery. David was not spared this either. Hardly had he reached Bahurim (Baurim), on the eastern side of the Mount of Olives, when he was met by the Benjaminite Shimer (MT *Šim'i,* Vulg. *Semei*), who cursed him as a "man of blood and worthless fellow" and threw stones at him (16, 5-13). Such shameful treatment was more than Abishai, son of Zeruiah, could bear. His blood began to boil: "Why should this dead dog curse the lord my king? Let me go over and take off his head" (16, 9). But David had a different answer. Here he attains his true heroic proportions, far beyond the measure of a normal man: "What have I to do with you, you sons of Zeruiah?" (16, 10).[58] Just as in the days of his

---

57. "From the mouth of Baal." Similar Babylonian names: Ša-pi-Bel — "from the mouth of Bel; Ša-pi-Marduk"— "from the mouth of Marduk." The Masoretes regularly replace the element "baal" with "boshet" (abomination). Mephibaal was five at the time of the battle of Gilboa. His nurse dropped him during the flight and he remained lame 2 S 4, 4.

58. The idiom "what is to me and you?" generally signifies the forceful rejection of interference: cf. Jos 11, 12; 2 S 16, 10; 19, 23. This usage is the key to our Lord's words in Jn 2, 4. Jesus emphatically rejects his mother's suggestion, which was based on a purely human appraisal of the situation, and then proceeds to render assistance in his own, wholly unexpected manner.

prosperity, so now in his moment of deepest degradation, David sees not men at work, but Yahweh himself. If Yahweh had ordained that Shimei is to humiliate him, there is no point in asking why (16, 10). He finds calm assurance in the hope that Yahweh will one day show him mercy instead of shame. In this respect, David recalls the figure of Job, who also placed everything in the hands of Yahweh: "The Lord gave, and the Lord has taken away; blessed be the name of the Lord" (Jb 1, 21). David's flight becomes a pilgrimage of penance. Interiorly, David will not be broken by this catastrophe. It turns him into an heroic penitent, such that his behavior is a puzzle beyond the understanding of his companions.

In forced marches — they had to reckon with immediate pursuit — the 40 km from the Mount of Olives to the Jordan ford near Jericho were quickly put behind them. Only here was it safe to stop for breath. Fording the river was no simple task. But on the other side, across the river, there was security. Here David could wait for the first reports about the political upheaval in Jerusalem (16, 14).

d) *Absalom's Seizure of Power* (2 S 16, 15-17, 23):

Hushai left the Mount of Olives and returned to the city. At the same time, Absalom was making his triumphant entry. The rebellious son and his fugitive father were only a short distance apart, upon their separate paths. The future fate of both father and son is now entrusted to the hands of the aged Hushai, who had to wage a gigantic duel with Ahibaal, with David's life and death hanging in the balance. Immediately after his entry into the city, Absalom convoked the new imperial council. What was his next step to be?

The rebel party was primarily interested in making any further reconciliation between father and son an absolute impossibility. If Absalom ever reconciled with David, then their treason could not go unpunished. It was Ahibaal who gave the diabolical advice that Absalom should immediately take possession of his father's abandoned harem. Ordinarily, such an act would have been a public expression of succession to the throne of an exiled or deceased monarch.[59] In this case, however, it was a question of father and son. Absalom did not shrink from accepting this advice. Accordingly, they pitched a tent for Absalom upon the roof, and Absalom went to his father's concubines in the sight of all Israel. A grotesque irony of fate. From this same roof terrace David had first began his adultery with Bath-Sheba. His sin came back to rest upon his own head (16, 20-23). If we are correct in our supposition that Ahibaal was Bath-Sheba's grandfather, then this advice was obviously tinged with vengeance. The violation of his granddaughter was now being paid for in full, by the shameful treatment of David's harem.

In an attempt to assure the rapid and complete destruction of David's cause, Ahibaal then proposed that the pursuit be taken up immediately, during that very night, in order to strike David before he had an opportunity to assemble his forces. The old man offered to lead the campaign himself. 12,000 men would certainly be enough to overpower David with his approximately 2000 troops. It would be best to avoid an open battle. A sudden, lightning-quick attack would completely scatter the royal forces. Once David himself was killed, the rest of the people would go over to Absalom and peace (Šālôm) would be established (17, 3).

The plan found favor with Absalom; but he wanted to hear the advice of Hushai as well. Ahibaal's proposals had been short, decisive, and confident of success. It would take no little persuasion to counterbalance his effectiveness. Hushai, accordingly, embarked upon a masterpiece of rhetorical art. By way of introduction, he admitted that Ahibaal was obviously a most extraordinary counsellor, but this time he had apparently decided upon a less than perfect plan. Ahibaal's reaction to this statement might well be imagined. It is obviously an easy thing to fall upon a crowd of fugitives and dispatch them; this time, however, it is no ordinary band of fugitives, but King David, the "man of battle" ('iš milḥāmâh), who would be aware of the danger and would thus be spending the night not in the open field but in a cave or some other hiding place. The proposed night attack would

---

59. De Vaux, Samuel, 198.

thus be a wasted effort. They would have to count on serious losses. David's men, the heroic young warriors, would be deeply embittered at the sudden change in their situation and they would fight like a she-bear robbed of her young or a wild boar driven into a corner. And if even a few of the attacking party were to fall, the news would travel quickly throughout the kingdom, creating a new panic, and popular sympathy would swing back towards David. Then everything would be lost. In such a situation, it was a mistake to resort to any uncertain expedients. They must be certain. Ahibaal's plan offered too little guarantee of success, and was thus to be rejected. It was better not to strike at once, better to have a little time, to consolidate their power, to organize the army; then success would be assured.

The faithful Hushai was successful in his artistry. Absalom took his advice and thus sealed his own doom. Ahibaal immediately realized that his game was lost. With cold deliberation he foresaw the likely consequences; he saddled his ass, rode home, made his will, and hanged himself.[60] — A perfect type of the traitor Judas.

Now it was the high priests' turn to keep faith with David. Hushai informed them of the council's decisions. They sent this information to En-rogel [61] with a maidservant, who could hardly arouse suspicion. There Jonathan and Ahimaaz, the two young sons of the high priest, were in hiding. They received the information from the maidservant and immediately set out upon their way to report to David. But they were observed and Absalom was informed. The pursuit was taken up immediately. The two young men reached Bahurim, on the eastern side of the Mount of Olives, where they hid from their pursuers in a cistern. The woman who owned it, with great presence of mind, spread a cloth over the cistern's mouth and scattered grain on it. When the pursuing party came to that very house, she told them that the two young men had already left and had probably

---

60. After the failure of their conspiracy against Ramses III, the parties to the plot all committed suicide. ANET 215.
61. South of Jerusalem, where the Kidron and Hinnon valleys intersect. Modern Bir-Ajûb, "the well of Job." DBS IV, 912.

reached the big water cistern.[62] As soon as the danger was passed, they came out from hiding and hurried along their way, bringing David the news he so eagerly awaited. Once again he was saved.

e) *The End of Absalom* (2 S 17, 24-29, 9):

Although Absalom had rejected the plan of immediate pursuit, this does not mean that he put off the decisive confrontation for any great length of time. At all events, the preparations may have been going on for some time, as the text seems to suggest at first reading: "Then David came to Mahanaim, and Absalom crossed the Jordan with all the men of Israel." If both operations took place simultaneously, the following would be the telescoped course of events: from the Jordan to Mahanaim is a distance of 40 or 45 km, which ordinarily required a march of two days. On the second day after his seizure of power, Absalom could thus have crossed the Jordan, and on the fourth or fifth day he would have reached the battle ground. This interval is much too short for both sides to have assembled their full forces. Upon the advice of Hushai, Absalom had actually assembled the military levy of all Israel (17, 24), and this took some days. Head of the army was Amasa,[63] Joab's cousin. This was a battle not only of son against father, but also nephew against cousin.

David lost no time. His old decisive ways are once again in evidence. With Mahanaim as his center, he organized the resistance. His lenient treatment of the Ammonites now stood him in good stead. In addition, there was spontaneous sympathy for the persecuted king. Shobi, King of Rabaath-Ammon, Machir of Lo-Debar, with whom Jonathan's son had found a welcome refuge (2 S 9, 4-5), and the otherwise unknown Barzillai brought "beds, basins, and earthen vessels, wheat, barley, meal, parched

---

62. The woman uses the word *mîkal*, which occurs only in this passage; Assyrian *mêkaltu* means "water reservoir." Bahurim must have been well known in antiquity. Bressan, 649.

63. Abbreviated form for *'amaś-yah*, "Yahweh has borne" (?) -- son of Abigail, David's sister.

grain, beans and lentils, honey and curds and sheep and cheese from the herd." The old warrior Joab once again proved to be a savior. In short order he had put together an army from nothing, an army that must have numbered several thousand men.

Although Absalom had done him immeasurable harm, David's love for his lost son had only increased. When the army, in companies and divisions, passed by the gates of Mahanaim in review, David's fatherly affection for Absalom appeared once again, and it must have shaken even the most seasoned of his warriors. He ordered his soldiers to spare the life of Absalom.

The decisive battle took place in the forest of Ephraim, in Gilead (Galaad).[64] Joab had relied upon the wooded terrain to overcome some of the imbalance between his own military strength and the superior forces of Absalom. Relying upon his vastly superior strength, Absalom joined battle on what was an extremely unfavorable terrain for his troops. He had no room to develop his plan of battle. "The forest devoured more people that day than the sword" (18, 8). In his wild flight, Absalom's thick hair caught in the branches of a large oak and he remained hanging there;[65] the mule he was riding passed on, and left him hanging betwen heaven and earth, unable to free himself.

When this was reported to Joab, he promised to give the man who killed Absalom ten shekels of silver and a suit of armor. But the man who reported it was unwilling to kill Absalom, and

---

64. The name has been interpreted as contemptuous by many authors: Ephraim was situated in the land west of the Jordan. But it is always possible for an Ephraimite clan to have migrated into Transjordania where it acquired a new territory to settle and even gave the country its name. The woods of Ephraim must be located not too far from Mahanaim. Modern es-Salt, which has preserved the Latin word *saltus* (woods), is some 20 km SSE of Tubel ed-Dahab (Mahanaim). Today there are only remnants of the ancient forestation.

65. The text does not make it clear how Absalom was left hanging. The general interpretation is: "by his hair." Others understand that he caught his head between the branches of the tree and was stuck there. A similar fate is recorded of the Abyssinian king Takia Haimanoth II. Gressmann, 179.

referred to David's express orders. Then Joab himself took
three spears and ran Absalom through. The dead body was
thrown into a grave and stones were piled up above it.[66] Then
Joab had the bugle sound pursuit. The battle had been decided
with Absalom's death, but for David this was no triumph. Quite
the contrary, when he heard of his son's death, he was deeply
moved, and went up to the chamber over the gate, and wept:
"Oh my son Absalom, my son, my son Absalom" (19, 1). This
outburst of grief expresses the whole tragedy of life. In view
of this family tragedy, David completely forgot the crisis of
the kingdom. The victorious warriors crept silently away as if they
had done something evil. Only Joab was able to bring David
back to the reality of the situation. David then took his position
at the city gates, to welcome home the returning troops. It was
a bitter victory, but David mastered his emotions and once again
set about the task of restoring order to the tottering kingdom.

This time we cannot say that his work was crowned with
success. All he could do was wait; he did not want to resort to
force. The rebellious party might come to its senses. To whom
was the nation to turn, if not to their king? Israel was certainly
prepared to receive David back. Diplomatic negotiations were
initiated; but there was some difficulty with Judah. It was the
tribe of Judah who had been most active in supporting Absalom's
rebellion. David charged the high priest in Jerusalem with the
task of feeling out the sentiments of Judah. By way of reconciliation, he promised to put Amasa, the leader of the rebel army,
at the head of his troops, in place of Joab. This was a bold
political maneuver, dictated by a spirit of compromise, but not
destined to any real permanence. The negotiations, however,
were successful: David once again won the hearts of the men

---

66. Absalom, during his lifetime, had already had a monument-pillar
erected to his memory, apparently a stone stele with his name en-
graved on it. This practice he no doubt borrowed from his Aramaean
ancestors. W. F. Albright, *The Religion of Israel* (1956), 121. —
The so-called tomb of Absalom in the Kidron Valley has nothing to
do with this monument. It is a product of the first century before
Christ. H. Vincent, RB 58 (1951), 362ff.

of Judah (19, 15). They came to escort him back into his
kingdom.

But precisely in this episode of crossing the Jordan, there
were new difficulties between the representatives of Judah and
the northern tribes of Israel (19, 41-44). The northern tribes
felt cheated. They felt that the king had been stolen from them
by Judah. The motive force in the rebellion had been only partially
Absalom's ambition in refusing to wait until his father's death
left him the throne. Such a case, in the ancient world, could
hardly be considered a rarity. But this rebellion had involved more
than personal interests within the royal house. In the last analysis,
it was the expression of tribal differences between north and
south. Even after Absalom's death, this wound remained un-
healed.[67]

On the way back to the capital, three episodes are recorded
as a counterbalance to the story of David's flight. Shimei and
Zibea, with troubled conscience, came to meet David (19, 16-
24). — Shimei had cursed David for a man of blood and was
afraid of punishment. David, however, magnanimously forgave
him. Zibea had lied to David, saying that Mephibaal had also
joined the rebel cause. David was magnanimous towards him
as well and divided the property between Mephibaal and Zibea
(19, 25-31). Most touching of all was the leave-taking from the
aged Barzillai at the Jordan (19, 32-41a).

2) REVOLT OF THE BENJAMINITE SHEBA (2 S 20, 1-22):

Even before David could reestablish his power, the quarrel
broke out again between north and south. Once again it was
clear that the royal power was not absolute, but rather dependent
upon the free allegiance of the tribes. David was an elected monarch. If he no longer satisfied the wishes of his electors, he was
faced with rebellion and secession. The northern tribes complained
that their king had been stolen by Judah (19, 42). The tribe
of Judah claimed ties of blood relationship to the royal house,

_____

67. Gressmann, 180.

while Israel, on the other hand, could point to a clear majority:
"We have ten shares in the king, and in David also we have
more than you. Why then did you despise us? Were we not the
first to speak of bringing back our king?" (19, 44). These
harsh slogans turn into equally impassioned battle cries for the
struggle between north and south. Even David could not manage to
settle their quarrel in time. "It was Sheba, of the tribe of Benjamin,
who first sounded the battle song which was to become the
Israelite Marseillaise; its political result was the split of the
northern Israelite tribes from David and his house"[68]:

> "We have no portion in David,
> and we have no inheritance in the son
> of Jesse;
> every man to his tents, O Israel" (20, 1).

It was at the Jordan that the men declared their allegiances.
David's return to Jerusalem did not take place under a lucky
star. Upon his arrival home, he set aside those concubines who
had been violated by Absalom and no longer went into them
(20, 3-4); but then his new preoccupation with the preservation
of his kingdom demanded all his attention. It soon became obvious
that entrusting Amasa with the supreme command of the military,
while it had been a clever move towards reconciliation, was not
a politically sound appointment. David sent Amasa off to put
down the revolt. In three days he was to summon all Judah.
In this he failed. Meantime, Sheba was threatening to become
more powerful than Absalom. Accordingly, David entrusted
Abishai with the command of his own personal bodyguard, the
Cherethites and Pelethites, and the troops of Joab. He was
to crush Sheba before he managed to make himself master of a
fortified city. But, in this new shift of power, what was the
position of Joab the discarded general? Abishai was, after all,
his brother; but would he consent to serve under the supreme
command of his cousin Amasa?

---

68. Gressmann, 180.

The nucleus of David's army, under Abishai, was already encamped at the "great stone" near Gibeon (Gabaon), when Amasa finally appeared with the new army. Job went out to meet him. As he went forward, his sword fell from its sheath, as if by accident. He picked it up with his left hand and, as he approached Amasa, he spoke these friendly words: "Is it well with you, my brother?" [69] With his right hand he seized Amasa's beard, and with his left he struck him a blow in the body, shedding his bowels to the ground, without striking a second blow (20, 10). Then a man from Joab's troop was ordered to stand by the corpse and cry: "Whoever is for Joab and David, let him follow Joab!" (20, 8-13). Once again, Joab had seized the upper hand. With his customary severity and dispatch, he cleansed the country-side of rebels. Sheba took flight, with the last of his faithful followers, towards Abel of Bet-Maacah.[70] This city is called a "mother in Israel" (20, 19),[71] that is, a district settlement upon which other cities and villages were dependent. Joab threw up a rampart around the city and undermined the walls. A wise woman (20, 16) provided the final answer. She called to Joab from the city walls and reproached him for trying to annihilate a "mother" in Israel. Joab demanded only the head of Sheba, and promised to depart as soon as he secured it. Within a short time, the head of Sheba was cast over the wall. They brought it to Joab, mounted on a pike, and he immediately sounded the signal to abandon the siege and then dissolved the army. They all returned to their own tents, but Joab returned to the king in Jerusalem (20, 14-22). He must have received a rather cold reception. Once again, as so frequently in the past,

---

69. Literally: "is peace (šālôm) with you, my brother?"
70. Modern Tell Abil, upon which the village of Abil el-qamḥ is built. In the ruins it is still possible to recognize the location of the ancient acropolis. Situated on the west bank of the Jordan, 10 km from Dan.
71. The term "mother-city" (metropolis) was current usage in Phoenicia as well. Coin inscriptions from Beirut: leLaodikea, 'em bi-knaʻan, "Laodicea, mother in Canaan"; leSidonâim 'em Kambe, Aphô, Kit, Ṣor, "Sidon, the mother of Kambe (Carthage), Hippo, Kittim, and Tyre." — E. J. Pilcher, A Mother in Israel PEQ 54 (1922), 323.

David owed Joab a great debt of gratitude. His strong hand had saved kingdom and crown. But at the same time he shuddered in the presence of this man of blood, who once again had walked over a corpse on the path to success. He was forced to recognize him and confirm him in his command. He left it to his successor to pay for the blood that had been shed (1 K 2, 5-6).

3) THE END OF SAUL'S POSTERITY (2 S 21, 1-14):

The account of the famine and the end of Saul's posterity comes from a different source than the family history narrated above, which was recorded shortly after the events. The Book of Samuel must have closed, at one time, with the list of officials in 2 S 20, 23-25. Only later the so-called appendix (chs. 21-24) was added, which contained six episodes from the time of David's reign. A similar historical appendix is to be found at the conclusion of the Book of Judges (Jg 19-21). These appendices provide us with a very conclusive insight into the development of the Old Testament book. Prior to its present form, several hands have been at work on it. Even though the episodes recorded in the appendix apparently merely add isolated narrative sections to the compact over-all construction of the Book of Samuel, it is still impossible not to recognize the hand of an artist. The six accounts (two narratives, two catalogues, two songs) were not added gradually or without plan; they are arranged according to the artistic principle of chiasmus:

1. The end of Saul's posterity (21, 1-14).
2. Four heroic deeds against the Philistines (21, 15-22).
3. The great psalm of thanksgiving (22).
4. The last words of David (23, 1-7).
5. David's heroes (23, 8-39).
6. Census and pestilence (24, 1-25).

The nucleus of this appendix is the great psalm of thanksgiving and the last words of David (3 + 4), framed by the heroic deeds of the Gibborim (2 + 5), and two tragic episodes from the time of David's reign (1 + 6). Such an arrangement cannot be the result of mere chance. The appendix, accordingly, was not added piece by piece; it was first outlined as an artistic whole.[72]

---

72. At all events, prior to the time of king Hezekiah, since Psalm 17/18 would hardly have been taken into the appendix if the collection of David's psalms had already been published. Bressan, 686. / O. Eissfeldt, *Einleitung* 1956, 336. / J. Schildenberger, *Studia Anselmiana* 27/28 (1951), 134, 145, refers the appendix to the original composition of the Book of Samuel.

It is not easy to determine when the three years' famine is to be dated. At all events, it must have been before the revolt of Absalom, since otherwise Shimai could not have reproached David for being a "man of blood." The famine was caused, as it so often was, by lack of the early rain in autumn and the late rain in spring (cf. 1 K 17, 1; 18, 1). The explanation of this catastrophic drought was not to be sought in natural causes; it was recognized as a sign of God's wrath and judgment. There must be some unexpiated sin among the people. But where? David inquired into Yahweh's will.[73] The answer was that there was an unexpiated blood guilt upon the house of Saul. Saul had killed the people of Gibeon (Gabaon), although, when the Israelites first took the land, Joshua had sworn to preserve their inviolability (Jos 9, 15). Now the four Canaanite cities actually formed a wedge between the northern and southern tribes. Accordingly, Saul disregarded Joshua's oath and, with his usual obstinacy, attempted to incorporate the four cities into his kingdom. His attempt did not meet with full success; only the inhabitants of Beeroth fled to Gittaim (2 S 4, 2-3). The other cities maintained their independence until the time of David.

David assembled the men of Gibeon and asked what they demanded as expiation for this blood guilt. They wanted neither gold nor property, only the blood of Saul's descendants,[74] and they demanded the number sacred to sacrifice, seven. David reserved the right to choose the victims, since he was obligated, by oath and covenant, to protect the descendants of Jonathan. Among the seven unfortunates were the two sons of Rizpah (Respha), Saul's concubine, and five of Saul's grandchildren through his first-born daughter Merab, who had once been promised to David in marriage. "He gave them into the hands of the Gibeon-

---

73. Bressan, 687, feels that the sentence "and David sought the face of Yahweh" is merely an indication of his expiatory prayers. The following verse, however, presupposes a formal interrogation (21, 1).
74. Among the Arab Bedouins, in cases of blood vengeance, the same formula was in use: "I want no money, but only blood." J. van der Ploeg, CBQ 13 (1951), 301.

ites, and they hanged [75] them on the mountain before the Lord, and the seven of them perished together. They were put to death in the first day of harvest, at the beginning of barley harvest" (21, 9). They were to remain hanging there until the beginning of the fall rains. To go unburied was considered the greatest curse.[77] Like an Israelite Niobe,[78] Rizpah spent four or five months keeping the birds of prey away from their victims. Finally, in autumn, David had the corpses of the sacrificial victims, together with the remains of Saul and Jonathan, transferred to the family burial plot in Sela,[79] in the land of Benjamin.

David's conduct has provoked a variety of opinions. "In the Orient, modern as well as ancient, the royal usurper could be expected to exterminate the last remnants of his predecessor's line, in order to eliminate any further claims to the throne. He would spare only those who were no threat to him; he would however, also protect himself against them, by incarcerating them or at least having them watched. David, too, had confirmed his sovereignty by blood. Ishbaal was treacherously put to death, the seven were sacrificed, the crippled Mephibaal was received at the royal court and thus rendered harmless. Shimei is perfectly justified in calling David a man of blood." [80]

But things do not seem to have been quite so simple. David

---

75. We translate freely "sacrificed," because the Hebrew verb *hôqîa'*, which occurs only here and in Nb 24, 4, is unclear; it can mean "expose, hang up, impale." P. Jouon, Bibl 7 (1926), 285.
76. Gibeon (modern el-Gib) had a sacrificial heights nearby, which is generally located on the Nebi Samwil, 2 km from the city. The mountain is 895 m in elevation, commanding the surrounding territory by some 150 m; even in pre-Israelite times it was the site of a Canaanite sanctuary in which Baal was most likely venerated as the source of fertility. The Israelites turned the ancient site into a "high place of Yahweh," and it was here that the tabernacle and altar of holocausts were established after the destruction of Shiloh. Solomon too offered sacrifice here (1 K 3, 4).
77. E. Dhorme, *L'idée de l'au-delà dans la religion hébraïque*, RevHistdesRel (1941), 113-142.
78. Bressan, 691.
79. Modern *Ḥirbet Ṣalaḥ*, Abel II, 453.
80. Cf. Gressmann, 143.

certainly did not have a hand in the treacherous murder of Ishbaal. He was obligated to Mephibaal by his covenant of friendship with Jonathan. The fact that he brought him to the royal court is not, in itself, suspect. The conduct of the Gibeon affair has too many facets to be attributed to a single author. David's kingdom, from the religious point of view, does not represent a unified picture. It embraced not only Edom, Moab, Ammon and Aram, but also included the ancient Canaanite cities in its midst. The Gibeonites had accepted faith in Yahweh, but they still remained largely faithful to their Canaanite convictions. As king, David had to respect the religious attitudes of his subjects.[81] It is certainly credible that the Gibeonites demanded a seasonal sacrifice to alleviate the famine.[82] But this fertility cult is not the only motive here; it is bound up with breach of a treaty and blood vengeance. In a Hittite text,[83] the high incidence of death in the country is likewise attributed to a breach of treaty. If, in addition, we take cognizance of the unconditioned law of blood vengeance,[84] fulfillment of which was regarded as an act of mercy towards the murdered relatives and not as an act of criminal outrage, then David's manner of behavior becomes much more understandable. At all events, he cannot be accused of deliberately exterminating Saul's surviving posterity. He had been magnanimous when Saul's life lay in his hands; why should he now act differently towards Saul's descendants? The forces which motivated him were fertility cult, breach of treaty, and blood vengeance. A gloomy chapter from a gloomy age.

---

81. H. Cazelles, *David's Monarchy and the Gibeonite Claim*, PEQ 87 (1955), 165-167.
82. A. S. Kapelrud, *König David und die Söhne des Saul*, ZAT 67 (1955), 198-205.
83. A. Malamat, *Doctrines of Causality in Hittite and Biblical Historiography, a Parallel*, VT 5 (1955), 1-12.
84. E. Merz, *Die Blutrache bei den Israeliten* (1916), 24. / J. Scharbert, *Solidarität in Segen und Fluch im AT und in seiner Umwelt*, I (1958), 88ff., 122: *Sippenhaftung Blutrache*. / J. Prado, *El exterminio de la familia se Saul*, Sefarad 14 (1954), 43-57. The account is theologically colored to absolve David of blood guilt.

4) CENSUS AND PESTILENCE (2 S 24):

The account of the census and the pestilence, by reason of its ancient religious preoccupations, is closely connected with the story of the death of Saul's descendants. In the former account, the great famine comes over the land because of Saul's breach of treaty; here it is David's own guilt that is responsible. In our modern age, we find it difficult to understand how a census could be interpreted as a sin against Yahweh. Moreover, we are informed that it was Yahweh himself who incited David to take the census of Israel and Judah (24, 1). We find it contradictory that Yahweh, on the one hand, should incite David to undertake the census and, on the other hand, should send the pestilence as an act of wrathful vengeance. But it is Yahweh, as the final cause of history, to whom everything is referred, good as well as evil. Only over the course of several centuries did religious thought in Israel undergo a species of differentiation and achieve greater depth. The Book of Chronicles, written at a much later date (5th to 4th centuries), accordingly ascribes temptation not to Yahweh, but to Satan (1 Ch 21, 1ff.).[85] But even in this more developed theological expression, we find evidence of the position which regards the census as a sin against God. This conception of things is based upon attitudes which are little explored in the experience of our modern cultures.

Throughout the entire world of the Ancient Semite, knowing was equivalent to exercising power or dominion over a person or an object. Counting flocks or populations, "in order to know their number," was equivalent to a claim of absolute and unlimited dominion. Such dominion, however, was proper only and solely to God, the Lord of all. Accordingly, a census of the people must be regarded as an arrogation of the divine prerogative of dominion, and condemned as an act of sacrilege.[86]

---

85. R. A. Scharf, *Die Gestalt des Satans im AT* (Zurich, 1948), 63-78.
86. This unwillingness to be counted, out of fear of divine punishment, is still to be recognized in various tribes of Africa and Arabia: cf. J. G. Frazer, *Folklore in the OT* (1923), 307-313: The Sin of Census.

David bitterly reproaches himself after the census. He brands his behavior explicitly as a sin, just like his adultery with Bath-Sheba: "I have sinned greatly in what I have done" (24, 11).

The prophet Gad, as Yahweh's representative, accordingly announces the divine punishment to come. David has three choices: three years of famine, three months at the mercy of his enemy, or three days of pestilence. David chooses the third, in the hope of God's mercy. The fact that 70,000 men perished in this pestilence is certainly credible; such plagues had been known to depopulate entire districts. The pestilence was not interpreted in terms of its natural causes. For our hygienic age,[87] it is so very easy to explain things. We need only isolate the germ or virus responsible for the plague and we can control it. The Bible takes a different view. We might indeed prefer to find greater cognizance of the natural elements involved; but even the most precise organic diagnosis would not yield the ultimate answer. The pestilence was a plague from Yahweh, executed by his destroying angel (24, 16). The plague was averted at the threshing floor of Araunah, outside the gates of Jerusalem.[88]

The pestilence narrative is constructed on a pattern similar to the deluge story: God's wrath (24, 1), the threat of punishment (24, 15), God's repentance (24, 16), the erection of an altar (24, 18). David buys the threshing floor from Araunah for fifty shekels [89] and erects an altar there. The chronist records that fire fell from heaven and consumed the sacrifice (1 Ch 21, 26). Thereupon, the destroying angel sheathed his sword.

---

87. A. Gemayel, *L'hygiène et la médecine à travers la Bible* (Paris, 1932), 82.

88. H. B. Rosen, *Arauna, Nom hittite?* VT 5 (1955), 319. To be derived from *arawanni*, "free, noble." Thus, Arauna would have belonged to the Hittite nobility. / E. Broegel, OrLitZ 39 (1936), 727, connects the name with the Indian god Varuna, who was familiar in Palestine during the Hyksos era. / B. Maisler, *EncMikr* I, 552, holds for a Hurrite derivation. *ewar* (*ewri*) "Lord, warrior." The no longer intelligible name was Hebraized by the addition of the theophoric element -*yah*. MT Arawna or Araw-yah.

89. 1 Ch 21, 25 records a much higher purchase price, 600 gold shekels.

It was the urgent need of the hour which prompted David to choose Araunah's threshing floor as a sacrificial site; but this also set the stage for the temple to be built upon the same location.

Though the account of the census is completely steeped in religion, it also has a great significance for secular history which we must not overlook. David has welded the loose tribal confederacy into a unified kingdom, which must be ruled and administered. In the construction of his centrally administered state, he was guided by Egyptian prototypes; the same thing is probably true of his census. A painfully accurate numbering of the entire population, with the head of each house obliged to confirm, under oath, the number of persons in his family, were available in Egypt, since the time of the Middle Kingdom, for drawing up the tax lists.[90] David entrusted this work to the energetic Joab. But even this seasoned warrior had some religious scruples. "May the Lord your God add to the people a hundred times as many as they are, while the eyes of my lord the king still see it; but why does my lord the king delight in this thing?" The king's word prevailed against Joab's scruples, and he carried out the census. The military commission was 9 months and 20 days at their work, just under 300 days. First, Transjordania was counted, from Aroer in the south to Hermon in the north. Then Joab turned towards the west, and proceeded into the territory of Sidon, in order to deal with the Palestinian hill and mountain country as far as Beer-Sheba (Bersabee). Within a short time, great work was accomplished. Upon his return, Joab could make this proud report to the king: "In Israel there were 800 thousand valiant men who drew the sword, and the men of Judah were 500 thousand" (24, 9): in case of war, a military levy of 1,300,000 men,[91] almost ten times the military power of Rome at the height of the empire under Hadrian,[92] and thus quite impossible. Where is the error?

---

90. R. Kittel, *Geschichte Israels*, 164, note 4.
91. Chronicles records even higher figures: 1,110,000 for Israel and 470,000 for Judah, a total of 1,580,000.
92. J. Meysham, PEQ 90 (1958), 25: at the time of Hadrian there were 30 legions with a strength of 180,000 men.

Conclusive in this problem are primarily the yields of Mari,[93] a city on the Euphrates which achieved its cultural climax before the days of Hammurabi, and was shortly after destroyed and covered by the desert sands. On the basis of the archive texts discovered there, we can presume that Mari enjoyed a highly developed centralistic state, and no little bureaucracy. The military forces were kept up by a system of regular recruiting. The name and city of each recruit was written on a clay tablet, which was to be sent to the central headquarters. In case of mobilization, the necessary information was thus ready at hand. Side by side with this centralistic and detailed recording of the citizens fit for military duty, which served as the registration system for a native and settled population, there was another method as well, more adapted to the nomadic Bedouins and semi-Bedouins. Thus, Jasmah-Addu gives the following order to the Binujamina: [94] "The king is going out upon a military expedition. Let all citizens, including the young, assemble. The *Sagagum* (*sheikh*) whose troops are not up to proper strength shall taste the wrath of the king. Give them this order. They do not need to be registered." — These are two quite different recruiting systems: a centralized form with the available recruits recruited by name, and the tribal system in which the individual *sheikhs* were responsible for filling their quota. From a further letter of Jasmah-Addu, we discover that the four tribes Ubrabu, Jahrii, Jahuri, and Ammani — these are individual parts of the great tribe of the Binujamina — together muster only 600 men, 150 men each.[95] It is hardly probable that this number includes all the able-bodied warriors between 20 and 45. Perhaps an equal number remain with their families and flocks. Whereas, in the centralized recruiting system, the soldiers are conscribed to serve, in military units, under an authority established by the king, the tribal levy system was adaptable in terms of individual place or origin. Veith [96] refers to this as a "genocratically organized conscription," such as was practiced among the Greeks and Romans in pre-republican times.

Now Israel, at David's time, was in a state of political and social upheaval. Prior to that time, the really basic political element had been the tribe (*šēbeṭ*), with the tribal chief (*nāśí*) at its head. The tribe, moreover, was broken up into various families and clans, which were ruled by the elders (*zᵉqēnîm*). In cases of war, a military leader (*šar*)

---

93. J. R. Kupper, *Les nomades en Mésopotamie au temps des rois de Mari* (Paris, 1957).

94. Archives Royales de Mari, (ARM), I, 6, 15-21.

95. ARM i, 42. / J. R. Krupper, *Le recensement dans les textes de Mari* (Studia Mariana) (1950), 99-110.

96. G. Veith, *Heerwesen und Kriegsführung der Griechen und Römer. Handbuch der Altertumswissenschaften*, vol. 2 (Munich, 1928), 258.

was appointed.[97] In our investigation of the Biblical numbers, in this passage, the decisive element revolves about the clans and families, which bore the name 'eleph. Whenever war broke out, the tribes all organized their 'alāphîm, that is, their clan and family levies. The strength of these basic military units can also be determined by recent findings. The garrison of Mari numbered 222 men, belonging to nine Gayum (Hebrew: goy). Each individual Gayum numbered only approximately 25 men. The military census lists of Alalah in Northern Syria reveal that, in the individual "districts," very small figures are actually involved: 3, 60, 17, 19 men.[98]

Evidence of the fact that, in the royal period, 'eleph was still used in the meaning of clan or tribe, is furnished by Saul's grim threat that he will hunt David down through all the tribes and clans ('alphê, NB not thousands!) of Judah (1 S 23, 23). With the reorganization of the army in the royal period, 'eleph takes on a new meaning in the military terminology: thousand. Solomon had primarily abolished the significance of tribal membership in his army; he had established troops with war chariots and built a standing army, in which tribe or clan origin was no longer a determining factor.

David's census encountered such fierce resistance precisely because the tribes regarded it as an attack upon their ancient hereditary rights. Since we arrive at impossible figures by translating the term 'eleph as thousand, we might suppose that the census was taken on the basis of the ancient tribal levy. The northern tribes number 800 'alāphîm, and Judah numbered 500. Now if each 'eleph contained an average of 10 men, then, in case of war, David could call upon not 1,300,000, but only some 13,000, which is quite in keeping with the Ancient Near East balance of power and population. The kingdom of Mari could put 4,000 men in the field, Syria 10,000, Eshnunna 6,000 men.[99]

---

97. R. de Vaux, Les Institutions de l'Ancien Testament, I. Le nomadisme et ses survivances (Paris, 1958), 21ff. / H. Cazelles, VT 8 (1958), 321.

98. G. E. Mendenhall, The Census Lists of Numbers 1 and 26, JBL 77 (1958), 65ff.

99. Ibid., 64. On this basis the battle of Gedeon is historically intelligible. He did not have 32,000 men, but only 32 'alaphim, "clan," from Manasseh for his victory against the Midianites. He had, thus, a total of 300 warriors.

The relatively larger number in Israel's army is a good indication of the importance and position of David's kingdom. Since the Aramaeans of David's time had also preserved the ancient tribal levy and had not yet formed the "modern" centralized state form, they also reckoned their military conscription in terms of clan or tribal units, and not in thousands. Accordingly, in the military expeditions described above, we have translated *'eleph* as tribal levy, thereby avoiding the fantastic numbers involved in the text and bringing it closer to probability. These are the only figures that can fit within the framework of Ancient Near East military history. The earlier interpretation which gives the high number of 1,300,000 and the total population of David's kingdom, can now be considered as evident exaggeration. Hand in hand with the conscription process, the ancient tribal boundaries must also have been reapportioned. It is quite possible that the military lists of David's army have had their influence upon the tribal lists in the Book of Joshua.[100]

Even though this census was carried out for political reasons and is to be evaluated positively in terms of our modern conception of things, this very fact clearly demonstrates that our modern attitudes cannot be too simply applied whole-cloth to the world of the Old Testament. In the outbreak of the pestilence and death of so many citizens, popular belief necessarily recognized a judgment from God. Such a popular-theological interpretation must not surprise us; the soul of the people is always inclined to search for a definite author at work behind these visitations; the fact that the author of the Book of Samuel incorporated this popular-theological interpretation into his work, thus making it his own, can only mean that, according to Israel's conception of things, God's absolute dominion could not be challenged in any quarter, without provoking a judgment of punishment and reprisal. Even such secular affairs as census, drawing up the conscription lists, establishing the boundaries, are all seen in the light of Yahweh's sole kingship.

---

100. A. Alt., *Das System der Stannesgrenzen im Buch Josua, Kleine Schriften* I (1953), 193-202.

5) "THE LAST WORDS OF DAVID" (2 S 23, 1-7):

The "last words of David," in their powerful poetic language and in their message which clearly points to the future, recall the "last words" of Isaac (Gn 27, 1ff.), Jacob (Gn 48, 10ff.; 49, 1ff.), and Moses (Dt 33, 1ff.). Gressmann [101] believes that the figure of the dying prophet is to be derived from a style already current at David's time. Accordingly, words which point to the future were readily placed into the mouth of the "dying David." The words are not from David himself; they would be the invention of a much later, post-Davidic age. The most recent dating would assign them to an author of the second century.[102] The obviously archaic character of the verses is explained by Mowinckel [103] on the grounds that the passage is to be explained as an artistic product, in which archaic elements of speech have been employed in order to effect an archaic tone.

These negative verdicts have been opposed, in more recent times, by a growing strength of contrary opinion, solidly in support of the Davidic origin of this prophecy. According to Procksch [104] we have, "in the last words of David," the most ancient messianic prophecy preserved. Albright makes a particular point against hyper-criticism when he says: "It is going much too far to deny the Davidic authorship of the short psalm at the beginning of 2 S 23. The age of this poem is authenticated by the fact that it begins with the same words as the two ancient songs of Balaam in Numbers 24. The significance of this passage is increased rather than weakened by the stubborn insistence of later tradition that a great number of the psalms were composed by David." [105] This short psalm, together with the prophecy of Nathan (2 S 7) represents the salvation-history climax of the Books of Samuel. The author of our book discovered the psalm, incorporated it into his collection, and entitled it with the words:

---

101. Gressmann, 185.
102. Dhorme (1910) quoted in Bressan, 714.
103. S. Mowinckel, *Die letzten Worte Davids*, ZAT 45 (1927), 30, 58.
104. O. Procksch in Kittel's THWNT IV (1942), 92.
105. W. F. Albright, *The Religion of Israel* (1956), 141ff.

"Now these are the last words of David." The text has seriously suffered,[106] but the broader outlines are still visible. Since a translation is the best commentary, we shall let the text speak for itself:

a) Prophetic Inspiration:

> The oracle of David, the son of Jesse,
>> The oracle of the man who was raised on high,
> the anointed of the God of Jacob,
>> the sweet psalmist of Israel:
> "The Spirit of the Lord speaks by me,
>> his word is upon my tongue.
> The God of Israel has spoken,
>> the Rock of Israel has said to me:

b) Sun King:

> When one rules justly over men,
>> ruling in the fear of God,
> he dawns on them like the morning light,
>> like the sun shining forth upon a cloudless morning,
> like rain that makes grass
>> to sprout from the earth.

c) David's Everlasting Covenant:

> Yea, does not my house stand so with God?
>> For he has made with me an everlasting covenant,
>>> ordered in all things and secure.
> For will he not cause to prosper
>> all my help and my desire?

d) Destruction of the Wicked:

> But godless men are like thorns
>> that are thrown away;
>>> for they cannot be taken with the hand;
> but the man who touches them

---

106. In this respect, it is advisable to consult a commentary. Bressan, 714ff.

arms himself with iron and the shaft of a spear,
and they are utterly consumed with fire.

Nathan's prophecy, over the course of the years, has come
more and more to maturity in David. An invincible faith in the
great future of his house bursts from this short song. The song
itself becomes a new prophecy. It is the spirit of Yahweh who
speaks in him, the word of God breathing forth into voice. The
first strophe is one of the classical passages of Scripture for belief
in inspiration. The second and third strophes belong together.
What the one expresses in imagery, the other says in clear words.
The leit-motiv is the same as in the prophecy of Nathan, the
covenant (*b^erît*), God's work determining human fate (*tôrat
hā'ādām,* 2 S 7, 19). The future of the house of David is far
removed from every human agency. Not without reason does
David call Yahweh his rock (*Ṣúr*), and thus his house is also
built upon the rock, so that the powers of evil cannot prevail
against it (fourth strophe).

Many scholars believe that the song is a direct messianic
prophecy.[107] The foreground of the singer's field of vision is occupied by the future figure of the great ruler to come, whose
arrival will radiate like the sunrise. Apart from the fact that
the text of the third strophe is highly contested, David's era
does not seem to have been mature enough for the concept of
a Messiah to come. God's promises refer directly only to the
everlasting reign of David's dynasty, which will produce good
and evil kings alike (2 S 7, 14). Only with the further development
of revelation, in the age of the great prophets, does the entire
hope of salvation gradually begin to concentrate upon a definite
future figure from the house of David. The song is thus messianic
in the broader sense, since every king of Israel is an anointed
(*māšíah*) a "messiah." David is thinking in dynastic terms; the
prophets are thinking in messianic terms. They gave his words
a deeper meaning. David was speaking only of the plants sprouting
from the earth and the glory of the sunrise. But in the prophetic

---

107. Bressan, 714.

preaching, the "sprout of Israel" becomes a title of honor for the Messiah to come (Is 4, 2; Zc 3, 8; 6, 12; Jr 23, 5; 33, 15). In retrospect, the aged priest Zachary realizes that the "rising from on high" has been fulfilled in the Incarnation of Jesus (Lk 1, 78). Even though David understood the prophecy in national, dynastic, and quite human terms, the growing faith in a Messiah king from the house of David develops, after a time, into the central dogma of the Old Testament Church, eventually finding its development, its profounder meaning, and also its necessary correction in the person of Christ.

The history of the Old Testament is, once again, the history of the development of revelation and faith. It would be a mistake to project clearly defined ideas back into an early age. David, in his age, remains bound up with the imprecise conceptions characteristic of his age, as we clearly see in his conduct towards the family of Saul or on the occasion of the census. Yahweh was for him "the warrior of Israel," [108] the God who makes his way in storm and thunder upon the cherubim, as the great psalm of gratitude in chapter 22 describes him.[109] His concept of God has many similarities with the Canaanite storm god.[110]

But despite all the similarities that can be pointed out by a comparative study of religions, we must not let our judgment be clouded. In David we have evidence of something new, something for which there is no Canaanite parallel or, for that matter, any parallel in the whole history of religion; his belief in the unicity of Yahweh and the everlasting power of his house. Monotheism and messianism are the distinctive marks of the new covenant which God first struck with David towards the turn of the first millennium before Christ.

---

108. H. Cazelles, *La titulature du roi David* (Mélanges-Robert 1957), 131-136 translates 2 S 23, 1, *ne'îm zemirôt yiśra'el* as "beloved of the warrior of Israel," that is, Yahweh. It is commonly rendered: "singer of the songs of Israel."

109. F. M. Cross and D. N. Freedman, *A Royal Song of Thanksgiving* (2 S 22), JBL 60 (1953), 161-169, demonstrate the great age of the Psalm on the basis of linguistic relationship with texts from Ugarit.

110. Albright, *The Religion of Israel*, 89ff.

SOLOMON IN ALL HIS GLORY

THE age of Solomon had made such a profound impression upon the memory of posterity as the climax of Israel's national history that Christ, in the Sermon on the Mount, could refer simply to "Solomon in all his glory" (Mt 6, 29). The histories which are available for our examination of the age of Solomon and the story of the divided kingdom, Israel and Judah, after his death, have a popular character. The two Books of Kings, as well as the Book of Chronicles, do not hold up very well under the judgment of purely secular history. The Books simply do not present any explicit picture of the economic, social, or even the political development of those days. The principle according to which the material was selected is a surprising one. For example, the reigns of Omri (1 K 16, 15-28) and Jeroboam II (2 K 14, 23-29), brilliant high-points in the national history of Israel, are presented, in the judgment of the author of the Books of Kings, as religious low-points, pointing to the imminent decline of the kingdom. How are we to explain the origin of such an evaluation, which clearly contradicts the principles and points of view taken by the secular historian? The answer is clear if we remember the fact that these two works are in no wise intended to present an explicit account of national history, but rather a theology of the history of the Old Testament people of God. It would be a mistake to demand more of an author than he means to give. Yet it is precisely this history-theology character that casts new light upon the events of the past, a task which even the most explicit presentation of secular history would be unequal to.

CHAPTER XII

THEOLOGY OF HISTORY

THE Books of Samuel were composed in the first dawn of the rise of the Davidic-Solomonic kingdom. Everywhere there is evidence of the joy of pure narrative, painting the exact picture of events, holding to the precise historical order of things. The Book of Samuel is redolent of the immediacy of the eye-witness who refuses to tamper with his material, who means only to paint David's rise to power in its actual course. It is, accordingly, no wonder that the Books of Samuel belong among the masterpieces of Ancient Near East historical writing.

The Books of Kings and Chronicles, on the other hand, have a quite different point of departure. "Looking upon the ruins of the Temple, in the sorry hovels of their exile, when they were devoid of all earthly potential, abandoned to the harsh realities of a graceless world, and dependent exclusively upon the grace of God — it was these days that saw a reevaluation and a transvaluation (of the national history) in the unfaltering light of God's own judgment." [1] After the destruction of Jerusalem and the decline of national power, it was a time to question every conviction. Upon the ruins of city and national pride, the author

---

1. Th. C. Vriezen, *Theologie des AT in Grundzügen* (1956), 40.

of the Books of Kings sets about his inexorable examination of conscience in the history of his people. It is easy to understand his lack of concern in portraying the glorious blossom of Israel's secular power in the kingship; his primary concern is with laying bare the fundamental causes that underlie the catastrophe. In the same way, the chronist holds up those ideals from the days of past glory that have been able to withstand the crucible of destruction and prove capable of furnishing strength and conviction to the returning exiles, to start again, Both works are thus theologies of history in the truest sense of the word. Such a genre of history can be written only by an inspired author, in whose specially endowed judgment the internal bonds and make-up of things stand open and revealed. For any other historian it would be an undertaking doomed to failure. Our author rejected what seemed important to the world, and glorified what seemed unimportant. The history of kingship in Israel, as he tells it here, is like the *Ecce Homo,* broken and wounded from crown to sole, delivered up to judgment. This fundamental preoccupation with the theology of history is always a necessary presupposition for understanding the special character of the Books of Kings and Chronicles.

Insofar as it is necessary for our presentation of the Davidic-Solomonic age, we must attempt to consider the most important introductory problems presented by these two books; we shall need to refer to them frequently as sources.

A) THE BOOKS OF KINGS

Commentaries: SAT: Gressmann 1921[2] — HSAT: Eissfeldt 1922 — BB: Landersdorfer 1927 — EB: Rehm 1949 — JerB: de Vaux 1949 — ClamB: Médebielle 1949 — SBB: Slotki 1950 — ICC: Montgomery, ed. by Gehmann 1951 — GarB: Garofalo 1951 — HBK: Ketter 1953 — JB: Sochman, Calkins 1954.

Introductions: Cornely-Merk 1940[12], 387 — 97 — Simon-Prado 1941[4], 254 — 258 — Höpfl-Miller-Metzinger 1946[5], 159 — 173 — Pfeiffer 1948[2], 374 — 412 — Kuhl 1953, 147 — 167 —

Eissfeldt 1956², 289ff, 339 — 362 — Weiser 1957⁴, 140 — 149 — Robert-Feuillet 1957, 435 — 464.

1) TITLE AND CONTENT:

The Greek and Old Latin translation grouped the Books of Samuel and Kings together into a single, unified historical work, the "Four Kingdoms" (βασιλειῶν τέσσαρα — regnorum libri quattuor). Jerome, in the Vulgate translation, broke with this tradition to the point of replacing the word "kingdoms," which seemed meaningless to him, by "kings" (quattuor regum), and thus recalled the Hebrew title: "liber Malachim, id est Regum tertius et quartus" [2] — a title which was not destined to last. The division into "Four Books of Kings" was taken over, in the years that followed, by those translations which are based on the Vulgate. The four books do indeed present a continuous history of Israel from the era of the later Judges down to the destruction of Jerusalem, but the two "Books of Kings" (Malachim — 3 and 4 Regum) are so different, in presentation and composition, from the 2 Books of Samuel (Samuhel — 1 and 2 Regum), that it is logical to go back to the names used in the Hebrew Bible and clearly distinguish the two works in their titles. 1 and 2 Regum have always been quoted as 1 and 2 Samuel, while 3 and 4 Regum are quoted as 1 and 2 Kings. The Book of Kings was originally a unified work and only in the Septuagint was it divided into two books, for technical reasons as in the case of the Book of Samuel. The point of separation can hardly be considered fortunate, since it interrupts the reign of King Ahaziah. The work can be divided into three principal divisions: history of Solomon (1 K 1-11), synchronistic history of the kingdoms of Israel and Judah up to the destruction of the Northern Kingdom (1 K 12 – 2 K 17), and, finally, the history of Judah down to the destruction of Jerusalem (2 K 18-25).

2) THE SOURCES:

For the presentation of their history which runs over the course of some 400 years, the author has made use of various written sources, which were still available in his day. Expressly quoted are: "The book of the history of Solomon" (1 K 11, 41), "The book of the history of the kings of Judah" (15 times, e.g., I K 14, 29), "The book of the history of the kings of Israel" (18 times, e.g., 1 K 14, 19). The designation of the historical works employed as "Book of the words of the days" — which we have

---

2. Liber Malachim ex interpretatione sancti Hieronymi (Rome, 1954). Critical edition of the Vulgate by the Benedictine Fathers of the Abbey of San Girolamo, Rome.

given simply as "history" — recalls the annals and chronicles which were composed in the royal courts of Babylonia and constantly brought up to date.[3] The works quoted, however, can hardly have been the official royal annals preserved in the archives of Jerusalem or Samaria, since, according to the author's indication, the books were available for everyone's inspection, and this could hardly be the case if they were official archives. This presupposes the fact that Israel and Judah had already witnessed the publication of works dealing explicitly with the history of the royal era, and that our author made use of what he considered the important material in writing our present history.

Side by side with the explicitly quoted works, the author had many sources at his disposal, sources whose existence we must reason to indirectly. The far-ranging account of the activity of the prophets Elijah and Elisha were no doubt a well developed body of literature in the prophetic circles before being taken over into the Book of Kings. In like manner, the precise details of temple construction and cult reform presuppose an earlier written version that was current in priestly circles. From these three streams of tradition, court, priesthood, and prophetic tradition, a new work now arises, a work which is not merely the mechanical addition of the various independent sources, but rather their regrouping and reworking into a higher unity which derives its form from the theology of history.[4]

3) COMPOSER AND DATE OF COMPOSITION:

The conclusion of the book suggests that it was composed during the exile; the account of the destruction of Jerusalem is followed by a reference to the special favor accorded King Jehoiachin around the year 560 B.C.: "He put off his prison garments, and every day of his life he dined regularly at the king's table" (2 K 25, 29). Since there is no mention of the end of exile here, we might suggest the lifetime of Jehoiachin, approximately 550 B.C., as the date of composition. But this argument is seriously weakened by the consideration that the account of his privileges might well be the addition of a later editor, just like the appendices to the Books of Judges and Samuel. It is perhaps better, accordingly,

---

3. Gressmann, AOT, *Chronologisch-historische Texte*, 331ff. / B. Maisler, *Ancient Israelite Historiography*, Isr. Expl. Journ. 2 (1952), 82-89, points to the fact that in the late Babylonian era there was a flourishing interest in the study of antiquity, and this led Israelite scholars to a reevaluation of their own historical backgrounds.
4. A. Jespen, *Die Quellen des Königbuches* (Halle, 1953) distinguishes between synchronistic and annalistic sources, which have undergone a priestly, nebiistic, and levitical redaction.

to let the Book of Kings come to a conclusion with the despairing lament over the destruction of Jerusalem, and date its composition shortly after the year 586 B.C. — Other scholars go further and date its composition as late as the outbreak of the deuteronomic reform stirred up by the prophet Jeremiah. Actually, there are very close linguistic and ideological relationships between the Books of the Kings, on the one hand, and Deuteronomy and Jeremiah on the other. Under the impulse of the newly discovered Law (621) a man who was very close to the prophet Jeremiah might have undertaken a revision of the history of Israel.

M. Noth [5] has invented a new name for the four "former prophets," that is, the Books of Joshua, Judges, Samuel, and Kings: "the deuteronomic history." The basic lines of tradition are the Yahwist and Elohist, familiar from Pentateuchal criticism, which have here been worked into a new framework by the deuteronomist. On the basis of historical analogies, we must conclude that ancient Israelite historical writing had begun when Israel had achieved its political climax, or even passed beyond this point, that is, at the time of David and Solomon or shortly afterwards. This position is greatly strengthened by the fact that those years saw the creation of works which make allowance for the historical awareness of the new nation.[6] In the present-day state of tradition, however, no one has succeeded in demonstrating a satisfactory and convincing principle of division between the two "source works" E and J. Accordingly, Weiser rejects the presupposition of a continual historical tradition running consistently through the Pentateuch sources and the Books of Kings.[7] — We thus reach the conclusion that the author of the Book of Kings apparently made use of the various sources at his disposal, but that these sources were reworked, at his own personal initiative, under the influence both of the deuteronomic reform and the destruction of Jerusalem, into a prophetic work of history. Since the book shows so many clear points of contact with the prophet Jeremiah, ancient Jewish tradition (Baba Bathra 15a) identified him as its composer. Although this cannot be demonstrated, we might not be too far from the truth of the matter if we attribute the composition to a disciple of the great Jeremiah, who, still reeling under the fury of destruction, undertook to examine the conscience of the national-religious history of his people.

---

5. M. Noth, *Überlieferungsgeschichtliche Studien* (1943).
6. Eissfeldt, *Einleitung* (1956), 297ff. "There are some grounds to substantiate the view that an already existing Book of Kings has been reworked, but the text cannot possibly be reconstructed" (358). Eissfeldt holds fast to the concept of a deuteronomic reworking, even though "it is impossible to achieve certainty in this respect" (361).
7. Weiser, *Einleitung* (1957), 147.

4) THE TEXT:

Arvid Bruno [8] considers the Books of Kings as a "great Hebrew epic," which glorified the national history of both kingdoms in rhythm and verse. In his efforts to substantiate this view, however, he had to stretch the text on a Procrustean bed, and introduce so many "emendations" that his thesis is, *a priori*, untenable. The text of the Book of Kings was actually fixed at a very late date. Prior to the second century before Christ, it shows great fluctuation. Evidence for this is the numerous variants between the Hebrew text and the ancient translations. We distinguish, accordingly, two text groups: with the Masora we have the Syrian Peshitta and the Latin Vulgate; the other group is made up of the Septuagint and the Vetus Latina. With such a fluctuating textual foundation, it is difficult to establish the original form of the text. In individual cases, we must refer to the commentaries.[9]

B. THE BOOKS OF CHRONICLES

Commentaries: HS: Goettsberger 1939 — TU: von Selms I 1939, II 1947 — EB: Rehm 1949 — ClamB: Marshall 1949 — SBB: Slotki 1951 — HBK: Bückers 1952 — ICC: Curtius and Madsen 1952 — ATD: Galling 1954 —JerB: Cazelles 1954 — IB: Elmslie 1954 — HAT: Rudolph 1955.

Introductions: Cornely-Merk 1940[12], 398 — 407 — Simon-Prado 1941[4], 258 — 263 — Höpfl-Miller-Metzinger 1946 — Pfeiffer 1948[2], 782 — 812 — Kuhl 1953, 314 — 324 — Eissfeldt 1956[2], 654 — 669 — Weiser 1957[4], 261 — 265 — Robert-Feuillet 1957, 719 — 730.

1) TITLE AND CONTENT:

Even more than the two Books of Kings, the two Books of Chronicles present a theology of history of the chosen people. Accordingly, when Jerome in his violent preface (*prologus galeatus*) suggests replacing the Hebrew title *Sēpher dibrê hayyāmîm*, "book of the words of the days," by the title *Chronicon totius divinae historiae*, that is, Chronicle of the

---

8. A. Bruno, *Das hebräische Epos. Eine rhythmische und textkritische Untersuchung der Bücher Samuelis und Könige*. 2 vol. (Uppsala, 1935).

9. W. Rudolph, *Zum Text der Königsbücher*, ZATW 63 (1951), 201-215.

Entire Divine History, this suggestion is the most concise and suitable expression of the central concept of the work. The Chronicle is a presentation of salvation history in its broader outlines. It is not intended to fill out the gaps in the Book of Samuel and Kings. This was the understanding of the Septuagint translators, who entitled the work *Paralipomena*, that is, things passed by or left out. This interpretation, however, does not do justice to the true *"Sitz im Leben."* Chronicles owes its existence to the religious and national crisis that followed the exile. If this is kept in mind, the ideal and conception of the work are easier to understand.

Just like Samuel and Kings, the present two Books of Chronicles are really one single book, as evidence the position of the final masora at the end of the second book. For technical reasons, the Septuagint broke it into two volumes, a practice which was transferred to the printing of the Hebrew text in the year 1448. Many modern scholars feel that Chronicles was originally one great unified work of history, together with Ezra and Nehemiah; the conluding verses of Chronicles are identical with the beginning verses of Ezra.[10] In addition to this, there is the similarity in style, vocabulary, and ideology, as well as the similar treatment of literary sources. In this theory, the four books are to represent the history of the kingdom of God from Adam down to the author's own day, a type of history which was highly favored in the historical compositions of the Middle Ages. But since Chronicles was admitted to the official canon later than the Books of Ezra-Nehemiah, the separation and transposition of the books took place already in antiquity. In establishing the dates of composition, we must not lose sight of the fact that we are dealing with a universal work of history which originally included Ezra-Nehemiah as well.

The contents can be divided into the following principal sections: 1 Ch 1-9: the time from Adam to David, almost exclusively in the form of genealogies; 1 Ch 10-29: David; 2 Ch 1-9: Solomon; 2 Ch 10-36: from the division of the kingdom to the exile, in which sections only the kings of Judah are treated.

2) THE SOURCES:

The chronist has thoroughly examined the sources at his disposal and chosen the elements that were in accord with his purpose. He refers the reader who might be interested in more precise information to the sources he himself has used. For political history, these were: "The Chronicle of King David" (1 Ch 27, 24), "The Acts of the Kings of Israel and Judah" (1 Ch 9, 1; 2 Ch 20, 34), "The Acts of the Kings of Israel" (2 Ch 33, 18), "The Book of the Kings of Israel and Judah" (2 Ch 16, 11;

---

10. Cazelles, *Chroniques,* 7ff.

25, 26; 28, 26; 32, 32) and finally the "Midrash to the Book of Kings" (2 Ch 24, 27). In 45 passages, the Chronicle runs parallel to the canonical Books of Kings.[11] In addition to these sources, the author had at his disposal the above named historical compositions; it cannot be accurately determined whether these names refer to different books or whether they are one and the same book quoted under various titles.

For the prophetic sections of his work, the chronist refers to the following sources: "Words of Samuel the Seer," "Words of the Prophet Nathan," and "Words of Gad the Seer" (1 Ch 29, 29), "The Prophecies of Ahijah of Shiloh," and "The Visions of Iddo the Seer" (2 Ch 9, 29), etc.; finally, "The Lamentations of Jeremiah" (2 Ch 32, 25). The rather free method of citing his sources makes it difficult to determine whether these references are to the canonical books or otherwise. One thing is, at all events, quite obvious: the chronist had many sources at his disposal which are beyond our reach today. His conscientious use of the Books of Kings would seem to guarantee that he is extremely faithful in his treatment of the lost sources as well.

3) AUTHOR AND TIME OF COMPOSITION:

The author of this great "salvation history from Adam to his own time" can be only approximately determined on the basis of the book's content. "The predominant motif is the history of the theocracy which is incorporated in the Davidic kingdom and in the post-exilic cultic community. The focus of interest is the temple of Jerusalem and its cult. On these grounds, the history of David, with the exception of Saul's death, and also the history of the Northern Kingdom is not specifically treated. David is presented, essentially, as the spiritual father of the temple building, preparing the plans down to the last detail, handing on money, building materials, plans and model to his son Solomon; even the organization of the music and the sung portions of the divine services in the temple is attributed to David the royal psalmist. As principal figures in this history, together with David and Solomon the temple builder, we find Jehoshaphat by reason of his efforts in behalf of the law of Yahweh, Hezekiah and Josiah as the kings who saw to the reform of the Yahweh cult. They are expressly and explicitly referred to as pious and spiritual princes as well as national saints. Whatever tends to destroy this good repute has been excised: for example, the family history of David and the unedifying circumstances of Solomon's succession to the throne — or else it is substituted by a more favorable account. In the presentation of human history, moreover, the activity of God is stressed by a process of immediate intervention in the course of human affairs, a form of presentation that is characteristic of sacred

---

11. Best studied in the synopsis to the Books of Kings and Chronicles produced by P. Vannutelli, *Libri Synoptici* VT (1931).

history." [12] In this way, the chronist attempts to prove the fact that the post-exilic "church" [13] is the genuine heiress of the divine revelation and promises of antiquity. His strong interest in the temple cult, priesthood, and law, suggests the likelihood that the author is to be sought among the re-appointed Levites of the second temple.

A point of reference for the probable dating of Chronicles is afforded by the contents. The Book of Chronicles concludes with the edict of liberation promulgated by the Persian King Cyrus in the year 538 B.C.; this presupposes that Chronicles was composed after the return from exile. Further points of reference are the genealogical lists of David's descendants, a list which is carried up to the end of the fifth century (1 Ch 3, 19ff.). Furthermore, the name of the Persian monetary unit daric (*'adarkôn* − 1 Ch 29, 7) is used already in the story of David, proof of the fact that the original meaning of the name, a reference to the Persian King Darius (d. 485) had already disappeared. Since, finally, the original continuity with the Book of Ezra-Nehemiah must be kept in mind, the earliest resulting date for the composition of Chronicles is the beginning of the fourth century.[14]

4) HISTORICAL VALUE OF CHRONICLES:

Pfeiffer [15] considers it a serious error to refer to the chronist as "a history writer." The historical content of his work is essentially available in the Books of Samuel and Kings. His own additions should rather be evaluated as "historical fiction." History is, in his hands, only a medium of composing "the first apology of Judaism." We need only imagine the insignificant Jewish community of Jerusalem towards the middle of the third century. We need consider only their extreme poverty and insignificance in the midst of the great empires that had formed upon the death of Alexander the Great, persecuted by the Samaritans who had built a new temple on Gerizim, the plaything of history. It was in this desperate situation that the chronist undertook his bold attempt to establish a clear proof against the pagans of Europe and Asia and against the rebellious Samaritans, that this tiny "Church" is the only true Church founded by God, that the temple is the only valid place in which God is to be found.

---

12. Weiser, *Einleitung* (1957), 261.
13. The ancient Israelite popular assembly *qahal* is translated as *ekklesia* in LXX; this is important background for the NT concept of church as "people of God."
14. Weiser, *Einleitung*, 263. / Eissfeldt, *Einleitung*, 668 goes back into the middle or second half of the 4th century. / Cazelles, *Chroniques*, 26, dates the composition in the Ptolemaic era (3rd century); likewise Pfeiffer, *Einleitung*, 815, around the year 250 B.C.
15. Pfeiffer, *Introduction* 806: "The First Apology of Judaism."

History is now enlisted in the service of this idea and the work proceeds from this one-sided point of view.

Weiser [16] is convinced that the Chronicle is not a historical work in the proper sense of the word, although it is impossible to deny the author's intention of using written sources to compose the history of the theocracy. "The realistic view of history is always clouded by spiritual and religious-cultic interests." Eissfeldt [17] also finds the Chronicles to be a "spiritual conception of history, alien to reality," the typical product of its age.

Obviously, we must admit that the Chronicle bears the stamp of its times, the post-exilic reform, and can thus be called a reform writing in the most proper sense of the word; it is obviously true that we are dealing with "spiritual history," but it is precisely this consideration which makes the Chronicles so valuable. It is not only a document of post-exilic spirituality,[18] but, precisely through this inexorable principle of choice and rejection, it gives a clearer picture of the basic lines of the Old Testament kingdom of God than we could ever achieve by even the most detailed political, economical, and social presentation of history. Finally, no book of the Old Testament is a history in the modern sense of the word; all of them bear some sort of theology-of-history orientation. If this element shows up more strongly in the Chronicles than in other books, this is no ground for attacking its credibility. The demonstration loses all contact with reality when the historical facts are referred to as mere pious fiction. It is within a disciplined historical frame of reference that the chronist presents a Biblical theology of the essence of the Old Testament "Church." [19] He is well aware of the fact that his presentation can create the impression of one-sidedness; that is why he constantly appeals to secular sources. These sources, unfortunately, are lost to us. Archaeology attempts to replace them by helping us to shore up this "spiritual presentation of history" with the discovery of secular facts. With this attitude and knowledge regarding their literary-history presuppositions, we can admit both the Books of Kings and the Books of Chronicles as reliable sources for our presentation of the history of Israel in the royal era.

16. Weiser, *Einleitung*, 264ff.
17. Eissfeldt, *Einleitung*, 665, 667.
18. Cazelles, *Chroniques*, 29.
19. W. Rudolph, *Zur Theologie des Chronisten*, ThLZ 79 (1954), 285. *Die Verwirklichung der Theokratie in Juda und Israel Ziel der Chronik.* / J. Botterweck, *Zur Eigenart der chronistschen Davidgeschichte.* TübThQ 136 (1956), 402-434 and *Vorderasiatische Studien*, Festschrift Christian (1956), 12-31. The ideal of the David kingship was to give Israel a living hope for the future.

CHAPTER XIII

THE BATTLE FOR SUCCESSION

THE account of the fight for succession to the throne (1 K 1—2) is still part of that masterfully written history of the family of David which makes up the greater part of the Second Book of Samuel.[1] David's fall and decline, as described in this passage, form the melancholy background for the ascendancy of the sun king Solomon.[2] David was almost 70 years old (2 S 5, 4). His hard life as a young man, his continuous wars, his constant work in the service of the kingdom, internal problems in the government and crisis in his own family — all this had worn down his strength.[3] Since he could no longer warm his own tired body, the court counsellors advised him to seek out a young maiden to stand before the king and care for him, to sleep in his bosom and keep him warm. "So they sought for a beautiful maiden throughout all the territory of Israel, and found Abishag from Shunem." [4] She was received into the king's harem but the king

---

1. De Vaux, *Rois*, 11: "Ce chef-d'oeuvre de la prose hébraïque a été rédigé du vivant de Salomon."
2. Garofalo, 28.
3. Rehm, 8.
4. Šunem, the modern Arab village of Solem or Sulâm, 11 km SW of Tabor. Many authors feel that Abishag is also the Shunamite of Song of Songs (6, 12; 7, 1). Garofalo, 29.

"did not know her" (1 K 1, 1-4).[5] No matter how energetic
and severe David can be as warrior and leader, when it comes to
his own children and family, he gives evidence of a certain ir-
responsible weakness. Against the rebellious Absalom he could
only use gentleness and kindness, to the point of absurdity; similarly, he could not bring himself to take a positive action against
the intrigues of Adonijah, Absalom's full brother and son of the
same mother Haggith, when, after Absalom's death, he seemed
to have a valid claim, as oldest son (1 S 20, 31), to succeed David
on the throne.

1) ADONIJAH'S ATTEMPTED COUP (1 K 1, 5ff.):

Adonijah was so certain of his succession to the throne that,
like Absalom before him, he equipped himself with horse and
chariot and assembled a personal bodyguard of 50 men. In his
ambition, he was unwilling to wait for his aged father's death;
he was prepared to seize the government. Like Absalom, he also
understood the value of giving his attempted coup a religious
disguise. No one could have any objection against a great sacrifice
to be offered by the Serpent's Stone, near the Rogel springs.[6]
Seen from his point of view, the attempted *coup d'état* had every
promise of success; even the aged general Joab, so often the
support of David's throne, and even the high priest Abiathar,
David's faithful companion since the days of his flight into the
wilderness, had decided in favor of Adonijah. Adonijah also in-

---

5. "To know" is a veiled reference to the marital sex act (Gn 4, 1).
6. Modern Bir-Ajûb, well of Job, 40 m deep, SE of Jerusalem, where
   the Hinnon joins the Kidron valley; also called "well of fire" because it was here that the priests concealed the sacred fire after the
   destruction of Jerusalem (2 M 1, 19). — *'eben hazzôhelet,* generally
   translated as the "Serpent's Stone." The name has survived in the
   naming of a rocky heights in the village of Silwan, *zahweileh,* not
   far from the spring of Rogel (En-rogel). Either the name has undergone change or else it is meant to refer to a large "rolled down"
   stone, which was used as a sacrifice stone. J. Simons, *Jerusalem in
   the OT* (1952), 158ff. — There is an elevation differential of about
   150 m between spring and city.

vited other princes and influential men of Judah to his sacrificial banquet. Solomon himself, together with the prophet Nathan, he deliberately slighted. When a quantity of sheep, oxen, and fatlings had been slaughtered, Adonijah was acclaimed king. They ate and drank and called out: Long live King Adonijah! (1 K 1, 25).

In this decisive hour, when everything seemed lost for Solomon, the prophet Nathan made his appearance. In a few brief moments, the wheel of history was turned once again. The sleeping lion David roused himself once more and made this most important decision, before closing his eyes forever. The scene takes place in the sick room of the aged king. Adonijah's accession to the throne did not only spell mortal peril to Solomon and his mother, but it also disregarded David's ancient oath and disposition that Solomon should be his successor. In order to clarify the perilous situation for the king, and to stir him to prompt and decisive activity, Nathan first sent David's favorite wife Bath-Sheba into his presence and put his words into her mouth: "Did you not, my lord king, swear to your maid-servant, saying, 'Solomon your son shall reign after me, and shall sit upon my throne?' " (1 K 1, 13). Bath-Sheba was admitted into David's presence. She reminded David of his oath, and announced that Adonijah had already been acclaimed king, and that, accordingly, both she and her son Solomon would soon be proscribed as criminals. While she was still speaking, the prophet Nathan was announced. According to court ceremonial, Bath-Sheba had to leave the room and now Nathan gave a more exact report, which opened the aged king's eyes. Could David actually have changed his mind and named Adonijah as his successor without having taken the prophet into his confidence? Then David had Bath-Sheba called back into the room where he renewed his oath that Solomon should be king after him.

In order to anticipate the over-hasty Adonijah, who was unwilling to wait for his father's death, a countermove had to be launched without delay. General Joab, together with the army, and Abiathar with part of the priesthood, had already decided for Adonijah. Solomon could count on the bodyguard under the command of Benaiah, the other half of the priesthood under Zadok, and the assistance of the prophet under Nathan. David ordered Solomon to mount his own mule [7] and go down to the waters of Gihon;[8] there the high priest was to anoint him "shepherd" (*nāgîd*)[9] over Israel and Judah (1 K 1, 35). Under cover of the bodyguard, Solomon rode the king's mule down to Gihon. Zadok had taken the horn of oil from the sacred tabernacle, and he proceeded to anoint Solomon as shepherd and king. The horns were sounded and the whole people cried out: "Long live King Solomon!" (1 K 1, 39). — Then all the people followed him up into the city.[10] "All the people went up after him, playing on pipes, and rejoicing with great joy, so that the earth was split by their noise." Solomon took his seat upon his father's throne and accepted the homage of all his faithful followers.

---

7. Mules appear in Palestine as the personal mounts of the upper class and nobility for the first time during the time of David (2 S 13, 29; 18, 9). The king's prerogative seems to have been a white she-mule. Garofalo, 34.

8. Gihon from *giāḥ*, "to spring up." Modern 'Ain Sitti Miryam (Mary spring), or, named after the long series of steps that lead down to it, 'Ain Umm ed-Darag ("well down the stairs"). Situated at the foot of the ancient city, from where Joab once made his way into the city.

9. J. van der Ploeg, *Les chefs du peuple d'Israel et leurs titres*, RB 57 (1950), 42-61, maintains that *naqîd*, "exalted," as distinguished from the secular kingship (*melek*) has a religious overtone as well, designating the king as Yahweh's chosen one. The finds from Ugarit suggest such an interpretation. Biblical *nagîd* is merely the Ugaritic *noqed*, and means simply "shepherd." On *nagîd*, cf., above, the account of Saul's anointing. Furthermore, both royal anointings take place near a spring; is this some indication of a sort of royal baptism? The royal terminology employed in Ps 2, 6, with the verb *nasak*, "to pour out," would seem to suggest the reading: "I have 'baptized' you king over Zion, the holy mountain." In Egypt, a ceremonial baptism of the Pharaoh was a regular practice (A. Gardiner, *The Baptism of Pharao*, JEA 1950, 3-12). *Ausführlicher bei*, H. Cazelles, VT 8 (1958), 323. Cf. R. de Vaux, *Les Institutiones de l'Ancien Testament* (1958). / Noetscher, BAK, Salbung, 109ff.

10. Difference in elevation: Gihon 645 m, Jerusalem 780 m.

When the conspirators got word of this — the two springs are only some 760 m from each other — they immediately gave up their cause for lost. "Each went his own way." Adonijah himself realized that his life was at stake. In his final despair, he fled into the sanctuary and embraced the horns of the altar.[11] Solomon promised to spare his life, on condition that he prove to be "a worthy man" (1 K 1, 52).[12]

2) DAVID'S TESTAMENT AND DEATH (1 K 2, 1-12):

When David felt that "he was about to go the way of all on earth" (2, 2), he transferred what was left of his religious and political power to Solomon. He urged him to fulfill his obligations to Yahweh, to walk in his ways, to follow his statutes (*ḥuqqâh*), his commandments (*miṣwâh*), his ordinances (*mišpāṭ*), and his testimonies (*'edût*). These categories obviously belong to the era of the deuteronomic reform, and, in this form, they could hardly have been spoken by David; their content, however, is a clear reference to the prophecy of Nathan. Fidelity to Yahweh will keep the throne strong, and the house of David will never be wanting for an heir. This is David's religious legacy to Solomon, a point of origin for the messianic salvation from the house of David.

The political legacy is surprising in its severity. Is it mere thirst for vengeance when David orders his son not to let the bloody deeds of Joab or the curse words of Shimei go unpunished? Joab had shed blood; he had assassinated two generals, Abner (2 S 3, 27), and Amasa (2 S 20, 10). The motivation for his con-

---

11. Both primitive and civilized peoples are familiar with the feeling that the fugitive should be regarded as secure from his pursuers in a sacred place. The OT recognized places of asylum: altars and cities specified by law (Ex 21, 14; Nb 35, 9-15), but excludes the man guilty of deliberate murder from the right of asylum (Ex 21, 4). — The horns of the altar, as excavations have demonstrated, are protuberances on the four corners of the altar surface, often further emphasized by a slight depression in the altar surface. Rehm 11. — Illustrations in Gressmann, AOB 444, 462-465.

12. Literally, "son of uprightness" (*ben-ḥayil*).

duct had, of course, been blood vengeance and fidelity to the crown, but still his gray head was not to go down to Sheol in peace (1 K 2, 6). David thus left an unsettled account behind, since during his lifetime he had felt too insecure in his position to take a stand against the sons of Zeruiah. Shimei had cursed David during the rebellion of Absalom; in the joy of his return to power, David had sworn by Yahweh that he would do no harm to Shimei. Antiquity was convinced of the all but infallible effect of curse and blessing. David necessarily considered Shimei's curse as a serious injury to him; but his own oath had made it impossible for him to punish Shimei. Solomon, too, could not act merely on his father's order in this affair; he had to wait for new grounds before he could proceed.[13] David's last hours are thus not darkened by his thirst for vengeance; it is rather justice, the first preoccupation of the true ruler. The villain is not to go unpunished. On the other hand, David does not forget, even on his deathbed, the faithfulness of Barzillai (2 S 17, 27-29; 19, 38). His son will be among those who eat from the king's table (1 K 2, 7).

Here is a final and true-life picture of the aged David, clearly based on the witness of reality. His faith in Yahweh was the very content of his life. Faithful to his friends even beyond the portals of death, inexorable where there was unexpiated guilt to avenge, but also too forbearing towards his own ambitious sons. The author of the Book of Kings does not idealize the figure of David. He records greatness and failings with like objectivity. "There is no basis here for doubting the historicity of the events recorded, even though the facts are stylized by the treatment of the artist." [14]

The account closes with a brief notice of David's death, burial, and the statistics of his reign: "Then David slept with his fathers, and was buried in the city of David" (1 K 2, 10). The precise location of the royal tomb can no longer be determined. An old pilgrim legend [15] locates David's burial place in the vicinity of Bethlehem, where modern guides still point out the

---

13. On blessing and curse, cf. J. Scharbert, *Solidarität in Fluch und Segen im AT und seiner Umwelt*, BBB 14 (1958), I, 135ff.
14. Gressmann, 193.
15. Garofalo, 39.

"Mausoleum of David." A tradition which dates from the ninth century locates David's tomb on the western hill of Jerusalem (800 m in elevation), erroneously called Zion. It is here that the Mohammedans venerated the tomb of Nebi Daud. Today this "Zion" is the object of an uninterrupted Jewish pilgrimage.[16] Christian pilgrims, too, visit the location en route to the Upper Room.[17] The archaeological exploration of Jerusalem, however, has definitely established the fact that the Zion of David's time was situated on the Ophel to the southeast. It is here that R. Weill, in 1913-14, carried on excavations which led him to believe he had discovered the tombs of the first thirteen kings of Judah. But the chambers he uncovered, cut deep into the rock, were completely empty.[18] There is great probability that the royal tomb lay beneath the city of David; but since so many catastrophes have occurred in this holy city, archaeology has not yet succeeded in establishing any definite proof. In New Testament times, pilgrims venerated a tomb of David whose position is presumed to be well known (Ac 2, 29). Herod had the entrance to the royal tomb faced with white marble.[19] With the destruction of Jerusalem in the year 70 A.D., all traces of this have disappeared, and the location of David's burial has been left to legend.

---

16. David's tomb is symbolically represented by an ancient stone sarcophagus, which was formerly covered with a green carpet on which was written the Koran verse: "David, you we have chosen to be the supreme ruler of the world; you will accordingly judge men in justice." Since the formation of the State of Israel, 22 crowns and pomegranates have been depicted on it, in memory of the 22 kings of David's dynasty. E. J. Finbert, *Israel (Guides Bleus)* (1955), 330.

17. Today along the boundary of the no-man's zone.

18. R. Weill, *La cite de David* (Paris, 1920). / A. G. Barrois, *Manuel d'Archéologie biblique,* Vol II (1953), 314ff. Because of the royal tombs, the water tunnel could not be engineered in a straight line, but had to be executed in an S-shaped curve through the mountain. Explicit treatment of this difficult question in the monumental work on Jerusalem by J. Simons, *Jerusalem in the OT* (1952), 194-225; The Royal Necropolis.

19. Flavius Josephus, *Jewish Antiquities* XVI, VII, 1.

3) SETTLING WITH THE CONSPIRATORS (1 K 2, 13-46):

Solomon followed the activity of his rival and half-brother Adonijah with great suspicion. Would he manage to fit into the role of rejected pretender to the throne and remain "a *worthy* man"? Grounds for taking measures against him were furnished by Adonijah himself, when he requested that the young Abishag be given to him as his wife. Even Bath-Sheba supported him in this request.[20] Solomon, however, was very angry: "Ask for him the kingdom also; for he is my elder brother, and on his side are Abiathar the priest and Joab the son of Zeriah" (1 K 2, 22). Abishag belonged to David's harem. Solomon, following the thinking of his time (2 S 3, 7; 12, 8; 16, 21), regarded any attempt against his harem as equivalent to an attack upon the crown. Whether Adonijah really had such intentions is questionable. Solomon, however, immediately had his brother put away by Benaiah, the commander of his bodyguard (1 K 2, 13-25).

After the rival had been disposed of, Solomon had to make himself secure against Adonijah's followers. Abiathar could not be put to death; he was, however, relieved of his office as high priest and exiled to Anathoth (1 K 2, 26).[21] The Book of Kings interprets this as the fulfillment of the threat which Yahweh once spoke against the house of Eli through the mouth of the young Samuel (1 S 2, 30-36). The office of high priest was now filled by Zadok, whose genealogy is carried back to the elder son of Aaron, Eleazar (Ex 6, 23; 28, 1; 1 Ch 5, 34; 6, 27).

Despite his gray hair, Solomon showed no inclination to spare the life of the aged general Joab, who had fled for asylum into the temple. He had him cut down in the sacred place by Benaiah. The blood he had shed was thus avenged: the blood vengeance had fallen upon his own head (1 K 2, 18-35).

---

20. The queen mother's special prerogatives explained in terms of the matriarchal make-up of early society. Parallels in the position enjoyed by the Hittite Tavanna. — Cazelles, VT 8 (1958), 103-106 points to similar practices in Ugarit.
21. A priestly city (Jos 21, 18), some 4 km NE of Jerusalem. Modern Ras el-Ḥarube, in the vicinity of the Arab village of 'Anata, which has preserved the ancient name.

All that remained now was the punishment of Shimei. Solomon could take no direct action against him, since David had sworn his inviolability; thus, he first ordered him to remain in Jerusalem, where he could be watched. Shimei lived here three years, completely withdrawn. One day, however, two of his slaves escaped into Philistine country. He set out in pursuit and caught them in the city of Gath. Upon his return into Jerusalem he was condemned to death, since he had disregarded the royal prohibition against leaving the city (1 K 2, 36-46).

Solomon thus succeeded in removing the elements which could threaten his position on the throne. His disposing of Joab and Shimei and the exile of Abiathar can find some justification, even in law; but the fact that Solomon disposed of his own brother necessarily casts some shadow upon his character. These first measures of the new ruler, however, clearly show that Solomon was not to be a weak and undecisive king, waiting for the favor of opportunity; he was a man of most energetic will who knew how to get around the obstacles in his path and, even though it meant the loss of popularity as a ruler, to make his way unfailingly to the goal he set. Only such a man was capable of undertaking the great building projects required to transform the kingdom of Israel from within.

CHAPTER XIV

THE SUN KING OF ISRAEL

SOLOMON was largely in a position to reap in peace what his father David had sowed in tears and sorrow. David was a warrior. Not only did he free Israel from all her enemies, but he won her a position of power in the midst of the fertile crescent that he would never again attain. This was the heritage into which Solomon entered and surrounded the young empire with such an abundance of glory, both within and without, that he can justly be called the Sun-king of Israel (cf. 2 S 23, 4). On the basis of Biblical sources, we are, unfortunately, not in a position to present the life and character of Solomon in all its living fullness, with all its bright points and all its shadows, as we can in the case of David. The Book of Kings makes numerous references to Solomon's building activity; "but the precise details of Solomon's building campaign can never equal the rich human content of David's life story." [1] Despite this, the description of Solomon's reign is still far removed from the monotonous schematization with which the later kings of Israel and Judah are treated. The individual blocks can always be fitted into a very significant picture of Solomon's time and character.

---

1. C. H. Gordon, *Geschichtliche Grundlagen des AT* (1956), 179.

1) "A WISE AND DISCERNING MIND" (1 K 3, 12):

Solomon's reign opens as a brilliant triptych [2] with two scenes that are described in the full detail of popular narrative: the sacrifice at Gibeon (1 K 3, 2-15) and the judgment of Solomon (1 K 3, 16-28).

In Gibeon [3] was located the sacred tabernacle erected by Moses, before which all sacrificial animals were to be slaughtered during the wilderness trek (Lv 17, 3ff.), together with the bronze altar of holocaust which also dates back to Moses' day (2 Ch 1, 3-5). On account of these objects, Gibeon was considered the legitimate place of worship where the prescribed daily sacrifices were offered (1 Ch 6, 17; 16, 39; 21, 29); it was thus a favorite place of pilgrimage. Solomon took cognizance of this fact and arranged for a great sacrificial banquet here. The "great high place" (1 K 3, 4) has been located in the vicinity of el-Gib, on the Nebi Samwil (900 m).[4] From this vantage point there is a magnificent view of the surrounding country, a vista which includes both the Mediterranean and the Dead Seas. Such high places were favorite settings for sacrifice among all the ancient people. The Prophet Amos (4, 13) sings of Yahweh as one who "treads on the heights of the earth." Solomon spent the night on the heights and there he had a visionary dream. Many authors [5] interpret this as an incubation or sacred sleep. There is some evidence that ancient pilgrims seeking divine direction would sleep in the sanctuary and look for a dream to make known the decision of the god they were visiting. Even though the dream plays a great role in the Old Testament,[6] the Bible does not offer sufficient material on which to reconstruct the practice

---

2. De Vaux, *Rois*, 7.
3. Rehm, 15.
4. A. Alt, *Neue Erwägungen über die Lage von Mizpa, Ataroth, Beeroth und Gibeon*, ZDPV 69 (1954), 1-27. Gibeon = *el-bire* order *ramallah*. / A. Fernandez, *Geografica*: el gran Bamah de Gabaon MiscBibl. Ubach (1953), 137-145.
5. S. Yeivin, *The High Place at Ghibeon*, Rev. de l'Hist. Juive en Egypte, 1 (1947), 143-147.
6. E. L. Ehrlich, *Der Traum im Alten Testament* (1953).

of incubation. For the man of the Bible as the Ancient Near East in general, the dream is not only the sounding board for the unresolved problems of the day; it is an open door to God's inspiration. "We have no grounds for doubting the antiquity of this account, any more than we would doubt the antiquity of the dream of the Sumerian prince Gudea, and we know for certain that the accounts of Gudea's dreams were actually composed in the form we have them during the time of his reign." [7] Solomon did not ask for long life, riches, and victory over his enemies, but for insight and vision in order to rule the people with justice. This choice pleased God so much that he promised to give him not only a "wise and discerning heart," but also all the other blessings for which he had not asked.[8] The word for "mind" is "heart" in the Bible, but there is no sentiment at play here; the heart is the organ with which man not only feels, but also thinks and makes decisions.[9] Where a man's heart is, there is the man himself.

The popular narrative of Solomon's famous judgment calls to mind nothing so much as a school example. Two prostitutes gave birth to children at the same time, and in the same house. On the third day, the one smothered her child in sleep and exchanged her dead child with the living child of the other woman, who was asleep and did not notice the exchange. Next morning they both began to quarrel over the living child. The decision was carried to the king himself. For lack of witnesses, a proper judgment was all but impossible. Solomon called for a sword, in his effort to determine the true mother of the child.

---

7. C. H. Gordon, *World of the OT* (1956), 180.
8. Cf. "Seek first the kingdom of heaven, etc ...." (Mt 6, 33).
9. O. Procksch, *Theologie des AT* (1950), 390, 395, 574. / H. Brunner, *Das Herz als Sitz des Lebensgeheimnisses* (Pap. Orbiney). AFO 17 (1954/55), 140-141. / *Das hörende Herz*, ThLZ 79 (1954), 697-700. The heart is the organ for the reception of divine directions; a fool is a man without a heart (Book of the Dead, ch. 125). / B. de Geradou, *Le Coeur, la Bouche, les Mains; Essai sur un scheme biblique. Bible et la Vie chretienne* 4 (1954), 7-24. There is no division of man into body and soul, but man is conceived of in terms of his distinct activities: thought, word, action: heart, mouth, hands, feet.

The true mother would gladly renounce her right to the child rather than see him killed.

Similar stories involving the quarrels over the real parentage of a child, with the truth of the matter being discovered by the willingness of the real mother to renounce her rights to the child in order to preserve his life or keep him from harm, are found in many other passages of world literature as well.[10] Gressmann [11] has collected 22 examples, largely from India. These examples, however, prove nothing, since they are more recent in origin than the Biblical narrative; in the whole of Asia Minor no single parallel has been discovered.[12] Solomon's reputation as a wise judge and ruler cannot have been unfounded. The "judgment of Solomon" must, accordingly, have some factual basis in a brilliant decision of the young king, which resulted in the open admiration of the good and the genuine fear of the wicked.

2) THE NEW ADMINISTRATION:

Solomon was not a revolutionary who felt impelled to do away with all existing forms. Wherever possible, he meant to build upon the foundations laid by David. The official court positions thus remained the same as before;[13] the occupants of the various offices remain partially the same, or else they are filled by sons and grandsons. The Egyptian secretary Shishai (or Shusha) was succeeded by his two sons Elihoreph (Elihaph)[14] and Ahijah; Elihaph has a genuine Egyptian name: "My god is Apis," whereas Ahijah's name, "My brother is Yahweh" would suggest his acceptance of the Yahweh cult.[15] The high priest Zadok had also died and was succeeded by his grandson Azariah (Yahweh

---

10. Rehm, 16.
11. In "Deutsche Rundschau" (1906/07). Quoted in Médebielle, 599.
12. De Vaux, *Rois*, 36.
13. See above, p. 221ff.
14. Thus LXX: Mt, however, Elihoreph.
15. Unless the final *h* is an archaic suffix of the third person, in the meaning: "his brother," which is then to be augmented by the addition of an Egyptian divinity. Garofalo, 50.

has helped). There is the new office of majordomo, who had to administer the greatly increased private and official household, as well as the office of chief district director, who was in charge of the twelve administrative directors in the various areas of the country. It is worth noting that, so far as possible, Solomon supported his reign by choosing officials from his own "household." Three such important offices as the post of chief district director (*'al hanniṣṣābîm*), majordomo (*'al habbayit*), and "friend of the king" [16] (*rē'ēh hammelek*) were entrusted to his three nephews, sons of Nathan, a son of David.

Throughout the whole time of his reign, David had treated the tribal organization as the basis of the official administrative units. But this no longer corresponded with the actual political situation; the Canaanite cities had also been incorporated into the kingdom. Like it or not, it was time to introduce a new order. In 1 K 4, 7-20 we have a list of the new district divisions. Albrecht Alt [17] has this to say regarding the historical value of this catalogue: "This sober and unpretentious document stands out in sharp relief from its literary surroundings; it stands there on its own feet, loosely incorporated into the account of Solomon's history, whose tendencies it is made to serve, without sacrificing anything of its own autonomy. The text has obviously suffered many mutilations and additions over the course of time; but these changes are easily recognized and they cannot disturb the reader's judgment as to the kind and quality of the document. The content that is to be found in the sober words of this catalogue is so opposed to all comparable elements of the Old Testament, so rich in individual characteristics, so independent of the otherwise current schematization, so completely in keeping with what we are led to expect, from other sources, regarding the historical situation of Solomon's age, that these objective observations force

---

16. The office of "friend of the king" (*re'eh hammelek*) is verified in other royal courts, as well. Corresponding positions are the *mudu* in Ugarit, the *ruhi* in Amarna, and in Egypt the *rḫ nśwt*. H. Cazelles, VT 8 (1958), 324.

17. A. Alt, *Kleine Schriften*, II (1953), 76-89: Israels Gaue unter Salomon.

us necessarily to conclude to the originality and genuinity of the account."

What we have here is not a physical description of Palestine in terms of its natural landscape, but rather a document of political geography, whose form and outline is just as strongly influenced by the events of history as by the physical formation of the country. Before David's great work of unification, the mixture of Israelite tribal territories and Canaanite city states is characteristic of Palestinian geography. The new kingdom had indeed succeeded in tearing down the ancient political framework, but allowed it to continue in the administration. To what extent? Five districts are identical with the ancient tribal boundaries: Ephraim, Naphtali, Asher, Issachar, and Benjamin (vv. 8, 15-18). The other seven districts had to be created new. Ancient Canaanite cities or natural geographical units were grouped together in the new administrative districts. It is possible that the twelve districts are here numbered according to the order of their military conscriptions; but the principle of order might also be a geographical consideration. The first three districts form the central mountain country of Ephraim with its neighboring districts (I — V); then follow the two Transjordanian districts in Gilead (VI and VII); next the list moves to the north and describes the Galilean districts (VII, IX, X) and ends with the southern districts (XI and XII). When we consider that the tiny country of Benjamin [18] has managed to assert its position as administrative district side by side with the much greater territory of the country of Ephraim, we are inclined to describe the entire district division as ultra-conservative rather than the work of an over-eager spirit of innovation. It is strange to note that Judah does not occur explicitly in the list of districts. Was it perhaps not included in the new administrational division of the state? The list concludes with these words: "And there was one officer over the land" (1 K 4, 19). But the word "land," without any further identification, always referred to the royal

---

18. Z. Kallai-Kleinmann, *The Town Lists of Juda, Simeon, Benjamin and Dan,* VT 8 (1958), 134-160.

tribal territory of Judah, as distinguished from the twelve districts of Israel. Similarly, the Assyrian title "governor of the land" means simply the administrator of the central province of Assur.[19] It is, however, possible that Judah is not expressly mentioned in the list simply because of the fact that David had already begun the process of administrative division in Judah.[20] What Solomon did, accordingly, was simply to apply the Judaean system to all of Israel. The newly created districts were to take turns in supplying the royal court, although it is not clear what measures were taken to equalize the burdens among the smaller and larger districts. The new administrative division shows, further, that both halves of the kingdom were treated differently. Only a powerful ruling personality could manage to bridge such a dualism; the kingdom was bound to split in two as soon as an incompetent man succeeded to the throne.

If the new administrative division was to be more than a provision of the royal chancery, then the necessary material for the proper functioning of the administration had to be provided. Solomon had "store-cities" (*'ârê hammišk^enôt*) established throughout the country (1 K 9, 19). "Archaeologists have discovered various places that were meant to serve as centers for this district administration. For example, in Beth-shemesh [21] one of the largest cities in the district, which was originally inhabited by the tribe of Dan, we have apparently discovered the residence of a district governor, although it has not been completely ex-

---

19. De Vaux, *Rois*, 38.
20. Proof for this is to be found in the presence of such "store-cities" dating from David's era (Lachish and Beth-shemesh). G. E. Wright, *Biblical Archaeology* (1958), 128.
21. Beth-shemesh, modern 'Ain-shemesh, located in the Soreq Valley, a Philistine border fortress, ancient cultic site of the sun god. Excavations in 1910 by D. McKenzie, PEF Annual 1 (1911), 41-94 (1912-13). In the year 1929 the excavations were continued by the Americans. E. Grant, *'Ain Shems Excavations*, Vol. 1-5, Haverford 1931 – 1939. – Comprehensive excavation account in Ch. C. McCown, *The Ladder of Progress in Palestine*, 1943, 144-147; A. Bea, *Archaeologische Beiträge*, Bibl 21 (1940), 429-437. – Description of the fortifications in Barrois, I, 152ff.

cavated. Near by were discovered foundations of a great building which must have had three long and narrow rooms. The walls are very thick, and the floor originally lay considerably higher than the present foundation. In the city of Lachish,[22] in the district of Judah, we have discovered similar remains. Once again, the official residence together with a building with thick walls and long narrow rooms. The palace stood on an elevated platform, which was filled with earth on the inside and reached a height of almost 7 m towards the west. The platform had a level surface of 32 x 32 m, which, in the centuries that followed, was increased to about 77 m .... As Albright has demonstrated, such buildings with their long narrow rooms, as they have been discovered here and there throughout Palestine, could only have been designed to serve as storehouses for the preservation of grain and other supplies. The thick walls and the raised floors are obviously meant to preserve the grain from spoiling. If this is the correct explanation — and it certainly seems to be the most probable — then we have an example of the 'store-cities' that Solomon is reported to have built." [23]

Solomon's building activity can be explored best of all in the city of Megiddo. Its natural position makes this city a key fortress. From here the great plain in the north could be controlled, and to the south the mountain passes across Carmel through the Wadi Ara could be kept under reconnaissance and guarded. The position of this important district capital has been completely lost to oblivion. According to Robinson's account, in the year 1852 the heights of Tell el-Mutesellim were a solitary wheat field. No one could suspect that this mound contained levels of ruins attesting to the presence of 25 cities. In 1903 Schuhmacher, working under the

---

22. Lachish, modern Tell-ed-Duweir, excavated in six campaigns from 1932 to 1938. The director J. P. L. Starkey was shot by Arab robbers on 1/10/1938. The publication of the valuable materials discovered has been the work of Olga Tufnell. *Offizielle Publikation der Welcome Expedition*: I. *Letters 1938* (*Torczyner*), II. *The Fosse Temple 1940* (*Torczyner*), III. *The Iron Age 1953* (*Tufnell*), IV. *The Bronze Age 1958* (*Tufnell*). Outline in Ch. C. McCown, *The Ladder of Progress in Palestine* (1943), 133-144; O. Tufnell, PEF 82 (1950), 65-80; 81-91; Stretch in Barrois I, 158ff.
23. G. E. Wright, *Biblical Archaeology* (1958), 127.

German *Palastinaverein,* began the excavation,[24] which was then continued in 1925 by the Americans, with the support of the Rockefeller Foundation. The Oriental Institute of Chicago proposed a 25-year plan. The whole hill was to be excavated, layer by layer, each stage precisely sketched and photographed. But excavators soon realized that such a method would take more than 50 years, and that the hill would thus be destroyed for later and better developed methods of investigation. The work was then restricted to the investigation of a few important areas, until, in 1939, the Second World War put an end to the undertaking. The excavations at Megiddo [25] are a perfect small-scale reproduction of the course of Palestinian history from 4000 to 400 B.C. From 400 B.C. onwards, the city fell completely into ruin, until finally the Arab farmers ran their primitive plows over the dead city and raised their wheat crops, without suspecting that the business of their daily livelihood was setting the groundwork for an unparalleled proof of the impermanence of human history.[26]

There is no doubt that David gave some attention to this strategically important city and renewed its fortifications. At all events, the ancient city was torn down by Solomon and completely rebuilt according to his new plan. The entire hill was girdled by a massive wall some 3.3 m (10 ft.) in strength. The city could be entered only from the north, through a complicated series of fortifications. The gate itself lay at a right angle. If the enemy attempted to storm the gate, they exposed their unshielded right side to the defenders all along the wall. First the outer gate must be passed, and then once again there was a right angle before reaching

---

24. G. Schuhmacher, *Tell el-Mutesellim* I, *Fundbericht* (Leipzig, 1908), II. *Die Funde* (*Watzinger*), (Leipzig, 1929).

25. C. S. Fisher, *The Excavation of Armageddon* (Oriental Institute Chicago, 4), (1929). / P. L. O. Guy, *New Light from Armageddon* (Or. Inst. Chic., 9), 1931. / G. Loud, *The Megiddo Ivories* (Chicago, 1939). / R. S. Lamon and G. M. Shipton, *Megiddo I* (Chicago, 1939). / R. S. Lamon, *The Megiddo Water System* (Chicago, 1935). Further literature: Ch. C. McCown, *The Ladder of Progress in Palestine* (1943), 171-191, 357. / G. E. Wright, *The Discoveries at Megiddo 1935-1939,* BA 13 (1950), 28-46.

26. Stratum I: Babylonio-Persian; II-III: Assyrian outpost for Galilee; IV: Age of Solomon; V: c. 1000 destroyed by fire and earthquake; VI: Philistine; VII-VIII: Egyptian control 1479-1150; IX-XIII: Hyksos era with doubly fortified walls; XIII-XVI: time from 2000-1800; XVIII: c. 2500; transition from Copper-Stone Age to Bronze Age; XIX: around 3500 and upwards: transition from cave dwellings to village settlement.

the entrance gate proper.[27] In the city itself, the most important building was the palace of the district officer, a strong and apparently two-storied structure. From the tower there was a good view of the whole city and surrounding countryside. One riddle was posed, for the first excavators, by the double rows of stone columns, which Schuhmacher interpreted as religious *maṣṣebes,* which must have belonged to a temple structure. Further investigation, however, showed that these stone columns had a very practical purpose. They were meant to carry the roof and at the same time horses were stabled in the area between the columns. The entire installation belongs to the royal stables established by Solomon at various locations in the kingdom. The plan of the stable has not altered considerably over the centuries: a passageway leads to the middle of the stable, with rows of stone mangers along either side. The calculations of the excavating party have assigned 450 as the approximate number of horses that could be stabled here.[28]

Excavations have also established Solomon's great building activity in other cities which are only names in the Bible. Among these are: Hazor, Gezer, Beth-Horon, Baalat, and Tamar; there is also a reference, without name, to "all the store-cities that Solomon had, and the cities for chariots, and the cities for his horses" (1 K 9, 15-19). Hazor is currently being excavated by Dr. Yigael Yadin (Hebrew University, Jerusalem).[29] In Joshua's time, Hazor was the most powerful city of northern Galilee, with a population of 40,000. Here too, Solomon took over the ancient Canaanite traditions, refortified the city, built a great governor's palace, and also erected large facilities to stable the mounts for his cavalry. The city of Gezer came into Solomon's power in a very surprising way. Up to that time, this ancient Canaanite city had resisted incorporation into the Israelite kingdom. But when Solomon married an Egyptian princess (1 K 3, 1), Pharaoh Psusennes II (c. 984-950) undertook a campaign against Gezer, which he conquered and destroyed, leaving it to Solomon as a gift on the occasion of the marriage. Solomon, thereupon, rebuilt the city of Gezer, on new plans, as a border fortress against the coastal plains.[30] The city of Baalath [31] was

---

27. Illustrations in G. E. Wright, *Biblical Archaeology,* 128, 129.
28. Illustrations of the ruins, reconstruction of the stables, as well as the palace in Wright, *ibid.,* 130, 131. — Also H. L. Haag, *Bibellexikon,* table 33, p. 1764. / A. Jirku, *Die Welt der Bibel* (great cultures of the past) (1957), table 83. Illustration and reconstruction.
29. Y. Yadin, *Excavations at Hazor,* BA 18 (1955), 2-11. *Further Light on Biblical Hazor,* BA 20 (1957), 34-47. Further account in *EncMikr* III (1958), 257-270.
30. With the excavations in Gezer we enter upon the age of scientific archaeological investigation in Palestine. R. A. S. Macalister here developed the methods that remained normative for all later archaeolo-

also treated as a border fortress. Beth-Horon, 25 km northwest of Jerusalem, was fortified to protect the road from Jerusalem to the sea. The same objective must have motivated the fortification of Tamar [32] along the southern boundaries of Judah.

By this new administrative constitution, the new district division, the erection of store-cities, border and trade-route fortresses, Solomon had given a completely new face to the kingdom he inherited from David. From the free confederation of the twelve tribes, he had formed a centrally ruled bureaucratic state. Hand in hand with this process, there was a quiet social revolution, the catastrophic effects of which were opposed by the great prophets. The secure patriarchal family bond, in which there was no great distinction between rich and poor, had gradually dissolved. Side by side with the new rich class and its extensive land holdings, we find the growing mass of the impoverished.[33]

gical work. The excavation account is in 3 vol.: "The Excavation of Gezer 1902-1905 and 1907-1909" (London, 1912). / Ch. C. McCown, *The Ladder of Progress in Palestine* (1943), 148-150. Fortification system with 5 sketches in Barrois I, 145-152. An Egyptian penetration as far as Gezer semes unlikely to Albright. Accordingly, he proposes, instead of Gezer in 1 K 9, 16, to read Gerar, modern Tell eš-Šeri'a, halfway between Beersheba and Gaza in the south, which could easily have been overrun by an Egyptian attack. His opinion is also argued by H. Schmoekel, *Geschichte des alten Vorderasien* (1957), 294 (Handbuch der Orientalisk II, 3). R and Z are easily confused in reading, but a comparison with the Palestinian campaign of Shishak (1 K 14, 25) makes the prospect of an Egyptian penetration as far as Gezer much less improbable.

31. Position uncertain, probably on the north bank of the Soreq Brook, on the hill of Mughar. Y. Araroni, *The Northern Boundary of Juda*, PEQ 90 (1958), 27-31, with geographical sketch.

32. Perhaps 'Ain Tamar (palm springs) on the southern end of the Dead Sea. 2 Ch 8, 4 reads, erroneously, "Tadmor in the wilderness," that is, the oasis Palmyra. Solomon's building activities certainly did not carry him that far.

33. J. Gray, *Feudalism in Ugarit and Early Israel*, ZAW 64 (1952), 49-55. From administrative document of the 14th century it is obvious that the tribal organization was breaking down and being replaced by a new economic scheme based on guilds and class. Claus Schedl, *Soziale Umschichtung im alten Israel*, BibLit 22 (1954/55), 205-208.

This process Solomon set in motion by the creation of forced labor. The old, established, non-Israelite population — Amorrites, Hittites, Perezites, Hivites, and Jebusites — became state slaves [34] obliged to regular and continuous forced labor on the public works (1 K 9, 20-21). 80,000 men are supposed to have been employed as stone cutters in the mountain quarries, and 70,000 burden-bearers (1 K 5, 15; 2 Ch 2, 16). In a somewhat similar manner, the foreign elements in the population of Egypt and Mesopotamia were also bound to forced labor. The free-born Israelites were to supply only the royal household and the military service (1 K 5, 13; 9, 22). As the building projects began to multiply and the number of Canaanite workers was no longer sufficient, Israelites were also drawn into the forced labor programs. The number of Israelites who had to do forced labor in Lebanon with the wood-cutters is recorded as 30,000 — 10,000 a month. Each of the forced laborers would spend two months at home and one month of forced labor away from home; this amounts to a full quarter of a year's vacation (1 K 5, 27).

The grand total of such laborers at Solomon's disposal was 180,000. The number does not seem to be exaggerated if we recall the many current building projects and the number of laborers regularly so employed throughout the Ancient Near East.[35] This army of laborers was organized along military standards (2 K 1, 9-14). Every 50 men were subject to a captain (*niṣṣābim*), making a total of 3600 captains who, once again, received their directions from 250 overseers or prefects (*sārê hannissābim*).[36] Such a mighty work levy the people could tolerate for a few years; but if it becomes an established precedent, as was actually the case in the long years of Solomon's reign, then

---

34. J. Mendelsohn, *State Slavery in Ancient Palestine,* BASOR 82 (1942), 14-17.
35. According to Herodotus, 360,000 men were required for the 20 years' work of raising the pyramid of Cheops. According to Pliny, 200,000 were needed to raise the Ramses Obelisk. Garofalo, 60.
36. The numbers are different in 1 K 5, 30 and 2 Ch 8, 10. The total number of overseers is, however, the same: 3850. It is not clear why the numbers were explained differently. Cf. F. X. Kugler, *Von Moses bis Paulus* (1922), 248ff.

it leads, sooner or later, to riot and rebellion. It is this utter exhaustion of the people's strength which is the fundamental reason behind the collapse of Solomon's empire shortly after the death of the willful and despotic building-master.

3) THE SOLOMONIC KINGDOM IN THE MIDST OF THE ANCIENT NEAR EAST:

The kingdom of Israel, under Solomon's reign, enjoyed a long period of undisturbed peace. The name *šelōmōh,* the "peaceful," was a fortunate omen for his people. Solomon's great empire was possible only because, towards the end of the millennium, the ancient kingdoms of Egypt, Asia Minor, and Mesopotamia had all collapsed.

In Egypt, Ramses III (1197 — 1165) had succeeded in breaking the attack of the sea peoples in a double land and sea battle before the very gates of his empire, thereby saving the Pharaoh's throne for a few more centuries. After his death, however, the royal power quickly dissipated. The eight Ramesside Pharaohs who followed (IV — XI) ruled only 80 years between them (1165 — 1085), from the eastern delta, in the "city of Ramses" (Tanis). It was under their reign that the last of Egypt's Palestinian holdings were lost for good. The Philistines established themselves along the coastal plains, and Israel penetrated into the mountain country. The last Ramesside was toppled from his throne by Smendes, who then founded the 21st dynasty (c. 1085 — 950). In ancient Thebes, the power of the high priest of the god Amon had continued to grow until eventually Herihor seized power in the south, thereby splitting Egypt into two administrative districts. The 21st dynasty presents a picture of the most extreme descendancy in Egypt, both with respect to political power and cultural collapse. Egypt's poor reputation abroad is best demonstrated by the historical novel of Wen-Amon,[37] who was sent by Herihor to procure cedar wood from Lebanon for the

---

37. Text in ANET (1950), 25-29; Galling, TGI (1950), 36-43; Gressmann, AOT 71-77.

processional bark of the god Amon. Wherever the Egyptian ambassador lands along the Palestinian coast, he is treated miserably; obviously the inhabitants of Syria are well aware of the former military greatness of Egypt and the god Amon, but this has vanished without leaving a trace.[38] Since the chronology of this era of collapse is a fluctuating thing, and the Royal Book does not present any accurate basis for dating (1 K 3, 1), the Pharaoh whose daughter Solomon married cannot be precisely determined. Probably it was Psusennes II (c. 984 — 950). Around the year 950 the Libyan Shishak,[39] the founder of the 22nd dynasty, took possession of the throne, united the divided empire, and set out to enforce the ancient claims in Palestine.

The obstinate opponent of Egypt in the era of the New Kingdom, the great empire of the Hittites in Asia Minor, no longer really existed towards the turn of the millennium. In the years of its blossom, under such energetic leaders as Šupiluliumaš (1380 — 46), Muršiliš II (1345 — 15), and Hattušiliš III (1282 — 50), Hittite Asia Minor had risen to the position of third power in the Ancient Near East, side by side with Egypt and Mesopotamia, and had begun to make increasingly more frequent inroads into the middle lands of the fertile crescent. After the battle at Cades on the Orontes, in the year 1296, the Nahr-el-Kelb (Dog River) formed the boundary between the Egyptian and Hittite spheres of influence in Syria-Palestine. Here, north of Beirut, where this mountain torrent from Lebanon reaches the Mediterranean in a narrow and precipitous crevasse, Ramses II made good use of the incomparable natural setting to have an inscription cut into the rock wall high above the sea shore, marking out the boundaries of each empire's spheres of

---

38. A. Scharff, *Geschichte Ägypten von der Vorzeit bis zur Gründung Alexandreias* (1950), 169.
39. 1 K 14, 25 written Shoshak: *Hebraized form of the Egyptian name Shoshenk or Sheshonk*. Cf. W. F. Albright, *New Light from Egypt on the Chronology and History of Israel and Juda*, BASOR 130 (1953), 4-8. On the basis of a lunar eclipse the reign of Shishak is dated as 935-914. / Cf. E. Vogt, *Expeditio Pharaonis Sošenq in Palestinam anno 927 B.C.*, Bibl 138 (1957), 234-236.

interest.[40] But in the great storm of the sea peoples, the mighty Hittite empire disappeared from the arena of history, and its capital city Hattusha was destroyed. Not too long afterwards, Phrygians settled on the ruins of the ancient city. The collapse of the Hittite empire created a political vacuum in the formerly Hittite districts of north Syria, and the void was filled by a long series of Hittite successor-kingdoms, the most important of which were Carchemish on the Euphrates and Aleppo in northern Syria.[41] In Babylonia the already weary rule of the Kassites comes to an end towards the turn of the millennium. The ancient Babylonian concept of world empire was now only a dream and not a real factor in history.[42] Assyria, too, had reached a low point in both internal and external politics. In the thirteenth century Assur had experienced an unheard of period of ascendancy. "At first it is only against their will that the kings of Egypt, Hatti, and Babylonia admit the petty king of Assur to the dignity of brother, but finally they can no longer overlook the clear facts of the matter. Among the great warriors on the Assyrian throne, together with Adad-Nirari I (1305 — 1274) and Salmanassar I (1273 — 44), Tukulti-Ninurta I (1243 — 07) is the most brilliant and fantastic. His was one of those natures who understand how to win control not only of material things but also the minds of men, forcing them to follow along their own path and will. From the territory across the Euphrates near Carchemish, he brought some 30,000 Hatti (Hittites) into the Assyrian country and settled them there, just as, after the conquest of Babylon, he attempted to transplant the spirit of this city, and thus its very great power, the god Marduk, in the form of his statue, from his sanctuary Esagila into Assyria. Nor was he content with the old capital city of Assur. Tukulti-Ninurta was the first of the Assyrian rulers to establish his own residence, Kar-Tukulti-Ninurta,

---

40. Ill. in Gressmann, AOB, Tafel LXV, LXVI.
41. M. Riemschneider, *Die Welt der Hethiter* (Grosse Kulturen der Frühzeit) (Stuttgart, 1955), 18-46.
42. A. Moortgat, *Geschichte Vorderasiens bis zum Hellenismus* (1950), 392; *Babylonien unter den Kassiten*, 332-348.

together with palace and temple, on the opposite bank of the Tigris, across from Assur." [43] Around the year 1250 the whole civilized country from Nile to Euphrates had still been organized under the sway of a mighty trinity, and three great ruling personalities had left their stamp upon it: Ramses II in Egypt, Hattušiliš III in Asia Minor, and Tukulti-Ninurta in Assyria. Towards the west, the newly self-coherent late-Mycenaean world of the Achaeans was exerting pressure upon this bloc. A few years later, this powerful construction which the then highest form of civilized humanity had managed to produce after centuries of bitter effort, was a pile of ruins.[44] The invasion of the Indo-Germanic sea peoples from north and west, and the inroads of the Semitic Aramaeans from the Syro-Arabian desert towards the turn of the millennium gave a whole new face to Asia Minor. Only in this hour of world history was it possible for a world empire to emanate from Palestine, whose sphere of influence now reached from the gates of Egypt to the great river (Euphrates). David had succeeded in conquering the Philistines, subjecting the small neighboring states of Edom, Moab, and Ammon, and in bringing the Aramaean principalities into subjection.[45] This was the secure heritage upon which Solomon now entered. When, accordingly, we read in 1 K 4, 24f.: "He had dominion over all the region west of the Euphrates from Tiphsah [46] to Gaza, over all the kings west of the Euphrates; and he had peace on all sides round about him. And Judah and Israel dwelt in safety, from Dan even to Beer-Sheba, every man under his vine and under his fig tree, all the days of Solomon" — This is a description of the two-fold

---

43. *Ibid.*, 380.
44. *Ibid.*, 384.
45. See above: "David's Wars against Aram." Cf. also A. Alt, *Das Grossreich Davids, Kleine Schriften*, I (1953), 66-75.
46. The word "River" always refers to the Euphrates. The expression *'eber hannāhār*, "otherside the river" is a technical term for the district west of the Euphrates; hence the later Assyrian provincial name *ebir nâri*. But since *'eber* can also mean not only "otherside" but "territory, region" as well, it would be better to simply translate, "from the land of the river . . . ." — Tapascus on the Euphrates (ford, from *pāsaḥ*, to pass over).

territory over which the Solomonic kingdom established its control: its sphere of influence lies over Syria and up to the Euphrates on the one hand, and the hereditary Israelite heartland from Dan to Beer-sheba.

Along the Mediterranean, the Phoenician cities had always managed to preserve their autonomy. The towering heights of Lebanon looked down directly upon the sea. The narrow strip of coastal land afforded too little living room; the Phoenicians had to turn to the sea. With its agricultural products of wheat and oil, Israel was a natural commercial partner for the coastal cities; in return, the Phoenicians were the masters under whom Israel approached the construction of her infant state. It is, accordingly, no wonder that between Tyre and Jerusalem, both under David and his successor Solomon, treaties of friendship were constantly being renewed (1 K 5, 15ff.).

Not only their geographical location, but also their historical development bound these two nations, Phoenicia and Israel, to each other. Phoenicia's expansion to the central and western Mediterranean was made possible only by David's suppression of the Philistines around 990/980. Prior to that time, the Philistines and their related and allied tribes had largely ruled the Mediterranean, as pirates, making frequent inroads into the Palestine-Syrian coast, as far as the Galilean hinterland. Based upon the two principal Phoenician port cities of Byblos and Sidon, the development of Phoenician mastery over the sea followed in quick tempo. In the Phoenician annals, Hiram I appears as a powerful personality, conqueror, builder, victor in several colonial uprisings. Under his rule, Phoenician power centered more and more upon the island fortress of Tyre (Heb: ṣûr, rock), which was rebuilt as a harbor and an impregnable fortress.[47]

4) TRADE AND MINING:

Even a cursory examination of a map of Asia Minor shows that Solomon had established his control over the middle part of the fertile crescent, and thus also controlled the entire trade

---

47. W. F. Albright, *The Religion of Israel*, 148ff.

which passed through his territory. Commerce in horses and chariots between Egypt and Asia Minor must have yielded considerable profit. Along the Arabian incense routes passed the vast treasures of the East. And the young commercial fleet of Israel returned, laden with gold, from its voyages into the fabled lands of Ophir. Finally, Solomon continued to promote the economic progress of his country by his continued exploitation of the mines.

a. *Commerce in Horses and Chariots*: (1 K 10, 28-29):

"And Solomon's import of horses was from *mṣrym* and from *qwh*. And the King's traders received them from *qwh* at a price. A chariot could be imported from *mṣrym* for six hundred shekels of silver, and a horse for a hundred and fifty; and so through the King's traders they were exported to all the kings of the Hittites and the kings of Syria." — This, the most ancient of the Israelite commercial records, sounds rather awkward. The very first sentence names the partners in the enterprise. But who are they? The ancient translations are unanimous in reading *mṣrym* as *miṣrayim*, that is, Egypt. But Egypt was certainly never famous for its horses. On the other hand, in the land of *muṣru*,[48] a territory in Cappadocia in Asia Minor, was famous for its horse breeding. The second name *qwh* was unintelligible to both the Masoretes and the Septuagint; MT punctuates *miqweh*, that is, "gathering," which it takes as referring to the traders; LXX reads the place names Tekoa near Bethlehem, which is also meaningless.[49] The Vulgate reading "de Coa" has been confirmed by excavation as a reference to the land of Quweh in Cilicia.[50] Quweh was a successor to the Hittite culture, continuing the ancient Hittite traditions of horse breeding.[51] King Azitawadda, in an inscription, boasts

---

48. Evidence for the existence of the Land of Muṣru: an account of the battle at Qarqar, where Israel mobilized 10,000 men, Muṣru only 1000, which would have been far too low a number for Misraim-Egypt. Also, the treaty of Bar-Ga'yah, King of Katka, with Matti'el, King of Arpad, and with both Muṣru and all of Aram. Since this is a Northern Syria treaty, the Muṣru must be assigned to the same general area. DBS V (1957), article Muṣur, 1468-74.
49. Further readings in the critical apparatus in BHK, *sub loco.*
50. W. F. Albright, *Cilicia and Babylonia under the Chaldean Kings*, BASOR 120 (1950), 22-25: Also treats the "Land of Khuwe/Cue," which reasserted its independence around 630 after the collapse of Assyrian power.
51. Among the "horse texts" from Boghazköi there was a book of instructions for training horses, by Kikkuli of Mitanni. Cf. A. Kleinasien,

of his many horses. Even at the time of the Persian King Darius, the country had to furnish 360 horses.[52]

Solomon thus carried on an active traffic in horses with both Asia Minor countries of Muṣru and Quweh. Verse 28 should, accordingly, be read: "Solomon's import of horses was from Muṣru (not Egypt) and Quweh. The chariots, on the other hand, were imported from Egypt (Miṣrayim),[53] which was famous for its metal working. The Pharaoh on his war chariot is a favorite decorative and representational motif.[54] A chariot could be had for 600 silver shekels, a horse for 150. A chariot was equal to the price of four horses.[55] The greater part of these horses and chariots Solomon used for his own garrisons and store-cities. He himself maintained 1400 war chariots with a complement of 12,000 men. Since the complement for each chariot was three men, the driver, the armor-bearer, and the warriors, these 12,000 men represent both the main body of personnel and reserves. The horse was thus used only in chariot warfare, not as cavalry. In addition to supplying his own needs, Solomon also delivered horses and chariots to the surrounding countries, apparently making considerable profit from the traffic. The fact that what were thus, to Israel's way

---

Handbuch der Altertumswissenschaften, Kulturgeschichte des AO, 111, Anm. 6.

---

52. E. Weidner, *Weisse Pferde im AO,* BA 15 (1952), 157-159.
53. In our version of the commercial situation, the consonants *mṣrym* refer to two different countries, Muṣru in the North and Egypt in the south. Since the northern Muṣru had already sunk into oblivion, verse 28 could no longer be properly understood. That countries in north and south could have the same name is clear from our more contemporary usage as well: the basic meaning of "mark, march," as a compound form in names of countries: it means "fortress."
54. Ill. in ANET 322-328: Seti I as warrior in Syria: 314-316: Thutmose IV in battle against the Asians; 332: triumphal return, on an ivory plaque from Megiddo.
55. The use of the horse as a draft animal has been, in modern times, largely discontinued by the increase of motorized transportation, but still a good draft horse will bring a high price. A war chariot was, thus, about as expensive as an automobile.

of thinking, gigantic military preparations consumed a great part of the national economy is another factor which contributed to the collapse of Solomon's empire.

b. *The Queen of Sheba* (1 K 10, 1-13):

The visit of the queen of Sheba ($\check{s}^eb\bar{a}'$) was not some fabled adventure from the *Thousand and One Nights,* but the predictable result of commercial objectives and interests. Since Solomon controlled the land-bridge between Asia and Africa, this ruler of the Arabian spice route was greatly interesting in securing her trade lines through Israel. "She gave the King a hundred and twenty talents of gold, and a very great quantity of spices, and precious stones" (1 K 10, 10), obviously in the hope of achieving corresponding commercial advantages which, however, are not mentioned in Scripture. The Queen had come with a great camel caravan. The domestication of the camel, a quite recent accomplishment, had opened up the desert as a commercial highway. The formerly widespread opinion [56] which held that the Sabaeans (Sheba) were a Bedouin tribe of northern Arabia who did not migrate southwards before the eighth century, must now be considered unsatisfactory on the basis of the most recent excavations. W. Phillips [57] who, in the most adventuresome circumstances, managed to uncover the capital cities of the long forgotten kingdoms of Kataba and Saba, buried in the desert

---

56. Z. B. Rehm, 37; Garofalo, 92.
57. W. Phillips, *Kataba und Saba. Entdeckung der verschollenen Königreiche an der biblischen Gewürzstrasse Arabiens* (1955), 97ff.; 150, 200ff. — The immigration of the Sabaeans from northern Arabia into Yemen is dated by Albright prior to 1200 B.C.; around 1000 camel caravans were common use throughout Arabia. The formation of the Sabaean nation has much in common with the tribal confederation of the Israelite tribes. The first kings of Saba called themselves Mukarrib, that is, "unifier," "striker of the covenant," since they had succeeded in confederating the various "divine communities, covenant communities, and patronal communities" into a religio-political unity. Cf. M. Hoefner, *War der sabäische Mukarrib ein "Priesterfürst?"* WZKM 54 (1957), 77-85.

sands of Yemen, maintained that the queen of Sheba (Saba) might have ruled over the Sabaeans during the time that they were still nomads; there is thus no grounds for locating them in north Arabia. After the taming of the camel, the use of the Arabian commercial route from Yemen through Mecca and Medina towards Egypt and Palestine was just as easy or difficult for the South-Arab Sabaeans of the tenth century B.C. as for the Arabs who were equally familiar with the use of camels as caravan animals. The existence of a queen of Sheba (Saba) around 950 B.C. becomes at least very probable on the basis of recent excavations, and at the same time inscriptions make it clear that, among the southern Arabs, a form of matriarchal society, and hence rule by a queen, has maintained itself well into historical times.[58]

c. *Caravans to Tarshish (?) and Ophir:*

After the stormy inroads of the sea peoples, it was primarily the Phoenicians who gradually brought the entire Mediterranean under the control of their navies.[59] They established trade colonies not only along the northern coast of Africa, in Sicily, and in Sardinia, but they also made their way to the Pillars of Hercules (Gibralter), as far as Tarshish in Spanish Andalusia.[60] A temple of the Tyrian city god Melkart testifies to the presence of a Phoenician trade colony in Cadiz. These lengthy voyages were made possible only by the fact that Phoenician ship-builders, towards the turn of the millennium, had discovered a new and much more sea-worthy way to build their vessels.[61] Even in these times, technology was the companion of new discoveries and conquests.

It is no longer possible to doubt the existence of this Spanish Tarshish, where gold and silver were to be found in abundance;

---

58. Phillips, *Kataba and Saba,* 98.
59. P. Bosch-Gimpera, *Phéniciens et Grecs dans l'Extrême-Occident,* La NouvClio 3 (1951), 269-296.
60. S. Bartina, *Tarsis, studia recentiora,* VD 34 (1956), 342-348.
61. J. G. Fevrier, *L'ancienne marine phénicienne et les découvertes recentes.* La NouvClio 1/2 (1949/50), 128-143.

Albright,[62] however, has also found an inscription in Pula on Sardinia with the name Tarshish, an area rich in bronze. It is no great surprise that the same name should come up in different surroundings: the name Tarshish is derived from the root *rašašu,* that is, "burn, smelt," and means simply "foundry." [63]

The Book of Kings (1 K 10, 22) records that Solomon, together with Hiram [64] of Tyre, attempted a commercial expedition with his fleet. In this, it was the Phoenicians who led the way. For Solomon, this meant the added advantage that by employing his own navy he could avoid the services of Tyre as middleman and find a cheaper route to the gold and silver from foreign mines. Does this mean that it was Israelite ships, sailing under the Phoenician flag, that made their way to the Mediterranean as far as Gibraltar? This is expressly stated in the later text of Chronicles: "For the king's ships went to Tarshish with the servants of Hiram; once every three years the ships of Tarshish used to come bringing gold, silver, ivory, apes and peacocks" (2 Ch 9, 21). Such combined expeditions are historically possible, but older texts would incline us to doubt it. The products which return on the "Tarshish ships" according to 1 K 10, 22, are gold, silver, ivory and apes,[65] all of which point, not to the west, but rather to the east. Accordingly, Gottberger has postulated the location of Tarshish in the east, in the neighborhood of Ophir. This, however, is not necessary. It seems rather that the "Tarshish ships" get their name not from the land of trade involved, but

---

62. W. F. Albright, *New Light on the Early History of Phoenician Colonisation,* BASOR 83 (1941), 14-22. Inscription published in Corpus inscriptorum semitarum I, 1, 191.
63. Garofalo, 98.
64. The name is also given as Ḥuram or Ḥirom. J. Friedrich, *Phönizische Namen in kyprischer Silbenschrift,* WZKM 52 (1953-1955), 90-92 demonstrates that the Hebrew *rām* corresponds to the Phoenician *rōm.* Phonetic laws have developed somewhat differently in the two languages. The full form is *'ahî-rām,* "My brother (God) is exalted."
65. The uncertain word *tukkiyyim,* which has generally been translated as "peacock," refers to a species of ape. *gf* and *ky*-apes were imported from the Land of Punt by the Egyptians. The Egyptian names passed over into Hebrew as loan words, retaining the article *t-* (*tu-ky*). Albright, *The Religion of Israel* (1956), 238, n. 18.

the particular form and style in which they are built (1 K 10, 22; 2 Ch 9, 21; 1 K 22, 49). These are "long-distance fleets," [66] as opposed to the smaller ships designed for coastal trade. If we retain the root meaning of Tarshish (foundry), we could perhaps call them bronze ships. The objective of these expeditions with the "Tarshish ships" was not the Mediterranean, but rather the fabled land of Ophir. This suggestion is further confirmed by the record in 1 K 22, 49 which states that King Jehoshaphat built Tarshish ships for his expedition to Ophir.

The ships sailed from Ezion-Geber [67] near Elath along the shore of the Sea of Reeds in the land of Edom (1 K 9, 26). They were "three years" on their way; that is, they departed in the fall, spent the summer in Ophir, and returned with the favorable winds of the following winter, one full year and two parts of a year in our reckoning (1 K 10, 22). Where, finally, are we to locate this fabled country of Ophir (1 K 9, 28)?

The excavations in Tell-Qasile at the mouth of the Jarkon north of Tell-Aviv in the year 1948 supplied the first extra-Biblical evidence for the name Ophir. Two ostraca were unearthed with the inscription: *zhb 'pr lbyt-ḥrn,* that is, "Ophir gold for Beth-Horon." [68] Regarding the location of Ophir, the most fantastic hypotheses have been advanced. Some authors have even thought of South America and the gold country of Peru; others locate it in Eastern Africa (Somaliland, Zambesi, Madagascar). Jerome located it in India. The Table of Nations in Gn 19, 29, in which Ophir is mentioned together with other South-Arab tribes, would seem to point to southern Arabia. Pliny [69] speaks of it as the source of the very precious *apyron*

---

66. G. Ricciotti, *History of Israel* I (1953), no. 385.
67. Probably modern Tell el-Helefi, 3.5 km NW of Aqaba, ancient Elath, today some 500 m inland. Ezion-geber is thus not identical with Elath; it refers instead to the "industrial quarter" with its foundries and shipworks. Ezion (*'ezion* — bush) and *geber* (proper name). A. Bea, Bibl 21 (1940), 437-445; explicitly treated in N. Glueck, *The Other Side of the Jordan* (1940), 89-113: Solomon's Seaport.
68. B. Maisler, *The Excavation of Tell Qasile*, BAM 14 (1951), 43-49. *Abbildung der Scherben* in *EncMikr* I (1955), 159.
69. Hist. nat. 6, 28, 38.

gold, natural gold which was acquired "without fire" (ἄ-πυϱον). The claims made by individual scholars have covered almost the entire South-Arabian coast: Yemen, [70] Hadramaut, even the Gulf of Oman, where there is a modern village with the name el-Ophir, 15 km south of Sohar; finally, attempts have been made to locate it in the Persian Gulf, where, according to Elamitic inscriptions, we find the name Apir-ti.[71]

The most obvious point of origin for identifying the position of Ophir are the ancient Egyptian sea voyages into the land of Punt under Queen Hatšepsut (1501 — 1480). She sent a flotilla of five ships into the incense land of Punt. This expedition has been immortalized in her temple tomb in Dêr-el-Baḥari. The relief carvings show how the incense trees were loaded onto the ships, and later planted in the temple of Dêr-el Baḥari. Apes and giraffes were also brought home by the expedition. The land of Punt, already mentioned in inscriptions of the Old Kingdom, can today, on the basis of zoologico-geographical investigations, definitely be identified with the modern Somali Coast.[72] Accordingly, we should not be too far wrong in locating Ophir along the African Somali Coast as well; from here the gold mines in the mountains of Fura could easily be reached. Perhaps, even the name of Africa is etymologically related to Ophir.[73] The fact that the seafaring merchants also returned with Indian specialties, including the famous sandalwood,[74] shows that there was a flourishing commercial trade with India, even though Solomon's ships did not actually call on the Indian coast. The quantities of gold which made their way into the country are the foundation for the luxury and great building

---

70. Strongly opposed, on grounds of South Arabian excavations, by W. Phillips, *Kataba und Saba* (1955), 99.

71. Various opinions compared in Garofalo, 92; Médebielle, 639.

72. A. Scharff, *Geschichte Ägyptens* (1950), 128. / W. Bissing, *Pyene (Punt) und die Seefahrten der Ägypter. Die Welt des Orients 3* (1948), 146-157.

73. Ouhir, Ofir, — afer — africa, cf. *EncMikr* I (1955); 163.

74. *'almuggîm* (1 K 10, 11), identified with the Sanskrit word *valguka*. Aromatic wood from the Malabar Coast. L'Ami du Clergé, 66 (1956), 535-537.

projects undertaken by Solomon. The Book of Kings (1 K 9, 28) speaks of 420 talents of gold,[75] that is, 17.388 kg.

David's conquest of Edom also had great consequences for Israel's "industry." It was this conquest that established Israel in her possession of the great copper and iron works in the Aqaba region. The investigations of Nelson Glueck [76] have demonstrated the existence of large and small foundries in various places. The fuel must have been brought in from a great distance, in the form of charcoal carried by camels and mules. The lack of a water supply suggests the possibility that many of these hearths were fired only during the rainy seasons. It is true that, in other locations along the Aqaba sink, much attention has already been given to the development of bronze working; but in Ezion-Geber Solomon had built a completely new "industrial city" from the ground up. The architects and engineers chose this desolate and apparently unfavorable location because of the prevailing favorable winds, positioning their foundries and hearths according to its prevailing direction. There was also a source of fresh water available. The bronze refineries employed a great number of workers, who obviously must have been forced laborers to be consigned to such an inferno. A second bronze refinery center lay in the Jordan trench near the city of Adamah between Succoth and Zarethan (1 K 7, 46). These commercial and industrial enterprises have earned Solomon the title which N. Glueck [77] translates into modern concepts: "copper king, shipping magnate, merchant prince, and a great builder."

75. Various numbers assigned: LXX 120, 2 Ch 8, 18, however, 450 talents.
76. N. Glueck, The Other Side of Jordan (1940): King Solomon's Copper Mines, 50-93. — Ders.: Three Israelite Towns in the Jordan Valley, BASOR 90, 2-23. — Foundry illustrated in G. E. Wright, Biblische
77. Glueck, ibid., 99.
    Archäologie (1958), 132.

CHAPTER XV

SOLOMON THE BUILDER

A) CONSTRUCTION OF THE TEMPLE

WHEREAS we are in a position to investigate Solomon's building activity from Ezion-Geber in the south as far as Hazor in Galilee by means of excavation, archaeology is of no use whatsoever in evaluating the greatest of Solomon's building feats, the temple in Jerusalem.[1] We are thus dependent almost exclusively upon the Biblical accounts, which can be illuminated and augmented only in a few particulars on the basis of other pagan cultic structures that are contemporary with the Bible. The later accounts of Flavius Josephus and the Mishnah[2] are no great help, since they were written with the Herodian temple in mind.

---

1. Even the mighty foundations for the modern Ḥaram walls, which the archaeology of the 19th century, ignorant of pottery chronology techniques, had ascribed to Solomon, can no longer be definitely assigned to him. For an explicit discussion of the problem, see J. Simons, *Jerusalem in the OT* (1953), 381-436: The Problem of the Temple. Excavations alone can give further answers in this respect, but they cannot be undertaken for the time being by reason of the political situation.
2. Flavius Josephus, *Jewish Wars* V, 5, 1-6; *Antiquities* 15, II, 1-3; Mishnah under Middot.

The building was made possible only by the commercial relationship that David had already established with Hiram of Tyre. The Phoenicians delivered cedar and cyprus wood from the forests of Lebanon; the trees were floated along the coast to the new Solomonic harbor of Tell el-Qasile [3] at the mouth of the Jarkon (1 K 5, 23). Hiram also supplied architects, artists, and technicians. The foundries of Ezion-Geber and the Jordan district supplied the necessary bronze. The merchants from Ophir brought the quantities of gold that were required for decorating the temple.

Ill. 3. Reconstruction of the Solomonic Temple (Wright, *Archaeology,* Ill. 92)

1) THE HOUSE OF YAHWEH

Although the construction of the temple is apparently described down to the least detail both in the Book of Kings (1 K 6; 7, 13-51) and in Chronicles (1 K 6 — 7; 2 Ch 3 — 4), it

---

3. Excavated by the Hebrew University under the direction of B. Maisler-Mazar, since 1948. Level IX was David-Solomon. A large administrative structure with several stories was uncovered. Identified with ancient Jaffa, a place name which, with the mouth of the river clogged by sand, made its way further to the south. Cf. *The Excavation at Tell-Qasile,* Jerusalem, 1951 = IsrExplJ 1 (1950/51), 61-76; 125-140; 194-218.

is hardly possible today to present an harmonious reconstruction.[4] Even the ancient versions already began transposing and emending many verses whose clear meaning had already been lost.[5] Some worthwhile additions are offered by the temple vision of the prophet Ezekiel, who was familiar with the Solomonic structure from his own personal experience (Ezk 40 — 41).

The threshing floor of Arauna, which David had already acquired as the site of the temple, had to be partially leveled and partially filled. Untouched, in this earth-moving activity, was the sacred rock upon which David had seen the angel of pestilence standing, the exact location at which he had offered the sacrifice of expiation. According to the testimony of the prophet Ezekiel (41, 18) the temple house stood on a prominence which surrounded it on every side, that is, a platform-like elevation, which was supplied with staircases. Like the sanctuary in the wilderness, it was divided into three sections: vestibule (*'êlam*), sanctuary (*hêkāl*), and Holy of Holies (*dᵉbîr*).

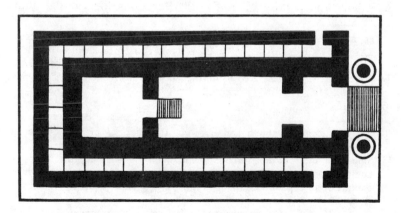

Ill. 4. Floor-plan of the Temple (*Westminster-Atlas,* fig. 31b)

4. The Israelites had no interest in the photographic aspect of things. In the whole OT there is not a single "photographic" description. It is not the finished product that is described, but rather its accomplishment, the actual construction of the building. Such a description produces a very vivid effect, but loses sight of the picture

The vestibule, *'êlam* or *'ûlam*,[6] was 20 cubits in breadth [7] and 10 cubits in depth. The Book of Kings does not record its height. In 2 Ch 3, 4 we find the unbelievable height of 120 cubits, approximately 60 meters. Was the chronist thinking of the pylons at the entrance to the Egyptian temple? The number is obviously exaggerated, if it has been correctly handed down.[8] I should suggest the possibility that the number 120 has arisen from a combination of the breadth and depth measures, 10 and 20 cubits. The uncertain text does not, at all events, authorize us to picture the vestibule of the temple according to the style of the Egyptian pylon. Although Egyptian influences can be abundantly established in the constructions of the Davidic-Solomonic kingdom, the Canaanite form of temple structure, as we shall later see, points in a quite different direction. The vestibule probably had the same height as the immediately adjacent chamber.

The *hêkāl* [9] adjoined the Elam with an identical breadth of 20 cubits, but it was 40 cubits long and 30 cubits high. The room was lighted by windows with recessed frames carried about the whole upper story (1 K 54).[10] Here was located the altar

---

as a whole. Cf. L. Knothe, *Zur Frage des hebräischen Denkens,* ZAT 70 (1958), 175-181. / G. E. Wright, *The Stevens' Reconstruction of the Salomonic Temple,* BA 18 (1955), 41-44. / Noetscher, BAK 280. / P. L. Garber, *Reconsidering the Reconstruction of Solomon's Temple,* JBL 77 (1958), 123-133.

5. Garofalo, 61.

6. Assyrian *elammu,* ante-chamber, from the root *'ûl* or *'êl,* "to be in front."
7. Since the units of measurement fluctuated between Egypt, Mesopotamia, and Canaan, De Vaux proposes the measures of 50 cm for a cubit. For an explicit treatment of the units of measurement, cf. Barrois II, 243ff.
8. Barrois II, 438, even supposes, for lack of a measurement indicating the height, that the Elam was an open court; but this is hardly possible.
9. Sumerian loanword *ê-gal,* "great house." In Assyrian it refers to the palace.
10. The technical term *ḥallônê šequphîm 'atumîm* is no longer clear. Vulgate translates: *fecitque in templo fenestras obliquas.* Where the windows "oblique" (*obliquas*) in the sense that the window housings

of incense, the golden table for the bread of the Presence, the lamp stands of pure gold, five on the south side and five on the north, before the inner sanctuary (1 K 7, 49). The walls were completely faced with cedar wood, so that no stone was visible, and the floors were covered with cyprus flooring. The cedar paneling was covered with relief work: open flowers, garlands and festoons, carved cherubim — and everything was abundantly overlaid with gold.

From the Hekal, steps led up to the two-winged door of olive wood, whose lintel and door posts formed a pentagon (1 K 6, 31), and thence into the "Holy of Holies," [11] the west room, or the room furthest to the rear, called $d^eb\hat{i}r$,[12] a cube-shaped room 20 cubits square, completely dark, without windows. The only light came from the gable door, which, moreover, was covered by a large curtain. Through the open doors it was possible to see, beyond this curtain, the carrying-stand of the

---

diminished towards the inside? Excavations have not uncovered any windows: they were made of wood and have, of course, decomposed. Still, on the basis of Egyptian and Assyrian two-dimensional pictures, we can get some idea of how they looked. There was an Egyptian harem window, with narrow grating, that could be secured and was not meant to be opened; there was also a Syrian window with wider grating, such that a man could put his head out the window; the window could also be opened. By reason of their position high up on the temple walls, the temple windows were surely not designed to be opened and closed. The Hebrew term in question does not mean to describe the type of window, but rather its location in the wall. Assyrian *šakkapu*, "door-lintel," *atmanu*, "living room"; i.e., the windows were installed over the main entrance and along the side walls. Galling, BRL 163.

---

11. Hebrew superlative form, with the repeated genitive: *qodeš-qodāšîm*, the sanctuary of sanctuaries, the holiest place.
12. Jerome refers to the root *dābar*, "word, speak" and interprets *dbîr* as *"oraculum"* (Vulg. 6, 4), or as *"locutorium,"* the seat of the oracle, the place where God speaks (Migne, PL XXVI, 476). A more likely interpretation is based on the derivation from the Arabic *dubr*, "back or reverse side, room"; or *dibra*, "west side of the sky, western room" — the temple fronting to the East. Cf. Garofalo 64; Médebielle, *Rois*, 610.

Ark of the Covenant, which probably occupied an elevated position [13] in the middle of the *debîr*.[13]

2) THE CHERUBIM

Over the Ark of the Covenant, two cherubim [14] of olive wood, 10 cubits in height, spread their wings, a span of 10 cubits each. With their inside wings they touched each other, and with their outside wings they touched the wall, thus spanning the entire area to a breadth of 20 cubits (1 K 6, 23-30). The text does not give any further description of the appearance of these two, five-meter tall colossi, because the style was familiar to readers of that time. A later author, Flavius Josephus,[15] was forced to admit that no one at his time could describe their appearance. Our investigations of the Ancient Near East, however, has enabled us to reconstruct something of the appearance of the cherubim in Solomon's temple.

Solomon did not invent anything new with the representation of the cherubim; he merely developed the idea of Moses in a gandiose and super-dimensional scale. Already on Sinai, Moses had two cherubim depicted, apparently in relief, on the mercy seat of the Ark of the Covenant (Ex 25, 17). Thus the cherub figure belongs to the ancient body of Israelite faith. It is possible, however, in this connection, to present surprising parallels from the cultures of Israel's pagan neighbors, illustrating both the similarity and dissimilarity between Biblical and extra-Biblical representations of the cherub.

The Hebrew word *kerûb, kerûbîm*, is related to the Accadian *karâbu*. Like the Hebrew word *bârak, karâbu* means to bless and also to pray or intercede. In the ancient picture writing, this concept was represented by a hand raised to the mouth, the classical Babylonian gesture of prayer

---

13. Based on Sir 49, 10 and 1 Ch 28, 18, which speak of the cherubim cart, many scholars feel that the Ark of the Covenant was erected on a cart or wagon. This is hardly possible, since it is the idea of a throne that is predominant.
14. A new summation of the evidence in DBS, V (1957), 161-186, article *Kerub*, by J. Trinquet.
15. *Antiquities* 8, 3, 3.

and blessing.[16] The present participle in the word *kāribu* (fem. *karibatu*) thus has a two-fold meaning; it can refer either to a person who prays and intercedes, or to something that blesses and protects. The Babylonian *kāribu* [17] were conceived of as intermediary creatures, tutelary spirits and genii, whose office it was to represent man in his relationship with the higher gods.[18] In the older pictorial representation, the intermediary *kāribu* is still presented as a man, whose divinization, however, is re-

Ill. 5. Kerubs, guarding a tree (Wright, *Archaeology*, fig. 134)

cognizable by the bull's horns on his head. Towards the end of the third millennium, we note the appearance of *kāribu* represented with wings, which are meant to symbolize the speedy certainty of their assistance and intercession. Only in the Assyrian and late Babylonian era do the elements of bull and lion make their appearance.[19] In this practice, the properties of the most outstanding creatures in the realm of nature are joined into a symbolic figure: the face is human, while the eagle supplies the swiftness, the lion represents majesty, and the bull is symbolic of invincible strength.

The *kāribu* thus had a two-fold office: intercession and protector. In order for them to better fulfill their office as intercessor, their statues were placed in the temples of the principal gods. This practice is expressly attested in three inscriptions: a) In the chronicle of King Nabû-mukîn-apli of Babylon (c. 990-995) we read of "a god *kāribu* at the right hand of the throne in the sanctuary." — b) We read of the Elamite King Teptiaḫar (c. 900) that, at the entrance to the temple of Susa, he

16. Cf. Latin *adorare*, "worship, adore"; composed of *ad-os*, "lift to the mouth."
17. In the strengthening form *karûbû;* most closely related to the Hebrew *kĕrûb*. Cf. P. van Imschoot, *Theologie de l'Ancien Testament*, I (1954), 128.
18. *Ibid.*, 127ff.
19. Médebielle, 613.

erected statues of *ka-ri-ba-a-li* (fem. plur. of *kāribu*), female tutelary divinities. The text also mentions *la-ma-az-za-a-ti*, female intercessory genii. c) The third text comes from Assarhaddon (681-669), and, together with the *laḫme*-gods, who were conceived of as sea monsters in the form of dragons and winged serpents, also mentions the *ku-ri-bi*, which were represented on both sides of the entrance into the Holy of Holies.[20] We conclude, accordingly, that in Mesopotamia it was customary to adorn sanctuaries with statues of tutelary genii, who, like the other gods, were conceived of as bi-sexual: *lamassu-lamastu, lahmu-lahamu, kāribu-kāribtu*. They were gods of lower rank and, corresponding to their name, they were intercessors in behalf of man, but also served as guardians of the sanctuary. The mixed creatures (human-lion-eagle-bull), which were erected as guardians in front of temples and palaces, were commonly called *šedu,* genii, tutelary spirits.[21] From the text quoted above it is also clear that the *kāribu* or *kurâbu* are to be numbered among the same category of tutelary genii, although one gets the impression that the boundaries between the two cannot always be sharply drawn in individual details.[22]

Egypt, too, is familiar with the tutelary spirit. On the sarcophagus of Tutankhamen we find "angels" in the form of human beings with outspread wings.[23] Similarly, mixed creatures, the sphinxes, keep watch before the temples. It is the Syro-Palestinian culture, however, that yields a form of representation which most closely resembles the Solomonic cherubim. On the sarcophagus of Ahiram of Byblos [24] is a representation of a royal throne, with winged lions with human faces standing at both sides. Three divine thrones have been discovered with the same pair of figures.[25] For Palestine proper, there is the ivory plaque of Megiddo [26] which depicts two winged lions with human faces flanking a royal throne. Further discoveries of the same type were made in Gezer, Taanak, and

---

20. DBS V (1957), 163.
21. B. Meissner, *Babylonien und Assyrien, II* (1925), 50. / G. Conteneau, *Manuel d'archéologie orientale,* II (1931), 699; III, 1184, 1254-1257.
22. B. Bonkamp, *Die Bibel im Lichte der Keilschriftforschung* (1939), 106 maintains that *kerûb* is a Sumerian loanword and means, "warrior, victor": hence its representation in the form of a monster designed to frighten off the enemy. — Possibly cognate with the Sanskrit *gribh,* the griffon of German fable; but this cannot be demonstrated. DBS V (1957), 162.
23. Gressmann, AOB 197.
24. Ill. DBS V (1957), 167.
25. Ill. DBS V (1957), 167, G. Conteneau, *La civilisation phénicienne* (1939), 122, 1477.
26. A. Jirku, *Die Welt der Bibel* (Grosse Kulturen der Frühzeit) (1957), table 63.

the royal caves in Jerusalem.[27] On the basis of these archaeological discoveries, we can conclude with certainty that the cherubim in Solomon's temple at Jerusalem were winged lions with human faces.[28]

Solomon had to import Phoenician artists for the construction and furnishings of the temple. These artists tried to exhaust the artistic possibilites at their disposal. Wright[29] might well have hit upon their real *Sitz im Leben* when he asks simply what these artists "had in stock." It would seem that this invasion of Phoenician art has something to do with Israel's defection from the pure Yahweh religion. Was Solomon's reign actually a primary epoch of religious syncretism in Israel?[30] We must not be too surprised by the external similarities in the pictorial representations. Despite all their similarity, the Biblical cherub is fundamentally distinct from the pagan conception. The Biblical texts present a closed picture of the nature and office of the cherub. They are the watch-men of Paradise (Gn 3, 24), but also the inseparable attendants to the apparition of Yahweh's glory (Ezk 1, 5ff.). Despite his absolute unicity, Yahweh is not a solitary God. Isaiah speaks of the seraphim who stand about God's throne and worship; according to Ezekiel the cherubim are the bearers of God's throne. Even though Ezekiel attempts to describe the cherubim chariot with images that border on the grotesque, he has simply produced a richer development of the more ancient and simpler religious conceptions. The cherubim are so properly a part of the epiphany of Yahweh, that he received the epithet "he who thrones upon the cherubim" (Ps 79/80, 2; 98/99, 1). When we read in Psalm 103/104, 3: "Who makest the clouds thy chariot, who ridest on the wings of the wind," — this is obviously equivalent in meaning to Ps 17/18, 11 (2 S 22, 11): "He rode on a cherub, and flew; he came swiftly upon the wings of the wind." If, accordingly, Yahweh is represented as riding his cherub chariot through the air, then the representation of cherubim in the Holy of Holies

---

27. DBS V (1957), 168ff.
28. W. F. Albright, *What were the Cherubim?* BA I (1938), 1-3.
29. G. E. Wright, *Biblical Archaeology* (1958), 134.
30. *Ibid.*, 138.

is more than symbolic. They represent the very presence of God, Yahweh thrones above the cherubim, with the Ark of the Covenant at his feet. There is thus established a perfect bond of connection between the universal sky-god and the covenant-God of Israel.

The Biblical cherubim are essentially distinct from the pagans'. They are not gods or demi-gods, with distinction of sex, but superterrestrial beings, surrounding the throne of Yahweh's apparition. That is why Solomon had cherubim carved in relief along the walls and on the doors, as an indication of the sacred presence of God. For the Bible, the cherubim are not a product of imagination; they are spiritual beings and realities. In order to make them somehow comprehensible in human terms, the Ancient Near East found a well suited pictorial representation in the figure of the genius. We could not, however, go so far as to say that Israel is dependent upon the pagan world about her for her representation of the spiritual beings which surround God's throne and carry out his commands. We must rather turn the question around and ask if perhaps it is not true that the pagan representations of tutelary divinities are a genuine presentiment of a truth which comes to clearer focus in revealed religion, purified of all polytheistic tendencies, properly subordinated to the one true God, who has revealed himself in Israel.[31]

3) THE "PILLARS OF THE WORLD"

The two pillars *yākîn* and *bo'az* which stood at the main entrance to the temple, did not carry the roof of a vestibule, but were independent and free-standing structures. Despite their precise description in the text,[32] it seems almost impossible to form a clear picture of their appearance. The dimensions are astounding: 18 cubits high, 12 cubits in circumference, hollow

---

31. The question of pagan influence explicitly treated in M. Vereno, *Vom Mythos zum Christos* (1958).
32. 1 K 7, 15-22; 41-42; 2 K 25, 13-17; 2 Ch 3, 15-17; 4, 12-13; Jr 52, 17-23.

on the inside, cast in bronze, four fingers thick.[33] The pillars were crowned by a "capitol" five cubits in height. With loving care, this "crowning" (kōtéret)[34] was adorned with all manner of artistic ornamentation. There were net-work (šebākîm), checker-work (gelilîm), chain-work (šaršerôt), lotus leaves (šôšān), and two rows of a hundred pomegranates (rimmônîm). What is the meaning behind this ornamentation?

One very worthwhile attempt at explanation has been proposed by Yeivin[35] who has gathered the sparse archaeological material from the tenth to the eighth centuries, including, among other things, clay models of small houses (temples?), whose entrance doors are likewise flanked with a pair of free-standing columns. The characteristic feature is the fact that these columns are crowned with a double capitol. Likely as not, the "crowning" of the Biblical pillars also consisted in a similar double capitol. The lower half was formed of four lotus leaves, while the upper half was formed in the shape of a semi-circular crown. The space between the two halves was occupied by the "chain-work" and the "pomegranates."

The pillars bore the names yākîn and bo'az (1 K 7, 21). Yākîn is an imperfect hiphil from the stem kwn, and it is fre-quently used in proper names[36] in an optative form: "May he erect, establish, preserve!" 'Bo'az, on the other hand, is a sub-stantive with preposition, and means "with power."[37] Scott[38] thought that both words were the initial words of longer in-scriptions. The text, however, offers no grounds for this con-jecture. It is more probable that both words are to be read as a single sentence. With lapidary brevity, they recall the great promise made to David's house. The prophet Nathan had pro-mised David in the name of Yahweh: "Your house will be firmly established (nākôn) for ever!" (2 S 7, 16, 26). God had built a "house" for David; and thus David's son Solomon builds a

---

33. The numbers are hopelessly corrupt: 2 Ch 3, 15 gives the height as 35 cubits.
34. Derivation from keter, "crown."
35. S. Yeivin, Jachin and Boaz PEQ 91 (1959), 6-22, with 8 photographs of the archaeological material and a sketch of the reconstruction.
36. Gn 46, 10; Ex 6, 15; Nb 26, 12.
37. Also used as a proper name. Rt 2, 1ff.
38. R. B. Y. Scott, The Pillars Jachin and Boaz, JBL 58 (1939), 143-149.

house for Yahweh, a house that will abide for all ages. The two words are at once prophecy and prayer: "(Yahweh) will (or rather: "May he") establish with power (temple and house of David)!" [39]

In addition to this prophetic interpretation of the pillars, we must also mention various interpretations which draw on the history of religion. Albright [40] is of the opinion that the pillars were originally large-scale candelabra. The "crowning" is also referred to as *gullâh* (1 K 7, 41), which Albright translates as "basin of a lamp stand," into which oil could be poured for illumination, or incense for burning. They would have been meant as an historical reminder of the pillars of smoke and fire from the days of Exodus. Albright refers to a painting on a grave in the Necropolis of Marisa in southern Palestine, which shows two such candelabra. The painting faded out shortly after its discovery. But this representation stems from Hellenistic times and offers no certain application to the Solomonic era; furthermore, the interpretation of *gullâh* as "basin" is not conclusive.[41] Interpreted on the basis of a different root, it can mean "protuberance, ball, as on the capitol of a pillar," which is its most obvious interpretation in the present connection. Finally, the incense stands excavated in Megiddo and Taanak [42] do not approach the height of the pillars.

Other authors claim that the pillars were sacred obelisks; but we should then expect them to have a different form. The obelisk comes to a point at the top, symbolic of the sun's ray and the sun god himself. Similar comparisons with Canaanite stone pillars (*maṣṣēbôt*), with the stylized sacred trees, or with the Jed pillars in Egyptian cult, lead to no more certain results. One fact appears to be certain, that both pillars, in addition to their ornamental purpose, which was to accentuate the temple façade, also must have had a symbolic meaning. They might be a remembrance of the nomadic era. When a man entered his wife's tent, it was customary to plant his spear in the ground, pointed downwards, before the entrance. This, apparently, was interpreted as the sign of his personal presence. In like manner, the pillars for the temple entrance might be a reference to the personal presence of God in the sanctuary.[43]

---

39. The no longer extant imperial terminology would suggest the translation: "(God) uphold (throne and altar) with power."
40. W. F. Albright, *The Religion of Israel* (1956), 164ff. / H. G. May, *The Two Pillars before the Temple of Solomon.* BASOR 88, 19-27, stands for incense offerings.
41. Cf. Gesenius-Buhl, *Hebr. Handwörterbuch*: *gullâh* III.
42. W. F. Albright, *The Religion of Israel* (1956), table 10.
43. S. Jeivin, *Jachin and Boaz*, PEQ 91 (1959), 21.

But since there is evidence of cosmic symbolism in other details of the Solomonic temple, it is likely that these two pillars are meant to represent the two pillars of the world, between which the sun rises every day.[44] On the occasion of the autumnal equinox, the rays of the rising sun would have shone directly into the sanctuary. Accordingly, the pillars would have their place in the realm of solar symbolism, which has left visible traces in the chronology of the Bible.[45]

Connected with the orientation of the temple towards the rising sun was, apparently, the new orientation of the Israelite calendar according to the Egyptian solar calendar. For the Davido-Solomonic kingdom, the ancient Canaanite agrarian calendar, which changed from one district to another, was no longer adequate. The strong reaction against this new calendar in the northern kingdom (a reaction we shall study later) under Jeroboam makes it seem very probable that it was Solomon who introduced the solar calendar together with the temple.[46]

---

44. Morgenstern, HUCA 6 (1929), 1-38; cf. Job 26, 11, "The pillars of heaven tremble . . . ."

45. II, 183, no. 7: chronology of the pre-history, solar rhythm. — Illustration of a temple with two pillars at the gate in Gressmann, AOB, 523. — Perhaps the solar hymn of Pharaoh Ikhnaton was reworked into Psalm 103/04 at about this same time?

46. The problem of the ancient Israelite calendar is brought up once again by the discoveries of the Dead Sea Scrolls. It had been previously known that the Book of Jubilees reckons in terms of a solar calendar. But it was regarded as the product of imagination. Today, however, we can recognize, more and more, that it is an echo of the ancient solar calendar which the Israelites adapted from Egypt with the help of the Phoenicians. The problem, today, is still too much in a state of flux to arrive at any definitive conclusions. The following are the most important views and treatments: S. Talmon, *Divergences in Calendar-Reckoning in Ephraim and Juda*, VT 8 (1958), 48-74; / A. Jaubert, *Le Calendrier des Jubilés et les jours liturgiques de la semain*, VT 7 (1957), 35-51; / J. B. Segal, *Intercalation and the Hebrew Calendar*, VT 7 (1957), 250-307; / E. R. Learch, *A Possible Method of Intercalation for the Calendar of the Book of Jubilees*, VT 7 (1957), 392-397; / E. Vogt, *Antiquum Kalendarium sacerdotale*, Bibl 36 (1955), 403-408. The solar year was familiar to the Israelites long before the lunar calendar.

Outside, on the two long sides and on the back side of the temple house, there were side chambers with three stories, three chambers in each story (Ezk 41, 6), which were used as treasuries and storerooms. The beams which supported the roof of these side chambers were carried by the temple walls on the inside, which was offset one cubit at each story. Above these side chambers were two windows for the temple proper.

The temple structure, elevated on its raised platform, was surrounded by a court (*ḥāṣēr*), which confined the limits of the sacred precept. As distinguished from the outer court, which was located at a lower elevation, this is called the inner court (1 K 6, 36), the upper court (Jr 26, 10), or the priests' court (2 Ch 4, 9). The walls of the court were built in a style which is still exemplified in structures dating from this period: [47] three courses of hewn stone and one course of cedar beams (1 K 6, 36). It was in this outer court that the altar of holocaust and the bronze sea were located.

4) THE "MOUNTAIN OF GOD"

The descriptions of the altar of holocaust, which represented the center and climax of Israelite worship, are, surprisingly enough, extremely few. One gets the impression that both Chronicles and Kings are more interested in the extraordinary. In describing the rather unimportant mobile stands for the lavers, 1 K 7, 27-30 takes up 12 long verses; the structure and appearance of the great altar of sacrifice, however, is more or less presupposed as well-known.

At the dedication of the temple, all the sacred objects of the tabernacle of the covenant were transferred. Those mentioned by name include: the Ark of Yahweh (*'arôn-yahweh*), the tent of revelation (*'ōhel-mô'ēd*), and all the sacred utensils which were in the tabernacle (1 K 8, 4). The bronze altar of holocaust (Ex 27, 1ff.), which was kept at Gibeon after the destruction of Shiloh, where Solomon offered a series of sacrifices shortly after his accession to the throne, is not expressly mentioned here,

---

47. Barrois I, 103.

although it must have already been transferred to the new sanctuary by that time; it was still being used on the occasion of the great dedication festival, but it proved to be too small (1 K 8, 64). As a mobile sanctuary in the wilderness it had served its purpose well; but for the new state sanctuary something new was required.

The statement that the king "consecrated the middle of the court" (1 K 8, 64) has been incompletely, not incorrectly, understood. It is not a reference to a secondary altar which was meant to supply the deficiencies of the former altar. Quite the contrary: these words describe the erection and consecration of the new Solomonic altar of holocausts, which was needed to replace the "bronze altar" of Moses. On the basis of this laconic description, it is, of course, impossible to reconstruct the altar. In 2 Ch 4, 1, this new Solomonic altar is also called the "bronze altar" (*mizbaḥ nᵉḥóśet*). This led to an identification of the Solomonic altar with the "bronze altar" of Moses, and the mistaking of one for the other.[48] But the dimensions of the two altars are basically different. Length, breadth, and height are 5:5:3 (Ex 27, 1) and 20:20:10 cubits (2 Ch 4, 1). The Solomonic altar of bronze was many times larger than the altar of Moses. The dimensions assigned by the chronist are in agreement, surprisingly enough, with the information furnished by the prophet Ezekiel (Ezk 43, 13-17). There is no grounds for writing off the information supplied by Ezekiel as visionary and thus unreal. He knew the destroyed temple from his own experience. The archaic terminology and the cosmic symbolism it implies make it doubly probable that in Ezk 43 we have an exact description of the Solomonic altar of holocaust.

In its external form, the holocaust altar is patterned after one of the most ancient altar forms of the Ancient Near East. It was a step-altar [49] in three distinct "ledges," in the proportion

---

48. The bronze altar of Moses, which is recognizable as such by the explicit reference: "which stood before Yahweh," was finally retired from service by Ahaz, who replaced it with an altar on the Assyrian pattern, which he had seen in Damascus (2 K 16, 14).

49. The question is clarified particularly by Albright, whose explanation

of 2:4:4 cubits; the total height was thus 10 cubits (c. 5 meters). The surface of the individual ledges was a square area of 16:14: 12 cubits. The various steps were offset by one cubit each, according to a progressive pattern of 8:7:6. The entire structure rested on a foundation of 18 cubits square, and one cubit in height.[50] This foundation bore the symbolic name: "lap (bosom) of the earth" (*ḥêq hā'āreṣ* — Ezk 43, 14, 17). The same expression *irat erṣeti* or *irat kigalli,* that is, "lap of the earth, lap (bosom) of the underworld," is found in inscriptions from Nebuchadnezar's time as a reference to the ground on which the royal palace or the temple structure was erected.[51]

Ill. 6. Altar of Holocaust (Wright, *Archaeology,* Fig. 93)

we have taken over in the discussions that follow. *The Religion of Israel,* 1956, 168ff. The Babylonian step towers were only step-altars on a much larger scale: H. J. Lenzen, *Die Entwicklung der Zikkurat* (1941), 56-60. — Likewise, in Egypt, since the time of the pyramids, there is evidence of step-altars.

50. The measurements given in Chronicles (10 cubits) and Ezekiel (12 cubits) are only apparently at variance. Chronicles is figuring only the height of the upper levels: 2+4+4= 10, and does not include the cubit taken up by the horns or the cubit of the foundation platform. The variation in the square measurements might be explainable in somewhat the same way, although the text does not present anything to work on here (Ch 20, Ez 18 cubits).

51. W. F. Albright, *The Religion of Israel* (1956), 169.

Even more conclusive for the symbolism involved is the name of the uppermost level, the altar proper, which is generally given, in the translations, as "altar hearth." This is rather a careful circumlocution for a no longer understandable word than it is a translation proper. The confusion dates back to the Hebrew manuscripts themselves, some of which read *'ari'ēl* instead of *har'ēl*.[52] "The mistaken notion that, etymologically, the first component of the word in question *'ari-'ēl* means "hearth," seems to be well nigh ineradicable. That the *har-'ēl* served as altar hearth is quite true, but there is nothing in the name itself to suggest such an interpretation." [53] The word *har-'ēl,* as it stands in the manuscript, means nothing other than "mountain of God." This Hebrew word might, however, well be a popular corruption of the Accadian loan word *arallû,* which refers both to the underworld as well as the mountain of the gods, that world mountain upon which the gods are born and reared. Such a borrowing should not occasion any particular surprise, since the word *hêkāl,* the name for the temple of Yahweh, is also borrowed from the Sumerian *e-gal,* "great house."

Babylonian temple towers were actually referred to as "mountain peaks" (*zikkuratu*) or, in Sumerian, as "world mountains" (*ḫursag* or *kur*).[54] The peoples of ancient Mesopotamia thought in terms of going out to meet their gods on step-altars and steptowers; and in the altar of holocaust Israel had its own "mountain of God," where Yahweh was to be found. The representation of God's mountain belongs to the general world picture of the Ancient Near East; just as the ancient conception of cosmic structure has its echo in the week of creation, in Genesis, neither must we be surprised to find an expression of the popular conception of the world mountain reflected in Israelite worship. This is not a question of a pagan borrowing or derivation, but rather a concept common to the cultural background of the entire Ancient Near East. The distinguishing characteristics, just as

52. BHK s.v.: five MSS read *'ari-'ēl.*
53. W. F. Albright, *The Religion of Israel* (1956), 243, Anm. 90.
54. *Ibid.,* 169.

in the case of the creation narrative, lie in the claim of Yahweh's unicity as creator of the world.

"Who shall ascend the hill of the Lord? And who shall stand in his holy place?" (Ps 23/24, 3). From the eastern side of the altar, steps led to the top of the "mountain of God," the altar of holocaust proper. When the priest offered sacrifice here, he stood with his face towards the Holy of Holies, where Yahweh throned above the cherubim. The four corners of the "altar hearth" bore four horns, each a cubit in length, as the symbols of the divine strength and power. In like manner, the peaks of the temple towers were adorned with four horns. The horns and probably also the "hearth" were of bronze, so that the reference to the altar of holocaust as a "bronze altar" is fully justified.

The interpretation of the three steps of the altar as a further symbol of the construction of the cosmos should not be cause for surprise either: "Lap (bosom) of the earth" (ḥêq hā'āreṣ), underworld; 1. story: earth-globe; 2. story: air; 3. story: mountain of God (har-'ēl). The step altar is a miniature representation of the larger cosmos. [55] Moreover, the symbolic value of the number twelve must not be overlooked. The har-'ēl has a square surface of twelve cubits; the distance from the ground to the peak of the horns is also twelve cubits. This is not simply playing with numbers. Quite the contrary: the mythical-symbolic form of thinking in which measure, number, and gradation can be the expression of a higher reality, is, in the history of human development, much earlier than the analytic and rational point of view which treats numbers and symbolism as so much idle speculation. Since Solomon called upon the Phoenician architects, "we can safely regard the form of the altar, together with its symbolism, as a borrowing from Phoenicia, where, in turn, it represented a more ancient Canaanite borrowing, going back to Mesopotamia." [56] But what has this "borrowing" turned into? There is no longer any trace of the Babylonio-Canaanitic pantheon. The external form of the step-altar, with its cosmic sym-

---

55. Cf. I, 290: Sumero-Babylonian pantheon.
56. W. F. Albright, *The Religion of Israel* (1956), 170.

bolism, is taken over, but filled with new content. The pagan mountain of the gods becomes the mountain of the one God Yahweh, and it is here that sacrifice and worship and homage are offered to him alone.[57]

5) THE "PRIMORDIAL SEA"

The numerous bloody sacrifices required a good deal of water for purification. Accordingly, Solomon had a "bronze sea" set up (1 K 7, 23-26; 2 Ch 4, 2-5), a large round basin of water, 10 cubits in diameter, 30 cubits in circumference, and 5 cubits high. It stood upon 12 oxen, 3 of which faced in each direction. Its brim was like the brim of a cup, "like the flower of a lily." It had a capacity of 2000 baths (according to 2 Ch 4, 5 about 3000), some 45 or 50 hectoliters, of water.[58] Barrois [59] feels that the dimensions must be exaggerated and doubts that the metal-casters of those days could have accomplished a work of such proportions. Transport of the finished product from the foundries along the Jordan all the way to Jerusalem is impossible, in view of the estimated over-all weight of 25 to 30 tons. But we must not underestimate the capacity of the technicians of that time. We need only think of the primitive means employed by architects to transport mighty blocks of stone from the quarry to the building site. If the individual components, the basin and the four groups of oxen, were transported individually, it would not be an impossible undertaking.

This sea (*yam*) did, obviously, serve some practical purpose, but here too, as in the case of the "mountain of God" of the altar of holocaust, there is a cosmic symbolism at work. This

---

57. Cf. the parallel with the creation narrative: the picture of the world is completely Ancient Near East, but thoroughly penetrated with monotheism. I, 24. The Biblical-theological content of the creation narrative. This might also serve as a pattern for missionary activity: when pagan forms of expression are symbolic, they should be retained, but "baptized."
58. De Vaux, *Rois*, 51.
59. Barrois II, 444.

interpretaton has been somewhat prematurely contested by Garofalo, but in view of the facts, it cannot be simply rejected.[60] At
all events, it is significant that it is referred to as "sea" (yam).
Why not simply the more prosaic term, water basin? The "temple
sea" of Jerusalem can hardly be distinguished from the Mesopo-
tamian apsû. This was the name for both the subterranean ocean
of fresh water, from which all life and fertility is derived, as well
as for a basin of sacred water which is set up in the temple.[61]
In the picture language of mythology, all cosmic sources of water
were conceived of as dragons, and accordingly represented in
pictorial art and epic. The Enuma-elish epic recounts the primordial struggle between Apsu and Tiamtû. These conceptions
were not restricted to Babylonia proper. Struggle with, and conquest over, the yammu (sea) and naharu (river) also played
an important role in Canaanite mythology.[62]

Even in Biblical poetry, the motif of battle with the sea
(yam) and rivers (nᵃharôt) finds a powerful echo. But here,
the dragon-slayer is not some Babylonian god or the Canaanite
Baal, but Yahweh himself: "Thou didst crush the heads of the
wounded dragon (Leviathan), thou didst give him as food for
the creatures of the wilderness. Thou didst cleave open springs
and brooks; thou didst dry up ever-flowing streams" (Ps 73/74,
13).[63] Just as these mythological battle motifs cannot be simply
struck from the Bible text as "pagan," neither can the cosmic
symbolism of the bronze sea be simply denied. Its presence
in the temple gives a mute acknowledgment of Yahweh as victor
over the chaos of the primordial sea. The twelve oxen, probably
bulls, which are arranged in four groups looking to the four cardinal points, obviously symbolize the four seasons, whose ordered

60. "Il mare salomonico era privo d'ogni simbolismo religioso," Garofalo,
74. / O. Kaiser, Die mythische Bedeutung des Meeres in Ägypten,
Ras Schamra und Israel. Dissertation (Tubingen). Cf. also: ThLZ
81 (1956), 156-158.
61. W. F. Albright, The Religion of Israel (1956), 166.
62. A. Jirku, Die Welt der Bibel (Grosse Kulturen der Frühzeit) (1957),
46: the myth of the battle between Baal and the Sea god Yam.
63. Cf. also Ps 92/93, 3; Is 51, 10; Jb 3, 8; 7, 12; 9, 8; 26, 12; Hab 3, 8.

succession is guaranteed only by Yahweh's mastery over the powers of chaos.[64]

Among the other temple utensils: cups, snuffers, basins, dishes for incense, fire pans, (1 K 7, 50) the most explicit and detailed description is reserved for the stands and lavers in which the water was transported (1 K 7, 27-39). A somewhat smaller model than that described in the Bible, likewise decorated with cherub motifs, has been discovered on Cyprus.[65]

6) YAHWEH'S KINGSHIP AND COSMIC SYMBOLISM

From the above description, we can gather that the Phoenician-Canaanitic symbolism was employed to a great degree in the Solomonic temple. The artist in charge was, of course, a Phoenician, Hiram of Tyre, son of a Tyrian coppersmith and a widowed woman from the tribe of Naphtali. For the plan of the temple itself, it had been customary to seek parallels in Egypt and Babylonia;[66] none of the archaeological discoveries, however, have offered any clear parallel. Now, thanks to the recent investigations of Möhlenbrink, Watzinger, and Wright, [67] the problem has been solved. "In the year 1936 the Oriental Institute of Chicago was excavating a small temple in Tell Tainat in northern Syria, dating back to the ninth century. When C. W. McEwan published the outline of the structure, it was immediately clear that the missing

---

64. In Ps 73/74 the description of Yahweh's victory over the sea dragons is followed by an allusion to Yahweh's establishment of the four seasons.
65. Representatives of the pan-Babylonian school have interpreted the sea as the sky-ocean and the twelve bulls as the twelve signs of the zodiac. But now we know that the 12 signs of the zodiac are a much later development; there were 17 figures in the original Babylonian zodiac. Cf. E. Weidner AFO 7 (1931), 170-178. / B. L. van der Waerden, *History of the Zodiac*, AFO 16 (1953), 216-230.
66. Cf. Galling, BRL 511: *Tempel, Sakralarchitektur des Vorderen Orients;* see also the comprehensive article by A. Alt, *Verbreitung und Herkunft des syrischen Tempeltypus, Kleine Texte* II (1953), 100-115.
67. K. Moehlenbrink, *Der Tempel Salomos* (1932); C. Watzinger, *Denkmäler Palästinas I* (1933), 88-95; G. E. Wright, *The Biblical Archaeologist* 4 (1941).

Syrian parallel had been discovered. This construction was rectangular and divided into three chambers, all connected together: a vestibule with two pillars in the front, a principal chamber and a cella with an elevated platform in the background. Its length was approximately two-thirds the size of the Solomonic temple, and the surface measurements were approximately two-thirds as large, so that the width of the structure was correspondingly larger. An important feature in which the temple of Solomon was similar to the Syrian structures of the iron age, was the use of wood to continue the inner walls above the orthostats. Carved ivories discovered in Megiddo (early twelfth century), Samaria (ninth century), together with the discovery of proto-aeolic pilaster in Megiddo (the tenth century on), Samaria (ninth century), and other places have recently cast new light on the interior ornament of the temple. It turns out to be specifically Phoenician, just as we must expect since it is the work of a Tyrian architect." [68]

Despite the constant reference to the similarity between the Solomonic temple and Phoenician architecture, pictorial art, and symbolism, we must be equally insistent, in our presentation, on the essential distinction between the two. Israel's God was different from the gods of the pagans. Side by side with Yahweh, there is no room for any other god. The symbolic language proclaimed him "sole ruler over all the universe." [69] In David's and Solomon's time, there was no longer room for any doubt as to the universality of Yahweh's rule and kingdom. The temple was constructed as a microcosmos, a miniature edition of the macrocosmos.[70] The "mountain of God," the "primordial sea," and the two "pillars of the world" proclaim him as master over all the world. His throne above the cherubim proves that Yahweh

---

68. W. F. Albright, *The Religion of Israel* (1956), 161ff. — P. 160, Temple and Palace of Tainat. / G. E. Wright, *Bibl. Archaeology* (1958), Fig. 91.

69. W. F. Albright, *The Religion of Israel*, 172.

70. G. E. Wright, *Bibl. Archaeology*, 142. / W. Vischer, *Du sollst Dir kein Bilnis machen. Festschrift K. Barth* (1956), 764-772. Tabernacle and Temple as symbolic image of the universe. / H. Vincent, *Le caractère du temple salomonien*, Mélanges bibl. — Robert, (1957), 137, 148.

is also Lord over all the powers above the earth. Faith in Yahweh's kingship has determined the temple structure down to its least details. It is from this point of view that the Yahweh-royal psalms must be understood. They are the liturgical expression of the same ideas that have taken on a mute eloquence in the stone and structure in the temple.[71]

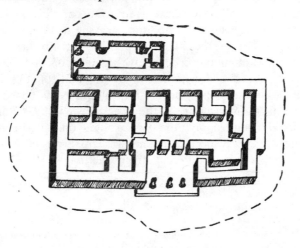

Ill. 7. Palace and temple of Tell-Tainat: Syria
(Wright, *Archaeology*, Fig. 91)

The fact that the earthly kings also have a significant role to play in this temple of the heavenly master of the world, Yahweh, is not surprising. In the Nathan prophecy (2 S 7, 14), the earthly ruler is called "son of God." [72] Earthly kingship is the mirror and participation of the heavenly. As Yahweh's representative — Yahweh had never said to any of his priests: "You are my son" — the king also has a special office in the sphere of worship. The regular sacrificial services were attended to by the priests; on extraordinary occasions, the king also appeared as the sacrificial priest of his people. Even externally he was

---

71. There is no grounds for dating the origin of the royal psalms as late as the post-exilic era.
72. Cf. above on the prophecy of Nathan, p. 196ff.

visibly raised above his, people. When he spoke his great prayer on the occasion of the temple consecration, Solomon was standing on a *kiyyôr* (2 Ch 6, 13), which has been incorrectly translated to mean altar.[73] Albright [74] has demonstrated that this is a Sumerian loanword, which means "foundation of the earth" (*ki-úr*). The Solomonic *kiyyôr* was a podium 5 cubits square and 3 cubits high. Here too we have Canaanite parallels. A king from Ugarit stands on just such a podium, praying to Baal.[75]

The position of the king in public worship has been the focus of new attention in the investigation of cult history. In Israel, he served a function similar to that of the kings of Babylon, who had to play a decisive role, at New Year's festival, in executing the ceremony of the "sacred wedding." But, as we have already pointed out, the Bible offers only fragmentary information in this respect. Kingship in Israel was a sacral kingship,[76] but essentially different from the pagan. The difference

---

73. Galling, BRL 21 (Altar).
74. W. F. Albright, *The Religion of Israel*, 171.
75. *Ibid.*, table 12.
76. G. Widengren, *Sakrales Königtum im AT und im Judentum* (Stuttgart, 1957). The Israelite king is supposed to have played the role of the god arising from the slumber of death and returning, on the New Year's feast. Opposed to this view is S. McCullogh, *Israel's Kings, sacral and otherwise*, ExposTimes 68 (1956/57), 144-148: Only rarely is a religious role assigned to the king. There is absolutely no further evidence for the existence of this Fall festival. Nathan's prophecy is thus a political concept and not a "mythical" myth. E. Kutsch, *Das Herbstfest in Israel*, Diss. Mainz 1955 shows that, neither before nor after the exile, was the Fall festival a festival of covenant renewal with a mythical character. The most convincing demonstration against the mythical character of Israelite kingship is advanced by J. Gray, *Canaanite Kingship in Theory and Practice*, VT 2 (1952), 193-220; on the basis of epic and administrative texts from Ugarit he shows that the idea of a divine kingship is nowhere to be found. In Israel's day, the Canaanite kingship had largely fallen into insignificance. If, accordingly, there are no clear traces of the mythical character of kingship in the pagan world of that time, we are all the less inclined to assume its existence in Israel, where it would be absolutely irreconcilable with faith in the unicity of Yahweh, who rules immutable over all the powers of nature.

is expressed primarily in the faith in God. Yahweh is not one of the dying and resurgent nature divinities. With respect to the kingship, the same basic leit-motiv is at work that we constantly see at play in the temple and its furnishings: Israel was not slow to adapt paagn borrowings; but they were always "baptized." Even the kingship as such was, for Israel, a pagan borrowing: "Appoint for us a king to govern us like all the nations" (1 S 8, 5). From the very beginning, however, the prophets, as the national conscience, were most anxiously concerned with the struggle to keep the pure form of Yahweh religion inviolate and unsullied by the introduction of the kingship they regarded as a pagan institution.

The adoption of pagan cult elements is always a source of great peril. Wright [77] refers to Solomon's reign as the primary epoch of religious syncretism in Israel. As long as the Yahweh cult was vigorous, the danger appeared to be in check. But in times of religious collapse and political weakness, the prospect of a defection to paganism was always Israel's greatest temptation, a temptation to which it frequently yielded. This also explains the fact that the cosmic symbolism of the temple had hardly any role to play in the later writings of the Old Testament, and has gradually passed into oblivion. It explains, further, how the king's position in official worship came to be more and more suppressed, until the cultic activity of a king came to be regarded, actually, as an offense against the divine ordinance (2 Ch 26, 16).

7) THE CONSECRATION OF THE TEMPLE

Upon completion of the building, Solomon invited the elders of Israel, the heads of all the tribes and clans and families, to celebrate the consecration of the temple at Jerusalem, and assist in the solemn transferring of the Ark of the Covenant from the city of David into the new sanctuary. The new temple area

---

77. G. E. Wright, *Bibl. Archaeology* (1958), 138. / M. Smith, *The Common Theology of the Ancient Near East,* JBL 71 (1952), 135-147. The similarity between OT and its pagan neighbors is based on the common psychological, social, and rhetorical patterns of expression.

lay some 50 m higher than the ancient Zion. It was the month of Etanim, the month of the "strong" (*'ētān*) rushing brooks, which coincides with the beginning of the fall rains, and thus corresponds to our September/October. The ancient Canaanite name for the month is explained in the text: "That is the seventh month." The transfer of the Ark took place during a "festival" (1 K 8, 2), which was apparently the feast of tabernacles, which was celebrated from the 15th to the 22nd of the seventh month.

A solemn procession, even more magnificent than the ceremony of David's time, accompanied the transfer of the Ark. Priests and Levites administered their sacred office. Before the Ark of the Covenant, as his father David had once done, Solomon now walked with the tribal princes and clan heads. Once again abundant sacrifices were offered all during the transferral. Arrived at the sanctuary, the priests deposited the Ark of the Covenant, with its two tables of the law of Sinai, between the cherubim in the Debir.

In human terms, everything possible had now been accomplished for the erection of the sanctuary. Many parallels in the history of religion have already been alluded to in the course of our investigation; but for one particular element there is no point of comparison. When the priests left the sanctuary, a cloud (*'ānān*) came down and the glory of Yahweh (*kᵉbôd-yahweh*) filled the room (1 K 8, 11). This miraculous account occurs in the midst of the otherwise quite human details, and thus deserves as much or as little credence as they do. It would be incorrect methodology to consider this miracle as anything other than historical, particularly since the other details of the account all fit in perfectly with conditions of that time and age. Here once again we strike upon the difference, the enigma, or the miracle of the Old Testament. Time and time again, we see the evidence of God's special intervention. The fact that the Kabod Yahweh appeared over the Solomonic temple clearly connects this episode with the apparition of Yahweh's glory at the Exodus from Egypt, and at the striking of the covenant on Sinai. Yahweh is the faithful God who keeps covenant and favor (1 K 8, 23). He both reveals and veils himself at one and the same time. He dwells in shadow (1 K 8, 12), beyond the grasp of human comprehension and invisible to human eyes. Heaven and the heaven of heavens (the highest heaven) cannot grasp him (1 K 8, 27), and still he has condescended to take up his abode in the temple of Solomon.

The prayer of seven petitions (1 K 8, 31-53; 2 Ch 6, 22-42) is a unique document for the ethical monotheism which was practiced in the temple at Jerusalem. The formulation of the individual petitions might well date from a later age, but the firm conviction of faith they express is in no wise contradictory to the concept of God preserved in the ancient text. David had already turned to Yahweh for refuge, help, and forgiveness in every circumstance of his persecuted existence: in danger from his enemies and in crisis of war, in pestilence and famine, after sin and in despair: and he had never been disappointed. The same attitudes are clearly evident in the "Solomonic" solemn prayer of the seven petitions.

With the consecration of the temple, the Old Testament history of salvation has arrived at another climax and turning point. From this time forward there are two "houses" firmly established, the house of Yahweh in the temple and the dynasty of the house of David. David had once wanted to build a "house" for Yahweh; he was refused. Only Solomon was allowed to complete the plan: "He will build a house to my name" (2 S 7, 13). Far more important than the human effort which erected the earthly temple is the omnipotence of God in human history, promising to establish the house of David for all time. Since the prophecy of Nathan, the two are inseparably linked in their fate, for better or for worse, a fact which is symbolically expressed in the names of the two temple pillars: "May he establish in strength (temple and throne)." It almost seems as if the course of history had stopped to catch its breath for a moment, as if lost Paradise had been restored. God once again dwells among men and is accessible upon his holy mountain. And yet, the glorious days of the temple consecration are colored by the uneasy sense of foreboding evil. God appeared a second time to Solomon in a dream (2 Ch 7, 11) to renew his promise but also to renew his threat. Temple and promise are no guarantee of magical invulnerability: "There shall not fail you a man to rule Israel . . . . But if you turn aside and forsake my statutes and my commandments . . . , then I will pluck you up from the land which I have given you; and this house, which I have consecrated for my name, I will cast out of my sight, and will make it a proverb and a byword among all peoples" (2, 7, 18ff.). Nathan, too, had spoken of a chastisement the way men chastize their children (2 S 7, 14).

Who, in these glorious days, could possibly have guessed that this chastisement would turn into the ultimate rejection of the political kingship of David's descendants and the destruction of the mighty temple itself? For, side by side with the decline of Yahweh's house, the house of David, as a political power, begins to disappear from history. In terms of salvation history, the consecration of the temple is an unheard of initiative on the part of God, greater than anything that has come before; he binds his word to a house of stone and cedar, and also to a house of flesh and blood. Just as before, in all the other splendid examples of God's initiative, it is man who fails his creator, and delivers both houses to their ultimate destruction. The temple will lie in ruins, and David's house will collapse (Am 9, 11). In terms of human politics, God's kingship cannot ever be carried out. How, then, is God's kingship to be established among men? Is there any real validity to the pledge he writes upon the temple pillars: "Firmly established in power"? — The question does not require a speculative answer; it must be answered only from the course of that human history in which the prophets make their appearance as God's spokesmen, proclaiming, far beyond the collapse of the earthly ideals of empire personified in the Davidic-Solomonic kingship, the arrival of a new ruler from the line of David, and the establishment of a new stage of God's eternal dominion over man.

B) PALACE CONSTRUCTION

The record of the palace construction is surprisingly brief, although it took thirteen years to erect. Only the House of the Forest in Lebanon is, more as a curiosity, described in greater detail (1 K 7, 1-8). Barrois [78] accordingly rejects every attempt at reconstruction of the palace as pure imagination and guess work. Galling,[79] however, feels that, nevertheless, some accurate picture can be arrived at on the basis of collating all the available material.

First of all, it is clear that temple and palace formed a unity. The buildings were constructed on the sacred rock upon which the angel of the pestilence had appeared and where David had offered sacrifice. Round about this rock the temple terrace was erected, sealed off by a wall which thus formed a sacred precinct.

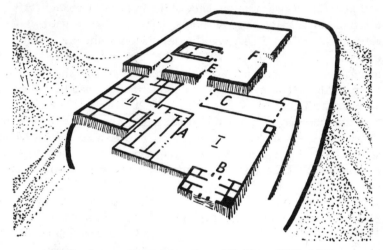

Ill. 8. Acropolis of Jerusalem (Galling, BRL 411)

A — Throne room (audience room)

B — Pillar hall

C — House of the Forest of Lebanon

D, E — Two entrances to the temple court

F — Principal entrance for the people

I — Public court

II — Private court with quarters for the royal family

---

78. Barrois II, 446: The reconstructions attempted on this base are of pure fantasy.

79. Galling, BRL 411.

The plan of the palace buildings was dictated by nature. In order simply to have a foundation for the structure, a great amount of stone and fill (Millo — 1 K 7, 10) had to be supplied first. Thus, the higher elevated temple terrace was adjacent, towards the south, to a second, lower, terrace which contained the palace buildings, grouped about two courtyards.

Fronting on the first courtyard was the House of the Forest of Lebanon (*bêt-ya'ar hall^ebānôn*), 100 cubits long, 50 cubits wide, and 30 cubits high. It took its name from the 45 cedar trunks, arranged in three rows, which served as pillars to support the roof and were thus a clear reminiscence of the Forest of Lebanon. Above the pillar hall there was, probably, an upper story with various cells and chambers. Regarding the disposition of these quarters, the only sure information we have is that the rooms were used as arsenals. It was here that Solomon kept the golden shields of his bodyguard, 200 large shields and 300 smaller shields, all richly adorned with gold (1 K 10, 16ff.; 2 K 20, 13; Is 22, 8; 29, 2). Some authors have supposed that the hall itself was used for great court festivals;[80] more likely, however, it was used for the court stables.[81] If this presupposition is correct, then we should have to presume that there was also an exit ramp, similar to the construction in the citadel at Sargon.[82]

Fronting upon this first courtyard were also the Hall of Pillars (*'ûlām hā'ammûdîm*) and the Hall of the Throne and Hall of Judgment (*'ûlām hakkisē*) (1 K 7, 6-7). The name Hall of Pillars, the text of which de Vaux[83] considers to be corrupted beyond hope, can most easily be explained in terms of the building style of the Hilani. "A *bît ḥilani* is an individual house, whose front side forms a supporting vestibule which, in its turn, is enclosed by chamber areas which need not be exclusively in the form of towers or turrets; the main room behind the vestibule can be in the shape of a square or a long or short rectangle."[84] The Biblical Hall

---

80. Médebielle, 615.
81. K. Moehlenbrink, *Der Tempel Salomos* (1932), 49ff.
82. Galling, BRL 411.
83. De Vaux, *Rois,* 49.
84. Fr. Wachtsmuth, "Was ist ein Hilani, *ein bît hilani?*" ZDMG 109

of Pillars was a rectangular room 50 x 30 cubits fronted by a vestibule with pillars. The structure can best be compared to a gateway giving access to the royal palace.

The dimensions of the throne room have not been preserved. The text records only the cedar paneling. It is here that the famous ivory and gold lion throne of Solomon was located.[85] Six steps led up to it and it was flanked by six lions on either side (1 K 10, 18ff.). On both sides of the arm rests there were also two lions. Solomon's lion throne is best pictured after the sample of an ivory plaque from Megiddo, which represents a king sitting on a throne borne by two lion-cherubs. Before him stands his queen, and behind her a lyre player, then a warrior who is escorting captive kings to audience.[86]

The private living quarters of the royal family were grouped about the second inner court. Here the women's quarters (harem) was also located. Perhaps the palace which Solomon built especially for the daughter of Pharaoh (1 K 7, 8) was also to be found in this area.

The new Solomonic temple and palace city was enclosed within an extension of the walls of the ancient city of David. The total city area was thus increased by some 10 hectares.[87] Within these more spacious accommodations there was ample room to develop the full magnificence of Solomonic court life. What a difference from the primitive citadel fortress of Saul, who lived like a peasant-king, and what a difference from the simple court life of David. The mighty buildings were an external proclamation of the mighty

---

1958), 66-73. The relationship between the pillars and the Hilani building has been noted already by Galling, BRL, 1937, 411. Cf. 1 K 7, 6: 'ab possibly related to Assyrian bēt appāti, "house with folding doors" (?)

---

85. Apparently this term means "with gilded ivory inlays," such as are known from Samaria and Megiddo. Cf. A. Jirku, Die Ausgrabungen in Palästina (1956), 61ff. / H. Th. Bossert, Altsyrien (1951), 1106-1121 (partim). / Grollenberg, Atlas of the Bible (1958), 211-217.

86. A. Jirku, Welt der Bibel (Grosse Kulturen der Frühzeit), (1957), table 63.

87. Rehm, 25.

changes in Israel's position in relation to the rest of the Ancient Near East. In Solomon's time, the court of Jerusalem was the most important political center in the middle of the fertile crescent. Through commercial enterprises and tribute payments, unheard of riches flowed constantly into the land (1 K 10, 14). The long reign of Solomon was blessed with universal peace. But already in the last years of the sun-king there were signs, on the one hand, that he had made too great demands upon his people's strength and, on the other hand, that he had failed to keep pace with the changing political situation which gradually led to the loss of his outlying provinces.

CHAPTER XVI

SIGNS OF COLLAPSE

1) PAGAN SACRIFICE IN JERUSALEM

IT is easy to lose sight of the fact that the Davidic-Solomonic kingdom represents a unified picture in neither national nor religious terms. The heartland was, to be sure, composed of the Twelve tribes of Israel with the temple of Yahweh at Jerusalem serving as the religious center and the royal palace as the political focus of the kingdom. But David's conquests had incorporated a circle of non-Israelite territories into the kingdom. These subjugated territories, from Edom in the south to the Aramaeans in the north, were never forced to accept the Yahweh cult. For the most part, they continued to worship their own national gods. It is only natural that these various peoples should introduce sanctuaries of their own gods into the national capital.

The manifold composition of the Israelite kingdom is mirrored most effectively in Solomon's harem. The harem is not only an expression of the power and wealth of a ruler; it is also the seal and mirror of his political success; commercial, alliance, and friendship treaties were always sealed by taking a wife into the royal harem, who was thus to be regarded as a sort of "court ambassador." Thus, the military crisis with Egypt (1 K 3, 1) was avoided by Solomon's marriage with a daughter of the Pharaoh: this was equivalent to a tactical recognition, by the ancient pharaonic kingdom, of Palestine's new position in the Ancient Near East. The taking of wives from Edom, Moab, and Ammon was calculated to bind the subject peoples to the court of Jerusalem by a more friendly tie than the threat of military power. The fact that there were also women from Sidon in Solomon's harem should not occasion any great surprise; since David's time there had been intimate ties of friendship and commercial exchange with the Phoenicians. Whether the Hittite women were national Hittites, or whether the term is merely used to designate the non-Israelite population of Canaan, cannot be determined with any real certainty. At all events, the ancient Canaanite cities would certainly have regarded it as an honor to have their women represented in the royal harem. It is surprising that the text mentions no Israelite wives of Solomon; this, of course, can be presupposed on the part of our author. In keeping with Solomon's great glory, the number of his wives must have been considerable. The actual figure is given in round numbers, which cannot be taken as an accurate count: 700 women of royal blood and 300 concubines.[1]

These foreign women brought their native gods with them; they had not renounced them upon their marriage. When Solomon established sacrificial high places for Ashtoreth, the goddess of the Sidonians, for Milcom the "abomination" of the Ammonites and Chemosh the "abomination" of Moab,[2] as well as for other

---

1. Many authors doubt the accuracy of the traditional number, although, in terms of Oriental attitudes towards numbers, there is no grounds for such doubt. Thousand means "a great number" which is also composed of the two universal numbers 700 and 300. Other authors suspect that the numbers in the Song of Songs are correct (6, 8): 60 royal brides and 80 concubines. Cf. the common usage: "Thousand and One Nights."

2. The name of the God of Ammon is handed down in two forms: Milkom (1 K 11, 5) and môlēk (11, 7), the second in reference to child sacrifice; hence the additional epithet, "abomination of the Ammonites." — New evidence for the interpretation of môlēk as child sacrifice, based on Punic inscriptions, in J. Hoftijzer, Eine Notiz zum punischen Kinderopfer. VT 8 (1958), 288: milk'dm bšrm btm, "a human sacrifice, of his own child, in complete state."

gods and goddesses on the mountain east of Jerusalem he acted not only out of weakness, giving in to the will of his harem, but also from political necessity and acumen. "The subjugated peoples must learn to recognize Jerusalem as a focal point. Idol-worship was further supported by the great increase in commercial relations: the merchant who came to Jerusalem brought with him the altar or image of his gods, to worship or to seal commercial contracts in his presence. Solomon's world politics thus necessarily increased the number of gods worshipped in Jerusalem."[4]

What was political acumen in terms of commerce and international relationships, is evaluated quite differently in the eyes of the Biblical theologian of history. He sees this cosmopolitan and liberal religious attitude as the underlying cause for the collapse of Solomon's empire. Israel and her kingship can only survive in terms of the covenant (*berît* — 1 K 11, 11). If this fundamental root of Israel's greatness is systematically gnawed away, then the splendid tree must, sooner or later, totter and fall. Solomon's religious politics encountered opposition primarily in the prophetic circles. The prophetic threat of the collapse of his kingdom (1 K 11, 9-13) does not come as a bolt from the blue.

2) MORTGAGE OF ISRAELITE CITIES WITH HIRAM

Despite Solomon's high annual income — "the weight of gold that came to Solomon in one year was 666 talents of gold,[5] beside that which came from the traders and from the traffic of the merchants, and from all the kings of Arabia and from the governors of the land" (1 K 10, 14-15) — despite this gigantic income, Solo-

---

3. These are not temple buildings, but rather the sacrificial high places (*bāmâh*) which are typical of the Canaanite worship. Located on the mountain of scandals, modern *gebel bâten el-ḥâwa*, south of Jerusalem.
4. Gressmann, *Geschichte* 218.
5. 666 is a general number for expressing the idea of "very much," when the speaker is not in a position to give more precise details. Because of the fluctuating value of modern monetary units, the determination of the original precious content of the coinage, and the differences in the purchasing power of money, it is impossible to attempt an adequate

mon's means were insufficient to defray the expenses of his great building projects and the maintenance of his royal court. King Hiram of Tyre had not only supplied Solomon with cedar and cyprus wood; he had also advanced him a loan of 120 talents of gold. As a mortgage against this loan, Solomon had to pledge twenty cities in Galilee (1 K 9, 10-14; 2 Chron 8, 1-2). But when Hiram saw the cities, he was not satisfied with the offer and sent word to his "brother" — in the Amarna letters kings also call each other "brother" — "What kind of cities are these which you have given me?" The answer is obvious: They are "as nothing" (k^e-bal) in comparison to what I have delivered to you. His disillusionment, like a true citizen of the Ancient Near East, he expresses in a mockery: "And he called the land Cabul." Hiram did not invent the name Cabul for this territory but rather reinterpreted the ancient place name, which could easily be understood as k^e-bal, that is, "as nothing."[6] Cabul is already mentioned in Joshua 19, 27 as belonging to the tribe of Asher. From 2 Ch 8, 2 we can establish the fact that the cities in question were returned and others were pledged as surety for the loan. The fact, however, that Solomon was prepared to mortgage his own country is obvious evidence of his great financial straits.

3) REVOLT OF EDOM

On the occasion of the extremely cruel and heartless subjugation of Edom by David's captain Joab, the young prince Hadad had succeeded in fleeing through Midian and Paran into the land of Egypt. Pharaoh offered him political asylum; Egypt was obviously interested in preventing Israel from becoming too powerful. Hadad thus enjoyed a favorable position in the land of the Nile: "Hadad found great favor in the sight of Pharaoh, so that he gave him in

---

picture of the amount involved. Cf. Rehm, *Die Bücher der Könige* (EB) (1949), 38.

---

6. A. Johnson, *1 K 9, 3, Etymologie von Kabul = "unjust," ein Witz-Wortspiel*, Expository Times 66 (1954/55), 32. The name has been preserved even today in an Arab village of the same name, 14 km SE of Acco.

marriage the sister of his own wife, the sister of Tahpenes."[7] Her son Genubath was raised in the Pharaoh's own household. After David's death, Hadad was no longer satisfied to live in Egypt. He went back to Edom, where he became a "satan" for Solomon, that is, an adversary who could not be forced out of the way. The course of their struggle is not recorded in the Bible. At all events, Hadad managed to secure a section of Edom, while the main route to the Gulf of Aqaba remained in the possession of the kings of Judah. Edom regained full autonomy only under the reign of Joram (1 K 11, 14-22; 2 K 8, 20).

4) THE REVOLT OF DAMASCUS

A second powerful satan, or adversary, appeared in the person of Rezon of Damascus. David had shattered the Aramaean alliance under the direction of Hadadezer of Aram-Zobah, and subjugated his kingdom (2 S 8, 3-6; 10, 15-19). Rezon had escaped this catastrophe by fleeing into the wilderness. There, like David before him, he lived as an outlaw chief. At a favorable opportunity, when the power of Solomon was growing weaker and weaker, he seized the city of Damascus,[8] expelled the officials established there by David, and made himself king. This was a most serious blow to Solomon's position in the Aramaean provinces, and a serious threat to the trade routes leading north. It is surprising that Solomon, despite his great military strength, did not undertake any counter-offensive either in Edom or in Damascus; he simply resigned himself to the gradual defection of his outlying provinces. Perhaps the long years of forced labor and official building programs had laid such a strain on domestic politics that he was not in a position to attempt any further military operation (1 K 11, 23-25).

---

7. *taḥpᵉneš* is not a proper name, but the title of the "great consort of the king" — *tᵉḥm(t) ns(wt) wr(t)*; thus, instead of *taḥpᵉneš*, we read *taḥmenis*. Cf. LXX *thekemeina*. / B. Grdseloff, *Takhpnès, Annales du Service des Antiquités de l'Egypt*, 47 (1947).

8. On the history of Damascus, the important oasis and commercial city on the edge of the wilderness, and its fluctuating position in the course of world history, see the explicit treatment in A. Barrois, DBS II (1934), 275-287.

5) THE REVOLT OF THE FORCED LABORERS

Jeroboam (Hieroboam), son of Nabath, an Ephraimite from Zeredah,[9] son of a widow named Zeruah,[10] soon appeared as the spokesman of the domestic opposition before the king. Solomon himself had been quick to recognize the extraordinary capabilities of this young man during the public building programs at Jerusalem, having put him in charge of the entire labor contingent (*sēbel*)[11] of the house of Joseph. In this position he soon managed to sympathize with the attitude of the workmen who were groaning under the heavy load they had to bear. Although the text does not specifically say so, the workers on the Millo in Jerusalem must have staged a rebellion. "Jeroboam lifted up his hand against the king" (1 K 11, 26). When Solomon, subsequently, attempted to have him put out of the way, he fled to Egypt, where the Pharaoh Shishak[12] offered him political asylum.

Not only did the social conditions gradually lead to a series of rebellions; in prophetic circles there was no sympathy at all with Solomon's liberal religious politics. His establishment of pagan sacrificial high places was a threat to the purity of the Yahweh cult.

---

9. Perhaps *dêr ghassane*, 8 km NE of Rama (Rentis), the town where Samuel lived (1 S 1, 1).

10. The name *serû'âh*, "the leper," which the Hebrew text records as the mother of Jeroboam, and the term prostitute (*pornē*) in the LXX, betrays the contempt of a later age towards Jeroboam, who, by his political and religious schism, had made Israel a "leper and a prostitute." Probably, like David's sister, her name was simply Zeruiah (Sarvia).

11. The word *sēbel*, with which 1 K 11, 28 refers to this office, is generally translated as "forced labor" and thus Jeroboam is assigned a position within the administration of the program of public works. It is to be noted, however, that the word means something like "bearing burdens," and is not the normal word for forced labor (*mas*). It is also unclear precisely which of the work projects he was placed in charge of. M. Noth, *Geschichte Israels*, 1950, 179. – Egyptian forced labor and attendant rebellions has been recently much illuminated by the discovery of a new papyrus: W. C. Hayes, *A Papyrus of the Late Middle Kingdom in the Brooklyn Museum* (1955).

12. Cf. Israel in the midst of the OT, above, p. 309ff.

These circles began to look to the young and very promising figure
of Jeroboam. The prophet Ahijah met him alone in the open country one day. He tore his garment — a large square of cloth which
was worn across the shoulders — into twelve pieces and told Jeroboam to take ten of them. This symbolic gesture he then explained
in words: Solomon's kingdom was to be torn to pieces and ten of
them would go to Jeroboam. The united kingdom was once again
to be dissolved into its ancient components: Israel and Judah.[13]
That such a political division would also entail a religious split
was not the intention of the prophet: quite the contrary. It was
expected that the future king of the northern kingdom would restore the Yahweh cult to its ancient purity and do away with the
pagan cult on the high places. But the unholy course of events, once
set in motion, took a quite different path. At all events, Jeroboam
set out for exile greatly strengthened by the promises he had received. Time could only work in his favor.

6) SOLOMON'S DEATH AND BURIAL

The author of the Book of Kings is very conscious of the fact
that he has not recorded everything of the life of Solomon. Anyone desirous of further information is referred to "the Book of the
Acts of Solomon" (sēpher dibrê šelōmōh — 1 K 11, 41). He gives
Solomon's reign as 40 years and closes his account with the epitaph:

---

13. The tribal division is not entirely clear. Ten tribes are to go to
Jeroboam and only the one tribe of Judah to remain to David's house.
What about the 11th tribe? Levi, who does not possess any land of
his own, is excluded as a 13th tribe. The remnants of the tribe of
Simeon were sympathetic to the Northern Kingdom, as the introduction of the bull-cult in Beersheba shows (Amos 5, 5; 8, 14). The
tribe of Benjamin remained faithful to Judah. The later Southern Kingdom actually comprised the tribal territories of Judah, Simeon, Dan,
and Benjamin; further, there are the Levites who immigrated from
the north; this makes a total of five tribes. — The prophecy can
hardly be brought into agreement with these facts: "Prophetische
Worte sind keine geometrische Formel und keine algebräische Gleich-
ung." — Prophetic oracles are not geometric formulas or algebraic
equations (Garofalo, 103). Ahijan was foretelling the division of the
kingdom, and assigning the larger half to Jeroboam.

"And Solomon slept with his fathers, and was buried in the city of David his father" (1 K 11, 43).

There can be no doubt as to the fact that Solomon was a most extraordinary ruler. Living at a favorable moment in world politics, he managed, in a lengthy and peaceful reign, to lend an unheard of magnificence to the kingdom which David his father had welded together with his sword. He is one of the boldest and most decisive figures in the annals of Israel's kings. He gave a new face to the kingdom he inherited from David. In an effort to weld it together into an unbreakable unity, he inaugurated a new district administration, built fortresses, made elaborate military preparations, advanced the position of agriculture, mining, business, and commerce, and gave the new nation a religious center in the temple at Jerusalem. In his foreign politics, he succeeded, by a carefully planned series of treaties and alliances, in bringing the entire commerce of the Ancient Near East under his control, so that the treasures of the most distant lands flowed into Jerusalem. All this he could never have accomplished had he not been a man of wisdom, sagacity, and determined will. His figure lives on in subsequent history as a nostalgic dream of Israel's most golden age. The best elements of Solomon become a type for the future Messiah.[14] That is why the Book of Chronicles records nothing of the dark side of Solomon's character.

"Of all this magnificence and glory, however, only very little has survived. Solomon never succeeded in establishing a really unified kingdom. As a result of his overly centralistic administration and the heavy load of taxes on his subjects, the separatist movement, which already existed at the time of his accession to power and which was founded on opposition between Israel and Judah, constantly gained ground; its progress was furthered by the efforts of certain prophetic circles who were in opposition to Solomon's religious tolerance. After his death, the kingdom fell apart. It was only his religious edifices which survived him."[15]

Since the Books of Kings are concerned with a theology of history, they present Solomon's religious failure as the most funda-

---

14. Cf. Mt 12, 42; Lk 11, 31.
15. H. Haag, *Bibellexikon* (1951), 1456.

mental cause of his collapse. Seen in this light, Solomon becomes a tragic figure, like Saul. Both men are broken by their opposition to God. It is only for David's sake that Solomon is left with even one "lamp" (1 K 11, 36), which, in the dark night of catastrophe that follows, is to preserve the light of David's dynasty for a new day to come.[16]

---

16. For a similar verdict, cf. Sir 47, 12-22.

CHAPTER XVII

DIVIDED KINGDOM AND
DIVIDED FAITH

THE death of Solomon, who, in the last years of his reign, was regarded more as a despotic tyrant, was an occasion of great hope for the northern tribes. They looked forward to a lightening of the forced labor and a relaxation of the tight rein of centralistic administration. Few rulers in history have had an opportunity equal to that enjoyed by Solomon's young successor Rehoboam (Roboam)[1] either to completely win or completely lose his subjects. But in his youthful folly and unbounded self-conceit, he himself stood in the way of a reasonable compromise and thereby lost not only the sympathy of the people, but also the greater part of his kingdom.

1) POLITICAL DIVISION

Despite the strength of David's and Solomon's reign, and their continued efforts to weld the tribal confederacy into a unified king-

---

1. Since *'am* can mean "relative" in the more narrow sense, as well as "people," there are also two interpretations: *rĕḥab-'ām*: taken as an imperative, "let the people be great and spacious." Or better, as perfect: "my relative (God) is great and spacious." *yorob-'ām*: "may he increase the people," or, better: "may my relative (God) increase."

dom, the deep-rooted consciousness of the two halves of the kingdom, Israel and Judah, had never disappeared. In Judah, Rehoboam
was immediately recognized as Solomon's successor. This is expressed in the brief statement: "And Rehoboam his son reigned in
his stead." But the succession to the throne was not such a simple
matter in the northern tribes; the hereditary dynasty is not yet
sufficiently established. The northern tribes still favor an elective
monarchy.[2] The decision was to be made at the official assembly
in Shechem,[3] "where all Israel had come to make Rehoboam king"
(1 K 12, 1f.).

Jeroboam (Hieroboam), from his exile in Egypt, had maintained close contact with his followers in Israel. The death of the
tyrant made possible his return. At the assembly in Shechem he
became the spokesman for the popular assembly of Israel (q^{e}hal
yiśrā'ēl). The attitude of the people is best reflected in the resolu-
tion passed by the assembly: "Your father made our yoke heavy.
Now therefore lighten the hard service of your father and his heavy
yoke upon us, and we will serve you" (12, 4).

_____

2. A. Alt, *Das Königtum in den Reichen Israel und Juda*, VT 1 (1951),
2-22. The Northern Kingdom retained the idea of a charismatic kingship, election by the prophet and ratification by the people. In the
Southern Kingdom the hereditary dynasty of David continued in
power.

3. šekem, "neck," named for its position between the shoulders of the
two mountains, Ebal and Gerizim, šakmi in the Amarna Letters. The
ruins of the ancient city are still to be found in the modern *tell
balaṭah*. In 1913/14, and, after the first world war, in 1926-1933, it
was excavated under the direction of E. Sellin. Galling, BRL 477; Haag,
Bibellexikon 1508, with abundant literature. Schechem must have
been settled as early as 2000 B.C. It was fortified with powerful walls
during the Hyksos era. Worthy of mention is the Temple of Baal of
the Covenant. Since Joshua renewed the covenant here shortly after
the entry into Canaan, the city must have quickly fallen into the
hands of the Israelites. After the second world war, the excavations
were carried on by the Americans. G. E. Wright, *The first campaign
at Tell Balātah*, BASOR 148 (1957), 11-28. Overall account of the
history of Schechem in the special publication of the *Biblical Archaeologist* 20 (1957): I. W. Harrel, *Schechem in extra-biblical references*,
II. W. Anderson, *The place of Schechem in the Bible*, III. G. E.
Wright, *The Archaeology of the City*.

The king asked for three days to consider the matter. The aged counsellors, who had already served under Solomon, had to admit that the yoke was, in fact, too hard and that a lightening of the work load was definitely in order. At the same time, they pointed out the far-reaching political effects of his first official measures as king; if he showed a ready understanding for his people's needs, he would win their hearts once and for all. But the younger counsellors, who had grown up together with him, advised the opposite: If you give in to the people now, you are lost for good. Show them that you are their master. They clothed their advice in a brutal figure of speech: "Thus shall you say to them, 'My little finger is thicker than my father's loins. And now, whereas my father laid upon you a heavy yoke, I will add to your yoke. My father chastised you with hooks, but I will chastise you with scorpions'" (1 K 12, 10-11).

Such harsh words were hardly calculated to soothe the righteous anger which had thus far been contained. Revolution broke out openly. The battle cry of the northern tribes, heard already once before, now echoed more ominous than ever:

"What portion have we in David?
We have no inheritance in the son of Jesse.
To your tents, O Israel!
Look now to your own house, David!"
(1 K 12, 16; 2 S 20, 1b).

Abandoned by all his good spirits, Rehoboam now added fuel to the fire; he sent his most unqualified man, Adoram, minister of the forced labor, to soothe the excited masses. When the people saw this man they hated, they turned upon him and stoned him to death. Rehoboam managed to leap to his chariot and thus escaped the fury of the mobs (1 K 12, 18). The work which David had so adroitly put together, had suddenly collapsed. In order to make a definitive breach with the house of David, the popular assembly of Israel elected Jeroboam king.

Rehoboam immediately set about forcing the northern tribes to obedience. He assembled a mighty army, attempting to win back with the edge of the sword what he had lost by the failure of his politics. But the word of God came to the prophet Semiah, who ex-

plained the defection of the northern tribes as the will of God and
the expedition was called off. Rehoboam, like it or not, was forced
to go along with him. Thus begins the unhappy history of the
divided kingdom.

Jeroboam used his time to consolidate his young kingdom.
First he built up Shechem as his capital. In order to have a secure
point of support in Transjordania, he also fortified Penuel. The
mention of his two residence cities shows that the Northern Kingdom, after its split from Jerusalem, had not yet found a new center.
Later kings ruled from Tirzah, until finally the descendants of
Omri established Samaria as the new capital of the Northern Kingdom, which it remained until the destruction of the kingdom.

2) DIVISION IN FAITH

The political defection of the northern tribes did not necessarily
have to lead to a religious split as well. But the centralizing influence of the temple at Jerusalem was too strong not to be taken
into account by the new rulers of the Northern Kingdom. On the
occasion of the annual pilgrimage feasts, the northern tribes would
once again experience their religious ties with the south and thus
reawaken their longing for the lost political unity. The prophets
had looked to Jeroboam for the restoration of the Yahweh cult
in all its purity, free from all heathen contamination. But politics
won out over religion and turned what was at first only a political
division into a national schism.

In this area, Jeroboam's work was extremely clever. He avoided
the appearance of revolutionary innovator in either political or
religious affairs. In his politics he defended the ancient separatist
rights of the northern tribes, and in religion he built upon the survival of ancient popular beliefs. He reestablished the ancient bull
symbolism. Even though Moses, in his holy anger, had shattered the
golden calf at Sinai, this popular religious representation must
have lived on in the people's imagination. The king made two calves
of gold and set them up, one in Bethel on the southern boundary,
and one in Dan on the northern boundary. His original purpose was
not to encourage defection from the Yahweh cult, no more than the
Israelites at Mount Sinai had meant to abandon Yahweh with their

golden calf. It was not the calves themselves that were to be worshipped; they were only a symbol of Yahweh who had his throne above them. But this was still a serious breach of the Ten Commandments, which strictly forbade any representation of Yahweh in material objects, and it was an open door to the rapidly developing Canaanization of religion in the Northern Kingdom. What distinction was there between Yahweh and Baal, if Yahweh too was to be worshipped in the vital power of the bull?

In his reestablishment of cultic high places, Jeroboam consciously builds upon the ancient tradition. The pre-Israelite population had offered sacrifice to their gods on the "high places" (*bāmôt*). The Israelites too, upon their arrival, worshipped Yahweh on such high places (1 S 9, 12; 10, 5; 1 K 3, 2; 18, 30). Until the time of King Josiah (c. 638-608), sacrifice was regularly offered outside Jerusalem, in keeping with the text of Ex 20, 24, which provides for a plurality of cult centers. Israel in the desert had only one altar and one sanctuary. This was a necessary result of Israel's structure as a tribal confederacy formed about the sanctuary of the tribal God Yahweh. After the conquest of Canaan and the territorial expansion of the people, this ideal of cultic unity could no longer be carried out. Accordingly, by way of concession to historical reality, sacrifice was frequently offered on the ancient, hereditary Canaanite high places. But with the building of the temple, the situation is different. Yahweh once again has a central sanctuary, with Yahweh himself enthroned above the Ark of the Covenant. Sooner or later, the cult of the various high places would have to be abrogated as contrary to law. The law of the unicity of cult center (Dt 12) is not to be interpreted as the invention of a later age; it is rather a return to the traditions of the desert wandering.

Jeroboam, however, would have nothing to do with the political implications of the institution of a central sanctuary; he took a firm stand in favor of the cultic high places which had become so firmly established in popular favor. In this he met with the opposition of the Levites, a great number of whom emigrated into the Southern Kingdom (2 Ch 11, 13). Thus Jeroboam was forced to reorganize the priesthood. 1 K 12, 31 is generally translated: "He also made houses on high places, and appointed priests from among all the people, who were not of the Levites." If Jeroboam had entrusted the priesthood to unqualified persons from the rank and file of the population, he could hardly have counted on the sympathy of his countrymen. Here too, he seemed to have proceeded along conservative lines: the words *miqqᵉṣôt hā-'ām* certainly does not mean "from the lower classes of the people." The Danites would certainly have not sent "lower class people," but rather the "ablest people" (*'ᵃnāšîm miqqᵉṣôtām* — Jg 18, 2) of their tribe to look for new territory to settle.[4] Accordingly, in connection with Jeroboam's appointment of the new priests, the word is not to be taken in any derogatory sense.[5] Jeroboam could point back to very ancient Ephraimite traditions. Already in the era of the Judges, a certain Micah had set up a graven image in the mountains of Ephraim, which probably means Bethel. The Danites stole this image and took it with them on their immigration into the new Dan, where they set up Jonathan, son of Gershom, as priest (Jg 18, 30); his genealogy is derived from Gershom, son of Moses. The descendants of this family were, at David's time, assigned to the temple in Jerusalem (1 Ch 26, 23-26; 24, 20, 22; 25, 20). Just as Moses' brother himself, Aaron, did not hesitate to take a stand in favor of the bull cult, his posterity was also perfectly willing to worship Yahweh under this symbol. This involvement with a Mosaic priestly family and the two cultic centers of Bethel[6] and Dan must have characterized Jeroboam's cultic reform, in the eyes of the people, as a restoration of the ancient faith rather than a religious innovation. Jeroboam had cleverly played the Ephraimite cultic tradition against the pan-Israelite centralism emanating from Jerusalem and won the first round of his quarrel.[7]

---

4. The word is used in its same positive sense by Joseph in Egypt, who selected five of his brothers to present to the Pharaoh (Gn 47, 2).

5. S. Talmon, *Calendar Reckoning in Ephraim and Juda,* VT 8 (1958), 52: "We cannot help but assume that Jeroboam's new priests were men of considerable social prestige."

6. A summation of the archaeological evidence and literary testimony on Bethel from the Old Bronze Age to the Arabic era, in J. L. Kelso, *Excavations at Bethel,* BA 19 (1956), 36-43. The temple was not discovered since it had been completely destroyed by Josiah.

7. *Ibid.,* VT 8 (1958), 51-53: Jeroboam's cultic reforms.

Breaking with the central sanctuary also necessitated a calendar reform, which helped to accentuate the religious schism. The ancient Israelite and Canaanite calendar was an agricultural calendar, regulated by the rhythm of sowing and harvest.[8] Since the Israelite annual festivals were, basically, agricultural festivals, they were also arranged on a seasonal basis. But the harvest ripens at various times in the various parts of the country, and thus there was some fluctuation in the festival calendar. It was only in David's and Solomon's kingdom that the calendar was centralized and regulated by the solar year. The festival calendar of Jerusalem was established as official and obligatory for the entire kingdom. According to this official calendar, the feast of tabernacles, which was also the consecration of the temple (1 K 8, 2), was celebrated in the seventh month. We read of Jeroboam that he "appointed a feast on the 15th day of the eighth month like the feast that was in Judah" (1 K 12, 32). This was no mere arbitrary innovation on the part of the new king; he was simply breaking with the centralized Jerusalem calendar and reintroducing the ancient Ephraimite agricultural calendar, since, in the northern mountain country, the harvest actually takes place a whole month later than in Judah.[9]

The postponement of the feast of tabernacles necessarily involved a different reckoning for the dates of the other feasts, especially Easter, on the basis of this new starting point. Under Hezekiah an attempt was made to reach a compromise on the Easter dating, but without success (2 Ch 30, 1ff.); according to the northern calendar, Easter was not to be celebrated until the second month. Only after the destruction of the Northern Kingdom could Josiah manage to establish the Jerusalem calendar for the remnants of the Northern Kingdom.[10] As long as there is a Northern Kingdom, there is a double festival calendar. Jeroboam succeeded in

---

8. Witness to this the farmer calendar of Gezer, which lists 8 months, 4 of them in the dual number (yrḥ and yrḥw), making a total of 12. The best summary, together with illustrations, in *EncMikr* II (1954), 471-474. The names of the months are: 1. Double month of "bringing home," 2. month of sowing, 3. month (double) of late sowing, 4. month of the flax harvest (?), 5. month of the barley harvest, 6. month of the other harvests, 7. double month of the pruning, 8. month of the fruit. — Gressmann, AOT 444, 609. / Noetscher, BAK 258.

9. If the completion of the temple in 1 K 6, 38 is assigned, by way of contradiction to 1 K 8, 2, to the 8th rather than the 7th month, this might be a dating from a different calendar. Both accounts refer to the same festival, celebrated in Judah in the 7th month and in the Northern Kingdom in the 8th month.

10. S. Talmon, *Calendar Reckoning in Ephraim and Juda*, VT 8 (1958), 58-63.

dissuading his subjects from the annual Jerusalem pilgrimage and directing the streams of pilgrims to the two newly established national sanctuaries.

Since Jeroboam, in both his political and his religious reforms, managed to rely upon ancient popular traditions in his protest against the court and sanctuary of Jerusalem, his reforms found willing acceptance in the northern tribes, thereby irremediably perpetuating the divided kingdom. The prophet Ahijah had expected great things from Jeroboam; he was to be a king after the heart and mind of Yahweh himself, not like Solomon who, in his folly, had broken with Yahweh. The course of history bitterly disillusioned the prophet. Jeroboam serves rather as an introduction to that long and sorry list of kings of the Northern Kingdom about which Scripture has the monotonous and thus all the more moving words of judgment to speak: "He did what was evil in the sight of the Lord, and walked in the way of his father, and in his sin which he made Israel to sin" (I K 15, 26, 34; 2 K 13, 2, 11 etc.).

The internal political and religious division was quickly followed by a sharp split in foreign policy. Under the blows of the Egyptian Pharaoh Shishak (Shoshenk) Israel lost the position of leadership achieved by David's military brilliance in the middle of the fertile crescent, and sank back into her former impotence. Shishak wanted to reestablish Egypt's ancient claims to sovereignty in Canaan, and, accordingly, fell upon the country with a powerful army. The Bible has recorded only the calamities which befell the kingdom of Judah. The Egyptians overran the border fortresses, setting villages and cities to the torch; they even marched against Jerusalem (1 K 14, 25; 2 Ch 12, 2-11). Rehoboam was able to save Jerusalem from siege and destruction only by plundering the treasures of Solomon and yielding them as tribute to the Egyptians. Solomon's gold found its way into the treasure chambers of the Pharaoh. Among other things, he had to surrender the two hundred golden shields. Rehoboam had them replaced by bronze shields, a sorry commentary on the sad change of Israel's military potential.

The true extent of Israel's humiliation is to be learned only from the extra-Biblical sources. Shishak had a great victory inscription carved into his temple at Karnak, listing a catalogue, apparently haphazard, of all the conquered cities from middle and northern Palestine, including some from Transjordania. It was only after the work of B. Mazar[11] discovered the key to the interpretation of this inscription that scholars were able to reconstruct the course of the Egyptian campaign. Shishak made his way along the ancient route through Gaza into Palestine. First he had to overcome the key fortress city of Gezer. After the fall of Gezer he made his way through Aijalon, Beth-Horon, and Gibeon, all names which are well known from the Philistine wars, and penetrated deep into the heart of the mountain country. From Gibeon it is only 9 km (6 mi) to Jerusalem. Shishak was satisfied with the heavy tribute, and left Jerusalem unharmed as he turned his attention to the northern tribes. Passing through Bethel and Shiloh he marched into the Jordan country, crossed the river, passed along the valley of the Jabbok River into Transjordania, and put the cities of Penuel and Mahanaim to the torch. He then turned westward once again, making his way across Beth-Shan into the great plains, where he conquered Taanak and Megiddo. Then, following the path of the earlier Egyptian armies, he crossed through the Wadi Ara and Carmel mountain range and penetrated the Plain of Sharon. After plundering the outlying districts, the Egyptian was able to turn his attention to the heartland of the Northern Kingdom; he took Shechem, the capital of the Northern Kingdom, as well as Tirzah and other cities. Richly laden with spoils, and leaving a humbled people in his wake, he marched back in triumph to the Nile. For Israel, this was the end of her great dreams of empire; the golden age was over.

The split kingdom initiates a catastrophic era in the salvation history of the Old Testament. Once again, one of God's great plans has shipwrecked. The idea of God's kingdom upon earth, symbolized in the earthly king as "son" and representative of God,

---

11. The city names must be read "boustrephedon," that is, the first line from left to right and the second from right to left, the third from left to right, etc., in the manner that a farmer turns his oxen (*bous* + *stroph*) in plowing a field. For an evaluation of B. Mazar's interpretation, cf. E. Vogt, *Expeditio Pharaonis Šošenq in Palaestinam 927 B.C.*, Bibl 38 (1957), 234-236.

had proved to be beyond the capacity of his human agents. Mere man, even as chosen and splendid a character as Solomon, was unequal to the divine potential. And still, over the fallen booth of David (Am 9, 11), shines the prophecy of the everlasting permanence of David's house (2 S 7, 14).[12] In what sense could this prophecy be fulfilled? What is the goal towards which God means to direct the history of his people and all humanity? It is as God's chosen interpreters of the confusion of human history, and as God's spokesmen to illuminate the future, that the great prophets now make their appearance, ushering in a totally new division in the history of God's kingdom on earth.

APPENDIX

THE CHRONOLOGY OF THE UNITED KINGDOM

The problem of chronology in the era of the kings is, according to R. de Vaux,[1] so difficult that the solution is, at the present time, all but hopeless. In order to arrive at even a basic understanding of the Biblical numbers, we must, from the outset, learn how to distinguish between salvation history chronology and the chronology of the secular scientific historian. The secular historian begins with the synchronistic data in the Books of Kings and Chronicles, where, together with the total number of the regnal years of any individual king, we are always precisely informed in which year of the neighboring kingdom a given episode took place. While these comparative dates are of the greatest value, they do not present any unified picture. The problem is discussed at greater length in the following volume, since it is primarily the dates of the divided kingdom that are concerned. The historian, however, has also tried to assign years and numbers to the days preceding the political division. Since he had no precise secular sources to work on here, he was left to the construction of a salvation-history chronology. The broader outlines of salvation form a numerically compact unity for him, a "cosmic year" according to the plan of God.

---

12. The kingship remained hereditary, in the Southern Kingdom, in the dynasty of David, while, in the Northern Kingdom, it became a political football in the play of power politics, with one short-lived dynasty after another on the throne. On the different form and history of the kingship in the two kingdoms, cf. A. Alt, *Das Königtum in den Reichen Israel und Juda. Kleine Schriften* II (1953), 116-134.

1. R. de Vaux, DBS IV (1949), 748.

1) RECKONING TIME IN TERMS OF THE "YEAR OF SALVATION":

The construction of the temple is an undeniable climax and turning point in salvation history. Hence its symbolic dating: "In the year 480 after the people of Israel came out of the land of Egypt, in the fourth year of Solomon's reign over Israel, in the month of Ziv,[2] which is the second month he began to build the house of the Lord" (1 K 6, 1). The temple is, accordingly, bound up retrospectively with the Exodus from Egypt and the erection of the tabernacle of the covenant in the wilderness. As we have already demonstrated in discussing the chronology of the patriarchal era, 480 is the symbolic number for a "cosmic year" of 12 generations of 40 years each. From Abraham's call to the events of Sinai, and from that time onward until the first and finally the second temple we are always dealing with a span of 480 years. This outline cannot be made to adapt to the data of secular history. These are not the numbers of the secular historian; they are salvation history impregnated numbers, designed to accentuate the climactic and turning points of salvation history. The number 480 represents a salvation history solar year. Whether there is any connection between this cosmic solar year speculation and the structure of the temple which was oriented towards the sun is not immediately evident.

When we compare the numbers assigned to the persons treated in this volume, from Eli down to Solomon, we note the surprising fact that the number 40 is predominant. Eli was judge in Israel for 40 years (1 S 4, 18). For Samuel we have no such number assigned, only the fact that he was judge in Israel throughout his life (1 S 7, 15). The interpretation of the corrupt text in 1 S 13, 1 by M. Noth,[3] according to whom Saul's kingship was an episode of only two years, has already been rejected as extremely questionable in our above treatment of Saul's days as king. The Book of Acts (13, 21), at all events, assigns 40 years as the length of Saul's reign. David reigned 7 years in Hebron[4] and 33 years in Jerusalem, again a total of 40 years (1 K 2, 11). And finally, the length of Solomon's reign over Israel is also given as 40 years (1 K 11, 42).

We can be reasonably certain that in all these cases we are not dealing with an exact statement of the actual regnal years involved but only a general statement involving the number 40, a number which encompasses the active years of a man's life between childhood and old age, and thus serves as the typical measure of a generation. The succession of generations from Eli, Samuel, Saul, David, down to Solomon, are presented, in terms of number symbolism, as 40 years for each individual. Since, moreover,

---

2. That is, in "the month of blossoming."
3. M. Noth, *Geschichte Israels* (1950), 153.
4. In 2 S 5, 4 the number is increased to 7 years and 6 months.

it has been established that this figure, the number of a generation, has been employed as the basis of the salvation history cosmic year — 12 x 40 gives a cosmic solar year of 480 years — we must necessarily conclude that the number 40 was never intended to serve as a secular and actual chronology of the early kings. These symbolic figures are no more intended to serve as a reliable chronology than the seven days of the week of creation are meant to serve as the basis for an accurate cosmology. Any system which takes these salvation history numbers in their "literal" meaning necessarily arrives at an impossible sequence of events, which clearly contradicts the actual course of history. But if the symbolic genre (*genus litterarium*) of these numbers is properly recognized, the difficulties automatically disappear. We no longer make greater demands of them than they are designed to bear. The error is not in Scripture, but in our unwillingness to deal with the symbolic force of Scriptural numbers.

We are perhaps too easily inclined to write off this number system based on symbolic cosmic years in terms of the Ancient Near Eastern preoccupation with numbers and number series. But these numbers were not written merely to satisfy the individual pleasure of the man who first penetrated the mystery of the numbers. They are rather the expression of a dynamic awareness of history. Their meaning becomes clear if we compare them with the ancient Egyptian picture of history. The ancient Egyptians drew one clear line of distinction in the formless nothingness prior to the creation of the world; after creation, however, their history runs in terms of periodic cycles, subject to an infinite series of repetitions. The idea of entelechy, the conviction that history is progressing towards a goal was unknown to them.[5] — The Semitic conception of the *'ôlām* expresses the same static concept of cyclic history.[6] In Egypt and in Mesopotamia there is much evidence of dating; but their scholars never arrived at one unified historical composition. Within the whole realm of the Ancient Near East, this one very questionable symbolic chronology system of the Bible represents the first great attempt at a dynamically charged synthesis of history. The world is not statically at rest. It is pushing on — or rather it is being pushed on by God — in succeeding series of cosmic years, towards a set goal and purpose, and this goal is the salvation of the world. The symbolic numbers are, accordingly, fundamentally salvation history numbers and can be understood and interpreted only from that point of view. Since this knowledge of salvation to come was proper to Israel alone, such a system of reckoning time accord-

---

5. E. Otto, *Altägyptische Zeitvorstellung und Zeitbegriffe, Welt als Geschichte*, vol. 14 (1954), 135-148.

6. E. Jenni, *Das Wort 'ôlām im AT, ZAT* 64 (1952), 197-248; 65 (1953), 1-35. The myths of the dying and resurgent divinities are also an expression of the concept of eternal renewal. Ch. Virolleaud, *Legendes de Babylone et de Canaan* (1949), 118ff.

ing to "the years of salvation" could only have been produced in terms of divine revelation. The suggestion that this cosmic-lunar-year-theology is somehow connected with the construction of the temple which is oriented towards the sun's rays, cannot, *a priori,* be rejected, especially since recent study has ascribed the introduction of the solar calendar to Solomon.[7] Once we have recognized these symbolic characters as a very unique expression of the theology of history, we must once and for all abandon them as the basis of any secular chronology. For this we must turn to other sources.

2) SECULAR CHRONOLOGIES:

We call attention first to two ancient datings for the building of the temple, which correlate this event with the foundation years of Rome, Tyre, and Carthage, as well as with the destruction of Troy.[8]

a. Flavius Josephus, *Contra Apionem* 1, 18, and *Antiquities* 8, 3, 1.
Building of the temple, 240 years after the foundation of Tyre.
Building of Tyre: one year before the destruction of Troy.
Troy destroyed in the year 1207 (Marble tablet of Paros).
(1207 + 1) − 240 = 968 B.C.: building of the Temple.

b. Flavius Josephus, *Contra Apionem* 1, 17 and Justin *Apology* 18, 6, 9.
Building of the Temple 143 years before the foundation of Carthage.
Carthage founded 72 years before Rome.
Rome founded in the year 753.
753 + 72 + 143 = 968 B.C.: building of the Temple.

Since the building of the temple was begun in the fourth year of Solomon's reign, this would identify the first year of Solomon's reign as 971 B.C. With the aid of the number 40 the following regnal dates can be drawn up: Saul: 1051-1011; David 1011-971; Solomon 971-931; division of the kingdom 931.

These numbers are only as valuable as the presuppositions upon which they are based. We have already demonstrated that the number 40 is without value as the basis for an actual chronology. The foundation years of Rome, Carthage,[9] and Tyre are imaginary figures, which, at the most,

---

7. J. Morgenstern, *The Calendar of the Book of Jubilees, its Origin and its Character,* VT 5 (1955), 34-76: Solomon, influenced by Tyrian examples, transformed the Canaanite agrarian calendar into a solar calendar of 12 months with 30 days each.
8. F. X. Kugler, *Von Moses bis Paulus* (1922), 172-179.
9. E. O. Forrer, dates the origin of Carthage between 673-633. *Festschrift-Dornseiff* (1953), 85-93. It was not until Tyre was seriously threatened by the Assyrian power that the "new city" (*qarti-ḥadašti*) was established.

can be accepted as approximations, but not exact dates. Since the basis for these dates is so questionable, the figures themselves can hardly be accepted as certain.

c. *Synchronism*:

For the time after the divided kingdom, there are some synchronisms with the Assyrian, Egyptian, and Phoenician history which offer definite points of departure for an accurate chronology. There are similar synchronisms for the time of David and Solomon: the treaty with Hiram of Tyre, the campaign of the Pharaoh Shishak; but their dates are uncertain. Excavation has yielded very valuable confirmation of Solomon's building activity, but no basis for a date. Unless some newer archaeological finds come to our assistance, we can arrive at only approximate dates for these years of Israel's history which are treated in the present volume.

New systems of reckoning, accordingly, are no longer based on the building of the temple; they take the political division of the kingdom as their point of departure, a point which can be determined on the basis of synchronisms. The year of the political division fluctuates between 945 and 922 B.C., with the greater probability favoring a date somewhere in the middle. Since some knowledge of the history of the divided kingdoms is necessary to understand these various points of departure, we can only offer the various proposed solutions here, while reserving their more explicit foundations for a future volume. A brief glance at the estimates listed below [10] is enough to show that the discussion is still

10. For proper orientation, cf. the series of recent estimates of the date for the division of the kingdom:
933: Schmoeckel, *Geschichte des alten Vorderasien* (Handbuch der Orientalistik), vol. II, (1957), 290. Most recent literature, 325.
932: M. Rehm, *Die Bücher der Könige* (EB) (1949), 7. / G. Ricciotti, *Geschichte Israels* (1952), #417.
931: R. de Vaux, DBS IV (1949), 748.
930: L. H. Grollenberg, *Atlas of the Bible* (1958), 81. / P. L. Lemaire and D. Baldi, *Atlante storico della Bibbia* (1955), 124.
929: P. Heinisch, *Geschichte des AT* (1949), 189.
926/925: M. Noth, *Geschichte Israels* (1950), 195: Solomon's death occurred in the course of the year Fall-926 to Fall-925. This is considered the first certain date in the history of Israel. G. Bressan, *Samuele* (GarB), (1954), 29ff. — Westminster-Atlas (1953), 7.
922: M. B. Rowton, *The Date of the Founding of Solomon's Temple,* BASOR 119 (1950), 20-22; Tempelbau auf das Jahr 959 angesetzt. / W. F. Albright, JBL 71 (1952), 247; BASOR 100 (1945), 16ff.
Opposed to this later dating is the position of S. Mowinckel, who

very much in a state of flux. It would be a mistake to hold with any one system. But we can produce the following series of reasonable approximations:

c. 1050: Destruction of Shiloh,
c. 1030: Activity of Samuel, last of the judges,
c. 1020-1000: Saul's kingship,
c. 1000-970: David, king of Judah, then king of all Israel, contemporary of Hiram of Tyre, the first year of whose reign can be established as 979/78 [11]
c. 970-930: Solomon in all his glory, the first years of whose reign are contemporary with Hiram of Tyre, and whose last years coincide with Shishak of Egypt (935-914?) [12]
c. 930: Political and religious schism.

The reader must bear in mind the fact that these numbers are only a working hypothesis, valid until new discoveries have made it possible to arrive at more precise dates.

---

proposes the year 929/928: Norsk Teologisk Tidskrift 56 (1955), 270-295 quoted in IZBG IV (1955/56), Nr. 1148.

11. J. Liver, *The Chronology of Tyre at the Beginning of the First Millennium B.C.*, IsrExplJ 3 (1953), 113-120. The weak point of this dating lies in the fact that the by no means definitely established year of the foundation of Carthage is reckoned as a determining factor; more convincing is a text of Salmanassar III presented here.
12. W. F. Albright, *New Light from Egypt on the Chronology and History of Israel and Juda*, BASOR 130 (1953), 4-11. Investigates the inscriptions of the Ethiopian kings in Kava, in which there is mention of a lunar eclipse in the 15th year of Rakelot II, which Albright identifies as the year 822; accordingly, Shishak's dates would be from 935-914.

THE GOLDEN AGE OF HEBREW LITERATURE

THE national, economic, and cultural ascendancy of Israel under David and Solomon led to a new intellectual orientation which left its stamp upon the literary productivity of the age. We need only consider the change in Israel's political circumstances. Ever since they first occupied the Promised Land, the Twelve tribes had lived in constant fear of their enemies, in a defensive position of alert against foreign invasion, deeply concerned with maintaining their national character and autonomy. David's victorious sword had dissipated all these threats. Israel was at last free to take her stand upon the lofty mountains and boldly face the four quarters of the world. Now was the time to reestablish her status in the world about her. It is this intellectual and spiritual reconstruction that the thinkers, poets, and historians, (together with the new political and military order) now begin to express by the creation of a new literature. The Davidic-Solomonic era is referred to as the "Golden Age of Hebrew Literature." [1]

---

1. R. H. Pfeiffer, *Introduction to the OT* (1948), 21 used the term "Golden Age" to include the time from Moses to the destruction of Jerusalem. W. F. Albright, *From Stone Age to Christianity* (1949), 292 would like to see the term somewhat reduced in its extension.

In our treatment of the Pentateuchal problem we made it clear, beyond the shadow of a doubt, that we attribute to Moses an essential role in the formation of the Jewish law. He is not only the political and religious unifier of the confederation of the Twelve tribes; he also supplies this new people with a written law for their future direction. In this same connection, we expressed the opinion that the patriarchal narratives, particularly the land promised to the seed of Abraham, could well have been a powerful motif for the exodus from Egypt. But at the same time we pointed out that the work of Moses was subject to the literary laws of tradition current in the Ancient Near East, in terms of which more ancient writings were regularly reworked and adapted to the character of a newer age.

It would be surprising indeed if the high period of the united kingdom had not left its stamp upon this work. In Israel we note the rise of a singular historical awareness, which has no single counterpart in the world of the Ancient Near East.[2] The horizon of the historian is not confined to the individual episodes of tribal history, merely succeeding each other without purpose or connection. His view has been broadened to include the universal, and he has included the history of all humanity within his presentation. From the creation of the world down to his own times, he points to the powerful activity of Yahweh in human history. History, for him, becomes theology, divine revelation. Although there is little agreement, among Protestant and Catholic exegetes, as to which sections are to be attributed, in detail, to the Yahwist, "the great narrator," all share the opinion that this work owes its present form to the Davidic-Solomonic era. "The historical composition of the Yahwist was created in a universe in which the most profound classical works of Egypt and Babylonia were well known."[3] The fact that the Mosaic law, which was promulgated primarily for the people during their wilderness trek, necessarily underwent a process of adaptation to a later age, and the fact that the cultic precepts

---

2. M. Noth, *Geschichte Israels* (1950), 193.
3. H. Cazelles: "Le jahwiste écrit dans un univers où circulent les oeuvres classiques les plus profondes de l'egypte et de la Babylonie." *Introduction à la Bible* I (1957), 348, hg. von A. Robert and A. Feuillet.

of those days were, correspondingly, reworked to accommodate to the demands of the newly constructed temple, cannot, on grounds of historical necessity, be simply rejected. Any well-informed scholar of today must necessarily recognize the claim that Moses' work has taken on a new literary form in the high era of the Davidic-Solomonic kingdom. The final form of the Pentateuch is, however, to be ascribed only to the era following the national catastrophe of the Exile.

In assessing the work of the Yahwist, we cannot say precisely what part is to be ascribed to the Davidic-Solomonic era, but the Books of Samuel were, at all events, written prior to the death of Solomon. The account of David's rise to power (1 S 16, 14 — 2 S 5, 10) and the description of his succession to the throne (2 S 7 — 20; 1 K 1 — 2) are pure masterpieces of historical writing. The historical value and literary genre of the Books of Samuel have already been treated in detail.[4]

Temple and palace make up the vital focus of the new kingdom. Each of these is the source of new literary creation. David, as "singer of the songs of Israel," created the psalms for the newly organized cult in Jerusalem; Solomon, on the other hand, stands as the founder and creator of the Wisdom literature and the love song. But neither the Book of Psalms nor the Book of Proverbs, nor the Song of Songs, in their present form, date back completely to the Davidic-Solomonic era. History has left its mark upon them. Still, as the following discussion will amply prove, they bear the marks of that glorious era which, with perfect right, has traditionally been referred to as the golden age of Hebrew literature.

---

4. Cf. above, chapter 3: The Historical Value of the Books of Samuel.

CHAPTER XVIII

"THE PSALMS OF DAVID"

Commentaries: HSAT: Bertholet 1923 / Gunkel 1926[4] / König 1927 / KAT: Kittel 1929[5], [6] / Peters 1930 / HAT: Schmidt 1934 / Wutz 1935 / BB: Herkenne 1936 / Calès 1936 / HBK: Kalt 1937[2] / SBB: Cohen 1945, 1950[2] / EB: Nötscher 1947 / Bonkamp 1949, 1956[2] / Podechard I. 1949, II. 1954 / ClamB: Renard 1950 / Steinmann 1951 / Kissane I. 1953, II. 1954 / JerB: Tournay, Schwab 1955[2] / GarB: Castellino 1955 / ATD: Weiser 1955[2] / BK: Kraus 1958.

Introductions: Cornely-Merk 1940[12], 473—485 / Simon-Prado II. 1940[2], 3—102 / Höpfl-Miller-Metzinger 1945[5], 255—272 Pfeiffer 1948[2], 619—644 / Kuhl 1953, 246—258 / Eissfeldt 1956[2], 101—145; 547—557 / Weiser 1957[4], 224—232 / Robert-Feuillet 1957, 586—621.

NB. For the sake of simplicity, the psalms are here quoted only in the Vulgate reference system, whereas elsewhere in these volumes both reference systems are noted, Hebrew and Latin.

A) POST-REFORMATION INTERPRETATION OF THE PSALMS

There is hardly any other book in the Bible which so clearly registers the ups and downs of various schools of interpretation over the course of Biblical exegesis as does the Book of Psalms. The present position of Psalms exegesis can hardly be evaluated without a brief retrospect over the intellectual struggles of recent centuries.[1] Synagogue and Church have both agreed in considering David as author of all 150 Psalms. This opinion was made possible by the fact that the Psalms were regarded, not in their literary variety, but in their theological unity. The Psalms were prayed as the book of Christ, the book of the Church militant, suffering, and triumphant. If this required the aid of allegorical interpretation, this was wholly in keeping with the attitude of taking Scripture as the word of God. The divine character of the Bible word radiated so powerfully before the eyes of exegetes and men of prayer alike that, against the brilliance of this light, all human distinctions of author and time of origin were completely lost sight of. During the whole of the first Christian millennium,[2] and even beyond that time, the Psalms were accepted not as a witness to the faith of the past, the expression of Old Testament piety; they were translated wholly and completely into the faith of New Testament and Church, and thus interpreted from the fullness of revelation. In the light of the goal attained by Christ's redemption, it was easy to lose sight of the long road over which the Psalms had made their way in the course of centuries.

Nor can it be claimed that the Protestant Reformation achieved any humanization in this conception. Quite the contrary. It viewed the entire Bible and particularly the Book of Psalms in the absolute light of God's illuminating spirit. Scripture thus assumed an absolute character which raised it above every influence of human

---

1. J. J. Stamm, *Ein Vierteljahrhundert Psalmenforschung,* ThR 23 (1955), 1-68. Most complete collection of literature on the psalms. More than 13 small-print pages of titles alone.
2. We need mention only the principal representative of the Latin Church: Ambrose (ML 26-27) who exerted the greatest influence for many centuries; on the Davidic authorship, cf. ML 41, 547ff. — Critical opinion, as expressed by Jerome, did not become a general attitude: *Breviarum in Psalmos* (ML 26, 821-1270). Petrus Salmon, *Das Problem der Psalmen, Text und Interpretation der Psalmen zur Zeit des hl. Hieronymus und hl. Augustinus,* Benediktinische Monatsschrift, Beuron, 30 (393-416).

criticism. In the Leipziger Disputation of 1519 we see this Protestant principle of Scripture at work: it is no longer the tradition which emanates from the Fathers of the Church, no longer the Pope or the councils — it is only Sacred Scripture which serves as source and judge (*fons et judex*) in all questions of faith and dogma. With his battlecry of *sola scriptura* Luther turned away from all human authority and based himself on a principle which lies outside the teaching tradition of the Church. God alone has authority. And God speaks through Scripture. The Bible is queen, *Regina*.[3] Luther oriented his fundamental attitude towards the Bible on the mystery of the Incarnation. This attitude is, in itself, nothing new. Already for Origen and his school it had been the golden key to a proper understanding of Scripture.[4] Luther's contribution is the actualization of the word of God, which, as a living form of address, becomes a constantly new experience. The man who reads the Bible is struck immediately and directly by the word of God, to the utter exclusion of all human intermediaries. This dynamic and christological understanding of Scripture produced one very characteristic result: in the place of exact and systematic dogmas of faith, we now have signalizing references to the mighty event.[5] And in this process, every human medium, be it ecclesiastical magisterium or scientific examination, is automatically excluded.

This radical principle, with its claim to absolute exclusivity, is tantamount to an epochal turning point in the whole of Protestant theology, which, by its rejection of the visible Church, which, as Mystical Body, belongs to the whole Christ, has lost its proper meaning and perspective, and, by sheer historical necessity, is driven from its fundamental divinization of the word to an equally fundamental humanization. The history of this process is best read in the story of the commentary on Psalms.

3. Hans-Joachim Kraus, *Geschichte der historisch-kritischen Erforschung des Alten Testaments von der Reformation bis zur Gegenwart* (1956), 4 (quoted as: Kraus, *Geschichte*).
4. Urs von Balthasar, *Geist und Feuer*. / G. E. Closen, *Wege in die Heilige Schrift*, 11-26; Das Mysterium der Hl. Schrift.
5. Kraus, *Geschichte*, 6ff. Also develops Calvin's position on Scripture.

1) WORD AND HISTORY:

The common characteristic of patristic exegesis lies in the fact that words of Scripture are interpreted from the fullness of the Church's awareness of faith. In terms of this perspective we find a plurality of scriptural senses, the literal or historical sense (*sensus literalis seu historicus*) and the spiritual or mystical sense (*sensus spiritualis seu mysticus*). It was this spiritual sense that furnished the scope for the Church's awareness of her faith to find expression. Theologians distinguish between the allegorical, tropological, moral, and anagogical meanings, according as the body of the historical word was interpreted in terms of traits and teachings that were messianic, end-time, or moral in character. The breach with the Church necessarily involved a rejection of the mystical sense of Scripture, in place of which the reformation exegesis established the supremacy of the literal sense. This immediately led to a new and more intensified preoccupation with the Biblical languages. "The languages are the sheath in which the sword of the spirit lies hidden. They are the vessel in which this draught is kept. . . . Thus it is certain that where the languages have not survived the Gospel must ultimately perish." [6] In this dawn of the humanistic spirit, such words fell on fertile ground. The door was opened to a one-sided literary-critical exegesis.

2) GOD'S SPIRIT AND HUMAN CONGENIALITY:

The Age of Romanticism offers a new approach to the experience of the Psalms. As opposed to the one-sided over-emphasis of the ancient classical approach, Herder discovered the voices of the people in their songs. His ideas were applied to the Psalms by Eichhorn (1752 — 1827), who developed the following guideline for their interpretation: "We must go back into the time in which each of these songs was first composed, we must become as familiar as possible with the situation, spirit, and the world of ideas proper to each individual poet." [7] "All those poets whose songs have been

---

6. Luther quoted in Kraus, *Geschichte*, 10.
7. J. G. Eichhorn, *Einleitung in das AT* (1787), I, 13.

assembled in the Book of Psalms have been denied the light of our age: they are content with the weaker light of their own times. Nowhere must we demand Christian morality or dogma or expect the sacred singers to have been figures of super-human sanctity."[8] The Psalms can be properly interpreted only by a man who approaches them with psychological congeniality. The strict principles of the age of the reformation are thus abandoned in the face of the principle of the congenial human spirit feeling its natural way into the soul of the Biblical poet.

The romanticist attitude of Herder is also shared by the *"Commentar über die Psalmen"* (1823) by W. M. L. de Wette (1780 — 1849). The Psalter is defined as a "collection of lyric poems." "The essence of lyric poetry is the immediate expression of feeling. And feeling is precisely the sphere in which the Psalms are most eloquent. Most of them are a living expression of a sympathetic and inspired human heart, the lyrical product of real human enthusiasm and spiritual exaltation."[9] The touchstones of romanticism, "feeling, spirit, heart," become the yardstick for the historical classification of the Psalms. Fresh and original expressions of feeling belong to the earlier age, while more formal and torpid forms are from the later era. According to these principles, de Wette produced the first analysis of literary genre, dividing the songs into hymns, popular songs, Zion and temple psalms, royal psalms, dirges and laments, and moral songs. He thus set the scene for an evaluation of the Book of Psalms in terms of literary history.

3) "PNEUMATIC EXEGESIS":

The "new momentum of discovery" did indeed break loose from the unyielding forms of Protestant orthodoxy, but, in its understanding of Scripture, it is still deeply rooted in the Protestant revolt. The Psalms are not merely the lyrical outpouring of a religiously attuned temperament; the human *gramma* is filled with the divine *pneuma*. As opposed to the one-sided philological-gram-

---

8. *Ibid.,* I, 18. Cf. also Kraus, *Geschichte,* 130.
9. De Wette, *Commentar über die Psalmen* (1817), Vorrede. / Kraus, *Geschichte,* 166.

matical interpretation, which sticks to the letter of the text, men like Tholuck (1799 — 1877) and Stier (1800 — 1862) demand a "pneumatic exegesis." The divine Logos has enlisted the aid of the human *gramma* and given it a "pneumatic" fulfillment. The "grammaticalistic sense" must thus yield to a *philologia sacra*. This reintroduces a theology or interpretation in terms of Scripture's clear involvement with faith, and approaches an approximation of the Catholic principle of Scripture. "The symbolism of the language of the spirit is much more an organic whole than any form of grammar; and the typicalism of the divine economy in both Testaments proceeds in a much more precise pragmatism than any form of history."[10]

This great and all-inclusive pneumatic element is referred to, in the words of the Old Testament exegete Franz Delitzsch (1813 — 1890) as "salvation history." [11] In the Psalms, we have half a millennium and more of the progressive realization, revelation, and understanding of salvation lying open before our eyes. "The new age of exegesis begins with that destructive theology of the second half of the eighteenth century which tore down without being able to rebuild. But this upheaval was not without issue: the denial of the divine and eternal element in Scripture has cast light upon its human and temporal character, the charm of its poetry, and, what is even more significant, the concrete reality of its history."[12] The nineteenth century stands under the mighty impulses which emanate from romanticism and which made possible a new understanding of the divine element in Scripture; these attempts towards a theology of the Psalms were overrun by radical, negative criticism, which entirely lost sight of the divine element in Scripture.

4) THE "DE-SANCTIFICATION" OF SCRIPTURE:

Friedrich Delitzsch (1850 — 1922), the son of an Old Testa-

---

10. R. Stier, *Auslegung der Psalmen* (1834). / A. Tholuck, *Übersetzung und Auslegung der Psalmen* (1843). / Kraus, *Geschichte*, 197-200.

11. Franz Delitzsch, *Psalmen* (1859/60; 5, 1894).

12. Ibid., *Biblischer Commentar über den Propheten Jesaja* (1879), XXXIII. / Kraus, *Geschichte*, 215.

ment exegete of the same name, in his impassioned battle against the Old Testament, attempted to unmask it as "the great delusion." "The chance remnants of the ancient Hebrew writings which we are accustomed to refer to as 'Old Testament' obviously contain much that is valuable in terms of profane history, culture, literature, and even the history of religion. Just like the Babylonian, Arab, Persian, Indian, and other Oriental literary products in poetry or prose, they are rich in linguistic beauties, in thought-provoking Wisdom literature, in deep philosophical contemplation, and in serious ethical principles. But all these Old Testament Books, from Genesis to Daniel, have absolutely no meaning at all in the religious sphere, for anyone who lives today, and especially for us Christians."[13] The so-called "Old Testament" is thus something the Christian Church and hence the entire Christian family could well do without. We might turn instead to a fuller contemplation of the deep thinking which our own national heroes of the spirit have evolved on the subject of the divine, the hereafter, immortality.

Harnack presents a bolder formulation of the same thesis: "The rejection of the Old Testament in the second century was a mistake which the Church at large did well to combat; to hold to it in the sixteenth century was a fate which the Reformation was not yet in a position to escape; but to preserve it in the nineteenth century as a canonical foundation of Protestantism is the consequence of a religious and ecclesiastical paralysis. . . . We must wipe the tables clean and give glory to the truth in confession and instruction; that is the mighty step which today — almost too late — is demanded of Protestantism."[14]

Today, however, such a judgment of the Old Testament is referred to as "poisoning the well"[15] a process which can only lead to unhappy consequences. After the exclusion of the principle of inspiration, it was only logical to put the Bible on a par with the "sacred scriptures" of other peoples. Excavations throughout the Ancient Near East and the initially one-sided evaluation of the

---

13. Friedrich Delitzsch, *Die gosse Täuschung* (1921), Schlussbetrachtung quoted in Kraus, *Geschichte,* 273.
14. A. V. Harnack, *Marcion* (1924), 127f, 222. / Kraus, *Geschichte,* 351.
15. Kraus, *Geschichte,* 279.

finds all contributed to a complete "de-sanctification" of the Bible. Delitzsch did not deny the fact that many Psalms and many passages in the Psalms breathe a truly religious spirit. But in order to understand them in a Christian sense, they would need to be reinterpreted and rewritten, and thus, fundamentally, falsified. They can, accordingly, no longer be a Christian prayer book. Whatever we find in the Bible was already expressed in Babel.[16]

Since the time of the Bible-Babel controversy, there have been many changes. The narrow horizon of Pan-Babylonism has been corrected, after its aggressive attitudes ended in catastrophe. Scholars learned to recognize not only the similarities but also the differences on both sides and thus achieved new insight into the independence of Old Testament literature and primarily the Psalms.

5) "SITZ IM LEBEN":

Far removed from any polemical purpose, and motivated simply as a man of science, Hermann Gunkel (1862 — 1932) elaborated a new approach to the Psalms.[17] Hebrew lyric poetry passed through various ages of piety, but this religious evaluation cannot serve as the point of departure for thorough examination. A literary material must be evaluated primarily against the laws of its own times, that is, the laws of literary history. A commentary on the Psalms could only be a piece of ancient Hebrew literary criticism. The exegete must, accordingly, make every attempt to examine his material in the light of its natural and native literary type. This automatically suggests the existence of a variety of genres. The scholar must go back to the psalm's place of origin, rediscover its "Sitz im Leben." Gunkel developed these ideas in his two volume work on the Psalms.[18] No longer content with the final editorial stage of the Psalter, he tries to penetrate back to the place and time of origin proper to each individual psalm: they were not produced

---

16. Friedrich Delitzsch, *Bibel-Babel*, I (1902), II (1904).
17. Fuller presentation in Kraus, *Geschichte*, 309-334.
18. Hermann Gunkel, *Die Psalmen, übersetzt und erklärt. Göttinger Handkommentar zum At, II*, 2, (1926). — "Die Einleitung in die Psalmen" (1933) was not completed during Gunkel's lifetime: it was published by J. Begrich.

in the study of a scholar; they had a concrete *"Sitz im Leben."*
When the 150 psalms are examined in this light, a variety of genres
are immediately evident: hymms, songs of Yahweh's enthronement,
individual and collective dirges, royal psalms, pilgrimage psalms,
wisdom psalms, etc. Gunkel attempts to interpret the psalms in the
light of their original place and time and circumstances of origin
and thus "let the psalms speak for themselves." The exegete is only
the guide and medium to point the way to the original source of
life. "My purpose, as it has always been, is simply to make the
poems speak. In this capacity, I have meant to be nothing more
than the mouth of times past: what the world of our ancestors
felt deep down in its heart I have attempted to explain to their
very different posterity in the words of our own language. Accordingly, I have strictly avoided all later, Christian, or modern
additions, no matter how deep and intellectually satisfying they
might be to our present age; from the steward we ask nothing of
his own invention, merely that he be found faithful; but on the
other hand, neither have I managed completely to conceal my
firm conviction that in this book, not everywhere but frequently
enough, we catch the sweet music of eternity, whose voice penetrates into our modern age and can never fully die away."[19]

By virtue of this natural feeling for his subject matter and by
the mastery of his language, Gunkel did indeed succeed in making
the psalms speak for themselves. But herein also lies the weakness
of his system. This is what he demands of the exegete: "Hours of
experience and practice are required before your own soul is
touched by the spirit of the past, before the melodies of antiquity,
which have long since died away in the storm of history, begin
to sound clearer and more distinctly, until they reecho in the heart
of modern man in all their ancient power and beauty."[20] Obviously,
the *norma normans* of his exegesis is a strongly subjective element,
a congenial and sympathetic feeling for the history of religion,
in which divine inspiration is an element sharply distinct from the
artistic inspiration of both the poet and his interpreter. Despite
all this subjectivity, it is Gunkel's abiding merit to have worked out

---

19. H. Gunkel, *Die Psalmen* (1926), VII.
20. *Ibid.*, VII.

the artistic literary forms (genres). The psalms are witness to the religious life of the Old Testament, developing in different places and at different times. This obstinate investigation into the *"Sitz im Leben"* must, sooner or later, lead to the discovery of cult as the vehicle and depositary of religious song in Israel.

6) CULT AND SONG:

Already in the year 1912 P. Volz, in his work *Das Neujahrsfest Jahwehs* (feast of tabernacles) stated that the Israelite people reached the climax of their national and cultic life in the great pilgrimage festivals.[21] It was the Norwegian Sigmund Mowinckel[22] who first motivated this research. His book *Psalmenstudien II: das Thronbseteigungsfest Jahwehs und der Ursprung der Eschatologie* (1922) posed the problem of cult in its full dimensions. Point of departure for his investigations are the "enthronement psalms" which reach their cult-dramatic climax in the enthronement ac-clamation "Yahweh is made king." The genre of "songs of Yahweh's enthronement" includes primarily Pss 46, 92, 95, 96, (97). As the *"Sitz im Leben"* for these songs, Mowinckel postulates an enthronement festival in honor of Yahweh, introduced in imitation of the annual enthronement festival of Marduk in Babylon. The content of this Yahweh festival is elaborately described: the myths of creation, dragon-conquest, exodus, and judgment all have a part to play. "The enthronement festival is the foundation day for God's kingdom, and the festival is a kingdom-of-God festival."[23] In taking his throne anew each year, Yahweh also renews his sovereignty and his kingdom. But since the reality was always far short of the ideal, the prophets projected this enthronement of Yahweh into the end-time. Mowinckel thus credits the prophet with a new position in cult.[24] There is a cultic reality which corresponds to the prophetic form of certain psalms. Priest-prophets, he claims, an-

---

21. P. Volz, *Das Neujahrsfest Jahwehs* (1921), 1.
22. More explicit account in Kraus, *Geschichte*, 364ff.
23. S. Mowinckel, *Psalmenstudien* II (1922), 211ff.
24. *Ibid.*, III (1923), *Kultprophetie und kultprophetische Psalmen*, 3.

swered the prayers of those who came seeking direction by the decisions of Yahweh. Mowinckel's ideas were taken up, in Germany,
and continued primarily by A. Weiser.[25] In his commentary on the
Psalms, he develops the cultic foundation of the Psalms and claimed
that they attained their climax in the cult of the covenant feast, in
the theophany of Yahweh, in the proclamation of the sacred name
and in the kingship of Yahweh.[26]

The new discovery of Israel's cult and the special place the
psalms occupy within this cult has obviously opened new vistas in
the interpretation and evaluation of Israel's rich collection of songs,
but in its one-sided over-emphasis, the derivation of psalm from
cult is false. The festivals alluded to: Yahweh's enthronement festival, festival of Zion, festival of the covenant, are more than questionable. This cultic interpretation can be accused of allowing its
judgment to be blinded by the Babylonian New Year's feast. The
fact that psalms had a significant role to play in Old Testament
cult can no longer be doubted; but apparent similarities in the history of religion must not lead to an over-hasty identification of
substance. The method of form history, with its energetic investigation into the *"Sitz im Leben,"* has yielded much fruit in Psalm
study, but it suffers from an over-evaluation of the comparative

---

25. A. Weiser, *Die Psalmen* I (1950), ATD, 11-17: "Die kultische Grund-
lage der Psalmendichtung," 18-20: "Die Psalmen im Bundesfestkult."
26. Mowinckel arranged the individual psalms within a cultic framework.
The poet and man of prayer who created these songs did not mean
to express his own personal religious emotions; he created them as
"formulae" for cult. His words of prayer were formulated in a personal
manner, of course, but put into the mouth of a "corporate personality."
S. Mowinckel, *Traditionalism and Personality in the Psalms,* HUCA
23 (1950/51), 205-231. — Mowinckel has defended this thesis in the
face of great criticism. "There were cult songs in Israel as long as
there was a cult." The title formula *"leḏāwiḏ"* would thus be a
reference to the king in his capacity as cultic functionary. By the same
author: *Psalm Criticism between 1900 — 1935,* VT 5 (1955), 13-33.
— Following Mowinckel's lead, the cultic interpretation of the psalms
has enjoyed a constant vogue. Thus, F. Willesen, *The Cultic Situation
of Ps. LXXIV,* VT 2 (1952), 289-306, takes the cultic drama of the
New Year Festival as the point of departure for his interpretation.

method, an over-stress ðf the cult element, and the many other prejudices common to the comparative study of religions.[27]

Individual studies have demonstrated that the presuppositions of a festival of Yahweh's enthronement are philologically untenable. *Yahweh mālak* is not an enthronement acclamation by which Yahweh's accession to his kingship is proclaimed, but rather an acclamation of worship to Yahweh already sovereign in the omnipotence of his kingship. And thus a magnificent and widely favored idea is proved to be untenable.[28] The same thing is true of the hypothesis of a covenant festival. Israel's existence is, to be sure, based upon the covenant, but this does not demonstrate the existence of a special covenant festival.[29] Even when the presuppositions of the cultic school have been shown to be inadequate, it is still their abiding merit to have cast new light upon the significance of cult as the vehicle of religious tradition and especially in the area of Israel's song. In terms of Biblical theology, their particular merit lies in their stress on an idea that was central to the Old Testament, Yahweh's kingship.[30] But here we are once again at the point of departure proper to the Reformation. In that age, oral tradition as the basis of scriptural interpretation was rejected; the form history and cult history school have now reestablished the position of oral tradition as an element at work in the formation of Scripture. We are very much aware of the fact that between the ecclesiastical and "cultic" concept of tradition there is a great difference — on the one side a principle of faith under the guiding

---

27. A. Robert, *L'exégèse des psaumes selon les methodes de la* "formgeschichtlichen Schule," Misc. bibl., B. Ubach, Montserrat (1953), 211-225.

28. J. Ridderbos, *Jahwäh Malak*, VT 4 (1954), 87-93. Interpreted not as a new factor, but the assertion of an established fact. Yahweh ·is king and exercises his sovereignty. / D. Michel, *Studien zu den sogenannten Thronbesteigungspsalmen*, VT 6 (1956), 40-68.

29. H. Bückers, *Zur Verwertung der Sinaitradition in den Psalmen*, Bibl 32 (1951), 401-422.

30. H. Gross, *Lässt sich in den Psalmen ein Throbesteigungsfest Gottes nachweisen?* Trierer Theologische Zeitschrift 65 (1956), 24-40, demonstrates that there was no question of one single festival, but that the fundamental credal statement of Yahweh's kingship was an element celebrated within the Pasch festival.

influence of the Holy Spirit, and on the other side a purely literary element of formation — but still this new evaluation of the place of tradition is, in terms of the history of ideas, well worth noting.

This brief historical conspectus, which can trace only the broader outlines, is still sufficient to demonstrate how the post-reformation currents of thought approached the interpretation of the Psalms. It was a pendulum stroke from one extreme to the other, from the reformer's pure insistence on the word of God to the completely desanctified word of man in the racio-biological interpretation. Between these extremes lies a wide range of special points of emphasis as stressed by the individual aspects of the schools of literary criticism, history of religion, form and genre history, and history of cult. Much was discovered that was new and important, but, by reason of the one-sidedness of its approach, much of this learning bore within itself the inevitability of its own demise at the hands of further investigation. The insistence upon pneumatic and salvation history interpretation only demonstrates the fundamental truth that the theological character of the Bible can never simply be lost sight of.

7) CATHOLIC INTERPRETATION OF THE PSALMS:

The Catholic interpretation of the Psalms, after the Reformation, was, not unlike the Protestant, subject to the various currents of thought characteristic of its age; it did, however, manage to avoid the strong fluctuation of Protestant studies, holding fast to the fundamental principle of the Bible as word of God. From the early years of this era we must point to the commentary on the Psalms by St. Robert Bellarmine (1542 — 1621), who laid great stress on the literal meaning, but, in keeping with the pace of his age, also developed an ascetical interpretation of the Psalms. It is not our purpose here to present a history of Catholic Psalm exegesis,[31] but merely to call attention to the more important commentaries.

---

31. Bibliography for the older Catholic Psalm commentaries in E. Ecker, *Porta Sion, Lexikon zum lateinischen Psalter* (1903), 3/217, 234. More recent bibliography in G. Castellino, *Libro dei Salmi* (1955), 34: Bibliografia generale.

In the period of monastic renewal, a position of great prominence is occupied by the five volume commentary on the Psalms by M. Wolter (1904 — 1907). G. Hoberg treated the Vulgate version of the Psalms (1906). *The Psalms, in Hebrew and German* (1911), by Nivard Schlogl, are, despite his arbitrary textual emendations, of some value even today, particularly for his metrical investigations and the beauty of his translations. In the series *Ecclesia orans*, we have the two volume work on the Psalms by A. Miller (1: Introduction, 2: Translation and brief exposition. 1925); his text is the most widely spread in Germany. The commentaries of the 30's are still strongly under the spell of literary and textual criticism: E. Kalt, *Die Psalmen* (1935), H. Herkenne, *The Book of Psalms translated and interpreted* (Benner Bibel 1936), J. Cales, *Livre des Psaumes* (2, 1936).

The Psalm commentaries that appeared after the war are written in a spirit of recognition and examination of recent Protestant investigation. The most explicit and best commentary is that of D. G. Castellino, *Libro del Salmi* (Garofalo-Bibel 1950), in which the form-history principle of division is thoroughly carried out on the basis of various literary genres: 1. individual dirge, 2. Psalms of confidence, 3. public dirges, 4. songs of thanksgiving, 5. hymns, 6. royal Psalms, 7. Zion Psalms, 8. Psalms of Yahweh's kingship, 9. liturgical Psalms, 10. wisdom Psalms, 11. various prayers. Somewhat in the same tone and spirit are the Psalm translations in the Biblical series which present only the text together with brief notes: "Fr. Noetscher, *Echter Bibel* 1947; E. Pannier — H. Renard, *Clamer-Bibel* 1950, R. Tournay, *Jerusalem Bible*. An explicit, three volume commentary has been written by E. Podechard, *Le Psautier* (Lyon, 1949 — 54), a two volume work by E. J. Kissane, *The Book of the Psalms* (Dublin 1953/54). The commentary of B. Bonkamp (1949, 1956) is characterized by a somewhat one-sided elaboration of Babylonian parallels.

This brief historical conspectus shows that the individual hypotheses, overstressed in a one-sided interpretation, are obviously false and necessarily lead to revision and correction by later scholarship. Once the one-sidedness has been done away with and the fundamental concepts have been clarified, these new insights into the structure and essence of the Biblical Psalms are of great value: they belong to the permanent treasury of Psalms interpretation. Without text criticism and literary criticism, without the history form and religion, without the investigation of cult, without archaeology and the literary history of the Ancient Near East, it is impossible to approach a proper explanation of the Psalms. The Psalms are the religious songs of the Ancient Near East. The word has, once and for all, become history. Nothing and nobody can relieve us of the burden of "profane exegesis."

A one-sided interpretation of the Psalms in terms of the world of the Ancient Near East means, however, not only the impoverishment but actually the loss of this word. The Psalms are not simply songs of any Ancient Near Eastern people; they are the product of the Old Testament people of God. Accordingly, in the dramatic evolution of the story of salvation, they also need a salvation history interpretation. Pneumatic exegesis is not merely a pious superstructure to the work of profane exegesis, a superstructure that could be just as well forgotten or neglected; without it the Psalms, as songs of the Holy Spirit, remain only half understood. If Luther, in his interpretation of Scripture, proceeds from the mystery of the incarnation, we must do the same. Scripture, as the word of God, is a divine-human mystery and, as such, it is image and likeness of the God-man himself, completely encompassed within all the conditions and qualifications of historical reality, and still participating in the immutability of the eternal God who has revealed himself in history. Now part of the Incarnation of the whole Christ is his Mystical Body, the Church. It would be a detraction of the person of Christ himself, if we attempted to interpret Scripture without respect to the Church's awareness of faith. More than any other book of Holy Scripture, the Church expresses her very essence in the daily prayer of the Psalms. The Psalms do indeed owe their origin to a definite moment in salvation history, and they are covered with the dust of their long journey; but the Church experiences them every day in new dimensions of life. It is not the congenial human-history understanding of the Psalms which is the decisive factor here; it is rather her faith in the God who is at work in human history, the God who has inspired the psalms and speaks in them as powerfully today as ever in the past. Still, mere reference to the "secure" property of faith, and a one-sided pneumatic exegesis which loses itself in barren theological speculation, would be just as much a betrayal of the reality of the word as would a total de-sanctification in terms of a purely human-history exegesis. It is in the attempt to construct a divine-human synthesis, an approach that involves neither one-sidedness nor unwarranted stinting of attention, that yields the key to the divine-human meaning of the Psalms.

B) EVOLUTION OF THE PSALTER

1) THE FIVE BOOKS OF PSALMS:

Why there should be precisely 150 Psalms can no longer be determined. The Septuagint contains an additional Psalm, 151, a song about David's battle with Goliath, but it refers to it as "outside the number of Psalms." The number 150 gives the impression of something arbitrary and deliberate. Some longer songs were sectioned, and other independent songs were joined together in order to preserve this number. It is on this basis that we encounter a different numbering in the Hebrew text on the one hand, and the ancient versions of the LXX and Vulgate on the other hand. Since Luther, in his translation of the Psalms, relied on the Hebrew text, while the Catholic Church held to the system of numbering adopted by the Septuagint-Vulgate translations, this sectarian difference of opinion has been reflected even in the numbering of the psalms.

The LXX considers Ps 9 + 10 as a single psalm, Ps 9, and rightly so, since it is an alphabetical song. Less felicitous is the joining of the two individual songs 114 + 115 to Ps 113. Joining these psalms together would create a total, in LXX, which was two psalms short of 150. In order to fill up the lacuna, two Hebrew psalms were split in two (116 = 114 + 115 and 147 = 146 + 147). As a general rule, the Hebrew (Protestant) numbering is one number ahead of the Greek-Latin (Catholic) system. But since the Greek translators of LXX worked on the basis of a Hebrew text, we must suppose that various systems of numbering were possible already on the basis of the Hebrew text.[32] In New Testament

---

32. The Talmud, influenced by the life span of the patriarch Jacob, counts only 147 psalms. Other systems of numbering in Ginzburg, *Introduction to the Masoretico-Critical Edition of the Hebrew Bible* (1897), 536, 725, 777.

times too, the numbering still fluctuates. Thus, e.g., in Ac 13, 33, our present Ps 2 is quoted as Ps 1.

These 150 psalms were subdivided into five books on the basis of their hymnal and liturgical concluding formulae (doxologies) (40, 14; 71, 18; 88, 53; 105, 48; Ps 150 as concluding doxology for the entire Psalter). This division is quite arbitrary, and apparently is an imitation of the five books of Moses. It certainly does not prove that the Psalter has evolved by a gradual combination of five separate books. Behind this mechanical division, we catch traces of other units, with whose help it is possible to reconstruct the evolution of the Psalter.

2) THE YAHWISTIC AND ELOHISTIC REDACTION:

When we examine the Psalms on the basis of which name for God they use, Yahweh or Elohim, the result is truly surprising. In Pss 1-40 the word Yahweh occurs 272 times (278 times, including titles and doxologies), while Elohim occurs only 15 times. In Pss 41-48 the ratio is just the opposite: 200 Elohim and 43 Yahweh. In Pss 89-150 the word Yahweh is again preponderant, 339 to 7 Elohim.

On the basis of the names for God, we must thus distinguish three collections: two Yahwistic (1-40; 89-150) [33] and one Elohistic (41-82). When we compare the psalms which are recorded twice (e.g., 13 = 52), we are drawn to the conclusion that the divine name Yahweh was deliberately written as Elohim by a redactor. Why and when this took place we cannot definitely determine. That the Elohim collection was meant for the Jews of the diaspora who, living in foreign territory, were not supposed to pronounce the sacred name of Yahweh, is not a particularly cogent argument; in the Book of Chronicles, even though it was written in Palestine proper, the name Yahweh is still changed to Elohim.[34] Other scholars maintain that the Yahweh psalms are national songs, while the Elohim psalms are universal and international in character: this is not a convincing argument either. On the basis of the divine names, only one point can be made with certainty: the Elohistic stratum is more recent than the Yahwistic. This can be established on the basis of a careful philological comparison of the double psalms (13 = 52; 39, 14-18 = 69). The division into five books was thus preceded by a Yahwistic and an Elohistic redaction.

3) COLLECTIONS OF PSALMS:

Within the Psalter, we can isolate groups of songs which are clearly recognizable as collections. The basic collection appears to have been

---

33. Psalms 83-88 make up a "Yahwistic anthology."
34. U. Cassuto, *La Genesi* (1934), 19, 23ff.

the "Psalter of David," and there was a Yahwistic Psalter of David (3-40, with the exception of 32) and an Elohistic collection of "the prayers of David" (*ṭephillôt*: 50-71).[35] That Ps 71, 20 once served as the conclusion to the collection is evident from the note: "The prayers of David, the son of Jesse, are ended." The two Davidic Psalters probably were joined together at one time, but they were later separated by the Psalter of Korah (41-48) and augmented by the Psalter of Asaph (49; 72-82).

This was not the end of the collection. David's psalms are scattered through the rest of the Psalter (85, 11, 102, 107-109, 121, 130, 132, 137-144).

A special collection is formed by the "royal psalms" (91-98), so named from the repetition of the acclamation *Yahweh mālak*, "Yahweh rules as king!" There are also the 15 pilgrimage psalms (119-133) and the Hallel songs (110-113; 115-117; 134, 135; 145-150), which all begin with the acclamation *hallelû-Yah* "praise Yahweh," which also occurs, in some cases, at the end of the preceding psalm.[36]

It is easy to see that the Psalter is not a compact unity. Many hands and many ages have contributed to its production. In order to form a proper judgment it is imperative to distinguish between the evolution of the Psalter as a collection of songs and the development of the individual psalms. The lowest date (*terminus ante quem*) for the completion of the Psalter as we know it is the year 200 B.C.[37] This date is based on the preface to the Wisdom of Sirach, in which Sirach's grandson and translator says that he went to Egypt in the 38th year of Ptolomaeus Euergetes II, i.e., 132 B.C., in order to translate the work of his grandfather Jesus Sirach. He goes on to say that his grandfather had been most zealous in studying the Bible in what later came to be its general division into three sections: "law, prophets, and writings"; i.e., that already at his grandfather's time, two generations before him, and thus approximately 200 B.C., the "writings," which include the Psalms, already existed. It is, moreover, possible to go beyond this minimum date. The Greek translation of Scripture, the LXX, was made between 300-250 B.C. LXX is in general conformity with the text and sequence of the Hebrew form, so that we are justified in the conclusion that the Hebrew Psalter must have been complete already by the year 300. As a maximum limit for composition (*terminus post quem*), we may assign the year 400 B.C., the time in which the Books of Chronicles were written. 1 Ch 16 is apparently an excerpt from Pss 95, 104, and 105, with the concluding doxology of the fourth book, which presupposes the existence of Psalms.[38]

---

35. Pss 65, 66, 70 have no notice of authorship; 71 is attributed to Solomon.
36. L. Finkelstein, *The Origin of the Hallel*, HUCA 23 (1953), 319, 337.
37. Castellino, *Salmi*, 10.
38. Dating from the Maccabean era, as represented by Pfeiffer, *Introduction*

By way of conclusion, it appears that the Psalter, as a collection of songs, represents the most precious ornament of the post-exilic "silver age of Hebrew literature." [39] This, however, does not yet determine the age of the individual psalms, which must always be the subject of a special investigation. In this area, the possibilities date back to the time of David and even beyond.

4) THE DATING OF THE INDIVIDUAL PSALMS:

Whereas former criticism tended to date the Psalms, in their totality, as the product of the post-exilic era,[40] the cultic school locates them in pre-exilic, even Canaanite times.[41] It is the unquestionable merit of this cultic exegesis that the psalms have "become much older." The truth probably lies somewhere between these two extremes.

It is certain that David reestablished the official cult when he transferred the Ark of the Covenant to Jerusalem. Not only did he himself play, dance, and sing before the Ark (2 S 6, 5, 14), but he also entrusted the guilds of musicians with the execution of the temple music (1 Ch 25, 1ff.). The author of the Book of Chronicles records their names: Asaph, Heman, and Ethan (who is also called Jeduthun). Ethan is further referred to as *'ezrāhî,* i.e., a "native," a member of the pre-Israelite Canaanite population. Now Syria-Palestine had long been regarded as a land of developed musical culture.[42] Like the Romans and the Greeks, David had managed to conquer with the sword, but he was perfectly willing to enlist the

---

(1948), is no longer admissible. Songs from this later era (the Psalms of Solomon and the Community Hymns from the Dead Sea) are of quite different character. Castellino, *Salmi,* 10; Tournay, *Psaumes,* 8; Albright, *The Religion of Israel,* 143, sums up his opinion as follows: "For the scholar . . . it is no longer possible to attribute the composition of psalms to the Maccabean Era."

---

39. Pfeiffer, *Introduction,* 639.
40. The best collection of sources for critical study, together with bibliography, in Pfeiffer, *Introduction,* 619ff.
41. Cf. above "Cultic Interpretation of the Psalms." S. Mowinckel, *Zur Sprache der Psalmen,* TLZ 81 (1946), 199-202 points to a pre-Israelite, Canaanite basis.
42. Albright, *The Religion of Israel,* 24, 142ff.

cultural supremacy of Canaan into the service of his own kingdom. An adaptation of the Canaanite temple music and a reworking of pagan songs for the Yahweh cult cannot be excluded as a working hypothesis. The discoveries of Ugarit have cast surprising light on the close relationship, in both content and language, between many psalms and non-Israelite cult songs.[43]

Cult songs are as old as cult itself. Now it is most difficult to actually suppose David's full authorship of all the 73 psalms attributed to him by the Psalter. The inscription *leḏāwîd* has been generally interpreted as an indication of authorship. Recently, however, clay tablets from Ugarit have been discovered beginning with inscriptions like *leba'al, lekeret, leakhat*, in which the particle *le* is followed certainly not by the name of the author, but rather the hero of the composition: Baal, Keret, Akhat. Accordingly, the particle *le* indicates only that a given psalm is part of a cycle of songs; the word *leḏāwîd* thus indicates belonging to a "collection of David's songs,"[44] without making any statement as to its author. On the other hand, we must also note that the 13 *leḏāwîd* psalms also make note of the situation in which David wrote or prayed them. Even though the historical titles and notes may well have been taken over much later from the Books of Samuel, they still point to the fact that the particle *le* was meant to indicate the name of the poet (*Lamed auctoris*).[45] The Hebrew particle *le* can mean

---

43. Albright considers Ps 67/68 as a hymn catalogue from the 13th/12th century, in the form of a list of initial lines or strophes. Some 30 poems would thus be catalogued here, similar to the Accadian and Sumerian hymn catalogues. "A Catalogue of Early Hebrew Lyric Poems" in HUCA 23 (1950) 1-39; also: *Religion,* 145. Even though this hypothesis has been vigorously contested, it is characteristic of much modern interpretation. A fuller treatment of Ugarit and the Psalms in Tournay, *Psaumes,* 47ff. Exegesis of the individual psalms in M. Dahood, in CBQ 16 (1954), 15019; 302. / R. T. O'Callaghan, *A Note on the Canaanite Background of Ps 82,* CBQ 15 (1954), 311-314. / *Echoes of Canaanite Literature in the Psalms,* VT 4 (1954), 165-176. / M. Tsevat, *A Study of the Language of the Biblical Psalms,* JBL Monographie, vol. IX (1955), 1-53. / R. Tournay, *En marge d'une traduction des Psaumes,* RB 63 (1956), 161-181.
44. Tournay, *Psaumes,* 13ff.
45. H. Cazelles, *La question du "lamed auctoris,"* RB 56 (1949), 93-101. / Eissfeldt, *Einleitung,* 555.

"by, for, over," and it could refer both to the poet and to the hero of his poetry; this means that the "songs of David" were either composed by David himself or put into his mouth by later poets. They are "songs of David" in a double sense, by or about David. Accordingly, the extremely sceptical position[46] which would attribute none of the psalms to David's authorship, is no longer justified. Archaeology itself has established the credibility of the obstinate tradition which regards David as the "singer of the songs of Israel" (2 S 23, 1).

The first creative epoch of psalm composition coincides with the "golden age of Hebrew literature,"[47] as the work of David and his temple guilds. The significance of public cult as the *"Sitz im Leben"* for most of the psalms must not be overstressed, however, since the festivals (enthronement, Zion, covenant) which have been postulated to explain their origin remain unsubstantiated hypotheses.[48] We must reserve a much larger area than the cultic school allows for individual "spiritual songs," even in the era of the kings. In the Psalter of David, the cultic element is a very meager one, since we are here dealing not with later cultic outlines, but with the living expression of a powerful poet, who "pours out his soul and his sorrow before God" (Ps 101).

The silver age of Hebrew literature was no less creative. It is in the religious enthusiasm of the great days of national restoration that we date the Zion songs (45, 47, 75). More than ever before, the repatriates looked to Zion as the focal point of their ancient faith. The Zion songs are songs turned prophecy, inspired by Isaiah (cf. Is 11, 9; 25 — 26; 14; 51, 17; 60; 62). The newly established cycle of pilgrimages gave rise to the pilgrimage songs (119 — 133).[49] It was the faith of the repatriates that gave the

46. Pfeiffer, *Introduction*, 627: "None of the Psalms could have been written by David."
47. Wright, *Archaeologie*, 117.
48. Eissfeldt, *Einleitung*, 119, §15: Kultlieder. Masterful synopsis of the cultic interpretation of the psalms, without any emphasis on the weak points of questionable character of the hypothesis.
49. L. J. Liebreich, *The Songs of Ascent and the Priestly Blessing*, JBL 74 (1955), 33-36 points to the close connection between pilgrimage

ancient songs of Yahweh's kingship (46, 92, 95 — 98) their new composition. The idea of God's kingship is not new. It was already clearly expressed in the building of Solomon's temple, where Yahweh was worshipped as the God and king who has his throne above the cherubim. New is only the actuality and the end-time stamp imposed upon the ancient songs of God the king. Subject to foreign kings, threatened in their very existence by their neighbors on every side, struggling for the preservation of their national and religious liberty — this Israel, now only a burning brand snatched away from the fire of ultimate destruction, relived, in reawakened glory, the theocracy of former times, which was to be accomplished anew at the end-time. After the collapse of the national kingship, the true title of king belonged to Yahweh alone (Is 40-45). When he comes to take possession of his kingdom, that is the end of all idolatry, ultimate victory over the pagans, formation of a universal kingdom of God. The Psalms of God the king are more a protest against the Babylonian festival of Marduk the king than they are an imitation of the songs. If Ps 92 sings of Yahweh's victory over the powers of chaos, this is no evidence for a festival celebrating Yahweh's enthronement; it must be taken, rather, as proof of the fact that the exiled Hebrews, suffering under the palpable impression of Babylonian cult and worship, had finally managed to truly recognize the triumph and ultimate victory of their king and God Yahweh, and to express this faith in their Psalm literature. The *"Sitz im Leben"* for the royal Psalms is thus the faith of the exilic and post-exilic community.[50]

To this same post-exilic period we must assign the Wisdom literature, with its rediscovery of the glories of the law. The Torah is experienced not as servitude, but as the Magna Carta of freedom. It radiates like the sun, and deserves to be contemplated day

---

psalms and priestly blessing (Nb 6, 24-26). The four concluding words of the blessing reappear in the psalms: "preserve, favor, bless, peace."

---

50. A. Feuillet, *Les Psaumes eschatologiques du règne de Jahve*, NouvRTh 73 (1951), 244-260; 352-363. The royal psalms of Deutero-Isaiah are not independent, and thus to be dated in the Persian era.

and night (Pss 1, 18, 118).[51] It is within the community of these
pious teachers of the law that we must also seek those men who
were responsible for the final collection of religious songs into the
Psalter that we know today.

Some seven centuries (1000-300 B.C.) have woven their religious convictions into the precious tapestry of the psalms, further
proof for the genuine incarnation of the Biblical word. The original body of songs, covered with the dust of centuries, was available to the final redactor who, inspired by the Spirit, rejected what
was unsuitable, and incorporated what seemed worth preserving
into the collection of the 150 Psalms. Only thus did the oft sung
songs of ancient Israel become the "songs of the Holy Spirit,"
songs that will be sung forever.

With the transition of Judaism into the Greek-speaking world,
a translation of the Bible, and particularly the Book of Psalms,
was an absolute necessity. The Greek translation of the Psalms, the
Septuagint, was the result of pastoral concern, and not a literary
preoccupation. This explains its many failings and shortcomings.
For example, the Hebrew perfects were simply, and quite mechan-
ically, translated as Greek aorists, the imperfects were translated as
futures, without respect to the quite different meanings conveyed
by these forms in the two languages. The Hebrew text which
served as the basis for the translation, already quite corrupt in some
passages, could only become even more obscure and enigmatic.
It is one of the great mysteries of history that the word of God was
destined to make its way into the Hellenic world through such a
sorry instrument. Despite their awkwardness, however, the Septuagint Psalms are a valuable witness to the state of the original text
at the time of the translation.

With the spread of Christianity into the Latin-speaking world,
there was a further need for a prayer text in the native language.
Once again it was not the scholars who set about translating the

---

51. A. Deissler, "Psalm 119 (118) und seine Theologie, Münchner Theol.
  Studien, 11 (1955), XX/1-347, ein Beitrag zur anthologischen Stilgat-
  tung im AT." Psalm 118 interpreted as an "anthology" of the old and
  an introduction to the new.

Greek Septuagint Psalter into Latin, enlightened by the canons of artistic taste. The translator, a missionary man no doubt, was concerned only with reproducing the Greek text as literally as possible. This old Italian translation (*Vetus Latina*) was revised by St. Jerome, on orders from Pope Damasus, on the basis of the best Greek codex available at that time. This revision is the text still used in the Roman Missal (*Psalterium Romanum*).[52] But when Jerome, in Palestine, became familiar with the text criticism of Origen (Hexapla), he revised the Psalter a second time, and this version became popular in Gaul (*Psalterium Gallicanum*);[53] this became the canonical text for the Roman breviary. In Bethlehem, Jerome undertook a third revision of the Psalms; this time he translated them completely new and independently on the basis of the original Hebrew text (*Psalterium iuxta hebraeos*),[54] a work which is of the greatest value for the history of the Psalm text, but which has found no application to the Church's liturgy. The progress of modern textual investigation prompted Pius XII to initiate a new Latin translation of the Psalms (*Psalterium Pianum*)[55] which was to preserve the traditional wording insofar as possible, but

52. New edition: Dom Robert Weber, *Le psautier romain et les autres anciens psautiers latins,* Edition critique (Collectanea biblica latina, vol. X), Rome, Abbey of St. Jerome (1953).

53. The monks of this same abbey have also edited the Psalm volume from the same series: *Die Mönche der gleichen Abtei edierten in der Reihe der Vulgataausgabe auch den Psalmenband: Biblia sacra juxta latinam vulgatam versionem ad codicum fidem . . . X. Liber psalmorum ex recensione sancti Hieronymi* (Rome, 1954).

54. New edition by Dom Henri de Sainte-Marie, *Sancti Hieronymi psalterium juxta Hebraeos. Edition critique* (Collectanea biblica latina, vol. XI), (Rome, 1954), Abbey of St. Jerome.

55. Promulgated by Moto proprio, March 24, 1945. This translation has given rise to a whole new series of commentary. The first German version by Claus Schedl, *Die Psalmen nach dem neuen römanischen Psalter übersetzt* (Vienna, 1946). On commission of the German Bishops' Conference, Romano Guardini published a "unified text" (Kosel, Munich). — There was also the translation of the Augustinian specialist Carl Perl (Styria, Graz), which enjoyed considerable success. A selection for younger readers, together with interpretation, in Claus Schedl, *Eine Feste Burg,* (Vienna, 1947). / A. Allgeier, *Der Liber Psalmorum cum Canticis Breviarii Romani* (Freiburg, 1949).

also to bring the text up to date in keeping with the results of modern scholarship.

C) THE PSALMS AS POETRY

1) RHYTHMIC LAWS:

Even though all tradition regarding Hebrew metric forms has been lost,[56] scholarship of recent centuries has elaborated metrical laws which are generally recognized as valid. It is primarily the element of rhythm which distinguishes poetry from prose. What is the rhythm employed by ancient Hebrew poetry? The Greek exegetes[57] simply applied the classical rhythmic laws of Greek poetry to the Psalms. Flavius Josephus presupposed that Moses had composed his song in hexameters. This is quite in keeping with the tendency to demonstrate the superiority of the Torah over Hellenic culture, but it is hardly in keeping with the laws of Hebrew poetry. The humanists also went back to classical patterns. Today, however, such attempts at interpretation have been widely abandoned as contradictory to the spirit of the Semitic language. Hebrew poetry is determined not on the basis of quantity, long and short syllables, but by a rhythmic accent. It was the work of Julius Lay[58] which showed the way: Metrical Forms of Hebrew Poetry, 1886. His ideas were incorporated and further developed by the rhythmic analysis of E. Sievers.[59] These scholars effectively set the general pattern for the rhythmic laws at work in the Psalms.

It was left to further investigation to establish whether this was a free rhythm of accent or a set schema. Bickell[60] made an analysis on the basis of Syrian poetry. Syrian verse consists of a determined

---

56. Eissfeldt, Einleitung, 66; §6: Logical and metrical division of Hebrew poetry, 63ff.
57. Castellino, Salmi, 17ff.
58. J. Lay, Grundzüge des Rhythmus, des Vers-und Strophenbaues in der hebräischen Poesie (1875). — Leifaden der Metrik der hebräischen Poesie (1887).
59. E. Sievers, Metrische Studien (1901).
60. C. Bickell, Metrices biblicae 1879. — Carmina VT Metrice 1882. — Die Dichtung der Hebräer 1882-1884. / G. Hoelscher, Elemente arabischer, syrischer und hebräischer Metrik, BZAW 34 (1920), 93-101.

number of *arses* and *theses*. The adaptation of the Syrian system to Hebrew poetry, however, proved impractical, since a strict syllable count cannot be demonstrated. The Hebrew does count the accented *arses,* but not the unaccented *theses*. Since each Hebrew verse falls into two halves or members, the accented syllables produce a rhythm of 2 plus 2, 2 plus 3, or 2 plus 4 (2 plus 2, 3 plus 3, 4 plus 4) or a composite measure (3 plus 2; 4 plus 3, etc.). In the lamentation (*qînāh*) it is this "elegiac pentameter" which is predominant; it is also called *qinah*-strophe (3 plus 2) (Pss 5, 18, 22, 34, 54, 64, 121, 125, 127).

The Hebrew verse line with its two rhythmic members never stands alone; it is always accompanied by a second parallel verse. The metrical unity is thus the double verse, the distich. This law was already recognized by R. Lowth in 1753 in his book *De sacra poesi hebraeorum* in which he refers to it as *parallelismus membrorum*.[61] The discoveries in Babylonian, Egyptian, and even Canaanite literature have shown that the poetry of the entire Ancient Near East was constructed according to this fundamental principle of *parallelismus membrorum*.[62]

Scholars distinguish three kinds of parallelism, a synonymous form, in which the second verse continues the same thought with other images:

"The heavens are telling the glory of God;
and the firmament proclaims his handiwork"
(Ps 18, 1);

antithetic, in which the second verse continues the thought of the first in an opposite figure:

"A wise son makes a glad father,
but a foolish son is a sorrow to his mother"
(Pr 10, 1);

61. *Praelectiones academicae* (Oxford, 1753).
62. A. Erman, *Die Literatur der Ägypter* (Leipzig, 1923), 9ff. / B. Meissner, *Babylonien und Assyrien,* vol. II (1925), 151-155. / Gressmann, AOT 241-281: *Babylonische Psalmen, Hymnen, Klagelieder, Gebete, Leichenlieder.* — ANET, 365-404, *Selection of Egyptian, Sumerian, Accadian, and Hittite hymns and prayers.* For the Canaanite world of that day, cf. G. Gordon, *Ugaritic Handbook,* 200ff.

synthetic, in which the idea begun in the first verse is further developed by new concepts:

"As a hart longs for flowing streams;
so longs my soul for thee, O God"
(Ps 41, 2).

In addition to this basic unity of the parallel double verse form, there are also principles of strophe formation, although in this respect it is no longer possible to establish a definite law. A strophe division can be clearly recognized when a refrain occurs in the song (Pss 41, 42, 45, 55, 98, 108) or, in the case of alphabetic psalms, when several verses begin with the same letter. Ps 118 is divided on the basis of the Hebrew initial letters, into 22 strophes of 8 double verses each. A further indication of the strophe division appears to be the word *selâh* which occurs 71 times in 39 psalms; its basic meaning is still contested.[63] According to the testimony of the Mishnah, in the second temple the psalm of the day was sung in three sections which were recognizable by the word *selâh*.[64]

2) HEADINGS AND TITLES:

All but 34 of the psalms have headings or titles in the Hebrew text, referring to author, type of song, musical accompaniment, time of composition, and liturgical usage. These titles must, at all events, be very ancient, since they were no longer properly understood at the time of the Septuagint translation and were frequently reproduced in a corrupted form.[65]

---

63. Interpretations of *selah*: daccapo, forte, interlude, pause, exclamation like Amen. Cf. Castellino, *Salmi*, 11ff.
64. N. H. Snaith, *Selah*, VT 2 (1952), 43-56. — Cites Mishnah, Tamid VII, 3.
65. The psalm titles have great historical value since they represent the conception of the earliest editors of the Psalter, but they are not a part of the inspired text. A. Vaccari, *Institutiones biblicae*, II, 2, *de libris didacticis* 16. / Jesús Enciso Viana, *Los titulos de los Salmos y la historia de la formacion del Salterio*, Estudios Biblicos 13 (1954), 135-165, compares the various titles with archaeological strata and thus constructs a history of the evolution of the psalter: the most ancient stratum is without titles, then come the royal psalms (90-103), then the Davidic collection, etc. Not too convincing.

The kind of song is indicated by the following expressions: *mizmôr* (57 times), derived from the stem *zāmar*, "to pluck," referring to a song designed for stringed accompaniment. The corresponding Greek word is *psalmos*, while *psalterion* refers to stringed instrument. Partially in connection with *mizmôr*, and partially alone, the word *šîr* (30 times) refers to the lyric-religious song, the title referring to its manner of delivery; under the term *maśkîl* (13 times), derived from *sākal*, "to be wise" are grouped the wisdom songs. The word *miktām* (6 times) has been variously explained: golden ornament (Luther), mystical song, song with the mouth covered (by the hand?). It is most probably related to the Accadian *kitmu*, a flute with keys (?). The word *šiggāyôn* (Ps 7, 1) might well correspond to the Accadian *šegû*, "dirge song." The general term *tephillâh*, "prayer," occurs only 5 times.

This short catalogue is sufficient to show that the Psalms are not lyric outpourings for private reading, but rather songs especially prepared for choral and musical presentation. This point is made even more strongly by an examination of the musical directions: 55 times we have the note *lammenasseaḥ*,[66] probably "for the choir master" or "for musical accompaniment." *Mizmôr* means "stringed instrument" in general. There are also instructions for the use of particular instruments, but with our incomplete knowledge of the ancient techniques of music, these cannot be satisfactorily explained. Thus, *neginôt* refers to accompaniment "with stringed instruments" [67] *mehilôt* "with flutes." Perhaps the enigmatic title for Ps 9 *mût labbēn* ("Die for the son!") contains a reference to the Egyptian oboe (*m't*) and the large Egyptian harp (*bnt*).[68] Pss 8, 80, and 83 were to be accompanied with an instrument which was played in the Philistine city of Gath (*'al haggittît*). The notice in Pss 6 and 11 *'al haššeminît* is not a reference to the "eighth voice" (that is, the basso), but to an eight-stringed instrument, and *'al 'alāmôt* is not a reference to "female voices," but once again to an instrument with some number of strings.

---

66. Piel participle of *nāṣaḥ*, "direct, lead, guide." Cf. 2 Ch 2, 1, 17.
67. Thorough examination of the musical terms in Jesús Enciso Viana, *Indicaciones musicales en los titulos de los Salmos*, Misc. bibl., B. Ubach, Montserrat (1953), 185-200. Translates *neginôt* as "in the manner of a folksong." Follet-Nober, *Zu altorientalischer Musik*, Bibl. 35 (1954), 230-238. / W. Auer, *Die Musikinstrumente im AT*, Collect. Bibl. (1953), 39-53. / J. Murray, *Instrumenta musica*, VD 32 (1954), 84-89. / H. Hickmann, *Terminologie musicale de l'Égypte ancienne*, Bull. de l'Inst. d'Egypte 36 (1955), 583-618 (together with a description of OT musical instruments). *lammenasseh* taken as an abstract: "with musical accompaniment."
68. Tournay, *Psaumes*, 9.

The psalm writer was not always concerned with the creation of a new melody for his work; there are frequent references to familiar melodies: "The hind of the dawn" (21), "lilies" (44, 68), "the dove on the far-off terebiths" (55) "do not destroy" (56-58, 74) etc. Since the basic melody is unfamiliar, the interpretation of the titles, which is different in practically every commentary, is most difficult.

Further titles refer to the liturgical use on particular days, thus Ps 91 "for the Sabbath." According to LXX: Ps 23 for the first day, Ps 47 for the second, Ps 93 for the fourth and Ps 92 for the sixth day. The Vulgate refers Ps 80 to the fifth day. The *Mishnah* (Tamid VII, 3) also lists Ps 81 for the third day, so that each day of the week has its own psalm, an echo of the prayer form of the synagogue. — L*e*hazkir, "for memorial" (Pss 37, 69) is a reference to its use at memorial sacrifices (Lev 23, 24), l*e*tôdâh "for the thanksgiving sacrifice" (Ps 99), and there is also a reference to the "temple consecration festival" (Ps 29). The liturgical character of the pilgrimage psalms (119-133) is self-explanatory. Similarly, the Hallel psalms had their place in the liturgy. The Jews distinguished a three-fold Hallel. The "little or Egyptian" (112-117) Hallel was prayed at the Passover in memory of the Exodus from Egypt, and on the yearly festivals. The "great Hallel" (134, 135) was sung on the Sabbath morning and on Easter morning. The third Hallel group contains Pss 144-150, and are called simply "morning prayer."

There are also inscriptions which refer to the Psalms' time of composition. Pss 7, 33, 51, 53, 55, 56, 58, 141 are attributed to the time of David's persecution by Saul; Ps 17 is David's song of triumph over all his enemies; Ps 59 is connected with the war against the Ammonites and Aramaeans; Ps 50 is a song of repentance after David's adultery with Bath-Sheba; Pss 3 and 6 date from the rebellion of Absalom. The value of these historical indications might be contested in individual cases; but at any rate they do represent the attitude of a very ancient age, which meant to have the psalm understood in terms of these incidents from David's life.

The Psalter unites songs of the most diverse poetic value, from the lofty ode with its lyric rhythm down to the almost prosaic wisdom song. We could hardly think of referring to the Psalms as the climax of the combined poetic creativity of the human race. But even without such a one-sided glorification, the Psalms retain their own value as poetry within the patterns of their surrounding culture. Compared with the Egyptian and Sumero-Babylonian compositions, the Psalms are not only the most recent blossom of Ancient Near Eastern poetical creation, but also the smallest. Israel has little to compare with the secular poetry of Egypt.[69] In comparison to the great abundance of Sumerian and Accadian hymns, the 150 Psalms are a very modest production.[70] But if this comparison with respect to material abundance finds the Psalms somewhat wanting, it does at least cast their fundamental otherness and their individual value in a new light. The Babylonian poet was too much the slave of his iron-bound poetic outline; the psalm writer, on the other hand, was free to create a new rhythm with its corresponding form, to reflect the spirit of a given mood. The Psalms are free of the polytheistic distortion of nature, and thus enjoy a much more open encounter with the things of creation, which are a song of God for them. The de-demonization of the world has freed the soul of the Biblical poet from his inhibitions and obstacles, teaching him to discover new styles and new songs which, even from the profane point of view, belong to the highest point of Ancient Near Eastern poetic creation.[71]

The crown of all Psalm studies would be a theology of the Psalms. In individual cases we must refer this to the commentaries.[72] But it is possible to examine three leit-motifs: nature, history, and end-time. — The one God who is celebrated in the Psalms is the creator of heaven and earth. The elements are at his service and reveal his glory (nature psalms)[73] (e.g., Pss 8, 18, 28, 102, 103). But it is not nature as such which interests the singer: the God of the universe is also the God of Israel and thus the God of history. He is the shepherd and guardian not only of the whole people, but of each individual person. History, with its succession of high points and low points, becomes an abiding revelation of God's

---

69. G. Gilbert, *La poésie égyptienne* (Bruxelles, 1949). / Th. H. Gaster, in JBL 74 (1955), 239-251.
70. A. Falhenstein and W. von Soden, *Sumerische und akkadische Hymnen und Gebete* (1952).
71. Castellino, *Salmi*, 24.
72. *Ibid.*, 25: *Teologia dei Salmi*. / Tournay, *Psaumes*, 41ff: *Doctrine du psautier*.
73. Among the nature psalms, Ps 103 assumes particular importance by reason of its similarity with the Egyptian hymn to the sun composed by Pharaoh Ikhnaton. Cf. H. Kruse, *Archetypus Psalmi 104 (103)*, VD 29 (1951), 31-43.

judgment and salvation (historical psalms: 104, 105, 114). History, however, is not without direction; it is working towards a goal and end, looking to the time when God will establish his kingdom through his Messiah (messianic and eschatological psalms 2, 21, 71, 109).

Obviously, we must not ever lose sight of the fact that these ideas were not, from the very outset, expressed in all their present clarity. They have grown from light to light. The imperfect concepts of the hereafter,[74] the one-sided evaluation of the present,[75] and the severity of the curse Psalms[76] are relics of an age in which Israel was still walking in night and in the shadow of death (Is 9, 1), but she had already begun to glimpse a mighty light. When Christ prayed the Psalms,[77] when Mary took her inspiration for the Magnificat from them (Lk 1, 46), and when the Church took them for her daily prayer, this only proves that, despite all its temporal shortcomings, the Psalter has a power that surpasses time, a power that can be explained only by the Holy Spirit who first inspired the Psalms and made them the songs of God's people in Old and New Covenant alike.

---

74. Tournay, Psaumes, 44.
75. B. Hall, The Problem of Retribution in the Psalms, Scripture 7 (1955), 84-92.
76. E. J. Kissane, The Interpretation of Ps 108 (109), The Irish Theol. Quart. 18 (1951), 1-8 attempts to avoid the problem by interpreting the curse words as merely a description of the misery of the godless; but this is not possible. The curse psalms are an actual attempt at an impassioned warding off of evil, and are thus to be interpreted from the point of view of God's judgment. They must be taken together with the judgment psalms, whose interpretation poses much less difficulty.
77. In temptation, Ps 90, 11 (Mt 4, 6); in his polemic with the Pharisees, Ps 109 (Mt 22, 44); on the cross Ps 21 (Mt 27, 46).

CHAPTER XIX

THE SOLOMONIC WISDOM LITERATURE

ON the occasion of his famous dream in Gibeon, Solomon had not prayed for wealth, long life, or power, but rather for "an understanding mind to govern the people" (I K 3, 9). As proof of the fact that this prayer had been heard and that Solomon had been endowed with extraordinary wisdom, the author next presents the account of Solomon's famous judgment (1 K 3, 16ff). Solomon's reputation for wisdom spread beyond the borders of his kingdom, so that even the Queen of Sheba (Saba) came to experience his wisdom (1 K 5, 9-14). In addition to this, 1 K 4, 29 — 34 affords a more precise insight into the nature of Solomon's wisdom: "And God gave Solomon wisdom and understanding beyond measure, and largeness of mind like the sand on the seashore, so that Solomon's wisdom surpassed the wisdom of all the people of the east, and all the wisdom of Egypt. . . . He uttered three thousand proverbs; and his songs were a thousand and five. He spoke of the trees, from the cedar that is in Lebanon to the Hyssop which grows out of the wall; he spoke also of peace, and of birds, and of reptiles, and of fish."

It is surprising to find no religious content in this catalogue, only nature wisdom. These facts are meant to establish Solomon's wisdom in its proper position, not as an isolated factor in the history of the Israelite mind, but as an obvious and deliberate orientation within a much larger scope: "His wisdom surpassed the wisdom of all the people of the east, and all the wisdom of Egypt." A. Alt[1] has already called attention to the surprisingly close relationship with Egyptian literature, especially the so-called *Onomastikon* (name book) of Amenope,[2] dating from around 1100 B.C. The scope of this work is indicated by its title which, fortunately, has been preserved: "Beginning of teaching . . . about everything that exists, that has been created by Ptah and given form by Thot, about the heavens and their ornaments, about the earth and all that is in it, what the mountains spew forth and what the flood waters, all things that Re looks upon, and everything that is green upon the earth." This declaration of purpose corresponds with the content of the entire writing, which begins immediately with a description of all created things in the sky, in the water, and on the earth, divine and royal persons, courtiers, officials, the various classes, callings, tribes, and types of people, even outside Egypt, the cities of Egypt itself, buildings and their parts, the countryside, the various grains and their products, food and drink, the butchering of cattle and various kinds of meat — a total, in the extant versions, of some 610 entries, a list which does not exhaust the original compass of the work. As the table of contents clearly indicates, this work is nothing more or less than an attempt at an encyclopedia of all learning, even if only in the form of a series of proverbs in a more or less ordered arrangement, in which the persons and properties of supra-human nature are treated just as amply as the phenomena of human life. Nowhere in this writing do we find rules, in the sense of the practical wisdom of life which had for centuries been so richly developed in Egypt; nowhere in the entire book is there a single such statement. This is all the more significant by reason of the fact that in its title, just like the other

1. A. Alt, *Die Weisheit Salomos, Kleine Schriften* II (1953), 90-99. The basis of our presentation.
2. Published by A. H. Gardiner, *Ancient Egyptian Onomastica* (1947), I, 24ff: II, 1ff. —H. Grapow, *Onomastica, In Handbuch der Orientalistik,* I. *Ägyptologie, 2. Literatur* (1952), 188.

books of practical wisdom for living, it is referred to as "teaching" (*sb'yt*).[3]

Such lists of encyclopedic content seem to have belonged among the established body of learned literature in Babylonia as well. The Sumerians, with their characteristic preoccupation with order and system, had already begun the creation of this "catalogue knowledge." A certain degree of influence by the Babylonian works can hardly be excluded in our judgment of the Egyptian Book of Names. Everything points to the fact that Solomon also cultivated this branch of Ancient Near Eastern science at his court in Jerusalem. Not only did he take over the ancient forms; he created something new by building the simple lists and catalogues into a whole series of proverbs and songs. This transformation of a literary genre is quite in keeping with our image of Solomon. He was concerned in every respect with promoting the cultural development and the powerful position of the kingdom he had inherited from his father David, to make Israel a power to reckon with among the ancient kingdoms. His activity in the international competition of the wisdom literature is to be explained in this connection. If he succeeded in creating something new in this area, it would mean an increase of prestige in other areas as well. The international reputation which the court of Jerusalem soon acquired is ample proof of his success in this enterprise. Israel did not simply achieve a mechanical adaptation of a body of culture common to the Ancient Near East; Israel assimilated and made important original contributions. The appearance of this new Solomonic literary style represents a step in Israel's emancipation from the heritage of her national past.[4]

But it was not only on the scientific plane that Solomon meant to bring his country up to date; he was also concerned with the cultural formation of his people. "The early era of kings was an era marked by the break with many patriarchal traditions, but at the

---

3. A. Alt, *Die Weisheit Salomos, Kleine Schriften* II (1953), 94. / S. Morenz, *Eine "Naturlehre" in den Sargtexten*, WZKM 54 (1957), 119-129.
4. *Ibid.*, 99.

same time it was an era of a completely new intellectual and cultural revolution, a sort of Enlightenment, that is, an era marked by the rise of cultural self-awareness. Man became aware of his intellectual powers and his rational capacity to put things in order; whole new dimensions of the world around him, dimensions which had not been perceived by the faith of his ancestors, now entered upon his field of vision."[5] The changes in external circumstances called for a new ideal of culture. This contemporary need was met by the older wisdom literature,[6] as it finds expression in the Book of Proverbs. The Proverbs of Solomon are not a mere chance collection of various proverbs and sayings; they are meant to sketch the guidelines according to which youth were to be educated in the national culture. Since it is always true that words move but examples impel, G. von Rad maintains that the story of Joseph in Egypt was sketched in terms of the ideal of the older wisdom teachings.

It is obvious that a court which was so concerned with the achievement of refined and courtly culture must have its courtly poetry as well. As to how far Solomon can be named as the composer of these "proverbs" and the author of the "Song of Songs" there is less clarity. It would be well to present a brief outline of the literary problems of both books.

A) THE PROVERBS OF SOLOMON

Commentaries: HSAT: Steuernagel 1923 — BB: Wiesmann 1923 — HAT: Gemser 1937 — EB: Hamp 1949 — SBB: Cohen

---

5. G. Von Rad, *Josephsgeschichte und ältere Chokma*, Suppl. VT I (1953), 120-127. / *Die ältere Weisheit Israels*, Kerygma und Dogma 2 (1956), 54-72: a) Rules for Living, b) Officials' schools at court, c) Ideals for formation, the example of Joseph in Egypt, d) Later pious thinkers theologizing on the subject of wisdom.

6. As distinguished from the later wisdom literature which developed under the influence of Hellenism after the Exile: Book of Wisdom (composed in Greek), Ecclesiastes (the Preacher), Jesus Sirach (Ecclesiasticus). The older wisdom literature is described in the supplement to VT III (1955): R. B. Y. Scott, *Solomon and the Beginnings of Wisdom in Israel*, 262-279. / D. Winton-Thomas, *Textual and Philological Notes on Some Passages in the Book of Proverbs*, 280-292. / A. R. Johnson, *Untersuchung zu māšal*, 170-182.

1952² — JerB: Duesberg-Auvray 1951 — ClamB: Renard-Busy-Weber-Spicq 1946.
Introductions: Cornely-Merk 1940,¹² 488 — 491 — Simon-Prado II, 1940,² 144 — 162 — Höpfl-Miller-Metzinger 1946,⁵ 315 — 325 (Patristic literature) — Pfeiffer 1948,² 645 — 659 — Kuhl 1953, 269 — 279 — Eissfeldt 1956,² 579 — 587 (Extensive bibliography) — Weiser 1957,⁴ 238 — 241 — Robert-Feuillet 1957, 624 — 641.

1) STRUCTURE OF THE BOOK:

Even a brief glance at the table of contents is enough to show that Solomon's proverbs have undergone a fate similar to the Book of Psalms. It is a collection of collections. The headings preserved in the text point to the existence of nine collections:

I. Ch. 1-9: The Schoolhouse of Wisdom.
II. Ch. 10-22, 16: Proverbs of Solomon (357 pithy sayings).
III. Ch. 22, 17-24, 22: Words of the Wisemen.
IV. Ch. 24, 23-34: Further Words of the Wisemen.
V. Ch. 25-29: Further Proverbs of Solomon, collected by the men of Hezekiah (128 sayings).
VI. Ch. 30, 1-14: The Words of Agur of Massa.
VII. Ch. 30, 15-33: Number Proverbs.
VIII. Ch. 31, 1-9: Words of Lemuel, King of Massa.
IX. Ch. 31, 10-31: The "Good Wife."

This division shows that, after the nine introductory chapters on the "school of wisdom" the Solomonic groups of proverbs (II and V) are two points of crystallization about which the later collections are grouped.⁷ The whole book gives the impression of a mosaic, in which the tessarae of the individual proverbs have been worked into an artistic unity which is faded and weathered in many places.⁸

The Book bears the Hebrew title *mišlē šelōmōh,* generally translated as "proverbs of Solomon." The word *māšal* is apparently derived from

---

7. The Greek Bible LXX has a different sequence: I, II, III, VI, IV, VII, VIII, V, IX, proof of the fact that the sequence was still in flux at the time of the Greek Septuagint translation in the third century.
8. G. R. Driver, *Problems in the Hebrew Text of Proverbs* (54 passages examined), Bibl. 32 (1951), 173-197. Critical edition of the Vulgate *Libri Solomonis,* i.e. Proverbia, Ecclesiastes, Canticum Canticorum ex interpretatione Sti Hieronymi (Rome, 1957).

the root "to rule, to guide, regulate,"[9] and means something like "rule of life." Because of its brevity of form, and its compact force of expression, the word *māšal* comes closer to our English "proverb," which is likewise drawn from the manifold experience of life and expressed in compact brevity. This ancient form of the proverb, the product of mother-wit and popular wisdom, later developed into the artistic forms of epigram, enigma, and parable.

"In terms of form, the author of the proverb shows a preference for the two-line verse (distich), with both members generally of equal length. Generally the two members will express contrast or opposition. It is the contrast between wise man and fool, the man who fears God and the man who ignores him, the upright and the wicked, which furnishes the inexhaustible theme. This confrontation of two types brings the hearer to an awareness of the fact that it is his duty and fate to choose between two ways. Other forms of proverb prefer the element of comparison (as—as; better — than), which stirs up the powers of interior vision and lends a plastic charm and ornament to the thought expressed . . . . The brevity and pregnant compactness of expression make it impossible to read over the proverb in haste. It must be read twice, three times, and its background must be examined, before we properly understand. We note that the ancient teachers took great pains in formulating the content of their doctrine, sparing neither labor nor wit, in an effort to say what they meant to say in such a way that they would hit the nail squarely on the head and their words of wisdom would stick fast in their hearers' mind." [10]

In the two Solomonic collections (II + V) it is the short two-line verse form which prevails: 375 proverbs in the first and 128 proverbs in the second collection. In the later collections added to the text, this briefer form of proverb has generally been developed into a rather lengthy instruction, and in the nine introductory chapters, it has taken on the form of a full-blown parable. There is, in every people, an abundant treasure of naturally developed human wisdom, expressed in pithy maxims. Has the Book of Proverbs simply drawn upon this wide stream of popular wisdom and included whatever seemed valuable in its collection? Is the Book of Proverbs to be attributed to the authorship of the great unknown and nameless composer, the "people"? It is no doubt

---

9. There are two roots for *māšal*, either "to rule" or to "be similar." It seems that later ages favored the meaning "to be similar" (hence "likeness"), whereas the more ancient age had most likely derived the meaning from "to rule." Duesberg-Auvray, *Proverb*, 8, Anm. 1. / J. Pirot, *Le Mašal dans l'AT*, Recherches de science rel. 37 (1950), 565-580. / A. R. Johnson, *māšal*, Sppl VT III (1955), 170-182.

10. H. Lamparter, *Das Buch der Weisheit, Prediger und Sprüche* (Calwer Verlagswerk) (1955), 162.

true that many very pointed and well phrased proverbs have their origin in the mouth of the people. "But the strict form of the proverb, together with its precise and refined diction, makes it obvious that we are dealing with the works of avowed masters — collecting, making original contributions, forging and polishing, working with the sharpened tools of their educated thinking, even producing new creations, until the proverb has attained its definitive form." [11]

Behind the Book of Proverbs, we must recognize the patient, careful, centuries-long effort and dedication of the "wisemen" (ḥᵃkāmîm). They are not so evident in Scripture as the prophets or the priests. They represent rather the secular element of Israelite culture, focusing upon the royal court. For the proverbs are dedicated to a very definite aim, the formation and training of a courtly class, government officials or district administrators or even the upper classes of the people. The wisemen sought to develop an ideal for guidance and instruction, which is in close sympathy with the medieval idea of reasoned temperance. Everything points to the fact that Solomon was not content with having produced the external splendor of his court in Jerusalem by building his magnificent palace; by his deliberate cultivation of proverb wisdom he left his spiritual and cultural stamp as well. Solomon's personal contributions to the Proverbs must not, accordingly, be underevaluated. In order to present a truer picture of the historical probabilities, we shall begin our interpretation of the Book of Proverbs with collection III, the "words of the wisemen."

2) APPROPRIATION OF FOREIGN CULTURE:

David had installed the Egyptian Scribe Shisha at his court, and his two sons served under Solomon. This man certainly drew not only upon the technical capacities, but also the cultural background of the Egyptian scribes, introducing both to the new and universally receptive capital city of Israel. Egypt was then in a position to look back upon a very ancient tradition of wisdom. From the interval between 2000 — 100 B.C. we have seven completely or almost completely preserved wisdom treatises, and

11. *Ibid.*, 163.

fragments of five others, in addition to our knowledge of six or seven titles of vanished works. The significance and importance enjoyed by these wisdom books in Egyptian antiquity is amply attested by the many quotations and references, as well as the fact that most of them have been preserved in several copies.[12]

The bearers of this wisdom tradition were the members of the ruling classes, in the old Kingdom the viziers, and the official administrators of the New Kingdom. Of the "teaching of Kagemmi" (Old Kingdom, 3 — 4 dyn.) we have only one example: "Instruction of the vizier for his children: Avoid faults of the tongue, cultivate good table manners, and do not stir up the anger of God." — "The teaching of Ptahhotep" (Old Kingdom, 5 dyn.) develops a professional ethics not only for the officials for whom he wrote, but for the whole body of citizens. Various rules of life are developed in casuistic form. Then Ptahhotep gives the proper behavior for each individual case. A good deal of space is given to the proper conduct towards superiors and men of higher rank; there are also table manners, proper behavior towards women, and a warning against pride. — "The teaching for King Merikare" (10 dyn.) is, on the one hand, a picture of the princely ideal as developed for his successor by an aged ruler, here put into the mouth of the father of Merikare; on the other hand, it is also a political document, written to justify a claim to the throne. — The "teaching of King Amenemhet" (12 dyn.) is similar to this. — The "teaching of Cheti, son of Duauf" (12 dyn.) sings the praises of the bureaucrat. The song discusses a long series of manual vocations and arts, and then comes to the conclusion that there is no calling in which one is not subject to commands and orders excepting that of public official. The corresponding advice is "Be a public official!" To guarantee the son's success in attaining this goal, the document proceeds to enumerate the rules of life that he must follow. — "The teaching of Ani" (18 dyn.), who calls himself simply "the scribe," is the product of the lower order of public officials. It is largely focused upon the ideal of the modestly retiring, reticent, discreet, pious,

---

12. Fuller account of Egyptian wisdom literature in *Handbuch der Orientalistik*, I: *Ägyptologie*, 1. *Literatur* (1950), 90-110.

grateful, and accommodating citizen. — By reason of its influence on the Solomonic Book of Proverbs, the "teaching of Amen-em-ope" (22 — 26 dyn.) is of the greatest significance. He was a highly placed official in the administration of landed property, and he presents the rich experience of his life in some 30 chapters. The focus of his teaching is divine worship and a system of morality which is always oriented towards God. God is the judge who brings everything to light, and who directs the course of human fate. The ideal of human education and upbringing, which is already announced as the purpose of the other wisdom literature, is expressed in much clearer form here. Two types are contrasted. The "firebrand" (*nnw*), that is, the man who is violent, passionate, bent on gain, without conscience, in a word, undisciplined; his opposite is the "taciturn" (*gr*), who is content, quiet, and mild mannered, and the "reserved" (*qb*), who can control his feelings. He is the man who is always master of the situation, able to hold his tongue, but who also has control of his interior self, and is not inclined to any form of excitement.[13] The same media of education come up in the Book of Proverbs as well: "He who restrains his words has knowledge; and he who has a cool spirit (*qar-rûᵃḥ*, "of cool spirit") is a man of understanding" (Pr 17, 27).[14]

The other Egyptian princely ideals and wisdom teaching may have had only indirect influence on Israelite thinking, but the 30 chapters of the teaching of Amen-em-ope were taken over into the "words of the wisemen" (22, 17ff.), sometimes literally, and sometimes in a free reworking.

At the beginning of his instruction, the wiseman admonishes his disciple: "Have I not written for you thirty sayings of admonition and knowledge, to show you what is right and true, that you may give a true answer to those sent you" (Prv 22, 20).

---

13. *Ibid.*, 96.
14. Text in Gressmann, AOT 33-46 and ANET 412-424. / L. Grollenberg, *A propos de Prov XVII*, 27 RB 59 (1952), 40-43. / A. Alt, *Zur literarischen Analyse der Weisheit des Amenem-ope*, Suppl. VT III (1955), 16-25. — E. Drioton, *Sur la Sagesse d'Aménémopé*, Melanges-Robert (1957), 254.

Amen-em-ope, on the other hand, closes his instruction with these words: "Contemplate these 30 chapters. They are a source of joy, the first of books, and they bring knowledge to the uneducated." — These two verses show how freely the Israelite wisdom scholar was to rework the Egyptian teaching. Although the commentaries are, in places, literal translations, still this Egyptian "guideline for a good public official" has given rise to a new work, thoroughly steeped in the individual spirit of Israel, a work which pursues the same objectives: a sense of justice, proper bearing, and good upbringing are the clear path to success; on the other hand, drunkenness, dissipation, and intercourse with the wicked are a great obstacle in the way of all progress.

These "directions for a proper public official," based on the Egyptian pattern, are continued in a small appendix in Collection IV, Ch. 24, 23 — 34: "Further words of the wise." This section points to the second cultural fund of the Ancient Near East, Mesopotamia. The Babylonian wisdom literature was, originally, an independent creation; but it could not escape the influence of Egyptian wisdom. Evidence of this is the Ahikar story, which has come down in various forms, but whose oldest text, written in Aramaic, goes back to Elephantine, an island in the Nile, and dates to the era around 500 B.C., although it has a much older tradition.[15] The ten Hebrew verses from Ahikar have been increased, in the Greek Septuagint, to fifteen, further proof of the fluidity of the text over a period of many years.

The Israelite sages did not hesitate to incorporate the wisdom literature of the Arab Bedouin tribes. In this category belong Collections VI, VII, and VIII: "The words of Agur, son of Jakeh, of Massa," "the words of Lemuel, King of Massa," and various number proverbs. Massa was a Ismaelite tribe in northern Arabia (Gn 25, 14; 1 Ch 1, 30). Concerning Agur, we know nothing apart from his proverbs. The name Lemuel becomes in-

---

15. Duesberg-Auvray, *Proverb* (JerB), (1951), 20. / C. J. K. Story, *The Book of Proverbs and Northwest Semitic Literature*, JBL 64 (1945), 319-337. Relationship with Ugarit and Aḥikar.

telligible on the basis of the Mari excavations, which have discovered the existence of a god Lim.[16] The words of Lemuel belong to the genre of princely education ideals; they hand down the teachings that Lemuel's mother entrusted to her son. — Finally, number proverbs, throughout the Ancient Near East, were a favorite means of impressing a truth upon the memory (Collection VII). Collection IX is not simply a praise of woman in general; it is the description of an ideal woman [17] and was meant to serve as a guide for young brides upon entering marriage. This leaves only the two great Solomonic collections and the introductory chapters.

3) THE SOLOMONIC COLLECTIONS (II AND V):

(Ch. 10 — 22, 16; 25 — 29)

In these collections we find one proverb after another, with no particular order or sequence in terms of theme or subject matter. The most varied and diverse thoughts stand right next to each other, frequently without a single word to suggest the connection between them. Yet, taken all together, they do present a compact picture of the human ideal. The most ancient proverbs are the result of daily experience of life. The ancient sages were good observers. With their sharp wit and clever minds they need only a few words to capture a scene from daily living that is typical for all times. For example, a scene from the street: "The poor use entreaties, but the rich answer roughly" (18, 23). Or "The sluggard buries his hand in the dish, and will not even bring it back to his mouth" (19, 24). Or "A continual dripping on a rainy day and a contentious woman are alike; to restrain her is to restrain the wind or to grasp oil in one's right hand" (27,

---

16. A. Jirku, *Das nomen proprium Lemuel (Prov 31, 1) und der Gott Lim,* ZAW 66 (1954), 151.
17. M. B. Crook, *The Marriageable Maiden of Prov 31, 10-31,* JNES 13 (1954), 137-140. — J. Obersteiner, *Die Erklärung von Prov 31, 10-31 durch Beda den Ehrwürdigen und Bruno von Asti,* ThPrQ (Linz), 102, (1954), 1-12.

15). The wisdom teacher is only describing, without offering any express praise or censure. His attitude must be determined from the subject matter.

But most of the proverbs have a quite different turn of direction. The wiseman steps out of the background and passes judgment on questionable behavior. The world is divided into two camps, good and evil, just and unjust, wisemen and fools. In fluid parallelism, he parades his subjects in pairs across the stage of life: "The Lord does not let the righteous go hungry, but he thwarts the craving of the wicked" (10, 3; cf. 10, 6, 7, 21, 26; 29, 6 — 11). On the side of the good man, as his instructor, there is "wisdom" (10, 21), advice (12, 15), patience and long-suffering (12, 16; 19, 11). Children are docile and full of respect (10, 1; 15, 20), women are prudent and retiring (19, 14; 18, 22). But the camp of the wicked is ruled by deceit (12, 5. 17; 13, 5), arrogance (13, 10; 21, 24); hypocrisy (26, 24 — 26); the children are poorly brought up (19, 26), and the women are without morals (21, 9).

More or less explicitly, there is one forceful thought that permeates the proverbs: Be good, cultivate wisdom, remain faithful to the ancient ideals (12, 11; 27, 23 — 27), bring up your children properly (13, 1; 15, 27, 1), and with strictness (13, 24; 22, 15; 29, 15). No motives are assigned for this line of conduct. Their excellence as guides for human behavior will be immediately obvious to the unspoiled human understanding. They are presented as an absolute imperative of human behavior.[18]

In addition, however, there are many proverbs which present the success of the good man as a motive for his proper behavior. The just man has success over the godless (10, 24; 28, 30; 12, 3); for he alone is on the way of life (10, 11; 13, 4; 16, 22); the way of the wicked leads to ruin (10, 16), and to death (11, 19). In terms of this principle, it is truth that wins out over falsehood, humility over pride, industry over sloth. A healthy faith in the success of the good lends an air of victorious certitude to these proverbs. Justice and well-being are almost synonymous. The

---

18. Duesberg-Auvaray, *Proverb,* 14.

problem of the man who suffers and is persecuted unjustly is hardly mentioned here. The wisdom literature is concerned primarily with a practical attitude towards life, an attempt to regulate the normal behavior of man, and this is established in terms of everyday experience. Wickedness, in the last analysis, must necessarily lead to failure. The success of the wicked and failure of the good is only an apparent success or failure; the day of reckoning will eventually come. This is the healthy and enthusiastic conviction of the proverbs.

Some surprise has been expressed as to the fact that the number of religious proverbs is proportionately quite small. Despite this fact, the proverbs do not preach a merely humanistic ideal of life, without reference to God. The religious foundation sometimes shows quite clearly. God is primarily a source of recompense and judgment. He blesses the good and annihilates the wicked (10, 3. 6. 27; 22, 12). He especially rewards truthfulness (12, 22), love (19, 17), a pure heart (22, 11), and honor (11, 1); on the other hand he rejects pride (15, 25), unjust judgment (17, 15), dishonorable conduct (20, 10). The foundation of all good behavior is wisdom, which proceeds from fear of God. It is a precious treasure (15, 16; 22, 4), the source of all good on earth (11, 29; 14, 26), the source of life (14, 27; 19, 23; 22, 4), and the very foundation of religion (15, 33; 16, 6).

All of human life is to be directed towards God from whom it has its origin (16, 4), towards God who directs the course of all the world (19, 21) and leads it towards its appointed goal (20, 24). Life is worth living only when we commit ourself entirely into the hands of God (20, 22; 29, 25).

4) THE HOUSE OF WISDOM (Collection I,' Ch. 1 – 9):

The life wisdom of the proverbs, so completely directed towards the practical, but at the same time deeply rooted in religion, achieves a particular depth and compactness in the introductory chapters. The motivation for human activity is no longer grounded in the daily experience of the wiseman's living; wisdom itself takes a stand above the earth and invites mankind to follow her. The exhortations of this section remind us of the stirring words of a prophet Isaiah or Jeremiah. The concept of wisdom (*hokmâh*) is deserving of particular attention.

Wisdom appears as a person, acting and speaking, demanding the full confidence of her human subjects (1, 23 — 25), inviting them to a banquet (9, 1 — 6), promising them fortune and happiness (8, 20 — 21). Wisdom comes from God himself. Like the *Logos* in the prologue of St. John's Gospel, wisdom is at once in God and outside God. She is older than the world and has a part in the work of creation (8, 22ff.), she guides and directs all things and only through her can kings and rulers exercise power. Her only desire is to be heard by men and to lead them to life (8, 35; 9, 11). In the Books of Sirach and "Wisdom" these ideas are further developed. Frequently it is difficult to determine the precise compass of this figure. Is it merely a personification, "dame wisdom" as opposed to "dame foolishness" (7, 1ff.), or is it actually a person? It is only in the retrospect of the Incarnation of the Word that we can understand the full significance of these texts.[19]

It is precisely these introductory chapters on personified wisdom that have led many authors to date the final redaction of the Book of Proverbs in the Hellenic era,[20] since these ideas must have developed only by contact with the Greek concept of *Sophia*. But the discovery of the Egyptian wisdom literature inclines one to be rather sceptical at this late dating. We might even suspect that the Greeks learned something of their *Sophia* from the ancient land of wisdom, Egypt.

It would be surprising if the Israelite wisemen had taken over only the Egyptian rules of life, and not their underlying conception of "wisdom." "The central concept of Egyptian wisdom is the *maat*, the 'right,' 'justice,' 'primeval order,' generally translated

---

19. R. Stecher, *Die persönliche Weisheit in den Proverbien Kap. 8*, ZkathTh 75 (1953), 411-451.

20. Weiser, 240: "From the post-exilic era, hardly before the 4th century." Eissfeldt, 582: "... rather late, not before the 4th or even the 3rd century." Pfeiffer, 659: "in the 3rd century."

simply as 'wisdom.' As a goddess, Maat belongs to the system of Heliopolis, where she appears as the daughter of the sun god. She develops as a principle of right order in all things, in times primordial. By the wicked attacks of Seth and his followers this primeval order was disturbed, and then reestablished by the victory of Horus. As the incorporation of Horus, every new king reestablished this right order, on the occasion of his coronation; a new state of Maat, i.e., of peace and justice, dawns anew. The object of the wisdom literature is to prepare the way for this principle of order which derives from God, and is thus impervious, by essence, to all human influence; it is to prepare the way for Maat, to pass it on . . . . It is idle to attempt a division between divine and human wisdom; there is only one truth which is valid in all the world, in the human sphere as in the divine. In like manner, every violation of this true order will provoke a like vengeance, which takes the form of failure in earthly life as well as in the life which immediately follows death with no fundamental breach or distinction, that is, at the time of judgment . . . . It is the province of wisdom to delineate this 'way of life' or 'way of God' in a series of individual precepts." [21]

The similarities between the Egyptian Maat and the Biblical *ḥokmâh* is apparent to even the most casual reader. Both incorporate the concept of an original world order which proceeds from God. Both court the allegiance of listeners or readers, in order to teach them the "way of life." We find the same laws operative here as in the building of Solomon's temple. Solomon did not hesitate to entrust the temple to the supervision of a Phoenician architect, and had it built according to "pagan" architectural motifs; and still it was the temple of Yahweh and not

---

21. H. Brunner, *Im Handbuch der Orientalistik*, vol. I. *Ägyptologie*, 2. *Literatur* (1952), 93. Somewhat surprising is the apparently monotheistic tendency of Egyptian wisdom literature. Man is responsible not so much to the individual gods as to the divinity itself, and his fate rests in the hand of God. A. H. Gardiner, *A New Moralizing Text*, WZKM 54 (1957), 43-44. Presents 20 rules of conduct for practical living, dating from the time of Ramses II, e.g.: "Have no care today for tomorrow, before it comes. Are not yesterday and today in the hand of God?"

a temple of Tyrian Baal. What is to keep the Israelite thinkers and poets from taking over the Egyptian concept of an original moral order in the world, the concept of Maat? It has lost nothing in the transition; in fact it has gained. Set free from the error of polytheism, it has taken on new light as the wisdom of the one true God. The conception of a moral world order as emanating from God was nothing new for the wisemen of Solomon's era. On Sinai, "the ten words" had proceeded from the mouth of Yahweh, and from that time forth they were to determine the life of the people and of each individual in all its circumstances and details. The proverbs of Solomon are nothing more than the application of the ten commandments to the most varied realms of daily living.[22]

Just as the New Testament borrowed many concepts from the world of Greek thought, and enlisted them in the new ideology of the Gospel, even so the Old Testament never hesitated to incorporate whatever elements were useful in the world about it, and to fill them with new spirit.

These considerations force us to assign Collection I (Chs. 1 — 9) to an earlier age than is normally suggested. The antiquity of the conception of the personification of wisdom in chs. 8 and 9 has already been noted by Albright.[23] He arrives at this position on the basis of a vocabulary comparison with Ugaritic sources, which point back to ancient Phoenician-Canaanite influence, which, once again, point back further to an Egyptian origin. At all events, the problem of Biblical wisdom must be reformulated in terms of its Egyptian borrowings.

---

22. The commentary of H. Lamparter, *Das Buch der Weisheit* (Calwer Bibelwerk) vol. 16 (1955) arrange the proverbs in the order of the Ten Commandments.

23. W. F. Albright, *From Stone Age to Christianity* (1949), 365ff. / *Some Canaanite-Phoenician Source of Hebrew Wisdom,* Suppl. VT III (1955), 1-55. / G. Lanckowski, *Beeinflussung des Christentums durch ägyptische Vorstellungen,* Z. f. Rel. und Giestesgeschichte 8 (1956), 14-32. The Amarna letters and Egyptian records attest to the fact that Israel was directly influenced by the Phoenician-Amorrite courtly style, and indirectly by the Egyptian. / W. Baumgartner, *The Wisdom Literature, The OT and Modern Study* (1951), 210-237. Points to the significance and limitations of extra-Israelite parallels.

Seen as a whole, the Book of Proverbs gives the impression of a mosaic, the product of various hands and various ages. The wisemen of Egypt and the Arabian desert vied with the wisemen of Israel in their description of true wisdom. The confrontation took place at Jerusalem: the Bible tells us that Solomon encouraged the study and development of wisdom literature at his court. The Bible explicitly speaks of his wisdom as surpassing that of all the sons of the east and the wisdom of Egypt (1 K 5, 9ff.). The extent to which the proverbs preserved in the two Solomonic collections actually reproduce the work of Solomon himself, and the extent to which they are "Solomonic" proverbs after the pattern of Solomon's creations, cannot, in individual cases, be clearly decided. The men of Hezekiah,[24] at all events, considered the collection of proverbs they made after the destruction of the northern kingdom as "Solomonic" (25, 1). Eissfeldt is very cautious in evaluating the contributions of Solomon in the Book of Proverbs: "It is quite possible that one or another proverb is actually the work of Solomon or was at least collected by him — and perhaps we cannot completely exclude the possibility that one or another of the collection goes back to him." [25] But if we evaluate the proverb literature within the broader outlines of the Solomonic era — Solomon's openness to world culture, the building of the temple and palace — then we cannot avoid the conclusion that he gave an entirely new face to his kingdom and his court, not only in terms of its material prosperity, but, — what is more important — in its spiritual and cultural advance, by the cultivation and promotion of the wisdom literature. The Solomonic Enlightenment was accomplished by the assimilation of the works of foreign culture. Just as Moses gave his people their law, and David produced their songs, it was Solomon who made available for later generations the books of wisdom. And just as later centuries made their contributions to the works of Moses and David, so also in the case of Solomon. One thing, however,

---

24. J. P. Audet, *Les Proverbs et Isaie dans la tradition juive ancienne*, Études et recherches (1952), 23-30. Maintains that Hezekiah is not the king, but a collector and editor.

25. O. Eissfeldt, *Einleitung* (1956), 586.

is common to all three: as creative men, inspired and enlightened by God himself, they set their stamp upon the ages to come and thereby achieved an imperishable monument for themselves in the history of God's people.

The postscript which one papyrus [26] devotes to the subject of Egyptian wisdom literature, is valid for the Bible's wisdom writing as well: "(These writers) have built no pyramids of bronze, no monuments of iron. They have managed to leave no heritage in the form of children to keep their name alive. But they have created a heritage to themselves in the form of the books they have composed.... A book is much more valuable than a tombstone with its epitaph, or a solid burial chamber. They made their tombs and pyramids in the hearts of those who call upon their name.... The man has perished, and his corpse is dust, and all his contemporaries have gone beneath the earth. It is the book which perpetuates his memory from mouth to mouth. A scroll is more valuable than a walled house, better than tombs in the western land; it is better than a well-founded castle, better than a memorial stone in the temple."

Applying this to Solomon, we should have to say that the temple he built went up in flames, his palace sank in ruins, and his mighty kingdom collapsed. What remains is only the wisdom of his "sympathetic heart," since it bears the stamp of that divine wisdom which has come down upon earth. Catholic liturgy applies the wisdom texts to the Blessed Virgin Mary, who, as Mother of the Word, truly deserves the title "Seat of Wisdom."

B) SOLOMONIC LYRIC: THE SONG OF SONGS

Commentaries: HSAT: Budde 1923 — BB: Miller 1927 — HAT: Haller (Die fünf Megilloth) — EB: Fischer 1950 — ClamB: Buzy 1950 — JerB: Robert 1951 — SBB: The Five Megilloth 1956 — *A. Bea,* Canticum canticorum, 1953 — *A. Feuillet,* Le Cantique des cantiques, 1953 — *R. Gordis,* The Song of Songs, 1954 — *H. Schmoekel,* Heilige Hochzeit und

---

26. Papyrus Beatty IV, Rs 2, 7 quoted in *Handbuch der Orientalistik,* I, *Ägyptologie,* 2. *Literatur* (1952), 110.

Hoheslied, 1956 — *F. Ohly,* Hohelied-Studien. Grundzüge einer Geschichte der Hoheliedauslegung des Abendlandes bis um 1200 n. Chr. 1958.

Introductions: Cornely-Merk 1940[12], 500—507 — Simon-Prado II. 1940[2], 103—143 — Höpfl-Miller-Metzinger 1946[5], 339—358 — Kuhl 1953, 281—284 — Pfeiffer 1948[2], 708—716 — Eissfeldt 1956[2], 596—605 — Weiser 1957[4], 241—244.

1) MYSTICAL AND MYTHICAL INTERPRETATIONS:

There is hardly another book in the Bible which has experienced such a variety of interpretations as the Song of Songs. And yet the form of its text is no worse than that of any other book. The words are just as clear. They are love songs, and they sing of the love between two young hearts. This very fact accounts for much of the difficulty. Can love songs, with their undertones of physical passion, have a place in Sacred Scripture? Rabbi Aqiba (d. 132 A.D.) was upset over the fact that the young men had sung portions of the Song in a tavern, as secular love songs.[27] Counting all the days since the beginning of the world there is no day so precious as that upon which the the Song of Songs[28] was first entrusted to Israel. All the other Scriptures are holy, he says, but the Song of Songs is the holiest of all.[29] It sings not of secular and profane love, but simply and solely of the love of Yahweh for his people. Yahweh is the bridegroom of the Song and Israel is the bridal people. On the basis of this fundamental conception, the individual stages of the love developed in the Song are all interpreted in terms of events within the compass of salvation history. This mystical interpretation dates back to the time before Christ, but it does not appear to have been generally recognized before the Jewish synod of Jamnia (90-95 A.D.) spoke out clearly in favor of the Song's place in the canon of Sacred Scripture.[30]

This mystical conception of the Song was taken over by the early Church, and carried further in terms of the further development of revelation. It was now interpreted as an expression of the love between Christ and his Church, between Christ and the individual soul, and,

---

27. Josephta, Sanhedrin XII.
28. *sir hassirim,* "song of songs," expression for the superlative, "most beautiful of all songs." Cf. "king of kings, vanity of vanities."
29. Mishnah, Yadaim 3, 5.
30. Survey of Jewish interpretation of the Song in P. Vulliaud, *Le Cantiques d'après la tradition juive* (1925).

finally, between Christ and his Blessed Mother. The great commentaries of the ancient and medieval Church are eloquent testimony to the mystical theology of the Song.[31]

Against this mystical interpretation of the ancient Church, we already have the voice of Theodore of Mopsuestia (350-428). He interpreted the Song as an occasional composition destined for Solomon's marriage with an Egyptian princess. This natural interpretation, devoid of all reference to a higher mystical sense, was officially rejected by the Second Council of Constantinople (553).[32]

In more modern times, we note a series of attempts to explain the Song in terms of ancient pagan myth. Thus, attempts have been made to demonstrate the influence of the Egyptian Osiris cult,[33] but these have not been convincing. Schmökel, in his book *Sacred Wedding and Song of Songs*,[34] attacks the problem from the point of view of the Canaanite culture. He regards the Song as a Palestinian-Syrian counterpart to the Babylonian Tammuz-Ishtar myth. "One puzzle has always been the completely unconnected and abruptly interrupted text of the Song. In this area we see Schmökel's original work at its best. He takes the bold step of completely analyzing and dismembering the text, which he then divides into three so-called scenes, in which he assigns the individual verses in turn either to a priest or a priestess (taking the place of a male or female divinity from Palestine-Syria), a chorus of men or a chorus of women. Schmökel thus succeeds in rebuilding the Song, which, in its present-day form, is completely disconnected and fragmentary, into cultic songs of a Palestinian-Syrian myth, analogous to the Babylonian

---

31. Origen, 2 sermons and 10 treatises, PG 13, 37-58; 13, 61-216. / Gregory of Nyssa, *Deus et anima*, PG 44, 755ff. / Beda Venerabilis, *Allegorica expositio in canticum*, PL 91, 1063-1236. / Bernard Clairvaux, *Sermones in Canticum*, PL 183, 779-1198. (86 ascetic conferences on religious life on the basis of the Song of Songs). — History of exegesis of the Song from Origen to the age of Bernard in: F. Ohly, *Grundzüge einer Geschichte der Hoheliedauslegung des Abendlandes bis um 1200* (Schr. d. Wiss. Ges. Joh. W. Goethe Univ., Frankfurt/Main, 1958). / A. Feuillet, *Le Cantique des Cantiques et la tradition biblique*, Nouv-RTh 74 (1952), 706-733.

32. P. Dubarle, RB 61 (1954), 68-69 questions the formal character of this decision.

33. N. de Jassy, *Le Cantique des Cantiques et le mythe d'Osiris-Hetep* (1914).

34. *Abhandlungen für die Kunde des Morgenlandes XXXII*, 1, Wiesbaden (1956). / H. Ringgren, *Hohes Lied und hieros gamos*, ZAW 65 (1953), 300-302.

Ishtar-Tammuz myth."[35] — Is it proper, however, to take such arbitrary liberties with an historical text, and force it to fit within the limitations of a pre-conceived idea? Although, in the course of our interpretation, we have frequently referred to the possibility of the adaptation of pagan culture, this pagan-mythical reinterpretation of the Song of Songs does not seem to be tenable, since there are other, simpler, and thus more probable solutions to the problem, solutions in which the text of the Song does not need to be submitted to a Procrustean bed.

2) COLLECTION OF POPULAR LOVE SONGS:

When, in the Age of Romanticism, a feeling for the value of popular songs had been widely reawakened, Herder interpreted the Song of Songs as a collection of popular love songs (*Lieder der Liebe* — 1778). This interpretation was based on the fact that in the preceding century Palestinian-Syrian love and wedding songs had been discovered which seemed to be very similar to the Song of Songs. The Syrian wedding songs were collected by Wettstien, who spent several years as consul in Damascus, and published in his book *Die Syrische Dreschtafel*.[36] The following observations bear repeating: "On the day before the wedding, the bride danced a sword dance, to the rhythm of a song, sung by the spectators, which described the beauty of her clothing and her physical charms (*waṣf*). For a week following their wedding, the young couple are feted as king and queen; a threshing table, set up on the threshing floor, serves as throne. In this 'royal week' a variety of songs are sung, among them another *waṣf*, a song which describes the charms of the young couple."[37] The marriage customs of the Arabian Palestine were gathered by G. Dalman, *Palastinischer Diwan* (1901), those of the Bedouin tribes by A. Musil, *Arabia Petraea* (III, 1908).

These comparisons with modern Oriental marriage and love songs demonstrate only that love is timeless and tends to express itself in like or similar forms of expression. More careful investigation of the style and literary genre of the Song of Songs forces us to conclude that the Song, with only significant exceptions, does not represent a popular love lyric: the dignified and measured language, the exquisite images, the free treatment of the theme — this all points to court circles in which

---

35. A. Jirku, *Besprechung des Buches von Schmökel*, ZDMG 108 (1958), 200.

36. *Zeitschrift für Ethnologie* 5 (1873), 270-302. — Neue Sammlung von S. Linder, *Palästinische Volksgesänge*, published by H. Ringgren (Uppsala, 1952).

37. O. Eissfeldt, *Einleitung* (1956), 600.

the love song was cultivated. The *"Sitz im Leben"* for the Song is to be sought not in myth or popular lyric, but in the courtly love song.

3) SOLOMONIC COURTLY SONG:

This raises the question as to whether or not a courtly love song is historically possible and credible in Solomon's court. The statement from the Book of Kings (1 K 5, 12) to the effect that Solomon composed 1005 songs may or may not refer to the Song of Songs, since the Biblical reference says nothing about the type of song involved. We are thus forced to turn to the contemporary pagan culture for a point of departure. In our discussion of the proverbs of Solomon we spoke of a sort of Solomonic Enlightenment. The Sun-King had opened the doors of the outside world to the cultural life of Israel. We have already alluded to the influence of Egyptian wisdom philosophy on Israel's literature. Are we to posit some such similar influence in the case of love lyric?

The greatest extant collection of Egyptian love songs is to be found on the recto of the so-called Papyrus Harris 500 in the British Museum. A second collection is contained in a papyrus of the museum at Turin. Further love songs have been discovered on the Ostraca, currently preserved in the museum at Cairo.[38] The London manuscript and the Cairo Ostraca date back to the 19th dynasty (1350 — 1200), the golden age of the New Kingdom, a time at which Egyptian culture was widely recognized as normative in Canaan and Phoenicia. The Turin papyrus is somewhat more recent, probably dating to the beginning of the 20th dynasty, about 1200 B.C. Further manuscripts have been unearthed in the tomb of Pa-Aton-em heb in Sakkarah (currently at Leiden) and from the Amarna era (1375 — 60) and in the tomb of Neferhotep in Thebes, all dating from the same time. A postscript to the Thebes papyrus states that the composition dates from the time of the 12th dynasty, approximately 1900 — 1800 B.C. This would indicate a long and continued cultivation of love poetry in ancient Egypt. These songs have been made

---

38. Gressmann, AOT, 30.

available to modern appreciation in a series of different translations.[39]

Both the depth of feeling and the power of linguistic expression in these songs makes a profound impression. "The expressive power of the Egyptian poetry at work in these songs
is of a very high artistic rank, and thus their most essential element
consists in the inseparable union between thought and feeling
and tone, which can be adequately experienced only by an immediate acquaintance with the Egyptian text." [40] The Egyptian
poet makes use of word-plays, chooses the best suited hieroglyph
forms which make the poetry a delight to the eye. All this, once
again, serves to show that the Egyptian love song is not a popular,
but rather an artistic song form. The discovery sites also point
to a circle of highly placed officials or nobility among whom the
courtly lyric was widely cultivated.

The Egyptian love song is obviously older than the Israelite.
Striking similarity between the two, however, suggests the conjecture that the younger Israel had taken up the Egyptian challenge in the field of courtly song as well. The Egyptian singers
speak of their beloved as "brother" and "sister." The same form
of expression is to be found in the Song of Songs (4: 9, 10, 12;
5: 1, 2). This form of reference was so unfamiliar to the Hebrew
mentality that the word "sister" later needed to be explained
by the addition of the word "bride." Moreover, the Egyptians, in
their poetry and in their painting, displayed a marked preference
for flowers, trees, vineyards, grapes, swallows, and gazelles;
nature, for them, is symbolic of the human soul.[41] Along the

---

39. Erman, *Literatur der Ägypter*, 303ff. / F. Dornseiff, *Ägyptische Lie-
    beslieder, Hoheslied, Sappho, Theokrit,* ZDMG 96 (1936), 589-601.
    / J. Spiegel, *Ägyptische Liebeslyrik.* In Handbuch der Orientalistik,
    I, 2 (1952), 164-167. / S. Schott, *Altägyptische Liebeslieder* (1950).
    / Hermann, *Beiträge zur Erklärung der ägyptischen Liebesdichtung.*
    (*Ägyptische Studien* published by Firchow, 1955, 118, 139.) *Altägypt-
    ische Liebesdichtung* (Wiesbaden, 1959).
40. J. Spiegel, *Ägyptische Liebeslyrik,* Handbuch der Orientalistik, I, 2
    1952), 158, note 36.
41. Other comparisons are quite conclusive in terms of comparative culture
    history. Cant. 4, 4: the neck of the beloved is compared to a tower of

Nile they sang this song: "Your beloved I remained, I am yours, like to a garden which I have planted full of flowers, full of plants with spicy fragrance." [42] And in the Song: "I come to my garden, my sister, my bride, I gather my myrrh with my spice . . ." (4, 12 — 5, 1; 6, 2). This delight in natural description is found nowhere else in the Old Testament, excepting for Ps 103/104, the great hymn dedicated to the marvels of creation; this psalm, too, is generally held to have been influenced by Egyptian solar poetry.

The first stirring of springtime is another motif which is compared to the first blossom of love: "The voice of the swallow sings and says: the land is so wonderful, where lies your path?" [43] And in the Song: "Arise, my love, my fair one, and come away; for lo, the winter is past, the rain is over and gone. The flowers appear on the earth, the time of singing has come, and the voice of the turtledove is heard in our land" (2, 10-13; 4, 1-5; 10 — 13; 7, 11-13).

Various attempts have been made to interpret the Song as a unified poetical composition. Bea [44] divides it into the following six sections:

1. Budding of love between bride and groom (1, 2 — 2, 7);
2. Growth and ripening of love (2, 8 — 3, 5);
3. Bringing home the bride (3, 6 — 5, 1);
4. Trial of love (5, 2 — 6, 10);
5. Beauty of the bride (6, 11 — 8, 4);
6. Final union (8, 5 — 8, 14).

David, with shields and "mural crowns." There is also some archaeological evidence, a sculpture from Cyprus (7/6th cent.), a housewife with a necklace: the uppermost strand being a chain of tiny shields, with second and third strands of "mural crowns." B. S. J. Isserlin, PEQ 90 (1958), 59-60.

---

42. S. Schott, *Altägyptische Liebeslieder* (1950), 56.
43. ANET 468.
44. A. Bea, *Canticum canticorum* (Rome, 1953). / R. E. Murphy, *Recent Literature on the Canticle of Canticles,* CBQ 16 (1954), 1-11. Verficht Einheit von Text und Autor.

Thilo [45] has also attempted to understand the Song as a unified lyric composition, describing, in balanced progression, the development of first love, betrothal, and marriage. But such a unified construction can be attempted only by a rather violent reinterpretation and by neglecting the frequent change in person, mood, and train of thought. In terms of subject matter, too, this conception of the Song is hardly tenable; the longing for complete union of love has already been reached at the very outset, and thus precludes a development of love in the proper sense of the word.[46] By reason of this same lack of internal unity, the interpretations of the Song of Songs as a musical pageant or a drama are hardly convincing. Such a conception is denied by the total lack of any form of dramatic development, or progressive treatment, and by the markedly lyrical character of the entire composition.[47]

The Song of Songs is best interpreted if, like the songs and proverbs, we regard it as a collection of various love songs. Whether the number of the songs is 25 or 28,[48] is difficult to determine. The text itself suggests many appropriate points of division. Corresponding to the nature of the love experience, the songs can be divided into songs of the maiden, songs of the young man, duets for both, songs of joy. That such songs should have been used in wedding celebrations is quite understandable, but this

45. Thilo, *Das Hohelied* (1921).
46. Weiser, *Einleitung* (1957), 242.
47. Watermann, *The Song of Songs*, translated and interpreted as a Dramatic Poem (1948) — has attempted to trace a dramatic development. Solomon is attempting to win the love of Abishag, and takes her to his court; but she resists all the allurements of court life and remains true to her beloved, a shepherd, to whom she is eventually betrothed at the end of the song. But this involves a certain violence to the text.
48. R. Gordis, *The Song of Songs* (1954). Arbeitet 28 Lieder heraus. / M. A. van den Oudenrijn, *Vom Sinn des Hohenliedes*, Divus Thomas 31 (1953), 257-280. Collection of individual songs, whose collector has given the work a unified style. F. Landsberger, *Poetic Units within the Song of Songs*, JBL 73 (1954), 203-216. Short songs arranged in series according to the proverb principle. S. Segert, *Die Versform des Hohenliedes, Charisteria Orientalia*, Prag 1956, 285-299. Collection of originally 32 small poems.

says nothing as to their origin. The idyllic background, so far removed from the harsh realities of life, the free relationship between the young people which is so unfamiliar in Ancient Near East society, the frequent change of locale, royal court, the shepherd's camp, Judah (Jerusalem, En-gedi) northern Israel (Tirzah, Carmel, Shunem, Sharon, Hermon, Amana, Senir, Lebanon), and even Transjordania (Gilead, Heshbon), — the keen appreciation for the beauties of the field, flowers, birds, gardens, vineyards, the expressive power evident in the description of deep human emotion, from the tender first stirrings of love to the quiet peace of ultimate union — all this points to a well developed and highly cultivated courtly lyric, and not to the creativity of popular love song.[49]

When we now consider the era of Old Testament history in which such a courtly love song could have flourished, the answer is quite clear. Investigations in literary criticism [50] can only establish the date at which the Song of Songs achieved its present form. The occurrence of Greek and Persian loan words and Aramaic influences brings the time of final redaction down as far as the Persian or even the Hellenistic era. The lowest date would be the first half of the third century.[51] Even during the Middle Ages, love songs enjoyed a life of several centuries, and were freely adapted to current forms of language and expression. That is why any investigation into the original date at which the Song first appeared will be pointless if it is based on a one-sided linguistic approach. The methodology of literary criticism must here be supported by an analysis of the history of tradition. Neither the uncertainty of the post-exilic era nor the catastrophic era of the destruction of the Northern and Southern Kingdoms was the proper soil to produce so tender a blossom as the courtly love lyric. In terms of the history of culture, the courtly lyric belongs to an era that has attained its maturity, an age that is already ripe for collapse. This corresponds best with the Solomonic era. The attribution of the "Book of Wisdom," which was written in Greek,

---

49. Pfeiffer, *Introduction* (1948), 713.
50. V. Hamp, *Zur Textkritik am Hohenlied*, BZ, NF 1 (1957).
51. Pfeiffer, *Introduction* (1948), 713, 197-214.

to King Solomon is a pure literary fiction; when the same claim is made for the Song of Songs — "Song of Songs, of Solomon" (1, 1) — this is the only true key to unlocking the riddle of its composition: Just as Solomon cultivated the pursuit of wisdom literature at his court in Jerusalem, he also promoted the development of the native love lyric, under the direct or indirect influence of Egyptian letters.

Just as we cannot claim that all the proverbs in the two Solomonic collections actually date from Solomon himself, neither can we ascribe all the love songs contained in the present text of the Song of Songs to the work of Solomon himself. It is sufficient that the first great impulse and encouragement for the cultivation of this literary style came from Solomon, thereby constituting him the troubador of Israel. After his death, the cultivation of this lyric form continued, developed and enriched with new form and styles. Our only anthology from this rich treasury of song is to be found in the present text of the Song of Songs.

4) PROPHETIC MYSTIQUE OF LOVE:

These secular love songs owe their acceptance into the canon of Sacred Scripture to the circumstance that they were reinterpreted under the influence of the prophetic love mysticism.[52] Yahweh is the true and only beloved and bridegroom of Israel (Ho 2, 2; Ezk 16, 8); Israel, as his espoused people and bride, has broken faith with him (Ho 2, 7; Jr 2, 20-25; 13, 27; Ezk 16, 15-34; 23, 2-8; 23, 11-21). Yahweh rejected Israel as an adulteress (Ho 2, 4-6; Jer 3, 8). But this rejection is not to last forever; he will turn Israel's infidelity into conversion (Jr 3, 7, 12-18;

---

52. D. Buzy, *Le Cantique des Cantiques. Exégèse allégorique où parabolique?* Recherches des sciences rel. 39 (1951), 99-114 — points out that the mystical preoccupation begins with Hosea, attains its most marked expression in Ezekiel, and continues to be cultivated after the Exile. / A. Neher, *Le symbolisme conjugale, expression de l'histoire dans l'AT*, RHPhR 34 (1954), 30-49. The personal exchange between bride and groom occasioned the application of the Song to God and people. History thus becomes a moving drama of love between God and man.

Ezk 3, 26-27). The idyll of the desert will bloom once more upon bride and bridegroom; God and his people will possess each other for all time (Ho 2, 16-17; 21-22).

Since the element of love symbolism came to play such a significant role in the prophetic preaching, it was only natural that the ancient Solomonic love songs should be rediscovered and reinterpreted, no longer in terms of earthly love, but as a symbol of the divine. When, accordingly, Rabbi Aqiba made such a strong protest against the profanization of the Song of Songs, against its being treated as a mere secular love song, and insisted that it is, instead, the most sacred writing in all Scripture, he is only witnessing to the synagogue's firm belief in the prophetic meaning of the Song.

In order to properly understand and interpret the Song of Songs, we must keep two points in mind: its origin as a courtly love song and its symbolic interpretation under the influence of the prophetic love mysticism. The Song of Songs, in its present form, is neither exclusively profane and secular nor exclusively spiritual; it is both in one. The songs which sing of earthly love could certainly never serve as the expression of divine love unless our earthly love, from the first beginning of humanity, were possessed of a divine spark. This is what the account of human creation says: "So God created man in his own image, in the image of God he created him; male and female he created them" (Gn 1, 27). It follows, accordingly, that in the relation of one sex to another, there is somehow an image and likeness of God. From the very beginning, this capacity to serve as image is stamped into the very essence of earthly love. When the troubador sings of the heights and depths of earthly love in a series of intoxicating images, he is thereby touching on the mystery of God's love, that divine love of which all earthly love is only an "image" (ṣelem). This idea runs through Deutero-Isaiah (62, 5) like a brilliant leit-motif, and it must also serve as our key to understanding the Song of Songs: "As the bridegroom rejoices over the bride, so shall your God rejoice over you."

Thus, in itself, it would be sufficient to regard the Song of Songs as the supreme expression of a marriage song, marriage being understood not as a secular institution, but rather as a mighty mystery. The songs would then be only an expression of what God himself put into the human heart when he created man.[53] Prophetic mysticism, however, seems to have been the decisive factor in winning the Song a place in the canon of Sacred Scripture. This makes the Song doubly precious. Its message is nothing less than an inspired proclamation of the fact that God is love. This point of view makes it possible to understand expressions which would otherwise be difficult to grasp. Yahweh is a "jealous God,"[54] who will tolerate no other lover (Ex 20, 5). The "covenant" loses its juristic impersonality; it becomes the expression of God's free and loving union with the world. Even the basic concept of "election" takes on new meaning. God's election of his chosen people is not merely a mechanical choice for a particular purpose; God's heart is beating in human history, as David says in his great prayer of thanksgiving: "Because of thy promise, and according to thy own heart, thou hast wrought all this greatness" (2 S 7, 21). Since salvation history is thus simply the progressive revelation of the ever greater love of God, it is only obvious that the Song of Songs must be given a deeper understanding and interpretation from the vantage point of revelation. The Christian interpretation in terms of Christ, the Incarnate Love of God, and the Blessed Virgin Mary, who, as the handmaid of the Lord, most fully answers the loving appeal of God and Christ, is only a very logical development. This is the basic reason why the Song of Songs has such a fascinating effect upon the exegetes of the ancient Church. Of the great bulk of Origen's commentaries on the books of the Bible; no one complete text has been handed down. Of his commentary on the Song of Songs, which embraced ten books, we have today only the first three books and a section of the fourth, and this not in

---

53. This opinion has been recently presented by A. M. Dubarle, *Le Cantique des Cantiques,* Rev. des sciences phil. et théol. (1954), 92ff. / J. P. Audet, *Les sens du Cantique des Cantiques,* RB (1955), 197-221.

54. A. Brunner, "Der eifersüchtige Gott," Stimmen der Zeit 76 (1950/51), 401-410.

its Greek original, but in the translation of Rufinus of Aquilea. There are many homilies on the Song, the first two of which have been translated by Jerome. In his prologue to these homilies, Jerome has this to say in his pointed, if somewhat barbed style: "If Origen has outdone all scholars in the other books, in the Song of Songs he has outdone himself." In the patristic era, there were many who drew abundantly upon this fertile source: Athanasius, Gregory of Nyssa, Theodore of Mopsuestia, Theodoret of Cyrus, and Maximus Confessor. The exegesis advanced by Origen is allegorical. In his two homilies, the bridegroom is interpreted as Christ and the bride as the Church. In his commentary, it is the individual soul, rather than the Church, which comes more and more into the foreground: Christ unites with the individual soul.[55] The allegorical interpretation of the Song of Songs, as developed by the Fathers, might, in many respects, seem quite artificial and arbitrary. We might prefer to interpret this Song in terms of its historical evolution rather than from the vantage point of faith and revelation. The interpretation loses nothing; rather, it grows in conviction.

The Song of Songs, as the product of courtly lyric, stands wholly within the human sphere, and must, in the last analysis, be so interpreted. But these earthly love songs achieve their highest consecration by the prophetic mysticism which assured them a reception into the canon of Sacred Scripture, and thus they can no longer sing only of the wonders of human love; they are, ever after, an expression of that divine love of which all human love is but a parable and likeness.

---

55. Patristic texts translated into English by R. P. Lawson, *The Song of Songs, Commentary and Homilies.* — Cf. ThLZ 83 (1958), 519. A similar fate was in store for Psalm 44/45. Originally a marriage song, it was reinterpreted along prophetic lines. Th. h. Gaster, *Psalm 45,* JBL 74 (1955), 239-251.

INDEX

Abiathar 131, 134, 288, 294
Abigail 190
Abiboam 190
Abishag 287
Abner 168
Absalom, rebellion 243ff
　family 243, 252ff
Achish 132
acropolis, Jerusalem 351
Adonijah, attempted coup 288ff
Adullam 133, 143
agricultural economy 209
Ahiba'al 232f, 251f
Ahijah 361
Ahikar romance 426
altar of holocausts 337f
　bronze 337f
Amalekites 79ff
Amasa 252
'amm, as divine epithet 190, 365
Ammon, war with 210
anointing 55, 91, 165
apes 318
Aramaeans 214ff
Arauna 263
Asahel 168
'ašĕrâh 31
Assyria 311
'aštārôt 29

ba'al, names compounded with 81,
　245, 248
Babylonia 311
bāmâh 31, 57, 369

ban 82ff, 144
Bath-Sheba 289
　adultery 230
battle cry 23, 32
bᵉ'ālim 29
beard, tear out 211
Bekaim 178
Belial 14
bᵉrît 175
Beth-El 370
Bethlehem 93
Bible-Babel controversy 392
blood, man of 248
blood vengeance 259, 261
booty division 159
bow song 159
bread of the Presence 128
bride price 117
buffer kingdom 68f
bull, symbol 212, 368

Cabul 358
Cades 310
calendar 335, 371
capital punishment 233
cart 26
catchword 116
cedars 218
census 262ff
Cherethites and Pelethites 246
cherubim 328ff, 353
child sacrifice 357ff
childlessness 10
chronology 71ff, 166, 219, 323,

chronology (cont.), 374ff
clan levy 23, 65, 75
concubines 80ff
congeniality 388ff
conjuring 148ff
copper, discovery 213
cosmic symbolism 340
covenant 115, 175, 204, 271, 445
    Ark of 22, 24, 127, 191
creator of heaven and earth 236
cremation 155
cult places 369
cult prophets 198
cult and song 394ff
cultural ideas, court 413ff
cup 140

Dagon 24
Damascus 216, 359
dance 193
David city 181, 187
    Elhanan 114
    Family 190ff
    last words 267ff
    name 96ff
    testament 291
debir 325
district of Solomon 302ff
division of kingdom 300, 365ff
Doeg 130
dream 298
duel 107
dust, strewn on head 240
dwarf 207

'eben ha'ezer 22
Edom 217, 358
El Valley 104
'eleph 23, 65, 74, 116, 137, 213,
    215, 265
Elhanan 112ff
En-dor 148
En-gedi 137
enthronement feast 394, 396
ephod 18, 129, 134ff, 195

eponymous officials 225
Euphrates 214, 310
Execration Texts 180
Ezion-geber 319

faith, splitting 368
family sacrifice 125
fate 205
fertility cult 261
fool 132
forced labor 36, 216, 224, 360ff
foreskins 118
foundations of the earth 346
friend of the king 30

Gad, prophet 263
garment, symbolic of person 138
Gath, literary 392
Gezer 306ff
Gibeah, excavations 54, 79
Gibeon, great stone 257
    pool 167
Gihon spring 183ff
Gilboa 147
Gilgal 67
goat — kebir 121
God's mountain 336
    throne 331
gods, Canaanite 29ff
Goliath 103ff, 113

Hada 30, 212
Hada'ezer 214ff
Hamat, battle 214
Hammurabi 175
hand (memorial) 84
Hanum 211
harem 84, 180, 190, 194, 250, 294,
    353, 366
Hazor 306
heads 77
heart 298, 299
    of God 203ff, 445
Hebrews 23, 146
Hebron 164

hêkāl 320
Helam, battle 214
heraldic animals 53
ḥerem 82, 145
heroes of David 190
Heroes, Book of 158
hieros gamos 15, 436
high places for sacrifice 31, 369
Hilani, architecture 352
Hiram 218, 318, 357
hokmah 431
hophsi 108
horn (*shophar*) 194
horns of the altar 291
horse trade 313ff
house 200
Husai 247

image — *ṣelem* 444
inspiration, prophetic 269
iron working 74, 208
Ishbaal 166
Ishtob 213
Ittai 246

Jabesh-gilead 63ff
Jebusites 182
Jeroboam 360ff
Jerusalem, archaeology 187
    capital 189
    name 179
    population 190
Jesse 44
Joab 167, 185, 257ff, 288
Jonathan 78, 114ff
Jordan ford 249
judgment of Solomon 299

Kenites 83
king and cult 345ff
king's baptism 290
    election 60ff
    law 35
    psalms 346
kingship, Israel 34

Philistines 34
Yahweh 343

lamed auctoris 404
lamentation 158
    dirge 155
land, possession of 22
Lebanon, residence 352
line, measure 209
literal meaning 388
love songs 434, 437
    mysticism 443
lunar year 335

Maat 430
Mahanaim 166, 243
Milkom 237
man of God 16ff
maṣṣēbôt 31
mazkir 222
measures of length 105
Megiddo 304
melek 58
Mephibaal 248
Messiah 13, 58, 206, 270
metal casting 341ff
metropolis 207, 257
mice 26
Michal 81, 118, 170, 194
Mizpah 29ff
miṣrayim 315
Moab 209ff
Molok 237, 356
money 64
month names 371
monument stones 33
mouth of Yahweh 85
musical instruments 100, 192, 412
musical play 440
Musru 315ff
mystical sense 388
Mysterium tremendum 192

Nabal 141
nābî 56, 59, 16

nāgîd 58, 290
Nahash 63
name book 419ff
Nathan 197, 234ff, 289
national consciousness 22
nature motif 440
Nazirite 11
Negeb 156
New moon 124
Nob 126
numbers 26, 65, 71, 215, 264, 358, 394

obedience 84
Ophir 317ff
oracle 61
oratorical art 250

palace architecture 350ff
parallelism of members 410
patriarchal state 61
Penninah 7
pestilence 262ff
Philistine army, composition 21
    cities 20
    professional soldiers 22
    wars 32, 72, 145ff, 176ff
Phoenician cities 313
pilgrimage psalms 406
Pillars, Hall of 352
pneumatic exegesis 389
possession 97
priest 192, 196, 223, 369
    and king 196
    apron 195
primordial sea 341ff
privy council 225
procession 192
promises, great 196ff
prophets, bands of 59, 202
psalms, book of 387ff
    collections 401
    development 400
    titles 411
Punt 320

purity, cultic 128

Qe'ilah 134ff
Quweh 306, 315

Rabbath-Ammon 210ff
Ramathaim 6
Ramses III 309
razzia 144
Rehoboam 244, 365
Rephaim 177
representative combat 167
Rezon 359
rhythm of psalms 409ff
Rizpah 169, 260
river, across the 312
road along the sea 208
rock 270
royal stables 352

Saba (Sheba) 224ff
sacrifice 259
sacrificial hearth: hearth of
    sacrifice 338
sacrificial heights 259, 298, 335ff
salvation history 89, 373, 390, 445
šalîm 181
Salt Valley 217
Samuel, name 11
Samuel, Book 39ff
sanctuaries to the dead 31
Satan 262
Saul, name 53
    posterity 258ff
saw 92
scorpion 367
scribes 224

Tamar 238ff
Tekoa 241
Temple construction 323ff
    consecration 347
    plan 234
    utensils 343

t^eraphim 120
theology of history 277ff
   of the psalms 413ff
throne, succession to 287ff, 365
throne room 352
thunder god 212
tôrat hā'ādām 204, 270
tribal levy 23, 65, 75
Tyre 218

unclean 233
underworld 151
Uriah 233ff
Urim, meaning 204
Uzza 192

vassal 143
victory song 116
vigil 66
vow 9ff

waist apron 193
war chariot 146, 315

games 167ff
hallowed 75
warrior of Israel 271
water systems 184, 237
weaver's beam 106
weights 73
wilderness of Judah 136
window 211, 326
wisdom literature, ancient 419
   Egyptian 424ff
   Solomonic 417ff
womb of the earth 338
word of God 18, 203ff
word and history 388
world pillars 332

Zadok 223, 246, 294
Ziba 248
Ziklag 144, 156
Zion 186, 293
Zobah-Aram 212ff
zodiac 343

GEOGRAPHY OF
THE OLD TESTAMENT

Map No. 1	The Syrian Trench
Map No. 2	Galilee — Hauran — North Transjordania
Map No. 3	Central Palestine
Map No. 4	Southern Palestine and Transjordania
Map No. 5	Roads Between Beer Sheba and Shechem
Map No. 6	Roads of Samaria and Galilee
Map No. 7	Roads of Sinai, Negreb, and Southern Transjordania
Map No. 8	Roads of Northern Transjordania
Map No. 9	Caanan and Neighboring Countries
Map No. 10	Tribes and Districts under Solomon, Neighboring Peoples
Map No. 11	Judah — Benjamin — Dan, Corresponding Philistine Territory
Map No. 12	Northern and Central Tribes, Corresponding Districts
Map No. 13	The Two Divisions of Transjordania
Map No. 14	Kingdom of Judah, Deportation to Babylon
Map No. 15	Palestine Under the Assyrian Empire
Map No. 16	Judah After the Exile, Samaria
Map No. 17	Kingdom of Herod, Neighboring Countries
Map No. 18	The Three Capitals: Shechem, Shiloh, Jerusalem

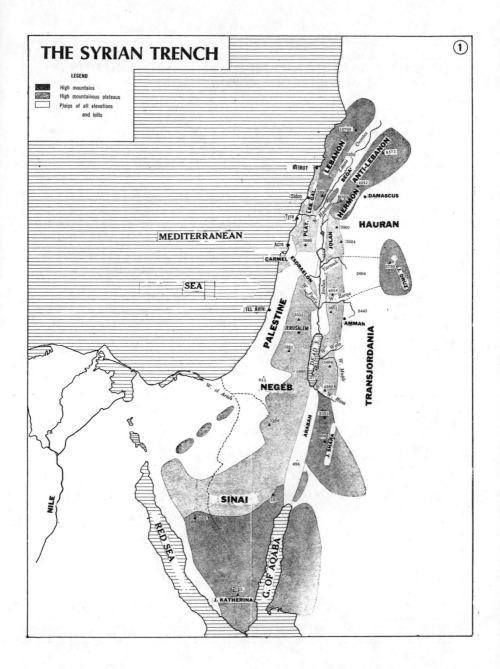

THE SYRIAN TRENCH

LEGEND

High mountains
High mountainous plateaus
Plains of all elevations and hills

①

LEBANON · 10700 · Orontes
ANTI-LEBANON · 8572
BEQA' · Litani · 3250
BEIRUT
HERMON · 4092
Sidon · 0392 · N. Hasbani · DAMASCUS
Tyre
PLAT. LEB. GAL.
HAURAN
JOLAN · 3907
MEDITERRANEAN · Acre · 3960 · 3024
CARMEL · 5750 · J. DRUZ
ESDRAELON · Yarmuk · 2604
SEA · W. Fara · Jordan · 4054 · W. Zarqa
TEL AVIV · 3651 · 2443
PALESTINE · 3333
JERUSALEM · AMMAN
DEAD S. · W. Wala
3221 · 3464 · W. Mujib
1660 · 1277
913 · 4260 · W. Hasa
NEGEB · ARABAH · 5353
3364 · 4044 · J. SHARA
494
TRANSJORDANIA

NILE

SINAI · 3183
5503

RED SEA · G. OF AQABA

8733
J. KATHERINA

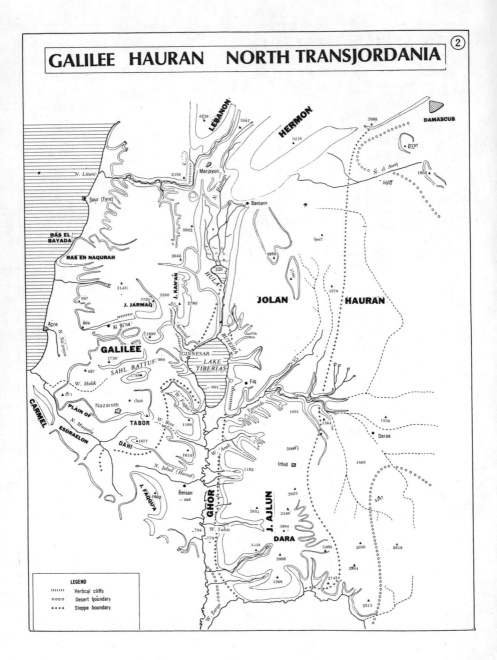

GALILEE HAURAN NORTH TRANSJORDANIA

②

LEGEND

'''''''	Vertical cliffs
○○○○	Desert boundary
++++	Steppe boundary

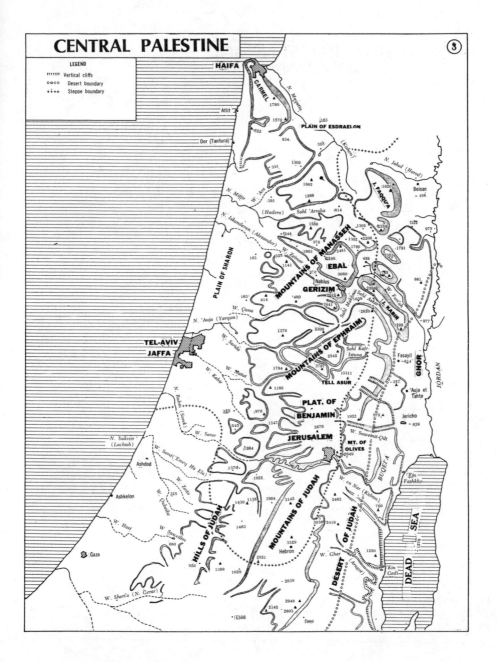

CENTRAL PALESTINE

LEGEND
- ⲧⲧⲧⲧⲧⲧⲧ Vertical cliffs
- ⲟⲟⲟⲟ Desert boundary
- +++++ Steppe boundary

HAIFA

CARMEL

Atlit

Dor (Tantura)

N. Muqatta

1780

1570

522

834.

PLAIN OF ESDRAELON

1183

325

(Kishon)

N. Jalud (Harod)

1302

531

1685

N. Misrir

W. Ara

391

1268

(Hadera)

N. Iskanderun (Alexander)

Sahl 'Arraba

814

1588

1244

976

W. Zeimar

1603

163

1325

1141

976

W. Zeimar

2481

2240.

EBAL

3060

MOUNTAINS OF MANASSEH

Nablus

GERIZIM

2519

163

814

2641

480

163

W. Qana

N. 'Auja (Yarqon)

J. FAQUA

1620

Beisan
- 488

N. Jalud (Harod)

1302

2350

975

1101

2208

1760

1791

488

2323

Sahl Makhna

Sahl Askar

2290

1630

2820

J. KABIR

661

W. Far'ah

1228

977

PLAIN OF SHARON

1370

2300

MOUNTAINS OF EPHRAIM

W. Sarida

W. Kahn

W. Matul

1784

1188

2542

2787

Sahl Kafr Istuna

3311

337.

TELL ASUR

Fasayil
- 814

GHOR

JORDAN

'Auja et Tahta

TEL-AVIV
JAFFA

N. Rubin (Sorek)

325

845

976

1247

PLAT. OF BENJAMIN

2679

1922

979.

Jericho
- 839

W. Suweinit-Qilt

JERUSALEM

1264

MT. OF OLIVES

2649

N. Sukreir (Lachish)

W. Sarar

W. Samt('Emeq Ha Ela)

Ashdod

1370.

1922.

W. Zeita

325

W. Qubeibe

W. en Nar (Kidron)

BUQEI'A

'Ein Fashkka

Ashkelon

N. Hasi

W. Souweilih

680

1430

1138

1904

3143

2463

760

MOUNTAINS OF JUDAH

3038

2019

DESERT OF JUDAH

1220

'Ein Gedi

DEAD SEA
- 1276

HILLS OF JUDAH

920

1389

1629

1463

3329

Hebron

2931

2639

W. Ghar

W. Ghar (Arugot)

Gaza

W. Sheri'a (N. Gerar)

2948

2803

2142

1300

1980

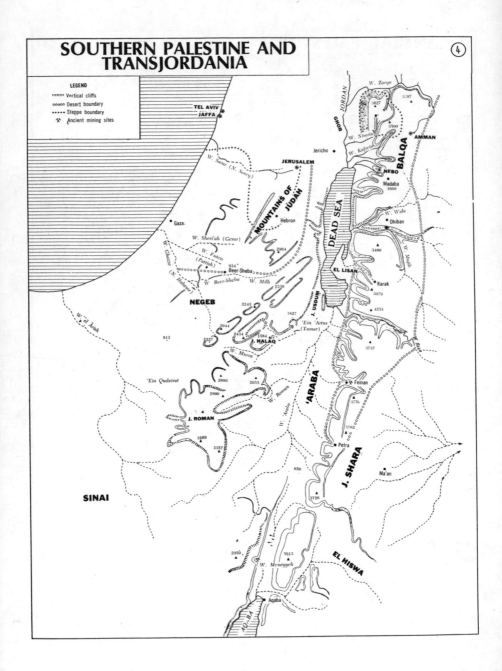

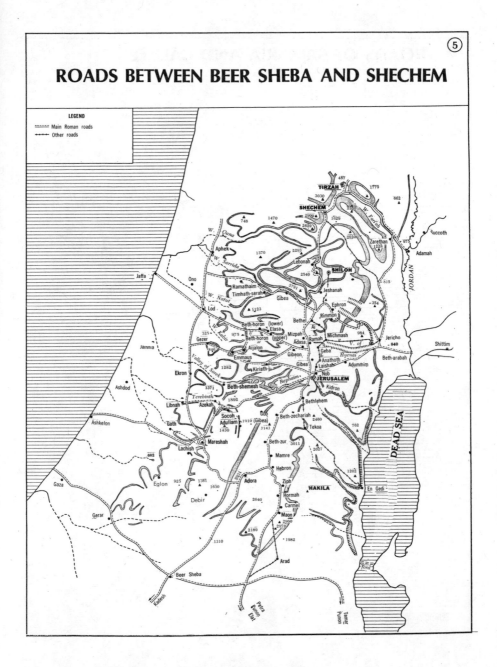

ROADS BETWEEN BEER SHEBA AND SHECHEM

⑤

LEGEND
----- Main Roman roads
-++- Other roads

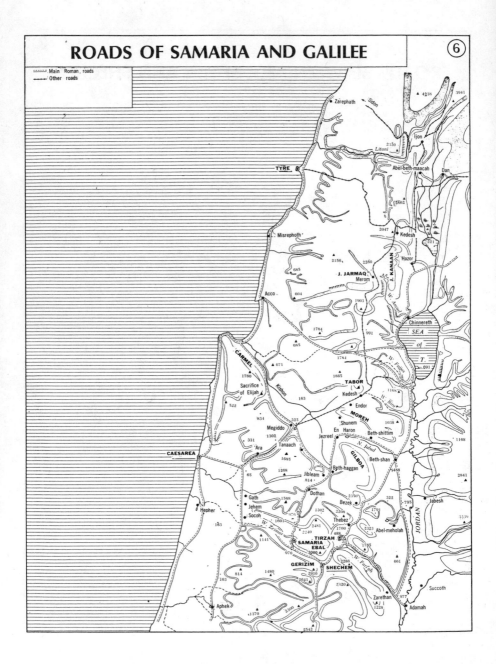

ROADS OF SAMARIA AND GALILEE

6

Main Roman roads
Other roads

Zarephath
Sidon
Ijon
2130
Litani
Abel-beth-maacah
Dan
TYRE
2562
Misrephoth
2047
Kedesh
Hazor
2156
2260
J. JARMAQ
685
Merom
J. KANAAN
Acco
604
1903
W. Amud
Chinnereth
1784
991
SEA
685
of
CARMEL
1784
W. Fejjas
T.
671
991
1780
1865
W. Bira
Sacrifice
Kishon
TABOR
of Elijah
163
Kedesh
1168
522
Endor
MOREH
834
325
Shunem
1038
Megiddo
1302
En Haron
Beth-shittim
Jezreel
N. Jalud
'Ara
Tanaach
GILBOA
Beth-shan
331
1685
1268
Beth-haggan
1488
CAESAREA
65
Jibleam
2841
814
1168
Dothan
Gath
1568
Bezek
322
795
Jabesh
Jehem
2150
179
1170
Socoh
1302
3200
Thebez
JORDAN
183
976
1603
1780
Abel-meholah
W. Zemar
2240
2481
488
Hepher
1141
TIRZAH
1793
SAMARIA
3060
EBAL
661
GERIZIM
2286
814
1480
SHECHEM
W. Far'ah
163
2910
2641
2320
Aphek
1370
2390
Zarethan
977
Succoth
1228
Adamah
2543

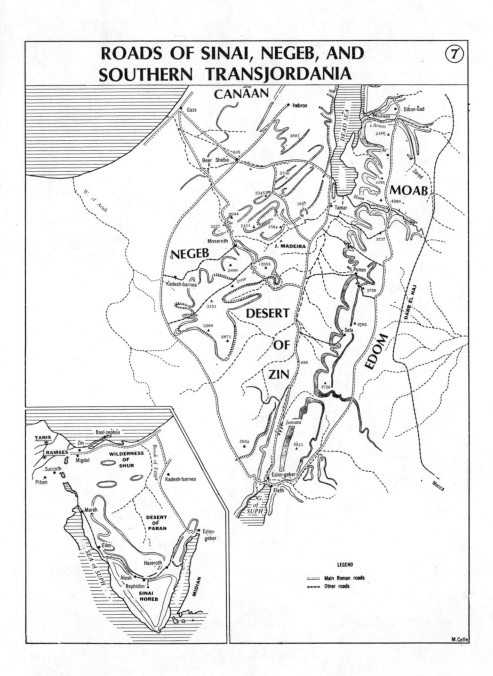

ROADS OF SINAI, NEGEB, AND SOUTHERN TRANSJORDANIA

⑦

CANAAN

Gaza · Hebron · Dibon-Gad

Arnon · 3460

At

2803 · 935 · Tered

Beer Sheba · 4058

2335 · MOAB

2245 · Hasa · 4260

1827 · Tamar

W. el Arish · 2044 · 1584

2237 · 2434 · 3737

Moseroth · J. MADEIRA · Punon

NEGEB · 2880 · 2655

Kadesh-barnea · 2090 · 3750

3351 · DARB EL HAJ

DESERT · 3260 · 5762

2871 · Sela

OF · 658 · **EDOM**

ZIN · 3726

Jotcata

2930 · 5013

Ezion-geber

Elath

G. · Mecca
of
SUPH

Inset map

TANIS · Baal-zephon

Zin · Brook of Egypt

RAMSES · Migdol · **WILDERNESS**
OF
SHUR

Succoth

Pitom · Kadesh-barnea

Marah

DESERT
OF
PARAN

Elim · Ezion-
geber

SEA of SUPH · Hazeroth

Alush

Rephidim · **MIDIAN**
SINAI
HOREB

DEAD SEA

LEGEND

------ Main Roman roads
←+++→ Other roads

M.Celle

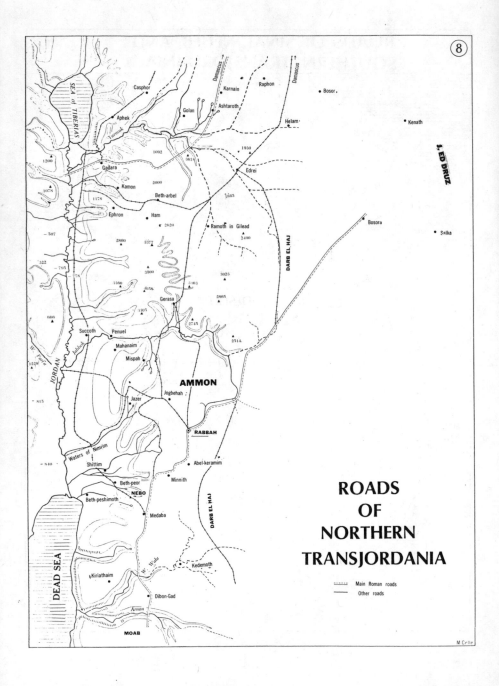

ROADS
OF
NORTHERN
TRANSJORDANIA

Main Roman roads
Other roads

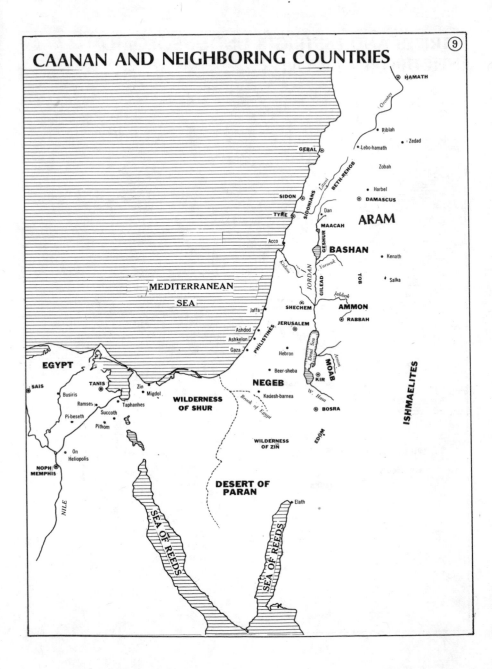

CAANAN AND NEIGHBORING COUNTRIES

⑨

HAMATH

Orontes

Riblah

Zedad

GEBAL · Lebo-hamath

Zobah

Litani

BETH-REHOB

Harbel

SIDON DAMASCUS

SIDONIANS

Dan

TYRE ARAM

MAACAH

GESHUR

Acco *Kishon* BASHAN Kenath

Yarmuk

JORDAN

GILEAD *Jabbok* Salka

TOB

MEDITERRANEAN

SEA

Jaffa SHECHEM AMMON

JERUSALEM RABBAH

Ashdod PHILISTINES

Ashkelon

Gaza Hebron Dead Sea *Arnon*

Beer-sheba MOAB

EGYPT NEGEB KIR

SAIS Zin ISHMAELITES

TANIS Migdol Kadesh-barnea

Busiris *Brook of Egypt*

Ramses Taphanhes WILDERNESS BOSRA

Pi-beseth Succoth OF SHUR EDOM

Pithom WILDERNESS

OF ZIN

On

Heliopolis

NOPH DESERT OF
MEMPHIS PARAN

NILE Elath

SEA OF REEDS

SEA OF REEDS

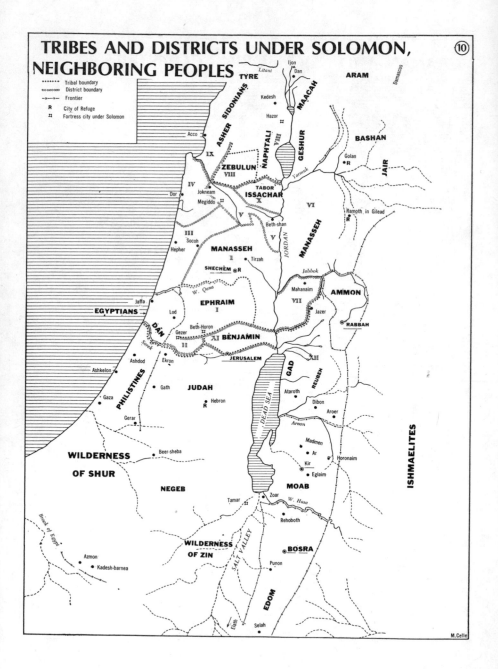

TRIBES AND DISTRICTS UNDER SOLOMON, NEIGHBORING PEOPLES

⑩

Tribal boundary
District boundary
Frontier
R City of Refuge
Fortress city under Solomon

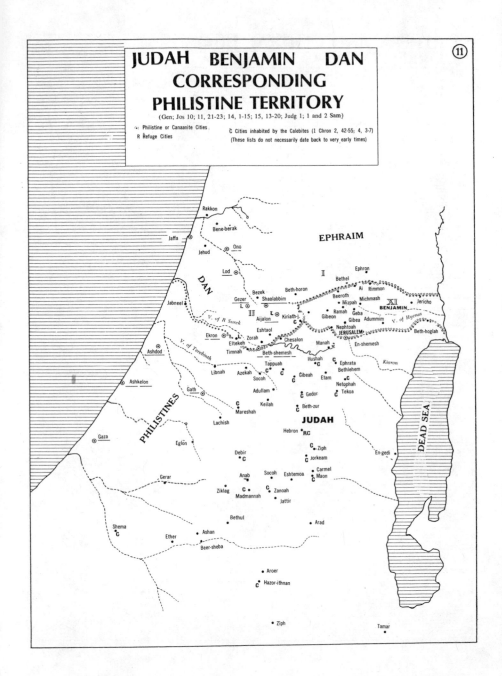

JUDAH   BENJAMIN   DAN
CORRESPONDING
PHILISTINE TERRITORY
(Gen; Jos 10; 11, 21-23; 14, 1-15; 15, 13-20; Judg 1; 1 and 2 Sam)

⊙ Philistine or Canaanite Cities
R Refuge Cities

C Cities inhabited by the Calebites (1 Chron 2, 42-55; 4, 3-7)
(These lists do not necessarily date back to very early times)

⑪

Rakkon

Bene-berak

Jaffa

Jehud

Ono

EPHRAIM

Lod

Ephron

Bethel

II

DAN

Bezek

Beth-horon

Ai   Rimmon

Gezer

Shaalabbim

Beeroth

Jabneel

Mizpah   Michmash   **XI**   Jericho

Ramah   Geba   **BENJAMIN**

V. of R Sorek

III

Aijalon

Kiriath-j.

Gibeon   Gibea   Adummim   V. of Hyenas

Eshtaol

Nephtoah

Ekron

Zorah

Chesalon

JERUSALEM   Beth-hoglah

Eltekeh

V. of Terebinth

Timnah

Beth-shemesh

Manah   En-shemesh

Ashdod

Hushah

Kidron

Tappuah

Ephrata

Libnah

Azekah

Socoh

Gibeah   Bethlehem

Ashkelon

Etam

Adullam

Netophah

Gath

Gedor   Tekoa

Keilah   Beth-zur

Mareshah

Lachish

JUDAH

Gaza

Eglon

Hebron   RC

PHILISTINES

Debir   C

Ziph

Jorkeam

En-gedi

DEAD SEA

Gerar

Anab

Socoh   Eshtemoa

Carmel

Maon

Ziklag   C

Zanoah

Madmannah

Jattir

Bethul

Arad

Shema   C

Ether   Ashan

Beer-sheba

Aroer

C Hazor-ithnan

Ziph

Tamar

NORTHERN AND CENTRAL TRIBES
CORRESPONDING DISTRICTS

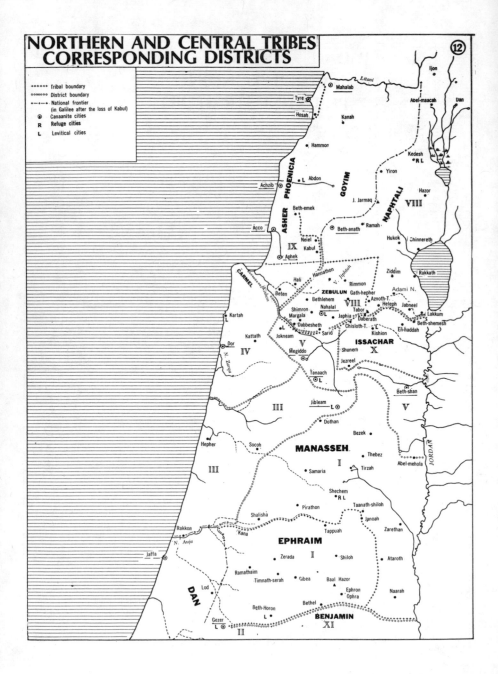

+++++	Tribal boundary
ooooooo	District boundary
+-+-+-+	National frontier
	(in Galilee after the loss of Kabul)
⊕	Canaanite cities
R	Refuge cities
L	Levitical cities

Litani

Ijon

Mahalab

Tyre

Hosah

Kanah

Abel-maacah   Dan

Hammon

Kedesh
R L

PHOENICIA

Abdon

L   Achzib

GOYIM

Yiron

Kishon

Beth-emek

Hazor

ASHER

Acco

J. Jarmaq

NAPHTALI

VIII

IX   Neiel

Beth-anath   Ramah

Kabul

Hukok   Chinnereth

Aphek

Hannathon

Hali

Rakkath

CARMEL

Beten

Rimmon

V. Jiphtah

Ziddim

Adami N.

ZEBULUN   Gath-hepher

Bethlehem

Aznoth-T.

Kartah

Shimron
Margala

Nahalal
O L

Tabor

Heleph   Jabneel

VIII

Japhia

Daberath

Lakkum

Dabbesheth

Chisloth-T.

Beth-shemesh

L   Joknem

Sarid

En-haddah

Dor

Kattath

V   Megiddo

Kishion

ISSACHAR

N. Zalmon

IV

Shunem

X

Jezreel

Taanach
O L

Beth-shan

III

Jibleam
L ⊕

V

Dothan

Bezek

JORDAN

Hepher

Socoh

MANASSEH

Thebez

III

Samaria

I

Tirzah

Abel-mehola

Shechem
R L

Taanath-shiloh

Pirathon

Janoah

Shalisha

Zarethan

Rakkon

Kana

Tappuah

N. Auja

EPHRAIM

Jaffa

Zerada   I

Shiloh

Ataroth

Ramathaim

DAN

Timnath-serah   Gibea   Baal Hazor

Ephron
Ophra

Naarah

Lod

Beth-Horon
L

Bethel

Gezer
L ⊕

BENJAMIN

II   XI

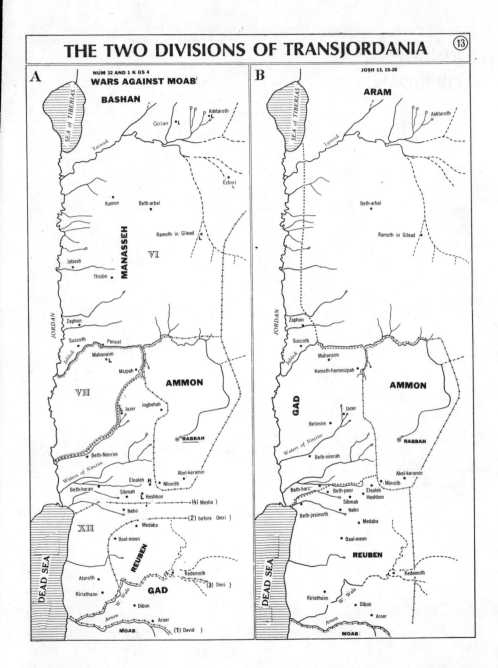

THE TWO DIVISIONS OF TRANSJORDANIA ⑬

A NUM 32 AND 1 K GS 4
WARS AGAINST MOAB

BASHAN

SEA of TIBERIAS

Golan · L
Ashtaroth · L

Yarmuk

Edrei

Kamon · Beth-arbel

MANASSEH VI

Ramoth in Gilead · L

Jabesh

Thisbe

JORDAN

Zaphon

Succoth · Penuel
Mahanaim · L

Jabbok

Mizpah

VIII AMMON

Jazer · Jogbehah

⊙ RABBAH

Beth-Nimrim

Waters of Nimrim

Elealeh · R
Beth-haran · Sibmah · Minnith
L Heshbon ——— (4) Mesha)
Nebo
——— (2) before Omri)

XII Medaba

Baal-meon

REUBEN

DEAD SEA

Ataroth · Kedemoth
Kiriathaim · GAD ——— (3) Omri)
· Dibon
Arnon · Aroer
MOAB ——— (1) David)

B JOSH 13, 15-28

ARAM

SEA of TIBERIAS

Ashtaroth

Yarmuk

Beth-arbel

Ramoth in Gilead

JORDAN

Zaphon

Succoth

Jabbok

Mahanaim
Ramath-hammizpah

GAD AMMON

Jazer

Betonim

⊙ RABBAH

Waters of Nimrim

Beth-nimrah

Abel-keramin

Beth-haran · Minnith
Beth-peor · Elealeh
Sibmah · Heshbon
Nebo
Beth-jesimoth

Medaba

Baal-meon

REUBEN

DEAD SEA

Kedemoth

Kiriathaim · W. Wala · Dibon
Arnon · Aroer
MOAB

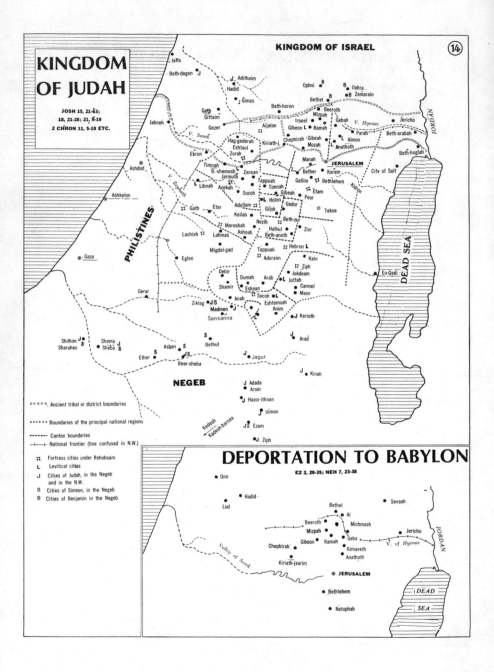

KINGDOM OF JUDAH

JOSH 15, 21-63;
18, 21-28; 21, 5-19
2 CHRON 11, 5-10 ETC.

KINGDOM OF ISRAEL

⑭

Jaffa
Beth-dagon J
J Adithaim
Hadid
Ophni B
Gimzo
Beth-horon
Bethel B
Ophra
B Zemarain
Beeroth
Irpeel
Mizpah
Jericho
Gath Gittaim
Jabneh
Aijalon
Gibeon L Ramah
Gebah
V. Hyenas
Gezer
Chephirah Gibeah
Parah
Beth-arabah
V. Sorek
Hag-gederah
Kiriath-j.
Mozah
Almon
Anathoth
Eshtaol
Ekron
Zorah
Manah
Beth-hoglah
Ashdod
Timnah
Zanoan
Bether
Karem
City of Salt
JERUSALEM
B.-shemesh
Jarmuth
Gallim
Bethlehem
Kidron
Ashkelon
Libnah
Azekah
Tappuah
Timnah
Etam
V. Zaphath
Socoh
Gibeah
Peor
PHILISTINES
Gath
Eter
Adullam
Holon
Gedor
Giloh
Keilah
Beth-zur
Tekoa
Mareshah
Nezib
Hebron L
Gaza
Lachish
Lahmas
Ashnah
Beth-anoth
Zior
Migdal-gad
Tappuah
Kain
Eglon
Adoraim
Ziph
Debir
Jokdeam
En-Gedi
Dumah
Arab L
Juttah
Gerar
Shamir
Eshean
Carmel
Ziklag JS
Anab
Socoh L
Maon
Madmen J
Eshtemoah
Sansanna
Anim
J Kerioth
J Arad
Shilhim JS
Shema J
Asban S
Bethul
Sharuhen S
Sheba S
J Jagur
Ether S
JS
Beer-sheba
J Kinah
NEGEB
J Adada
Aroer
J Hazor-ithnan
J Dimon
Kedesh
Kadesh-barnea
JS Ezem
J. Ziph

ooooo. Ancient tribal or district boundaries

++++++ Boundaries of the principal national regions

------- Canton boundaries

—x—x— National frontier (line confused in N.W.)

⊞   Fortress cities under Rehoboam
L   Levitical cities
J   Cities of Judah, in the Negeb
     and in the N.W.
S   Cities of Simeon, in the Negeb
B   Cities of Benjamin in the Negeb

DEAD SEA
JORDAN

DEPORTATION TO BABYLON

EZ 2, 20-35; NEH 7, 23-38

Ono
Hadid
Lod
Bethel
Ai
Senaah
Beeroth
Michmash
Mizpah
Geba
Jericho
Chephirah
Gibeon
Ramah
V. of Hyenas
Kiriath-jearim
Azmaveth
Anathoth
⊛ **JERUSALEM**
Bethlehem
Netophah

Valley of Sorek
JORDAN
|DEAD|
|SEA|

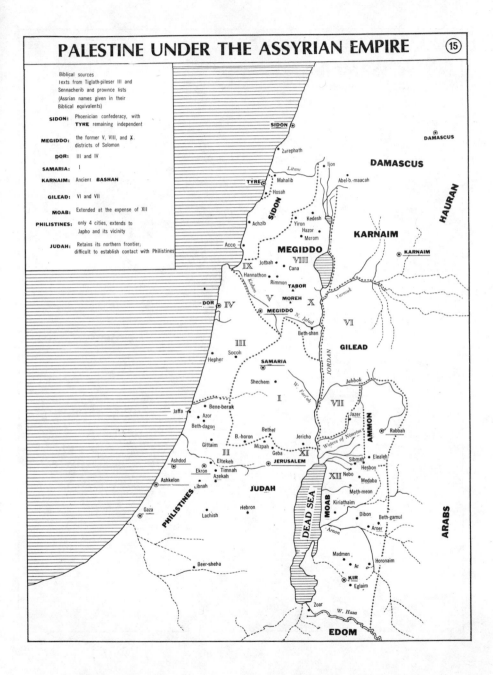

Biblical sources
Texts from Tiglath-pileser III and
Sennacherib and province lists
(Assyrian names given in their
Biblical equivalents)

SIDON: Phoenician confederacy, with **TYRE** remaining independent

MEGIDDO: the former V, VIII, and X. districts of Solomon

DOR: III and IV

SAMARIA: I

KARNAIM: Ancient **BASHAN**

GILEAD: VI and VII

MOAB: Extended at the expense of XII

PHILISTINES: only 4 cities, extends to Japho and its vicinity

JUDAH: Retains its northern frontier; difficult to establish contact with Philistines

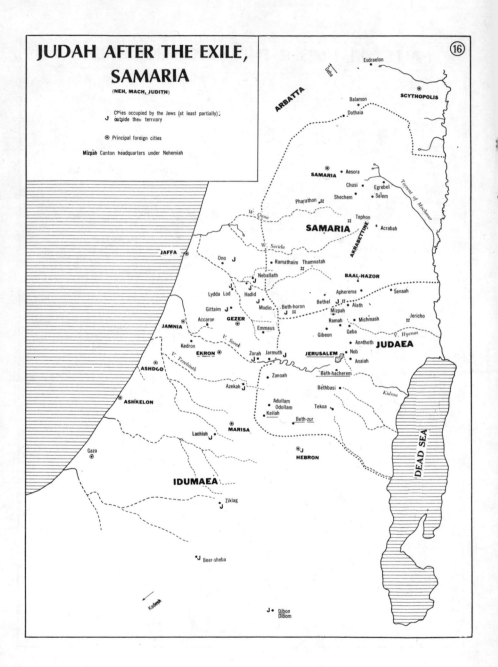

JUDAH AFTER THE EXILE, SAMARIA

(NEH, MACH, JUDITH)

J Cities occupied by the Jews (at least partially), outside their territory

⊙ Principal foreign cities

Mizpah Canton headquarters under Nehemiah

16

Esdraelon

SCYTHOPOLIS

ARBATTA

Geba

Balamon

Dothaia

Torrent of Mochmur

SAMARIA · Aesora

Chusi

Egrebel

Shechem · Salem

Pharathon

Tephon

SAMARIA

Acrabah

AKRABETTINE

W. Qana

W. Sarida

JAFFA

Ono J

Ramathaim Thamnatah

Neballath

BAAL-HAZOR

Lydda Lod Hadid

Apherema · Senaah

Gittaim J

Modin Beth-horon

Bethel J

Aiath

Mizpah

JAMNIA

Accaron GEZER

Emmaus

Ramah · Michmash

Jericho

Gibeon

Geba

V. Hyenas

Kedron

EKRON

V. Sorek

Zorah Jarmuth J

JERUSALEM · Nob

Anathoth

JUDAEA

Anaiah

ASHDOD

V. Terebinth

Zanoah

Beth-hacherem

Azekah J

Bethbasi

Kidron

ASHKELON

Adullam
Odollam
Keilah

Tekoa

Beth-zur

DEAD SEA

Lachish

MARISA

Gaza

HEBRON

IDUMAEA

Ziklag

J Beer-sheba

Kadesh

J · Dibon
Dibom

KINGDOM OF HEROD   NEIGHBORING COUNTRIES

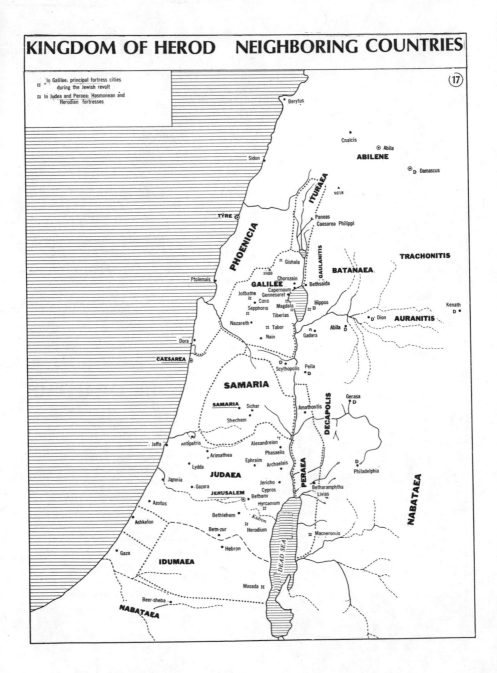

In Galilee: principal fortress cities during the Jewish revolt

In Judea and Peraea: Hasmonean and Herodian fortresses

(17)

Berytus

Cnalcis

Abila

ABILENE

Sidon

Damascus

ITURAEA

9218

TYRE

Paneas

Caesarea Philippi

PHOENICIA

GAULANITIS

BATANAEA

TRACHONITIS

Gishala

3920

Chorozain

Ptolemais

GALILEE

Capernaum

Bethsaida

Jotbathe

Gennesaret

Cana

Sepphoris

Magdala

Hippos

Kenath

Tiberias

Nazareth

Tabor

Dion

AURANITIS

Nain

Gadara

Abila

Dora

CAESAREA

Scythopolis

Pella

SAMARIA

SAMARIA

Sichar

Gerasa

Shechem

Amathontis

DECAPOLIS

Jaffa

Antipatris

Alexandreion

Arimathea

Phasaelis

Ephraim

Philadelphia

Lydda

Archaelais

Jamnia

JUDAEA

Gazara

Jericho

PERAEA

NABATAEA

JERUSALEM

Cypros

Betharamphtha

Bethany

Livias

Azotus

Hyrcanium

Bethlehem

Kidron

Ashkelon

Beth-zur

Herodium

Macnerontis

Gaza

Hebron

DEAD SEA

IDUMAEA

Masada

Beer-sheba

NABATAEA

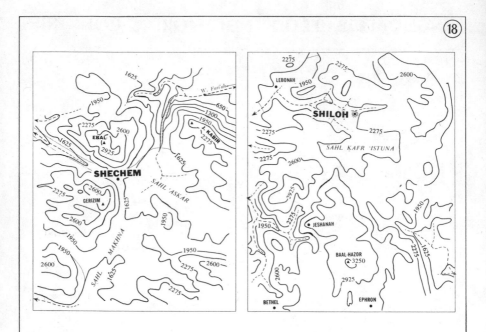

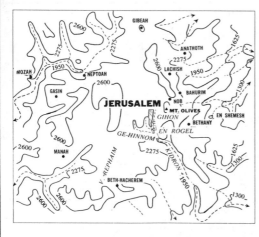

THE THREE CAPITALS

SHECHEM: Good soil, easy communications to
North, East, and West; no natural defenses.

SHILOH: Good soil, difficult communications
in all directions; natural defenses.

JERUSALEM: Mediocre soil, easy communications
to North and South, difficult in other directions; natural defenses.

Geological Morphology

Hard Limestone: vicinity of **SHILOH** and West of **JERUSALEM**

Soft Limestone: East of **JERUSALEM**

Soft Limestone with overlying nummulite: West of **SHECHEM**

▨ Plains or alluvial valleys.